British Political Though

British Studies Series

General Editor JEREMY BLACK

Published

Alan Booth **The British Economy in the Twentieth Century**
Glenn Burgess **British Political Thought, 1500–1660: The Politics of the Post-Reformation**
John Charmley **A History of Conservative Politics since 1830** (*second edition*)
David Childs **Britain since 1939** (*second edition*)
John Davis **A History of Britain, 1885–1939**
Gary S. De Krey **Restoration and Revolution in Britain: A Political History of the Era of Charles II and the Glorious Revolution**
David Eastwood **Government and Community in the English Provinces, 1700–1870**
Philip Edwards **The Making of the Modern English State, 1460–1660**
W. H. Fraser **A History of British Trade Unionism, 1700–1988**
John Garrard **Democratisation in Britain Elites: Civil Society and Reform since 1800**
Brian Hill **The Early Parties and Politics in Britain, 1688–1832**
Katrina Honeyman **Women, Gender and Industrialisation in England, 1700–1870**
Kevin Jeffreys **Retreat from New Jerusalem: British Politics, 1951–1964**
T. A. Jenkins **The Liberal Ascendancy, 1830–1886**
David Loades **Power in Tudor England**
Ian Machin **The Rise of Democracy in Britain, 1830–1918**
Alan I. Macinnes **The British Revolution, 1629–1660**
Alexander Mordoch **British History, 1660–1832: National Identity and Local Culture**
Anthony Musson and W. M. Ormrod **The Evolution of English Justice: Law, Politics and Society in the Fourteenth Century**
Murray G. H. Pittock **Inventing and Resisting Britain: Cultural Identities in Britain and Ireland, 1685–1789**
Nick Smart **The National Government, 1931–40**
Howard Temperley **Britain and America since Independence**
Andrew Thorpe **A History of the British Labour Party** (*third edition*)

British Studies Series
Series Standing Order
ISBN 0–333–71691–4 hardcover
ISBN 0–333–69332–9 paperback
(*outside North America only*)

You can receive future titles in this series as they are published by placing a standing order. Please contact your bookseller or, in case of difficulty, write to us at the address below with your name and address, the title of the series and the ISBN quoted above.

Customer Services Department, Macmillan Distribution Ltd
Houndmills, Basingstoke, Hampshire RG21 6XS, England

British Political Thought, 1500–1660

The Politics of the Post-Reformation

Glenn Burgess

First published 2009 by
PALGRAVE MACMILLAN

Palgrave Macmillan in the UK is an imprint of Macmillan Publishers Limited,
registered in England, company number 785998, of Houndmills, Basingstoke,
Hampshire RG21 6XS.

Palgrave Macmillan in the US is a division of St Martin's Press LLC,
175 Fifth Avenue, New York, NY 10010.

Palgrave Macmillan is the global academic imprint of the above companies
and has companies and representatives throughout the world.

Palgrave® and Macmillan® are registered trademarks in the United States,
the United Kingdom, Europe and other countries.

ISBN-13: 978–0–333–57410–2   hardback
ISBN-10: 0–3330–57410–9   hardback
ISBN-13: 978–0–333–57411–9   paperback
ISBN-10: 0–333–57411–7   paperback

This book is printed on paper suitable for recycling and made from fully
managed and sustained forest sources. Logging, pulping and manufacturing
processes are expected to conform to the environmental regulations of the
country of origin.

A catalogue record for this book is available from the British Library.

A catalog record for this book is available from the Library of Congress.

10 9 8 7 6 5 4 3 2 1
18 17 16 15 14 13 12 11 10 09

Printed and bound in China

For Aubrey

Contents

Preface

This book has been a long time in the making, and over this period debts too numerous to record have been incurred. Many are, in effect, noted in the footnote references to the work of the many scholars from whom I have learnt. This book has been written on the basis of my own direct encounter with the primary sources, but it would be misleading to pretend that that encounter has not frequently been shaped and guided by the work of other scholars.

Over the years in which I have been working on this project I have often drawn inspiration from academic friends and colleagues, and from collaborators on other projects with which I have been involved. In many cases, they have been more important in suggesting ideas and maintaining morale than they are probably aware. Particular thanks are due to these people, notably Trevor Burnard, Conal Condren, Colin Davis, Robert von Friedeburg, Simon Hodson, Mark Knights, Howell Lloyd, John Morrill, Charles Prior and Jonathan Scott. I should also thank, for patience well-tested by the time it has taken me to bring this work to completion, Terka Acton, Sonya Barker, and others at Palgrave; and my superb copy-editing team, Valery Rose and Jocelyn Stockley.

As always, the most heart-felt thanks go to those who (unlike the others mentioned) have had to endure my working on the project and my talking about its frustrations night as well as day, namely my wife Amanda Capern and my son Aubrey, to whom the book is dedicated. Their support has been unflagging.

Working on a subject that has taken me beyond the areas of my own greatest expertise makes me more than usually aware of the inevitable limitations the book will have, notwithstanding the advice and guidance I have received from others. All errors and misjudgements remain, of course, my responsibility. All quotations from primary sources follow the spelling and punctuation of the edition cited, though I have silently corrected errors and very occasionally modified punctuation in the interests of clarity.

Introduction

'Every true history is contemporary history,' Benedetto Croce once said: 'however remote in time events there recounted may seem to be, the history in reality refers to present needs and present situations wherein those events vibrate'.[1] The truth in these remarks has become particularly apparent during the writing of this book. A draft of an early (and longer) version was completed as long ago as 2000; eight years later its central theme, an examination of the interaction of religious belief and political ideas, seems newly topical. Religious fundamentalism, zeal and enthusiasm have erupted forcefully into modern politics. One of their consequences, terrorism, is widely (though possibly exaggeratedly) seen as the greatest contemporary challenge to global political stability. Though terrorism is arguably a distinctively modern phenomenon, the disturbing impact of religious extremism on politics is not. Early modern Britain, during the post-Reformation period, was a place in which religion posed reiterated threats to social and political order. Historians are now beginning to draw the parallels between our world and that of the Reformation;[2] but it should be clear both that there can be dangers in this, if we lose sight if the differences, in our efforts to find the similarities, and that the process can unsettle many of our deeply ingrained perceptions of the past. On the whole, historians of early modern England and Scotland have shown more sympathy for Protestants than for Catholics, and a willingness to see religious radicalism as a liberating and progressive force. Radical Protestant thinkers in the seventeenth-century British civil wars and the English Revolution have, for example, often been seen as forerunners of modern liberals, socialists, or democrats. It is not difficult to see why; but it may be troubling to note that they can as readily be seen to be the forerunners of modern religious fundamentalists, sometimes with political ideas to match – ideas that were rooted in a willingness to disturb the political order in the pursuit of God's cause. This book examines these ideas in the contexts provided by their own times.

It is organised around two concepts, each lightly deployed: the concept of a confessional polity, and the concept of religious war. The book does not assert that England or Scotland were confessional polities after the Reformation – in both cases there was room to contest the proposition, and (perhaps more importantly) even those who might want to think that they lived in a confessional polity could disagree vehemently over what sort of confessional polity it was. Nor does the book assert that the British civil wars or the English Revolution were (just) religious wars. Rather it uses these conceptual poles to orient its major themes.

It is helpful to pose the question, was the post-Reformation state a confessional polity? Contemporaries gave no clear answer. The same people might suggest different answers on different occasions, partly for tactical reasons. There were very different conceptions about what a confessional polity might and should look like – the term can be understood as essentially contested – and there were those very interested in denying that it was a confessional polity at all. Elizabethan and Jacobean conformists could argue that the English state was not a persecuting confessional state, since it condemned only traitors and not heretics; Catholics might be forgiven for having a different view of the matter. Furthermore, different confessions had different views of what form a polity ought to take, and how confession and politics should be aligned. Later sixteenth-century Scotland, for example, saw bitter divisions between the king and many of his subjects over the value of episcopacy and the role of the monarch in relation to the church. In using the concept, I am not making assertions about the nature of the polities, but providing a point of contention around which to organise material.

The same is true with religious war. Whether the British wars and the English Revolution were or were not parts of a war of religion it is not my purpose to decide. Indeed, it is not easy even to decide what the question might mean. But clearly, different contemporary people would have given very different answers. For some, religion was paramount, though whether for good or ill was another matter. For others, a struggle for civil liberties may have been more important. Even if the war was a religious one, there might be serious differences about what this meant. Oliver Cromwell in 1655 said of the Civil War that 'religion was not the thing at the first contested for, but God brought it to that issue at last . . . and at last it proved that which was most dear to us'; but by 'religion' he meant here liberty of conscience, and was not asserting that the war was initially secular.[3] Others could read the nature of the conflicts differently. For all, though, the question of how confession and public life interacted was a pole around which discussion occurred, and for everyone issues that we can relate to the idea of religious war shaped their responses to and understanding of the events they lived through.

These concepts shape this book. To that extent it has a story to tell, and it emphasises the interaction of religion and politics. But it aims to do more than just that. It also provides readers with broad discussions

of the major political thinkers of the period that it covers. There are
extended accounts of 'canonical' political thinkers (for England:
More, Hooker, James I, the Levellers, Hobbes, Harrington; for
Scotland: Knox, Buchanan, James VI, Craig, Rutherford), and sometimes it ranges a little beyond its core organising principles to do so. A
wide range of other texts is also discussed or mentioned. On the whole,
I have preferred to deal with fewer writings, and to be able to say something of substance about them, though this is a principle not observed
too rigorously. The selection of writers to include will inevitably be
controversial – no two scholars would make the same choices. My
guiding principles have been to choose those who most help to provide
contexts within which to situate the canonical writers, and to discuss
those figures who are prominent in the historiography of political
thought. This subject, 'political thought', I have defined conservatively
– that is to say, this is a book about those writers who wrote about
English and Scottish civil politics. It certainly argues that these writers
and thinkers were driven, in good part, by post-Reformation concerns,
but the book remains one about political thought, not theology.
Similarly, it is not a book about literature, though this is not to deny
that Spenser, Shakespeare, Jonson and Milton (as a poet) were political thinkers of a sort. Although the book is largely organised in a
chronological way, this is a little misleading, and in places mini-essays
trace themes forwards or backwards from the chronological scope of
the chapter in which they are found. In short, this is a book organised
and shaped by a thesis; but it is not a thesis that intends to strait-jacket
the book, or to prevent it from providing a general introduction to
British political thought in the post-Reformation period.

   A word is needed about the word 'British' in the title of the book. I
take it to mean England and Scotland, considered both in parallel as
two different post-Reformation polities, and in their interaction. When
I first began to work on the project I envisaged that it should cover
Ireland as well, and that it would be possible to write about British
political thought as a fully integrated history. Over time, I came to
think differently.[4] Ireland is undoubtedly important to the politics and
conflicts of the Tudor and Stuart multiple polities, but the history of
Irish political thinking is not only less well understood than British
(though recent work is doing much to rectify this), it is also very different from that of the other kingdoms – more different from both than
they are from one another. Scottish and English political thought, even
though in both cases developing within cultures that were strongly if
not exclusively Calvinist, need to be understood in good part as constituting two separable, though overlapping and intersecting, histories.
In part, so far as the themes emphasised in this book are concerned,

the differences owe a lot to the very different Reformations experienced by the two kingdoms, and to the very different polities that emerged. England possessed a church by law established; the Scottish kirk after 1560 could be thought by some to be characterised by a 'religion, established neither by law nor parliament'.[5] For these reasons, and contrary to my original intention, the Scottish and English material in this book is largely treated separately (though not entirely so, as the years around 1603 and after 1638 demonstrate); and I am aware that the difficult problems of organising this parallel account have not been perfectly solved. One day, it will be possible to write a full account of the interaction of political thinking in the three kingdoms of Ireland, Scotland and England, though not as a single story; but I came to the conclusion early in this project that this time was not yet upon us. It would be easier now than it seemed in the 1990s, and it would be a source of pride to me if this book were to inspire someone to attempt such a task.

My central subject, then, is the way in which Scottish and English political thinking was marked by the impact of religion (above all, of the Reformation) on the affairs of the commonwealth and its government. The Reformation established or brought to new prominence three important themes in the history of political thinking. First, there was the relationship between religion and political allegiance or obedience. Was it necessary for a ruler to be of a certain faith or to display Christian virtues in order to have a proper claim to the allegiance of his subjects? Was a ruler's heresy a proper ground for rebellion against her or him? In contrast, Renaissance political thought had been largely unconcerned with questions of obedience and resistance; and, although resistance theorists (almost always members of religious minorities) did make extensive use of arguments developed by the medieval Conciliarists, they nevertheless went much beyond their pre-Reformation predecessors in the uses to which they put these ideas. Furthermore, once the question of obedience was raised, it began to spill beyond the bounds of religion, as religious minorities extended their case for resistance to include more secular legal and constitutional arguments.

A second theme was much more obviously an old medieval problem now possessing a renewed urgency. What was the nature of a church, and what was its relationship to secular authority? To put it differently, what should a Christian polity of a particular confessional identity actually look like? In Protestant countries many old answers to these questions ceased to be viable after the Reformation, causing people to find new ways of defending the legitimacy of their church. In doing that, they inevitably were forced to rethink the nature of church–state relationships. Closely related to this was a theme that ran throughout the political thought of the sixteenth and seventeenth centuries. The British rulers found themselves with more than a set of domestic churches to keep in line: they were also compelled to rebut Papalist arguments. The need to confront the political thought and political claims of the Roman Catholic church was one of the most important forces shaping the pattern of early modern political thought.

The third problem that compelled attention was perhaps the most significant in the long term, while being the least significant in the short term. Should a ruler tolerate religious diversity amongst his people? Was religious uniformity necessary for religious stability? For a long time most English protestants continued to insist on uniformity; and it was not until after 1660 (how long after I do not specify) that the extent of religious diversity became so great that there could be little doubt that the church, at least in England, would be forced to reach some accommodation with it.

In developing these three themes this book will in effect be claiming that the period from the 1530s through to the Restoration was one in which thinkers were struggling above all else with the legacy of the Reformation. It was a post-Reformation period in much more than a chronological sense. The book will also suggest that, in seeing the period in this way, we shall be able to get a fresh view of such subjects as 'absolutism', 'revolution' and 'radicalism', which can too readily be seen in an inappropriately secular way. Thus one further claim will also be advanced: it is only when we see the seventeenth century alongside the sixteenth, only (that is to say) when we appreciate the unity of the post-Reformation period, that we are able to see the seventeenth century accurately. The complex dialogue between politics and religion did not obligingly end when this book does, but an important phase in that dialogue was completed, not so much with the Restoration of the Stuart monarchy, as with the long and alarming shadow cast over the future by the bitter conflicts of England's and Britain's wars of religion.

This is, of course, not the only way of approaching a history of early modern British political thought. But it does capture the centrality of religious matters to political thinking in the period, and does capture some of the essential things that define the period. Other histories with other themes can be written;[6] but this one, I would claim, at least takes us to one of the essential themes in the history of early modern British political thought.

Prologue: Humanism and Political Thought before the Reformation, 1500–30

'Such is the unity of history that anyone who endeavours to tell a piece of it must feel that his first sentence tears a seamless web.' These are the words of Frederick William Maitland, one of the greatest of English historians. The web being torn in this first chapter is that which connects early modern English and Scottish political thought to the past, to the political thinking and the culture of medieval Latin Christendom, and of the Greek and Roman worlds before that. The Reformation exploded in a European world discovering new ways of relating to its heritage, especially the classical heritage, and this humanist movement had begun to transform English political thought in the early sixteenth century. Humanism had an impact in Scotland, too, but less obviously on Scottish political thought. This prologue will explore the impact of humanism on early Tudor political thought, and more importantly look at some of the discontinuities – *and continuities* – between humanist and Reformation political thought. The first two chapters of the book will then examine the political ideas of the English and Scottish Reformations.

Humanism and the Best State of a Commonwealth

The word 'humanism' has been a troublesome one. It may be taken to refer generally to the development of approaches to rhetoric and scholarship that based themselves firmly on the emulation of classical examples and authorities. The effect of humanism on political writing was complex and diverse, and two general points need to be stressed. First, Renaissance political thinking was not by any means simply a product of humanism. Certainly, humanists contributed to the defence of the 'liberty' of the city-state republic in *trecento* Italy, and especially formulated a much-discussed civic and republican ideology in early *quattrocento* Florence and elsewhere; but so, too, did jurists and scholastic philosophers contribute to the formation of civic ideologies. And, secondly, though humanism has been particularly associated, thanks to the work of Hans Baron, with the emergence of a new patriotic civic

1

ideology, justifying the independence and republican institutions, initially of Florence ('civic humanism') and ultimately of other places, it is clear that humanism was broader than this. Humanist intellectuals were able and willing, using classical rhetorical and literary tools, to defend princely as well as republican states, and to defend a life of contemplation as well as the active life of the self-ruling republican citizen, or of the merchant.

Thus, by the beginning of the sixteenth century, when its impact was becoming very apparent north of the Alps, humanism was clearly not a simple ideology, but rather a complex set of topics and terms. Humanism could be divided not just into political varieties (republican and princely), but, more usefully, it was divided by its allegiance to different classical writers and traditions. Much humanist political writing, including civic humanist writing, was essentially Ciceronian in orientation – one recent scholar has termed this strand 'neo-Roman',[1] and it adapted the political values of *Romanitas* to the circumstances of early sixteenth-century European cities and states. This could involve many things, but among the central themes of this strand of northern humanism were the application, to the monarchies of the north, of classical ideas of 'mixed' government (the idea that the best form of government fused elements of the three good forms – monarchy, aristocracy and democracy); the exploration of the idea of counsel, in part as a way for intellectuals and scholars to find for themselves a sort of Ciceronian civic life that could be lived even in the political circumstances pertaining within a territorial monarchy; and the elaboration of a powerful critique of the values and functions of the feudal aristocracy, conducted with reference to the humanist idea that *vera nobilitas*, true nobility, rested on virtue not lineage, and conducted partly because the nobility were accused of cultivating the arts of war rather than the more important arts of peace.[2]

But within the classical heritage the values of the neo-Roman tradition could be challenged using ideas drawn from Greek writers, especially Plato.[3] The pattern is, of course, complicated. Most humanists were eclectic, drawing on a variety of models, and the most important of the early northern humanists, Desiderius Erasmus, drew on Ciceronian and neo-Roman ideas as well as on Greek ones. But, at least as we approach the intellectual context of More's *Utopia*, it is true to say that Erasmus and the circle of intellectuals around him questioned or modified civic humanist and neo-Roman values in at least two important ways. *Utopia* dramatised that questioning, and it did so by pitting Greek Platonic ideas (advocated by More's character Hythlodaeus) against Roman Ciceronian ones (advocated by the character More – referred to in this account by the Latin version of the name, Morus, to distinguish him from his creator). One suspects that the value of the book for More and his friends lay as much in that questioning as in the provision of straightforward answers.

Thomas More and some other Erasmians posed two questions to the neo-Roman tradition. First, should citizens (but above all, intellectuals) involve themselves in public affairs as advisers to princes, or should they avoid public life? In this sense, More and others questioned the superiority of the civic life, the *vita activa*. Secondly, was the existence of private property compatible with what the sub-title of *Utopia* refers to as the *optimus status reipublicae*, the best state of a commonwealth.[4]

Civic humanism had extolled the importance of an active civic life for the maintenance of 'liberty', meaning both the independence of the state as a whole, and the freedoms of its citizens. (Those freedoms could include their right to secure private property.) Greek and Roman authors had complex and sometimes ambiguous views on the subject, but a dividing line can be discerned, for example between Cicero and Plato. Cicero was, in essence, a defender of the active life. While unwilling to denounce the Stoic ideal of the tranquil life led in seclusion from public affairs, Cicero nonetheless stressed that those naturally fitted to doing so ought to win office and engage in public affairs. How else could a city be adequately ruled? (Cicero, *De Officiis*, I, 69-73). Plato, in contrast, was of the view that public affairs were such that the wise man should steer clear of them. He idealised a polity in which either philosophers became kings, or kings became philosophers (*Republic*, 473c–d). His own experience with Dionysius of Syracuse suggested that when the wise only advised, their advice was insufficient to reform corrupt rulers (*Epistles*, VII). In the dialogue of *Utopia*, More ironically used the *Republic* in defence of the Ciceronian ideal, urging that a situation in which philosophers advised kings was a step towards this view.[5] But Plato did not himself seem content with such an intermediate position (*Republic*, 496c–497c); and More's character Hythlodaeus pointed to the lesson that Plato himself had discovered at Syracuse. Plato's message was taken to be that, if the ideal could not be achieved, then nothing was achievable, and the philosopher should avoid public life. This was mirrored in the 'moral absolutism' displayed by Hythlodaeus.[6] The preference for a private life also drew strength from another of the Greek philosophers, who declared the contemplative and largely solitary life of philosophic contemplation to be that which gave the greatest happiness (Aristotle, *Ethics*, 1177a–b). In Greek philosophy, the highest good for human beings was *eudaimonia* (happiness), and this had no necessary connection with a life of political or civic engagement (though perhaps some involvement in society was inescapable – see Aristotle, *Ethics*, 1178b 6–7).

Clearly intertwined with this question of involvement in public affairs was another one: was it possible to achieve political reform in a corrupt world, and (if so) how should a wise man act in order to bring about that reform? Hythlodaeus's argument that reform was impossible was encouraged by his view that the wise man should speak only the complete truth, but would be ignored when he did so. There was an alternative Ciceronian argument. This held that the view that significant reform was impossible rested upon a mistaken notion as to how it would best be achieved. If the philosopher was uncompromising, and spoke the truth regardless of circumstances, he would get nowhere. But if he offered counsel that was sensitive to context and followed the rules of rhetorical *decorum* (and, if he was prepared for reform that fell short of achieving the ideal), then there was cause for hope. Cicero's *De Oratore* pointed out that a speaker must adapt his style to the character of his audience (III.lv.211–12; also Cicero, *Orator*, XXVII, 74). A wise man cannot always act with complete decorum, but must strive to act (and speak) in as seemly a fashion as circumstances will allow (*De Officiis*, I, 114). Sometimes it was necessary for those giving advice to trick men into doing the right thing because a more direct approach would fail (Quintilian, *Institutio Oratoria*, II.xvii.28–9; III.viii.38–9). Circumstances sometimes prevented us from doing only good things, and in such situations one followed the Roman proverb *minima de malis*, choose the least evil option (Cicero, *De Officiis*, III, 102–5) – though it was important to make sure that one had identified correctly what the lesser evil was. Hythlodaeus, and before him the Greek philosophers, seemed at times to reject public life because they were unwilling to follow this guidance. They set their sights uncompromisingly high. Thus *Utopia* contrasts the inflexible *philosophia scholastica* of Hythlodaeus with the *philosophia civilor* (civil philosophy) of Morus (94–7), as we shall see.

Erasmus's own views on these subjects were complex.[7] On occasion he clearly endorsed the ideas of the Latin rhetorical theorists,[8] and, like More, he spent some of his life in the service of princes. Indeed, it can be argued that his writing, rather than exploring the clash between the Ciceronian and the Platonic views of counsel, exemplifies a fusion of both perspectives.[9] He shared Plato's belief that the king should be a philosopher, contrary to the opinions of the 'idiot courtier'. Consequently, Erasmus's view of the education, training and virtues needed to produce a good prince is so demanding that it engenders doubts about the possibility of ever seeing them in the actual world. The doubts are reinforced by the fact that Erasmus so frequently conjured a picture of the corruption of royal courts, and (in particular) was so aware of the dangers of courtiers and counsellors who would corrupt through flattery.[10] The words that More gives to Hythlodaeus can read like a warning to Erasmus that he cannot have it both ways: Plato and Cicero do not fit together as easily as he might assume.

One of the things about which Hythlodaeus was reluctant to compromise was the iniquity of private property. This is the second major way in which *Utopia* conducts a Platonic interrogation of Ciceronian and civic humanist principles. Cicero's political principles, as they appear in *De Officiis*, rested upon an understanding of justice that was closely connected to the private ownership of property. He was concerned to reconcile the Stoic principle that all men are part of a wider world or community with a powerful endorsement of private property rights.[11] Thus he declared that it was the primary duty of public officials to ensure that private men were not deprived of their goods by public acts. This was because the point of forming political communities in the first place was to ensure that men could hold their property securely (*De Officiis*, II, 73). Plato, in contrast, was insistent that the proverb 'the property of friends is common property' applied to all of society. The best-arranged polity was one in which private ownership did not exist (*Laws*, 739c–e), though Plato recognised that this was excessively demanding, and that landed property in the second-best form of polity would need to be portioned out. Nonetheless, even here, men should see their property as but a portion of the common property of the whole society (*Laws*, 740a). Erasmus discerned the affinity between Plato's views and those of the New Testament. The first proverb collected in his *Adages* from the 1508 edition onwards was *Amicorum communia omnia*, friends hold all things in common. He noted that Plato had used the proverb in his defence of the principle of common ownership, and added that 'nothing was ever said by a pagan philosopher which comes closer to the mind of Christ'.[12] Hythlodaeus also linked communism with the message of the gospels (218–21). Erasmus was even more emphatic in the introduction to the *Adages*, urging that if communism existed, 'war, envy and fraud would at once vanish from our midst' and thus the chief purposes of Christ would have been achieved.[13]

More's *Utopia* was centrally concerned with exploring (more, perhaps, than deciding between) these different humanist responses to political and civil life. *Utopia* was written over the years 1515–16,[14] and the full title of the work, 'On the best state of a commonwealth and on the new island of Utopia' (3), identified the basic interpretative problem with the book. Was Utopia itself 'the best state of a commonwealth' (*optimus status reipublicae*)? Broadly speaking, Hythlodaeus answered yes, Morus no; while what More himself thought is much debated. Hythlodaeus (said to have been a traveller after the fashion of Plato, with a strong preference for Greek learning over Latin) represented the Platonic strains in the Erasmian synthesis; Morus represented the 'civic' strains.[15] But *Utopia* appears to be an insider's analysis of the humanist world, the work of a friend asking his friends to consider further some of the implications of what they thought.

Book I of *Utopia* established the conversational context for Hythlodaeus's account of the Utopian commonwealth that would occupy the bulk of Book II. Its central subject matter was whether the wise man should live as an adviser to princes.[16] Giles began the discussion by expressing his surprise that Hythlodaeus was not in the service of a prince, revealing his 'Ciceronian assumption that the natural use to which knowledge and ability should be put was in political service as a counsellor to a king, and that the proper way of benefiting oneself and one's friends was through public service.[17] Morus took a similar line: 'if you could bring yourself to devote your intelligence and energy to public affairs, you would be doing something worthy of your noble and truly philosophical nature even if you did not much like it' (53). Morus argued that the philosopher should serve in public life by becoming counsellor to a king.[18]

Hythlodaeus was not persuaded, and began a complex *structural* analysis of the problems involved in counselling kings and in the achievement of social justice, these two things being tightly linked. The structural character of this analysis is important, for it constitutes one of the ways in which *Utopia* is a critique of any humanists naive enough to believe that if only power were in the hands of good and wise men, social justice could be achieved.[19] Thus Hythlodaeus suggested that 'the public would still not be any better off if I exchanged my contemplative leisure for active endeavour'. Good men make little difference, first because 'most princes apply themselves to the arts of war, in which I have neither ability nor interest, instead of to the good arts of peace', and secondly because those who advise kings are full of conceit and therefore are strongly opposed to innovation, for any suggestion that things have not been well-conducted for some time will reflect badly on the advice they have already given to the prince. They always wanted to follow 'custom', though Hythlodaeus cuttingly commented that this reverence for custom did not stop men from ignoring the best examples that the past has left us (53–5). Thus, not only a king's sense of the purpose of his rule, but the nature of his court and councils, suggested that the wise man could have no impact for good in public life.

Hythlodaeus, as the good rhetorician that he was,[20] supported his argument with vivid examples, drawn from events that supposedly occurred in the household of John Morton, Lord Chancellor, cardinal and archbishop of Canterbury, in the late 1490s. Thomas More had himself served in Morton's household and respected him greatly.[21] One evening a lawyer at Morton's dinner table spoke approvingly of the policy of executing thieves, but was puzzled that in spite of all the executions, theft remained rife. Hythlodaeus was not in the least puzzled. In a long speech he explained the folly of putting thieves to death, and analysed the root causes of poverty and theft. Capital punishment was both unjust, because 'too harsh in itself', and ineffective,[22] because it failed to realise that theft arose from poverty and nothing could deter a starving man from theft. It was the utmost folly and cruelty to punish thieves severely while doing nothing to alleviate the poverty that made them into thieves in the first place (57). Some of the poor were so because they could not work rather than because they would not. Many noblemen (themselves 'liv[ing] idly like drones off the labour of others') maintained in idleness large bands of servants and retainers. These men, when surplus to requirements or when ill, became thieves because they were untrained for any useful employment (57–9). '[S]oft and flabby because of their idle, effeminate life', such men could do nothing but steal (61). In these remarks Hythlodaeus was giving vent to one of the major themes in northern humanist writing, the attack on the values of the traditional landed nobility made in the name of *vera nobilitas*, true nobility. True nobility came from virtue (*virtus vera nobilitas est*), not from wealth or lineage.[23]

Hythlodaeus identified another cause of poverty, especially notable in England. 'Your sheep,' he informed Morton and the other diners, 'that commonly are so meek and eat so little; now, as I hear, they have become so greedy and fierce that they devour men themselves. They devastate and depopulate fields, houses and towns' (63). Hythlodaeus was referring to the loss of common rights in land and the conversion of arable land into pasture, both of which might result in a form of depopulating enclosure, whereby common or arable land was parcelled up into fields used for grazing sheep.[24] The surplus population had little choice but to steal in order to live. To make their plight worse, enclosure also raised the price of food and wool, so that the poor could neither eat nor make cloth, and the root cause of all this was the 'crass avarice' of the rich (65). The lesson was obvious, 'Certainly, unless you try to cure these evils, it is futile to boast of your justice in punishing theft' (67).

Hythlodaeus's speech was not well received by most of those present, but Morton himself invited him to continue his discussion with an account of how theft should be punished. The figure of Morton complicates the message by listening attentively and eagerly to what Hythlodaeus was saying, rather than dismissing his comments as a radical threat to the customary way of doing things (67–9).

Hythlodaeus responded with an account of the Polylerites (= people of much nonsense). They punished theft not with death (not even the Mosaic code did that) but by demanding restitution paid to the victim of the crime, and by putting convicts to work as 'slaves' under reasonably mild conditions. Punishment was for life, though a few criminals were pardoned every year. Hythlodaeus describes this as 'mild and practical', a punishment intended 'to destroy vices and save men' (71–5).

The lawyer, and most others at the table, held that the system Hythlodaeus had described 'could never be established in England without putting the commonwealth in serious peril' (75). Morton disagreed, and again intervened in the discussion in a way that cast doubt upon the points about counsel that Hythlodaeus was trying to illustrate. It was impossible to tell whether such a system would work, he commented, until it was tried. And he suggested an experiment, using criminals temporarily reprieved from death, adding that the system of control outlined by Hythlodaeus might also be tried out on vagabonds. Hearing their master's opinion, the others also changed their minds (75–7). Thus Hythlodaeus outlined a radical alternative to the existing system of justice, based on an even more radical diagnosis of the causes of theft; and the king's most powerful counsellor had suggested trying the proposal out. Presumably, Hythlodaeus was too blinded by the sycophancy and stupidity of the lawyer and his friends to observe properly that his message was well received where it mattered.

Hythlodaeus drew the lesson from the events he had recalled: the behaviour of the lawyers and other diners showed 'how little courtiers would value me or my advice'. Morus's response, we can now see, made perfect sense, brief though it was. 'I by no means give up my former opinion; indeed, I am fully persuaded that if you could overcome your aversion to court life, your advice to a prince would be of the greatest advantage to the public welfare.' He even invoked Hythlodaeus's own philosopher Plato, suggesting that having philosophers assist kings was one step on the way to the ideal situation in which kings were philosophers or philosophers kings. Morus's comments, not Hythlodaeus's, capture what was actually shown in the Morton episode: court life was distasteful, but there were good individuals like Morton who could nonetheless make a difference and counteract the folly of others. Hythlodaeus, however, did not see this, and reverted to a Platonic and Erasmian moral absolutism. Plato correctly foresaw that if kings were not philosophers then no advice in the world could be of any use to them, because they would have been 'infected with false values from boyhood on'. Anyone proposing good laws would be scorned or banished (81–3). Whether or not that verdict was true, it was not what was shown by events at Morton's table. Hythlodaeus gave other examples of unconventional advice that might be given, and Morus again agreed that such advice would not be listened to (29–34) but he did not abandon his civic Ciceronian perspective. Instead he accused Hythlodaeus of being a poor rhetorician, for his counsel lacked appropriateness or decorum. Which is to say, that Hythlodaeus was guilty of the same fault, though in a different way, as his critics at Morton's table. Morus even went so far as to accuse Hythlodaeus of behaving like a scholastic philosopher rather then a humanist rhetorician in supposing 'that every topic is suitable for every occasion', that is in not fitting his message to circumstances (95–7). More positively, Morus advised Hythlodaeus to adopt 'an indirect approach, you must strive and struggle as best you can to handle everything tactfully – and thus what you cannot turn to good, you may at least make as little bad as possible'. You cannot 'make everything good unless all men are good, and that I don't expect to see for quite a few years yet' (97). A philosopher might not achieve all that he might want in politics but it did not follow that his only proper course of action was to try to do nothing at all: counsel offered according to the rules of rhetorical decorum would have some effect. The Morton example suggests that we should follow Morus in rejecting Hythlodaeus's attitude to counsel.[25]

Was the wholesale indictment of the injustice of modern European states that Hythlodaeus expressed justified, or was it just another example of his tendency to overstatement? We have already seen that Morus briefly endorsed what Hythlodaeus had said at Morton's table, suggesting that the latter's indictment of the modern world was valid. But if so, could advice as radical as was necessary succeed, even if offered with appropriate decorum? Hythlodaeus thought not: if he told people what was really needed to sort out social problems and create a true commonwealth, as in Plato's republic or in Utopia, 'those institutions . . . would seem alien because private property is the rule here, and there all things are held in common' (99).[26] They resemble in this respect the teachings of Christ himself and 'are far more alien from the common customs of mankind than my discourse was' (99). Given this, Hythlodaeus urged, what was the use of counselling a king? He cited Plato's similar verdict, that in the actual world philosophers should have nothing to do with the corrupt and corrupting world of politics – a verdict Plato gave immediately before beginning to construct his portrait of the ideal philosopher-king (*Republic*, 496d–e). The example of Utopia, like the precept of Plato, demonstrated that equality, justice and good government could not exist unless private property was abolished (101–5), and no counsel, however decorous, was likely to achieve that. Morus contented himself with defending private property using a set of standard Aristotelian and Roman arguments against Platonic communism (105; Aristotle, *Politics*, 1262b–1264b).[27]

Book I initially undermined Hythlodaeus's credibility, but these later exchanges partially undid that work. In them Hythlodaeus raised a genuine problem: if Morus was right – and we are led to believe that he was – about the rhetorical conventions for giving effective counsel, then was it possible within those rhetorical conventions to give counsel of a sufficiently radical and systemic character? Morus doubted whether communism was really needed as a remedy for injustice and poor government, a position that would enable him to escape the need for offering radical advice at all. So the questions that Book I of *Utopia* posed to Book II turn out to be these. Should kings be counselled that they cannot achieve perfect justice without instituting communism? Or, to put it another way, is communism essential to the *optimus status reipublicae*? If kings should be advised of the importance of communism, would that counsel have any effect?

Book II of *Utopia* consisted almost entirely of Hythlodaeus's account of the island, its people, and their manners and institutions. Only on the last page or so did the dialogue between Hythlodaeus and Morus resume, and even then, after spluttering briefly into life, it ended because Hythlodaeus was too tired to continue. Hythlodaeus's account of Utopia is almost wholly admiring – his only reservation appears to be a worry that the Utopians are 'too much inclined' to the Epicurean view that happiness consists of pleasure (159) and he concluded his account of their moral philosophy with the explicit statement that he was describing, not defending, their principles (179). Thus the structure of the work makes it difficult for the reader to see Utopia through the eyes of anyone but Hythlodaeus. Did More, therefore, intend us to share the traveller's enthusiasm for the island he had visited, as Hexter and others suggest? Is Utopia a straightforward model of the *optimus status reipublicae*? Hythlodaeus was to conclude that Utopia was the 'commonwealth which I consider not only the best but indeed the only one that can rightfully claim that name' (241). Should we believe him? Or has Book I warned us that we are facing an example of the unreliable narrator?

Utopia, on Hythlodaeus's account, was an island republic, made up of 54 city-states, each with its own agricultural hinterland and its own governor (a figure who is best seen as a republican magistrate). Utopia as a whole had only one institution, an assembly consisting of three representatives from each city. It met once a year. The governor of each city, elected from amongst the scholars for life by the syphogrants (or phylarchs), each representing thirty households, was advised by a senate of tranibors (or head phylarchs), each representing ten phylarchs or 300 households. To maintain a rough equality in household sizes, adults could be transferred between them, or transferred to other cities. If the total population grew too great, then people could be exported to colonies on the mainland. The inhabitants of the 54 closely similar cities lived in large households (10–16 adults, mostly blood relations). They dined in communal halls, each of which served fifteen households. The Utopians operated a moneyless economy. Heads of households and the stewards of the halls took what they needed from the warehouses in the four market-places, in which the goods produced by the households were pooled. Surplus produce was given at no charge to other cities if needed. The Utopians traded with other peoples, though the only thing they lacked themselves was iron. Few traders came to Utopia itself, for the Utopians preferred to keep the conduct of trade in the hands of their own people. They traded by extending credit to other peoples, and frequently did not call in the debts incurred to them. Utopia only needed gold and silver in time of war. To show their contempt for these otherwise useless metals, they stored their gold and silver reserves in the form of chamberpots, or chains and shackles for slaves. The Utopians had no great love of labour (179–81), but (with a few exceptions – officials, scholars, priests and ambassadors) labour was compulsory for all.

In several different ways this was a highly controlled world in which nothing was private. Political discussion was permitted only in the senate of tranibors or the 'popular assembly' in which the syphogrants met. Private discussion of public affairs was a capital offence (123). Houses were open and unlocked, 'so there is nothing private anywhere'. Houses were exchanged by lot every ten years (119). Clothing was uniform, and two-year stints of agricultural work compulsory for both men and women (125, 113). Utopians were in practice free to travel to other cities, but permission was always required, so that no one could avoid work by travelling. It was the function of the syphogrant to ensure that no one escaped her or his duty to labour, though the burden of labour was light (six hours a day). All citizens laboured, but consequently all could have a fair share of leisure time after supper. However, there were restrictions on how one's leisure could be spent. Sloth and roistering were not permitted; attending public lectures and other intellectual activities were the most common and most favoured form of recreation. As much time as possible was released for cultivation of the mind, a situation possible only when the rest of life was rigorously disciplined. This portrait of a controlled society is confirmed by the fact that Utopia had inhabitants who were not citizens. These slaves (Utopian criminals, foreigners condemned to

death abroad, prisoners of war and immigrants) performed the most
unpleasant labour (185–7, 193, 139). In short, 'nowhere is there any
chance to loaf or any pretext for evading work; there are no wine-bars,
or ale-houses, or brothels; no chances for corruption; no hiding places;
no spots for secret meetings'. Furthermore, 'since they share everything equally, it follows that no one can ever be reduced to poverty or
forced to beg' (145).[28]

Morus was less convinced that this was an ideal commonwealth than
Hythlodaeus, expressing grave doubts about 'their methods of waging
war, their religious practices . . . [and above all] the basis of their whole
system, that is, their communal living and their moneyless economy'
(247). It is worth considering each of the areas he identified.

Utopia presented several differently-targeted messages about war.[29]
The Utopians refused to make international treaties, because they
accepted that their conduct should always by guided by the (Stoic)
principle that all human beings were united by reason and nature,
which bonds transcended the superficial and artificial division of
humankind into separate nations. 'The Utopians think . . . that the
kinship of nature is as good as a treaty, and that men are united more
firmly by good will than by pacts, by their hearts than by their words'
(201). This principle was not just Stoic: it was also one of the foundation stones of the Erasmian critique of war, though the principle of
transnational unity became for Erasmus primarily the Christian faith.[30]
Much of the attitude to and practice of war by the Utopians flowed
from this. 'They utterly despise war as an activity fit only for beasts, yet
practised more by man than by any other animal' (201). Victory in
battle was deemed inglorious, and a bloody victory something of which
to be ashamed (201, 205). The Utopians would go to war 'only for
good reasons' (201), but if war became necessary they conducted it 'in
such a way as to avoid danger, rather than to win fame or glory' (205).
The passage in which this statement is elaborated can only be read as
an Erasmian satire on the aristocratic warrior elite of early sixteenth-
century Europe. The Utopians, to win a war, thought nothing of
encouraging assassination and treachery amongst the peoples they
opposed. Using bribery where possible, they stirred up dissension and
encouraged pretenders to the thrones of their enemies. The point of
this was, of course, to assert that war was best waged so as to win with
the minimum cost in human life. No one should pride himself on a
proficiency in an activity best avoided, and, if unavoidable, best won by
cunning not military prowess. So much for Europe's aristocracy with its
perverted notions about what constituted a noble life.

But there are places where Utopian practices and principles might
seem to conflict with both the Christian humanism of Erasmus and

their own Stoicism. The most obvious example of this occurred in Hythlodaeus's account of the Utopian employment of mercenaries. A sensible reluctance to see their own citizens killed led the Utopians to rely heavily upon mercenaries. They used especially for this purpose the Zapoletes, an avaricious people who would change sides for financial gain, but nonetheless fight furiously for the highest bidder (209). The Utopians did not care how many of them got killed, and would be pleased 'if they could sweep from the face of the earth all the dregs of that vicious and disgusting race' (211). So much for Stoic brotherhood. In general, the Utopians were prepared to pursue their own particular interest ruthlessly. When they did not use mercenaries, they preferred to put into battle the soldiers of their friends and allies rather than risk the lives of Utopians (211). When required to form colonies for the export of surplus population, they were willing to make war on any native inhabitants who refused to live under Utopian law (137). Zapoletes were not the only people whom the Utopians seemed prepared to treat badly. We are told that 'they go to war only for good reasons: to protect their own land, to drive invading armies from the territories of their friends, or to liberate an oppressed people, in the name of compassion and humanity, from tyranny and servitude' (201–3).[31] All of this endorsed humanist views, including the idea of liberal interventionism, but it is not so clear that the Utopians always lived up to the theory. Of their wars against the Alaopolitans, Hythlodaeus laconically commented, '[s]o sharply do the Utopians punish wrong done to their friends, even in matters of mere money' (203).[32] Life mattered more than money, it seemed, only if you were a citizen of Utopia.

Hythlodaeus, accepting that the Utopians were Stoics in their belief in a natural law uniting all of humanity into a common fellowship, failed to appreciate that their attitude to warfare seemed to question the principles that they professed. Stoicism was widely taken to be the pagan moral philosophy that most thoroughly anticipated Christianity, so for the Utopians to be portrayed by More as hypocritical Stoics must raise doubts about whether one should accept that Utopia was, to all intents and purposes, intended to be a truly virtuous and therefore truly Christian commonwealth (and thus a device for shaming the ostensibly Christian societies of early sixteenth-century Europe).[33] This poses problems for an alternative interpretation too. Quentin Skinner has suggested that although Utopia was not a truly Christian community it nonetheless still represented the best state of a commonwealth. His argument rests on a distinction 'between the optimal conduct of public affairs on the one hand and the optimal conduct of one's own individual life on the other'.[34] The Utopians had achieved the former but not the latter. The problem created by the account of the Utopian conduct of warfare, however, is that it might suggest that the moral errors of the Utopians were not confined to the private sphere, but spilled over into the public.

It is worth turning to look more closely at the Utopians' moral and religious beliefs, about which Hythlodaeus himself had reservations. Their fundamental principle, to which they were 'too much inclined', was the Epicurean one 'that all or the most important part of human happiness consists' in pleasure (159). In standard Epicurean style, they distinguished between higher and lower pleasures, as well as between true and false ones, and gave pride of place to pleasures of the mind rather than pleasures of the body (esp. 167, 173–9). In general, Utopian moral beliefs were a mixture of Stoic and Epicurean elements, the equal of those of the most enlightened Greek philosophers. They were also aware of the need for a theological structure to support moral practice, an awareness that suggests that the Utopians were themselves aware that their own philosophical beliefs were by themselves an insufficient basis for a moral life (161–3). This may, indeed, suggest that a society with access to the true faith (i.e. a Christian society) should be able to surpass in moral virtue that of the Utopians. Reason led them to a belief in an immortal soul, and in the idea that men would be rewarded or punished in an afterlife for their conduct in this one (161). It led them, less securely perhaps, to monotheism; and it led the wisest of them to a conception of an unknowable and incomprehensible divinity not unlike the Christian conception (219–21). But it led them no further. As a result, the Utopians were tolerant in religion. This was a mark of the imperfection of their society, not of its moral superiority. Lacking an adequate grounding for religious belief (i.e. the Christian revelation), they could not behave otherwise. For the sake of peace and religion, Utopians were free to practise and believe what religion they liked, provided that they did so without a zeal that might upset others of a different view. Only those who denied the mortality of the soul or the guidance of events by providence were in a different category. Those beliefs made them unfit to be citizens, and they were unable to hold civic office (223–5). There was public provision of religion, conducted by priests (231, 131). This public worship concentrated on the agreed essentials of belief, and citizens were free also to engage in private sectarian worship (235).

A sign that this moral and religious belief structure might not be perfect is that it supported a number of practices that we might assume to have been abhorrent to More (though Hythlodaeus passed them by with little comment), including broad religious toleration,[35] suicide and voluntary euthanasia (187), divorce (191), and the appointment of women priests (231). The implication would appear to be that a society organised according to even the best and most rational non-Christian principles must be imperfect. But that trite conclusion can hardly have been the central point that More wished to make.

The clue to the ultimate message of *Utopia*, and to the ironical masterstroke with which the book ended, lies in other passages on Utopian morality and religion. The Utopians' belief that pleasurable life constituted happiness did not lead them into purely selfish attitudes. In particular, they remained obedient to public laws because these 'control the distribution of vital goods, such as are the very substance of pleasure' (165). Furthermore, when introduced to the Christian message by Hythlodaeus, many Utopians rushed to embrace it. This, of course, further identified them as virtuous pagans, already primed by reason to be receptive to the moral truths inherent in the Christian message. But Hythlodaeus tells us, also, that they were greatly taken by the fact 'that Christ encouraged his disciples to practise community of goods, and that among the truest groups of Christians, the practice still prevails' (219–21). The Utopians built communism into their moral principles, recognising that without it access to a happy life could not be possible for everyone in the community; and they valued Christianity because it seemed consonant with that judgement.

This prepared the ground for what is a stunning reversal of expectation in the final pages of the book. More had gently questioned Hythlodaeus's credibility through Book I, and even in parts of the account of Utopia in Book II. In the final dialogue, Morus correctly and precisely identified the passages in which the Utopian realities betrayed Hythlodaeus's enthusiasm, singling out as 'my chief objection' Utopian communism, 'the basis of their whole system'. He defended his objection by saying that communism 'alone utterly subverts all the nobility, magnificence, splendour and majesty which (in the popular view) are the true ornaments and glory of any commonwealth' (247). Now, at the very last, he too is betrayed by his own words, for 'the popular view' was undoubtedly the wrong one, in this case.[36] A central feature of the humanist attitudes shared by More was precisely the wish to subvert commonly accepted ideas of nobility, magnificence, splendour and majesty.[37] Read in that light, Morus's comment amounted to the claim that, if one seriously wished to achieve this subversion, then instituting of communism as practised by the Utopians was the means of doing so. Utopian communism was the thing that linked together the central themes of *Utopia*. True nobility (*vera nobilitas*), as opposed to the perverted forms of nobility based on breeding, wealth and property, was a product of virtue. Utopia was so constructed that its people broadly displayed the characteristics of true nobility, and it achieved this in good part by suppressing and ridiculing traditional ideas of splendour and majesty (fine clothes, the pointless amassing of a useless metal like gold). But at the core was Utopian communism, which did away with both poverty and pride, causes of theft and of ideas of false nobility respectively. Only on this basis could genuine social justice be achieved, and people valued and rewarded for their virtue and merit rather than for their power and wealth. Utopia was a society ruled by the best and wisest, not by the wealthiest or those with the most impressive lineage. In the end, *Utopia* endorsed the Platonic view that community of property was necessary to the achievement of social justice, even as it questioned the Platonist view on the superiority of the contemplative life over the active, and endorsed a Ciceronian view of counsel.

Hythlodaeus declared that Utopia was such a 'commonwealth which I consider not only the best but indeed the only one that can rightfully claim that name'. He condemned those societies that made much of the ideal of a commonwealth without possessing the substance, societies in which 'men talk all the time about the commonwealth, but what they mean is simply their own wealth'. In most societies men pursued their own interest; in Utopia, they pursued public business because there was no private business. In both cases men were only responding sensibly to the system within which they lived. 'And in both places people are right to act as they do. For elsewhere, even though the commonwealth may flourish, there are very few who do not know that unless they make separate provision for themselves, they may perfectly well die of hunger' (241). In Utopia all people could live 'joyfully and peacefully, free from all anxieties'. Their families and descendants would be equally well provided for. Hythlodaeus contrasted the Utopian situation with that pertaining in European nations, in a passage that returned to the central theme of *vera nobilitas*. Christian Europe was a place in which honour and nobility were acquired by those who contributed least to the common welfare.

> What kind of justice is it when a nobleman, a goldsmith, a money-lender, or someone else who makes his living by doing either nothing at all or something completely useless to the commonwealth, gets to live a life of luxury and grandeur, while in the meantime a labourer, a carter, a carpenter, or a farmer works so hard and so constantly that even beasts of burden would scarcely endure it? (243).

This was surely 'an unjust and ungrateful commonwealth', which rewarded 'parasites' (including the 'so-called gentry'), while ignoring the welfare of those whose work was essential to the very existence of the commonwealth itself. To make things worse, the rich in such societies exploited public laws to oppress the poor, so that they came to be 'nothing but a conspiracy of the rich, who are advancing their own interests under the name and title of the commonwealth'. Were it not for the 'serpent from hell', pride, men would long ago have seen that it was in the interest of all to live as the Utopians lived (241–7).

Clearly there is some truth in the view that 'the underlying thought of *Utopia* always is, *With nothing save Reason to guide them, the Utopians do this; and yet we Christian Englishmen, we Christian Europeans . . . !*'[38] Utopia was not Christian in belief or practice, and not all of the Utopians' moral beliefs, or the social and political practices sustained by those beliefs, were acceptable in Christian eyes. Though Utopia might represent the best society that could be achieved on the basis of unaided reason, it was therefore not the best of all possible societies, a fact that made the satirical effect of the work even more pointed. Yet there was a sense in which Utopia nonetheless did represent the best state of a 'commonwealth'. It is perhaps the wittiest aspect of a very witty book that the central component of Hythlodaeus's Utopian vision of a commonwealth was paradoxically endorsed by Morus's rejection of it. We need to *take seriously*, if not fully to accept, the possibility that private property was the key obstacle to the achievement of social justice.[39] As a work addressed to a contemporary humanist audience, *Utopia* therefore invited consideration of the claim that only radical structural change could achieve the sort of commonwealth that many humanists admired. It was a warning to fellow humanists, telling them of the way in which their radicalism could be blunted by a willingness to compromise with the existing social order and its defence of private property. In this it rejected central features of Roman and Ciceronian republicanism, and emphasised the Greek ideas hostile to private property that Erasmus himself had shown sympathy for.[40] If men were serious about the achievement of social justice, then they would need seriously to consider the abolition of private property. *Utopia* was an invitation to a debate, not an attempt to end one.[41]

But when debate had been concluded, policies produced, would radical counsel be listened to? It is hard to be certain of the answer. If not, then the work served to raise doubts about the *attainability* of a genuine commonwealth, returning us to Morus's recognition that the point of counsel was not to achieve perfection but to make the world as little bad as possible. We might, with Alastair Fox, take this as a product of More's 'sense of the absolute insolubility of the human dilemma', the impossibility of satisfying an idealistic demand for perfect justice. More, through Morus, committed himself to a life of action, not because he was sure that action would achieve the best result possible, but because he was sure that inaction would not.[42] On that reading, *Utopia* might be said to convey a tragic sense of the gap between what ought to be and what can be.[43]

Utopia was a work of playful seriousness, and it explored (at least implicitly) themes that were to be central to post-Reformation political thought. It raised questions about whether the best state of a commonwealth had to be a Christian society, and whether social justice was attainable naturally even in societies without access to the Christian revelation. By implication, it seems to have concluded that to a very considerable degree it was. It also portrayed a pagan community that practised a considerable degree of toleration for all but atheists. The playfulness with which this was done did not last the Reformation. That the Utopians practised religious toleration might be taken as a mark of the imperfection of Utopia. Lacking access to the one true faith revealed by Christ through his life and through the scriptures, the Utopians had no authoritative basis on which to build religious uniformity. They did insist on as much uniformity as reason could justify. In the more relaxed atmosphere before the Lutheran schism, More's tone on the subject was visibly less anxious than it was to become, though it would be wrong to portray him as moving from an advocacy of toleration to a rejection of it.[44] Nonetheless, the tone of post-Reformation humanism was very different (though early Protestantism did produce some voices in favour of tolerance too).[45]

By the 1530s it was being emphasised again that unity and uniformity were necessary to political order,[46] and it was Thomas More who gave the fullest defences of intolerance and persecution in Henrician England.[47] 'For neuer', he argued, 'shall y^t cuntre long abyde wythout debate and ruffle / where scysmes & factyouse heresyes are suffered a whyle to grow.' Heresy always resulted in 'dystruccyon and manslaughter'. It must, then, be dealt with, and 'yf it happely be incurable, then to the clene cuttynge out ye parte for infeccyon of the remanaunt' are all judicial officers bound.[48] Tyndale (against whom More was arguing) had, of course, presented in 1528 a Lutheran argument for absolute obedience to princes. More was not impressed. Heresy was always seditious. All 'scysme and dyuisyon must nedes moue and prouoke [sedition] amonge any people y^t are of dyverse sectis', because this division will 'cause them . . . though they rebelled not agaynste his person, yet to breke the peace and quiete of his cuntre, and rune in to the daynger & parelle of hys lawes'.[49] The persecution of heresy was necessary to preserve the souls of both the heretics and those exposed to their heresy. Was, asked More, killing people for heresy 'harde and vncharytable'? No, because persecution was undertaken by good princes 'for preseruacyon not of the fayth onely / but also of the peas amonge theyr people'.[50] It was an act of self-defence by the faithful. The heretic, especially the lapsed heretic, was a person whose 'conuersacyon were peryllouse among crysten men', a threat to the faith of others.[51] Mercy would be an act of folly, for the heretic would 'with the spredyng of his errour infecte other folke'.[52] Of an anonymous heretic, captured in possession of works by Tyndale, More commented that

> both two [the books and the man] burned togyder / wyth more profyte vnto his soule then had ben happely to haue lyued lenger & after dyed in his bedde. For in what mynde he sholde then haue dyed our lorde knoweth / where as now we know well he dyed a good crysten man. And when he wyste well his reuocacyon coude not saue his body: yet reuoked he his heresyes and abhorred Tyndals bokes for to saue hys soule.[53]

This was a different world from the world of *Utopia*, a world with more pressing concerns than that of the conversationalists who had met to hear Hythlodaeus's account of his travels. The Utopians might have been prepared to allow a discussion of rational religion; the later Thomas More was not.

Commonwealth Ideals and the Reformation

But all was not discontinuity at the Reformation. The idea of the common weal or 'commonwealth' explored in *Utopia* was a central component of early modern political thought, with a long life ahead of it. In humanist hands, it expressed ideals of social justice, and a conception of the nation separable from its identity as a monarchy. The word 'commonwealth' itself – an inheritance from the fifteenth century – was a controversial one. The Erasmian Platonist Sir Thomas Elyot, for example, objected to the use of 'commonwealth' as a translation of '*respublica*' (he preferred 'public weal') precisely because it implied 'that everything should be to all men in common, without discrepance of any estate or condition'.

> if there should be a common weal either the commoners only must be wealthy, and the gentle and noble men needy and miserable, or else, excluding gentility, all men must be of one degree and sort. . . .

In this latter case, Elyot added, 'a new name [ought to be] provided', for the term 'commonalty' (*plebs*, at least for Elyot), which was at the

basis of 'commonwealth', functioned only in contradistinction to other
categories of degree.[54] Utopia was, of course, a 'commonwealth' in
exactly the sense so abhorrent to Elyot,[55] if understood as demonstrating that only the abolition of private property could create a true
commonwealth.[56] Elyot's concerns did not prevent others from
making extensive use of the term, and some of these other thinkers
also questioned the idealism or lack of political depth and insight to be
found among their fellow humanists, most notably Thomas Starkey.[57]
'Commonwealth' came into its own in discussion of the social basis for
and social impact of government. Over the fifteenth century, even
more in the early sixteenth, the term came to be associated with
reform, and to acquire its links with an explicitly humanist ideal of
respublica.[58]

Starkey's *Dialogue between Pole and Lupset*, unpublished until 1871 but
probably written on the eve of the Reformation, between 1529 and
1532,[59] is a remarkable work, more radical than *Utopia* if only in the
sense that it lacked More's pessimistic sense of the difficulty of bringing
about substantial change. Starkey laid down a dramatic programme of
reform. Like *Utopia*, the *Dialogue* began by debating the merits of the
vita contemplativa and the *vita activa*, translating this debate into terms
relevant to the English monarchy – whether to lead an active life as a
counsellor and adviser to a king – and it strongly contrasted Platonic
and Ciceronian views of the subject.[60] Lupset advanced standard
Ciceronian humanist arguments in favour of the active life. Men were
born for 'perfayt cyvylyte, & not to lyve to theyr own plesure',[61] 'idul &
slomeryng', and he argued that Aristotle demonstrated that the good
life should combine both knowledge and action. Virtue and learning
are of no value unless shared and used for the good of all (3–4). Pole in
contrast noted that 'old & antique phylosopharys forsoke the medelyng
wyth materys of commyn welys & applyd themselfys to the secrety studys
& serchyng of nature as the chefe thyng wherin semyd to rest the perfec-
tyon of man . . .' (3). Pole's position here came close to that of
Hythlodaeus. In many actual circumstances, counsel was useless and
would go unheeded. Lupset admitted that there might be some truth in
the point, but – correctly recognising the provenance of the arguments
he was listening to – he warned against the folly of standing by and
allowing the commonwealth to go to ruin simply because it never lived
up to the model of 'platos commyn wele' (16). In any case, England was
now ruled by a noble prince, and the time was therefore propitious for
a life of political involvement (16–17). Pole agreed. He would do what
he could to establish and maintain a true commonweal, beginning with
a consideration of the reforms needed to achieve that end (17).

Thus agreed, the two developed an account of the ideal commonwealth that led into a diagnosis of the failings that prevented England from matching that ideal, followed by a detailed set of reforms that would, so far as possible, repair those deficiencies and bridge the gap between the ideal and the actual. The *Dialogue* would show how 'thes abusys both in custum and law may be reformyd and the treu commyn wele a mong us restoryed'.[62] A 'veray & true commyn wele' was 'no thyng els, but the prosperouse & most perfayt state of a multytud assemblyd togyddur in any cuntrey cyty or towne governyd vertusely in cyvyle lyfe according to the nature & dygnyte of man' (38). Three things were necessary to the existence of this true commonweal: the people and the body politic had to be 'helthy, beutyful & strong abul to defend themselfys from utward injurys'; they had to be nourished with life's necessities; and they had to 'lyve togyddur in cyvyle ordur, quyetly & peasybly passyng theyr lyfe, ychone [= each one] lovyng other as partys of one body, every parte dowing hys duty & offyce requyryd therto . . .' (38).

The force that could be acquired by the term *common weal* (or *commonwealth*) is apparent in two respects. First, it served both as a descriptive term and as an ideal. Like the Greek *polis* for Aristotle, the common weal was the last stage of an historical sequence that began with men who 'waneryd abrode in the wyld feldys & wodys' like 'brute bestys'. Certain men of 'gret wytt & pollycy wyth perfayte eloquence' then began 'to persuade the rest of the pepul to forsake that rudnes & oncomly lyfe' and to live instead in cities and towns. This view, which gave orators and oratory a key role in the formation of civil communities, was Ciceronian. Although these early communities did not display 'perfayt cyvylyte', eventually, 'by perfayt eloquence & hye phylosophy' – a distinctively Ciceronian harmony of rhetoric and philosophy – a common weal was created, in which the rulers sought to act for the profit of all and not their own private benefit (35–6). And yet, this historical process was also strongly teleological, so that the common weal was (again like the *polis*) not just the last of a sequence of social formations, but the best. It was an ideal. Every commonwealth had constantly to exert itself to live up to the ideal embodied in its name, to provide the perfect civil and political life for its inhabitants. Secondly, the term embodied a *social* dimension, requiring a distribution of goods that would leave the entire body politic well nourished, and encompassing ideals of social justice. It is this feature of Starkey's work that has made it plausible to interpret it as the inspiration for a whole range of social reforms in the 1530s, from regulations concerning horse-breeding to intervention in the cloth industry.[63]

Nonetheless, Starkey pulled some of his punches. Though he claimed that he had not dealt with the subject of true nobility (143), the work says much of relevance to that central topic of humanist discussion. Most humanists unequivocally accepted that *virtus vera nobilitas est.* Typical might be Elyot's statement that some men were originally accorded superior dignity 'more for remembrance of their virtue and benefit, than for discrepance of estates'.[64] The children of these men, educated in virtue, thus also came to possess it. By this means some – but only some – allowance was made for lineage. However, 'nobility is not after the vulgar opinion of men, but is only the praise and surname of virtue', even though 'the longer it continueth in a name or lineage, the more is nobility extolled and marvelled at'. Starkey went even further in abandoning any anti-aristocratic implications of humanist ideas of *vera nobilitas*. He proposed an education for the nobility 'in vertue & lernyng but also in al featys of warre', so that they would be fitted for 'al cyvylyte and polytyke rule' (125). He even proposed that *only* the nobility should be trained in Roman law (128). Starkey also reinforced the linkage between nobility, property and lineage. After a discussion of elective and hereditary monarchy, Pole launched an attack on the practice of primogeniture in the inheritance of private property as repugnant to a true commonweal. Lupset replied that the practice was essential to the 'pollycy & hole ordur of thys our reame' (73). He emphasised especially that the people needed superiors to keep them in order, and this would not be possible if the break up of landed estates led great families to decay (74). This would 'take away the foundatyon & ground of al our cyvylte'. In particular, the abolition of primogeniture would 'bryng in the ruyne of al nobylyte & auncyent stokkys, for yf you from the nobyllys onys take theyr grete possessyonys, or mynystur any occasyon to the same you schal in processe of yerys confude the nobyllys & the commynys togeddur' (74). Pole was persuaded only in part, accepting the need for primogeniture among the nobility only (princes, dukes, earls and barons), and on condition that provision was made for the welfare of younger sons (75). Other measures agreed by Pole and Lupset would have further strengthened the landed base of the nobility. The entailing of estates was to be confined to the nobility, so that 'base' families could not build up estates beyond their station (76). The custom of wardship pertaining to lands held by knight's service (a tyrannical custom imposed by the conqueror in 1066) was to be abolished, in part because lords did not see to the 'bryngyng up in le_rynyng & vertue' of their wards (76–8). The passage may remind us that Starkey had not altogether lost sight of the link between virtue and nobility, but there is no doubt that these measures would also have strengthened the control of the nobility over their own property.

Counsel, commonwealth, true nobility: these were central humanist themes, and there was another to be found in Starkey's *Dialogue*, the preference for a mixed government. While socially, Starkey may have mitigated the potential radicalism of his commonwealth ideals, constitutionally he did not. His 'aristocratic constitutionalism' led him to develop a set of political and constitutional proposals evincing a distinctly lukewarm attitude to the institution of monarchy. Starkey was an eclectic writer, but he drew particularly on a humanism of strongly Venetian stamp, acquired in Padua, and on Parisian conciliarism, mixed with an obvious interest in the English baronial political traditions of the middle ages.[65] All of these influences and interests conspired to give Starkey a strong interest in the use of conciliar authority to limit and control royal authority.

'[M]ost wyse men . . . affyrme a myxte state to be of al other the best, & most convenyent to conserve the hole out of tyranny' (120). Mixed government meant, for Starkey, the rule of laws and not of men's wills. Though he laid great stress on unity, order and obedience, Starkey nonetheless recognised that 'tyranny in al commynaltys ys the ground of al yl, the wel of al myschefe & mysordur the rote of al sedycyon & ruyne of al cyvylyte'. Princes were imperfect men. Few, if any, matched the requirements of a perfect prince. To prevent tyranny a mixed state was needed, in which 'the lawys, whyche be syncere & pure reson wythout any spot or blot of affectyon, must have chefe authoryte, they must rule & governe the state & not the prynce after hys owne lyberty & wyl'. Only in mixed government was one part of the government restrained by the others. '[F]or when any one parte hath ful authoryte yf that parte chaunce to be corrupt wyth affectys . . . the rest schal sufur the tyranny therof.' The great need in England was, therefore, that 'the authoryte of the prynce must be tempered & brought to ordur' (120). Starkey provided details of the aristocratic institutions that would fulfil this need. He noted first that 'our old aunceturys' had 'ordeynyd a comustabul [constable] of englond to conturpayse the authryte of the prynce and tempur the same, gyvyng hym authoryte to cal a parlyament in such case as the prynce wold run in to any tyranny'. To ensure that he too was restrained, 'the connestabul schold be hede of thys other conseyl wych schold represent the hole body of the pepul wythout parlyament & commyn counseyl'. This council would be paramount in one area, 'to see un to the lyberty of the hole body of the reame & to resyst al tyranny'. The council would consist of the constable, earl marshal, high steward and lord great chamberlain, with four judges, four citizens of London and the bishops of London and Canterbury (121, 112), and would 'have autoryte of the hole parlyament in such time as the parlyament were dyslove' (112). It should itself possess the authority to summon a proper parliament when necessary (121, 112), and 'to see that the kyng & hys propur counsele schold do no thyng agayne the ordynance of hys lawys & gud pollycy' (112–13). Furthermore, the king's ordinary council (which ought to be appointed by the constable's council[66]) should consent to all acts of state, so that the realm would be free from tyranny and 'in true lyberty'. The council should also possess wide powers in the distribution of honour and office, and inferior magistrates ought to be accountable to it (113; cf. 121–2). These councils, with their aristocratic bias, would take over much of the traditional role of parliament, which 'schold never be callyd but only at the electyon of our prynce, or els for some other grete urgent cause concernying the commyn state & pollycy' (112).

This conciliar mechanism effectively reduced the king of England to the position of the Venetian doge. But Starkey went even further than that, strongly intimating a preference for elective monarchy over hereditary. The very idea of a true commonwealth demanded mixed government and elective monarchy. Commonwealth required the unity of all parts and their fusion into a single whole.

> [so] the state of a prynce where he ys chosen by fre electyon most worthy to rule, ys . . . chefe & princypal judgyd of wyse men for the mayntenance & long contynuance of thys commyn wele & polytyke rule in any commynalty. (39)

Elective monarchy was an essential mechanism for ensuring that a community was not ruled by only a part of itself, for the benefit of the part rather than of the whole. The subject of elective monarchy was discussed several times in the *Dialogue*. In the fullest of these discussions it was suggested that the English monarchy was not only hereditary but also arbitrary (67–8). The problem lay in the combination rather than in either feature alone. '[T]hat cuntrey can not be long wel governyd nor maynteynyd wyth gud pollycy, where al ys rulyd by the wyl of one not chosen by electyon but commyth to hyt by natural successyon' (68). Kings who inherited their office were seldom worthy of it. The solution was, then, either elective arbitrary monarchy, or hereditary limited monarchy. The former would recognise the fact that it was, indeed, the 'most perfayt & excellent state of pollycy & rule, to be governyd by a prynce' when that prince excelled 'in wisdome & vertue'. That situation did not exist in a hereditary monarchy, and it was therefore 'no thyng expedyent to commyt to them [hereditary kings] any such authoryte & pryncely powar, wych ys to syngular vertue & most perfayt wysdome only due & convenyent' (68). With an hereditary king it was best instead 'to restreyne from the prynce such authryte, commyttyng that only to the commyn counseyl of the reame & parlyamente' (69). This in fact reduced the prince to true liberty, 'for as much as to folow reson ys veray true lyberty'. Hereditary princes should be bound to the laws, because they were not possessed of perfect reason, 'wych obedyence [to the reason embodied in law] ys indede true lyberty' (69). After much reiteration of the arguments, Pole and Lupset agreed that England would be best with a hereditary monarch, limited by conciliar (and, less importantly, parliamentary) institutions. That conclusion was reached largely because it was accepted that election of the prince might produce 'cyvyle warre sedycyon & dyscordys', thus destroying two of the essential requirements of a commonwealth, 'unyte & peace'. Nonetheless, this argument was clearly signalled as leading to a less than ideal conclusion. A perfect commonwealth would have an elective prince, but sadly 'our pepul be of that nature that yf they had such lyberty surely they wold abuse hyt to theyr owne destructyon' (71). Hereditary monarchy was, as Pole put it, not the ideal, but only the lesser of the two ills actually achievable – either order on the basis of succession or disorder on the basis of election (72). The limitations on the monarch, which we have already examined, became necessary because of the necessity of accepting this less than ideal situation (123).

Starkey's *Dialogue*, like More's *Utopia*, was intended as an account of a true commonwealth, in which men could lead fully active and civil lives, displaying their virtue and concern for the welfare of all. Whereas More gave the edge to Platonic arguments about property, and developed an overt hostility to the values of a traditional nobility, Starkey's work was Ciceronian and Roman in its key features, an example of civic humanism. In both commonwealths there was emphasis laid on order, unity and obedience; but both of them implied substantial criticisms of the society and politics of early Tudor England. The vision they presented was richly reformist. Even Starkey's *Dialogue*, its aristocratic politics notwithstanding, was full of criticisms and suggestions about economic matters – education, trade, consumption, employment, building, enclosure, legal practices, the quality of the clergy.[67] But Starkey's powerful critique of traditional monarchy and other features of the Tudor world, all in the name of commonwealth, was to be far less evident in the humanist writing that followed the Reformation, including Starkey's own.

It has been suggested that the Henrician reformation of the 1530s took away much of the reforming bite of early Tudor humanism.[68] Thomas Cromwell, the royal minister who dominated the 1530s, certainly made use of humanist intellectuals (Starkey included) to write in defence of government policy, but his patronage deflected their interest away from social and political reform – away, even, from any very full conception of the civil life of a commonwealth – toward the themes of royal supremacy, sovereign authority and obedience. More broadly, it might be argued, two forces undermined the early Tudor commonwealth ideal. Protestantism, with its simple division of people into the elect and the reprobate, encouraged not social reform but a draconian disciplinarian and authoritarian response to social problems. The poor were to be blamed for their own poverty. Secondly, the nature of humanism itself changed. Beginning with Elyot's *Book Named the Governor* (1531) there developed a new 'court humanism'. This 'deprived [the commonwealth ideal] of its radical thrust', making it instead 'monarchical, centralized, authoritarian, hierarchical'. In short:

> The ideal of the commonwealth which had developed under the influence of Christian humanism in the opening decades of the century as a radical critique of the Tudor polity was transformed in mid-century, through the influence of protestantism and court humanism, into the Tudor polity's ideological bulwark.

How adequate is this verdict on the fate of the early Tudor commonwealth ideal? There is certainly much evidence to support it. The propaganda works written by humanist scholars for Cromwell in the later 1530s, for example, showed a very muted version of the commonwealth ideal, as we shall discover in the next chapter. Witness the definition of a commonwealth employed in Richard Morison's *Remedy for Sedition*. 'A commonwealth is . . . nothing else but a certain number of cities, towns, shires, that all agree upon one law and one head, united and knit together by the observation of the laws.'[69] The term has been denuded of all its idealistic and critical potential, while the stress on order and obedience has become predominant. Order, too, predominated in the statement that a commonwealth is 'worthy his name when everyone is content with his degree, glad to do that that he may lawfully do, gladder to do that which he seeth shall be for the quietness of the realm'.[70] It might almost be said that for Morison the active and civil life consisted in obeying with unusual alacrity. A commonwealth required 'those that are of the worser sort to be content that the wiser rule and govern them',[71] thus putting the conventional humanist view that the wise should rule into a form that emphasised the subordination of the 'worser sort'.

Nonetheless there is a risk of overemphasising the contrasts. Among earlier commonwealth treatises, Edmund Dudley's places the root of his tree of commonwealth in the king, who chooses the virtuous men that will help to rule it.[72] This is little different from Morison's position, suggesting that it may be fairer to see the conservative dimension of commonwealth language as constantly present – the term as essentially contestible – rather than a development of the period from 1530 to 1560. More important questions, however, surround the account described above of the fate of the commonwealth ideal. 'Commonwealth' remained powerfully connected with ideals of social justice in the reign of Edward VI, and if we look beyond the elite to the politics of popular rebellion, it helped inspire or legitimate rebellion in 1549.[73] As we shall see in the next chapter, protestant preachers at the high point of the English Reformation, the period before Edward's death in 1553, themselves gave eloquent expression to ideals of fairness and justice, ideals of social reform, and did so invoking visions of a commonwealth understood as a properly Christian (protestant) society, while even earlier radical political ideas were enunciated by a few protestants.[74] Recent work has also demonstrated that key civic humanist themes – the superiority of *negotium* to *otium*, the ideal of active citizenship, virtue as the source of true nobility, the superiority of mixed government, the importance of civil education – retained a constant presence in English political writing through the late sixteenth and early seventeenth centuries. They did not simply fade away.[75] But in one respect Bradshaw poses a challenge that those recent scholars who have examined the civic humanist and republican elements of Elizabethan and early Stuart political culture have not fully met. They have tended to assume or to suggest (and not always with explicit argument) that civic humanism, if it existed, was likely to do so in alliance with the subversive, critical and anti-monarchical dimensions of political thought, eliding it into 'republicanism'. This is not obviously so. We need to remain alert to the sense in which civic humanism could also serve – in Bradshaw's words – as 'the Tudor [–Stuart] polity's ideological bulwark'. Either way, we must remain alert to the continuities that stretched forward from pre-Reformation humanism; we must remain careful not to tear Maitland's seamless web.

Part I Political Thought and Confessional Polities, 1530–1640

Part 1   Political Thought and Confessional Politics 1620–1640

1 Royal Supremacy and the Obedience of Subjects: the Political Thought of the English Reformation, 1530–53

The Reformation focused attention on a very different set of problems from those that had occupied early humanists. It is not that an interest in 'commonwealth' issues disappeared, and many protestant writers, especially from the 1550s onwards, were interested, in their own fashion, in the same question that Thomas More had enigmatically considered – what is the best state of a commonwealth? But in the immediate aftermath of the Reformation other matters were more pressing. The Scottish case will be considered in the next chapter; here we will consider the ways in which the English Reformation compelled attention to defending the royal supremacy, and its claims on the obedience of subjects. By the end of Henry VIII's reign ambiguities had become apparent in the notion of the royal supremacy itself, while in the brief reign of Edward VI, English evangelicals developed the theme of commonwealth into a new protestant vision of the Godly society.

The Henrician Reformation and the Royal Supremacy

In 1534 Henry VIII was recognised by statute to be supreme head of the English church (26 Hen. VIII, c. 1); two years later the situation was tidied up with an Act abolishing the authority of the bishop of Rome in England (28 Hen. VIII, c. 10).[1]

The arguments that underlay the king's assumption of the supreme headship over the church were best and most famously expressed in the preamble to the 1533 Act of Appeals (24 Hen. VIII, c. 12):

Where by divers sundry old authentic histories and chronicles it is manifestly declared and expressed that this realm of England is an empire, and so hath been accepted in the world, governed by one supreme head and king having the dignity and royal estate of the imperial crown of the same, unto whom a body politic, compact of all sorts and degrees of people divided in terms and by names of spirituality and temporalty, be bounden and owe to bear next to God a natural and humble obedience; he being also institute and furnished by the goodness and sufferance of Almighty God with plenary, whole and entire power. . . .[2]

One historian has commented that it is in the consequences of these words uttered and acts made in the name of Henry VIII 'that we find the enduring problematics of English political thought for the next three centuries'. They established the conception of England as an autonomous sovereign state. That sovereignty was 'to be defended and debated through civil wars, dissolutions and revolutions to the end of the English *ancien régime*'.[3] The Henrician reformation – a process as much jurisdictional as theological – brought to the forefront concepts and problems that were very different from those discussed by the earlier Tudor humanists. They would remain central to English political debates and conflicts throughout the period covered by this book.

The ideas that culminated in Henry VIII's taking of the headship in 1534 originated in response to the divorce crisis as early as 1530. Frustrated by the inability of various steps designed to end the king's marriage to Catherine of Aragon, his advisers began to look at a solution to the problem that would not require the pope's approval. Some of these advisers may well have cared considerably less about the divorce and more about religious and ecclesiastical reform, but it was the divorce crisis and the king's growing involvement with Anne Boleyn (and her eventual pregnancy) that gave them leverage over Henry.[4] At the end of the 1520s Henry had a team of scholars – Edward Foxe, Thomas Cranmer, Edward Lee and Nicholas de Burgo – working on the tactics required to obtain his divorce. Two of them, Foxe and Cranmer, assembled in 1530 a manuscript compendium of historical materials that could provide the basis for arguments supporting Henry's claims to a divorce. It was shown to the king, who annotated it, in September 1530. The collection, which is known as the *Collectanea satis copiosa* ('adequately abundant collections'), widened considerably the approach being pursued.[5] The early strategy of the scholars was summed up in the *Gravissimae atque exactissimae illustrissimarum totius Italiae et Gallicae Academiarum censurae* (1531), translated into English as *The determinations of the moste famous and moost excellent uniuersities of Italy and Fraunce, that it is so unlefull for a man to marie his brothers wife, that the pope have no power to dispence therwith* (1531).[6] These works concentrated on the rights and wrongs of the proposed divorce, and the pope's authority in this particular matter. But the materials assembled in the *Collectanea* related to much more fundamental questions about the relationship between spiritual and temporal authority, though as

Bernard points out, the anti-papal implications of Henry's position were inherent from the start.[7] The precedents and authorities collected in the *Collectanea* served as the basis for the measures of 1533–4, and for a propaganda campaign elevating the king's authority within the church which extended throughout much of the 1530s.[8] The new phase continued the search for a solution to the divorce crisis that would not be dependent on papal authority; but it did so by advancing the view that the English church was an autonomous component of the universal Catholic church, and existed under the spiritual headship of an imperial monarch. *English Church Autonomous*

Where did the trains of thought emerging from the *Collectanea* came from? An answer commonly given is that they represented the English reception of a *Lutheran* theory of the divine right of kings.[9] The best known English work presenting a Lutheran view of kingship to an English audience was William Tyndale's *Obedience of a Christian Man* (1528), though the ideas can also be found in other works, especially Robert Barnes's *Supplication unto the Most Gracious King Henry VIII* (1534). The latter cleared the space for a view of temporal and spiritual authority as operating in parallel, each of divine right and supreme within its given sphere; but neither having any authority to interfere with the proper operation of the other. Thus, the temporal power, which 'God has committed ... to kings, dukes, earls, lords, barons, judges, mayors, sheriffs, and to all other ministers under them', is to be used only to 'regulate the commonwealth with all the worldly affairs pertaining to it'. Obedience to the temporal power was a religious duty, required 'not only (as Paul says) for avoiding punishment, but also for conscience' sake, for this is the will of God'. This implied even a duty not actively to resist tyrannical or unGodly rulers. Faced with a command contrary to right and law 'our charity must suffer it'. But there was an exception – 'provided it is not repugnant to the gospel or destructive of faith'. The view that temporal and spiritual power operated in distinct parallel spheres required the maintenance of strict boundaries between those spheres. While the spiritual authority had no law-making powers, equally the temporal could not act against God's word. In general cases of injustice, 'you may resist with a good conscience, if you can do so through reasonable means, without sedition, insurrection, or disruption of the peace ... but in no case may you resist with sword or hand, but you must obey'.[10] But even the religious duty to obey God before man was regulated by the duty to maintain civil order. So in the extreme case of 'a prince that condemns God's Word', Barnes still advised that subjects should pray and try to persuade the king to behave differently. But, if unsuccessful, 'they shall keep their Testament with all other ordinances of Christ and, if they

Barnes → Obedience

cannot flee, let the king exercise his tyranny. Under no circumstances shall they withstand him with violence but suffer patiently all the tyranny that he imposes on them both in their bodies and in their property.' Vengeance must be left to God; but, equally, no one should 'deny Christ's truth nor forsake it before the ruler'. Between a rock and a hard place lay the site of martyrdom. Barnes scorned the alternative solution to this situation, which he attributed to the bishops, of deposing the king.[11]

There do seem to be some obvious lines of connection between these Lutheran ideas and the arguments of Henry VIII's publicists in the 1530s. This will become clearer as we consider those writings produced in the wake of the Act of Supremacy. There was a shared stress on the importance of temporal order, on the doctrine of passive obedience in the face of tyranny, and on divine right kingship; a shared concern to ensure that the clergy present no threat to temporal authority in its own sphere. In particular, Henrician propagandists adopted a distinctively Lutheran and protestant emphasis on the connections between the word of God and obedience to the king. As recently emphasised, the defence of the royal supremacy was 'not just couched in terms of jurisdiction', but 'harnessed the rhetoric of Erasmian humanists . . . [and] of protestant reformers'.[12] This public defence, however, came *after* 1534 rather than before; and it does not seem that Lutheran doctrines were essential to the intellectual developments that actually brought about the royal supremacy.[13] There was a coherence to the Henrician position, but it was not a coherence that can be captured by identifying it with either Protestant or Catholic arguments.[14] Furthermore, there are a number of crucial objections to seeing the political teaching of the Henrician Reformation simply as part of the Lutheran diaspora. Firstly, the connection rests entirely on the similarity of ideas and not on the demonstrable use by Henrician propagandists of Lutheran sources. But, secondly, that similarity is not as great as may at first appear.[15] The Henrician publicists were, for a start, mostly Catholic rather than Lutheran in their theology. While the Lutherans believed in a true invisible church of the faithful, which was imperfectly present in those visible churches in which the faith was correctly preached, the Henrician writers remained committed to an idea of the visible Catholic church, of which the English church was a particular and autonomous part. Furthermore, it is not at all obvious that the Henrician imperial kingship and royal supremacy matched at all closely the strict separation of temporal and spiritual spheres advanced by the Lutherans. The major intellectual source for Henrician views of the church seems to have been late medieval conciliar theory rather than Lutheranism.[16] This leads to a third and final

point. Historians' recovery of the crucial importance of the *Collectanea*
seems to undermine the Lutheran interpretation and to strengthen
that view which sees developments of the 1530s as rooted in longer-
term trends in English legal and ecclesiastical thinking. This is not to
deny any broader European intellectual influence, but rather to
suggest that such influence was exerted by pre-Lutheran medieval
sources. The precedents and arguments collected in the *Collectanea*
would appear to point us both to conciliar theory, and to two other
developments. First, there was the important medieval assertion that
kings were emperors in their own realm (*rex in regno suo est imperator*).
The claim to an imperial crown, which Henry VIII made from his
coronation ceremony onwards, could be understood to be a claim to
possess the same rights over the church as the late Roman emperors.
In the late medieval context, there was nothing unusual about a king
mounting such a claim. It was a device ready to hand when needed in
the 1530s.[17] A second development underpinning the ideas of the
1530s was the growing assertion from before 1485 of the supremacy of
English law over canon law.[18] In this view, all the canon law of the
church was permitted a place in the realm only under the over-arching
control and direction of English common law. Any conflict between
canon and common law ought to be settled in favour of the latter,
which was as much an instantiation of the divinely ordained principles
of nature and equity as any law of the church.[19] Viewed as a continuation of this approach, the royal supremacy was a claim that the church,
except in so far as it exercised a purely spiritual authority in Christ's
name, was within the *imperium* or empire of the king in much the same
way that all other bodies in the realm were. However, as we shall see
later, this tradition had a marked tendency to view the imperial authority of the English monarch as something exercised by due process
through the law. In such a view the highest authority in church and
state was the king-in-parliament, not the king alone. This common-law
approach, then, resulted in the view that the royal supremacy was a
parliamentary supremacy, not a personal one, and it operated within
the same legal restrictions as those governing the king's exercise of his
temporal *imperium*.

This new thinking, fashioned from the material of the past that had
been collected, did not lead immediately to the construction in
published writings of a theory of imperial royal supremacy; it is
nonetheless true that arguments tending to such a conclusion can be
found as early as 1530–1, in the *Collectanea*, and hints of it are evident
in pamphlets of the early 1530s.[20] These include *The Glasse of the Truthe*
(1532), which urged English ecclesiastical authorities to reject 'the
Pope's law' and to acknowledge that 'by God's law, they be bound to

the obedience of their prince, and to seek also the quietation and peaceableness of this realm, which ought to be regarded more than any man's law . . .'.[21] The *Articles Devisid by the Holle Consent of the Kynges Most Honourable Counsayle* was a simple and blunt statement of the official doctrine lying behind the events of 1533. This too was innocent of any doctrine of royal supremacy, but argued from the supposition that the church was under the authority not of the pope but of the General Council, and from a theory of divine right kingship. The king was subject to the spiritual authority of the church in England, which was largely autonomous within a Catholic church subject to the supreme authority of a general council. Within his realm, the king faced no rival political or coercive authority; still less was he subject to any authority (including spiritual) from outside his realm.

The key works, though, were the pamphlets in defence of Henry VIII's imperial authority and the royal supremacy published from 1534 on. The 'first wave' consisted of three works: Richard Sampson's *Oratio qua Docet Anglos Regiae Dignitati ut Obediant* (oration teaching the English obedience to the kingly dignity – 1534),[22] Edward Foxe's *De Vera Differentia Regiae Potestatis et Ecclesiasticae* (on the true difference between regal and ecclesiastical power – 1534);[23] and Stephen Gardiner's *De Vera Obedientia, Oratio* (oration on true obedience – 1535).[24]

Sampson's was the simplest and shortest of these works, little more than a set of bald assertions. His universal Catholic church was one in which the pope had no power *extra provinciam*. In England he possessed no more power than the archbishop of Canterbury had in Rome.[25] The king, not the bishop of Rome, was the vicar of God.[26] Most of the work was given over to an attack on papal primacy, and an examination of the scriptural and patristic authorities relating to it. But the conclusion was simple. 'The word of God is to obey the king, not the bishop of Rome.'[27] The king's authority was of God; that claimed by the bishop of Rome was not. The changes introduced in England, including the recognition of Henry's headship in the church, were the commands of God, because they were the commands of the king, God's minister on earth, to whom supreme power had been given by God's word.[28]

What Sampson's defence did not provide was any sense of what exactly the nature of Henry's royal supremacy was. Foxe's *De Vera Differentia* was a little – but not much – more forthcoming. The work was very much a digest of the *Collectanea*, of which Foxe had been the chief compiler. It assembled the chief authorities for the royal supremacy – scripture, especially the Old Testament, patristic writings, and English historical precedents – and presented them with minimal elaboration.

Nonetheless, the outlines of an argument are clear enough. The universal church acted through agencies created by its members, in particular through a general council.[29] It did not act through the bishop of Rome. Christ certainly gave to the apostle Peter the keys of the kingdom of heaven, and on him built his church (Matthew 16.18–19). But St Peter here represented the universal Catholic church, not the pope.[30] The superiority of bishops to other priests came 'more of custome than by any ordinaunce by the lawe of god'. '[A] prest and a Byshop . . . be al one' and both were in any case 'subjecte unto him that is made the hed governeoure'.[31] Bishops and priests alike had from God authority but not dominion (or empire).[32] That is, they all had an essentially equal spiritual authority, but no political or temporal authority. Each province of the church was autonomous in jurisdiction.[33] The church and its priests had no power of coaction or compulsion. They could exercise spiritual authority only on those willing to be converted and to submit themselves to it. By contrast, a king's power 'maketh them [subjects] obediente and subjecte with feare or drede', and was exercised over men whether they were willingly subject to it or not.[34] A priest had authority 'to admonishe, to exhorte, to comforte, to desire, to teche, to preche, to mynyster sacramentes, charytablye to rebuke, to blame or finde faute with'; only kings could make laws binding in conscience and impose temporal punishments.[35] The papacy, of course, had claimed to be the source under God of the temporal authority of kings, and by claiming also the right to take that authority away from kings when they thought it fit to do so, '[T]hey take upon them dominion of al thinges which by ryght can take dominion of nothinge.'[36] Such dominion belonged by divine right only to kings,[37] and it included a sphere of authority in spiritual matters. Like the Christian emperors Constantine and Justinian, imperial monarchs 'dydde take upon them the cure and busines that they dyd make ordinaunce to the people of the ordering & reserving of Sacramentes & spirituall thinges'. More specifically, they could invest bishops with authority, and make laws concerning such spiritual matters as 'fornycacion, adultery, baptycm, baudry, [and] heresy'.[38] In short, the church in England operated under the imperial and autonomous jurisdiction and regulation of the king as supreme head, and its priests exercised a spiritual authority, through the sacraments and through their powers of persuasion, that was common to the whole of the Catholic church. Foxe provided limited guidance on the boundary between the king's authority and that of the church. How far did the king's authority in spiritual matters extend?

For an answer we might turn to the most intellectually distinguished of the first-wave defences of the royal supremacy, Gardiner's *De Vera Obedientia*.[39] Gardiner began with a theology of obedience. 'I thinke /

that to obeye truly / is nothing elles / but to obey unto the truthe. And God is *the* truthe . . . '.[40] Faith itself required obedience, because obedience was an acknowledgement of God's will, which was in turn the core of faith in God. The purpose of this obedience was therefore for man to 'be drawne . . . to atteyne that truthe' found in Christ.[41] This fundamental precept quickly became linked to civil obedience: the requirement 'to obey both him [God] and al them / whom God commaundeth him to obey for his sake'.[42] So that men could display their obedience more readily, God 'substituted men . . . as his vicegerentes', and to them he did 'require obedience / which we must doo unto them with no lesse frute / for Goddes sake / than we shoulde doo it . . . immediatly unto God him selfe'. This applied above all to princes, 'representours of his Image unto men', who 'excelle amonge all other humayne creatures';[43] it also applied to husbands and masters. But the king was the highest human authority, and always to be obeyed when his commands conflicted with those of any other human authority.

Gardiner next considered whether the divinely instituted authority of kings extended also over religious matters. Did the recognition by parliamentary consent of the king's supreme headship of the church conform to God's law?[44] There was in this recognition, Gardiner answered, 'no newely invented matter' but simply a clearer expression of 'the power perteinyng to a prince / by Goddes law'. The act of parliament was necessary because of the prevalence of false ideas about papal supremacy.[45] No one doubted that the king was head of the realm of England and thus ruler of all his subjects 'of what condicion so ever they be / whether the[y] be Jewes / Barbarianes / Saracenes / Turkes or Christianes'. But the church in England was simply the congregation of those subjects who were Christian and thus part of the broader 'communion of christen people'. In the same way there was a church of France, of Spain, and so on, each with their own supreme head on earth.[46] Thus those who asserted that the king was head of the realm of England but not head of the church of England simply claimed 'that the kinge is the heade of the unfaithfull / and not of the faithfull'.[47] But this was absurd. Even infidel kings represented the image of God on earth; their authority did not diminish when they became Christian.

Gardiner's argument had some obvious weaknesses. It might be argued, he recognised, that no one denied that kings should be obeyed; yet, still it might be thought that there were limits to the obedience that could be demanded. The reply was simple: those passages of scripture in which God's command of obedience to kings was revealed were all innocent of any suggestion of limitation (Romans 13.1–5; 1

Peter 2.13–17; Matthew 22.17).[48] Obedience must be 'not questioning nor inquiring'. If kings asked too much, then God would one day judge them.[49] Even the fact that God committed the government of the church 'to the apostles / and to those that succede in their rowmes' did not diminish the royal supremacy in the church. One needed to distinguish 'preeminence' from that spiritual government that consisted in 'teaching / and the ministerie of the sacramentes'. The former was the king's authority, the latter the authority of priests. But this did not mean that kings had purely temporal and not spiritual authority, for Christian kings existed to lead their people to truth, with a duty to ensure that they led good lives. This gave kings jurisdiction over the moral behaviour of all of their subjects, lay and clerical.[50] Old Testament examples showed that 'a kinge ordayned of God . . . shoulde take charge of spiritual and eternall affaires / before and rather than corporal maters / and thinges that shall perishe in time'.[51] They were required to see that their subjects formed 'a worthye and an acceptable people unto the lorde'.[52] The emperor Justinian, indeed, had made laws 'concerning the glorious Trinitie / and the catholike faith / of Bishoppes / of men of the clergie / of heretiques / and others'.[53] Gardiner especially stressed the imperial authority to decide what constituted heresy, 'the chief and principall poynt of office'.[54]

Gardiner completed his argument with a consideration of the authority of the bishop of Rome. He denied that kings had ever accepted that the pope was God's vicar on earth and head of the universal church.[55] Like all other bishops, the bishop of Rome had from God only the authority 'to fede and bring up the people / within their dioceses committed to their spirttual [*sic*] charge / with the ministracion of the worde of God / and of his sacramentes'.[56] Old Testament examples showed that 'the power of Princes / . . . [was] above even the highest priestes of all'.[57] By the New Testament, priests were commanded

> not to beare rule / but to be in subjeccion / not to commaunde princes / but to . . . be under their power and commaundement / not only whan they commaunde thinges indifferent / . . . but also whan they commaunde thinges not indifferent / so they be not wicked. . . .[58]

Not even Christ's grant of the power of the keys to St Peter was an adequate basis for papal primacy, for it implied only Christ's recognition that Peter was the best of his apostles, not a grant to him of any supremacy in authority.[59] Whatever spiritual authority Christ may have granted to priests, it did not entitle even the best of them to deny their subjection to the king.[60] The bishop of Rome was without any authority in England, where the head of the church was the king.[61]

Sampson, Foxe and Gardiner presented accounts of the royal supremacy that were very similar. Their arguments rested on two planks, the divine right of kings, and a distinction between the universal Catholic (but not papal) church and particular churches (such as the English). There was one interesting difference among them: Gardiner alone made almost nothing of conciliar authority in the universal church, being content simply to leave it under the headship of Christ. In this he turned out to be prophetic of future trends.[62] In 1536 the pope called the council of Mantua, an act which threatened to call the English bluff. If they wanted to appeal Henry's matrimonial dispute to a general council, here was their chance. In response, English polemicists denied even general councils any authority in ecclesiastical matters over the king; and thus left the universal church with no authority whatsoever over the particular churches of which it consisted. A good example of this sort of argument is to be found in an anonymous piece of government propaganda from 1538. In the early church the apostles and their successors were 'the hyghe rulers in all the sayd concylles'; but following the conversion of kings, this authority became theirs.[63] General councils had authority to declare the faith of the universal church and to determine what was in accord with scripture (though no authority at all to encroach on the jurisdiction, civil and ecclesiastical, of kings); the authority coercively to enforce their declarations belonged to princes.[64] Thus, whatever a council might declare, 'the correction and refourmation . . . they muste commytte to kynges in every countreye, and to theyr lawes'.[65] Furthermore, non-essential matters, such as the determination of religious ceremonies and vestments, not being commanded by scripture, were within the king's jurisdiction, not that of a general council.[66] The anonymous author was – like all of the Henrician propagandists – an adamant critic of claims to papal primacy; but he extended his attack on the papacy to include a rejection of their authority to call a general council. Such authority now resided only in those who had ecclesiastical jurisdiction, that is, kings and princes, who must 'charitably agree' amongst themselves in order to do so.[67] Others went even further, most notably Thomas Starkey in his *Exhortation* of 1536:

> al suche thinges as be decreed by princely authoritie, to goddis worde nothynge contrarye, we are by goddis worde bound, after they be receyved and stablyshed: to the whiche we must gladdely be obedient with humilitie, ye though they be contrary to suche thynges, as be propowned by generall counsell and assemble . . . [because a]

counsell generall and universall assemble of all chrysten nations, be
a thynge not necessary to the conservation of Christes fayth and
doctrine. . . . [68]

Kings were the authority that Christians were bound to obey, and so
'such thinges as be propouned by general counsell & assemble, be of
none authoritie among the people in any countrey, tyl they be
confirmed by princely power and common counsell'.[69]

This position on general councils came to be accepted as authoritative for the Church of England as founded in Elizabeth's reign.[70] The
official Henrician statements of ecclesiology were silent on the subject,
but their implications were clear enough. *The Institution of a Christian
Man*, usually known as the *Bishops' Book* (1537), though never authorised by the king, was an authoritative statement of doctrine produced
by a committee of bishops and clergy. Its commentary on the ninth
article of the Apostle's Creed ('I believe that there is one holy and
catholic universal church') provided a summary of the ecclesiology
underlying the royal supremacy. It distinguished the universal church
from the particular churches. The former, under the headship of
Christ, had 'a mere spiritual unity'. The particular churches, of which
the church of Rome was but one, were all autonomous, 'equal in power
and dignity', and all with different 'outward rites, ceremonies, traditions, and ordinances, as be instituted by their governors, and received
and approved among them'.[71] There was little room here for a general
council, and even less in the authorised revision of the *Bishops' Book*,
issued in 1543 as *A Necessary Doctrine and Erudition for Any Christian Man*,
but usually known as the *King's Book*. It bluntly stated that the unity of
the universal church was reflected in no authority but that of Christ.
There was no human authority or (by implication) institution above
the governors of particular churches. Thus,

> every Christian man ought to honour, give credence, and to follow
> the particular church of that region so ordered (as afore) wherein he
> is born or inhabiteth. And as all Christian people, as well spiritual as
> temporal, be bound to believe, honour, and obey our saviour Jesus
> Christ, the only Head of the universal church, so likewise they be, by
> his commandment, bound to honour and obey, next unto himself,
> Christian kings and princes, which be the head governors under him
> in the particular churches. . . . [72]

The only space left for general councils was to function with the
consent of the kings who governed the particular churches of
Christendom.

So what exactly was the scope claimed by Henry VIII's publicists for his royal supremacy? The general situation was clear from the legislation of the 1530s, and from the official formularies of faith that we have just encountered.[73] Following the medieval canonists, a distinction was drawn between two different aspects of ecclesiastical authority, a *potestas ordinis* (power of order) and a *potestas jurisdictionis* (power of jurisdiction). The former consisted of the truly sacramental authority of the church, and could be exercised only by a priest. The latter included the power to excommunicate, to reject men proposed to have the cure of souls in a particular place by lay patrons, and to regulate the ceremonies, rites and ornaments used in divine service.[74] Much of the manner in which this *potestas jurisdictionis* was employed, however, as well as certain other powers of jurisdiction, were derived from human law, and could be called back by kings into their own hands.[75] Nonetheless, some powers of jurisdiction (most notably the power to excommunicate) could only be exercised by a priest. On the other hand, others, including the power to determine doctrine and decide cases of heresy, could, as we have seen in several writers, be claimed for the king. Thus the king was granted what canonists called the *potestas jurisdictionis in foro externo* or *jurisdictio fori* (power of jurisdiction in external matters – including authority over heresy and doctrine, as well as over public morality and the regulation of matters concerning religious worship that were left undetermined by scripture), but not the *potestas jurisdictionis in foro interno* or *jurisdictio poli* (power of jurisdiction over conscience – including the power to excommunicate, to hear confession, and to impose penance).[76] This, it might be added, was a Catholic rather than a Lutheran or protestant position, in that the latter effectively denied that there was such a thing as *potestas jurisdictionis* at all. The contrast is readily illustrated. Whereas the Henrician position gave the prince authority to decide cases of heresy, the Lutheran denied it to him. Only priests had authority to deal with heresy, and as they lacked any worldly authority, they could deal with it only by spiritual means.[77] The Henrician royal supremacy over the English church-state was not a Lutheran idea, whatever elements it may have drawn from Lutheran sources.

Was there *any* effort made to claim for Henry VIII the right to exercise the genuinely sacramental authority of the church, the *potestas ordinis*?[78] On the whole it seems there was not. The semi-official statement denied that it was any part of the royal office 'to preach and teach, to administer the sacraments, to absoyle, to excommunicate'.[79] No one, for example, suggested that the supreme head of the church could administer by right of office the sacrament of the eucharist. But on one matter, the ordination and consecration of priests and bishops, indubitably an aspect of the *potestas ordinis*, there is some doubt. The example often cited of an attempt to claim such authority for the king is that of Edward Foxe; but the evidence is ambiguous.[80] Perhaps the most strikingly elevated claim for Henry VIII's ecclesiastical authority came from no less a figure than Archbishop Cranmer. In 1540 a number of questions were put to the bishops about the sacraments. The most interesting responses again related to the sacrament of Orders.[81] In response to the question 'Whether the apostles lacking a higher power, as in not having a christian king among them, made bishops by that necessity, or by authority given them by God?', he broke through the careful distinctions that we have found in others.

All christian princes have committed unto them immediately of God the whole cure of all their subjects, as well concerning the administration of God's word for the cure of souls, as concerning the ministration of things political and civil governance. And in both these ministrations they must have sundry ministers under them, to supply that which is appointed to their several offices.[82]

That came close to suggesting that the clergy were nothing more than ministers of the king, from whom they derived all the power and authority that they exercised. Cranmer backed away slightly from the full force of this opening as he added more detail, and suggested only that the clergy were 'appointed, assigned, and elected in every place, by the laws and orders of kings and princes'. None of the three verbs implies the conferral of *potestas ordinis*. But caution: in the early church, because there was no Christian magistrate, congregations were forced to appoint clergy by 'uniform consent', based often on the advice of those 'replete with the Spirit of God'.[83] There was nothing in scripture to show that only bishops could make a priest. Indeed, '[s]o may princes and governors also, and that by the authority of God committed to them', just as the people as a whole had appointed clergy in the early church. This did not mean that kings could consecrate priests – consecration was not anyway a necessary part of their appointment. Nonetheless, 'christian princes, and other laymen unconsecrate' may, especially where they find themselves amongst infidels with no consecrated bishops at hand, 'make and constitute priests'.[84] There may in all of this have lurked a potential for the development of a theory of sacramental kingship; but it was to remain an untapped potential.

'Not persued

An Ambiguous Legacy

The central place given to a theory of the divine right of kings and to an anti-papal royal supremacy in the 1530s provided a legacy that was to be squabbled over for the rest of the period covered by this book. The squabbling was particularly troublesome because it resulted in a set of ambiguities that resided at the very core of the English church-state – ambiguity that could be exploited by conformists, as well as exposed by critics. Among those ambiguities, two were crucial. First: was the royal supremacy vested in the king alone or in the institution of king-in-parliament? Second: what did the royal supremacy imply about the relationships between church and state, or between religion and politics? Both of these questions remained contentious through to the revolutions of the following century, and beyond.

King and parliament

Ambiguity was built into the very heart of the Henrician reformation. The legislation of 1533–4 did not confer imperial authority on the king; it merely recognised that by God's law such authority was invested in the king. Parliament did not create or authorise the royal supremacy. Nonetheless, it can be argued that in using parliament to reform the church, Henry VIII and Thomas Cromwell, willy nilly, established the ideas of parliamentary omnicompetence and parliamentary sovereignty, which became obviously triumphant by the reign of Elizabeth.[85] They certainly did the former. That parliament was seen as competent to legislate on all matters after the 1530s cannot be doubted. What is less certain is whether the king was obliged to legislate only through parliament on all considerable matters of church and state. In particular, was he obliged to regulate the church through parliament? According to one authority, the ambiguity in this area 'was not really cleared up until after the Glorious Revolution'.[86]

There is little sign that the initial defenders of the royal supremacy – Sampson, Foxe and Gardiner – viewed it as a parliamentary supremacy. Ecclesiastical jurisdiction was, for them, invested in the person of the king by God's law. Because this jurisdiction was in fact, though not in theory, a new thing, there was no defined institutional machinery for its exercise. This contrasted with the king's temporal authority, which was in practice limited by the apparatus through which it was exerted. Perhaps the neatest indication of the personal nature of the royal supremacy was the fact that it very quickly came to be delegated to Thomas Cromwell as Vicegerent in Spirituals – a personal power of the king's thus freely created the means of its own exercise.[87] None of this should suggest that the early publicists were theorists of arbitrary monarchy, if we mean by that term a monarchy legitimately able to make and break laws or impose taxes at will. It may be that the raw materials of such a theory existed. The *Collectanea Satis Copiosa*, for example, intriguingly converted a famous maxim of the thirteenth-century legist Bracton from the claim that the king was 'sub Deo et sub lege, quia lex facit regem' [beneath God and the law, for the law makes the king] to 'sub Deo. Non sub lege, quia Rex legem facit' [beneath God but not the law, for the king makes the law].[88] But when the chief apologist for a 'personal' royal supremacy was questioned by Thomas Cromwell, he denied any suggestion that he supported arbitrary monarchy. Cromwell, whose work for the king in the 1530s was largely conducted by employing the legislative authority of king-in-parliament, was perhaps teasing Gardiner for the king's entertainment, though this was not quite how Gardiner recalled the matter. Gardiner recounted the story in a letter of 1547 to Protector Somerset, in which he gave his opinion about 'whether the King may commaund against an act of Parliament'. The 1539 Act of Proclamations (later wrongly believed to have been an attempt to make the king's authority to legislate through proclamations the equal of parliament's legislative capacity) was, said Gardiner, actually intended to authorise nothing 'made contrary to an act of Parliament or Common Law'. However:

> The Lord Cromwell had once put in the Kinges our late sovereigne lordes head to take upon him to have his will and pleasure regarded for a lawe; for that, he sayd, was to be a very kinge. And therupon I was called for at Hampton Court. And as the Lord Cromwell was very stout, 'Come on my Lord of Winchester,' quod he (for that conceat he had, what so ever he talked with me, he knewe ever as much as I, Greke or Laten and all), 'Aunswer the King here,' quod he, 'but speake plainly and direccly, and shrink not, man! Is not that,' quod he, 'that pleaseth the Kinge, a lawe? Have ye not ther in the Civill Lawe,' quod he, '*quod principi placuit*, and so fourth?' quod he, 'I have somewhat forgotten it now'. I stode still and woundered in my mind to what conclusion this should tend. The King sawe me musing, and with ernest gentelnes sayd, 'Aunswere him whether it be so or no'. I would not aunswere my Lord Cromwell, but delivered my speache to the King, and tolde him I had red in dede of kings that had there will alwayes receaved for a lawe, but, I tolde him, the forme of his reigne, to make the lawes his wil, was more sure and quiet. 'And by thys forme of goverment ye be established,' quod I, 'and it is agreable with the nature of your people. If ye begin a new maner of policye,

how it will frame, no man can tell; and how this frameth ye can tell;
and [I] would never advise your Grace to leave a certeine for an
uncerteine'.[89]

The king's advisers might amuse themselves by discussing the exact
nature of his personal supremacy; but the increasing willingness of
common lawyers to argue that the law of the church was regulated by
the higher authority of the temporal law could lead to places that
neither Gardiner nor Cromwell wished to go. Well before the dramatic
events of 1533–4, Christopher St German had examined 'the power of
the parlyament concernynge the spiritualtie and the spiritual jurisdiction' in his *Newe Addicions* to *Doctor and Student* (1531),[90] but his thinking had developed further by the time he produced *An Answere to a
Letter* (1535),[91] purportedly a reply to a letter inquiring about his
opinion on the royal supremacy.[92] The reply began with a clear statement of the basics, of the sort to be found in the other Henrician publicists. Parliament in 1534 recognised the king's supremacy, but granted
him nothing new. The king had already possessed 'all such power over
his subjectes spirituall and temporall / as to a kynge belongeth by the
lawe of god'. After 1534 'he had the same power without alteration'.
The king's authority did *not* include 'any authority that our lorde gave
only to his apostels or disciples / in spirytuall ministratyon to the
people'. Any grant of authority to the king in such matters, even by
parliament and convocation, would be rendered void by God's law.[93] St
German of course accepted that 'parliament may nothinge do against
the lawe of god'.[94] However, the real problem was not the king's
encroachment on the church. The medieval church had deliberately
obscured the boundaries between its authority and the spiritual
authority of the king. It had claimed as exclusively spiritual functions
things that were within the king's jurisdiction. To avoid this encroachment, St German defined the king's authority negatively, by specifying
what was excluded from it: '[t]he consecration of the sacrament of the
auter [alter] / the makynge of absolucyons / the gyvyng of orders / &
the ministratyon that saynt Paul speke of ad Corin. iiii . . . wherby he
understode princypally the ministratyon of the sacramentes'. These
powers were reserved to priests and bishops, though if they were
'neglygente in doynge their ministration to the people / the kyng
might commaunde them to do it'.[95] Among the powers usurped by the
clergy had been jurisdiction over 'avoutrye [= adultery] / fornicacyon
/ symonye & usury', and the regulation of marriage, tithes and wills.[96]
   Soon, St German sounded more novel notes. Once the supreme
headship of the church was declared in statute 'it is nowe a lawe of the
realme / and must be judged accordynge to the groundes and rules of

the lawe of the realme'.[97] He applied this principle in discussing the interpretation of scripture. The basic rule laid down by St German for dealing with difficult questions of interpretation was that the advice of learned clergy should be sought.[98] However, some passages of scripture concerned the authority that was properly attributed to the church and the clergy, and priests could not be trusted to interpret these. They were interested parties.[99] So in the last resort the only safe principle was that when there were doubts about any scriptural text such that they became the occasion of dispute and conflict, 'that in all these cases / kynges and princes shal be judges / & have power to pacyfye all such unquyetnesse'.[100] St German went further. It was agreed, he said that the Catholic church expounded scripture. But the church did not consist just of the clergy; it included also 'emperours / kynges & princes / with their people', and so 'may the emperoure / kynges & princes *with their people* expounde it'.[101] This definition of the church meant, indeed, that neither the clergy alone nor kings alone could interpret scripture. Since the universal church could not be assembled to interpret scripture, it followed that:

> kynges & princes whom the people have chosen & agreed to be their rulers . . . and which have the whole voyces of the people / maye with theire counsell spirytuall & temporall make exposycyon of such scripture as is doubtfull.[102]

King-in-parliament, operating with the consent of the people, provided scriptural interpretation binding on the congregation of a particular church (but not on anyone else). God had thus provided that 'by obedyence to their princes', people's doubts about the meaning of scripture could be resolved.[103]

St German's analysis was reinforced in a passage referring to Sir John Fortescue's fifteenth-century description of the kingdom of England as a *dominium politicum et regale*.

> And here it is to be noted / that there be two maner of powers that kynges and princes have over theire subjectes: The one is called / Jus regale / that is to saye a kyngely governanunce: And he that hathe that power maye with his counsell make lawes to bynde his subjectes / and also make declaration of Sc[r]ypture for the good order of his subjectes / as nede shall requyre / for appeasyng of varyance. The other is called / Jus regale politicum / that is to saye a kynglye and a polytyke governaunce. And that is the most noble power that any prince hath over his subjectes / and he that ruleth by that power / maye make no Lawe to bynde his subjectes without their assent / but

by their assent he maye so that the lawes that he maketh be nat agaynste the lawe of God / nor the lawe of reason: And this power hathe the kynges grace in this Realme: where he by assente of his lordes spirytuall and temperall: and of his commons gathered togyther by his commaundement in his parlyamente maye make lawes ty bynde the people. And of those laws there nedeth no procla-mation / bicause they be made by all the people / for the parliament so gathered togyther / [the people][104] representeth the estate of al the people within this realme / that is to say of the whole catholyque churche therof. And why shuld nat the parlyament then whiche representeth the whole catholyke churche of englande expounde scrypture rather than the convocacyon whiche representeth onely the state of the clergy. . . . [105]

The position represented essentially a combination of the key Henrician idea of a particular church, coinciding with a secular realm, with a Fortescuean interpretation of the English polity as one both 'regal' and 'political'. There was in the Christian world no higher juris-diction than that of the princes who held supremacy in the particular churches. But in kingdoms like the English, that authority, in both its temporal and its ecclesiastical aspects, was exercised 'politically', with the consent of the realm given in parliament.

We should probably avoid over-interpreting the gap between St German and other writers. Though Henry VIII's publicists deployed a theory of the divine right of kings, and some of them seem to have seen the royal supremacy in the church operating in a personal rather than a parliamentary way, they were not necessarily advocates of kingship above the law.[106] Henry VIII himself admitted in 1542 'that we at no time stand so highly in our estate royal as in the time of Parliament'.[107] The competence of the early Tudor state enlarged enormously, and not just because of its increased control of the church.[108] Franchises in which the king's writ did not run were incorporated into the normal jurisdiction of the king's law (1536), as were the Principality and Marches of Wales (1536, 1543). Royal authority over Ireland was – at least in aspiration – extended when Henry became king (rather than lord, as hitherto) of Ireland in 1541. Attempts were made, too, to increase the economic and social functions of state authority, most obvi-ously in the steps slowly taken by statute to build a ramshackle system of poor relief. But all of this, remarkably, was done on a basis of enhanc-ing the authority of common law and parliament, and by these means enhancing the authority of the king. They were not justified by any theory of royal absolutism. But ambiguity fatally remained with regard to the proper mode for exercising the king's authority in the church.

Politics and religion

Pre-Reformation political assumptions had been built on the idea and (to a degree) the reality of religious uniformity. In the post-Reformation world, religious uniformity disappeared. As a result, the truism that obedience was owed to God before man became suddenly a time bomb ticking away at the heart of the body politic. The idea was not new; but its implications were now more immediately destabilising. The result of this in political thinking was a struggle between approaches to the ordering of the polity that could in many diverse ways be seen to pit the 'political' against the 'religious'. Broad positions developed. One combined a minimally-defined comprehensive view of the church with an emphasis on the overriding importance of maintaining political order. Its basic strategy was to avoid linking political obedience to confessional identity, and to construct theories of obedience to the state that could transcend religious diversity. Another tended to a more exclusive definition of the church (meaning not the whole realm but just the Godly), and it made secular authority into the handmaid of that church. In extreme cases it placed loyalty to the faith above loyalty to the church. It could result in the view that obedience to the state was conditional on its confessional identity. Much of the most explosive political writing of the period – Marian resistance theory, much of the thought of the Scottish Reformation, the radicalism of the English Revolution, much Covenanter thought – was of this sort. These were arguments for the priority of religious objectives over civil ones. They witness the explosive incursion into politics of religious principles, and sometimes even the denial of any real identity to a realm of politics. These ambiguities, too, fuelled future conflicts.

It could be argued that the capacity to conceptualise a realm of politics with its own autonomy and rules was a weapon that most readily served the purposes of kings trying to pacify the conflicts created in the aftermath of the Reformation. Civic humanism was arguably the conceptual framework that could most readily be used to defend the political realm, through its idea of the active life, which resulted in a theory of mixed government. For this reason civic humanist ideas could be co-opted by rulers, and were so co-opted throughout the sixteenth and seventeenth centuries. The process can be exaggerated. There were civic humanists who were resistance theorists (George Buchanan); there were others for whom any genuine *vita activa* was made impossible by the corrupt attitudes prevailing at the Elizabethan or early Stuart courts. After the Reformation, when More's search for a true commonwealth might be replaced by the search simply for peace and order in an ideologically divided world, civic humanism could be adapted to this new search.

These trends first became evident in the 1530s.[109] Thomas Cromwell used a number of humanist intellectuals as propagandists in the later 1530s, notably William Marshall, and the Paduan-educated duo Thomas Starkey and Richard Morison.[110] Marshall was significant primarily for his translation of Marsilius's *Defensor Pacis* (1324), which appeared in 1535 under the title *The Defence of Peace* as part of Thomas Cromwell's propaganda campaign. Marsilius's work was perhaps the most important medieval defence of the rights of temporal rulers against the pretensions of the papacy.[111] Many of Marsilius's arguments were well suited to employment in defence of the Henrician supremacy. He denied to the clergy any temporal jurisdiction and thus gave no toe-hold for any clerical claims to authority over princes, he denied the authority of the pope over the whole church, and he denied that there was any divinely ordained distinction between priests and bishops. All of these were key Henrician arguments. Marsilius based his arguments on the view that the only authority to impose binding laws on a community was possessed by those to whom the community had itself given the authority. Marshall's translation reduced the importance of consent in the argument, particularly by removing Marsilius's preference for elective monarchy over hereditary, and by institutionalising popular consent as parliamentary consent. Even then, Marsilius's text was altered to ensure that parliament was not credited with 'full legislative autonomy, [but] . . . acts as executor of the king's will'. Marsilius was manipulated so that he came to argue that the king alone possessed *imperium*, or coercive jurisdiction, but that he made law with the consent of his subjects through the institution of parliament. The prime intention of Marsilius's work was to show that to ensure peace, unity and order in civil communities the pretensions of the papacy had to be resisted. While, for Marsilius, this led to a defence of the authority over the church of the Holy Roman Emperor (and in it, of general councils), for Marshall the major beneficiary of these arguments became the king. Peace and order required acceptance of the idea that all imperial authority exercised in the realm resided in the king.[112]

These themes were expanded in other propaganda works of the late 1530s. Thomas Starkey, for example, observed in 1536 that England was now plagued by such 'disobedience and diversitie of opinion' that it had been led 'to great confusion, and to the great breche of christian unitie'.[113] His *Exhortation* was a remedy for these problems,[114] and it was built upon the concept of *adiaphora* or things indifferent, meaning 'all suche thynges whiche by goddis worde are nother prohibyted nor commaunded, but lefte to worldly polycie, wherof they take their ful authoritie'.[115] The last phrase gave the game away. Unlike Lutherans, Starkey used the concept of things indifferent not to indicate a sphere of liberty for Christians, but to indicate an area where the civil authority was free to regulate matters as it chose.[116] When civil rulers commanded things indifferent, then the people 'are to them bounde, ye by the vertue of goddis owne worde'.[117] A particular strength of the argument was the way in which secular obedience was itself rooted in theology. This was a valuable strategy, with a long future in conformist political thought. Starkey reduced the essentials of the faith to those specified in the Nicene Creed.[118] Thus he defined 'christen cyvilitie' as 'generalle knowledge of thynges necessary joyned with mekenes', resulting in 'gyvynge obedyence to common authoritie' in all matters indifferent.[119] One of the chief causes of disunity and disobedience was the superstitious mistaking of inessentials for essentials.[120] The great advantage in stressing that civil authority commanded only in the sphere of things indifferent was that there could then never be any clash between the duty of obedience and the requirements of conscience.[121] Of course, rulers might overstep the boundary, and demand things that God had forbidden, which demand ought to be 'boldely disobeyed with al constancy'; but Starkey made little of the point, emphasising instead the importance of obedience over the pretended claims of conscience.[122]

Starkey's argument for the overriding claims of civil order and obedience was not 'irreligious'; it rested neither on any divorce between religion and politics, nor on the triumph of secular values over religious ones. The claims of political obedience were defended as something obvious to those who understood rightly the Christian faith. There were two manners of living, Starkey argued. One was 'hevenly spirituall and godly' and was based on the word of Christ laid down in scripture, the other was 'civile, natural, and worldely' and based on natural reason.[123] Although the latter was common to all peoples irrespective of faith, nevertheless, amongst Christians they 'must perfitly agree'.[124] Together they produced that 'christian civilite', of which we have already heard mention, the foundation of which was the principle that 'to all suche thinges, as by common authoritie are stablished and founded, without repugnance to the spirituall unitie and manifeste doctrine of Christe, the people must ever be obedient'. This principle was indeed a 'manifest commandement' of Christ.[125] Obedience for Christians was a product not of fear but of the virtue of love and charity.[126] Furthermore, any aspect of the spiritual life might also be altered 'by good order & Policie', unless clearly determined by scripture. This included 'al rites & constitutions ecclesiastical'.[127] We are reminded of Starkey as author of the humanist *Dialogue* when we are told that this principle required the abolition of papal supremacy before 'a very and true common weale' could be re-established in England.[128] This commonwealth, united in obedience, would be determined by 'common consent' – like St German, he saw the supremacy as parliamentary – laws for religious and temporal matters. So, 'without scruple of conscience' the people could be obedient to all acts concerning the reformation of religion made 'by common authoritie here in our countrey'.[129]

Sir Richard Morison presented a similar theory, though with special emphasis on patriotism, the duty of all men 'to serve theyr contreye'.[130] He drew upon classical examples to suggest the need for 'spending bodyes, goodes, and lyves to[o], for theyr countreys sake'.[131] Extensive examples followed of the self-sacrificing service men had given to their countries. This might, perhaps, remind us of the civic humanist origins of patriotism, love of country or *patria*, invoked here by Starkey in defence of the Henrician reformation. The appeal to country was particularly effective against the papacy, something most clearly revealed in Morison's sardonic comments on his one-time patron Cardinal Pole's treachery in saying '*Roma mihi patria est*' – Rome is my native country.[132] The first duty imposed on those who would serve their country was obedience to authority, for '[o]bedience undoubtedly is the knotte of al common weales, this broken they must nedes runne al heedlonge to utter destruction'.[133] There is a dramatic gap in Morison's writing between the civic humanist language of public-spiritedness, and the fact that the only activity he required of subjects was obedience. Morison took his patriotic rhetoric to great heights – Cressy, Poitiers and Agincourt were remembered[134] – even identifying the cause of England with the cause of God. The English might face the world, but '[t]hey can not be to[o] fewe, that have god on their side'.[135] Classical examples of patriotism smoothly gave way to Old Testament examples of fighting God's cause under the leadership of a 'godly prynce'.[136] '[W]ho soo is leadynge his subjectes to the knowlege of goddis worde . . . may wel assure hym selfe, that god woll assyste him.'[137] The civic humanist language with which Morison began echoed ever hollower as he embraced fully a theory of divine right kingship. The king 'is our kynge, our ruler, by the wyll and ordinance of god, he is goddis minister, unto whose charge god hath commytted this realme, the governement is his, by goddis appoyntment, our dueties, to obey and serve him by goddes comaundement'.[138] The English were of 'one realme . . . one harte, one fydelitie, one allegiance'.[139] By the end, the sacrifice of goods and bodies required of the public-spirited man was not so much for the safety of the country as for 'his hyghnes preservation'.[140] Morison closed with the injunction, 'Let us fight this one fielde with englyshe handes, and englyshe hartes, rest, peace, victorie, honour, welth, all is owers.'[141] This is a long way removed from the 'common weal' envisaged by earlier Tudor humanists, perhaps even by Morison himself, in less fraught times.

It is worth noting that Morison's writings constitute one of the earliest attempts to employ the writings of Machiavelli in an English context. Historians have a perennial fascination with tracing the influence of Machiavelli.[142] What is worth noting, for it suggests a general warning about playing this game, is that Morison's familiarity with Machiavelli did not lead him to adopt any of the distinctive features of Machiavellian politics, whether these be deemed a preference for republican government or a ruthless amoral approach to politics. Machiavelli provided precepts and historical examples that could be used for various purposes. But Morison's writings used humanist language, whether derived from Machiavelli or elsewhere, in ways quite distinctly related to the post-1536 English context in which he wrote. The history of intellectual influence is not a history of doctrinal transmission but of creative use (and abuse). That is why it is possible to suggest that English Ciceronian humanism could become a bulwark of the Tudor state.[143]

Thus the immediate effect of the Henrician reformation, evident especially after the crisis year 1536 in which the Pilgrimage of Grace posed the most serious internal threat faced by a Tudor monarch, was to encourage political writers to search for a theory that would emphasise obedience to the king. The simplest such theory was the divine right of kings, with its emphasis on absolute obedience.[144] It was presented starkly by Morison, more complexly by Starkey, but in both cases was intended to provide the basis for a political loyalty that would be immune to any outside considerations. The king of England was 'a full king' with no human superior.[145] Adoption of this theory required even those writers influenced by civic humanist perspectives to turn away from ideas that had been tenable before 1530. A divine-right king ruled subjects rather than citizens. To the extent that there was any citizenship evident at all in the later writings of Starkey and Morison, it consisted in a patriotic duty to serve king and country. The language used by Morison and Starkey remained, at least in places, recognisably humanist, but it was a language now employed to bolster obedience to the civil magistrate. It did so in conjunction with the view that the king's authority was ordained of God, thus solving any potential conflict between religious duty and political obedience by the device of making obedience into a religious duty. But not everyone would accept this synthesis. The Henrician polemicists were keen to develop an all-encompassing theory of obedience seen as a religious duty; but in future decades ambiguities became exposed, especially over the question of just how far a (Christian) duty of obedience could apply to rulers manifestly irreligious or heretical, or manifestly harmful to their people in other ways. But before these conflict lines became apparent, the English Reformation was to develop a stage further, though even in this, obedience was to remain a central concept.

Obedience and Reform in the Reign of Edward VI, 1547–53

Dominated throughout by men with a commitment to evangelical reform, the brief reign of Edward VI saw more thorough-going attempts to destroy the old faith than had that of his father; it saw too, efforts, rather patchier in their success, to build a reformed church and society that would place England briefly in the vanguard of an international reformed movement.[146] A set of political ideas was readily developed to shape and to buttress this endeavour.[147] At the core of these ideas was the concept of 'true order', requiring both godly rulers who would support the true faith, and the creation of a godly commonwealth based upon realisation of the ideals of Christian charity. A godly king, according to John Hooper 'must . . . see their subjects instructed in the first table [i.e. their religious duties] . . . [and must aim] to live well himself, and to observe mercy and justice, to punish vice, and to extol virtue'.[148] The commonwealth as a whole ought to be founded upon principles of justice and charity if it were to be considered truly *reformed* according to God's word. Charity, as Hooper explained, 'is a fervent desire and earnest study to do well unto all men, yea, even with the hurt of him that doeth it', and it embraced social justice so that it was uncharitable to 'diminish the goods of our neighbours, whether they be of his body or his soul'.[149] Social justice did not require a Utopian community of goods, but it did require something more than selfishness. The great preacher Hugh Latimer advised in 1552 that:

> things are not so common, that another man may take my goods from me, for this is theft; but they are so common, that we ought to distribute them unto the poor, to help them, and to comfort them with it. We ought one to help another. . . . [150]

But true order required one thing more: obedience. Subjects were commanded to obey their rulers, except where this clashed with their duties to God. Then they were to follow God but in the expectation that they would quietly suffer the king's wrath.

True order always meant, for the evangelicals, more than simply obedience. It has rightly been said that 'the ungodly magistrate threatened true order far more than did the legitimate disobedience of the godly subject to him'. For Edwardian evangelicals 'the service of God' always took precedence 'above all worldly considerations'.[151] Nonetheless, circumstances encouraged a growing emphasis on the subject's duty of obedience. Above all, the 'rebellions of commonwealth' of 1549, in which the language of commonwealth was appropriated to demands of social justice for the common people, encouraged the clerical establishment to emphasise the obedience owed to kings.[152] They had much on which to build. As early as 1528, William Tyndale's *Obedience of a Christian Man*, adopting the Lutheran separation of the 'two regiments' – church and state – had both declined to allow the king any ecclesiastical functions, while making him unchallengeably supreme in the temporal sphere.[153] 'God', Tyndale declared, 'hath made the king in every realm judge over all, and over him is there no judge. He that judgeth the king judgeth God; and he that layeth hands on the king layeth hand on God. . . . If the king sin, he must be reserved unto the judgment, wrath, and vengeance of God.'[154] In his 1547 speech at the coronation of Edward VI, Thomas Cranmer declared, after outlining the duties imposed by God upon kings, that:

> I openly declare before the living God, and before the nobles of the land, that I have no commission to denounce your majesty deprived, if your highness miss in part, or in whole, of these performances, much less to draw up indentures between God and your majesty, or to say you forfeit your crown with a clause, for the bishop of Rome, as have been done by your majesty's predecessors, king John, and his son Henry of this land.

Kings were God's annointed automatically, and not by virtue of the rites of coronation. The bishop of Rome had no authority 'to condition with monarchs', though the clergy did have a duty to 'declare what God requires at the hands of kings and rulers'.[155] Thus protestants were greater respecters of the rights of kings than Catholics, and they accepted that the king had no earthly superior.

It is no surprise, then, that Cranmer, in the wake of the rebellions of 1549, could assert that 'Though the magistrates be evil, and very tyrants against the commonwealth, and enemies to Christ's religion; yet the subjects must obey in all worldly things, as the Christians do under the Turk. . . . How ungodly then it is for our subjects to take the sword, where there reigneth a most Christian prince, most desirous to reform all griefs.'[156] John Hooper, writing a little later, suggested that the king was 'bound to be obedient unto the law, and unto God, whereas the laws be not contrary to the law of God and the law of nature'. In all civil matters, kings were to be obeyed 'simply, without exception', unless their commands 'repugn and be contrary to the law of nature'.[157] Nonetheless, even when kings' commands contravened God's law (in spiritual matters) or natural law (in civil matters), and obedience was rightly withheld, active resistance remained unconscionable. Resistance was a 'damnable iniquity' and only God could punish magistrates and kings.[158] Kings undoubtedly had duties to serve the common weal, and to further the true faith;[159] but it was not for their subjects to ensure that those duties were well performed.

Perhaps the best known of the tracts published in the wake of the 1549 rebellions was John Cheke's *The Hurt of Sedition* (1549). Cheke, appointed in 1544 tutor to the future Edward VI, was a distinguished Greek scholar and early convert to protestantism. His work received a wide audience later in the century as a result of being incorporated into the 1577 and 1587 editions of Holinshed's *Chronicle*. Cheke sought to encourage the duty of obedience, both social and political. Combining the two, he stressed that we need 'to obey our kinge fayth-fully, and to serve in our owne vocacion lyke subjectes honestlye'.[160] The 'rable of Norfolke rebelles . . . pretende a common welth', Cheke noted, but these rebels failed to notice that true commonwealth could only effectively be sought in an orderly fashion. In all countries, 'some must rule, some must obey, every man may not beare lyke stroke, for everye man is not lyke wyse'. For ignorance of this, 'ye that seke the commune welth, have destroyed the commune welth'.[161]

Such a doctrine was of rather less comfort after 1553, even less after 1556 when Cranmer and Hooper had been martyred, when Cheke had been compelled to abjure his protestantism, and when England was ruled no longer by a most Christian prince, but by a prince more desirous, it seemed, of creating than of reforming griefs. Nevertheless, abandoning the doctrine was not easy. Not only did martyrs like Cranmer set a powerful example of non-resistance, but evangelicals came to pride themselves that *obedience* was a duty much dearer to them than to their Catholic opponents, identifying doctrines of resistance and tyrannicide with popery, and by the seventeenth century with the Jesuits in particular. The next chapter will trace the development of political ideas among English protestants who found themselves suddenly living in adversity, and above all it will look at the ideas of the Scottish Reformation, required from the start to justify reformation without the reliable support of royal authority.

2 Resistance and Commonwealth: the Political Thought of Marian England (1553–8) and the Scottish Reformation (1560–80)

Stressing royal supremacy and obedience to the monarch served English protestants well until 1553. During these years, it seemed to most that the purposes of God would be better served if they worked with their monarch rather than in opposition to him. The accession of a Catholic monarch in 1553 changed that. Furthermore, the situation was very different in Scotland. Protestants remained aware of the dangers of becoming linked with political disobedience – a sin they were generally inclined to associate with Catholics – but Scottish Protestantism could, in the end, only be firmly established against the wishes of temporal rulers. The actions needed to bring this about needed justification. The political thinking of the Marian exiles and the Scottish reformers should not be seen simply as circumstantial or opportunistic – the result simply of contingencies. Their theories of resistance were attempts to justify actions independent of the crown *without* justifying rebellion on a scale that would reduce the world to anarchy, and their political arguments were often tightly integrated with their views of God's purposes, his relationship to his human creation, and the nature of the churches that furthered his purposes on earth. Nonetheless, it is also true that political theories were not precisely *dictated* by theological and ecclesiological premises. There remained a looseness of fit, and circumstances inevitably shaped the ways in which political conclusions might be drawn from religious presuppositions.

The Marian Exiles

On 6 July 1553 Edward VI, aged only fifteen, died. For a few days the succession lay in doubt; but by 19 July there was no question that Mary Tudor was queen. No longer was there a safe haven for protestants anywhere in Britain. Certainly, the persecution of protestants in England that followed 1553 had not been, and was not to be, matched by anything similar in Scotland, where the regent, Mary of Guise,

Marian Exiled

pursued a more conciliatory policy. Even so, John Knox was already in England, exiled from his native Scotland; and after 1553 he accompanied many Englishmen into continental exile. This group of Marian exiles, mostly settled in Frankfurt and Geneva, was to produce by the end of 1558 an important body of political writing. It formed one of the earliest and most extreme attempts by protestants in the reformed Zwinglian–Calvinist tradition to develop a defence of forcible resistance to secular authority. In spite of this, as one recent scholar has said, 'the significance of their political thinking has too often, and unreasonably, been overshadowed by that of continental Protestants'.[1]

The England of Edward VI had become a country officially securely protestant, but it was not necessarily one in which enthusiasm for the reformed faith was firmly established among the population as a whole.[2] Nonetheless, the reversal of the nation's official faith under Mary was a traumatic event for the committed protestant minority. About eight hundred went into exile.[3] They did so conscious (like many other European protestants) of the uphill struggle in which they had been involved, the struggle to make an entire people into genuine protestants. But, more than that, the exiles were conscious that the English had now abandoned the road to Godliness along which they had been marching. They had not the excuse of ignorance that others might claim. England's political elite, assembled in parliament, had severed themselves from Rome in the 1530s and then embraced reformed religion by 1552. Now, with embarrassingly little principled concern, they returned their souls to papal care.[4] Thus, not only were the English collectively apostates – worse, perhaps, than infidels, or even heretics – but their 'lesser magistrates' (nobility, members of the Commons, other public officials) had by 1555 shown themselves to be an unlikely source of opposition to the forces of Antichrist. Yet, it was usually to just this group of lesser magistrates that protestant resistance theorists looked for aid. The return to Rome had been accomplished with impeccable observation of the legal and constitutional proprieties. The lesser magistrates had given their consent. From exile, the situation looked bleak. From where would come the means to return the nation to the true (reformed) Christian faith?

The situation seems one precisely calculated to turn people's minds to the thought of violent resistance by the people at large. But, as we have seen, before 1553 English evangelicals had firmly and almost universally accepted doctrines of non-resistance and passive suffering in the face of any hostility from secular authorities. There were, therefore, few native protestant traditions on which the exiles could draw to support a theory of resistance either to the crown or to heretical authorities generally. The early English protestants were far from unique in their attitudes to political authority. Theirs had also been the prevailing opinion amongst Continental protestants. In most places, protestants very quickly came to need the support of secular authorities to achieve their goals, and they naturally took immediate steps to appear as supporters of the rights of rulers. They were even more concerned to distance themselves from acts of rebellion or sedition. Luther, for example, vehemently condemned the uprising of German peasants in 1525 and was concerned to distinguish his position from that of the anabaptists, perceived by many to be fomenters of anarchy. As early as 1523, his important tract *Secular Authority* proclaimed a stern doctrine of obedience to the powers that be. Calvin, who with his followers came, from the time of the Marian exile onwards, to exert a powerful influence on English thought, was scarcely less compromising. All commands of the ruler should be obeyed; any resistance was resistance of God.[5] This applied even to wicked kings, who were to be obeyed as reverently as good ones.[6] There were qualifications to this. Obedience to God always came first, and that might require one passively to disobey a ruler, and quietly to suffer the punishment for such disobedience.[7] Furthermore, in a passage much exploited by later Calvinists, Calvin added that where there existed any 'popular magistrates established to restrain the licentiousness of kings' – as, for example, the Spartan ephors or the Roman tribunes of the people – then they did indeed have a duty of 'resisting the licentiousness and frenzy of kings' because appointed to do so by God's ordinance. Calvin speculated that the three estates might bear this function in modern kingdoms.[8]

In context the sentence reads most naturally as a minor qualification to Calvin's doctrine of complete obedience. It might be construed as saying that, where there were institutions or persons (lesser magistrates) established to moderate the rule of the king, then they could perform their functions without sin. Such institutions or persons were not excluded from the general rule commending obedience to authority but were constituted by God to share in that authority. The result of such an argument, fully revealed in the Elizabethan period, was to encourage people to examine the constitutional differences between states. In some there might well be institutions through which the supreme ruler could be controlled, if not resisted.

In any case, the basic thrust of Calvin's authoritarian position was clear, and it left little room (as his early followers appreciated) for resistance theory. It is scarcely surprising, then, to find that when the exiled John Knox probed Bullinger (Zwingli's successor in Zurich) in 1554 about the legitimacy of resistance, he received unhelpful answers.[9] The evidence suggests also that Calvin himself became unhappy with the British exiles' increasing attachment to resistance theory.[10] Both Calvin and Beza found themselves after 1558 having to explain away the unfortunate hot-headedness of Knox and Christopher Goodman to the new queen, Elizabeth, and her chief minister, Cecil.[11] One can well understand why in 1564 Knox was to refuse to canvass Calvin's opinion about the legitimacy of resistance (largely on the doubtless true ground that his own mind was already made up!).[12]

Nevertheless, the exiles were not entirely without precedents for resistance to secular authority. After 1529 the protestant princes and cities of the Holy Roman Empire found themselves increasingly opposed to, and by, the authority of their (Catholic) Emperor, Charles V. The Lutheran propagandists, including Luther himself, not surprisingly began gradually to move away from the uncompromising authoritarianism of the early and middle 1520s.[13] The most important and influential statement of this developing Lutheran resistance theory was the *Confession* (*Bekenntnis*) produced in 1550 to defend the continuing resistance of the city of Magdeburg to the Emperor.[14] The document forms, in effect, a summary of Lutheran resistance theory as it had developed in the 1530s and 1540s; and it is possible that the British exiles of the 1550s may have looked to it for inspiration.[15] This may be particularly true of Knox, who employed in his *Scottish* writings a 'lesser magistrates' theory of resistance similar to that of the *Confession*, as we shall see. In the great debate on resistance in the General Assembly of the Scottish Church (1564), Knox would cite the document, though there is no hard evidence of his earlier acquaintance with it.[16]

However, Lutheran resistance theories rested on two key arguments, one the duty to God of constituted 'lesser magistrates' to perform their allotted functions, the other a private-law argument for self-defence. This had more extreme potential: it seemed to imply (as some were troubled to realise) that any individual could resist an unjust ruler, for it was based on the proposition that all individuals had the right to repel unjust violence done to them.[17] Although it is impossible to prove direct lines of influence between the Lutherans and the Marian exiles, the similarity of argument is striking. This more radical line of argument is to be found in the English writers, Ponet and Goodman. Such a theory admirably suited the English situation, for it enabled those calling for resistance to abandon their reliance on the 'lesser magistrate', who by 1555 had clearly failed. Instead, appeal could be made directly to 'the people' (of God), whose willingness to suffer martyrdom showed them to be a more likely agency of the return of Protestantism.[18]

Resistance
Theories

The three great resistance tracts of the Marian exiles, John Ponet's *Shorte Treatise of Politike Power* (1556), Christopher Goodman's *How Superior Powers Ought to be Obeyed* (1558), and (much less overtly) John Knox's *First Blast of the Trumpet against the Monstrous Regiment of Women* (1558), all utilise something like a private-law argument for resistance.[19] But, just as importantly, they need to be understood primarily as sectarian religious documents. In all of them constitutional and legal considerations are subordinated to religious priorities. — simi law but sectarian

The earliest of the three works was Ponet's *Shorte Treatise*. It provides a good illustration both of why the Marian exiles were forced to adopt private-law (and natural-law) arguments from self-defence; and – in doing this – how their writings were shaped (or mis-shaped) by circumstance. Ponet's book was deeply fractured, its coherence impaired and its course of argument deflected, by the necessity of fitting his principles to the political realities of Marian England.[20] The *Shorte Treatise* contained a civic humanist defence of mixed government, and defended as well the right of people to choose a form of government that best served their needs. Ponet portrayed a situation in which God, after the Flood, instituted politic government; but whether government 'shal be and remayne in one person alone, or in manie, it is not expressed, but lefte to the discrecion of the people to make so many and so fewe, as they thinke necessarie for the mayntenaunce of the state'. Nonetheless, human experience showed that one form of state was generally better than the others: 'wher all [rule] together, that is, a king, the nobilitie, and commones, [there is] a mixte state: which men by long continuaunce have judged to be the best sort of all. For wher that mixte state was exerciced, ther did the common wealthe longest continue.' However, the other forms were legitimate, and all served (or should serve) the same purposes, 'the mayntenaunce of justice, to the wealthe and benefite of the hole multitude'. 'And when they sawe, that the governours abused their autoritie, they altred the state.'[21]

One might expect from this that Ponet would have gone on to develop a theory of 'lesser magistrates' resistance. If the polity were mixed, then it should follow that the nobility and commons had legitimate public roles that they could deploy independently of the crown, perhaps even using those powers to change the form of the state. That, however, is not at all what Ponet went on to say. His analysis of the mixed state soon unravelled; and, in fact, his most virulently hostile remarks were aimed at England's parliamentary elites. It was true that in places like England the existence of parliaments meant that 'nothing could be done without the knowlage and consent of all'. For this to mean anything, though, councillors and members of parliament were required 'not to neglecte their duetie, or to deceave the people of the trust and confidence, that was put in them'.[22] By 1556 the English nobility and gentry had failed. Placed 'in trust', 'to make lawes and statutes to the advauncement of Goddes glorie, and conservation of the liberties and common wealthe of their countrey', they had selfishly ignored their charge. Their duties – 'to redresse, reforme and heale' – were utterly neglected.[23]

After this introduction Ponet proceeded to discuss some important questions. Did kings possess 'absolute power'? Were they subject to God's law and to the positive laws of the land? What was the extent of obedience owed by subjects to kings? Did kings have ultimate ownership and disposal of the property of their subjects? The answers given to these questions built into an imposing picture of limited monarchy, restrained by human, natural and divine law. Rulers were not absolute, but constrained to performing certain functions, 'to maintene justice, to defende the innocent, to punishe the evil' (sig. C1). The king was, in both his public and his private capacities, as subject to God's law as any other man. Among many other things, therefore, kings were forbidden from committing idolatry (sigs C2–C2v). To support the contention that kings were bound by the positive laws of their own communities, Ponet drew on Roman law, citing the *Lex Digna Vox* (*Codex* I.14.4): 'It is a worthy saïeng . . . for the Maiestie of him that is in autoritie, to confesse that the prince is subjecte to the lawes' (sig. C6). Furthermore, he suggested, natural law decreed that the commonwealth depended on equality, which equality required that all be equally subject to the rule of law – and 'all' included the king (sig. C6v). Not only equality was necessary for the endurance of the commonwealth: 'every commun wealthe [is] kept and maintened in good ordre by Obedience' (sig. C8). Nonetheless, there were tight limits to that obedience. Civil power did not extend to 'the soule and conscience of man', but only to his body and temporal concerns (sig. D1v). When secular rulers ignored this, and commanded things contrary to God's laws, then the duty of subjects was clear. They must flee or suffer (sig. E6). Their task was 'to doo Goddes commaundementes before all mennes, to please God rather than men' (sig. E6v). In obeying God before man, it was necessary 'to abide all losses, bothe of body and goodes' (sig. E7v). Finally, Ponet argued that kings were God's stewards, and consequently one of their functions was to protect the property of their subjects (sigs F7v–F8v).

So far, Ponet had developed a far from uncommon or extreme view of the English monarchy as limited by law, protecting the property of its subjects, to be obeyed in all temporal matters, and to be disobeyed only passively when its commands are unjust. Certainly, there was in all of this little preparation for the doctrine of tyrannicide that was advanced later in the book. A reader of the book, ignoring the early attack on England's parliamentary elites, might well gain the impression that here was an author who trusted in the formal and informal restraints built into English law and public institutions, an author who, like so many earlier protestants, did not believe that active resistance was necessary or desirable. Such a reader would soon be disabused of that opinion. Embarking on a discussion of whether it was lawful for a tyrant – a king who came to the throne 'either by usurpacion, or by election or by succession' but abandons the commonwealth and 'seketh onli or chiefly his owne profit and pleasure' (sigs G1v–G2) – to be deposed, Ponet quickly abandoned the terrain of positive law. Accepting that 'ther is no expresse positive lawe for punishment of a Tyranne among christen men' (sig. G3), he turned instead to biblical and historical precedents and to that natural law known even to the pagan philosophers. English history recorded the depositions of Edward II, Richard II and Henry IV (sig. G3). The same practice occurred in the church itself, where canon lawyers, basing their arguments on natural law, had recognised that evil popes 'maie be deprryved by the body of the churche' (sig. G4). It surely followed from this that kings and emperors, 'abusing their office, [might] be deposed and removed out of their places and offices, bi the body or state of the Realme or common wealthe' (sig. G5). Again, this suggested a 'lesser magistrates' theory of resistance, in which the realm would be led in a collective act of deposition by its elected or natural leaders. Such a conclusion might be suggested by Ponet's earlier remark that deposition was acceptable when performed by 'those that have the just autoritie' (sig. G3v). In England, indeed, there seemed once to have been a person with just such authority, 'the highe Constable of Englande, unto whose autoritie it perteined, not only to summone the king personally before the parliament or other courtes of judgment . . . but also upon juste occasion to committe him unto warde' (sig. G5v).

We seem still to be with the classical mixed state (adapted here to explain the medieval English inheritance of baronial resistance to the crown), in which there existed the institutional means to thwart the wicked designs of tyrants. But when Ponet came to decide the question of whether or not tyrants might be killed, all of this was, in effect, swept aside. Their understanding of the principles of natural law led the ancients to revere those who had slain tyrants (sigs G6–G7), 'wherof came the name of Nobilitie . . . [b]icause they revenged and delivered the oppressed people out of the handes of their governours, who abused their autoritie, and wickedly, cruelly and tirannously ruled over them' (sig. G7). What, though, if the nobility failed to fulfil its duty? Ponet's hesitant answer was provided in a crucial passage, which contained powerful reference to the private-law principle that individuals might repel unjust violence done to them:

> Ethnikes [i.e. pagans] . . . thinke it lawful for every private man (without respecte of ordre and time) to punishe evill: [while] . . . the lawes of many christiane regiones doo permitte, that private men maie kil malefactours, yea though they were magistrates, in some cases: as whan a governour shall sodainly with his sworde renne upon an innocent, or goo about to shoote him through with a gonne, or if he should be founde in bedde with a mannes wife, or goo about to defloure and ravishe a mannes daughter: much more if [he] goo about to betraie and make awaie his countrey to forainers, &c. Nevertheles forasmuche as all thinges in every christen common wealthe ought to be done decently and according to ordre and charitie: I thinke it can not be maintened by Goddes worde, that any private man maie kill, except (wher execucion of just punishment upon tirannes, idolaters, and traiterous governours is either by the hole state utterly neglected, or the prince with the nobilitie and counsail conspire the subversion or alteracion of their contrey and people) any private man have from special inwarde commaundement or surely proved mocion of God . . . or be otherwise commaunded or permitted by common autoritie upon juste occasion and common necessitie to kill.   (sigs G8–G8v)

The last section of this applied *exactly* to Mary's reign. She was patently a tyrant and idolater; she was a traitor by virtue of her marriage to Philip II of Spain; the nobility and council conspired with her: necessity thus decreed, even if God did not, that any private individual could slay her. Where justice was not executed on princes, there could only be 'a most corrupte, ungodly and vicious state' which must suffer the fate of Sodom and Gomorrah (sig. H3).[24]

There were signs of at least three different political arguments in Ponet: that England was a mixed state, so well ordered that resistance would hardly be necessary; that lesser magistrates could resist the supreme magistrate; and that private-law theory justified tyrannicide. One might suspect that Ponet was driven to this last extremity by the desperate situation in which he wrote. Furthermore, in judging Ponet as a *political* thinker, we do him a disservice. What mattered to him was that Mary was an idolater, that prince, parliament and prelates together 'banish[ed] the sacred testament and Gospel of God' from the land, and introduced the 'power of the Romishe Antichrist in to

Englande again' (sig. I6). His thought may have had inconsistencies but it was not incoherent. Its coherence lay, rather, in its religious conviction, in the search for political weapons that could be pressed to serve in God's cause. Obedience to human laws was not automatic. The fact that a law was made by properly constituted authorities did not make it right, and every individual Christian had to examine the substance of a law before obeying it.

> It is not the mannes waraunt that can discharge the[e], but it is the thinge it self that must justifie the[e]. It is the mater that will accuse thee, and defende thee. . . . And therefore christen men ought well to considre, and weighe mennes commaundementes, before they be hastie to doo them, to see if they be contrarie or repugnaunt to goddes commaundementes and justice: which if they be, they are cruell and evill, and ought not to be obeyed.   (sig. D3)

Persecution was God's way of finding out who would put that advice into practice (sigs E5v–E6). The principle came close to founding government in grace rather than nature (and that is what Richard Hooker was to take as the essence of the political threat posed by Puritanism). That is to say that Ponet, though he never explicitly espoused such a view, at times suggested that only Godly rulers were to be obeyed, that only true Christians could rule over true Christians. The contrast with earlier English protestants was marked. Hooper, for example, had argued that in seeking to obey, subjects must 'look upon the power and authority of the higher powers, and not upon their manners'. The necessity of obeying God before man was, of course, accepted; but for Hooper it appeared as but a minor qualification to his basic position.[25]

This is one of the key themes in the history of post-Reformation political thought. The basic view that religious duties were, in the last resort, more important than political duties was more significant than its occasional development into resistance theory. It was at the heart of Elizabethan and early Stuart Puritanism, but it was not a new view, and it was shared by conformists and Catholics, as well as puritans. In the post-Reformation situation, marked by the *de facto* disappearance of religious uniformity, the belief took on a more immediate significance. It was now easy for groups and individuals to feel that their religious duties might actually lead them into direct or indirect conflict with the state. Defences of obedience did not quarrel with the proposition that God must be obeyed before man; but suggested only that the areas in which God's commands might clash with the king's were rather fewer than Catholics, puritans and presbyterians might believe. Most puri-

Religious priorities [marginalia]

tans after 1558 were not, as we shall see, resistance theorists; but the fundamental attitude that led Ponet and other Marian exiles to their espousal of resistance persisted throughout the period of this book.

There is no mistaking Ponet's religious priorities. Nonetheless, his work more than that of the other exiles contained elements that could be employed by more secular-minded thinkers. In contrast, Goodman and Knox wrote in ways that made them look thoroughly inadequate if we insist on seeing them primarily as *political* rather than as religious thinkers. Goodman's *How Superior Powers O[u]ght to be Obey[e]d* began as a sermon delivered to the exile community in Geneva, and formed a scripture-based treatise on religious duty.[26]

Goodman [marginalia]

Like Ponet, Goodman employed a private-law argument for resistance. When rulers become tyrants and murderers, 'then are they no more publik persons, contemning their publik auctoritie in usinge it agaynst the Lawes, but are to be taken of all men, as private persones, and so examyned and punished'.[27] Thus princes became subject to the rule that individuals could defend themselves from the unjust violence of others. But in Goodman's use of it, this argument was utterly subsumed within a religious argument which suggested that, in certain circumstances, resistance was not so much a right of self-defence as a duty demanded by God. Goodman's was a treatise on 'true obedience' (9, 14); but *true* obedience was owed to God not man. It was 'what God him self requiereth of us, and what he commandethe to be geven also to men'.

True "obedience" [marginalia]

Goodman's diagnosis of the English situation was similar to Ponet's. Counsellors, 'whose office is to brydle the affections of their Princes . . . in geving such counsele as might promote the glorie of God', have instead allowed the 'wicked Jesabel' Mary 'to raigne over us in Goddes furie'. In so doing they have 'betrayed Christe, their countrie, and them selves' by betraying the nation to the Spanish. The nobility were no better. They had 'turned their nobilitie to open shame amongst all nations' and become 'instrumentes of impietie, and destroyers of their native countrie, which firste were ordayned in Realmes to stande in defence of trewe religion, lawes, and welthe of their nation'. They too ought to have been 'a brydel at home to their princes', but were not; they too were 'charged by their office' with the role of defending 'the people of God' (34–5). The list of those who had willingly become the ministers of tyranny went on: justices, mayors, sheriffs, bailiffs, constables, jailers, and even 'the residue of the common people' who followed the lead of their superiors (36–7; also 95).

What, then, could be done to end the reign of the impious Mary Tudor? Goodman answered that question by, first, making it perfectly plain where the Christian Englishman's duty lay. God had to be obeyed before man. God required of his people a number of things. First, they must allow only Godly rulers to reign: 'they [must] chose suche a kinge, as the Lorde dothe appoynt, and not as they phantasie' (p. 49). The cards were rather stacked against Mary, for among the principles to be followed in electing a Godly ruler were that he must 'hat[e] unfaynedlie al papistrie and idolatrie' (51); and that there be care to avoid 'that monster in nature, whiche is the Empire and governement of a woman' (52). Goodman took the principle of elective monarchy some considerable distance. At the death of Edward VI, the English ruling elites ought to have asked themselves who was fittest to rule over them. The law of God, which required a Godly prince, took precedence over the merely human laws of succession (54–5). Secondly, ② when magistrates who attempted to introduce idolatry and oppression were elected, 'then are they no more to be obeyed in any commandements tending to that ende' (59). To obey princes against God is 'playne rebellion' (60; also 43–4); to disobey men who act contrary to God is true obedience.

At this point Goodman introduced a crucial twist into his argument. It was not enough merely to refuse to obey unGodly commands. 'God requireth more at our handes, that is, to withstande their preceptes, in doing the contrary: every man according to his office and estate wherin God hathe placed him' (63). At one step, then, we move from the world of passive (dis)obedience, to a world in which God required people to take positive action in order to ensure that his will was performed. That meant, among other things, acting 'to save, preserve, and defende, as well the goodes as the persones of our brethren and neghbours' (70). From there it was easy to conclude that true obedience was 'to resiste man rather than God' (84). Goodman was not entirely clear about what exactly might be entailed by this active resistance; but there was no mistaking the general thrust of a passage such as this:

Kill Mary!!!

> both by Gods Lawes and mans, she [Mary] oght to be punished with death, as an open idolatres in the sight of God, and a cruel murtherer of his Saints before men, and merciles traytoresse to her own native countrie.   (99; also 104)

Kings who were merely bad, as Saul was, were not to be actively disobeyed, as David did not lift up his hand against Saul. For resistance to be justified, a monarch had to have contravened *God's* law:

> where as the kinges or Rulers are become altogether blasphemers of God, and oppressors and murtherers of their subjectes, then oght

they to be accompted no more for kinges or lawfull Magistrats, but as private men: and to be examined, accused, condemned and punished by the Lawe of God, whereunto they are and oght to be subject, and being convicted and punished by that Lawe, it is not mans, but Gods doing.   (139–40)

What, it might be asked, justified a queen's subjects in acting as the executors of God's law in imposing punishment on her? In answering that question we can gain much insight into the politically subversive potential built into some key features of Christian, and especially of Protestant, doctrine. Goodman was quite explicit that it was not just 'inferior Magistrates' who possessed a duty to oppose idolatry, but the common people (145–8). Every individual human being is a rational creature, not a brute beast, and therefore not suited for blind unquestioning obedience (except, of course, to God) (148–9). Individuals possessed, like all creatures, a God-given natural tendency to preserve themselves (and that included being able to ensure their eternal salvation), and it was only proper that they be allowed to exercise it (158–9). But the argument that gave people more than a simple right to defend themselves was based on the concept of *covenant*.[28] The covenant made by God with his people through Moses was an 'example [that] ought never to departe from the eyes of all such as are, or would be Gods people' (163). A people who covenanted with God to be his people promised to obey his laws, to 'be governed onely by Gods Lawes' (163, marg. note). Christians, for whom Moses was replaced by Christ, were as much bound to God as the Israelites; and each individual Christian became a covenanted part of God's people through baptism (165–6). Thus all Christians, regardless of their worldly status, were individually bound to God, and individually responsible for ensuring both their own obedience to God's law and the obedience of their brethren. No subject was so subjected that he could claim the excuse of following orders. God required more; Christians promised more in their baptism and profession of faith (170).

From here it was easy to conclude that the failure of lesser magistrates to stand out against Mary's restoration of Catholicism was in itself no excuse for the common people's remaining submissive. If the nobility would not take on the role, then 'God him self ... [will] be your Capitayne' (180). Every individual had *promised* to God that he would ensure execution of divine law (180–1). Idolaters, whether emperors, kings or queens, must all 'dye the death' (184). When lesser authorities failed, 'God geveth the sworde into the peoples hande, and he him self is become immediately their head' (185). These passages, together with some that have already been quoted, amount to a clear suggestion that each individual Christian had a duty to commit tyrannicide, to slay oppressive and idolatrous rulers (as Sir Thomas Wyatt attempted to do in 1554; pp. 202–4). A final chapter counselled the common people, now abandoned by their superiors, to accept willingly the cruel suffering that might well accrue from trying to fulfil their religious duties. God would see that they were more than rewarded for their suffering.

Goodman's argument, much more even than Ponet's, was a religious one. It is true that he did draw on private-law arguments; but they were *religious argument* clearly subordinate to his chief concern with the duties owed by a Christian to God. Ponet's conclusions were, in fact, not much different; though he showed a much greater interest in more obviously political and legal matters than Goodman. John Knox's *First Blast of the Trumpet* was much closer in idiom to Goodman's work than to Ponet's. The same was less true of his writings directed to a Scottish audience, as we shall see; and this helps to make clear that the (English) Marian exiles were pushed into their religiously-based resistance theories largely by the need to find arguments that could fulfil two conditions. They needed to provide the foundation for a *general* call to arms against Mary; and they needed to avoid any reliance on the leadership of lesser magistrates. Religious argument fulfilled those conditions. It enabled one to move beyond the confines of private-law argument to envisaging a situation in which all Christians, equal in their subordination to God, were equally called upon to execute divine law on its transgressors. Furthermore, it could be argued that in the reign of Edward VI the people of England had collectively covenanted with God, and so could now be called upon individually to perform the duties that followed from the covenant.

Goodman also sought to remove the main obstacle in the way of such a theory. Earlier protestants, like Tyndale, Cranmer and Hooper, had relied heavily (as we have seen) on Romans 13 in order to argue that Christians had a duty to show complete obedience, passive if not active, to secular authority. They had all, implied Goodman, misinterpreted the scripture. The higher powers to whom St Paul had commanded obedience were only those instituted by God. Tyrants were not of God's ordinance, and so lay outside the scope of the command. Rightly understood, Romans 13 was aimed at those early Christians who (like the sixteenth-century anabaptists) believed that Christians were automatically exempt from obedience to all secular authority (108–10).

Knox[29] did not discuss that particular text in his *First Blast*, and like Ponet he ranged more widely than Goodman, using also classical, Roman law and (to a limited degree) historical evidence. That fact is misleading. For in spirit Knox was much closer to Goodman. He offered no analysis of civil politics, and the *First Blast* was a work written entirely in the prophetic mode. Knox saw himself as one of those people raised up by God to testify to the truth.[30] Knox's concern was with God's will revealed in his law. That law overrode all human laws and customs (42). The testimony of the Fathers – of Tertullian, Ambrose, Augustine and Chrysostom – was of no value except as a corroboration of Knox's own interpretation of scripture (15). Knox's discussion of the way in which the rule of women entailed 'the subversion of good order, equity and justice' (22; also 8) turned out not to lead into any examination of the civil sphere on its own terms, for order and justice themselves were founded on obedience to God's will (22, 30–1). The effective core of Knox's argument was, in fact, given in the opening few pages of his tract.

The regiment (or rule) of women was contrary to God's will as communicated to all men through nature, and to his revealed will communicated through the scriptures. Whereas the illegitimacy of women's rule was a (minor) theme in Goodman's writing, in Knox's it was central. He demonstrated his argument, first, by examining the views of those 'men illuminated only by the light of nature' (11). Relying on citations of Aristotle and of the *Digest* of Roman law, Knox showed that the ancients condemned the rule of women. Secondly, he turned his attention to the scriptures and showed that both the decrees of creation and God's punishment of women for the sin of Eve disallowed all women from exercising public authority (12–13). In addition, the injunctions of St Paul led to the same conclusion (13–15). '[A] woman promoted to sit in the seat of God, that is, to teach, to judge or to reign above man, is a monster in nature, contumely to God, and a thing most repugnant to His will and ordinance' (15). That, in essence, is all that Knox wanted to say.

There are, however, two further aspects of his argument that we need to consider. It appears that, in making his case, Knox was concerned more with the English queen Mary Tudor than with the Scottish regent Mary of Guise (who had ruled in the name of her infant daughter Mary Stewart since 1554). Knox's Preface clearly directed his *First Blast* against the Tudor queen (3), and though he did refer to the Scottish situation from time to time (24–7, 39, 40–1), it was always alongside some discussion of the English. Indeed, Knox was clear that the English, who had had so much opportunity in Edward VI's reign, had gone further in rebellion against God than the Scots (26). This primarily English focus of the work, and the desperate situation in which Knox (like Ponet and Goodman) thought the English to be, accounts for the desperate bluntness of Knox's conclusions. What was to be done about Mary Tudor? In God's judgement, Mary's rule was without legitimacy, He would ensure that someone would at some point execute that judgement (46–7). In particular, the nobility must

> acknowledge that the regiment of a woman is a thing most odious in the presence of God. They must refuse to be her officers because she is a traitress and rebel against God. And finally they must study to repress her inordinate pride and tyranny to the uttermost of their power. (43)

Tyrannicide

That last sentence sounds ominous enough; but Knox became even more explicit. The nobility, estates and even the common people had a duty before God 'to remove from authority all such persons as by usurpation, violence and tyranny' do possess authority; and 'to pronounce and then after to execute . . . the sentence of death' on any who support her (44). Within all of this, the sound of the trumpet-call to tyrannicide can be heard clearly enough.

The second theme that deserves elaboration concerns Knox's attitude to the Godly magistrate.[31] His so-called theory of resistance should be seen primarily as the reverse side of Knox's very high ideal of true magistracy. The true magistrate, as much as the true pastor, was ordained to do God's work. He had 'to know the will of God, to be instructed in His law and statutes and to promote His glory with his whole heart and study'. His duties included the punishment not just of civil misdemeanours, but also of 'such vices as openly impugn the glory of God as idolatry, blasphemy and manifest heresy taught and obstinately maintained' (29). Using Old Testament examples, Knox could conclude that 'the office of the king or supreme magistrate hath respect to the law moral and to the conservation of both the Tables' (30). Christian communities had a duty to remove magistrates who did not perform these tasks. We must be careful not to let Knox's virulent misogyny obscure from us the fact that he objected to women rulers simply because they were a sub-group of the broader category of unGodly rulers.[32] No such flawed thing could be an adequate instrument of God's will. The sub-structure of Knox's general position is clearly laid out in his plan for the never-written *Second Blast* (three were intended). No person who is a 'notorious transgressor of God's holy precepts ought to be promoted to any public regiment' over 'a people professing Christ Jesus and His eternal verity'. Should, by some error or mischance, such person come to rule, then those who gave them authority had a duty to 'depose and punish' them.[33]

Knox's writing shows us clearly that the resistance theory of the exiles was scarcely a *political* matter at all. None of them, not even

What king should be

Ponet, deduced a right of resistance from political, legal or constitutional analysis. Resistance was a sudden violent incursion of religious priorities into the political domain. Their attention was given to the question of Godly and unGodly rule. Their insistence that true magistracy consisted in the rule of a Godly prince who would act as a faithful servant of God's will made politics in any narrow sense redundant. The Marian exiles' desperate plight led them to espouse theories that destroyed the autonomy of the political realm. Theories of this sort were to have only a very restricted place in English political thought after 1558. The resistance theory of the English Civil War, for example, was to be of a markedly different character. Scottish political thought, however, was a another matter.

I disagree → their ideas are political but justified in religious terms

The Scottish Reformation

The Scottish Reformation, in dramatic contrast to the English, was brought about by a revolt of the nobility against the authority of the crown.[34] By 1559–60 it had gained the strength officially to reform the nation's church. Mary of Guise, the regent since 1554 (and in practice influential since her daughter's accession as a minor in 1542), adopted a much more conciliatory policy towards Protestantism than Mary Tudor. Thus, when five protestant nobles signed the First Band of the Lords of the Congregation on 7 December 1557, in which they covenanted to 'apply our whole power . . . to maintain, set forward and establish the most blessed Word of God and His Congregation',[35] they naturally hoped at first to work with her rather than against her. Naturally also, they kept their distance from the tactless and inflammatory rhetoric of John Knox, who did not return to Scotland until May 1559.

Treaty of Cateau Cambrésis

Two events transformed this situation. The death of Mary Tudor, and the accession of the protestant Elizabeth (1 November 1558), made it much less safe for Mary of Guise to take an indulgent attitude to Protestantism. In consequence, the protestant strategy of trying to persuade her fell apart. Internationally, the Treaty of Cateau-Cambrésis (April 1559), which brought a cessation to the long struggle between Habsburg Spain and Valois France, left the way open for the French king to devote his attention to destroying protestant heresy in Scotland. From 1559 that French king was Francis II, husband of the Scottish queen Mary Stewart. The resultant situation certainly helped the spread of protestant allegiance amongst the nobility and lairds of Scotland, as the reformed faith became identified with the task of freeing Scotland from the threat of French domination. The Lords of

Reform Parliament

the Congregation, now much increased in number, declared in October 1559 that Mary of Guise was suspended from her authority, and invested it instead in 'the great council of the realm'. In 1560 the Congregation's rebellion, with essential English aid, proved triumphant. The French abandoned Scotland, and on 1 August 1560 the first meeting of the Scottish Reformation Parliament took place. Its crucial act was the destruction of papal jurisdiction in Scotland. Following the death of Francis II (5 December 1560), Mary Stewart returned to rule a formally protestant Scotland in August 1561. By that time the First Book of Discipline, written by six reformers including Knox, had begun the task of reconstructing the kirk along reformed lines. The first of Scotland's three Reformation rebellions had, it seemed, removed all obstacles to reform.

The political writings produced by the Reformation in Scotland between about 1556 and 1560 showed a marked contrast with those of the Marian exiles. While political circumstance plays a considerable role in explaining the difference between Scottish and English thought, it may also be the case that the contrasting intellectual traditions of the two countries are significant. On the face of it, Scottish political thought of the fifteenth and early sixteenth centuries would not seem to provide fertile ground for the development of resistance theory. Late medieval Scottish kings, like their English counterparts, wore the closed imperial crown; and in consequence the monarchy itself came to symbolise, more than any other institution, the jurisdictional independence of Scotland, in particular its independence of the English claims to feudal overlordship. Not surprisingly, perhaps, there was little sign in Scottish thought, between the Declaration of Arbroath (1320) and the early sixteenth century, of the doctrine that tyrannical kings might be deposed. Monarchs were held to be morally responsible for the welfare of the community but not accountable to it.[36]

Different

To some degree, however, that situation is modified by the fact that there was a considerable influence in early sixteenth-century Scotland of the conciliarist political thought developed by Scholastic theologians, the Scotsman John Mair (or Major) above all.[37] Conciliar thought developed in the context of the Great Schism (1378–1417), during which Western Christendom was split by the existence of rival claimants for the papal throne. To help settle that dispute, theorists began to advance a variety of arguments that had in common the proposition that in some way the entire body of the church, acting through a general council, was superior in authority to the pope. Thus the General Council would, amongst other things, be able to decide who should be pope in the event of any quarrel over the matter, and might even be able to depose popes whose title was uncontested.[38]

Conciliarism

Developed in an ecclesiological context, conciliar thought was
nonetheless readily transferable to secular politics. Though the conciliar movement proper dissolved after 1449, conciliar theory remained
alive amongst Scholastic philosophers well into the sixteenth century,
especially at the University of Paris, where Mair taught from 1505 to
1518, and again from 1525 to 1531. It seems to have formed one of the
crucial sources for (so-called) 'Calvinist' resistance theory.[39] One of
the key figures in its survival was John Mair.[40]

Much of the sub-structure of Mair's political thought has to be
reconstructed from his theological writings;[41] but in his *History of
Greater Britain* (1521) we can find some very pointed political writing.
Mair made very clear the implications of his application of conciliar
principles to the Scottish monarchy. In defence of Robert Bruce's
claim to the Scottish throne, Mair asserted that John Balliol 'showed
himself . . . unfit to reign, and justly was deprived of his right . . . by
those in whom alone the decision rested'. Who had the authority to
make such a decision? '[A] free people confers authority upon its first
king, and his power is dependent upon the whole people'.[42] The
whole people thus exercised authority, in certain circumstances,[43]
over their king (just as the whole church did over the pope). Robert
Bruce's title derived from the fact that 'the whole people united in
their choice of' him (214). The people here does not, of course, mean
some sort of democratic majority, but what a Scholastic theologian
like Mair would call the *valentior et sanior pars*, the better and wiser
part: 'it is from the people, and most of all from the chief men and the
nobility who act for the common people, that kings have their institution' (215).

Mair rejected the idea that only disaster could follow from this view.
He suggested that 'only with the greatest difficulty could kings be
driven from their kingdom . . . 'tis a harder thing than you think to rob
a rightful king and his posterity of his kingdom'. Certainly there were
cases in which subjects 'rightfully deposed them, for foul vices of which
these showed no mind to be corrected'. But a king who was 'corrigible'
was only to be dismissed 'when their deposition shall make more for
the advantage of the state than their continuance'. Even then, 'a
solemn consideration of the matter by the three estates, and ripe
judgment passed wherein no element of passion shall intrude' was
necessary before kings were deposed (219). In civil politics the three
estates assembled in parliament served the same role that the General
Council served in the church. In addition to choosing and punishing
kings, the three estates had the right to consent to taxation, and were
to be the sole judges of when necessity might require extraordinary
taxation (347–8, 352). Mair went out of his way to make such a doctrine

sound non-threatening and non-subversive. For too 'slight a cause to dismiss and depose a king is nothing else than to make an easy opening for the horns of rebellion against the state' (308); while 'it is naught but fitting to punish with severity that many-headed monster, an unbridled populace, when it rises against its head' (302; cf. 375–6). Deposition might in some circumstances be justified, but only when it maintained rather than subverted the existing social order.

There was an obvious similarity between Mair's application of conciliar theory and what we know as a lesser-magistrates theory of resistance. In both, the nobility and chief officers of the realm were vested with an (emergency) power to punish, possibly to depose, errant rulers; this authority they had because they acted as the virtual representatives of the entire community. It is difficult to be sure of Mair's influence on later writers, but worthy of note that Mair, during his time at St Andrews in the 1530s, might have taught John Knox, and he certainly taught George Buchanan in Paris.

The first of Knox's important political writings aimed at a Scottish audience was the *Letter to the Regent* (Mary of Guise), which first appeared in 1556, and reappeared with substantial additions in 1558. It was in the form of a petition, seeking to persuade Mary that she should reform the church, and therefore implicitly recognising her authority. Indeed, it went out if its way to magnify that authority, attributing to Satan (for example) the principle that 'no civil magistrate [ought to] presume to take cognition in the cause of religion, for that must be deferred to the determinations of the church'.[44] The crown itself was responsible for religion, and could not shuffle off the responsibility to the prelates. Nor could it avoid responsibility by arguing that the multitude were happy with the existing religion, or that change in religion produced instability. Both points might be true, but were overridden by the command of God (58–60, 64). Knox, of course, pursued this line of argument because he wished to suggest that Mary had the authority to grant the petition of protestants that 'our doctrine be tried by the plain Word of God, that liberty be granted to us to utter and declare our minds at large in every article and point which now are in controversy' (53). The work thus reflected a situation in which petitioning an accepted authority seemed a more likely path to success than tyrannicide. Admittedly, not every petition warned its recipient of 'damnation and death' at God's hand (55), or reminded her that the death of her two sons and husband in close succession was a sign of God's anger at her idolatry (66–7). Nonetheless, this was tactlessness, not revolution. The surest sign of Knox's avoidance of the extreme position adopted in the *First Blast* was that he did not assert the complete illegitimacy of women's rule, contenting himself instead with pointing out to Mary that 'seldom it is that women do long reign with felicity and joy'. God ensured that they reign over men only 'in His wrath and indignation' (65).

In the *Letter*, Knox promised to treat elsewhere of the power that God had given the nobility and others to deal with religious matters (60). He was referring to perhaps the most important of his 1558 tracts, the *Appellation* to the Scottish nobility and estates. The *Appellation* began by mentioning two ideas: the need for a general council of the (protestant?) churches, and the need for the nobility and estates adequately to perform their duties as lesser magistrates. The two ideas were, in fact, closely intertwined, making the work a much more complex and sophisticated political tract than is sometimes acknowledged.

The term 'political tract' might, however, be deemed inaccurate as a label for Knox's *Appellation*. Like all of his writings, it is a religious work, in good part a work of ecclesiology rather than of civil politics. It is important to remember that the *Appellation*, like the *Letter*, was also a petition,[45] in which Knox sought the aid of the nobility to ensure that he be given, in spite of the death penalty passed on him *in absentia* by the Scottish bishops, the chance to rebut the charge of heresy laid against him in 1556. Throughout the tract, Knox's object of attack was neither the regent nor the child queen, but the church hierarchy (e.g. 97, 111). Much of the tract was taken up with arguing the position that it was legitimate to appeal to civil authorities on a religious matter. The doctrine that the clergy should be exempt from civil jurisdiction was deemed to be a popish Antichristian blasphemy (105–9). The 'reformation of religion' was a task entrusted to the 'civil magistrates and nobility' by God. Civil authorities had a wide range of religious duties, especially when the clergy failed to perform theirs (86–7). Indeed, at one point Knox seemed to find 'princes' (in which term he included lesser magistrates, like the nobility) the final (human) court of appeal: 'I am in your hands and cannot resist to suffer what ye think just' (78, expounding Jeremiah 26.14). Nonetheless, for the nobility to refuse to defend the innocent (i.e. Knox) was rebellion against God (75).[46]

Knox obviously could not hope that an appeal to the authority of the crown would help him much, hence his appeal instead to the nobility and the estates (and, in a separate *Letter to the Commonalty* appended to the *Appellation*, to the common people). The portions of the work most cited by historians of political thought are the passages in which Knox dealt with the objection that only the king, the chief magistrate, and not the nobility had the authority and duty to care for the faith and to reform it (91). The nobility were roundly informed:

Your duty is to hear the voice of . . . God, and unfeignedly to study to follow His precepts who, as is before said, of especial mercy hath promoted you to honours and dignity. His chief and principal precept is that with reverence ye receive and embrace His only beloved Son Jesus, that ye promote to the uttermost of your powers His true religion, and that ye defend your brethren and subjects whom He hath put under your charge and care (94–5).

The chief magistrate, of course, had the same duties. Knox then asked what might happen when the chief magistrate refused to perform those duties. His answer was clear. The prophet Ebedmelech spoke out in defence of the innocent (Jeremiah 38.9), '[a]nd the same I say is the duty of every man in his vocation, but chiefly of the nobility which is joined with their kings to bridle and repress that folly and blind rage'. If they fail, 'they provoke the wrath of God against themselves and against the realm'. They could be certain 'that God will neither excuse nobility nor people, but the nobility least of all, *that obey and follow their kings in manifest iniquity.* But with the same vengeance will God punish the prince, people and nobility' (96–7).

It might make sense to label this argument as, at heart, putting forward a lesser-magistrates theory of resistance; but only with some important qualifications. Knox was not asking the nobility to assault directly the authority of the crown. He was asking them to protect him against the clergy, whether the chief magistrate did so or not. The nobility were to perform their duties even when the crown did not perform its own, but there was no suggestion that the crown should be punished or called to account for its failure to be on the side of truth. Certainly, Knox said also 'that none provoking the people to idolatry ought to be exempted from the punishment of death' (p. 98); but if that were a threat to Mary of Guise, it was a threat for the moment left dormant. In addition, Knox was concerned entirely with the performance of duties imposed by God. He showed little interest in what might be called secular tyranny (if, indeed, the concept would have any meaning for him).

Knox, as Jane Dawson has pointed out, carefully distinguished between the Scottish and English situations.[47] The general principle was clear: 'The punishment of idolatry doth not appertain to kings only, but also to the whole people, yea, to every member of the same according to his possibility' (102; also 99). This time he did indeed proceed to make the point that God had made the nobility 'as bridles to repress the rage and insolence of your kings whensoever they pretend manifestly to transgress God's blessed ordinance' (102). At this point, however, Knox began to distinguish between different circumstances. First, there was the contrast between peoples who were not formally Christian and those who were; secondly, there was a distinction between those who were deluded or falsely Christian (i.e., lived under papal domination) and those who had at some time publicly bound themselves to the true Christian faith. The first of these distinctions marked off Scotland and England from the pagan gentile nations, in which the Christian was bound to call idolaters to repentance, but not to punish them (102). The second distinction, however, separated the English and Scottish cases. The Scots were bound, like the Israelites under the Mosaic covenant and like all formally Christian peoples to speak out against idolatry; but in formally papist countries, 'where all are blinded', 'no ordinary justice can be executed, but the punishment must be reserved to God and unto such men as He shall appoint [i.e. to particular inspired individuals?]' (104). The English situation was quite different. In the time of Edward VI, they 'received God's perfect religion', but now had fallen away. 'Unto such a number, I say, it is lawful to punish the idolaters with death if by any means God give them the power' (104). That meant – as Knox explicitly said – that the nobility and people of England were bound, by having 'solemnly avowed and promised to defend' true religion, to resist the Jezebel, Mary Tudor, and also 'to have punished her to the death' (104; cf. also, 111–12). It is notable that Knox's use of the concept of covenant was different from Goodman's. Whereas the latter built a theory of resistance directly on the idea that all Christians as individuals were covenanted with God and obliged to enforce God's law in some circumstances, Knox accepted that individual Christians in a Christian society were bound to speak out, not actively to resist. Every baptised Christian had *some* duty to care for religion (104), but what that meant in practice varied from place to place. The duty of tyrannicide imposed on the English people derived from the covenant entered into by the nation as a whole, committing them to promises that had not been made by all Christians. After 1553, falling away from their commitments, the English became apostates.

The *Appellation* has been read as advancing a theory of individual popular resistance of the sort found in Ponet, Goodman and the *First Blast*. Knox was quite explicit, however, that God imposed a duty to punish idolatry on lesser magistrates, on 'the whole body' of the people, and on individuals only according to their 'vocation' and 'possibility' (99, 102). The *Letter to the Commonalty* elaborated on that. Their vocation and possibilities meant that their role was largely passive. They should (and must) listen to Knox's arguments; they could provide true preachers for themselves when others failed to do so; and could protect those preachers from persecution. They had a duty to bear witness against tyranny.[48] Of course, even here Knox was demanding an awful lot; but he was not demanding what we might call resistance. Subjects must perform their religious duties while remaining essentially subjects. When speaking of them in a more active role, Knox added that they should act while 'concurring with your nobility' (116). Underlying his argument was a strong stress on the essential equality of all Christians. Regardless of their station, all Christians had the same general duty to serve the faith. This spiritual equality contrasted with – but also co-existed with – their civil *in*equality (118). And it was that inequality that helped to differentiate the particular requirements imposed by Christian duty on individual believers. As Knox might have said, 'from each according to his abilities'.

It makes sense to call this position ecclesiological, perhaps even conciliarist, because Knox was concerned not with the civil commonwealth but with the church, including both clergy and laity. Essentially, the *Appellation* asked what the lay members of the church should do when the clergy failed to ensure the propagation of true religion. The answer that Knox gave was an extension of the conciliarist answer to the question of papal inadequacy. The whole body of the faithful and every individual had duties to preserve the true faith. Those duties were activated by the failure of the clergy. The body of the church was superior to its clergy.[49] The initial stage of Knox's 'appeal' against the unjust sentence that the bishops had passed on him was 'to a lawful and general council'. From those countries in which Protestantism had advanced – Germany, Switzerland, Denmark, Poland – there had come an entirely appropriate wish for an appeal against the Antichrist to 'a lawful and general council wherein may all controversies in religion be decided by the authority of God's most sacred Word' (74). Knox appealed to the nobility for interim protection, to last until such time as his case could be heard by a more appropriate authority. In doing so, he granted the nobility religious authority within their own 'dominion'; but it was an emergency and subordinate authority, necessary until Scotland joined the international protestant fold and could participate in a general council of the sort that Knox wanted. In short, Knox advanced not so much a political theory as an ecclesiology in which the lesser magistrates served as the policemen for the (temporarily) absent authority of a general council, and overrode the perverted authority of the clergy.

Knox's thinking in 1558 reflected closely a Scottish situation in which there was great reluctance directly to confront the authority of the regent. His strategy had moved on a stage, from petitioning Mary of Guise herself to petitioning the nobility, in the hope that they might be willing on their own to confront the clergy and set about the task of

Reformation. But this was still not a theory of resistance to secular authority, and contrasted sharply with the tactics that Knox was simultaneously advocating for the English situation. There he demanded nothing less than the slaying of Mary Tudor, and allowed any individual who cared to try to set about the task. Furthermore, Knox's political thought reflected a situation – again markedly contrasting with that of Marian England – in which it was still possible to hope that the lesser magistrates, the nobility, would be the agents of Reformation and the destroyers of idolatry. This emphasis on the central role of the nobility runs through Reformation Scottish political thought, and continues on to that third noble revolt in the name of religion in 1638.

In May 1559 Knox returned to Scotland, where his preaching and propaganda helped to bring about the Congregation's attempt to destroy the authority of the regent. But an interesting change came over the Congregation's self-justificatory arguments during 1559 and 1560.[50] They began in strongly Knoxian vein (indeed, much of the Congregation's propaganda was probably written by Knox); but by the time of the Congregation's suspension of the regent in October 1559 some new themes had clearly emerged. In their letter to the regent of May 1559, the Congregation made clear their fundamentally religious justifications. They feared that they might need to defend themselves with the sword 'against all that shall pursue us for the matter of religion, and for our conscience sake'; they promised obedience only 'provided that our consciences may live in that peace and liberty which Christ Jesus hath purchased till us by His blood, and that we may have His Word truly preached and holy sacraments rightly ministered unto us'. Without that, 'we firmly purpose never to be subject to mortal man'.[51] In the letter to the nobility produced at the same time, the protestants characterised themselves as engaged in a struggle 'to remove idolatry' and 'to erect the true preaching of Christ Jesus' (152). They promised divine punishment of those who refused to obey God's clearly expressed law in these matters. 'If ye obey the injust commandments of wicked rulers, ye shall suffer God's vengeance and just punishment with them' (154). When Christ's church was victorious, then those who refused to help it to victory would be excommunicated, to their eternal loss (155).

By August there were signs of change. The same theory of religious disobedience was, indeed, reiterated (166–7); but greater public prominence was now given to the argument that the Congregation was acting in defence of the Scottish 'commonwealth', the identity and existence of which was being threatened by the regent's French ties. These arguments appealed to those who 'bear natural love to their country', and will defend their 'commonwealth, and the ancient laws and liberties thereof' (159). The document suspending the regent in October 1559 relied heavily on this patriotic language of 'commonwealth', which had acquired crucial connections to the idea of Scottish 'freedom' – that is, national independence – and to the ideal of good kingship. It enabled the Congregation to portray itself as the defender of Scotland's historic identity, and as loyal to the institution of monarchy in so far as it served the common good.[52] The regent was suspended for her 'enterprised destruction of their said commonweal' and for bringing about a 'manifest conquest of our native rooms and country' by bringing in 'strangers'. This would 'suppress the commonweal and liberty of our native country . . . make us and our posterity slaves to strangers forever . . . [and would be] very prejudicial to our sovereign lady, and her heirs' (171–2). The regent was deposed in an action that defended Scottish freedom, and defended the rights of Queen Mary and her heirs. The Congregation's propaganda, issued in the name of the 'nobility, barons and burghs', also portrayed their own role in the most traditional terms. In contrast to the 'strangers' on whom Mary of Guise relied, the native aristocracy were 'born counsellors . . . by the ancient laws of the realm', men 'touched with the care of the commonweal' (174). They were not so much God's lesser magistrates as the kingdom's.

This propaganda, which contrasted dramatically with Knox's religious arguments, was well suited to the situation of 1559. It drew on traditional Scottish themes, thus offering a broader appeal than the highly sectarian and divisive arguments of Knox; and it enabled the Congregation to tap the fears engendered both by the regent's heavy reliance on French aid, and by the marriage of the young queen to the French dauphin in 1558. In portraying the Congregation as *defenders* of crown and kingdom, it helped to make it possible for William Cecil to manoeuvre his queen, Elizabeth I, into giving the essential English aid to the Scots. Elizabeth was, naturally, very reluctant to support revolts against legitimate monarchs; and unlikely to be much persuaded by the views of a man who had denounced the regiment of women as monstrously unnatural. The Scottish Reformation became a patriotic act.

In 1561, following the death of her husband, Mary Queen of Scots returned to her subjects. Trapped by their own propaganda, the now-triumphant protestants had no choice but to accept her authority. Nonetheless, the situation was clearly an unstable one, with protestant ministers especially troubled by the queen's continued practice of Catholic worship in the midst of her protestant kingdom. In the General Assembly of 1564 an important debate took place over whether the queen might be deprived of the Mass against her will. The

queen's secretary William Maitland of Lethington rebuked the irre-
pressible Knox for his turbulent denunciations of the queen. Knox not
only defended his attacks on the queen's idolatry, but once again reiterated his belief that unGodly rulers should not be obeyed. Romans 13
commanded obedience only to good rulers. Wicked princes might
therefore be resisted without neglect to the ordinance of God. Only
just power was irresistible (191–2). Knox asserted, too, that it was not
enough merely to refrain from obeying unjust rulers. A more active
pursuit of righteousness was required by God (193). Idolaters – a category that included the queen – ought indeed to die the death; and the
people at large had the right to execute God's law on them (195; also
204). Scotland, now a protestant country, no longer had any excuse for
allowing idolatry in its midst (197). With that remark we see that Knox
was, by the mid-1560s, applying ideas to Scotland that in 1558 had
fitted only English circumstances. Their public professions had bound
the Scottish people to the most rigorous enforcement of God's law.

The General Assembly reached no decision, but Knox's account
suggests that his own arguments were not exactly victorious (204–9).
When in 1567 Mary was forced to abdicate, and replaced by her infant
son James VI, the major tract written in defence of the revolt, George
Buchanan's *De Jure Regni apud Scotos* (On the Law of Kingship among
the Scots) was very different from anything that Knox might have
produced. It was rather closer, however, to the arguments presented by
another of the speakers in 1564, John Craig, who suggested that 'every
kingdom is, or at least should be, a commonwealth, albeit that every
commonwealth be not a kingdom'. As such, it was essential to preserve
the laws against tyrants (207–8). Craig and Buchanan might both be
read as adding a further extreme twist to the commonwealth language
of 1559–60.[53]

Mary was forced to abdicate in 1567 for her adultery, not her idolatry, and there is no doubt that her mishandling of relations with the
Scottish nobility was as important a factor in her downfall as her
Catholicism. Nonetheless, religion remained central to the perception
of events, and Buchanan's defence of the proceedings of 1567, though
not itself primarily a religious work, was to become deeply embedded
in the minds of later Scottish protestants. Presbyterians within the
Scottish kirk, above all Andrew Melville, appear to have 'rapidly inter-
nalized' the politics of Buchanan,[54] while David Hume of Godscroft's
1605 work on the British Union would pick up many of the themes in
Buchanan's writing.[55] Though Buchanan did not publish the *De Jure
Regni* until 1579, the evidence suggests that it was written very soon
after Mary's deposition in 1567, and may have been circulating in
manuscript as early as 1569.[56] As McKechnie long ago pointed out,

there is a certain paradox about the way in which Buchanan's writing became a canonical Calvinist–presbyterian text, for it says nothing at all about the authority of the church *vis-à-vis* secular rulers.[57]

George Buchanan was one of the great humanist intellectuals of the later sixteenth century. He was a Latin poet, dramatist and historian admired by fellow scholars across Europe. He was a late convert to Calvinism, and his political thought arguably shows few distinctively Calvinist features. Instead, the *De Jure Regni* can be read as a key work of classical republicanism, important in transmitting Renaissance ideals into the seventeenth century.[58]

Buchanan appended to the *De Jure Regni* some lines from Seneca in which was portrayed the Stoic ideal of kingship. The true king displayed constancy, and was swayed from the right path neither by ambition nor by the 'fickle favour of the restless mob', neither by wealth and prosperity, nor by fear or death.[59] This, with much else in the dialogue, goes a long way towards suggesting that the *De Jure Regni* can – at one level – be read as a *speculum,* a contribution to the 'mirror of princes' *genre,* based on a distinctively Stoic ethic.[60] At one point near the end of the dialogue, 'Maitland' accused 'Buchanan' of advancing a position 'excessively Stoic and rigid'.[61] Severe it certainly was. Kings and laws alike should be 'hard and unyielding', recognising that even 'God does not wish us to take pity even on the poor in administering justice'.[62] Law was for Buchanan so much identified with reason, and so essential to the subjugation of passion, that he allowed little place at all for an equity that might mitigate the rigours of justice. Kings should be free from the sway of passions, their actions fully under the control of reason. All men were subject to the two monsters of anger and lust, and it was the function of law to ensure that in the case of kings, those passions were controlled by reason.[63] For a king, the law was 'a curb on his passions'.[64] Seneca's 'Stoic king' was certainly the ideal, but it was also an imaginary and unattainable ideal.[65]

But of the many classical authors used by Buchanan, it was not Seneca but Cicero who did most to provide him with the core of his argument. The *De Jure Regni* is less a Stoic *speculum,* and more the outline of a Stoic commonwealth built on a Ciceronian plan. Because the individual monarch could not be trusted to follow severe reason rather than his passions, then the community (through its laws) needed to ensure that he was externally compelled to perform the virtuous actions that he lacked the virtue naturally to perform.

What sort of monarch did Buchanan want? At one point 'Maitland' accused 'Buchanan' of 'praising the republics [*republica*] of antiquity, and the Venetian commonwealth'.[66] The reply was most interesting:

I do not think it matters much whether the person who rules is called king, doge, emperor or consul, provided that it is remembered that he is placed in office for the sake of maintaining justice. So long as the authority is lawful, there is no need for us to argue about its name. The man whom we call the doge of the Venetians is nothing other than a lawful king. Likewise, the first consuls retained not only the insignia of kings, but also their authority.[67]

The chief magistrates of a commonwealth were, then, true kings in the sense that Buchanan used that term. Furthermore, the Roman emperors were *not* included in the 'pattern of kings which we described'.[68] Nor were the Old Testament kings of any relevance, for they were not created by their citizens as true kings were, but acquired their authority directly from God.[69] 'Buchanan' did admit that some tyrants, in fact, ruled well enough to be counted as just kings – this category included the Roman emperor Vespasian, Alexander the Great, and Hiero of Syracuse[70] – but it is difficult to avoid concluding that Buchanan thought that really the *only* true kings were those who exercised magisterial authority in republics, or who ruled in a similar sort of way. His praise of the ancient Scottish monarchy was certainly eloquent;[71] but it was not post-feudal kingship that Buchanan extolled. The Scottish king was portrayed as the chief magistrate of a republic.

The Scottish kings, in Buchanan's world, ruled not subjects but citizens (*cives*), who sometimes acted as a people (*populus*). Their *regnum* was referred to in the more general passages of the dialogue (in spite of its title) as a *civitas* (a city, or – more helpfully – a community of citizens).[72] This terminology reflected more than Buchanan's attempt to discuss the Scottish monarchy in good Ciceronian Latin. It was essential to the course of his argument, and may indeed help us to sort out some obscurities in that argument.

The most obviously Ciceronian portion of Buchanan's writing was his account of the origins of political communities. His principal source appears to have been Cicero's *De Inventione*, I.ii.2–3, on the basis of which Buchanan asserted that originally 'men lived in huts and even in caves, living a wandering, nomadic existence without laws or settled habitations, and that they gathered together as their fancy took them or some common convenience and advantage inclined them'.[73] But this 'solitary wandering life' was less suited to men than a social existence, into which men were driven in part by 'expediency' (*utilitas*), looking to their own benefit. Expedience was not, however, at the root of the matter. There was also a certain force of nature such that, even when the attractions of expediency are absent, they nevertheless willingly assemble together with creatures of their own kind. . . . [We] see this force so deeply imprinted in man by nature that were someone to have in abundance all those things which are meant to ensure his safety or to please and delight his sole, he would still think his life disagreeable without human intercourse.[74]

'Maitland' then asked 'Buchanan' what was meant by 'nature' in this context. Buchanan replied that it meant nothing other than 'that light divinely shed upon our minds' (*quam lucem animis nostris divinitus infusam*). This light was the law of nature, and it enabled men to distinguish between things wicked or dishonourable (*turpis*) and things 'honest' or honourable (*honestus*).[75] It was, thus, not orators or lawgivers who brought men into society, but ultimately God himself, 'for like Cicero, I think there is nothing on earth more pleasing to the supreme God . . . than those communities of men bound by the law which are called commonwealths [*civitates*]'.[76]

This account of the origins of civil communities laid the ground for two things that were important to Buchanan's subsequent argument.[77] First, it avoided making man into an animal so naturally social that he could not live outside of communities. While men might have been driven into society for their own individual benefit, they were also impelled by their natural moral sense to seek for *honestas* in the framework of civil communities. Thus *consent* came into the picture. Men chose to join communities; they were not driven – still less commanded by God – to join them. Secondly, Buchanan's account provided a moral framework for politics. Societies were created by men seeking both *utilitas* and *honestas*; they therefore existed for furthering what was most 'honest', which meant (above all) the common rather than individual good. The principle was summarised in the 'Ciceronian maxim . . . *Salus populi suprema Lex esto* [Let the welfare of the people be the supreme law]'.[78] The civil community was not just created *by* men; it was created *for* men. In consequence, 'kings are created, not for themselves, but for the people [*populus*]'.[79]

That principle was reinforced by Buchanan's brief history of political forms, very similar to Cicero's account, which had been intended in part to portray the emergence of popular government in communities like Rome that had originally been monarchies.[80] Buchanan, indeed, pointed the message with his most extensive direct quotation from Cicero, in which it was argued that the Romans first appointed virtuous kings to protect the poor and weak against the wealthy and powerful. Laws and kings were for the same purpose, and the people would be content with the rule of a just prince; but when princes were unjust then laws were created, so that everyone was treated equally.[81] The first kings, these men outstanding for their virtue, reigned by their wills without laws. But such a situation was dangerous when monarchs were no longer men of outstanding virtue, but ordinary people no better than others.[82] At that point law became absolutely necessary.

Buchanan's analysis of the nature of law and its development was indebted to Plato's *Statesman*. Kingship was an 'art', and a sensible king – like a physician[83] – followed the rules and principles of his art. Just as physicians sought to use their art to restore to its proper health and temperament the human body, so rulers used theirs to restore health to the civil body. Such health was achieved through *justice*.[84] The art of ruling, therefore, had justice as its goal. Early kings, citizens of 'outstanding distinction', possessed the skill of their art more or less automatically; but later kings were not necessarily of outstanding virtue (though still chosen by the citizens from amongst themselves). 'Buchanan' at this point posed an interesting question: since it was not popular election that made a physician, but the skill to practise his art properly, was the same true of kings?[85] In answering this question affirmatively, Buchanan was able to explain why kings were subject to law. The rules or precepts of any art were called laws. Therefore, 'the Civil Lawes seem to be certain Preceptes of Royal Art'. A king could then be defined as someone who understood and followed these laws. That did not necessarily mean that kings had to be (like lawyers) fully learned in the precepts of the law, but rather that they possessed that capacity to rule in accordance with law that Buchanan called the faculty of 'prudence' [*prudentia*]. Practice was more important than precept.[86] Kings did not, therefore, have arbitrary power; but were restrained by laws 'to show him the way when he does not know it or to lead him back to it when he wanders from it'.[87] It is important to recognise that although Buchanan did indeed think that all true kings were *elected*, it was not the fact of election that defined kingship. Kings were defined as those with the prudence to rule lawfully, so that (as we have seen) even usurpers could come to be accounted true kings. This argument, more importantly, opened the way for Buchanan to say that tyrants were not kings at all, because in breaking the law they displayed openly their lack of prudence.

That did not, however, quite settle the matter. Before examining tyranny and tyrannicide, Buchanan devoted much attention to the problem of actually enforcing and institutionalising the king's subordination to law. The problem arose from two facts about law. There was sometimes the need for new ones, to cover new situations; and written laws were inflexible and required equitable moderation. That meant that there was a need for a law-maker and an interpreter of law. However, if the king were entrusted with such a task, then his subordination to the law would amount to nothing, for he would be able to remake it or to twist it to serve his own interests. Buchanan, as has been noted, had little time for equity (in the technical sense) and seems to have thought that the judiciary gave the law all the flexibility that it needed.[88] That still, however, left the problem of law-making. A law was 'what the people [*populus*] have enacted following a proposal made by someone with the right to propose it'. This was a thoroughly Roman understanding of the nature of statute law (*lex*), as Buchanan acknowledged. Clearly, it implied that the people were 'the makers of the laws'.[89] But 'Maitland' feared that making the laws rather than the king rule would subject the monarch to excessive fetters. In reply, 'Buchanan' emphasised that the rule of law meant that the people would

> be allowed to dictate to him [the rule they had chosen] the extent of his authority, and I require him to exercise as a king only such right as the people have granted him over them. Nor do I wish these laws to be imposed by force, as you interpret it. Rather I believe that, after consultation with the king in council, a decision should be taken in common matters, which affect the common good of all.[90]

This final function was given to the people, immediately raising the spectre of the multitude, the many-headed beast (*bellua multorum capitum*), incapable of rule because of its rashness and inconstancy.[91] 'Buchanan's reply has been much discussed.

> I have never thought that this task should be left to the judgement of the people as a whole [*universus populus*]. Rather, as is roughly our own practice, selected men from all estates [*ordines*] should meet with the king in council; then, once a 'preliminary resolution' has been drawn up by them, it should be referred to the judgement of the people.[92]

Commentators have suggested that Buchanan might here have been proposing something like the modern referendum, or that he was giving to the people sovereign power not intermittently but as a regular, institutionalised arrangement.[93] Neither interpretation seems entirely satisfactory, though it is hard to be sure precisely what Buchanan meant. The passage does seem to constitute a 'republican' reading of Scottish constitutional practice, drawing a loose parallel between Scottish institutions (parliament, and the smaller body that formulated legislation submitted to it, the Committee of the Articles) and the institutions of ancient Athens. The parallel was far from exact, and seems to have rested on a notion of virtual representation – i.e. that the involvement of the people in this process was not direct, but exercised by those qualified by their virtue to be accounted the people's representatives.[94]

Yet, it was not these virtuous lesser magistrates alone who could curb tyrants: any individual had the authority to bring tyrants to justice. A great variety of arguments were used to buttress that conclusion; but the central one rested upon the definition of a true citizen. In punishing a tyrant, the individual citizen was enforcing the decision of the entire citizenry, while his very performance of tyrannicide showed him to be a true citizen living the *vita activa et civilis*. There is no doubt that Buchanan drew on whatever intellectual sources he could find to support his extreme conclusions, including both private-law arguments and conciliarism. It was only, however, the argument from true citizenship that clearly supported the position that Buchanan held. Private-law arguments were excessively anarchic, lacking the communitarian controls important to Buchanan; conciliarism, however, was excessively aristocratic, too much inclined to view most individuals as subjects rather than citizens.

Tyrants, who ruled for their own benefit rather than that of their subjects,[95] 'are not joined to us by any bond of civility or common humanity but must be adjudged the most deadly enemies of God and man'.[96] They were not men but wolves or dangerous beasts, and 'whoever kills them benefits not only himself but the whole community'.[97] In this there are more than hints of the private-law argument that a tyrant, acting without public authority, might be resisted by every individual, just as individuals had the right to repel any other force unjustly used against them. Later, this became explicit when Buchanan pointed out the significance of the fact that 'a thief may be killed at night in any circumstances, but in daytime only if he defends himself with a weapon'.[98] At this earlier point, however, Buchanan did not explicitly go on to advocate tyrannicide. After examining various objections to his argument, he returned to the question of what should be done with tyrants, in an important passage over which there has been some debate.[99] Tyrants could be called to judgement before the people. This did not require the unanimous verdict of the whole people, but only of the 'greater part' of them (*maior pars*). A free people (*liber populus*), or citizenry, acting in this way had the same power over its rulers as the Roman Tribunes or the Spartan Ephors.[100]

What, however, defined the *maior pars*? Some have thought that Buchanan referred to a simple numerical majority (and have portrayed him accordingly as a proto-democrat); others have taken the view that Buchanan referred, like Mair before him, to what Marsilius called the *valentior pars*. If so, that would make his theory a typical lesser-magistrates resistance theory, similar to that of some of the Huguenot writers. Such a theory would tend to vest the authority to resist tyranny not in the people as a whole but in the better people, that is to say, in the aristocracy. In fact, neither reading of Buchanan seems quite correct. Central to his understanding of what the term *maior pars* meant was a concern with the nature of true citizenship. There was a numerical element, 'for injustices if tyrants can affect many, but their favours concern few'. Very likely, then, most people would be hostile to them. More importantly, though, those who *did* support tyrants were in any case betrayers of their own communities (and by definition, not good citizens).

> Who then are to be counted as citizens? Those who obey the laws and uphold human society, who prefer to face every toil, every danger, for the safety of their fellow countrymen rather than grow old in idleness. . . . So if citizens are reckoned, not by number, but by worth, not only the better part but also the greater will stand for freedom, honour and security.[101]

With its emphasis on public-spirited virtue, on actions undertaken for the collective good of the commonwealth (i.e., patriotically) and not out of self-interest, and on the fame and recognition acquired by such actions, Buchanan's brief account of citizenship is clearly derived from the central features of the Ciceronian account of the commonwealth. True citizens were, in a sense, defined by their willingness to defend the public good against tyrants. That defence went even to the extreme of single-handed tyrannicide, which we can now see as defensible primarily as an extension of the active political role played by true citizens. When collective action against the tyrant was not undertaken, the individual citizen had sufficient public authority alone to bring the tyrant to account. A citizen could do what a subject could not.

Buchanan employed a number of arguments to prove that tyrants were 'public enemies', outside the law and the bonds of citizenship, and that citizens had a duty to destroy them in defence of the public good. The most discussed argument is the assertion that there was a 'mutual paction' (*mutua pactio*) between a king and the citizens, constituted by oaths of obligation on the one side, and the king's coronation oath on the other.[102] A tyrant broke the terms of this pact, and thus became an 'enemy' (*hostis*, also *hostis publicus*) who could be slain by any citizen. Buchanan cited the approval that communities gave to tyrannicide in classical times, portraying the act as virtuous and rational.[103] But the defence of a collective public capacity to discipline tyrannical rulers, and of single-handed tyrannicide, rested primarily on a conception of the Scottish realm as a commonwealth in which all of the citizens – a category distinguished from the multitude by the fact that its members displayed the civic virtue of public spiritedness – had an active political capacity. Tyrannicide was the most extreme consequence of this position, and the person who performed it gave the ultimate proof of his right to be thought a true citizen.

Buchanan wrote to defend the deposition of Mary Stewart before a European audience. The resulting work was aimed, therefore, at the only Europe Buchanan knew: the international humanist confraternity of scholars. In spite of its occasional discussions of the Scottish polity, the work, therefore, was very much a general humanist political treatise, designed to provide a Ciceronian reading of the Scottish situation. Implicitly, as much as explicitly, the *De Jure Regni* portrayed the Scots as blessed with a tempered monarchy, like the Venetians or Rome in the days of the consuls. Much less than any other work examined in this chapter was the *De Jure Regni* a *livre de circonstance.* Or rather, its circumstances were much broader, European rather than English or Scottish; and the resulting work is the only British resistance tract of the period that is not primarily a sectarian work, written by an insider for insiders. It is one of the most sophisticated and original works of political thought produced in sixteenth-century Britain, though historians have only just begun to appreciate its manifold riches. Perhaps his immediate successors were not so slow in appreciating Buchanan, for it is notable that one of the few works produced in Jacobean England in defence of the classical theory of mixed government cited Buchanan. The earliest work that John Toland was, at the end of the seventeenth century, to admit to his republican canon was John Hall's *Ground and Reasons of Monarchy Considered* (1650), a work that based its arguments on analysis of Scottish monarchy. It is also surely more than coincidence that the earlier and more republican of Algernon Sidney's two major political writings gave such prominent place to the portrait of an ideal king contained in Seneca's *Thyestes*.[104]

Ponet, Goodman and Knox were all primarily religious rather than political thinkers. Their arguments rested on an understanding of God's commands, and upon a strong sense that the welfare of the civil or political community was of much less importance than the requirements of the faith. Knox, Goodman and Ponet subordinated all things to God. God required that rulers should not be oppressors, heretics or women, and no Christian people had the right even to tolerate such rulers. The people were very much conceived as subjects, both of God and of the monarch; and in all cases the argument rested on the fact that they were God's subjects first and the monarch's second. Buchanan's approach was quite different. God played no direct role in his argument. The people were not subjects but citizens, and they acted not in obedience to God but in protection of their own welfare. It is this emphasis on the active role of all citizens that both made Buchanan's political thought genuinely *political*, as well as linking it to the civic humanist tradition. Buchanan apart, what the Calvinist resistance theorists show us is that one immediate consequence of the Reformation was that in certain circumstances the political realm could be subject to the frighteningly destabilising force that arose from its complete subordination to religious ends. The major task of conformist political thinkers lay in controlling and restraining this dizzying capacity of religion to erode the very foundations of civil politics and civil order.

Disagree : England → their motives were political (or mixed w/ religion)

Agree : Scotland → Buchanan not religious at all

3 Lawful Conformity and its Critics: Political Thought in Elizabethan England, 1558–1603

The death of Mary I and the accession of Elizabeth I on 17 November 1558 immediately transformed the situation within which English political writers worked. After the brief aberration of the Marian years, the Protestant cause was once again on the side of the monarch – and *vice versa*. From 1558 through until the Civil War there developed a persistent polemical tendency to associate English Protestantism with loyalty, obedience and monarchy; and to associate Catholicism with disobedience, resistance, even republicanism. Conformist Elizabethan writers developed a complex picture of the English polity as a law-governed, orderly political community, unified by an absolute loyalty to a limited monarch. By far the most sophisticated expression of such a view was to be found in Richard Hooker's *Of the Laws of Ecclesiastical Polity*, publication of which began in 1594. In Hooker this emphasis on law was extended even to the queen's supremacy over the church, which came to be seen as something normally exercised through legal channels, like her civil authority.

Dissenting voices, from within the protestant camp and from outside it, challenged some of the ideas that supported the English church-state. Most did so with restraint, careful to avoid looking as if they were fostering disorder. Nonetheless, the resistance theories of the Marian period (and of the Scottish and European Reformations) were never entirely forgotten, though they were often repudiated; and, throughout the later sixteenth century, echoes of them can occasionally be heard, sometimes in unlikely places. Civic humanism, too, remained a powerful contributor to later sixteenth-century political language.

Conformist Protestantism

John Knox's *First Blast of the Trumpet against the Monstrous Regiment of Women* (1558) could not have been published with worse timing. A few months after it appeared, in the spring, its main target Mary Tudor died, and the 'wicked Jezebel of England' was replaced by another woman – a Protestant one.[1] Knox's fellow exiles rushed to repudiate his rash remarks, while he himself wrote an apologetic letter to the new queen. In it he asked that the circumstances in which he wrote should be taken into account. He was not an enemy to Elizabeth, but a friend. Divine dispensation had made for her an exception to the usual rules of nature, so in consequence Knox accepted 'your Grace's just regiment, provided that ye be not found ungrateful unto God'.[2] This was hardly an apology, and certainly not a retraction of the basic point.[3] (Goodman, too, was viewed with great suspicion in the new reign, and was compelled to recant his earlier political views in 1571.)[4] The headlong rush to repudiate Marian resistance theory must have been further fuelled by the fact that Catholic propagandists quickly seized upon the theme of protestant disloyalty. John Martial in 1566 contrasted Marian protestants with Elizabethan Catholics, among whom '[t]here is no blast blown against the monstrous regiment of women ... there is no word uttered against due obedience to the sovereign'.[5]

Aylmer

The earliest published response to Knox's arguments was written by his fellow-exile, the future bishop of London John Aylmer.[6] His *An Harborowe for Faithfull and Trewe Subjectes* (1559) announced a number of themes that were to prove central to Elizabethan political thinking. Recent historians have naturally been much interested in what the Knox–Aylmer debate can tell us about attitudes to women and women's authority in the early modern period, though their difference was not, on this question, very great.[7] Indeed, Aylmer's case rested on admitting the *general* inferiority of women to men, especially in public life. Elizabeth's rule might therefore be a great danger to England, *if* it were true that:

> the regiment were such, as all hanged uppon the Kinges or Quenes wil, and not upon the lawes wryten: if she might decre and make lawes alone, without her senate. If she judged offences accordinge to her wisdome, and not by limitation of statutes and lawes: if she might dispose alone of war and peace: if to be short she wer a mere monark, and not a mixte ruler.[8]

Personal qualities mattered little

The English polity was governed by law, and as such possessed the strength to tame even the worst ruler. The personal qualities of a monarch mattered not a jot, for she did not exercise personal rule. Not even having a woman on the throne could deflect the operation of English government from its steady course.

Aylmer drew upon the claims made in the fifteenth century by Sir John Fortescue that English government was as much 'politic' as it was 'regal', buttressing his argument with humanist emphasis on the rule of laws rather than of men, and on mixed government.[9] England was a nation 'where neither the woman nor the man ruleth. If there be no tyraunts, but the lawes. For as Plato saith . . . That cytie is at the pits brinke, wherein the magistrate ruleth the lawes, and not the lawes, the magistrate.'[10] Such an arrangement was produced by a mixture:

> The regiment of Englande is not a mere Monarchie, as some for lacke of consideracion thinke, nor a meere Oligarchie, nor Democratie, but a rule mixte of all these, wherein ech one of these have or should have like authoritie. Thimage whereof, and not the image, but the thinge in dede, is to be sene in the parliament hous, wherin you shal find these 3. estats. The King or Quene, which representeth the Monarche. The noble men, which be the Aristocratie. And the Burgesses and Knights the Democratie. . . . [I]f the parliament use their privileges: the King can ordein nothing without them.[11]

Aylmer is an important place to begin the discussion of Elizabethan thought for two reasons. The humanist language that he employed was less evident in later writers, yet the case of Aylmer may remind us that humanism played an important role in the capacity that English thinkers were to show hereafter for conceiving of their polity as a law-governed one.[12] English political thought remained throughout the period bi-polar: it was a realm that found unity in the monarch, but equally it was a 'commonwealth' that might have some existence and life of its own – and not just a commonwealth, but a Godly commonwealth, serving the purposes of God. Aylmer portrayed the rule of a queen as legitimate if she were well counselled, and that counsel came from bishops as well as from lay counsellors.[13] We are now learning from a number of historians the extent to which even 'establishment' figures were willing to envisage, should the kingdom find itself on the death of its monarch without an acceptable protestant heir, an emergency capacity in the commonwealth to act without its head and remedy the situation.[14] The men of Aylmer's generation seem to have been at ease with ideas of mixed monarchy, repudiated by most from the 1590s onwards.[15]

The best-known portrayal of the Elizabethan commonwealth was Sir Thomas Smith's *De Republica Anglorum*, published in 1583, but written in the 1560s. Most governments, Smith argued, were mixed, and the pure forms (monarch, aristocracy and democracy) were seldom to be found. Nonetheless, they usually took their designation from the part that dominated.[16] The appropriate form of government was dictated by circumstance, not by the inherent superiority of one form. Forms were changeable (62–4). In England's case, there was little doubt that the government was a monarchy (56). But it was also a 'commonwealth', 'a society or common doing of a multitude of free men collected together and united by common accord and covenauntes among themselves' (57). Kingship emerged from patriarchal authority, even though the civil societies over which kings ruled were formed by 'common and mutuall consent'. Smith rooted this patriarchal authority less in a divine command, and rather more in the simple natural affection that people possessed for their ancestors (59–60). English kings did not exercise all of their authority alone, but made laws and imposed taxes only in parliament. They could declare war and peace on their own authority, and could choose their own officers. Justice was administered by established institutions and procedures (88, 85). This account of the royal prerogative was uncontroversial, but there is no doubt that it was founded on a conception of England as a mixed and tempered monarchy, in which the 'commonwealth' shared in some of the essential functions of government. Smith explained how this was possible with his account of parliamentary representation. Certainly, the prince was 'the life, the head, and the authorities of all thinges that be doone in the realme of England' (88); but that realm was also a 'commonwealth', in which 'the most high and absolute power . . . is in the Parliament'. Therein, 'in peace and consultation where the Prince is to give life, and the last and highest commaundement', the nobility, the bishops and the commons are 'present to advertise, consult and shew what is good and necessarie for the common wealth'. Laws thus made are 'the Princes and whole realmes deede: whereupin justlie no man can complaine, but must accommodate himselfe to finde it good and obey it'. In this way, parliament 'representeth and hath the power of the whole realme both the heade and the bodie. For everie Englishman is entended to bee there present, either in person or by procuration and attornies. . . . And the consent of the Parliament is taken to be everie mans consent' (78–9). This commonwealth might be seen, as more explicitly by Aylmer, to be a Godly commonwealth.[17]

A second important feature of defences of the English monarchical church-state was revealed also in Aylmer's work. Knox's *First Blast* posed a simple question: how could you defend the rule of an admittedly inadequate ruler (i.e. a woman)? Aylmer's answer was to deny that the ruler's personal capacities mattered. That answer, however, was extendable. If it did not matter that your monarch was a woman, then it did not matter that he or she was a sinner, even a heretic. Government was founded in nature and not in grace. God might hate sinners and heretics. He might even hate women. But that divine disapproval did

not remove a person's title to rule, for political life was natural, open
to all human beings, not just those of whom God approved. Nature,
Aylmer suggested, required 'the preservation of the whol' (sig. C3).
Since there were many examples of women rulers preserving their
commonwealths, it must follow that there was a role for women to
serve in this way: 'what so ever preserveth common wealthes, and
destroyeth them not: is not againste nature, but the rule of women
hath preserved common wealthes, ergo, it is not against nature' (sig.
D2). A ruler's particular personal qualities become unimportant. What
mattered was her or his ability to preserve the community. Coupled to
this was the argument that the peculiar nature of the English polity
made it particularly resilient in the face of less than ideal monarchs.
Both of these themes – the foundation of politics in nature rather than
grace, and the peculiarities of the English polity – were central themes
in Elizabethan conformist political thought.

Lying beneath these more sophisticated arguments was a reinvigora-
tion of a theme running from Tyndale through the reign of Edward VI,
and inhibiting the development of resistance theory under Mary: the
association of Protestantism with obedience to the ruler.[18] As Aylmer
put it, Christian subjects had 'to be in every wise obedient to Gods
lieutenaunt our sovereign . . . everye man in hys callyng'. If not, God's
wrath would be provoked, 'to poure downe his vengeaunce upon us',
possibly even by sending a tyrant to rule.[19] The theme was repeated
endlessly. The maintenance of political order was thought to demand
either willing obedience, or a willing suffering of the penalties for
refusing to obey. Even tyranny was preferable to the anarchy that came
from active disobedience or rebellion. 'Is there any greater disorder
than rebellion?' was a question clearly intended by its author, Thomas
Norton, to be rhetorical.[20] '[A] rebell is worse then the worst prince,
and rebellion worse then the worst gouernement of the worst prince
that hitherto hath beene.'[21] Yet it was also pointed out that without this
obedience all men would be worse off. As the homilies put it,

> Take away Kings, Princes, Rulers, Magistrates, Judges, and such
> estates of GODS order, no man shall ride or goe by the high way
> unrobbed, no man shall sleepe in his owne house or bedde unkilled,
> no man shall keepe his wife, children, and possession in quietnesse,
> all things shall bee common, and there must needes follow all
> mischiefe, and utter destruction both of soules, bodies, goodes, and
> common wealthes.[22]

The legal writer Richard Crompton made the same point by quoting
Cicero. Without government 'no house, no Cittie, no nation nor

mankind, nor the nature of things [i.e. the natural world], nor the worlde it selfe can stand'.[23] Using the common analogy between the state and a ship, Norton summed up the point: 'The common weale is the ship we sayle in, no one can be safe if the whole do perish.' The safety of the queen ensured the welfare of all, 'the whole realme having interest in hir life, by which we all lyve, and can not live well without her'.[24]

The duty to obey was, of course, more than simply a product of self-interest. God had instituted magistracy and commanded obedience to it. '[T]he Scriptures of the holy Ghost . . . command us all obediently to bee subject . . . to the Kings Majestie' and to all others in authority. Romans 13 provided a summary of Christian politics, to be taken quite literally.[25] However, God's institution of civil government was general, made to all human beings through the law of nature, and not particular to Christians. Thus, in his exegesis of Romans 13, Crompton pointed out: 'Here is no exception of Turke nor Infidell, of the wicked and ungodlie Prince, more then of the Christian and vertuous King.'[26] Obedience was owed regardless of the ruler's personal qualities.

The earliest formal defence of the Elizabethan church-state, Bishop John Jewel's *Apologia Ecclesiae Anglicanae* (Latin, 1562; two different English editions, 1562, 1564) succinctly encapsulated this thesis of protestant loyalty to established authority.[27] It also introduced a second theme that we need to note, and which will be further examined later in this chapter. Catholics, Jewel noted, accused protestants of being 'men of trouble', who 'pluck the sword and scepter out of kings' hands', 'arm the people', and 'destroy the laws' and property. Jewel took comfort from the fact that the same charge had also been levelled at Christ and his Apostles.[28] In neither case was it justified. The writings of protestants clearly 'put people in mind of their duty to obey their princes and magistrates, yea, though they be wicked'. They have 'overthrown no kingdom . . . disordered no commonwealth'. In all places where protestants have succeeded (from Saxony, England and Scandinavia to Switzerland and the free cities like Frankfurt and Nuremburg), the rulers and people 'continue in their own accustomed state and ancient dignity' (58). Jewel contrasted that with the pope's claim to exemption from civil authority, and his claims to make and unmake emperors and kings (59–62). Thus it was protestants and not Catholics who taught and practised the principle 'that we ought so to obey princes as men sent of God; and that whoso withstandeth them withstandeth God's ordinance' (63).

In a later chapter Jewel introduced a second anti-papal argument, by suggesting that parliament and convocation together constituted a church council (104). The papist wrongly tried to exclude the prince and other civil magistrates from church councils (113–14). But, in fact, the prince 'hath the charge of both tables committed to him by God' and ought to be – in Isaiah's words – a 'nurse of the church' [Isaiah 49.23]. All of the early councils had been called by the Emperor (whose imperial authority modern kings had now acquired), who often participated in them, and we find that on occasion civil magistrates even passed sentence on priests for heresy (115–19). It followed that the prince had an extensive range of ecclesiastical duties, and thus an extensive ecclesiastical authority, denied by papists (119). Two things should be made clear: first, that this argument suggested that the prince's authority in religion was exercised through parliament and convocation; and, secondly, that, as one would expect, it did not attribute to princes any of the functions of priests.

But even the seemingly straightforward conformist doctrine of obedience was not without its subtleties and ambiguities. Two demand particular comment. The doctrine was one that demanded obedience not just to kings but to all of those in authority, and to the laws too. That is a matter of some importance given the strong tendency in English political thought, especially that produced by those trained in common law, to emphasise the belief that English monarchs were in some sense bound to rule by the law. Obedience was owed, in conscience, to 'the powers, their ordinances, and lawes', to 'Kings, Princes, Rulers, Magistrates, Judges'.[29] 'By me kings reign', God may have said (Proverbs 8.15); but he also said, or implied: 'thorow mee counsellers make just lawes, thorow mee doe princes beare rule, and all judges of the earth execute judgement'.[30] There may have been in this doctrine of obedience something that we can call the divine right of kings (and of all constituted authority); but it was not inevitably an absolutist doctrine. It commanded a general obedience to authority and law; but it did not specify how, in the English case, authority was in detail constituted. It did not determine the relationship between the king and the law, or between the king and his counsellors or officials. A second point follows closely behind. Balancing the subject's duty to obey (passively or actively) there was a stress on the king's duty to rule well and justly. Even the homilies managed to hint at this, indicating that 'the Magistrates ought to learne how to rule and governe according to GODS Lawes'.[31] They also made it clear that not all rulers did learn: 'when the wicked doe raigne, then men goe to ruine. ... A foolish prince destroyeth the people, and a covetous King undoeth his Subjects [Proverbs 28 and 29]'.[32] Naturally, the homilies made it very plain that even wicked rulers were not to be resisted; but they did not obscure the fact that kings had a duty to rule well, and were answerable to God if they failed in that duty. Nor did they hide the fact that the sufferings caused by evil rulers could be considerable. The doctrine of obedience might have been bleak and uncompromising, but it did not hide from unpleasant realities. Many other writers built on this foundation. Notwithstanding the increasing marginalisation of arguments in favour of resistance to tyrants in the period, it was a commonplace to suggest that tyrants were usually brought to account in this life. The colourful adventurer George Whetstone was uttering no more than a cliché when he said of tyrants that 'we seldome reade of any that raigne long, and of as few that die peaceablie';[33] but Whetstone nonetheless remained a powerful advocate of the doctrine of non-resistance.[34]

Upon this basic doctrine was built a much more complex body of ideas, aimed at a more learned audience, and ready to point to the peculiarities of the English polity. Nowhere, indeed, was the political sophistication of the Elizabethan conformist clergy more apparent than in their ability to support both a doctrine of non-resistance at home and the struggles of Continental protestants against their temporal rulers (particularly the Dutch struggle against Spain). In performing that task they made much of ambiguities within doctrines of obedience.

The conformist defence of the Elizabethan church-state was most fully laid out by John Whitgift in his debate of the early 1570s with the presbyterian Thomas Cartwright (1572–7), a debate known as the 'admonition controversy'.[35] To Cartwright's query whether 'the church be not in as great danger when all is done at the pleasure and lust of one man', Whitgift responded: 'Not so, if that one do govern by law.' He elaborated:

> There is neither prince nor prelate in this land that ruleth 'after their pleasure and lust', but according to those laws and orders that are appointed by the common consent of the whole realm in parliament. . . .[36]

While Whitgift was scornful of popular government,[37] and there is no sign that he was ever tempted to derive the authority of princes from popular consent, he nonetheless recognised the role of consent in the quotidian government of the realm. In this he was not untypical of many conformist English political writers through to the Civil War. What was important for them, in the end, was to discuss the nature and origin of authority in ways that both avoided a reliance on the lust and will of princes, while avoiding also any suggestion that princes shared authority, or were accountable to any other human authorities for any misgovernment that they might commit. A few writers achieved that goal by grounding authority in consent (Richard Hooker); but most, by combining divine right monarchy and the rule of law.

Whitgift, in contrast to Aylmer, was keen to reject the humanist ideal of mixed government, to which Cartwright appealed as the best polity for the Church, and which he claimed to be the nature of the English civil polity. But Whitgift was very typical of both Elizabethan and early Stuart writers in being careful to reject this view in ways that nevertheless preserved the principle that in England the monarch's naked will was subordinated to his or her laws and exercised through regular intermediate institutions. Certainly, the 'three kinds of governments may be mixed together'. But the form of government remained 'according to that which most ruleth, and beareth the greatest sway'. In England, 'although all the states be represented [in parliament], yet, because the judgement, confirmation, and determination resteth in the prince, therefore the state is neither "aristocraty", nor "democraty", but a "monarchy" . . . '.[38] England was a pure monarchy (and a monarchy by divine right at that); but not a tyranny. The monarch made laws – but in parliament; ruled – but by law; and governed – but not in person. When bishops decided matters of religion, and judges matters of law, 'yet is not the authority of the prince thereby abridged'.[39]

The works of the other great conformist writers before Hooker, Thomas Bilson and John Bridges, showed a similar ability to switch between simple all-inclusive statements of the duty to obey magistrates, and more nuanced analyses of the peculiar distinctiveness of the English polity. That is to say that they brought together the divine right of kings and a form of English 'constitutionalism'.[40] Bilson, for example, preached in 1603, at James I's coronation, a classic example of divine-right theory, in which he emphasised that kings were 'gods by Office, Ruling, Judging, and Punishing in Gods steede, & so deserving Gods name heere on earth'. Obedience to them was required in conscience; they wielded the sword; and to them taxes and tribute were due.[41] These were the moral commonplaces of divine-right theory, and should not be seem as incompatible with the more complex arguments of Bilson's earlier work, *The True Difference betweene Christian Subjection and Unchristian Rebellion* (1585). That work combined expressions of divine right and the irresistibility of English monarchy, with expressions of support for many beleaguered foreign protestants. 'Princes be supreme, that is superior to all, and subject to none but only to God'; all were subject to their sword 'not only by suffering, but also by obeying'.[42] Christians were, of course, to obey God before man; but the model to follow in this was provided by the early Christians, who even when persecuted by evil princes, 'earnestly adjured all christians to be subject to them in all other things, and even in those thinges which were commaunded against God . . . to indure the Magistrates pleasure, though not to obeie his will' (506).

Not all constitutions, however, were identical; and in some places (Venice, Milan, Florence, Geneva) there was no sovereign hereditary prince, and the people shared in authority. Here a magistrate 'may be resisted and recalled from any tyrannous excesse, by the generall and publike consent of the whole state where hee governeth' (513). Bilson distinguished between princes 'elected and limited' and princes 'succeeding and absolute' (514), the latter including the kings of England, Scotland, France and Spain. He therefore rejected Goodman's case for resistance to Mary Tudor (516). Thus resistance was never generally allowed by the law of God, but was allowed 'by the lawes of the Lande in some places' (517). All of this, though, 'is nothing to Princes that inherite, nor to subjectes that are absolutely bound to obey: as in this Realme and some others they bee' (517).

Even in proper monarchies, 'neither will I rashly pronounce al that resist to be rebels: cases may fall out even in christian kingdoms where the people may plead their right against the Prince and not bee charged with rebellion', as when princes try to 'change the forme of the common wealth, from imperie to tyrannie'. Such kingdoms were ruled by 'publike lawes, which afterward the princes themselves may not violate'. Indeed the superior power need not be a prince at all, but could be of any form, as the laws of particular polities determined. Even in hereditary monarchies, there might be agreed conditions: 'the people might preserve the fundation, freedom & form of there common-wealth, which they forprised when they first consent to have a king' (520).[43]

Catholics, Puritans and the Casuistry of Obedience

The conformist divines and establishment lawyers clearly believed that they were responding to a challenge laid down by critics of the English crown and (just as importantly) church-state. Two groups of critics stand out: papists and puritans, neither entirely happy with the royal supremacy or with the English church-state in which they lived.

One consequence of this was the advocacy of resistance theory. In the case of Catholics one might focus on their support for the papal deposing power (direct or indirect); in the case of puritans, on their role in keeping alive the Marian exiles' arguments about the right of a people to call to account their own rulers, in certain circumstances. It is possible to exaggerate the political subversiveness of both groups, but there were undoubtedly extremists among them.[44] Richard Greaves has seen Puritan principles as 'an amalgam of traditional, conservative values and potentially revolutionary ideals'.[45] *Mutatis mutandis*, the same may be true of those of Catholics.[46]

Many historians are reluctant to label too neatly religious groups in Elizabethan and early Stuart England, and disinclined to see any simple correlation between religious groups and political ideas. Contemporaries were much less hesitant. The Catholic propagandist John Floyd, for example, wrote in 1620 that there were in England three opinions concerning 'Princes Authority, and their subjects Allegiance'. Puritans, he alleged, 'wil have *God* without *King*, or else such a King that must depend on the peoples beck'. The 'politicians' (for which, read conformists) will 'have no more Christianity then Parlamentary decrees breath into them'. They will have '*God* so longe, and no longer then the *King* shall please'. Finally, there were Catholics, who will have both God and King. To the latter they will 'give all Allegiance and subjection as farre as Religion and conscience will permit'.[47] The bias is unmistakable, but so are a number of familiar contentions about the political thought of the period. Puritans were associated with a populist politics that overemphasised religious duties and underemphasised political ones; conformists were theorists of the church-state established by law; Catholics attempted to maintain a political loyalism within a context of recognising that their duties to God and His church came first. There is more than a grain of truth in all of these propositions, as we shall see, though they are also in part polemical myths; but what is interesting is the overall framework. Christians – all of them, of all persuasions – inescapably had a double set of duties, religious and political. Equally, they all said that the former were the more important. Yet from this agreement arose many divergent views. This chapter will assess the commitment of both papists and puritans to some variety of resistance theory, but also argue that the dangers posed by confessional difference went beyond direct political resistance. The very principle that God and the king were both owed allegiance – *and in that order* – posed an ever present potential for subversion, even sometimes among conformists themselves. The principle retained a frighteningly destabilising potential fully realised in the Civil War.

Catholic resistance theory

The Elizabethan establishment was in no doubt about the dangers posed by Catholics. William Cecil, Lord Burghley, himself wrote the key defence of the regime's treatment of them, published in 1583, three

years after the arrival in England of the first Jesuit missionary priests.
Cecil's argument was simple: Catholics were executed in England only
as traitors and not for their religion. England was not a confessional
state. Those Catholics who lived peacefully in the realm were allowed to
die peacefully. Treason occurred in two ways: on the one hand, the
pope in his bull *Regnans in excelsis* (1570) had excommunicated
Elizabeth, releasing her subjects from their allegiance, and encouraging them to treasonous rebellion; on the other, seminary priests were
entering the country specifically to foment rebellion. Nonetheless,
these men when apprehended by the authorities were 'not being dealt
withal upon questions of religion, but justly by order of laws, openly
condemned as traitors'.[48] The execution of the seminary priest
Edmund Campion in 1581 was justified by 'the ancient temporal laws
of the realm', and not dependent on any 'new laws established, either
for religion, or against the Pope's supremacy' (7–8). Cecil was able to
list a good number of prominent Marian Catholics whose political
loyalty meant that they were undisturbed by the Elizabethan régime,
though they remained Catholic (9–13). Even when, after 1570 and
Regnans in excelsis, some of these men and others became more of a
security threat, they were examined 'without charging them in their
consciences or otherwise by any inquisition to bring them into danger
of any capital law, so as no one was called to any capital or bloody question upon matters of religion, but have all enjoyed their life as the
course of nature would' (11–12). This belief that the English state did
not conduct 'inquisitions' was central to English self-identity, and given
classic formulation in Francis Bacon's words:

> her Majesty (not liking to make windows into men's hearts and secret
> thoughts, except the abundance of them did overflow into overt and
> express acts and affirmations) tempered her law so, as it restraineth
> only manifest disobedience in impugning and impeaching advisedly
> and maliciously her Majesty's supreme power, and maintaining and
> extolling a foreign jurisdiction.[49]

The Spanish, in contrast, 'by the device of their inquisition', had been
brought low, especially by the loss of much of the Low Countries. They
had failed to learn that a 'rigorous and strainable inquisition' was as
dangerous as 'indulgence and toleration'.[50] This view of England as
not a confessional state was, of course, self-serving, and others could,
explicitly or implicitly take a different view in different circumstances.[51]

The idea that papists were *ipso facto* also traitors was not new. Thomas
Norton had suggested that Catholics believed that the pope has 'the

authoritie of both swordes, spirituall and temporall, the one in exercise, the other in power: to have the disposition of all the crownes of
Christian Princes ... to have power to geve leave ... to subjectes to
rebell against the Prince, to depose the Prince, disherite and destroy
him'.[52] It was on the same sort of claims that Cecil also rested his case,
neither man being too fussy about the finer points of the doctrines that
they attributed to their adversaries.[53] Cecil charged the pope – and all
who accepted his claims – with attempting to usurp an authority,

> by his bulls and excommunications ... at his will in favor of traitors
> and rebels to depose any sovereign princess, being lawfully invested
> in their crowns by succession in blood or by lawful election, and then
> to arm subjects against their natural lords to make wars, and to
> dispense with them for their oaths in so doing, or to excommunicate
> faithful subjects for obeying of their natural princes, and lastly to
> make open war with his own soldiers against princes moving no force
> against him.[54]

The queen bent over backwards to avoid punishing Catholics, but who
could deny her right to seek legal execution of those more active papal
agents who 'secretly allured her subjects to new rebellions' (34), or
who taught 'the people to disobey the laws of the realm' (35–6)? They
were all traitors, even if they were not all armed and ready for rebellion
(37–9).

  William Allen's *True, Sincere and Modest Defence of English Catholics*
(1584) attempted to vindicate Catholics from these charges.[55]
Underlying its arguments was a strong sense that the idea of a national
church was an absurdity. It resulted in 'making a king and a priest all
one, no difference between the state of the Church and a temporal
commonwealth'. He went on. 'It maketh one part of the Church in
different territories to be independent and several from another,
according to the distinction of realms and kingdoms in the world. And
finally it maketh every man that is not born in the kingdom to be a
foreigner also in respect of the Church.'[56] Commonwealths were many
and several; the church was one. That principle enabled Allen to make
some show of loyalty to the queen's temporal authority, while denying
utterly both her spiritual and ecclesiastical authority. '[T]here is a great
difference to say she is not to rule the bishops in causes ecclesiastical
or in matter of ministering the sacraments, preaching, and doctrine,
and to say that she is not queen or governor over the clergy, or that
priests or ecclesiastical persons be not her subjects.' The clergy were,
indeed, bound 'to order and obedience of their kings and to observe
their temporal and civil laws made for peace, tranquillity, and tempo-

ral government of their people and to do them all honor and service in that behalf' (114).

Yet, while the separation of church and commonwealth seemed to guarantee the prince supreme temporal authority on earth, the subordination of commonwealth to church constantly undermined that supremacy. It was, indeed, a feature of times 'of disorder and error' that 'faults done against the prince, or so said to be done, are more odious and punishable than whatsoever is directly done against God'. There is 'more ado about Caesar's tribute than about God's due'. The proper condition for any country was that of Marian (or pre-Reformation) England, 'when God and His Kingdom had the first place, the terrene state the second' (118). The religious indifference that underlay the contrary situation was evident in Elizabethan England, where the pretence that Catholics were not persecuted for religion (even though that religion was believed false) was indicative of a government that 'care[ed] not ... what we believe' (118–19). Stressing the temporal loyalty of priests, Allen nonetheless embraced whole-heartedly the very doctrine that was so abhorrent to Cecil.[57] He embraced it on the grounds that the commonwealth ought to serve the church and was subordinate to it; and he denied that acceptance of the pope's indirect deposing power could be called treason.[58] There was no treason in the proposition 'that the Pope hath power to excommunicate or deprive a prince in case of heresy or apostasy, and consequently to absolve his subjects from their oath and obedience to him; or to stand in defense of themselves and the Catholic faith against him', and rulers only rule rightfully when they 'reign for the advancement of God's truth and kingdom in earth, which is His Church' (129–30).

Even protestants accepted the rightfulness of 'resisting of princes in magistrates in cause of religion ... [and] the subjects' taking of arms for their defense in such a case' (134) (though they applied the principle wrongly). Allen used the protestant writers to show, on the one hand, that there was a general Christian belief that religious considerations trumped political ones, in the last resort; and on the other, that Catholic theorists of the papal deposing power had developed principles that could be used to give effect to this belief in an orderly and proper fashion, in contrast with the anarchic subversiveness of protestant resistance theory. He cited in support of his general claim, Calvin, Beza, Zwingli, Goodman, Knox, Luther, and the Confession of Magdeburg (134–8). The English, he added for good measure, had also supported the Dutch Revolt and the Scottish resistance to Mary (138–9; cf. 192–5). The lessons followed clearly. Even 'the present divinity of England' itself allows that 'a prince lawfully invested and anointed may be . . . for matter of religion, resisted by his subjects'. Yet the protestant examples showed also that Catholics possessed a greater 'quietness of nature, love of order and obedience, and . . . detestation of garboils, stirs, and troubles' (139–40). The crucial difference was that protestants resisted on the basis of 'their own deceitful wills and uncertain opinions without rule or reason', while Catholics, in contrast, 'do commit the direction of matters so important to the Church' (142–3). It was a telling point, accurately exposing the weak-point of many protestant theories of resistance. They could seldom (outside the Holy Roman Empire) rely upon public authorities to lend legitimacy to their rebellions, and consequently had to spend much time explaining why the consequence of their ideas was not simple disorder or chaos. '[I]t is not decent,' said Allen, hammering the point home, 'that inferiors should determine at their pleasures of their superiors'. All Christians agreed about 'deposing and resisting kings for religion'; but Catholics and protestants nonetheless remained separated 'as far as reason and conscience differ from fury and frenzy' (143).

To suppose, Allen argued late in his book, that the English Imperial church-state, created by annexing all ecclesiastical jurisdiction to the crown, was an improvement on the medieval monarchy ('half kings in their own realms') was a mistake. There could be no peace and stability on earth unless the commonwealth were subordinate to Christ and his church. The English monarchy, in seeking to make itself stronger, was undermining the foundation of its own rule (215–16). Drawing upon Old Testament precept and medieval example, Allen constructed a model for the arrangements proper to Christian kingdoms. He admitted at the outset that princes were 'not subject to superiors temporal' (146). That, however, was the source of a problem, rather than the solution to one, for it ran the risk of subjecting countries to a ruler whose objectives were never more than worldly. England was under threat of a Turkism that would trample all spiritual concerns, which were properly to be uppermost, under the feet of base temporal interests (171). The solution to this difficulty lay in recognising that all Christian kingship was conditional upon faith. There was a

> condition . . . implied in the receiving of any king over the people of God and true believers forever, *videlicet*: that they should not reduce their people by force or otherwise from the faith of their forefathers and the religion and holy ceremonies thereof, received at the hands of God's priests and none other.   (152)

In Christian kingdoms church and state were 'joined, though not confounded', so that the civil was 'subordinate, and in some cases subject to the ecclesiastical' (156). Ecclesiastical power, though it 'immediately and directly concerneth not our temporal affairs', nonetheless does so 'indirectly (and as by accident) . . . so far as it is requisite to our soul's health and expedient for the good regiment thereof and the Church's utility' (154). That is why the pope did have the capacity 'to intermeddle indirectly with temporal princes' in matters concerning 'injury of the Church and true religion' (175). The pope could authorise resistance.

Allen's work might justify the view of Cecil and others that Catholic theories of papal authority were a dangerous form of resistance theory; but there was a diversity of Catholic voices, and considerable complexity of response amongst the Catholic community as a whole.[59] In the same year that Allen's *Defense* appeared there was published another reply to Cecil, one of the most famous of all works of Catholic propaganda, usually known as *Leicester's Commonwealth* (1584), a defence of the claims of Mary Queen of Scots. It contained no defence of the papal deposing power – indeed, implicitly rejected the idea – and contained a general defence of religious toleration, arguing along the lines of the French *politiques*, that the stability of the commonwealth did not require complete confessional uniformity.[60] On such a basis there was no room for any suggestion that the pope could depose heretical rulers (in any case, the chief obstacle was not the monarch but her evil counsellors). Any idea that the papacy might have direct temporal authority was forestalled by the assertion that the English crown was 'holden of no superior upon earth but immediately from God himself' (158).

One objection to Mary's succession to the English throne was her religion. A Catholic queen would cause chaos if she inherited a protestant kingdom. But, *Leicester's Commonwealth* argued, Mary's experience well equipped her to rule a kingdom divided into three religious groups (papists, protestants, puritans – 65–72). She had already 'in government of her own realm of Scotland permitted all liberty of conscience and free exercise of religion to those of the contrary profession and opinion, without restraint' (168). That, it turned out, was exactly what was required in England. The tract was frank in its recognition that some English Catholics were indeed traitors, and rightly persecuted as such (70).[61] There was equal frankness, though, in the claim that much of the persecution of Jesuits and other seminary priests was mistaken. They were the wrong target. The government needed to identify who the actual traitors were, those whose ambition made them discontented. Religion was not a consideration in this identification. Both puritans and papists would, no doubt, prefer 'to have the chief governor and state to be of his religion if he could'; but that did not push them into the category of traitors, in the sense of men who 'attempt or treaty against the life of the prince or state' (67–8). One thing in particular held men back. Love of country in most cases overrode confessional allegiance. People did not rebel for their faith because 'the fear of servitude under foreign nations may restrain them from such attempts' (69). The best policy was not to deepen religious divisions by persecution, but to exploit the bonds that attached men to their country and which, therefore, fostered unity. The task was to cultivate a situation 'where difference in religion breaketh not the band of good fellowship or fidelity' (182–3). Persecution brought 'matters finally to rage, fury, and most deadly desperation', while a 'sweet qualification or small toleration' served to enhance 'quietness, safety, and public weal', as in Germany, Poland, Bohemia and Hungary (184). Tolerance and moderation 'would content all . . . parties among us for their continuance in peace . . . [and] a temperate obedience to the magistrate and government for conservation of their country' (185).

John Bishop, in 1598, was another who denied the pope's authority to depose princes and authorise rebellion against them, on the grounds that it would be very likely lead to the realm's conquest and oppression by a foreign prince. That was not made more palatable by the thought that the foreign prince would be Catholic.[62] He attacked the notion that the pope had any authority, direct or indirect (though he did not explicitly distinguish the two), over princes; while, at the same time, he accepted that the pope did wield an ecclesiastical jurisdiction independent of secular authority. Bishop's use of *Doctor and Student* has led some to identify his position with that of St German and other Henrician publicists,[63] but that is misleading. Bishop was careful to make it clear that the English crown, unlike the papacy, did not possess spiritual authority and ecclesiastical jurisdiction. He drew a very sharp division between the two kingdoms, the spiritual and the temporal. Bishop, unlike Allen, though, refused to subordinate one to the other. Each was supreme in its own sphere. Directly rejecting the arguments of Allen and Sander, Bishop affirmed that the church had only 'a spirituall government'. Though the prince was subject to the pope and the church 'in causes and censures ecclesiasticall' (62), though the pope was the king's spiritual judge and superior (56), none of this was of temporal effect. Were the pope to excommunicate a heretic king, that act would not have the effect of deposing him or of releasing his subjects from their bonds of allegiance.

More extreme than anything published earlier, however, was Robert Persons' *Conference about the Next Succession to the Crowne of Ingland* (1594).[64] In 1592 Persons had suggested a view that was entirely

destructive of the English church-state, rooted in a vision of a differently configured politico-religious order. A king's title to rule was
dependent on his faith: 'if any Christian prince fall from the Catholick
faith ... he himself thereby, doth forthwith, both by Divine and
Human Law, though the Pope do no way censure him, fall from all his
Authority and Dignity, and his subjects are freed from all their oaths of
allegiance ... and so they may, nay and ought ... pull him down from
the Throne'.[65] Aspects of this verdict were to be comprehensively
developed in Persons' greatest work, which has been declared,
'arguably the best political work written by an Englishman between
More's *Utopia* and Hobbes's *Leviathan*' (excluding Hooker).[66] Its dual
emphasis on the faith and on the political rights and duties of the
people enabled Persons to escape the matrix that confined many
Catholics to defending or rejecting papal political authority.[67]

Persons' starting point was the claim that hereditary succession
('propinquity of birth or blood alone') could not be a sufficient principle for determining who should rule, though he admitted that in
usual circumstances it was 'the best of al other wayes'. What if the next
in blood were mad, or infidel? Clearly, he or she should be excluded
from the succession. '[N]o reason or law, religion or wisdom in the
world, can admitt such persons to the goverment of a common wealth
by whom no good, but destruction may be expected to the same, seing
that goverment was ordeyned for the benefit of the weale publique and
not otherwise.'[68] From this beginning Persons very quickly deduced
the essential framework of his entire argument. There had to be other
conditions that any successor needed to fulfil. '[T]hes condicions must
be assigned and limited out by some higher authority then is that of
the Prince himselfe, who is bounde and limited therby.' This higher
authority, however, could not be the laws of nature or God, for in that
case they would be 'both immutable and the selfe same in al countries'.
History clearly demonstrated the contrary. The conclusion that
Persons set out to explore at length was 'that every particuler countrey
and common wealth hath prescribed thes condicions to it selfe and
hath authority to do the same'. Society and government in general
were ordained by God and nature 'for the common benefit of al', as
Aristotle had shown, yet the form of government, the extent of its
authority, all the principles of succession were all 'ordayned by the
particuler positive lawes of every countrey' (i, 2–4). Not only did the
commonwealth choose its own mode of government, but it 'hath
[authority] ... also to limite the same with what lawes and conditions
she pleaseth' (i, 12–13).

Having established his basic premises, Persons turned to consider
monarchical government in more detail. Aristotle, Seneca and

Plutarch had all concurred in believing monarchy 'to be the most excellent and perfect' form of rule, though (in Aristotle's case) a king was accepted with the qualification 'that he governe by lawes' [cf. Aristotle, *Politics*, 1286a, 1287a-88a] (i, 15–16). Monarchy was not only the best form of government, as being most similar to God's government of the universe, it was also the one with the fewest inconveniences. Especially was it better than democracy, 'a beast of many heades' as Cicero called it; while aristocracy (a blend of the other two, in Persons view) was not untainted with the same problems (i, 18–20). Nonetheless, the authority of all monarchs rested on 'mans election and consent', so that it was true to say that monarchy was 'both a humane creature, and yet from God' (i, 17). Yet, though the government of kings might mirror God's rule itself, the worldly ruler remained 'a man as others be', 'subject to errors in judgment . . . [and] to passionat affections in his wil'. The commonwealth therefore created remedies to counteract those defects.

The first remedy was law. Following Aristotle [*Politics*, 1287a], Persons argued that 'a Prince ruling by law is more then a man, or a man deified, and a prince ruling by affections, is lesse then a man, or a man brutified' (i, 22). The second remedy consisted of councils and counsellors. Some, like the English parliament were so constituted that without them 'no matter of great moment can be concluded', but a king also has 'his privy councel, whom he is bounde to heare' (i, 23–4). The result was that there were nowadays 'no simple monarchies' because 'al are mixt lightly with divers pointes of the other two formes'. In England there was a queen (monarchy), her counsellors (aristocracy) and the commonalty represented in the lower house of parliament (democracy). All of these 'limitations of the Princes absolute authority' originated in the authority that the commonwealth had 'above their Princes for their restraint to the good of the realme' (i, 24). Persons cited ancient and modern examples to show that all commonwealths possessed the authority to temper over time the power of their kings (i, 25–8). The most 'absolute' of all European monarchies were those of Spain, France and England; yet even amongst them there were significant differences. The English monarch was more limited in authority than the others, 'for that every ordination of thes two kings, is law in it selfe, without further approbation of the common wealth, which holdeth not in England, where no general law can be made without consent of parlament' (i, 29). With regard to the succession, on the other hand, the monarchs of Spain and France were more tied by the principle of automatic hereditary succession being limited to the closest in blood to the present ruler (i, 29–32).

Commonwealths could also 'disposesse them that have bin lawfully put in possession, if they fulfil not the lawes and condicions, by which and for which, their dignity was given them'. Of course, that must not be allowed to authorise all sorts of violent tumults, and so this capacity was confined to 'urgent causes' and had to be exercised 'by publique authority of the whole body' (i, 32–3). Private men, certainly, were to obey their king 'in al that lawfully he may commaunde' once he was settled into office, and ought not to examine his title to rule (i, 34–5). The authority to punish and remove monarchs was vested in the whole commonwealth, just as 'the whole body is of more authority then the only head' (i, 38). Old Testament examples of this authority in action included the rightful slaying of Saul and Amon [1 Samuel 31; 2 Kings 21]; and numerous other examples could be found, including English ones (John, Edward II, Richard II, Henry VI, Richard III) (i, 56–62).

Persons summarised his fundamental contentions about the authority of kings, and its limits, in these terms: *limited*

> . . . the cheefest reason of al, and the very ground and foundation in deede of al kings authority among christians . . . [is that] the power and authority which the Prince hath from the common wealth is in very truth, not absolute, but *potestas vicaria or delegata* . . . power by commission from the common wealth, which is given with such restrictions, cautels and conditions . . . as if the same be not kept, but wilfully broken, on ether part, then is the other not bounde to observe his promise nether. (i, 73)

It was also permissible, by canon and civil law, to break an oath to obey kings when obedience could lead to one's own and the commonwealth's destruction, that is 'to the notable damage of the weale publique' (i, 74–6). Drawing upon the standard sources for anti-tyrannical literature (Plato, Aristotle, Cicero; Bartolus' *Tractatus de Tyrannia* [mid-fourteenth century]), Persons affirmed that the good king ruled 'according to equity, oth, conscience, justice, and law', while the tyrant ignored them all (i, 78–9). The true king accepted the principle of the *lex digna vox* (*Codex*, I.i.14) that '[i]t is a spech worthy of the majesty of him that reigneth, to confesse that he is bound unto the lawes', while the tyrant followed the principle of Caligula, recorded by Suetonius (Calig. ch. 23), that 'al things are lawful unto me and against al men without exception' (i, 78–9). All Christian kings promised at their coronation to rule as true and lawful kings and not as tyrants; and that – as we have seen- is a promise to which the commonwealth and its 'officers' could keep them by use of the sword (i, 79–80) – though this was to be done only 'uppon urgent necessity and dew deliberation' (i, 81).

The duties of English kings were well laid out in their coronation oath: they will 'beare revereence and honor unto almightie God, and to his Catholique church', and 'will administer law and justice equally to al, and take away al unjust lawes' (i, 116).

Persons *Conference* was a tract on the succession, intended (as the application of its principles in the second half made apparent) to undermine James VI's claim to succeed Elizabeth. There was no explicit call to resist the queen, and the chief purpose was to show that propinquity of blood alone did not make a monarch. There was inevitably an element of popular choice, of agreement, even if in most cases the nearest in blood was automatically the recipient of the people's approbation (i, 119–21). Three chapters (i, chs vi–viii) were devoted to elaborating those points, mostly by example. Admitting again that generally hereditary succession was to be preferred to election, Persons nonetheless stressed that in special circumstances strict hereditary succession ought to be and could be flouted. Most particularly, where the heir to the throne was 'unfit or pernicious to governe' he ought not to succeed (i, 126–9). '[T]his', he added, 'hath bin the custome and practice of al kingdomes and common wealthes from the beginning.' The system that all countries had adopted had the best aspects of succession and election combined (i, 130). Though there was a sort of *prima facie* assumption that the heir apparent would succeed to the throne, it remained the case that kings only became kings on coronation, not when their predecessors died, and only when they had been crowned was allegiance owed to them (i, 131–3). Numerous examples in which the commonwealth had modified the succession were piled up (the English ones are at i, 178–95). They all demonstrated that, though 'propinquity of bloode is a great preheminence towards the atteyning of any crowne', yet the commonwealth are 'bound to consider wel and maturely the person that is to enter, and to pass him over if they judge him to be 'an enimye or unfitt' (i, 196).

Persons' emphasis on the coronation oath enabled him to lay particular stress upon the king's duty to uphold the faith (e.g. i, 202, 209). A people should choose as their ruler a person most likely to fulfil the duties of kingship. Those duties were encapsulated under three headings: religion, justice, chivalry. But the first of these was of key importance. While 'in former tymes the prince and the people were alwayes of one and the same religion', nowadays it was 'the principal difference and chiefest difficultie of al other' (i, 203). It was also the most important of a king's duties, for the 'first cheefest, and highest ende' of all commonwealths was to help to achieve for its members 'the supernatural and everlasting [felicity] of the soule' (i, 203–4). To fail in religion was the worst offence that a ruler could commit; and 'want of religion'

was the best ground on which to deny the right of an heir apparent to succeed to the throne (i, 212). Furthermore, as 'ther is but one only religion that can be true amongst christians', it was a damnable sin to allow someone of a different religion from oneself to become the ruler of a Christian people (i, 214–16). One was bound in conscience to resist such a development, even when one's conscience was erroneous, for all men were required to do what their conscience demanded of them. The endpoint of its argument was simply that a king's title to rule is dependent on his faith.

There was, then, certainly resistance theory amongst Elizabethan Catholics, some of it mounting a wholesale attack on the Protestant church-state. At one extreme, Catholic writers were advocates of an alternative confessional state; but, just as conformist protestants could both affirm and deny an identity of church and state, so there were Catholics also willing to separate confessional allegiance and political loyalty. Confessional states might not exist, but the aspirations behind the ideal remained the subject of debate in endless permutations.

Puritanism and political thought

Puritanism, it has been said, has been seen in at least two different ways, as 'merely the zealous face of orthodox reformed Protestantism' or as 'an altogether more sinister phenomenon; a socially-divisive, semi-separatist movement . . . that threatened "order" as it was conventionally defined in both church and state'.[69] We do not, though, need to choose between a puritanism always on the 'road to revolution', 'capable at any time of assuming a politically active form in response to challenge or opportunity',[70] and the idea of a puritanism that was politically quiescent (or even enthusiastically 'imperial'[71]), for two reasons. First, there was no *necessary* connection between religious identities and political thought during the period 1558–1640. Throughout England and Europe there was a reservoir of political ideas (resistance, loyalism, toleration, absolutism), and though there may have been strong affinities between certain ways of thinking and particular religious groups (with ecclesiology often the link), nonetheless the relationship was flexible and contingent. More to the point, puritans and conformists *shared* crucial ideas, including the view of England as a (Godly) commonwealth, and the view that the purposes of this commonwealth might not in all circumstances be best served by unswerving loyalty to a monarch. There were other calls on one's allegiances.

Emphasis on the ties that bound puritans into a religious mainstream cuts two ways. While it can make puritans look more like conformists, it can also serve to make conformists look more like puritans.[72] In seeing puritans as integrated, we do not need to assume that we are committed to seeing them as politically innocuous. Rather, there was a subversive potential built into the very core of the Elizabethan establishment. It existed in the ideas shared by protestants (indeed, by sixteenth-century Christians generally) rather than in those that distinguished puritans from the rest. It so happened, however, that circumstances were such that this potential was most activated within English Protestantism amongst some of those people whom we call puritans, and it is amongst them that its political consequences were at first most visible.

This section will explore the most extreme dimensions of this by charting two features of puritan political thought, resistance theory and the presbyterian idea of the two kingdoms. Older accounts of puritan political thought had no hesitation in asserting that it was dominated by resistance theory (sometimes, it was claimed, in 'democratic' varieties).[73] It is clear that such a view needs very severe qualification. Even the most politicised of Elizabethan puritans, the presbyterians, initially pursued a strategy, outlined first in the *Admonitions* to parliament of 1572, that looked for reform by statute, with the queen's agreement. That helps to explain the fact that early presbyterianism reveals little effort to build on the central Marian theme of the covenanted Godly nation, a concept that certainly *could* be used to justify the coercion of monarchs who failed to perform the tasks to which they and the people were together covenanted.[74] In much puritan thought, the idea of the Godly Nation was to be used not against monarchs, but for them. Godly Nations would be led by Godly Princes, and the covenant that bound them together therefore seldom took on the sort of political edge that could prove a route to resistance theory. There was a shared identity with an English nation understood as covenanted with God in the fulfilment of his providential purposes, a view often attached to the name of John Foxe, whose *Actes and Monuments of Matters most Special and Memorable* appeared first in 1563, and in later editions in 1570, 1576 and 1583.[75] Resistance theory of any kind is hard to find among the major figures involved in the drive for further Reformation. Nonetheless, it was by no means absent altogether. Laurence Humphrey, for example, who had been an exile in Mary's reign and became Regius Professor of Divinity at Oxford in 1561, gently endorsed a lesser-magistrates theory of resistance: 'I do not deny . . . that sometimes it is permitted for lower magistrates to oppose higher ones and even for a private citizen to do so, if he happens to be a private citizen whom God raises up.' There comes a point when the covenant with God must be kept 'even if kings rage and the world collapses or even heaven itself falls'.[76] In his work on the duties of a nobility, Humphrey was careful to stress that no ordinary person could lay hands upon a tyrant, but that it was the duty 'of the most and best' to 'minister justice, to bridle tirannie, to maintaine the lawes'.[77] None of this was very explicit, and in both works there was a strong countervailing stress on the subject's duty of obedience.

More significant was Dudley Fenner's *Sacra Theologia*, an important work of systematic puritan covenant theology that was presented to the world with a preface by Thomas Cartwright. Subjects, in Fenner's view, had basic duties 'willingly to employ themselves in publick chardge and affairs', and 'willinglie [to] yeeld Tribute [and] Custom'. Nonetheless, monarchies had a tendency to degenerate into tyrannies, in which a single ruler 'treadeth under foot the lawes and right of the kingdom'. Tyrants were, conventionally as well as for Fenner, of two sorts, tyrants without title and tyrants in practice. With regard to the former, '[s]uch a one, it is lawful for every private man to resist, and also, if he be able, to kil him'. Fenner may have been a little unusual in allowing individual tyrannicide in such a situation, but it was not uncommon to accept that usurpers could be resisted. Less typical was the view that when ruled by a tyrant in practice, 'they that have that authoritie, as the Ephori or princes of the kingdome or a publick assemblie of al estates and degrees in the land, either peacablie, or by force of armes and war, [must] quite dispossess and remoov'. There were two key principles or 'laws' concerning the conduct of these Ephori, who were defined as 'the Confederates of the kingdom [*regni socios*], or the kinges counsellers':

> First that al of them jointly, or anie of one of them severallie as need shal require, both by woord and al lawful meanes, do reduce and cal back the king unto his dutie, whenas he shall either subvert the religion and worship of God, or oppress either the church or common wealth. The second that they faithfullie consult and advise what thinges are behoofull and profitable not onlie for the king but for the kingdom in like manner: and that they do with courage and bouldness persist in urging and enforcing the thinges consulted of until they be established, and that themselves in al lawful and equal thinges be obedient and subject.

Fenner did not dwell on unpleasant details, but the implications were clear enough. Clear also was the fact that undergirding the argument was the appeal to covenant. Kings were bound faithfully and without deceit to 'keep the Covenantes and league [*foedera*] towards God and the people, the lawes and statutes of the kingdom'.[78]

Humphrey and Fenner may be considered isolated cases. But resistance theory was also kept in circulation for a wide (and far from exclusively puritan) audience by the marginal glosses of the Geneva bible. First published in its entirety in 1560, the Geneva bible was mostly the work of William Whittington and Anthony Gilby. It went through close to two hundred editions before the Civil War, making it possibly the most widely read book of its day. The political principles revealed in the work's marginalia stressed, not surprisingly, that kings and magistrates derived their authority from God, and were therefore expected to rule in a Godly fashion [2 Peter 2.11]. They consequently had duties to protect the church, and to use their authority to create a Godly community [Isaiah 3.14; Daniel 3.29, 6.24; pref. to Deuteronomy]; they could not legitimately oppress the church [Psalms 94.20]. Even wicked rulers, however, were ordained by God, as a punishment to wicked peoples. That might seem to leave no space for resistance. While God must be obeyed before man, even infidel princes should be obeyed in civil matters. There were two exceptions suggested, however, to the principle that people should deal with tyrants by prayer. God might specially appoint individuals to perform acts of tyrannicide; or there might exist 'magistrates', all of whom obtained their authority from God, who could use that authority to check an erring king. As a general rule, the people, whether considered individually or collectively, had no right to use the sword against their divinely-appointed rulers. The Geneva bible thus countenanced, in passing almost, a 'lesser magistrates' theory of resistance, of the sort that could be derived from Calvin's *Institutes*. It did not elaborate at all on the circumstances in which this resistance might be appropriate, or the institutional structures through which it might be exercised.[79]

By whatever means, resistance theory retained its intermittent place in puritan thought into the seventeenth century. Perhaps the most significant and elaborate discussion of the subject was in Andrew Willet's *Hexapla: That is, A Six-Fold Commentarie upon the . . . Epistle . . . to the Romans*, printed for the University of Cambridge in 1611 and reprinted in 1620. Willet's explication of the key political passages in Romans 13 was heavily indebted to the commentaries and other writings of earlier reformed protestants, especially Calvin, Peter Martyr and Paraeus. The verdict that Willet reached was extremely cautious, but he came after many distinctions had been made, to cite the opinion of Paraeus 'that the inferiour Magistrates being subjects, may defend themselves, the Commonwealth, and the Church, and the true faith, even by force of armes against a Tyrant' under certain conditions. These conditions amounted to the need for such resistance to be the only way of protecting 'lives, bodies, and consciences'; and for it to be conducted moderately and without revenge (592). 'God forbid', Willet concluded, 'that the Commonwealth and Church should be left without remedie, the former conditions observed, when either havock is made of the Commonwealth, or of the Church and religion' (592–3).

'Inferior magistrates' resistance theory clearly persisted through the Elizabethan and into the early Stuart period. It was expressed generally in the context of systematic explorations of theoretical principles and biblical commentary (Fenner, Willet, the Geneva bible), and seldom in contexts where it seemed to have direct and immediate practical application. Arguably, this phenomenon is of relatively little significance precisely because there is so little evidence to suggest that puritans during this period seriously entertained the idea of using resistance theory to justify acts of resistance. Resistance, it has been said, was a 'safe ... topic ... when it was not aimed at the Queen or others in authority in England'. Even the writings of conformists, as we have seen, might confirm the view that '[a]iming it at foreigners was condoned'.[80] Much more important was the presbyterian idea of the 'two kingdoms', which reveals much about broadly shared assumptions concerning the relationship between matters of conscience and civil politics.

The presbyterian attempt to persuade queen and parliament to further reform the church effectively began with the *Admonitions* of 1572. In the second of these, Thomas Cartwright strongly denied the charge 'that we despise authorite, and contemen lawes'. Far from despising it, they wanted to ensure that authority operated effectively across the full range of its duties. The requirements of the faith may be laid down in scripture, but 'it is hir majestie that by hir princely authoritie shuld see every of these things put in practise'. Without civil authority to support it, the church 'may and must keep God his orders'; but in those circumstances it would have to do so 'always in troubles and persecution'.[81] The remarks capture well the ambiguities built into the political stance adopted by the presbyterians. They had a very exalted view of the civil authority, requiring it to perform a range of religious functions and to regulate and support the church (as did conformists). Yet they also separated sharply the church from the commonwealth, and gave to the former the capacity to act for its own purposes independently of secular authority. On the other hand, the church had no right to trespass on the proper sphere of the civil power. In his subsequent debate with Whitgift (the Admonition controversy), Cartwright expressed the implications of this position in very well-known words. While Whitgift 'thinketh that the church must be framed according to the commonwealth, and the church-government according to the civil government', this was 'to say, as if a man should fashion his house according to his hangings'. In reality ' the commonwealth must be made to agree with the church, and the government thereof with her government ... the commonwealth coming after must be fashioned and made suitable unto the church'.[82] The prince's position gave him special and important functions in the church; but she was nonetheless one of its members and not its head. Challenged by Whitgift to defend his preference for 'the mixed estate' (of which he thought England an example), Cartwright hedged his bets on the commonwealth; but emphasised the crucial difference between it and the church. Even if 'it be granted that the government of one be the best in the commonwealth, yet it cannot be in the church. For the prince may well be monarch immediately between God and the commonwealth; but no one can be monarch between God and his church but Christ.'[83] As a member rather than the head of the church, a prince was subject in religious matters to its authority. This doctrine of the 'two kingdoms', then, separated church and commonwealth; but it also subordinated one to the other. Certainly, 'we ought to be obedient unto the civil magistrate which governeth the church of God in that office which is committed unto him, and according to that calling'. However, the magistrate must govern the church 'according to the rules of God prescribed in his word'. They are both nurses and servants to the church, and 'as they rule in the church so they must remember to subject themselves unto the church, to submit their scep-tres, to throw down their crowns, before the church'. This did not mean 'that the church doth either wring the sceptres out of princes hands, or taketh their crowns from their heads', but rather 'that, what-soever magnificence, or excellency, or pomp, is either in them, or in their estates and commonwealths, which doth not agree with the simplicity ... of the church, that they will be content to lay down'.[84] The spheres of church and commonwealth were separate; but there was no doubt about which was the more important. The implication was plain, though its detailed application was not, that where their purposes clashed, the church's took priority.

A church, Cartwright explained, could *exist* without a magistrate, but that did not mean that magistrates were not important, for 'the church cannot be in quiet, in peace, and in outward surety, without a godly magistrate'. Conversely, this did not make the church into a monarchy. Indeed, it 'is governed with that kind of government which the philosophers that write of the best commonwealths affirm to be the best' – i.e., a mixed government – as was England itself, 'in respect of the queen her majesty, it is a monarchy, so, in respect of the most honourable council, it is an aristocraty, and, having regard to the parliament, which is assembled of all estates, it is a democracy'.[85] There was undoubtedly a political edge to this,[86] though it may be that Cartwright employed these terms because he believed them to be an uncontentious description of English government (as they had been, for example, when Aylmer used them).

Travers

The fullest elaborations of the institutionalised disciplinarian schemes of Elizabethan presbyterianism were in the writings of Walter Travers, *A Full and Plaine Declaration of Ecclesiastical Discipline* (1574) and *A Defence of the Ecclesiastical Discipline* (1588). Confident that the charges of 'Rebellion, destroyinge off common wealthes, confusion, Anabaptisme' levelled against himself and other presbyterians would be discovered to be false, Travers presented himself as a loyal petitioner.[87] Nonetheless, he began his defence of Godly discipline with some interesting reflections on government in general. Travers tackled a very common subject: the danger to a society of changing the political structure with which it began. '[A]ll humaine societies . . . can be preserved . . . [only with] some certeine manner of government and discipline. The most flourishing and longest lasting societies have been those 'which first of all were sette in goode order off government / and afterwardes kepte the same without any alteracion or chaunge'. The overthrow of Athens and the decline of Rome were examples of this process. The church, too, was a human society, 'a certeine societie and companye off suche as professe the trewe service off God'. God was its lawgiver, and it was only at its peril that the laws which God had instituted were changed. The preaching of the gospel, which had been restored with the Reformation, was not sufficient sign of the church's health, for that health could not be long preserved without the original discipline. Without a renovation of ecclesiastical discipline, it could only be a matter of time before sickness and calamity returned.[88] This appeal for the church to engage in what Machiavelli called a *ridurre ai principii*,[89] a return to original principles, is implicitly an account of the church as a political society with its own lawgiver and laws, separate from that of the commonwealth.

Return church to original principle

What principles, then, governed the interaction of church and commonwealth? Travers insisted on a strict separation of function. Magistrates dealt only with matters relating 'to our life and to our goodes', just as bishops dealt with 'spirituall matters and cure [?] of sowles' and 'hath no charge off the common wealth / nor off the state off this life'.[90] Indeed, precisely to prevent 'contention or striffe', God separated church and commonwealth 'by a most great distance'. There was no clash between the magistrate and the church, because the latter could not impose 'cyvill punishement / as off goodes or off body'.[91] This was a separation of types of authority more than of church and commonwealth:

[T]he civile and ecclesiasticall societies, powers, administrations and regimentes, are distinct and diverse one from another. For the civile is of God only, it is onely temporall and civill: yea, even when they deale with things ecclesiasticall, yet is it but civilly, and is given by civill constitutions. The other is of our Saviour Christ as mediatour, it is meerely ecclesiasticall and spirituall, and even in civill things dealeth but in a spiritual maner, and is bestowed by an ecclesiasticall maner of calling appointed by our Saviour Christ for that purpose. . . . [I]t is playne that the perfection of the one state and power dependeth not uppon the other.[92]

Unfortunately the separation of church and commonwealth was impaired when the bishops (especially the bishop of Rome) attempted, and with much success, to usurp the terrain of the magistrate. In stark contrast, the Apostles had refused to hold any civil office.[93] Travers coopted the authority of 'empyre' to reduce the bishops to their proper place.[94] He was not to be the last puritan to attack the bishops on the ground that they undermined royal authority.

For Travers, as for Cartwright, the church was a mixed polity, in which the one (God through Christ), the few (the elders), and the many (the whole church) each participated in ruling.[95] The prince was not the holder of any ecclesiastical office, but a member of the church; but one with a particular duty to use his civil authority to establish, protect and maintain the true church of God (to which he was as 'a duetifull childe'[96]), though he had no authority to rule in any ecclesiastical matters, not even in matters indifferent, it would seem.[97] He was, therefore, subject to the church's authority, exercised (like his own) by divine right. Magistrates were committed to the care of the church like other Christians, and 'must also as well as the rest submit them selves and be obedient to the just and lawfull authoritie off the Officers off the churche'. Church authorities ruled not according 'to ther owne will / but only accordinge to this word and commandement' of Christ, and therefore 'the princes and Monarches off the world shold geve upp their sceptres and crownes unto' them in spiritual matters. Within its own sphere of authority, the church could question 'thinges established . . . by authoritie' or 'ordeined by the civill Magistrate', for the alternative would have meant the perpetual continuation of 'poperie and paganisme'. Members of the church, therefore, obviously 'are charged . . . to further as much as by any godly meanes, agreable to our callings . . . the further reformation of our Church',[98] a duty quite separate from the subject's duties within the commonwealth.

Thus the principle of two kingdoms had a powerful polemical ambivalence, which was reflected in the use made by Travers of the clash between the Emperor Theodosius and St Ambrose.[99] At one point, 'it was a story about the ambition of bishops; at another, a quite different story about the proper and willing subjection of the prince to ecclesiastical discipline.[100] Presbyterians were thus able to present themselves as defenders of royal authority (against the bishops) and loyal subjects *within the commonwealth*,[101] at the same time as they openly subjected the prince to the rigours of ecclesiastical discipline. These points are of considerable importance. They show us, first, that the political thought of Elizabethan presbyterians was quite different from that of many Marian exiles. The idea of the 'two kingdoms', church and commonwealth, was as antipathetic to any religiously-grounded resistance theory as it was to the royal supremacy in the church. A queen's civil authority was not affected by her status as Godly, heretic or infidel. As a result, what interest the Elizabethan presbyterians showed in resistance theory was an interest in a *civil* form of resistance, in which specially constituted 'lesser magistrates', holding office within the commonwealth, not the church, could lawfully act to restrain a tyrant. There is less sign after 1558 of any continuation of the characteristic forms of Marian resistance theory. This may help to explain why in 1642 we find the puritan clergy who defended parliament's resisting Charles I unwilling to develop the view that they were justifying a religious war, and relying instead on a 'secular' theory of resistance by constituted lesser magistrates.[102]

The casuistry of obedience

Casuistry was developed earliest by Catholics, but came also to have an important place in puritan and conformist approaches to politics.[103] It has been given a good working definition by the *Oxford English Dictionary*: 'that part of Ethics which resolves cases of conscience, applying the general rules of religion and morality to particular instances in which "circumstances alter cases", or in which there appears to be a conflict of duties'. At the core of casuistry was the need to fit together valuable principles and intractable circumstances. It has been said that the first work of 'Protestant casuistry' written in England was Christopher St German's *Doctor and Student*, yet as late as the Civil War, English protestants of various types were lamenting that casuistical divinity was inadequately developed among them, leaving a need to draw on the well developed but deeply flawed casuistry of the papists.[104]

Casuistry tended to become politically significant in circumstances of religious persecution. Such circumstances posed to believers a series of questions concerned with reconciling their accepted duties to God, to their church, and to the civil sovereign. Most people who contemplated resistance (whether passive or active) did so in sorrow more than in anger (or so they said), because it involved precisely this sort of casuistical calculation. All accepted the importance of obedience and order, and were predisposed therefore to consider any acts of resistance dangerous if not sinful. Casuistry came into its own when called on to adjudicate between the conflicts between two duties each of which had good claims on the conscience. Casuistical divinity is important, even if it did not lead directly to the production of complex political theories, because it is a paradigmatic expression of the post-Reformation condition in which men and women were potentially caught between conflicting public duties with no easy way of avoiding the conflict.[105]

Elizabethan Catholic casuistry tended towards political non-resistance.[106] Discussion aimed at the laity focused instead on the legitimacy of 'church papistry' and on the acceptability of misleading investigating authorities about one's recusancy – could a Catholic avoid punishment for recusancy by outwardly conforming to the established church? Could a recusant, when questioned, conceal his Catholicism? There was a general need to balance the imperative to shun heretics (which meant that there was little direct approval of church-papistry) with the practical need not to provoke outright persecution of Catholics (which meant that confessors were encouraged to take a compassionate and indulgent attitude to church papists).[107] The product of this interaction was a body of casuistry that concentrated on such subjects as religious inter-marriage, employment and landholding, presenting to benefices, and religious observances – the day-to-day problems that would confront the Catholic who took seriously his duty to shun the heretic.

In protestant eyes there were three disturbing features in Catholic casuistry. It used the distinction between 'mortal' and 'venial' sins to build an unacceptably indulgent and lax moral code; it had an economical relationship with the truth, allowing people to use equivocation or mental reservation to give misleading answers under questioning (to protestants that amounted to the encouragement of lying);[108] and it allowed disobedience to the civil magistrate, or even tyrannicide (by which, of course, Catholics were taken to mean the murdering of good protestant monarchs). These more controversial features of Catholic casuistry had some limited foundation in fact, mostly in the casuistical instructions aimed at the missionary priests, though the appearance of laxity seems likely to be given by *any* attempt in writing to codify and discuss the mitigating circumstances in which strict observance of moral rules might not reasonably be expected.

And certainly, the general protestant charge of untruthfulness is false, for it was their horror of the direct lie that led Catholic casuists to search for other ways of enabling the individual sinlessly to escape persecution.[109] Furthermore, on the subject of political obedience, the casuistical texts gave little justification for protestant calumnies. Some of the Continental casuistic authorities did allow limited space for resistance theory – and, of course, the Spanish Jesuit Juan de Mariana was eventually to give credence to the idea that the Jesuits supported tyrannicide,[110] but the records of Elizabethan Catholic casuistry tell a different story. A nice illustration of the fine balance achieved in the attitude to public authorities is found in the advice that Catholics did not sin if they paid tithes to protestant ministers, but 'that it is most lawful and most holy to defraud heretics of such payments' if the opportunity arises.[111] Catholics were, on the whole, to be advised not to hold any public office (on the grounds that they might be required to persecute co-religionists), but were able, even after her excommunication, to obey Elizabeth in all political matters. It should be added that on this last subject, whether Elizabeth should be obeyed, the verdict ended, rather ominously, with the remark that 'there is a further comment on this case which must be given in secret'.[112]

The protestant horror at Catholic equivocation, or 'lying', may have been connected to the official justification for persecuting them. They were, it was said, condemned not for their private beliefs or their faith, but for treason. At the trial of Robert Southwell in 1595, at which the subject of equivocation and mental reservation first entered into public discussion, the chief justice commented that 'yf this doctrine should be allowed, it would supplant all Justice, for we are men, no Gods, and can iudge but accordinge to [men's] outward actions and speeches, and not accordinge to their secrette and inward intentions'.[113] The distinction between public acts and private faith, on which the official justification for persecution rested, would be destabilised if private faith itself allowed men to lie about their public actions and speeches. The words perhaps betray a fear that Catholic deceit might force inquisitorial methods upon the English government.[114]

Perhaps the most characteristic feature of puritan casuistry was its anticatholicism.[115] It may be this need to keep a visible distance from Catholic casuistry which explains why puritan casuistry appears often so distant from actual circumstances. The writings of the first puritan to *publish* extensively on the subject, William Perkins, have a rather abstract air to them, and too frequently reiterate the general principles rather than consider their practical application. He was reluctant to risk getting his hands dirty. It seems likely that Perkins' two casuistical treatises, *A Discourse of Conscience* (1596) and *The Whole Treatise of Cases of Conscience* (1606),[116] attempted to codify a body of oral puritan casuistry already widely practised.[117]

In his *Discourse of Conscience,* Perkins defined *conscience* as a knowledge, shared by man and God, of the good or evil of particular actions. It was 'a little God siting in the middle of men[s] hearts, arraigning them in this life' (5–7, 9).[118] The conscience was bound to judge by God's word presented in scripture. The most immediate duties that it imposed were to gain knowledge of scripture, to obey God even in suffering or dying, and to accept the true faith (10–11). Perkins used the latter duty to suggest the unacceptability of any religious pluralism (11). What if a man were subject to two conflicting duties? The paradigm example of this presented by Perkins was the conflict of obedience to God with obedience to the magistrate. Naturally, and like everyone else, Perkins suggested that the former always took priority (11), just as we had a duty to offend our neighbour rather than to offend God (12). The implications of such a doctrine all lay in the details. These may become clearer when we have taken into account that in Perkins' view neither human laws, oaths nor promises properly bound man's conscience (22). This is scarcely a new or a startling view, for it largely restated Calvin's own opinion that human laws could not bind the conscience, and was in any case kept on a tight leash. In response to the argument that in Romans 13.2 it had been declared that obedience to the civil magistrate was required 'for conscience sake', Perkins replied that this was true only after a fashion. Magistracy was certainly 'an ordinance of God', and '[f]or bodie and goods and outward conversation' subjection was due without question. But this did not amount to 'a subjection of conscience to mens lawes'. One sinned by civil disobedience only because one broke God's law, not man's: 'now thus breach is not properly made because mans law is neglected, but because Gods law is broken which ordeineth magistracie, and withall bindes mens consciences to obey their lawfull commandementes' (26–7). Even in matters indifferent, human law bound only in so far as it served a 'good end' (28). On the other hand, liberty of conscience, granted to God through Christ, guaranteed that the conscience could not be bound except by 'such laws and doctrines as are necessarie to salvation' (31; also 44–5). Furthermore, human authority was fallible, 'subject to ignorance and errour', so it was unreasonable to suppose the conscience could be bound by the flawed laws that it created (32). Perkins framed his case with sufficient breadth to address all human authority, concluding that 'wholesome [human] laws' were binding in conscience 'by vertue of an higher commandement' (Romans 13.1). These laws were such as were 'not against the laws of god, and withall tend to maintaine the peaceable estate and common good of men' (33). Men were bound 'in conscience to obey their governours *lawfull* commandements' (33; emphasis added).

Perkins, notwithstanding his casuistry, was committed to a very high view of civil and royal authority. He emphasised that rulers had a duty imposed on them by God to mitigate the severity of human laws in some cases, but *both* the power to make laws *and* the power to mitigate them were 'put into the hand of the magistrate by God himself'. Kings were, indeed, 'gods upon earth', and 'God ... hath given to kings ... not only to command and execute his own [i.e. God's] laws, commanded in his word, but also to ordain and enact other good and profitable laws of their own for the more particular government of their people, and to be helps for the better executing of God's laws: and also to annex a punishment and penalty to the said laws ... '.[119] '[T]he King is honoured, because in his Majestie and state, he carried a resemblance of the power and glorie of God; so as that which is said of God, may be also spoken of him' (236). Nonetheless, all human laws were made 'with reservation of libertie of conscience', which they could not take away (199). Obedience itself was, of course, required (again 'in all things lawfull and honest'), and even 'though punishment bee wrongfully, and most unjustly imposed by rulers, yet it must be borne without resistance, till we can have our remedie' – a remedy presumably from the hands of God (238–9).

Significant in this are not Perkins' conventional views on the duty to obey earthly rulers, but the force with which he reiterates the (also conventional) priority of duty to God before man. Evil human laws, commanding what God had forbidden, 'men are bound in conscience not to obey' (34). There was no sin inherent in breaking human laws. This led Perkins to add a middle category, between breaking and keeping the law, of doing something *beside* the law, an act wherein 'wee shall omit the doing of any law'.[120] Such acts may be done without breach of conscience. They were acceptable provided: (1) they did not hinder the (good) end for which the law was made; (2) in so far as possible, no offence was given; and (3) there was no contempt of the law-maker (35). Perkins' example was deliberately innocuous (opening a city gate to allow in a harried friend when commanded not to open the gates to enemies); but it takes little insight to see that these principles allow an individual to make some judgement about whether the civil magistrates' laws were in conformity with God's, and even to judge whether obeying them served the common good better than not doing so.

Perkins constructed a system of conscience in which the duty of men to God obviously overrode all other duties, and which correspondingly placed a reduced value on obedience to civil magistrates. It clearly allowed that in some circumstances conscientious disobedience to the magistrate was permissible, or even obligatory. Casuistical writing was important for the clarity with which it articulated this widely shared belief, as well as for the hesitancy with which it drew practical conclusions from it. Hesitant or not, Perkins made it clear that obedience to the civil magistrate must for all genuine Christians be to some degree a conditional thing.

Perkins defined English protestant casuistry. Those who wrote after him (William Ames, Joseph Hall, Robert Sanderson, Jeremy Taylor, and Richard Baxter) wrote in the mould he had established because it 'so well reflected the Protestant mainstream in . . . [its] moral instruction'.[121] The casuistical attitude underlay much political thinking and debate in England.[122] It is this as much as any 'underground' tradition of resistance theory that explains the readiness of men to judge that, in certain circumstances, they had a conscientious duty to refuse to obey the commands of their civil rulers in order that they might better obey their God. Furthermore, this was a broadly protestant and not just a puritan attitude. The most prominent Elizabethan figure to have been caught in the classic casuistical situation, between conflicting duties to God and monarch, was Archbiship Grindal, suspended from authority in 1577 for refusing to suppress 'prophesyings'. In his own words to Elizabeth, 'I rather choose to offend your earthly Majesty than to offend the heavenly majesty of God.'[123] As Sir Walter Mildmay observed, 'his conscience did assure him that they [prophesyings] were necessary . . . and he was fully persuaded never to find mercy at God's hands if he should confess the contrary'.[124]

Other phenomena of the Elizabethan political world might also be considered as phenomena of the casuistical mode in which people were driven by conscience to do things that they would in other circumstances consider improper. Here we might consider the Bonds of Association of 1584, which defined 'an essentially protestant political nation and ascendancy' by threatening resistance to any future monarch who acquired the throne, whether deliberately or not, by means of harm perpetrated on the body of Queen Elizabeth.[125] The chief duty imposed by God on kings that was identified in the Bond of Association was 'to preserve them [their subjects] in the profession and observation of the true Christian religion, according to his holy worde and commaundementes'. Those who took the oath constituted by the Bond of Association did so to ensure the continuation of 'peace, welth, and godly government', and in so doing were prepared to envisage the temporary dissolution of civil authority until it could be reconstituted by sworn protestant bands of private subjects.[126] The desperation to avoid a Catholic succession which underlay this oath, also led Burghley and other councillors (faced with Elizabeth's unwillingness to settle the succession) to envisage a thirty-day interregnum during which parliament would continue to sit under the guidance of an enlarged privy council, and would determine the succession.[127] Behind this lay a willingness to subordinate the usual laws and principles of succession to the higher goal of preventing a Catholic tyranny from being erected in England. It belongs less to a world of anti-monarchical republicanism and more to a world in which conscience might drive one to unusual measures in emergencies. Casuistry provided the framework within which we can understand a world in which even the most conformist of people might be driven to acts of disloyalty. There was a long future to this: much of the political thought of the 1640s was casuistical in character,[128] and as late as the Glorious Revolution, beyond the period of this book, the Tory reaction to James VII & II can be understood as a casuistical defence of resistance to royal command. Loyalty to the church overrode loyalty to the king, and thus the most royalist of all seventeenth-century political groups helped to usher James VII & II into exile, and to shut the door behind him.[129]

Richard Hooker and the 1590s

The last decade of Elizabeth's reign was marked by a final effort to suppress the presbyterian strands within English puritanism. Star Chamber and other courts were used to prosecute ministers involved in the *classis* movement, while at the same time a small number allowed their hostility to the established church to drive them into outright separation. The tone of the decade was often ugly, and a number of writers naturally continued the work of Whitgift in reply to presbyterian argument. Most typical, perhaps, was the argumentative thuggery of Richard Bancroft. His polemical characterisation of his opponents was generally crude, portraying them as a threat to social and political order:

> The world now a dayes, is set all upon liberty. . . . You shall finde it, a great matter amongst those that have beene travailers, and it is their usuall discourse, vz. what a notable thinge it is to live in *Venice*. There, (forsooth) every gentelman liveth with as great libertie as the *Duke* himselfe. They have noe Earles, no Barons, no Noblemen of whome their Gentlemen should stand in awe. . . . Be there not some in the world (and yet none *Anabaptistes*) that will say: what is a gentleman, but a man? And am not I in behavious as gentle as he? And for my manhood, as good a man as he?[130]

As part of this portrayal, Bancroft always linked the puritans (implicitly, at least) to the political subversion constituted by resistance theory.[131]

Much the most famous product of this period, though, was the very different work of Richard Hooker. There has been a tendency to see Hooker as impartial, balanced, moderate, tolerant, a writer above the fray; the 'judicious Hooker', inventor of the Anglican *via media*. In context, though, the polemical character of his writing is obvious. Patrick Collinson, writing on the 1590s, has suggested that for Hooker scholars, '[t]he question will be, not how such a calm, reflective book could have been written against such a backcloth, but how calm and reflective it really was'. If we want to find a genuine proponent of toleration in the 1590s, then we should look to Francis Bacon. His reflections of the period did espouse a *politique* case for toleration in ways that Hooker's did not. In broader context, though, Hooker was unusual in the 1590s, a period when many conformist views were turning away from ideas of mixed polity and constitutionalist understandings of English monarchy, and also finding ways, contrary to Bacon's claims, of making windows into men's consciences.[132] Hooker, by contrast, can be seen as 'the first to integrate the claims of the common lawyers into a general political theory', recognising in constitutionalist ideas 'the implications of a consent-based legal theory'.[133]

Even in Hooker's case, we should not be trapped into imagining that the polemic and the reflective are opposed or mutually exclusive categories. Hooker's polemic was of a high order, and he recognised that an effective response to puritan argument would require the careful establishment of first principles. As Collinson again puts it, 'presbyterianism itself had been only a superficial symptom of a more general malaise, which was a mistaken view of the relations of Scripture, reason, and church'.[134] Hooker's polemic therefore went well beyond Whitgift's simple insistence on the importance of obedience to established authority, and attempted to explain to puritans why their conscientious scruples were insufficient to justify nonconformity.[135]

Hooker's Preface to *Of the Laws of Ecclesiastical Polity* provided a polemical characterisation of his opponents, and the rest of the book was a response to the menacing figures that he created in it. Recounting the emergence of presbyterian church discipline in Calvin's Geneva, Hooker praised Calvin, and recognised that the discipline that he established in Geneva was well suited to its circumstances. 'This device I see not how the wisest at the time living could have bettered, if we duly consider what the present estate of Geneva did then require.'[136] His emphasis was on the circumstances that led Calvin to do as he did; but, asked Hooker, 'what argument are ye able to show, whereby it was ever proved by Calvin, that any one sentence of

Scripture doth necessarily enforce these things'? (Pref.ii.7, 139). He argued instead that the reformed churches had adopted a variety of disciplinary forms, the implication being that they were all of equal legitimacy (Pref.ii.9–10, 140–2). And yet there were many now who thought that Calvin's discipline was the only one acceptable. How could they be persuaded otherwise?

Hooker certainly recognised the need for genuine conscientious persuasion, making a point that was later to become the central argument of Locke's theory of toleration: 'whatsoever we do, if our own secret judgement consent not unto it as fit and good to be done, the doing of it to us is sin, although the thing itself be allowable' (Pref.iii.1, 143). Hooker argued that God required men in dispute to agree among themselves on an authority that could give a judgement on the matter that would bind all parties to its acceptance. God was 'not the author of confusion but of peace'. Therefore disputes would have to be settled, and to that end 'God did then allow them [in obedience to such judgements] to do that which in their private judgement it seemed, yea and perhaps truly seemed, that the law did disallow' (Pref.vi.3, 168). It is a striking passage, reminiscent of Hobbes more than Locke; and it leaves Hooker uncomfortably poised between the modes of persuasion and authoritative judgement – 'not that I judge it a thing allowable for men to observe those laws which in their hearts they are steadfastly persuaded to be against the law of God: but your persuasion in this case ye are all bound for the time to suspend' (Pref.vi.5, 170). He wished to persuade; but equally he wished to show puritans that there was, in all reason, an authority that had to be obeyed, whether it was in the right or they were. '[P]eace and quietness there is not any way possible, unless the probable voice of every entire society or body politic overrule all private of like nature in the same body' (Pref.vi.6, 171). Hooker was still able to maintain the emphasis on conscientious persuasion, for his point was to persuade that there was no necessary reason – i.e. one that would bind the conscience – justifying disobedience to properly established authority in matters of church government (Pref.vii.1–3, 171–2).

Hooker attacked the puritan's intellectual capacity to deal with the subject of church government. But in doing so, he made an important distinction between those matters that were clear and simple, even to the unlearned, and those that were not, and which required expert knowledge to understand. The former covered all 'things absolutely unto all men's salvation necessary, either to be held or denied, either to be done or avoided' (Pref.iii.2, 143). But many other matters were obscure, and, as with difficult matters of law, we required 'professors of skill in that faculty be our directors' (Pref.iii.2,

144). Many of those who advocated presbyterianism possessed only a superficial knowledge of the subject. Hooker drew a direct parallel with civil politics:

> If it be granted a thing unlawful for private men, not called unto public consultation, to dispute which is the best state of civil polity, (with a desire of bringing in some other kind, than that under which they already live, for of such disputes I take it his meaning was [Peter's in 2 Peter 2.12];) ... is there any reason in the world why they should better judge what kind of regiment ecclesiastical is the fittest? (Pref.iii.4, 145).

Hooker diagnosed the core problem with presbyterians as their perfectionism. They blamed on the established form of (ecclesiastical) government all 'the stains and blemishes found in our state; which springing from the root of human frailty and corruption, not only are, but have been always more or less, yea and (for anything we know to the contrary) will be till the world's end complained of, what form of government soever take place'. Then, of course, they 'propose their own form of church-government, as the only sovereign remedy of all evils' (Pref.iii.8, 147). Lurking beneath these comments is the claim that the presbyterians demanded a degree of perfection and purity in worldly things (including church government) that was simply inappropriate to the fallen condition of mankind. Unless the puritans were willing to base their arguments on reason, disputable by others, then they claimed for themselves a knowledge of God's will to which no ordinary human being could attain. Scripture was 'plain' only concerning 'the principles of Christian doctrine'. On other matters, including discipline, it was 'more dark and doubtful' (Pref.iii.10, 150–1).

The reason that should be followed in discussing matters of regiment was an historical reason, the sort of reason that was capable of deciding which forms were best suited to which circumstances. The puritans claimed Apostolic precedent for presbyterianism. For all his much-famed love of tradition, Hooker was capable of appreciating the need to change things. '[I]t is the error of the common multitude to consider only what hath been of old, and if the same were well, to see whether still it continue; if not, to condemn that presently which is, and never to search upon what ground or consideration the change might grow.' The puritans failed to consider 'how for the times of the Church, and the orders thereof may alter without offence'. Even Apostolic institution was not proof that something remained useful and fit in the present:

True it is, the ancienter, the better ceremonies of religion are; howbeit, not absolutely true and without exception: but true only so far forth as those different ages do agree in the state of those things, for which at the first those rites, orders, and ceremonies, were instituted. In the Apostles' times that was harmless, which now being revived, would be scandalous, as their *oscula sancta* (I, 159). *No change*

In his sermon on the nature of pride, Hooker argued that 'the greatest part of that confusion whereof Christianity at this day laboureth' lay in the failure to distinguish properly between 'the way of nature, and the way of grace'.[137] It was with this fault in particular that Hooker charged the puritans. They made the commands of God revealed in scripture to be the measure of all things, and therefore failed to leave *No reason* any natural space within which human beings might construct polities and societies using their own reason.

Hooker's counter-argument to the puritan confusion of the realms of grace and nature had three essential components. First it drew a careful distinction between the two realms, accepting the absolute importance of scripture in the realm of grace, but arguing that reason was the crucial authority in the realm of nature. Secondly, it treated the church, viewed as a community, and its organisation and governance, as matters primarily falling within the realm of nature and not of grace. Hooker understood the church as, at one level, a political association much like any other. His account of it was therefore rooted in the principles of reason embodied in the law of nature. And thirdly, his understanding of the nature of political societies, including the visible church, was based on Roman-law corporation theory, and the understanding of consent and representation contained therein. For that reason, though many have been inclined to link Hooker with Locke, his political thought more nearly resembles that of Hobbes.

Scripture, not reason, gave saving knowledge; but in other spheres there were other sources of authority, above all, reason. Natural reason, and the laws it discovered, could never lead men to salvation, their highest goal; that required 'a way which is supernatural' (II.xi.5–6, 258–62; also II.viii.3, 331–2). This situation was a product of the Fall, which had left men with a natural desire for salvation but no natural means to attain it. '[M]an having utterly disabled his nature unto those means hath had other revealed from God, and hath received from heaven a law to teach him how that which is desired naturally must now supernaturally be attained' (I.xii.3, 264). Scripture was perfect for the end for which it was given, salvation; but there was no need to suppose therefore that it provided exhaustive guidance in all matters (II.viii.5, 332–5).

But the puritan claim 'that scripture is the only rule of all things which in this life may be done by men' (II, title, 286) was false. God communicated his will to humankind in others ways, too (II.v.7, 308–9). The first book of the *Laws* enumerated the variety of laws that had been given them. For Hooker, laws were essentially principles of regularity and order designed to enable all things to achieve their proper purposes. 'That which doth assign unto each thing the kind, that which doth moderate the force and power, that which doth appoint the form and measure, of working, the same we term a *Law*. So that no certain end could ever be obtained, unless the actions whereby it is attained were regular; that is to say, made suitable, fit and correspondent unto their end, by some canon, rule or law' (I.ii.1, 200). Hooker acknowledged that this conception of law was broader than that accepted by many, who 'apply the name of Law unto that only rule of working which superior authority imposeth' (I.iii.1, 205). There were three chief categories of law: the eternal law (which guided even the works of God, who imposed it on himself, and on which all other laws depended – I.ii.6, 204); the law of nature, and the divine law revealed in scripture (I.i.3, 200).[138]

It was the law of nature that mattered most for Hooker's political thought. The law of nature was of two sorts, one, observed unwittingly, maintained the order of the natural world (I.iii.2, 206–8); the other, imposed on voluntary agents, included the law of reason. Again, we should remember that in identifying the laws of nature and reason, and the spaces in which they rather than scripture were our chief guides, Hooker was examining simply another way in which God gave instruction to his creation. 'Nature therefore is nothing else but God's instrument' (I.iii.4, 210; also I.viii.3, 227). It gave to men desire for 'the continuance of their being', and for continuation 'by offspring and propagation' (I.v.2, 216); but, as voluntary agents, it also left them untied, so 'that it is in our power to leave the things we do undone' (I.vii.2, 220). Human action was the product of 'Will [of which the object] is that good which Reason doth lead us to seek'. Actions not guided by this rational Will were the product of Appetite (I.vii.3, p. 221). Thus 'discovering in action what is good' was the function of reason; for which reason 'the Laws of well-doing are the dictates of right Reason' (I.vii.4, 222). This law of reason, which is sometimes called the law of nature 'meaning thereby the Law which human Nature knoweth itself in reason universally bound unto', 'is such that being proposed no man can reject it as unreasonable' (I.viii.9, 233). Nonetheless, it was never certain that groups of men would follow the law of reason, for 'lewd and wicked custom' – Heathen idolatry was

Hooker's example – might gain sway over whole societies and obscure the truth from them (I.viii.11, 235).

These laws of reason formed the basis for social and political organisation. The law of reason bound all men, including those living outside society, but it nonetheless revealed that 'we are not by ourselves sufficient to furnish ourselves with competent store of things needful for such a life as our nature doth desire, a life fit for the dignity of man'. It therefore instructed us 'to seek communion and fellowship with others', and thus 'was the cause of men's uniting at the first in politic Societies, which societies could not be without government, nor Government without a distinct kind of Law from that which hath been already declared' (I.x.1, 239). It was reason that disclosed to men the need to create civil societies, and to provide themselves with human laws to govern such societies. There were two foundations for 'politic societies', 'the one a natural inclination, whereby all men desire sociable life and fellowship; the other, an order expressly or secretly agreed upon touching the manner of their union in living together'. The latter of these foundations has sometimes been discussed in relation to the 'social contract' theories of Hobbes and Locke;[139] but Hooker's next sentence seems to make it clear that he was referring to the laws themselves, which in some manner flowed from the consent of the society itself.[140] 'The latter is that which we call the Law of a Commonweal, the very soul of a politic body, the parts whereof are by law animated, held together and set on work in such actions, as the common good requireth' (I.x.1, 239).

Hooker was talking about human or positive law as the bond of politic societies; and he struck at this point an Augustinian note. 'Laws politic' must presume 'man to be in regard of his depraved mind little better than a wild best'; and must ensure that, notwithstanding this inward corruption, his 'outward actions' are 'no hindrance unto the common good for which societies are instituted' (I.x.1, 240). Not surprisingly, given this depravity, before there were civil societies men lived in a dreadful state (I.x.3, 241). To end this they, by composition and agreement amongst themselves, erected 'government public' and subjected themselves to it (I.x.4, 241–2). Consent was crucial to Hooker's understanding of politic societies. For 'peaceable contentment . . . the assent of them who are to be governed seemeth necessary'. In human societies (and in contrast to the natural power of fathers), 'all lawful power [must come] . . . by consent of men, or immediate appointment of God' (I.x.4, 242). No particular form of government was required, 'Nature tieth not to any one, but leaveth the choice as a thing arbitrary,' though men came quickly to see that they were much safer ruled by laws than by the will of one person (I.x.5, 243–4). Human laws were subordinate to the laws of reason, serving to make clearer some of the more obscure principles of reason (I.x.5, 244). They would have been unnecessary were it not for the corruption of the Fall (I.x.13, 251). Human laws were either *mixedly* human or *merely* human. Those in the former category imposed duties already required by the law of reason, while 'merely' human laws created new duties. They were not however, divorced altogether from the law of reason, for 'the matter of them is anything which reason doth but probably teach to be fit and convenient'. It was a matter of expediency, and here Hooker was referring to that reason mentioned in his Preface, which discerned the probable fittedness of measures to particular circumstances (I.x.10, 248–9).

Hooker's second key move was to treat the visible church as a form of 'politic society' (I.x.11, 249), a 'sensibly known company' (III.i.3, 339). Even subdivided by their external professions into the Churches of Rome, England and so on, these societies 'must be endued with correspondent general properties belonging unto them as they are public Christian societies', of which the chief was 'Ecclesiastical Polity'. By that term Hooker meant broadly 'both government and whatsoever besides belongeth to the ordering of the Church in public' (III.i.14, 352). There was, however, no one proper form of church government demanded of them all: 'the necessity of polity and regiment in all churches may be held without holding any one certain form to be necessary in them all' (III.ii.1, 352).

It is worth noting that Hooker's defence of episcopacy sat a little uneasily with his general assertion of the indifferency of church polity.[141] Like many around him in the 1590s, including Thomas Bilson, Richard Bancroft and Hadrian Saravia, Hooker accepted that episcopacy was instituted by Christ with the Apostles. This would appear to constitute a theory of *jure divino* episcopacy that directly contradicted Hooker's claim that forms of church polity were rooted only in the positive law of the church (especially VII.v.2, 157; VII.iv.1–3, 151–4; also VII.i.4, 143). Hooker, indeed, confessed to having changed his mind on the matter; but came to believe that although episcopal authority derived from the apostles, 'yet the absolute and everlasting continuance of it they cannot say that any commandment of the Lord doth enjoin'. Therefore, the church 'hath power by universal consent upon urgent cause to take it away, if thereunto she be constrained through the proud, tyrannical, and unreformable dealings of her bishops'. Hooker, for good measure, said of the bishops:

Let them continually bear in mind, that it is rather the force of custom, whereby the Church having so long found it good to continue under the regiment of her virtuous bishops, doth still uphold, maintain, and honour them in that respect, than that any such true and heavenly law can be shewed, by the evidence whereof it may of a truth appear that the Lord himself hath appointed presbyters for ever to be under the regiment of bishops, in what sort soever they behave themselves (VII.v.8, 163–6).

These passage harmonise to some degree with Hooker's demonstration, in the third book, that the fact that God through scripture was the author of a law did not mean that the law was immutable (III.x.1–8, 384–91). But this does not altogether solve the problem. The emphasis in the third book is clearly that laws must be mutable so that they can fit circumstances, and Hooker made it plain enough that the church, just as much as the temporal commonwealth, was a politic society. He also, throughout the *Laws*, said enough to make it clear that polity must be a mutable thing. He emphasised flexibility, mutability and diversity in political arrangements to a remarkable degree. All communities formed their own polities by consent. Episcopacy was only one component of the church's polity, and Hooker was happy enough to treat the others in a different way from the way he treated bishops. All of which makes his gestures towards a theory of *jure divino* episcopacy anomalous. Scholars are probably right to say that Hooker does not exactly contradict himself, but there is a marked disjunction in tone between the opening books and the seventh. Even so, Hooker's rehearsal of the *jure divino* argument was in itself unusual. It is true that no theorist of *jure divino* episcopacy argued that the institution was immutable or an absolutely necessary mark of the true Church. Nonetheless, Hooker's account is of a markedly different tenor, even in the seventh book, for its very willingness to emphasise the mutability of the institution, for its agreement that, in a sense, episcopacy did rest on custom, and for its willingness to contemplate the possible inadequacy of bishops.

Having established that the church was a politic society, Hooker's third key argument was to understand political societies as forms of corporation, crucial to understanding what Hooker did with the principle of government by consent. In the Preface, Hooker laid down a maxim that was later to form part of the authorisation theory used in Hobbes's *Leviathan*:[142] 'A law is the deed of the whole body politic, whereof if ye judge yourselves to be any part, then is the law even your deed also.' It was the power of the whole community:

The lawful power of making laws to command whole politic societies of men belongeth so properly unto the same entire societies, that for any prince or potentate of what kind soever upon earth to exercise the same of himself, and not either by express commission immediately and personally received from God, or else by authority derived at the first from their consent upon whose persons they impose laws, it is no better than mere tyranny.   (I.x.8, 245–6).

The emphasis was upon the will of the body politic, or corporation, as a whole. The consent of which Hooker wrote did not mean that the individual members of a community had to be consulted regularly, or indeed at all. '[N]ot only they give [consent] who personally declare their assent by voice sign or act, but also when others do it in their names by right originally at the least derived from them'. In many assemblies and parliaments, we give our assent 'by reason of other agents there in our behalf.' It was not always apparent how consent had been given. Even absolute monarchs (whatever Hooker may have meant by that term) had consent:

[W]hen an absolute monarch commandeth his subjects that which seemeth good in his own discretion, hath not his edict the force of a law whether they approve or dislike it? Again, that which hath been received long sithence and is by custom now established, we keep as a law which we may not transgress; yet what consent was ever thereunto sought or required at out hands?   (I.x.8, 246)

Hooker's understanding of the corporate nature of bodies politic helped him out in this matter. He argued, in essence, that the political arrangements of a community, whether or not they allowed for active consent in law-making, could be understood to have the consent of the community's members. Therefore, as in Hobbes, the acts of the sovereign were the acts of all his subjects, who were virtually represented by their sovereign. We are at no man's command save by our own consent. But:

we do consent, when that society whereof we are part hath at any time before consented, without revoking the same after by the like universal agreement. . . . [T]he act of a public society of men done five hundred years sithence standeth as theirs who presently are of the same societies, because corporations are immortal; we were then alive in our predecessors, and they in their successors do live still. Laws therefore human, of what kind soever, are available by consent. (I.x.8, 246)

Whatever political arrangements we live under, we can be supposed to do so by our own consent.

In the eighth book, Hooker applied this general understanding to the English church and commonwealth. Hooker's starting point was a rejection of the presbyterian theory of the 'two kingdoms'. The puritans believed that 'the church and the commonwealth are corporations, not distinguished only in nature and definition, but in substance'. Hooker accepted the analytical distinction, but not the notion that church and commonwealth must be permanently severed and separated from one another. '[T]he name of a church importeth only a society of men, first united into some public form of regiment, and secondly distinguished from other societies by the exercise of Christian religion.' In England, all who were members of the commonwealth were members of the church, and *vice versa*. There was no reason to maintain strict separation between the two corporations. '[W]ith us one society is both the Church and the commonwealth . . . our Church hath dependency upon the chief in our commonwealth' (VIII.i.7, 340).

Hooker's main concern was with the monarch's ecclesiastical supremacy. This he carefully defined:

> the prerogative of calling and dissolving greater assemblies, about spiritual affairs public: the right of assenting unto all those orders concerning religion, which must after be in force as laws: the advancement of principal church-governors to their rooms of prelacy: judicial authority higher than others are capable of: and exemption from being punishable with such kind of censures as the platform of reformation doth teach that they ought to be subject unto.   (VIII.ii.1, 341)

He was emphatic that this supremacy gave the crown no spiritual powers, and no personal authority to decide matters of doctrine (VIII.viii.1, 431; cf. VIII.vi.5, 400–1).[143] It was a mistake to suppose that royal authority served only temporal ends: kings could help serve the Christian faith (VIII.iii.2–4, 363–6). Much, though, rested on the argument that in England, church and commonwealth, though distinct corporations, were in effect the same:

> in well-ordered states and commonwealths [religion] is the first thing that law hath care to provide for. When we speak of the right which naturally belongeth to a commonwealth, we speak of that which must belong to the Church of God. For if the commonwealth be Christian, if the people which are of it do publicly embrace the

true religion, this very thing doth make it the Church, as hath been shewed. So that unless the verity and purity of religion do take from them which embrace it, that power wherewith otherwise they are possessed; look, what authority, as touching laws for religion, a commonwealth hath simply, it must of necessity being Christian have the same as touching laws for Christian religion.   (VIII.vi.6, 402–3)

This makes it very clear why corporation theory and consent were integral to Hooker's polemic. The two together gave him the ability to argue that laws were made for any politic society (including churches) by whatever authority it had recognised. Without this, it would have been considerably more difficult for Hooker convincingly to reach the conclusion that the church was subject to royal authority (as opposed to distinct authorities of its own).

In locating supremacy and dominion in kings, Hooker was not indicating that they were superior to the law, especially in those places where the law gave them their power. With reference to those places in which the king's authority was derived from law, Hooker cited Bracton: 'rex non debet esse sub homine, sed sub Deo at lege', the king is not under man, but under God and the law (VIII.ii.3, 342).[144] His account of kingship was not intended to undermine the rule of law. '[S]o is the power of the king over all and in all limited, that unto al his proceedings the law itself is a rule. The axioms of our regal government are these: "Lex facit regem": the king's grant of any favour made contrary to the law is void; "Rex nihil potest nisi quod jure potest"'; law makes the king, and the king can do nothing that the law cannot do (VIII.ii.13, 353). The result was a very complex theory of royal authority. To have 'real sovereignty', kings needed to have 'supreme power in the greatest things'. Nonetheless,

> I am not of opinion that simply always in kings the most, but the best limited power is best: the most limited is, that which may deal in the fewest things; the best, that which in dealing is tied unto the soundest, perfectest, and most indifferent rule; which rule is the law. (VIII.ii.12, 352)

There were various ways in which societies might come into subjection – by force or conquest backed by divine providence, by special divine appointment, by human choice – but the result was approved by God. 'By what means soever it happen that kings or governors be advanced unto their states, we must acknowledge both their lawful choice to be approved of God, and themselves to be God's lieutenants, and confess their power his' (VIII.ii.5, 343–4). 'Unto kings by human right, honour by very divine right, is due' (VIII.ii.6, 345). Kings appointed by these different means had different degrees of power. Some, like conquerors, had no limits except 'the law of God and nature'; but those who ruled by 'compact' or consent had varying powers, as revealed both in 'the articles ... of compact at the first beginning', and 'whatsoever hath been after in free and voluntary manner condescended unto, whether by express consent, whereof positive laws are witnesses, or else by silent allowance famously notified through custom reaching beyond the memory of man'. By this means of 'after-agreement' even monarchs who acquired authority by force had been tamed (VIII.ii.11, 350–1).

In the case of England, constitutional arrangements helped to ensure that the king ruled by law, in church and commonwealth. This was an example of a polity in which 'the highest governor hath indeed universal dominion, but with dependence upon that whole entire body, over the several parts whereof he hath dominion' (VIII.ii.7, 346). In England, this dependency was institutionalised in representative bodies; and thus Hooker located sovereignty in king-in-parliament (and king-in-convocation), rather than in the king alone.

> The parliament of England together with the convocation annexed thereunto, is that whereupon the very essence of all government within this kingdom doth depend; it is even the body of the whole realm; it consisteth of the king, and of all that within the land are subject unto him: for all are there present, either in person or by such as they voluntarily have derived their very personal right unto. (VIII.vi.11, 408–9)

The king's 'supremacy of power' in law-making 'resteth principally in the strength of a negative voice'. The king did have certain prerogatives that he could exercise in person – declaring war and peace, regulating commerce – but other things 'the king alone hath no power to do without consent of the lords and commons assembled in parliament'; his power has been 'abridged' and 'restrained' by positive law and custom (VIII.ii.17, 357). Hooker linked all of this to his corporatist understanding of civil societies, in which the laws made were the act of all members of the society considered corporately. It is clear from Hooker's general theory that this would always be true, even where constitutional arrangements produced an absolute monarch who made laws without consent. It just so happened that in England, there was an institutionalised role for consent.

The corporative character of Hooker's also enabled him to defend limited monarchy (for England, at least), *without* defending resistance to erring monarchs. Hooker hoped that erring monarchs would see the harm they were doing, and correct it, 'but surely without their consent I see not how the body should be able by any just means to help itself, saving when dominion doth escheat. Such things therefore must be thought upon beforehand, that power may be limited ere it be granted' (VIII.ii.10, 350). In another context, he noted: 'The king is not subject unto laws; that is to say, the punishment which breach of the laws doth bring upon inferiors taketh not hold on the king's person; although the general laws which all mankind is bound unto do tie no less the king than others, but rather more' (VIII.ix.3, 448–9). This last was the essential point made in sermon after sermon that preached the divine right of kings.

In many respects, Hooker's political thought was out of kilter with the 1590s.[145] The mood of a period of economic trouble, renewed court faction, and religious repression may have been better reflected in the blunt writings of Richard Bancroft. It may also be the case that, in his religious doctrine, Hooker initiated the development of an *avant garde* conformity that was to culminate in Laudianism.[146] Yet his political thought was not as apart from the 1590s as some of this might suggest. One feature of his writing – the absence of any explicit link between his constitutionalist account of English monarchy and the idea of mixed government – was a notable feature of late Elizabethan and Jacobean political thought. There was in this period a marked rejection of the humanist idea of mixed government, which even in the early Elizabethan period had still found impeccably conformist adherents (Aylmer). The idea was a risky one, however, in a period of religious civil war or conflict, for there was a danger of it creating authorities not dependent on the monarch. For this reason (and for others, including, as Michael Mendle has shown, the way in which it risked undermining the place within the commonwealth of the clerical estate[147]) it came to be rejected in favour of the view that kings held an unmixed sovereign power. The king's unmixed sovereignty might well be limited, as in Hooker. He possessed certain absolute prerogatives, but many important matters could only be done with parliamentary consent. The king was irresistible; his authority unmixed – but he was still limited by laws and institutions to which he or his predecessors had agreed.

Richard Hooker provided one account of a sort of English confessional state, united under the authority of the royal supremacy, and united too by the rule of law, resting on consent. But during the Elizabethan period there had been others who challenged royal supremacy, and contested whether any commonwealths were confessional states. At least some Catholics were animated by a very different vision of what a confessional state might be. Even amongst conformists, there were occasions when separating confessional and political allegiance seemed important, and there were voices, especially in the 1590s, calling for a church-state more intrusive on private conscience than Hooker might allow. The patterns are complex – there is no simple answer then or now to the question of whether the Elizabethan polity was or was not a confessional one – but what is clear is the massive potential for conflict and disruption that was stored in these matters.

4 Peaceful Politics? Jacobean and Caroline Britain, 1590–1640

The reigns of James VI & I after his accession to the English throne in 1603 witnessed the greatest stability that Britain saw between the Henrician reformation and the early eighteenth century, making all the more startling the speed with which Charles I was able to bring about the destruction of political order across the British kingdoms, and in Ireland too, from 1638. The intellectual foundations for this stability were, however, complex. A shared acknowledgement that the British polities were made peaceful by the conformity of all – kings and subjects – to lawful and regular government, and to a church established by law, was certainly a major ingredient, but this position could mask (or accommodate) considerable divergence over the precise interpretation of what lawful government in church and state might mean, and how kings might be constrained to follow it. Where was authority located in a polity governed by law? And – just as pressing – to what extent did stability require England and Scotland to become *one* polity (possibly ruled by *one* code of law) after 1603?

James VI & I and Divine Right Kingship

James VI's political thinking was formed in the Scotland of the 1580s and 1590s. Accordingly, it can be understood in a number of interrelated contexts, in relation to the political thought of George Buchanan and its reception by Scottish presbyterians, to the two-kingdoms political theory of Presbyterianism, and to the king's concern about his future succession to the English throne.[1] There is relatively little in James's work that looks like a *specific* response to Buchanan, though clearly their views of kingship are utterly incompatible.[2] *Basilikon Doron*, though, certainly contains harsh words about 'puritan' ministers, and was attacked for them by one of the key advocates of Presbyterianism, Andrew Melville, and condemned at the 1599 Synod of Fife.[3] James had clashed with Melville in 1596, and was then informed:

> I mon tell yow, thair is twa Kings and twa Kingdomes in Scotland. Thair is Chryst Jesus the King, and his kingdome the Kirk, whase

subject King James the Saxt is, and of whase kingdome nocht a king, nor a lord, nor a heid, bot a member! And they whome Chryst hes callit and commandit to watch over his Kirk, and governe his spirituall kingdome, hes sufficient powar of him, and authoritie sa to do, bathe togidder and severalie; the quhilk na Christian King nor Prince sould controll and discharge, but fortifie and assist, utherwayes nocht faithfull subjects nor members of Chryst.[4]

With this argument in mind, James warned his son against the 'Puritanes, verie pestes in the Church and common-weill of Scotland' (78). This group posed a special problem in Scotland because of the character of the Scottish reformation. It had been 'made by a popular tumult & rebellion' rather than 'proceeding from the Princes ordour (as it did in England)'.[5] The result was that the Scottish reformers became wedded to 'a Democratik forme of gouernement' (74). They believed '[t]hat all Kings and Princes were naturally enemies to the liberty of the Church, and could neuer patiently beare the yoke of Christ' (76). Naturally, for its government they instituted 'Paritie in the Church', this being 'the mother of confusion & enemie to Vnitie, which is the mother of ordour; by the example whereof in the Ecclesiasticall gouernement, they think (with time) to draw the politick and civil gouernment to the like' (76–8). Such an ecclesiastical government 'can not agree with a Monarchie' (78–80).[6] The point was, of course, that expressed in the famous epigram uttered by James – twice, for good measure – at Hampton Court in 1604: 'No bishop, no king'.[7]

The *Trew Law*, the clearest expression of James's view of divine right kingship, was in contrast a less overtly engaged work, though it might be understood as a contribution to the debate on succession to the English throne that followed the publication in 1594 of Persons' *Conference about the Next Succession*. That work greatly troubled James, and his own insistence that God transferred rights to the crown by the principles of succession can be read as a response. But the preface and opening pages of the *Trew Law of Free Monarchies* were explicit attempts to transcend particular contexts. They sought to gain authority over the reader by appearing above dispute. 'I onely lay downe herein the true groundes . . . without wasting time vpon refuting the aduersaries.' To preserve his beloved country from 'endles calamities, miseries, and confusions', James had taken up his pen;[8] but he had done so not with a mind to 'answering the contrarie propositions', but simply to inform his subjects of 'the mutuall duetie and alleageance betwixt a free and absolute *Monarche*, and his people' (60).

The duties of kings and of subjects were each discussed in relation to scripture, to the fundamental laws of Scotland, and to the law of nature

(60). Almost immediately, James brought into the discussion the king's coronation oath, in which '[t]he princes duetie to his subjectes is . . . so openly confessed'. In it three duties were outlined. Kings must 'maintaine the Religion presently professed within their countrie, according to their lawes, whereby it is established'; they must 'maintayne all the lowable and good Laws made by their Predecessours'; and they must 'mainteyne the whole Countrie, and euery state therein, in al their ancient priuiledges, and liberties' (60–1). All of this was 'the cleerest ciuill and fundamentall law'. The same duties were to be derived from God, who made the king his 'lieutenant' so that he could 'vpon the peril of his soule . . . procure the weale of both soules and bodies, as far as in him lieth, of all them that are committed to his charge' (61–2); and from natural law, which made the king a father to his people, whose 'chiefe joy ought to be in procuring his childrens well-fare' (62).

Turning to the allegiance of subjects to their king, James began with scripture. Just as he had already made use of the coronation oath, taken by some writers to justify resistance, so he now began a lengthy exegesis of 1 Samuel 8.9–20, far from being the most obviously monarchist of scriptural passages. Both of these moves are indicative of James's essential argumentative strategy: the construction of what we might call the worst-case scenario. By emphasising both the demanding duties imposed on kings and the vast extent to which they often failed in fulfilling those duties, James was showing how bad things could get. Yet even in these unpromising situations, he would demonstrate, no justification for resistance could be found. James explained that the warnings given by Samuel when the people of Israel asked God for a king were 'to prepare their hearts before the hand to the due obedience of that King, which God was to give vnto them, what might be the intolerable qualities, that might fal in some of their Kings, therby preparing them to patience, not to resist to Gods ordinance'. Yet James was in no doubt that the kingship Samuel portrayed was 'tirannie, and oppression' (64). It was a kingship that broke the principles of equity and justice (65–6). The people, thus forewarned, were bound to obedience not only by the ordinance of God, but by their own 'willing consent', having asked God for a king with their eyes open to the possible ill consequences. The people had declared: 'we wil take the good and euill of it vpon vs, and we will be content to bear whatsoeuer burthen it shall please our King to lay vpon vs' (66). As no Christian king could be more tyrannical than that portrayed by Samuel, and no Christian people could claim greater liberty than that possessed by the Jews, it followed that in no Christian nation was resistance to kings permissible (67). Naturally, therefore, St Paul had commanded in Romans 13, Christian obedience even to the tyrant Nero (68–9). The king, 'Gods Lieutenant in earth', was himself answerable and accountable only to God (69).

The Bible seemed to make it clear that tyrants could not be resisted, but what did the laws and customs of modern realms permit? In Scotland, whatever the situation in other times and places, kingship originated in conquest. After Fergus, coming from Ireland, had conquered the barbarous inhabitants of Scotland and reduced them to peace and order, a situation was reached in which that king (later his successors too) 'made lawes by himself' and held dominion over all the lands of his vassal-subjects (70–1). Is not this an arbitrary king who can give laws and tax without consent? Perhaps; but the crucial point is that James was not claiming to be able legitimately to exercise such authority. The real value of the historical argument he had constructed was revealed when he remarked:

> So as if wrong might be admitted in play (albeit I graunt wrong should be wrong in all persons) the King might haue a better colour for his pleasure, without further reason, to take the lande from his lieges, as ouer-lord of the whole, & do with it as pleaseth him, since all that they hold is of him: then, as foolish writers say, the people might vn-make the king, & put an other in his rowme. But either of them, as vnlawful, and against the ordinance of God, ought to be alike odious to be thought, much lesse put in practize.   (71)

This passage made clear James's essentially *defensive* purpose. The fact that kings pre-dated laws and parliaments, both of which in origin derived from the king's will, was not being employed to justify arbitrary kingship. Arbitrary authority was as sinful as resistance. The point was, though, that – leaving aside sin – a legal case could much more readily be made for arbitrary kingship than for resistance. Because the king was the fount of all legitimate civil authority, it was utterly inconceivable that there might exist any authority that could be turned against him. This was an argument *against* resistance, not an argument *for* arbitrary rule.

This reading is reinforced by much else that follows in the *Trew Law*. For example, it is said that parliament made law only on the king's authority; and, whereas he had authority to make law in other ways, it had no authority to make law without his concurrence (71). That is, in context, surely a way of saying that there was no rival source of authority to the king's in the realm, not that kings could do what they pleased without parliament. James, indeed, made that point about as explicitly as was possible: 'For althogh a just Prince will not take the life of any of his subjects without a cleere law: Yet the same lawes, whereby he taketh them, are made by himselfe, or his predecessors. And so the power flowes alwaies from himselfe' (72).

The conclusion that resistance was never legitimate was reinforced by a consideration of natural law, which established the king as *pater patriae* (father of the fatherland – this language was in part aimed at the patriotic claims made by defenders of the Scottish reformation). He was therefore owed by his subjects all the respect and obedience that children naturally owed to their fathers (74–5). In conclusion, James dealt with a number of possible objections to the argument that he had presented, and it is useful to discuss these in relation to one matter that I have not so far mentioned. James had argued that kings ought to obey their own laws, as well as rule by them; but that they were not bound to do so except by their own wills. It is important to note his distinction between ruling by and obeying (the latter referring, his examples suggested, to obeying them as a man rather than as a king). But even so, the exact force of his claims that 'the King is aboue the law', that he might mitigate and suspend parliamentary laws, and that he was not subject to the law, is hard to gauge (72–3). There are two possible readings. Either these are claims for arbitrary authority, or they are again *defensive*, designed to rule out the possibility that a king could be brought to account for any failure to rule lawfully, and not intended to assert anything more positive.

James was careful to distance himself from any suggestion that he might be approving of wicked kings. His only concern, he emphasised, was to suggest that the wickedness of kings did not mitigate the wickedness of any rebellion against them (76–7). He admitted that, in fact, God might on occasion make use of wicked rebels to punish wicked kings, but again emphasised that this did not suffice to legitimate rebellion in general (78). A little later that point was further refined. James denied that 'whatsoever errours and intollerable abominations a souereigne Prince commit, he ought to escape al punishment, as if thereby the world wer only ordained for kings, & they without controlment to turne it vpside-down at their pleasure'. Not only would they eventually be punished by God – 'the sorest and sharpest Schoolemaister' – but, in reality, tyrants would indeed face rebellion, stirred up by God, in this life. James's point was to tell Christian subjects to eschew the wickedness of rebellion. The matter could be left to God and his sinful agents (81). Two things are made clear in this: first, kings were not unlimited; secondly, their wickedness would not go unpunished. But there was in the *Trew Law* no argument for arbitrary kingship. The work was explicitly designed to avoid endorsing the view that kings could act as they liked, and it did not – perhaps deliberately –

deal with the scope and limits of legitimate royal authority with enough detail and specificity for us to be at all sure what James thought on the subject.

James examined carefully the meaning of the coronation oath, often used as ammunition by defenders of resistance. These people interpreted it (he noted) as a 'mutuall paction and adstipulation . . . [or] contract bound vp, & sworn betuixt the King, & his people' whereby 'if the one part of the contract or the Indente be broken vpon the kings side, the people are no longer bound to keep their part of it, but are therby fred of their oath' (78–9). James's reply was not quite what we might have expected, and revealed very clearly his own carefully crafted use of the reciprocity *motif.* He denied that the coronation oath formed a contract of this sort – one with 'such a clause irritant' – but accepted that the king made at his coronation a promise before God to his people. That might be seen as a sort of quasi-contract, but in the civil law no party to a contract could judge of breaches of it. To enable the people to act when they believed the king had broken his coronation oath was, therefore, contrary to the principles of justice, making 'euery man . . . both partie and iudge in his owne cause'. God was the only judge of such a breach; and therefore God was the only person who could legitimately impose punishment on the king (79). Maintaining his rhetoric of moderation, James argued that the king could not judge of any breach of duty by his people, and was therefore not justified in treating as an 'vtter enemy' a rebellious people. He should punish only the principal wrong-doers, not 'practize the wrack of his whole people & native cuntry' (80). The king's ultimate authority, in any case, was derived from birthright not contract, and so no breach of contract could result in loss of his authority (80–1). Once again, this was an argument that served clearly to deny any ground for resistance theory.

James was not, then, a theorist of 'arbitrary' monarchy. His writing always seemed to presuppose a binary opposition between good and bad kingship, between law-abiding kings and arbitrary tyrants, a theory most fully developed in *Basilikon Doron.* Most of his contemporaries thought in similar binary terms: kings either ruled lawfully or they were tyrants. Given this, it is hard to make much use, in interpreting James, of the term 'absolutism', if that is taken to mean a form of monarchy somewhere between the arbitrary and the limited. He distinguished no such category. Rather, James provided an account of the nature of responsible, law-abiding kingship, and it is doubtful whether he could even have formulated for himself the intention of advancing an 'absolutist' theory as distinct from a theory of limited monarchy. The key concern for James was that monarchs were not *accountable* to their subjects. This, the intention he could have formulated, and did, was to correct some misapprehensions about the nature of law-abiding kingship, in particular the mistaken view that such kingship implied the right of subjects to resist tyrants. Tyranny, or arbitrary kingship, was not legitimate; but, equally, subjects were powerless to check a tyrant's rule.

James's reign in England undoubtedly saw the theory of divine-right monarchy in flourishing estate, as preachers repeatedly echoed their new Scottish king's known approval of this form of political theology. A very nice example of the *genre* is a 1614 sermon by William Goodwin, Vice-Chancellor of the University of Oxford, and a royal chaplain. The work was published at the royal command. Like much else published in the middle years of the Jacobean period, the sermon was in part a contribution to the Oath of Allegiance controversy, in which the king of England defended the rights of all Christian kings against the usurpations of the bishop of Rome.[9] The central thrust of Goodwin's argument was to refute the view that the papacy had the authority to release subjects from their obedience to the king. He targeted especially the claim that 'if the Prince fall from God, the people must fall from him, nay they must resist & take Armes'.[10] Goodwin was happy enough to admit that kings who were idolatrous, heretical or apostate might deserve censure from the church, and that in spiritual matters priests were the king's superiors. But he erected a very sharp distinction between civil and temporal authority, and argued that no ecclesiastical censure had any temporal consequences, except on the authority of the prince (pp. 36–7, 45–6). It was entirely within this framework of religious polemic that Goodwin (very briefly) explained the nature of royal authority. Kings were, he argued, exempt, in a sense, from their own laws. Very clearly, though, this argument was presented in such a way that its target was obvious. Goodwin had no interest in releasing kings from the expectation that they should rule according to (positive) laws; he did very much wish to release them from the coercive jurisdiction of any other human authority. This was the normal terrain on which divine-right theory operated.

Thus Goodwin preserved a very traditional scholastic distinction between the directive and the coercive force of law as it applied to a king: 'No man may stir an Hand or a Foot without him . . . *ipse solutus Legibus*, himselfe exempted from his lawes, nor from the *direction*, and Observance of them, but from the *Punishment* and penalty of them' (38). A king who broke the law was not punished, but Goodwin, citing the *Digna Vox* from the *Digest* of Roman law, added:

> It is a speech, and an act worthiest an *Emperour*, to oblige and bind himselfe to his lawes: it is a speech & practice unfitting the authority

of any earthly power to say, if hee transgresse I will chastice him. (38)

We need to remember that James himself, faced with the teachings of Buchanan and later with the threat of popular assassination on papal authority, had very good reason to develop arguments that disallowed any coercion that might be used against kings, whether by popes or by the king's subjects. It was necessary, in the course of such argument, to argue that a king who broke the law could not be punished. Thus kings were, to that extent, 'absolute' or *legibus solutus*. The difficulty came in controlling the consequences of this argument, in preventing it from spilling over into a theory of arbitrary monarchy in which kings were able to make law and impose taxes willy nilly. From the evidence of their writings, neither James nor Goodwin wished to develop this more aggressive argument. Both did all they could to reassure their audience that even irresistible kings should and would rule lawfully. The theory of divine right was a theory about the duty of obedience; it was much less frequently a theory that said anything about the specific nature of royal authority.

A useful summary of the typical Jacobean divine-right position is a short dialogue, published first in Latin and then in English, in 1615. The teaching of this 'Religious Treatise' (probably written by Richard Mocket) was endorsed by James in a proclamation of 8 November 1615.[11] The pamphlet was an exposition of the Oath of Allegiance. This should remind us that the position worked out by James and his advisers as a response to international Catholic defences of papal authority could also serve as a neat summary of approved political theology for a domestic audience. It is crucial to understanding the largely uncontroversial nature of the position (amongst English protestants) that this bedrock of anti-Catholicism is appreciated. The entire strategy lay in insisting that all protestants accepted the duty of loyalty to temporal authority, and the inclusiveness of this position was more than wishful thinking. Divine-right theory appealed to more than just conformists as a summary of the politics of Protestantism.

Mocket's *God and the King* rested on a detailed account of the threat to the English crown posed by the papal claim that, as heretics, neither Elizabeth nor James could command the civil allegiance of true Catholic subjects. Catholic sedition was portrayed as poor reward for the reasonable and patient efforts of the English crown to allow them as much liberty as was compatible with order.[12] In response to the most serious of Catholic plots, that of 1605, the king imposed the Oath of Allegiance, in which Catholics (and other subjects) were required to swear full allegiance to the king and to deny that the pope or any other

human authority had power to depose him (21–5). Mocket resolved
the subject matter of the oath into two propositions, and it is these that
he devoted the remainder of the tract to defending. The first was that
the king, 'receiving his authority only from God . . . hath no superiour
to punish or chastice him but God alone'; the second, 'that the bond
of his subjects in obedience unto his sacred Majesty is inviolable, and
cannot be dissolved' (31). In defending the former of these propositions, Mocket found little need to enter into specifics. It is perhaps
worthy of note that, in citing Bracton in support of his case, he
managed to omit reference to the king's subjection to the law as well
as to God (37); yet the general tendency of the discussion was to free
kings from the *punishment* or coercive force of human law (39). Much
more space, naturally, was given to the temporal superiority of the
king's authority to that of priests (47–60), and to the papacy's usurpation of authority over the Emperor (60–5). In defence of the second
proposition, Mocket laid great stress on the duty to love and honour
even princes who were tyrannical or impious (67–73). To them obedience was to be yielded 'from the heart' (77). Repentance and prayer
were the only legitimate weapons against tyranny (88–9). Neither
heresy nor apostasy in a prince could have any more effect in freeing
subjects from their duties of allegiance than tyranny and impiety
(78–9). Particular consideration was given to excommunication, and
Mocket showed that it could not serve to undermine the allegiance
owed to a king (82–3).

God and the King said almost nothing directly about the nature and
scope of royal authority, or the king's relationship to law and constitution. It was not that sort of book, and is in this way typical of much
divine-right theory. It takes ingenuity to make Mocket's tract into an
extremist statement; nonetheless, that is what was provided by the
Jesuit priest John Floyd. He put together an impressive attempt to show
that Mocket's *God and the King* ran counter to the moderation and
good sense of the best conformist writers (including King James
himself). The result was a reading of the tract that managed to portray
its highly-generalised and widely acceptable arguments as examples of
an extreme theory of arbitrary monarchy. Floyd pointed out that
Mocket dangerously sought to 'disclose the mysteries of the Regall
Prerogative', contrary to James's own advice of 1616. Following
Bancroft, Floyd linked evangelical zeal with 'rebellion and . . . hatred
to Monarchy'.[13] In response to the fact that they could never be
assured of the loyalty of protestant zealots, kings usurped a power to
settle religious controversy that they did not rightly possess (11–12),
with the result that those who sought reform were required to abandon
their civil allegiances (12–13). Protestants, not Catholics, were the real

threat to the authority of kings; it was they who claimed the right to resist kings who were tyrannical or irreligious (13–16). Since about 1603, though, things had changed a little: now the puritans accuse Catholics of favouring resistance while they 'extoll Royall authority above the skyes' (16). This new position, appearances notwithstanding, was as dangerous to princes as the old one had been. In exalting royal authority, it made slaves of subjects. In doing that, it made monarchy intolerable to its subjects. In such books as Mocket's, 'whilest they extoll him [the king] above measure to the state of absolute Lord & God upon earth, as it is hatefull to the subject to see himself abased, & put to a more miseralbe condition, then the bondage of slaves'. And even slaves possessed rights by the law of nature that they 'may defend by force against even their owne Masters that shall violently and unjustly invade them' (19). Of course, Floyd assumed that Mocket would have rejected any individual right of self-defence against violence. In fact, many Royalist writers against 'resistance', both in England and on the Continent, accepted the existence of such a right. Floyd wilfully confused this matter with the question of whether there existed any coercive jurisdiction over kings.

In Floyd's reading, Mocket's doctrine was both new and extreme, and calculated to destroy public affection for kings by reducing the people to 'bondmen' unable to defend their 'national' or their natural freedoms. A king might forbid subjects from marrying, or slaughter them (20–1). Mocket 'makes kinges more absolute then other Protestants doe' (50). It is hard to judge this a fair reading of Mocket, but it does reveal the difficult tightrope on which these Jacobean divine–right theorists were compelled to walk. They needed to defend the freedom of kings from coercive jurisdiction, while at the same time they needed to avoid any suggestion of defending tyranny, arbitrary power, or even any suggestion that kings were free to rule without regard to the positive laws of the realm. Their position was always vulnerable to the sort of hostile redescription that Floyd provided (and which was to flourish in the 1640s[14]).

In portraying Mocket's divine-right theory as extremist, as tantamount to a theory of arbitrary monarchy, Floyd was able to make it seem that his own view was the only reasonable alternative. 'Without question the generall voice of humane kind is, that Commonwealthes have power to make Princes, and upon just reason to unmake them.' The view was held by all Christian divines, even puritans, even 'our English conformants', a point demonstrated with reference to Bilson and Hooker (35, 32–3). Only if there is a way of punishing errant kings can they rightly be said to be restrained. This was a dangerous position, opening up the possibility that subjects might on a whim decide to destroy their kings, and reduce the commonwealth to chaos (78). The great advantage of the Catholic position, in Floyd's view, was that, in giving central place to church and pope, it was able 'to remove the life and state of Kings as much as may be, from popular rahnes' (81). It steered a 'moderate course betweene *Scilla* & *Charibdis*, without declyning to favour, in their doctrine, either the rashnes of common people, or the cruelty of tyrannous Princes' (81–2). This moderation was achieved by allowing to kings extraordinary powers and freedom from law, while accepting that 'for crymes exorbitant which tend to the destruction of the whole state' kings might be deposed (82–3). Such deposition had to be preceded by public judgement, given 'by the whole magistracy and nobility of the Commonwealth, or by the far greater part thereof' (86–7). Finally, 'a Christian Commonwealth may not proceed against their Christian Prince, though he be a tyrant, without the advise and consent of the supreme Pastor of their soules'. This applied not just in cases of heresy and apostasy, but in cases of oppression too (91). Thus, a course was steered between tyranny and popular tumult. Kings would be disciplined in an orderly fashion. Of the three groups now in England, only Catholics accepted allegiance to God *and* king: puritans 'wil have *God* without *King*', while the 'Politicians, who have no more Christianity then Parlamentary decrees breath into them . . . will have *King* without *God*, or at least . . . *God* so longe, and no longer then the *King* shall please' (139–40).

In the clash between Mocket and Floyd, a real and substantial difference has become overlain with differences that are the product of polemical stereotyping. The actual difference is between the view that there is on earth no coercive jurisdiction over kings, and the view that there are earthly institutions capable of exercising such jurisdiction (the magistracy of a commonwealth, or the church), giving subjects authority over their rulers. But the way in which these opponents constructed one another adds confusing layers to the picture. Floyd's sustained redescription of Mocket blurred the line dividing a theory of moderated but unaccountable monarchy from a theory of arbitrary monarchy. Floyd was engaged in an attempt to push Mocket off the tightrope on which he was balanced.

The Regal Union and the Ancient Constitution

James VI's accession to the English throne in 1603 brought him and his political ideas into a foreign world, and in so doing helped to transform that world in important ways. The early years of his reign were very much shaped by his wish to encourage 'further union', whatever exactly he might have meant by that phrase. James found a number of writers willing to praise the ideal of Anglo-Scottish union, and one willing to elaborate in relation to it a sophisticated body of political thought. Thomas Craig of Riccarton was, undoubtedly, the most important writer associated with the Anglo-Scottish union debates.[15] The crucial issues that emerged concerned the relationship of kingship, law and national identity. Was England's identity, so bound up with the common law, implicitly subverted by union with Scotland? Did the Scottish king's adherence to divine right kingship constitute another threat to English law?

Craig produced around the year 1603 a number of important political tracts, all of them remaining unpublished until later. He defended James VI's title to the English crown (against 'Doleman') in a work dated 1603; and he wrote in support of the union plans of 1604, for which project he was one of the Scottish commissioners. But he also wrote against the view that Scotland was a feudal dependency of England, and, very clearly, the union that Craig defended was a union between two sovereign or imperial nations, of equal status. In important ways, the intellectual underpinning for his other, more topical, writings was formed by yet another work that he left in manuscript, his treatise on the feudal law, *Jus Feudale* (published 1655). Craig was a lawyer by profession, educated in civil and canon law at the University of Paris, and versed in the intellectual techniques of French legal humanism.

Craig's work is particularly interesting for the way in which it brings a developed sense of royal sovereignty (informed by a reading of Bodin) into contact with a humanist understanding of the historical development of feudal law and Scottish custom. In this respect his nearest English counterpart was Sir John Davies, intellectually cruder than Craig, but similarly interested in the juxtaposition of royal sovereignty and legal custom. Craig brought together both community-centred and sovereign-centred perspectives on the nature of the polity: they fused most notably in his understanding of the term *civitas*. Societies originated in the joining together of people for their mutual defence and safety. The communities so formed operated on a basis of consent. There was both an 'implied covenant', whereby 'the individuals composing the community became bound to co-operate not only for the primary purpose of repelling attack from without but also for that of securing, within their own borders, respect for mutual rights',[16] and a more general sense in which the community operated by consent. On that latter basis Craig asked 'what is common citizenship but the expression of an agreement on the part of a plurality of households to co-operate in submitting the regulation of their affairs, both private and common, to some system of order established by common consent?' Citizens 'live in subjection to a common code of obligation, and under common social institutions, while the state [*civitas*] is an aggregation of diverse kindred or social units owing allegiance to one sovereign authority' (I.1.3–4, p. 2). *Commonwealth* would be a better equivalent for Craig's *civitas* than *state* (the term used by his modern translator), for it more clearly blends communality and sovereignty. Craig appropriated the Latin term *civitas* and the language of citizenship that went with it, while making it clear that the citizens of any commonwealth were by definition subject to a single sovereign authority. They formed a community on a basis of consent, but in so doing created a sovereign to whom they were subject.

Thus, when these communities came to need a mechanism for enforcing communal rules, they resorted to 'the appointment by general consent of the most highly esteemed member of the community to deal with offenders and evil-doers, and to decide between neighbours as might be just' (I.1.4, p. 4). All kings were, in origin, judges. There was no proper code of law by which these early judges and kings ruled. They followed natural equity (I.1.5, p. 5). It is notable that, from their very inception, kings were seen by Craig as fountains of justice: once they were established, all law and justice came from these sovereign figures. From the commercial interaction of communities there developed a law of nations, and this came to supplement natural equity (I.1.6, p. 7). Then, because succession struggles were extremely dangerous to the commonwealth, monarchies often became hereditary (I.1.7, pp. 7–8).

This situation could not prevail forever. As manners declined, so justice became corrupted. Judgements favoured the rich over the poor. To remedy this, written law (*lex* in contrast to *jus*, which had prevailed earlier) was introduced. This made judgements clearer, and provided an impartial measure for disputes between rich and poor, powerful and weak (I.1.11–12, pp. 12–13). Though frequently law was made 'by vote of public assemblies', things were done differently in monarchies 'because in them the sovereign was the supreme author of legislation' (I.1.14, p. 16). Thus, once monarchy was established, the sovereign's command functioned in the place of the consent or will of the people.

This emphasis on monarchical sovereignty ran through all of Craig's works. The chief reason for his emphasis on monarchy appears to have been a Bodinian insistence that divided sovereignty was harmful: monarchy embodied the principle of unitary sovereignty. Thus, Craig's discussion of the term *civitas* in his union tract noted that '[i]n such a state [*civitas*] if there be two rulers of similar power and equal following, or if two chief men, inordinately turbulent, arise and pursue each other with persistent war and rancour, either they will betray their country to the enemy, or their rivalry will destroy it'.[17] Monarchy was the form of government least prone to the danger of divided sovereignty, and it was therefore the best form of government, and rooted more directly in the law of nature than other forms.[18] Monarchy was 'of a Divine Original, ordain'd of God'. It was directly instituted by God (amongst the Jews) and that could be said of no other form of government (6, 10). There were qualifications, of course. The monarchy to which Craig referred was the 'most excellent' form of government only 'where there are faithful Councellours, and the Laws duly obey'd, which two things still attend the most Imperious Monarchy' (6). Indeed, Craig noted that while princes were sovereign law-makers, they were only so in a sense:

> When I speak of a Prince, I mean a Prince in the Parliament or great Court of the Kingdom. For then he has the Rights of Majesty more eminently, because otherwise he cannot make a Law, that obliges the Subjects, nor impose Taxes upon them.   (123)

Kings ought to obey the laws, especially when they had sworn to do so; but only they could *make* them (127–9, 162). In part, the discussion derived from Bodin (129), but Craig more clearly sided with the view that kings were bound by law.

Throughout his writings, Craig seemed to have some difficulty in maintaining a stable balance between his populism and his theory of divine right. Working in the Scottish conciliarist tradition, he seems always to have believed that polities rested on consent and the popular will, even while emphasising the sovereignty of the king as a Bodinian lawmaker. One extraordinary passage brings the tensions to the surface:

> [A]lthough political power has always resided ultimately in the people, who can choose the form of government they prefer, and have often overthrown ill-doing tyrants, yet in all the long centuries of the world's existence, monarchy has been accepted by nearly every people as the most perfect form of government, and continues to this day.[19]

Presumably this needs to be read in the light of the view advanced in *Jus Feudale* and elsewhere, that monarchy was created by the people for their own needs, but, once created, sovereignty resided with the king:

> at first, the Election of a King seem'd to be in the people, yet when once they had chose him, they hereby transferred to him whom they

elected and to his Posterity, all their Power and Right; So that they could not make a new Election, nor alter the Government or make Innovations: they lost all that power.[20]

His reference to popular resistance to tyranny sits a little oddly with his own hostility to Jesuit theories of deposition;[21] but it may be that he thought that tyranny, in dissolving the bonds of the community, returned power to the people as a whole (e.g. 120–1).

In all of his political writings, Craig applied these general theories to Scotland and England. In his discussion of the union of crowns, brought about by James VI's accession to the English throne, he clearly saw the monarchy as the key unifying principle for the British polity. This made sense, given Craig's awareness that a single locus of sovereignty was necessary to the constitution of any *civitas*. Nothing was 'more baneful than divided authority, nothing more useful and beneficial than monarchy'. The ancient Britons had many kings, but this plurality 'rendered impossible any common interest, and subjected the island the more easily to the Roman yoke'. The lesson for 1603 was readily drawn: the 'well-being of Britain depends solely upon this, that her government should be under a single head and direction'.[22] Craig was not here envisaging Brtish unity as the simple creation of a new state (*civitas*). Rather the two kingdoms should form 'a single body [*corpus*], almost [*quasi*] a single commonwealth [*civitas*]'.[23] The task facing the two kingdoms in 1604 was to find measures whereby 'two kingdoms, each possessed of sovereignty, may come together under the rule of one king so that the two become one'.[24]

Craig identified 'eight essentials to a complete and perfect union'. They were 'uniformity in religion, laws, customs and language, common rights, a single government pursuing a consistent and impartial policy, identical discipline. The same coinage, weights and measures, and, above all, the same name.' Uniformity could mean different things to different people, and the use of the term in regard to the union can be confusing. 'Uniformity' in this context did not usually mean identity in all particulars, but general concordance and compatibility. Thus, Craig's chapter on law was a discussion of whether the laws of the two kingdoms needed to be consistent with one another (*consonantia*), not whether they should be identical in all particulars.[25] In all of the eight areas Craig pointed out either existing compatibilities, or the policies that could build compatibility. He could point to the religious similarities between the nations. They might differ in 'forms of public worship', but there was 'certainly no cardinal point of doctrine on which the two churches disagree, nor does the one challenge what the other maintains' (286–7). That last phrase may reveal something more of what Craig meant by uniformity: it was important that arrangements in one country did not undermine the legitimacy of those in the other. Language, too, was another point of compatibility (287–9). Their currencies could easily be harmonised (294). It was important that equal access to offices and dignities was allowed, for '[i]f such a union is to be formed as is wont to exist between fellow citizens and townsmen, public posts ought to be open to all' (333–4). This position was supported with marginal references to the *Corpus juris civilis*, and it seems to be another point at which Craig's civilian training and Latin conceptual vocabulary led him into an understanding of the polity as constituted in part by the participation of its citizens through the holding of public office. He was emphatic, too, that the name of both kingdoms should give way to that of 'Britain', and he carefully replied to the fears of the English House of Commons on this point. His argument rested on the assumption that, in becoming king of Britain, James would cease to be king of England (408–9, 407). In the union, no new kingdom would be created; it was 'rather the resumption of a condition previously existing, the healing of a division' (402–3).

But it was law that mattered most, and it was law that received the most sophisticated discussion. It is clear from his conclusions that Craig did not envisage a union in which the two sovereign kingdoms would lose all separate identity. They would form (or re-form) a single British *corpus* under the king, but retain within limits their separateness. Each kingdom would, for example, retain a separate parliament (466). In the matter of law, Craig did not envisage rapid or wholesale change. It was necessary 'that each nation be governed in accordance with its own laws and customs; that no change be made in them . . . without the express sanction and approbation of either kingdom' (465). This powerful aversion to legal change was shared both by opponents and by supporters of the union. Henry Spelman warned that the dangers run by a lawful monarch who attempted to alter laws were shown by the 'experience of all ages and the present case of the King of Spaine with the lowe cuntryes'.[26] '[L]aws were never in any kingedome totallie altered without great danger of the evercion of the whole state,' was Dodderidge's verdict.[27] Sir John Hayward, an important English supporter of perfect union, rejected the view that all alteration of law was dangerous. But even he made it clear that change should be both minimal and gradual. That was all that was needed, for in his view the steps needed to make English and Scottish law uniform were not great.[28] Francis Bacon, perhaps the king's key English adviser on the union question, seems to have adopted a similar view, stressing the need for 'uniformity in the principal and fundamental laws both ecclesiastical and civil';[29] but suggesting, too, that any change was risky, and would need to be carried out slowly.[30]

Craig's position was not far removed from that of Hayward and Bacon. He argued that it was not necessary 'that the two kingdoms should submit to identical laws and systems', especially since changing laws was 'a fruitful source of trouble . . . [and] often changes the character of the state itself' (303). He argued instead that the laws of England and Scotland were already very similar; and that careful further harmonisation would be possible in some things. Underlying these arguments was the history of law that Craig had worked out most fully in *Jus Feudale*.[31] In that work, Craig portrayed the emergence of feudal tenures among the barbarian tribes that had conquered the Roman Empire. From the fifth century onwards, the chiefs among these people conquered lands and then parcelled them out to their soldiers in return for service. At first, these servants held land only at the will of their lord, but over time tenure came to be granted for life; and then it became fully hereditary (initially, in Capetian Gaul). Vassals began to treat their lands as their own, using them without regard to the wishes of their lords. A complex system developed, in which some held land directly from their king, while others held it from a lord who was in turn the king's vassal. The relationship between superiors and vassals was recognised in the oath of fealty, and it was a characteristic feature of the feudal system that superiors exercised jurisdiction over their vassals.[32] Feudal law was rooted in these practices, and grew alongside them. Originally the feudal law was purely a customary law, but it began to be reduced to writing under the Carolingian emperors, eventually being reduced into one general body of law (I.6.1–2, pp. 71–3). The feudal law became part of the law of every European kingdom. Craig was aware that this emphasis on the development of a customary code of law, seemingly independent of royal authority, seemed to contradict the principle that 'law-giving is an attribute of sovereignty'. He squared the circle by arguing that 'the sanction of princely approval . . . was also the true source of the authoritative character of the Books of Feus' (I.6.7–9, pp. 77–9). Nonetheless, the argument made it clear how Craig was able to hold together in his work an emphasis on law as a development from the customary practices of communities, and an emphasis on legal sovereignty. The latter gave formal authority to the former.

The feudal law spread all over Europe, and formed the basis for the law of real property in both Scotland and England (where it was called common law). Craig argued that feudalism reached England as a result of the Norman Conquest (I.7.1–6, pp. 81–4), and that the English common law was a hybrid, a product of the 'successive conquests of

England'. English law 'is highly composite, being in part Brythonic, in part Saxon, in part Danish, in part Norman, and in part also feudal' (I.7.9, pp. 86–7); but clearly it was the feudal element that predominated, especially in the law of real property. The highest form of law in England was statute (I.7.12, p. 90); and in a sense this also was a product of the Conquest. The English parliament was founded by Henry I in response to demands for the restoration of Saxon rights and laws. By establishing parliament, Henry was able to resist the demand for restoration. The institution thereafter gave particular form to the nature of sovereign authority in England. To its 'deliberations all amendments upon existing laws and institutions, as well as proposals for new legislation were referred; but in doing so he [the king] reserved to himself the sole right of calling it together, and the sole power of giving effect to its measures by royal assent' (I.7.11, p. 88). The common law was subordinate to the statutes made by parliament; but where there was no relevant statute, common law was invariably followed. English kings were sworn, at their coronations, to administer and preserve it (I.7.13, p. 90).

The feudal system arrived earlier in Scotland and was found there in purer form (I.8.1–3, pp. 99–101). It was on this basis that Craig was able to argue that there was a fundamental harmony between the laws of England and Scotland. He distinguished carefully between *jus* and *lex*.[33] The former referred to fundamental legal principles; the latter to particular laws. England and Scotland shared the same *jura*, derived from the *jus feudale*, but not the same *leges*. '[T]he same legal principles happen to prevail in both countries, yet their municipal laws are different' (I.8.4, p. 103). In Scotland, as in England, statutes 'passed by the three estates of the realm with the royal assent' were the laws of highest authority (I.8.9, p. 106). Indeed, statutes were the only genuine form of written law in Scotland. Beyond that there was legal custom, 'the settled course of legal decision', and beyond that the principles of the feudal, civil and canon laws (I.8.1217, pp. 109–12). Scotland lacked some of England's legal richness, and had no exact equivalent of the common law.

In the *De Unione* Craig built on this historical analysis to show two important points. First, although the English believed their law to be purely indigenous, the key principles of England's law of landed property derived from the feudal law and were imposed at the Conquest. The key principles of the Scottish law of landed tenure derived from the same feudal source, and were therefore largely compatible with those of England. Both the nature of the fief, and the pattern of feudal tenures were shared between the two countries (309–11, 312–20). Craig noted of the principles of English common law, 'it will be easily observed that the greater part of them are derived from the *jus feudale*', and 'do not differ much from ours' (322, 321). His second point was that the feudal law, which provided England and Scotland with the same fundamental legal principles (*jura*) notwithstanding their different laws (*leges*), could provide a basis for further harmonisation. It already underpinned both legal systems. Thus, '[s]hould the attempt be made to bring them into harmony, it would be necessary to revert to the sources of feudal law, that is . . . to the Norman code, in whose idiom the laws of England were and still are written'. And, if that was not sufficient, then one should go further back to find a common point before English and Scottish law began to diverge. '[I]f the ancient Norman code cannot provide us with a harmonious system we must go even further back to the feudal code whence that of Normandy was derived, and find in it, somehow, the basis of agreement' (327–8). Thus, Craig concluded that there was less difference between English and Scottish law than commonly supposed, and that there was no 'reason to despair of the possibility of . . . harmonising the legal systems of the two peoples' (328). What he sought was harmony, not identity in all particulars. The union would leave to each people its own customs, just as the regions of England itself had their own customs. And change would, of course, come carefully.

In making these points Craig developed an account of English legal and constitutional history that would have been immensely controversial within England itself. Nonetheless, in the debates on union there were those who advanced views similar to his, albeit without the historical sophistication. It is notable that in the account of English law in *De Unione*, Craig directly attacked the historical self-understanding of English lawyers. Making the point that English common law largely derived from the *jus feudale*, he added 'though the English conceal the fact and profess to believe that their laws are of purely indigenous growth' (322). He noted, too that '[o]ur English neighbours are far out in their reckoning in their belief that their legal system is indigenous and unlike those of other countries (311; also 305–6). Craig seems to have written this work mostly in 1605, and it therefore forms part of a broader critique of English common-law assumptions articulated in response to the union in these years. The English House of Commons had vociferously rejected any change in the name of the kingdom, from England to 'Great Britain', largely on the ground that it would have the same effect as a conquest. English law would be annulled, and with it the barriers that preserved English liberties from the prerogatives of kings. It was widely argued, with reference to the seventeenth chapter of Sir John Fortescue's *De Laudibus Legum Angliae*, that English common law was unchanging, and had persisted unchanged since the time of the ancient Britons. Edward Coke had already made much of the point in 1602,[34] but in 1607 he noted that 'some of another Profession' remained unconvinced.[35] He was, no doubt, referring to civil lawyers, two of whom had (in the union debates) advanced views of English law compatible with Craig's and incompatible with Coke's – John Hayward and Alberico Gentili.

Hayward rejected directly the view (Coke's interpretation of Fortescue) 'that the laws of England were never changed since the time of Brutus; not only in the peaceable state of the realme, but not by any of the severall conquerors thereof'. Such an idea was 'sutable but with artlesse times'.[36] His own view was compatible with Craig's that English common law was compounded of the laws of many conquering peoples, and had undergone dramatic change at the Conquest. It can be argued that it was in these debates that the idea of the ancient constitution, the principle that English common law was 'fundamental' and could not be altered without threat to the nature of the polity itself, came into its own. This attitude, though it came, by the late 1620s, to be useful in warning Charles I not to abandon traditional legal ways of governing, was in origin (and makes more sense as) an idea of national identity, designed to repulse the supposed efforts of a Scottish king to modify English common law, to ward off the threat of a Scottish 'conquest'.[37]

The idea of the ancient constitution certainly developed over time. John Selden more or less explained away the early stress on Fortescuean immutability. For him, as for many of the more sophisticated legal scholars, the truth lay with Craig's view that 'the *Saxons* made a mixture of the *British* customes with their own; the *Danes* with old *British*, the *Saxon* and their own; and the *Normans* the like'.[38] In Selden's view the law of England was constantly changing. Like all law codes, it was rooted in the law of nature. All laws were equally old, and equally to be seen as local variations on natural law, even though they had diverged over time (18). Thus, if anyone asks:

> *When and how began your common laws?* Questionlesse its fittest answered by affirming, when and in like kind as the laws of all other States, that is, *When there was first a State in that land, which the common law now governs*: then were naturall laws limited for the convenience of civill societie here, and those limitations have been from thense, increased, altered, interpreted, and brought to what now they are; although perhaps (saving the meerly immutable part of nature) now, in regard of their first being, they are not otherwise then the ship, that by often mending had no piece of the first materialls, or as the

house that's so often repaired, *ut nihil ex pristina materia supersit,* which yet (by the Civill law) is to be accounted the same still.   (19)

There was here no sense of the law as unchanging, but a strongly developed sense of the way customs were refined over time. There was also an awareness, shared with Craig but not found in all common lawyers, that law was the product of a *state.* Although Selden was always interested in custom and its evolution, he tended to see law primarily as the product of state action. Nonetheless, it should be noted that Selden did (sometimes) share the common lawyers' strong emphasis on legal continuity, and the refusal to see English law as ever having been altered on the authority of a conqueror;[39] and that even he, as in 1628, could work politically with those who wanted to assert, against Charles I, that the laws of England had been and remained immutable.[40]

Even Coke grew more sophisticated over time. While his early writings, referred to above, emphasised the all-too-simple Fortescuean point that English law must be perfect because it had remained unchanged through many conquests and changes of ruler, his later views were more sophisticated. When he began publishing the *Institutes* in 1628 he was able to blend together an awareness of the way in which custom evolved over time, perhaps derived from Sir John Davies, with the seemingly incompatible view that English law was perfect (and immutable?) because it was reason itself:

> *Nihil quod est contra rationem est licitum* [nothing contrary to reason is lawful]. For reason is the life of the Law, nay the Common Law itself is nothing else but reason, which is to be understood of an artificial perfection of reason gotten by long studie, observation and experience and not of every mans naturall reason, for *nemo nascitur artifex.* This legall reason *est summa ratio.* And therefore if all the reason that is dispersed into so many severall heads were united into one, yet could hee not make such a law as the Law of England is, because by many succession of ages it hath beene fined and refined by an infinite number of grave and learned men, and by long experience grown to such perfection for the government of this Realme, as the old rule may be justly verified of it *Neminem opportet esse sapientiorem legibus:* No man (out of his owne private reason) ought to be wiser than the Law, which is the perfection of reason.[41]

Even in this formulation we can sense the degree to which this is a doctrine of national identity, finding in the customary law of England the key to the character and essence of its polity,[42] though of course even in 1607 Coke was able to turn this against a king who had been provoked by his archbishop to claim a right to judge his subjects in person.[43] James I himself eventually came to accept a key political point behind this argument. He had accepted in 1604 the principle that 'fundamental laws' of neither Scotland nor England should be altered by the union. Judging from *The Trew Law of Free Monarchies*, James used this term in a narrow sense, meaning the basic principles that structured the polity, and particularly those that related to royal succession and sovereignty. These were the laws that Bodin identified as *lois royales* or *leges imperii*. But by 1607 James had come to recognise that the English understood something else by this term 'fundamental law'. For them it was linked to a point that Thomas Craig had recognised. The English believed that 'their kings at their coronation solemnly promise[d] to respect as unchangeable and inviolable' the common law.[44] That is to say, the English came to believe that the common law was a fundamental law, inviolable and the source of the identity of the English polity itself. James came to see this:

> Their [i.e. the Scots'] meaning in the word of Fundamentall Lawes . . . [was to] intend thereby onely those Lawes whereby confusion is avoyded, and their Kings descent mainteined, and the heritage of the succession and Monarchie, which hath bene a Kingdome, to which I am in descent, three hundred yeeres before CHRIST: Not meaning it as you doe, of their Common Law, for they have none, but that which is called IUS REGIS.[45]

James was here recognising an important difference between the ways in which his two sets of subjects viewed their own legal identity. He clearly learnt something from the union debates, with their assertion that the entire common law must be seen as fundamental and inviolable.[46]

An awareness of this fact ought to inform our reading of James's famous speech of March 1610, which registers a shift in his thinking since 1603. When he came to the throne, he held a view that made law dependent on his own will. Of course, even in the 1590s he still reassured subjects that this would not make the legal order unstable or subject to arbitrary royal intervention; and, of course, he never abandoned the view that kings made law, not *vice versa*. But he did come to recognise that the English common law was a 'fundamental law', through which he was bound to deal with his subjects' property:

> [A]s a King, I haue least cause of any man to dislike the Comon Law: For no Law can bee more fauourable and aduantagious for a King, and extendeth further his Prerogatiue, then it doeth: And for a

King of England to despise the Common Law, it is to neglect his owne Crowne. . . . [Civil law has a place, but] reseruing euer to the Common Law to meddle with the fundamentall Lawes of this Kingdome, either concerning the Kings Prerogatiue, or the possessions of Subiects, in any questions, either betweene the King, and any of them, or amongst themselues, in the points of *Meum & tuum.*[47]

Read in the light of the resonance the term 'fundamental law' had acquired in the union debates, and in the light of James's crucial admission in 1607, these words cannot be dismissed as empty pleasantries. They are a detailed and direct attempt to say to his English critics that James was 'bound' to rule by the common law. The word 'bound' is his, though typically the binding was also done by himself: kings 'bound themselues within the limits of their Lawes' (184). But the commitment was unequivocal: 'euery iust King . . . is bound to obserue that paction made to his people by his Lawes' (183). The very fear to which James was responding – that he preferred the civil law to the common law, and would replace one with the other – was a fear rooted in fears of legal subversion expressed during the union debates. Many English critics of union, unlike Craig, saw Scotland as a country dominated by civil law. Again in 1616 James affirmed that:

the inheritance of the King, and Subiects in this land, must bee determined by the Common Law, &c; and that is, by the Law set downe in our forefathers time, expounded by learned men diuers times after . . . [o]r else by Statute Law. . . .   (209–10).

James renewed his coronation oath to maintain the law, by which he meant 'the Common Law of the Land, according to which the King gouernes, and by which the people are gouerned' (208). The crucial point is to recognise that in these statements he was referring to the common law as a fundamental law, and thus accepting, albeit in part for tactical reasons, the English lawyers' view that the common law constituted the English polity.

This might suggest to us – as indeed might the example of Thomas Craig – that there was no inherent incompatibility between elevated views of royal authority and views emphasising the way in which English common law was rooted in the customary habits of the people. They might seem to involve opposed views – royalism *v.* populism, descending theory *v.* ascending theory – but there were ways of holding them together. Nowhere is that more apparent than in the thought of Sir John Davies. Davies, like Coke, developed a view of the English common law that drew both on the idea that it was *custom*, and on the idea that it was *reason*.[48] On the one hand,

> the *Common lawe* of *England* is nothing else but the *Common custome* of the Realme: And *a custome* which hath obtained the force of a lawe, is alwayes said to bee *Ius non scriptum*, for it cannot bee made or created, either by Charter, or by Parliament, which are actes reduced to writing, & are alwayes matter of *Record*, but being onely matter of *fact*, and consisting in use & practise, it can bee recorded and registred no where, but in the memory of the people.[49]

On the other hand, 'Certeine it is, that *lawe* is nothing but a rule of reason.' All human reason, we are told, is 'pliable', and it was the function of custom to ensure that the law of reason was adapted to the particular circumstances of individual commonwealths. This had worked so well in the case of England that 'there is no *art* or *science* that standeth uppon discourse of reason, that hath her *Rules* & *Maximes* so certeine & infallible, & so little subject to divers interpretation as the common lawe of England' (sig. *4).

What were the political implications of Davies's views? The emphasis on *popular* customs and the absence for the common law of any lawmaker might suggest that Davies's views were anti-monarchical. Law was not the command of the king; it was essentially rooted in the consent of the people. There are other passages that reinforce this impression. Customary law was 'the most perfect'. Whereas written laws 'are made either by the edicts of Princes, or by Counselles of estate, are imposed uppon the subject before any Triall or Probation made, whether the same bee fitt & agreeable to the nature & disposition of the people . . . a *Custome* doth never become a lawe to binde the people, untill it hath bin tried & approved time out of minde' (sig. *2).

There were, though, countervailing emphases in Davies's discussion. He noted, for example, that the common law 'doth excell all other lawes in upholding a free *Monarchie*, which is the most excellent forme of government, exalting the prerogative royall, and being very tender and watchfull to preserve it, and yet maintining withall the *ingenuous liberty* of the subject' (sig *2v). This not only uses James's term ('free monarchy'), but could be read as a gloss on the king's 1610 speech. Yet it remains a remarkable feature of Davies's account of the law that it betrayed no interest whatsoever in law-making. It did not ask whether the king made the law, or the law the king. Clearly, Davies was strongly inclined to see the rule of law as necessary for the ordering of a commonwealth. Without justice, 'there would bee nothing certeine, nothing sure, no contracts, no commerce, no conversation among men, but all

Kingdomes, & states would bee brought to confusion, & all humane society would be dissolved' (sig. *9). And yet, this justice that told the king how to rule also flowed from the king. Justice was the chief of moral virtues. A king was 'the cleare fountaine of Justice' and all kings 'sitt uppon Gods owne seate when they minister Justice unto the people'.

Thus a king by divine right administered God's justice. The particular national laws that rendered justice suitable to the circumstances of individual communities might have evolved from communal practice, but their continuing authority derived from the king. They were still the king's laws. Davies's position seems a very sophisticated version of the commonplace truism that God made kings, but also gave them duties to perform, of which justice was the paramount. Between kings and justice there was, in Davies's view, the common law, which matched the general requirements of justice to the particular needs of the English polity.

This view could easily be taken for the argument that kings were made by the law and subject to it; but such a reading of Davies is hard to square with his other major piece of political writing. His *Question Concerning Impositions* was not published until 1656, but seems likely to have been written in response to parliamentary objections to impositions in 1610 and 1614.[50] In this work, Davies set out to demonstrate the legality of impositions – charges that the king had levied upon goods involved in international trade 'by vertue of his Prerogative onely, without Act of Parliament'[51] – according to common and statute law, and also to the law of nations and the civil law. His argument rested on the claim that the law recognised that all 'absolute' kings had certain discretionary prerogatives reserved to them. This meant that there were some things that kings could do simply on the basis of their 'absolute' prerogatives, with no need for further legal authority. There was a problem in using this general argument to justify impositions. Such a position might seem to result in the claim that kings had an absolute right to tax, that is they were allowed to take from subjects without consent their lands and goods. It is not surprising, given his understanding of the nature of common law and its capacity to preserve the rights and property of subjects, that Davies did not wish to advance this more dramatic claim. He was, therefore, very careful to circumscribe the argument that he presented. There were two ways in which he did this. First, he argued that because impositions concerned a levy on *international* trade, they were not simply regulated by the domestic law of England, which applied only within the realm. '[T]he Law of Nations also is in force in such cases, especially wherein the King himself, or his Subjects, have correspondence or commerce with other Nations who are not bound in those cases by the Municipall Laws of *England*' (pp. 4–5). This worked two ways: it meant that Davies had greater freedom to apply the general precepts of the law of nations to the case, but it also meant that any conclusions that he reached carried no direct implications for English *domestic* politics. If, by the law of nations, kings could impose duties on international trade, it in no way followed that kings might therefore tax their subjects at will.

The second key point was to specify, at least so far as it was relevant, the particular points in which the king retained his absolute authority. By the law of nations, the king had 'absolute and unlimited power in all matters whatsoever'; but over time had agreed to bind himself to the rule of law, while 'retaining and reserving notwithstanding in many points that absolute & unlimited power which was given to him by the Law of Nations'. The result was that the king had two sorts of powers, absolute and limited:

> the King doth exercise a double power, *viz.* an absolute power, or *Merum Imperium*, when he doth use Prerogatives onely, which is not bound by the positive Law; and an ordinary power of Jurisdiction, which doth co-operate with the Law, & whereby he doth minister Justice to the people, according to the prescript rule of the positive Law.   (30–1)

The important thing was to be clear about which things were included amongst the king's absolute prerogatives. Davies mentioned a number of them. Some were uncontroversial, things accepted as within the discretionary authority of the king by more or less everyone, such as 'absolute power in making War, Peace, and Leagues' (8–9, 30, 101), the power to pardon (30), the power to regulate the coinage (32–3, 101), or the authority to appoint judges and magistrates, and to distribute honours (102). Undoubtedly, Davies's claim that absolute authority extended to the regulation of international trade, though it was neither new nor unusual, was controversial; yet it remains important to note that this claim explicitly disavowed any suggestion that the king had any *general* authority to impose taxes by his absolute power.

It is worth examining closely how the two general moves in Davies's argument are applied to the particular subject of impositions. Although English common law was quite capable of regulating internal trade (13), its jurisdiction did not extend over the seas. Therefore the common law itself accepted that international trade was to be governed by the 'law merchant', a branch of the law of nations (16–17). The king of England, like *all* kings, had an absolute authority to govern trade and commerce (89–90). This meant that any common-law protection for the subjects' property rights did not necessarily apply to merchandise involved in international commerce. 'Suppose it be admitted,' Davies hypothesised,

> that by the positive Law of the land Taxes and Tallages may not be laid upon our goods within the land, without an Act of Parliament, yet by the Law of Nations, and by the Law Merchant, which are also the Law of *England*, in cases of Merchandizes the King of *England*, as well as other Kings, may by vertue of his Prerogative, without Act of Parliament, lay impositions upon Merchandizes crossing the Seas, being goods whereupon the Law doth set another character than goods possessed in the land.   (18–19)

In other places where Davies cited laws other than the common law, such as the civil law, he went to some length to make it plain that his remarks did not carry any implications for those things that properly fell within the jurisdiction of English municipal law (24). His 'hypothesis' might sound a little reluctant, but elsewhere Davies was perfectly clear that 'the Right of Free-hold and all Inheritance, and all Contracts reall and personall, arising within the Land, are left to be decided by the positive Law of the land'. This contrasted with 'the Government and ordering of Traffique, Trade, and Commerce' (here including internal trade), which 'doth rest in the Crown as a principall Prerogative' (32). Explicit consent in parliament was necessary to allow kings to tax property in most cases, but the law (to which subjects implicitly consented) allowed kings in some circumstances to take subjects' property. The circumstances were clear and particular, and included the right to levy impositions (96–8). Davies spent much space indicating that all English kings had exercised an arbitrary prerogative to levy customs duties, concluding that King James, naturally enough, believed himself 'to be seized of this Prerogative' at his accession (73).

Davies's argument had two poles, and this enabled him triumphantly to declare that the king of England was as 'absolute' as any in Europe, while at the same time declaring that the English were less burdened by arbitrary exactions than other subjects. At one pole lay the law of nations, in which were rooted the prerogatives of all kings. All were, in origin, equally arbitrary, but had by their own grace modified their arbitrariness over time. It was important to Davies, as it was important to James, to assert that the English monarchy was the equal of any in Europe. '[T]he King of *England* is as absolute a Monarch, as any Emperour or King in the world, and hath as many Prerogatives incident to his Crown' (161). Of their own accord, the kings of England had refrained from the financial exaction of other monarchs. The king of England now used his financial prerogative *only* 'in laying

Impositions upon Merchandizes crossing the Seas . . . and not upon any other goods which are bought and sold within the Land'. Davies continued, emphasising at the other pole the security of English property rights, governed only by the common law: 'neither doth he by his absolute power alone, impose any Tax upon Lands or *Capita hominum* [the heads of men], or *Capita animalium* [the heads of animals], or upon other things innumerable' (148).[52]

Thus in both the works we have discussed, Davies stressed the peculiar English balance between prerogatives and liberties. Together these writings asserted that the common law recognised absolute royal prerogatives rooted in the law of nature or nations, while the king recognised the rights and property of his subjects as enshrined in the common law. Common lawyers did not often explore the ways in which the law of the land was underpinned by the law of nature or of nations; but they were not unaware of the fact. Even Sir Edward Coke appreciated that kings ruled by natural equity before there were any laws, and that allegiance to them was rooted in natural not positive law; but that did not prevent him from believing that the law itself came to limit what kings could do.[53] The essential point of Davies's defence of Jacobean impositions was to assert royal claims without invoking any general absolute or extra-legal authority to tax or to be free of the law. This is altogether typical of the way in which James's policies were presented and defended. These policies were said to be lawful and customary, and it was denied that they overrode the law of the land. We need not believe that James I turned overnight into a Coke or even a Davies in order to accept that both he and his publicists made every effort to ensure that they defended policies in ways that would not offend the assumption of many lawyers and gentlemen that domestic matters were to be regulated by the common law. Herein lies a sort of consensus: not a consensus in which everyone believed the same thing, but a consensus in which the theoretical bridges that connected the land of divine-right monarchy with the land of common law were kept in good repair. James's accession and his plans for Anglo-Scottish union might have been seen to constitute a threat to English law, encouraging strongly legalist interpretations of the English polity; but the degree to which these interpretations were incompatible with divine-right monarchy remained subject to negotiation.

Critical Voices

Divine right and ancient constitution were fundamental conceptual poles in the early Stuart period, justifying and explaining the nature of monarchical authority in church and state, and it is clear that they need not be seen as so inherently antagonistic that revolution must inevitably have followed from their clash. But historians have rightly pointed out that the political thinking of the early Stuart period nonetheless contained elements that could, in the right circumstances, be deployed in extremist argument, whether by defenders of a kingship impatient of any limits, or, by the early 1640s, by those urging armed parliamentary resistance to the king. Three such elements will be considered here: (1) classical and 'neo-Roman' arguments; (2) patriarchalist and other justifications of unlimited monarchy; (3) continued questioning of the nature of the royal supremacy in the church.

Civic humanism

One of the most fruitful texts for the exploration of the significance of humanist ideas on early Stuart political thinking has been a parliamentary speech delivered in 1610 by Thomas Hedley. The speech was an intervention in the debate on the legality of impositions, and in contrast to Davies, Hedley was convinced of their illegality. He, too, rooted his arguments in common law, for the 'question [was] determinable onely by the common lawe of England'.[54] It is one of the interesting features of the speech that it gave considerable time to a consideration of precisely what the nature of the common law was. The answer was that it was reason tried by time, 'a reasonable usage, throughout the whole realm, approved time out of mind in the king's courts of record'.[55] It was reason in customary form.[56] The speech is interesting simply for the way in which it developed this account of the common law, but recent scholarship has also directed attention to the arguments that underpin its construction of a common-law case against the prerogative right to impose additional customs duties.

At one level, Hedley drew explicitly on both Cicero and Tacitus, especially in understanding the basis for the common law's defence of property rights. Hedley considered 'the ancient freedom and liberty of the subjects of England', which were confirmed by Magna Carta, and which the common law balanced against the sovereignty of kings. In this way, England had the benefit both of 'an absolute monarchy and of a free estate', as Tacitus had portrayed the Rome of the Emperors Nerva and Trajan.[57] In considering the liberty of subjects, Hedley was concerned primarily with property rights, effectively underpinning a common-law perspective with ideas drawn from Roman writers. He drew most obviously on Cicero's insistence that commonwealths were instituted primarily to protect private property, and so it was the first duty of those in charge of public affairs to ensure that private property rights were not infringed [*De Officiis*, II.73].[58] Furthermore, Hedley pointed to the importance of property owning in making a man 'fit to do service to his country in war . . . [or] peace', invoking the argument (both classical and Fortescuean) that the independent property-owning Englishman made a better soldier than the French peasant.[59] He drew, then, on the Roman ideal of the armed citizen, whose property, protected by the commonwealth, enabled him to serve that commonwealth in war.[60]

Beneath even this level of argument, however, Hedley drew implicitly upon one of the fundamental distinctions of Roman law, the distinction between freedom and slavery, in order to argue that, if the royal prerogative could be permitted to infringe private property rights, then subjects were not free but slaves.[61] To be free was to be able to do as one pleased, while to be a slave meant that you were subject to the will or power of another [*Institutes*, I.3]. A subject whose property rights could be infringed at the will of the king was, therefore, not free because, regardless of whether or not the king chose to interfere with his property, the subject remained always dependent on him for its enjoyment. In Hedley's words, if a person's 'lands and goods [are] not absolutely their own but in the absolute power and command of another', then they are no better than 'bondmen'.[62] In this condition, they will lose the desire to accumulate wealth, given that it will always lie in the power of someone else to deprive them of it, and so the commonwealth will cease to have a property-owning independent and armed body of subjects on whom to draw. A commonwealth of free subjects was, therefore, one in which no one could be deprived of his property without his own consent, and so a king who possessed any discretionary power over property destroyed his subjects' property rights regardless of how he used that power. In this way a king, not in one blow but over time, will 'unjoint the whole frame of this so ancient, honourable and happy state, so prudently compact of the sovereignty of the king and the liberty of the subject'.[63]

In Hedley these neo-Roman propositions were in the service of what was essentially a common-law argument, serving to provide it with a set of theoretical underpinnings from which one might deduce that English common law was a set of rational principles proven by time to ensure a healthy balance of absolute monarchy and the freedom of subjects. But the ideas of Tacitus, Cicero and others could be used to support a considerable range of positions. Francis Bacon, a royal adviser and servant through most of James's reign, provided Ciceronian justifications of the active political life. For humankind, 'the conservation of duty to the public ought to be much more precious than the conservation of life and being'.[64] Discussing the rivalry between the claims to superiority of the active and the contemplative life, Bacon sided with Cicero in rejecting Aristotle's case for the supremacy of the contemplative life, '[f]or all the reasons which he bringeth for the contemplative live are private'.[65] For the same reason, Bacon rejected all of those, like the Epicureans, whose ethics 'are manifest to tend to private repose and contentment, and not to point of society'. A particular target was the great Stoic moralist Epictetus, who 'presupposeth that felicity must be placed in those things which are in our power, lest we be liable to fortune and disturbance', whereas actually it was 'much more happy to fail in good and virtuous ends for the public, than to obtain all that we can wish to ourselves in our proper fortune'.[66] But Bacon was also aware of Machiavellian and Tacitist arguments that encouraged the wise man to understand the evils of the political world, and perhaps even to seek to turn them to his advantage. In often-quoted words he remarked:

> So that we are much beholden to Machiavel and others, that write what men do and not what they ought to do. For it is not possible to join the serpentine wisdom with the columbine innocency, except men know exactly all the conditions of the serpent; his baseness and going upon his belly, his volubility and lubricity, his envy and sting, and the rest; that is all forms and natures of evil. For without this, virtue lieth open and unfenced.[67]

Thus his discussion of what made kingdoms great was, by and large, a Ciceronian argument for the cultivation of a people's civic and martial virtue; but it did occasionally have more ambiguous touches, becoming Machiavellian in the other sense of embracing a morally doubtful reason of state. In particular, he indicated that a people fought better in wars that they believed just. Therefore, rulers ought to ensure that the wars they fought had 'just occasions (as may be pretended)'; they needed justifications 'at least specious'.[68]

Whereas Bacon co-opted these ideas to the service of kings, others used them for contrasting purposes. Thomas Scott, indefatigable puritan polemicist against the Stuart foreign policies of the 1620s, was an open admirer of the Dutch republic. He commended both its government, in which there was wide public discussion, and its godliness and toleration, even of Jews, infidels and heretics. Toleration meant that the resources of all could contribute to the public good. They 'are a *Common-wealth*, and so want that absolute power over their members, which *Monarchies* have and may use. . . . Neither are they apt or desirous to presse the conscience too strictly, since *God himselfe saves no man against his will.'* The Dutch republic was explicitly likened to the ideal commonwealths of Plato and More, and Scott portrayed Dutch government as mixed, with the States General holding the balance between prince and people, 'as our Parliaments in England use to doe'.[69] Just as remarkable were the lectures given in Cambridge in 1627 by the University's first professor of history, the Dutch Calvinist Isaac Dorislaus. The lectures were given on Tacitus's *Annals*, and in them Dorislaus, while doing his best to praise English monarchical government, nonetheless praised tyrannicide, and seemed to lodge with the people a continuing right to take sovereignty back from their rulers.[70] The lectures caused a rumpus that split Cambridge along religious lines, Calvinists versus anti-Calvinists, a fact that emphasises the way in which the *use* of political arguments, if not their substance, was strongly conditioned by confessional allegiance.

Perhaps more significant than these extreme fringes of early Stuart political discourse was the potential for extremist use that inhered in arguments that could in some circumstances appear innocuous. An example might be found by considering the relationship between ideas of the 1610s and those to be found in a pamphlet appearing in October 1642, *The Vindication of the Parliament and their Proceedings*, a defence of parliament's 'defensive war' to prevent the 'reducing of the Government of this Kingdom, to the condition of those Countries, which are not governed by *Parliaments* and *established Laws*, but by the *will* of the *Prince* and his *Favourites*'.[71] Like Hedley, the author of this tract was concerned that subjects not be reduced to slavery. He made explicitly the point that whenever a person was 'at the mercy' of a king, regardless of whether he 'impoverish or enrich [him] . . . kill him, or keepe him alive', then he or she was in a condition of slavery. The question 'whether slavery or liberty?' was one of three fundamental to the issues in dispute in 1642.[72] But unlike Hedley, this writer was not concerned to use these arguments to buttress a common-law position. He would not trouble to search for precedents, being no lawyer, but was interested in the lawfulness of parliament's cause 'as farre as the *Law* of *Nature*, the *light* of *humane Reason*, and *experience*, and my small *knowledge* in *Religion*, will dictate unto me'. Thus freed from a position subordinate to the common law, the principle could be deployed with much less constraint and in defence of more extreme positions. This is a model for what happened to political ideas by the early 1640s. The collapse of confidence in common-law restraints on misgovernment led some to turn instead to natural law and to arguments from reason rather than from tradition.[73]

Patriarchal kingship

The 1620s, which saw a few puritans pushing their political arguments towards the extreme, also witnessed changes in royalist argument. For the most part, as we have seen, the theory of the divine right of kings was not a theory of arbitrary royal authority. It remained true, even in the 1620s and 1630s, that most of the time the policies of the crown were defended in ways that tried to avoid subverting the traditions of common law and legally limited government; but there is no doubt that in the atmosphere of the later 1620s and the 1630s there were some who pushed their arguments towards defences of arbitrary power.[74] It can be difficult to discern a clear difference between 'absolutist' and other positions, for almost all theoretical arguments, whether based on consent or on divine right, whether jurisprudential or theological, even humanist theories,[75] could support either position. There was also no clear division between theories of limited and unlimited monarchy. Almost everyone accepted some moral limitation (to distinguish kings from tyrants); almost no one suggested that the king was subject to the coercive force of ordinary positive law. For most, kings were limited by law, but those limits were not coercively enforced, though (as I have suggested elsewhere) this did not mean that there were not more oblique ways of imagining their enforcement.[76] It is worth, therefore, exploring in detail an example of someone who did clearly push divine-right theory towards a defence of arbitrary kingship.

In 1626, Charles I imposed a forced loan to pay for the same ill-considered foreign policy that in its earlier phases had so infuriated Thomas Scott. A preaching campaign was organised in 1627 to expound the moral duty of people to pay tribute to their rulers.[77] Two of the preachers involved, Robert Sibthorpe and Roger Manwaring, aroused considerable hostility with their efforts. They showed, bravely or rashly, both a willingness to deduce specific political consequences from general moral positions and a systematic denial of the qualifications usually made or assumed to divine-right argument. Manwaring,[78] for example, accepted – as did everyone – that, if 'any *King* on the world should command flatly against the Law of God', a subject should refuse to perform that command and suffer quietly the consequences. But Manwaring made it equally clear nothing of the sort applied to commands that were unlawful in the narrower sense. Commands in 'opposition to the originall Lawes of *God, Nature, Nations* and the *Gospell*' might be passively disobeyed; but otherwise even commands 'not correspondent in every circumstance, to Laws Nationall, and Municipall' could not by any subject 'without hazard of his own

Damnation' be so much as questioned.[79] This combination of specificity with a refusal to make even the slightest qualification pushed the
argument towards the extreme. Manwaring left no doubt that the legality or otherwise of the king's commands were entirely irrelevant. 'All
the *significations* of a *Royall pleasure*, are, and ought to be, to all *Loyall
Subjects*, in the nature, and force of a *Command*' (63). With fatal lack of
caution, Manwaring argued that the duty to pay taxes to the king was
quite independent of the mode by which they had been imposed.
Parliamentary consent to taxation was unnecessary. Of parliaments,
Manwaring wrote that 'they were not to contribute any *Right* to *Kings*'
in matters of taxation, but existed 'for the more equall *imposing*, and
more easie *Exacting* of that, which, unto *kings* doth apertaine, by
Naturall and *Originall Law*, and *justice*; as their proper *Inheritance*
annexed to their *Imperiall Crownes*, from their very births' (pp. 67–8). It
mattered not whether 'every of those Circumstances be not observed,
which by the Municipall Lawes is required' (68).

Much the same was true of Sibthorpe's sermon *Apostolike Obedience*
(1627), which deduced, as its sub-title made plain, specific *legal* or
constitutional conclusions from the fundamental precepts of divine
right kingship: 'shewing the *Duty* of *Subjects* to pay *Tribute* and *Taxes* to
their *Princes*, according to the *word of God*'. We are fortunate in having
some indication of how the sermon could be read, because archbishop
Abbot refused to license it for the press, and then produced a defence
of his refusal. He took exception, for example, to Sibthorpe's claim
that the prince's first duty was 'to *direct and make lawes*'.[80] Abbot
commented, 'There is no Law made till the King assent unto it; but if
it be put simply to make Laws, it will make much startling at it'.[81] There
was a sense in which Sibthorpe was correct; but he failed, no doubt
deliberately, to make it clear what that sense was. A parallel was drawn
with events in 1610, following the similarly unguarded sermon by
Samuel Harsnett, bishop of Chichester.

> King *James* was constrained to call the Lords and Commons into the
> Banqueting-house at *Whitehall*, and there his Majesty calmed all, by
> saying, *the Bishop only failed in this, when he said, The Goods were Caesars*;
> he did not add, They were his according to the Laws and Customs of
> the Country wherein they did live.[82]

In Sibthorpe's case, the problem was as much what he failed to say, as
what he actually said. Shorn of the usual qualifications, and applied to
the specifics of royal taxation policy, the moral platitudes of divine-
right theory acquired a dangerous edge.

We now know that the most extreme defender of monarchy during the early Caroline period was the Kentish gentleman Sir Robert Filmer.[83] His works have long been treated as products of the 1640s, or of the years immediately prior to the Civil War, but his *Patriarcha* can now be dated to the years around 1630, in which context it can be seen as an attempt to develop the notion of king as patriarch precisely to refute the attempts of men like Thomas Scott to invoke patriotic language against the king's foreign policy.[84] Around February 1632 Filmer tried, and failed, to gain permission from the press licenser Georg Weckherlin to publish the book. Weckherlin had sought the king's advice on the matter, though we do not really know why the king was reluctant to see Filmer in print.[85] The book is remarkable for its succinct clarity and its ruthlessly consistent pursuit of a powerful argument, untroubled by qualifications. *Patriarcha* aims to refute a claim that Filmer attributed primarily to the scholastics, especially Suarez and Bellarmine, but which was taken over by such protestants as Buchanan, and underpinned some arguments by English Catholics. This opinion was that:

> Mankind is naturally endowed and born with freedom from all subjection, and at liberty to choose what form of government it please, and that the power which any one man hath over others was at the first by human right bestowed according to the discretion of the multitude.[86]

Those holding such a view were guilty of 'never remembering that the desire of liberty was the cause of the fall of Adam' (2). Filmer replied to them in three ways. He indicated why this attempt to root political authority in popular consent was impossible; he presented an alternative account of the basis of political authority; and he refuted with respect to English law and constitution the particular implications that flowed from the populist theory.

Filmer's critique of consent theory was the best part of his argument.[87] He was remarkably acute in spotting the weaknesses in his opponents' position. Filmer asked those who believed that supreme power was originally in the people 'if their meaning be that there is but one and the same power in all the people of the world, so that no power can be granted except all the people on earth meet and agree to choose a governor?' (19). Clearly, this would be impossible, for the entire population of the earth could never have met to agree on their political arrangements. Not surprisingly, therefore, Filmer was able to quote Suarez as saying that power was originally in all the people, 'but a little while after the creation men began to be divided into several commonwealths'. But this would not do either. How was it that 'this distinct power comes to each particular community when God gave it to the whole multitude only, and not to any particular assembly of men'? Did the multitude ever meet to parcel up the earth into distinct commonwealths? If not, then every attempt to found a commonwealth would unjustly take from the multitude as a whole some portion of its common property; it would be 'a mere usurpation upon the privilege of the whole world'. There was no reason or proof provided for supposing that groups of men could, at their own discretion, divide themselves into separate commonwealths. However, even if there were such a power, the argument still did not work. '[W]as a general meeting of a whole kingdom ever known for the election of a prince? Was there any example of it ever found in the whole world?' Such a thing was an impossibility (20).

Filmer did not stop with that. He recognised that some might argue that the consent needed was not that of every individual but only of a majority, or of a minority and the rest by proxy, or of a minority and the rest by tacit acceptance. But, he suggested, none of this would do. Certainly, in 'politic human constitutions' majorities might carry a decision; but this could not be so in nature. '[U]nless it can be proved by some law of nature that the major, or some other part, have power to overrule the rest of the multitude, it must follow that the acts of multitudes not entire are not binding to all but only to such as consent unto them' (20–1). If men were born equal and free, then nothing but their own consent could hinder in any way their freedom. And there is no way that every man's consent to the political and social arrangements of the world could ever have been gained. It was equally fanciful to suppose that the multitude had ever given their proxy to others. And as for the argument from tacit acceptance, it would entail the 'ridiculous' proposition that 'every prince that comes to a crown, either by succession, conquest or usurpation, may be said to be elected by the people' (21).

If consent theory did not work, then how did political authority come into existence? Filmer's answer to that question provided the title of his book: the authority of kings was identical to the patriarchal authority of fathers. This was what we may call a 'hard' form of patriarchal theory, going well beyond the commonly drawn analogy between royal and patriarchal authority. Nonetheless, Filmer's form of patriarchalism was by no means his own invention, and has a history in English political thought that goes back at least to the 1590s and Hadrian Saravia.[88] In Filmer's view, 'Adam was lord of his children, so his children under him had a command and power over their own children, but still with subordination to the first parent, who is lord para-

mount over his children's children to all generations.' Thus, none 'can
be free from subjection to their parents'. This subjection was the same
as political subjection. 'And this subjection of children is the only foun-
tain of all regal authority, by the ordination of God himself' (6–7).
Filmer traced this patriarchal authority from Adam to Abraham, and
again amongst the descendants of Noah after the Flood. The division
of the world into continents (Asia, Africa and Europe) was familial, a
division amongst the three sons of Noah, and that provided a model
for subsequent divisions into particular commonwealths (7–10). The
difficulty in this position lay obviously in bridging the gap between Old
Testament patriarchs and modern kingdoms and states. In what sense
was it plausible to consider modern rulers as patriarchs? Filmer did his
best. 'It is true, all kings be not the natural parents of their subjects, yet
they all either are, or are to be reputed as the next heirs to those
progenitors who were at first the natural parents of the whole people,
and in all their right succeed to the exercise of supreme jurisdiction'
(10). The 'are reputed' suggests, of course, that there was no way of
proving the succession of Adam's heirs; and Filmer was in the end
forced to admit virtually anyone into the position of a patriarch. If they,
one or many, wielded political authority, then they must hold patriarchal authority. Thus, 'whether the prince be the supreme father of the
people or but the true heir of such a father, or whether he come to the
crown by usurpation, or by election of the nobles or of the people, or
by any other way whatsoever, or whether some few or a multitude
govern the commonwealth', the authority wielded was still the 'right
and natural authority of a supreme father'. Patriarchal right always
existed, even though 'by the secret will of God, many at first do most
unjustly obtain the exercise of it' (11). This was an unhappy conclusion, but for Filmer it was necessary to refute any suggestion that the
people at large could ever have had power. They were born into subjection. Even when no heir to patriarchal authority could be found, power
did not escheat to the people but 'to the prime and independent heads
of families, for every kingdom is resolved into those parts whereof at
first it was made' (10–11).

  From this patriarchal foundation, Filmer drew the conclusion that
monarchy was the original and only proper form of government.
Monarchies were inherently superior to republics. For long there was
'no other sort of government but only monarchy', which provided 'the
best order, the greatest strength, the most stability and easiest government', things found 'in no other form of government'. Republics, that
is, 'new platforms of commonweals were first hatched in a corner of
the world, amongst a few cities of Greece, which have been imitated by
very few other places'; and the turmoil that established them 'proved

most bloody and miserable to the authors of them, happy in nothing but that they continued but a small time' (24). All popular governments began in sedition, and continued in disorder (27–9). The evils of tyranny were less than the 'civil butchery' found in popular states (30). Even a tyrant knows that 'though he be a god, yet he must die like a man, and that there is not the meanest of his subjects but may find a means to revenge himself of the injustice that is offered him' (31). In any case, tyranny was much less frequent than men imagined (33). Naturally, Filmer was keen to reject theories of mixed monarchy – an utter absurdity that would convert monarchies into democracies (31–2) – and of resistance – even if kings made pacts with their people, the people could not be judges in their own case (32–3).

The third part of Filmer's argument dealt with the view held by some that, though kings were not dependent on the people, they were inferior to human positive laws. It was at this point that Filmer came to engage with some of the specifics of English law. The very idea that kings might be subordinate to law was, for Filmer, absurd. Kings predated laws, and, in the beginning, their wills were law. They had 'unlimited jurisdiction' (37). Filmer cited King James's discussion of 1 Samuel 8, but he wrongly attributed to James the view that 'it is right for kings to do injury' (36). James's point, as we have seen, had only been that it was wrong to resist kings who did injury. The coronation oath did not bind the king to obedience to the laws of the kingdom. He was bound, perhaps, to keep 'upright' laws; but 'what laws are upright, and what evil, who shall judge but the king?' (42–3). In some cases, even the king's commands contrary to divine law were to be obeyed (43–4). Particularly telling in this was Filmer's deconstruction of the very widely held view that kings were subject to the directive but not to the coercive force of law:

> That familiar distinction of the schoolmen, whereby they subject kings to the *directive* but not to the *coactive* power of laws, is a confession that kings are not bound by the positive laws of any nation – since the compulsory power of laws is that which properly makes laws to be laws, by binding men by rewards or punishment to an obedience; whereas the direction of the law is but like advice and direction which the king's council gives the king, which no man can say is a law to the king. (40)

In England even the customary common law was the command of the king, and 'the prerogative of a king is to be above all laws' (44–5). All power of jurisdiction remained inherent in the king's person, and he retained an 'absolute and indefinite power' of justice to correct the common law (47–9). In all courts, the king could personally exercise the powers he had delegated to his officials (56); and that verdict applied to parliament as much as to any other court. Filmer argued that the English parliament had a post-Conquest origin, and that the Commons was not originally a part of the institution (pp. 53–5). The privileges claimed by the people in parliament were not natural to them, but were liberties of grace (55). Quoting King James, Filmer indicated that laws were made in parliament 'by the king alone at the rogation of the people' (57). Assemblies 'do not share or divide the sovereignty with the prince, but do only deliberate and advise their supreme head, who still reserves the absolute power in himself' (32). It was not the first parts of this statement that mattered, but the last. Could the king alone override the laws he made in parliament? Filmer argued that he could, whether alone, through his counsel or through his judges (57). In origin, at least, there was little difference between a proclamation and a statute (59). Filmer refrained from saying that there remained no difference, but the point seemed to be implied (59–60). He painted a general picture of parliament as an institution that was and ought to be willing to take guidance from the king, and his council and judges (60–4).

It was not the generalities – the claim that kings were above the law – that made Filmer such an extremist, but the particular ways in which he applied and interpreted this widely-accepted view. He went out of his way to invest in the king absolute or arbitrary powers operating outside and over the institutions and laws of England, and he ruthlessly avoided any hint of qualification to his arguments. In this he closely resembled Thomas Hobbes, the first version of whose political thought was constructed before the Civil War (*The Elements of Law*, 1640). This will be examined in a subsequent chapter. Even in the 1640s, though, most royalists were not Filmerians or Hobbesians.

Royal supremacy

It was in Scotland, following the attempt to impose by royal authority a new liturgy in 1637, that the rule of the Stuart monarchy began to unravel. Arguably the first overt defiance of its legal authority – first of many – was the refusal in 1638 of the General Assembly of the Scottish kirk to accept the king's order to dissolve, in defiance of his 'Constantinian' authority to summon and dissolve ecclesiastical assemblies, one aspect of the royal supremacy in the church. The General Assembly went on to attack the royal supremacy as a whole, and episcopacy. James VI & I had outlined his own view of royal ecclesiastical authority in his *Meditation* on verses from the gospel of St Matthew

(1620), a work specifically designated in its preface as a counterpart to *Basilikon Doron*. Kings rule 'as *mixtae personae* . . . being bound to make a reckoning to God for their subiects soules as well as their bodies'. Of course, they 'ought [not] to vsurpe any point of the Priestly office, no more then the Priest should the Kings, for these two offices were deuided in *Aarons* Priesthood'. Kings were 'to ouersee and compell the *Church* to do her office, to purge all abuses in her, and by his sword (as *vindex vtriusque tabulae*) to procure her due reuerence and obedience of all his temporall subiects'.[89] James could even imply the view that he was a subject of the church, within its own sphere. In his first contribution to the Oath of Allegiance controversy, he asserted 'I . . . neuer did, nor will presume to create any Article of Faith, or to bee Iudge thereof; but to submit my exemplarie obedience vnto them, in as great humilitie as the meanest of the land'.[90] He precisely enumerated the facets of the royal supremacy (in England):

> to gouerne their Church, as well as the rest of their people, in being *Custodes vtriusque Tabulae*, not by making new Articles of Faith, (which is the Popes office as I said before) but by commanding obedience to be giuen to the word of God, by reforming the religion according to his prescribed will, by assisting the spirituall power with the temporall sword, by reforming of corruptions, by procuring due obedience to the Church, by iudging, and cutting off all friuolous questions and schismes, as *Constantine* did; and finally, by making *decorum* to be obserued in euery thing, and establishing orders to bee obserued in all indifferent things for that purpose. . . . [91]

Other conformists were also cautious about giving kings authority to determine matters of doctrine. Richard Field, for example, while affirming royal authority to call together religious assemblies, believed that matters of doctrine were for (clerical) experts: 'we do not attribute to our Princes with their Civill Estates, power newly to adjudge any thing to be heresie without the concurrence of the State of their Clergy, but only to Judge in those matters of faith, that are resolved on, according to former resolutions'.[92]

But even a supremacy carefully designed to preserve clerical authority was too much for some, especially to those clerics who did not have the King's ear. James VI, in his long battle with Melvillean Presbyterians, ensured statutory recognition in Scotland both of his authority to summon and dissolve church councils (the General Assembly above all) in 1606, and of the royal supremacy in 1610. The ecclesiastical policy for which he used his authority was problematic enough at times;[93] but it was his son, Charles I, who in using the royal

supremacy during the 1630s to buttress deeply controversial ecclesiastical policies in Scotland and in England, provoked challenges to it in
both kingdoms.[94]

Nonetheless, right through the 1630s, most English puritan critiques
of the church remained politically loyalist, though Scott, Dorislaus and
others make us aware of other more disturbing possibilities. Certainly,
anti-puritans did their best to make their opponents look as subversive
as possible. Peter Heylyn, for example, in his assault on Robert Burton,
did his utmost – in the style of Bancroft – to make the careful anti-epis-
copal casuistry of his opponent into a resistance theory. But there was
not much there.[95] Heylyn, for example, cited Burton's use of the coronation oath as implying a conditionality in kingship – true enough in
some senses – but he did not note that Burton's demonstration of the
point was a lengthy citation from King James's 1610 speech, and that
this portrayed a king who would 'bind himselfe to maintain the lawes
of his Kingdome'.[96] There is no doubt that for Burton, God imposed
duties on kings who ruled as his vicegerents, including the duty to
preserve the people's liberties. Furthermore, 'those that would
perswade Kings to rule in a terrible and formidable manner, as over a
sort of slaves' were to be condemned for undermining the proper
'filial' love that subjects should have for their rulers (43). The work
has, at its heart, a consideration of the relationship between duties
owed to God and duties owed to kings, but it also sought to brand as
Jesuitical those who encouraged kings to seek more power, especially
in religion, than was compatible with God's will. Burton came close to
denying kings the authority to innovate in religion, and was certainly
opposed to *jure divino* episcopacy (e.g. pp. 65–8). At issue was primarily
the authority vested in kings as part of the royal supremacy over the
church, not the king's civil authority. On the matter of the command
to ministers to read the Book of Sports, contrary to their sabbatarian
views, Burton argued that 'the Ministers . . . that refuse to read the
Booke, doe not therein directly disobey the King'. However, one of his
reasons for this was that 'no wise and honest man, can ever imagine,
that the King should ever intend to commaund that, which mainly
tends to the publicke dishonour of God, and his Word, to the violation
and annihilation of the holy commandement touching the Sabbath, to
the alteration of the Doctrine of the Church of England . . . and consequently to the destruction of the peoples soules. For this were against
all those solemne royall Protestations of the King' (56). This edges
close to a position in which aspects claimed for the king's ecclesiastical
supremacy are rejected as matters that go beyond his legitimate authority, even while his civil authority is maintained intact. This is a distinction that would be hard to maintain for long, and Burton's painful

casuistry is not untypical of the attitude with which many were to confront the Civil War.

The Scots, drawing on similar intellectual resources but refracting them through different political and ecclesiastical traditions, pursued a more direct line. Their response to the 1637 liturgy soon escalated into a direct confrontation with the king's (ecclesiastical) authority. The Scottish National Covenant of 1638 implied a very different model of kingship from that of James VI (& I), 'a limited monarchy co-existing in a theocratic state', in which allegiance to the king was 'conditional and contingent on the king fulfilling his prescribed role as the "godly magistrate"'.[97] The Covenant formed a band of 'mutual defence and assistance ... in maintaining the true religion and His Majesty's authority',[98] while making it abundantly clear that it was the former that took precedence. In its pursuit, civil war was to erupt.

Part II Political Thought and Religious Revolution, 1640–60

5 Resistance and Royalism in the British Monarchies

The advent of rebellion in Scotland in 1638, and in Ireland in 1641, and then Civil War in England from 1642 together produced a massive outpouring of political writing. The pamphleteering that effectively initiated the 'pamphlet wars' of the early 1640s was that of the Scottish covenanters, who flooded England with pamphlets justifying their actions against the king's ecclesiastical policies.[1] The results were spectacular: the average annual output of the London presses in the period 1588–1639 was 459 items; in the decade 1630–9 the average was 624; but the output in 1640 was 848 items, rising to 2,042 in 1641 and 4,038 in 1642: 1642 was to be the peak year for publication output in the whole period 1640–60.[2] This massive growth in printed pamphlets and other materials has led some historians to argue that the period of the British and English Revolutions witnessed the birth of a 'public sphere': 'the invention of public opinion', and the foundations of a democratic culture, were the result not of ideas and doctrines favouring new political forms, but of changes to 'communicative practice' to which printing was central.[3] This interpretation is challengeable, not least because the output of the presses was as much 'propaganda' as 'public opinion', and did as much to manipulate and constrain as to liberate public opinion.[4] Whatever view one takes on this matter, it is clear that politicians felt the need on an unprecedented scale to 'talk to the people', to persuade, even if they felt less need to listen to them; it is also clear that Parliamentarians and Covenanters did this with less unease than Royalists, who were more fearful of the consequences of addressing the people.[5] This chapter is an examination of political ideas, not print culture, but the printing context helps us to understand why the 1640s were unlike any earlier period for creativity in forms of writing and for rapid intellectual innovation, and cultural transformation.[6]

In the early 1640s, Scots Covenanters and English Parliamentarians developed two distinctive bodies of thought justifying their actions. Their arguments had much in common, but were also in some respects distinct from one another. Covenanter thought, more or less from the beginning, contained explicit argument for the right of God's people in matters of faith to act against their king in obedience to God's commands. In contrast, most English puritans adopted a casuistry that tried to reconcile loyalty to God and king, and within this to find ways of describing their action as involving no challenge to the monarch's legitimate authority. These contrasts were not absolute, and over time English political thought began to diversify. As well, the Solemn League and Covenant, which in 1643 brought Covenanters and Parliamentarians into military alliance, also provided both groups with a common focal point for political argument. Both groups also confronted similar arguments for loyalty to the monarch (though the opportunities for expressing monarchical loyalism in Scotland quickly dried up), and naturally their responses were often along similar lines, drawing in part on a common Reformation heritage of ideas.

Covenanter Political Thought

There are two themes that give the thought of the Covenanters its particular character.[7] First, the Scots, facing a king resident in and deriving the bulk of his power from another kingdom, were compelled to deal with the question of the relationship between the kingdoms of Scotland and England; and secondly, the Scottish rebellion was much more clearly and overtly defended as a war of religion than the English initially was. The framework within which these themes were explored was established by the National Covenant (1638) itself. That document laid down the basic aims of those who opposed the ecclesiastical policy of Charles I. They were organising 'a general band for the maintenance of true religion, and the king's person'. The greatest emphasis was placed on the defence of the true religion, but nonetheless the Covenanters would uphold 'the majesty of our king'. Their difficulty lay, of course, in the fact that their king was an enemy to what they considered to be the true faith.[8]

The early Covenanter political pamphlets, the most important of which were probably the work of Alexander Henderson,[9] were forced to confront this problem. Early statements denied that the Covenanters were 'seeking to overthrow his Majesties regall power under the false pretences of religion'; and portrayed their actions as conforming to the traditional ways of protesting against royal actions:

> It is our delight to obey his Majesties just commands, and is farre from our hearts to contemne any of his Majesties commands, although unjust, or, to protest mutinously against then: But to protest in a faire way, and as beseemeth dutifull subjects, is a course customeable, legall and ordinarie, and in some cases so necessarie

for preservation of right, and preventing of evil, that at sometimes it cannot be omitted, and at no time can give just offence.[10]

Nonetheless, even in early 1639 allusion was made to a set of arguments that justified the people's acting independently of their monarch – the natural right of self-defence, 'the Covenant betwixt the people and God, by the end for which Magistrates are ordained of God', 'the mutuall contract betwixt the King and the people at the Coronation'.[11] Alarming words, for these were allusions to some of the key themes in the resistance writings of Buchanan and his contemporaries.

As things developed by 1640 into a situation of war against the king of Scotland and his English army the defence of resistance became more prominent, but it was coupled with an insistence that the cause in which the Covenanters were engaged was a religious one. In defence of armed incursion into England, they portrayed their cause as 'this great work of Reformation'; their 'present Expedition' was 'one of the greatest and most notable parts of this wonderfull Work of GOD'.[12] They were called to it 'by that same divine providence & vocation which hath guided us hitherto in this great businesse'.[13] The cause was a Godly one, and from its Godliness it acquired much of its legitimacy. Their actions were acts of necessity, their greatest purpose to preserve religion.[14] This appeal to necessity[15] avoided the need to provide a full theoretical justification; but at least one pamphlet elaborated their position more fully. One argument was:

> From the Covenant betwixt the people and God; and for the people and Magistrate are joyntly bound in Covenant with God for observing and preserving the Commandements of the first and second Table, as may be seen in the books of *Samuel, Kings,* and *Chronicles*: And as the fault of the people would not excuse the Magistrates negligence, so the fault of the King would not excuse the people if they resist not his violence pressing them against the Covenant of God. This argument is strongly pressed by sound and religious Politicians.[16]

This was not the only argument – there was also an argument from self-defence, and from the 'mutuall contract betwixt the King and the people' – and nor was it original to the Covenanters. The covenant in question had been thoroughly explored in the Huguenot resistance tract, the *Vindiciae contra Tyrannos,* and less thoroughly in some of the British resistance theories of the 1550s. But it was a characteristic and central feature of Covenanter resistance theory to appeal to the idea of a covenant between God, king and people which gave the people not a right but a duty to resist the king's assaults upon God's religion. The same themes figured in the work of Samuel Rutherford, but before we turn to him, a second aspect of Covenanter political writing needs to be considered.

Before the outbreak of the Bishops' Wars the Covenanters could deny any intention of invading England.[17] After they had done so, however, they developed an interesting account of their relationship with their neighbour. In a study of their political actions, David Stevenson has examined the Covenanters' attitude to Britain, attributing to them a desire for 'federal union'. There may be room for quibbling about the details of his account, but the Covenanter pamphlets did develop some sort of federal or confederal approach.[18] Their position was founded upon an acceptance of national independence. They objected to the English prelates, who wished 'that we should no more be a Church or Nation'.[19] They appealed to 'patriots', in both England and Scotland, who would defend their religion and liberties.[20] Ruled by an absentee king, they had no option but to take extreme measures, for there was a 'difference put between the King resident in the Kingdome, and by opening his eares to both parties, rightly informed, and the King farre from us in another kingdome, hearing the one partie, and mis-informed by our adversaries'.[21] Ultimately, this compelled an invasion of England, and led the Covenanters to adopt a further objective of reforming the English church. But even in this, care was taken to respect the independence of the English nation. 'Scotland shall be reformed as at the beginning, the Reformation of *England* long prayed and pleaded for by the Godly there, shall be according to their wishes and desire perfected in doctrine, worship and discipline.'[22] 'According to their wishes', for the Covenanters insisted that they had no quarrel with the English people and parliament, but only with 'the *Canterburian* faction'.[23] Like many Scots throughout the early modern period, the Covenanters had a powerful sense of themselves as an independent nation. They wished, certainly, that 'the Lord shall be one, and his Name one throughout the whole Iland'; but this religious unity would occur with the willing consent and agreement of two independent peoples.[24]

Though it had its own distinctive features, the Covenanters' resistance theory nonetheless was in other respects broadly similar to that of the English Parliamentarians, reflecting in part their common European heritage. The nearest thing to a résumé of Covenanter thought was Samuel Rutherford's *Lex, Rex* (October 1644). There is no doubt that much of what appeared in that bulky work could have been written by a Parliamentarian, though its title specifically declared it to be a justification 'of the most necessary Defensive Wars of the Kingdom of Scotland, and of their Expedition for the ayd and help of their dear Brethren of England'. Much of the early portion of the book was concerned to discriminate the senses in which it was true that royal authority came directly from God, from those in which it was false,[25] and to discriminate the true from the false senses in which royal authority was from the people. From there, Rutherford was able to consider the relationship between royal authority and popular authority. The whole discussion was conducted abstractly, in terms applicable to all kingdoms.

Rutherford's work was a reply to Maxwell's *Sacro-Sancta Regum Majestas*, which appeared early in 1644. For Rutherford, civil society was rooted in natural instinct, and thus in God as creator. But men were created free:

> If all Men be born free . . . there is no reason in Nature, why one Man should be King and Lord over another, therefore . . . I conceive all jurisdiction of Man over Man, to be as it were Artificiall and Positive, and that it inferreth some servitude, whereof Nature from the womb hath freed us.[26]

This did not prevent Rutherford from admitting that there were a number of senses in which royal (and all other) authority came directly from God. 'God ordained the power', '[t]he Office is immediately from *God*'; but men have 'the designation of the person' (9, 16). Nonetheless, the people designated their ruler in ways that made his power both limited, with 'banks and marches to the exercise', and conditional, 'that they may take again to themselves what they gave out, upon condition, if the condition be violated' (10). In principle, communities were free to choose any form of government for themselves, for none was naturally superior to the others (51). In the case of monarchy, it ought properly to be elective, though it was permissible for people to tie themselves *conditionally* to an hereditary monarch (80, 77). Thus power resided ultimately in the kingdom. By this Rutherford did not mean in the people at large. In Scotland and England the community's power was vested in parliament (58, 146). They had power from God, independently of the king (174–6), and could 'unmake' kings who become tyrants (177). The community always reserved to itself some power: 'the community keepeth to themselves a power to resist tyranny, and to coerce it' (61, 151), though this power was not to be used against every act of royal injustice (63–4). The people were not permitted to create an absolute – for Rutherford the term meant 'arbitrary' – monarch by their consent (81); and nor could they enslave themselves by consent (119–20). People did not have absolute power over themselves, and so could not give it to others (184–5). The king's oath gave him a legal contractual obligation to perform the duties of his office (96–7), and the people might compel his compliance (101). The king had thus only a fiduciary power, or power of trust, and there were many things he could not do (124). He had no right, for example, to his subjects' property (120–2, 161). He was subject even to the coercive force of the community's laws (231–2). King's who failed in their trust 'may be resisted by defensive Wars, at the commandment of the Estates of the *Kingdom*' (260). It was, however, wrong to kill kings. Their abuses of authority could be resisted, but they nonetheless remained kings and their office was inviolate (265–8, 273).

Arguments like this, a version of an 'inferior magistrates' resistance theory, were common in England as well. But there were themes in Rutherford's writing that, although part of the Covenanter tradition, were much less common in English resistance theory, at least before the impact of the Solemn League and Covenant. In particular, he allowed to the people a right to pursue the true faith quite independently of their king: 'the people may swear a Covenant for Reformation of Religion, without the King'. Indeed, 'to renew a Covenant with God is a point of service due to God, that the people are obliged unto; whether the King command it, or no' (250). The people made the king a king on condition that he rule according to God's word (105). This understanding of the role of the people of Scotland as a covenanted people justified their actions in defence of the faith, regardless of the king. The English from the start could see their cause as religious, whether defensive or as the pursuit of further Reformation, but they were much cagier about deriving political and legal legitimation of their actions from religious presuppositions. Clearly for Rutherford though, the twin goals of the Scottish National Covenant had come apart:

> The *King*, as a man, is not more obliged to the publick and regall defence of the true Religion, then any other man of the land; but he is made by God and the people *King*, for the *Church* and people of *God*'s sake, that he may defend true Religion, for the behalfe and salvation of all. If therefore he defend not Religion for the salvation of the soules of all in his publick and royall way, it is presumed as undeniable, that the people of *God*, who by the law of nature are to care for their own soule, are to defend in their way, true Religion, which so nearly concerneth them and their eternall happinesse. (100)

The same understanding was extended to explain the Covenanters' incursion into English affairs. They were obliged 'to help our bleeding sister Church', for the two countries shared one Lord, one faith and one baptism (381).

> And beside the union in Religion . . . we sayle in one ship together, being in one *Iland*, under one *King*, and now by the mercy of God, have sworne one Covenant, and so must stand or fall together. (382)

English Parliamentarians

Gradually during 1642, England edged closer to a Civil War, which is conventionally taken to have begun on 22 August, when the king raised his standard at Nottingham. The first significant battle, Edgehill, did not, however, occur until 23 October. By stops and starts hostilities began; by stops and starts, even before the cold war became hot, Charles's opponents were forced to confront the tricky question of how they could make a case for the legitimacy of their actions that might have some hope of persuading significant numbers of people. This need to *persuade* in itself dictated that the political theories that the Parliamentarian spokesmen produced attempted as much as possible to appeal to shared and conventional principles, and would avoid wherever they could intellectual innovation or the appeal to new (and therefore divisive) principles. Though modern historians have (rightly) returned to emphasising the religious impulses that led men into civil war, some even emphasising that the Civil War was a 'war of religion', it is a striking fact that few of the important pamphlet defences of Parliament during the early phases of the first Civil War (1642–6) actually defended its actions simply on religious grounds. There are certainly some historians who have credited those puritan ministers who wrote in defence of Parliament with a theory of holy war.[27] Most of parliament's important early defenders – the chief exceptions are Henry Parker and William Prynne – were divines, men like Charles Herle, Philip Hunton, Jeremiah Burroughes, Herbert Palmer and William Bridge. In fact, though many did indeed think that they were fighting in a religious cause for God's purposes, most of them were keen to distance themselves from the idea that parliament's war with the king was *legitimated* simply by its religious objectives or intentions. It was legitimated as a *legal* religious war, in defence of the church (or faith) by law established.

We have to search amongst the anonymous tracts, such as *Powers to be Resisted* (December 1643), or R. W.'s *The Anatomy of Warre* (November 1642), for a real defence of something that we could call religious war. The direct avowal of religious war in the latter – 'War is lawfull when it is for Religion, and the Republickes good' (11) – stands in marked contrast to the hesitancy of others. '[W]e acknowledge we must not resist for Religion; if the Laws of the Land be against it,' Jeremiah Burroughes admitted.[28] Charles Herle agreed that a religious cause was no justification for resistance: ''tis not the cause, 'tis the constitution of the government, reserving in its coordination a power of resistance in order to its preservation'. In short, as Herbert Palmer put it, 'our case is of a Civill State'.[29] The legitimacy of resistance to the king thus depended upon the argument that parliament was acting in defence of the civil community, not of the church or the true faith.

But what was it that gave to parliament (or, more accurately, the two Houses, the Lords and Commons) the right to act for the whole community even against the commands of the king himself? In detailing the answers to this question, we shall discover most clearly the powerful compulsion felt by Parliamentarian publicists to make their case as conventional as possible. It has been said that during the 1640s English political thought moved from an emphasis upon history and custom (the ancient constitution) to an emphasis on reason and nature, and that this change to political rationalism was a necessary (if not sufficient) condition for the emergence of political radicalism.[30] Examining Parliamentarian arguments using this history–reason distinction is an enlightening enterprise, and one that will help us to answer the question with which the present paragraph began.

Henry Parker, a barrister of Lincoln's Inn, is usually taken to be the Parliamentarian writer with the clearest – and the hardest – head. Even so, he was careful to present a case for the parliament that was as conventional as possible. Early in his tract *Observations upon Some of His Majesties Late Answers and Expresses* (2 July 1642), Parker appealed to general principles, to reason and nature: 'The Charter of nature entitles all Subjects of all countries whatsoever to safety by its supreame Law.' The very next sentence, though, returned us to the laws of England:

> But freedome indeed has divers degrees of latitude, and all Countries therein doe not participate alike, but positive Lawes must everywhere assign those degrees. The great Charter of England is not strait in Priviledges to us, neither is the Kings oath of small strength to that Charter . . . yet it confirms all Lawes and rightfull customes.[31]

It is a common pattern: the general appeal to universal rational principles is modified as those principles are seen to work through, not against, the law of the land. Such an understanding of the relationship between natural reason and positive law was typical of common-law thinking.[32] William Prynne, another common lawyer, after stating the general principle that the community as a whole possessed an authority superior to that of its ruler, soon abandoned his 'foreign authorities' to show that the principle was also 'the resolution of some eminent ancient lawyers of our own'. This pattern we can restate as a rule for successful polemic: wherever possible, show that the principles to which you appealed were part and parcel of the positive laws of England.[33] The effect of following the rule was to make more arduous the path to political radicalism. Whereas the *principle* that the people chose their rulers and might discipline them when they erred could be taken to dangerously democratic conclusions (see below), this radical potential could be negated by the assertion that *English* law and precedent placed this power to check an erring ruler in the two Houses of Parliament. On the whole, it was precisely such an argument that the Parliamentarian propagandists advanced.

Before examining their argument, it is worth pointing out that the polemical rule we have identified was far from being unbroken in the period, and was treated with less respect by some than by others. As early as 26 May 1642 the two Houses issued a Remonstrance in which they forthrightly declared that:

> If we made any presidents in this Parliament, we have made them for posterity; upon the same or better grounds of reason and Law then those were upon, which our Predecessors first made any for us, and as some Presidents ought not to be rules for us to follow, so none can be limits to bound our proceedings, which may and must vary according to the different condition of times.[34]

Yet, earlier the same month (19 May) they had rested content with the altogether safer principle that their actions were justified 'not by any new Law of their own making . . . but by the most ancient Law of this Kingdome, even that which is fundamentall and essentiall to the constitution and subsistance of it'.[35] We might say that, while there was much pressure to argue as conservatively as possible, this was offset by some irritation at the constraints thus imposed on what could be said.

To make the case that parliament could restrain an erring monarch, though, its defenders were required to replace the diffuse and particularist common lawyer's conception of the English polity with a more succinct analysis that tackled directly the question of how exactly

power and authority were distributed at the centre. This more
succinct analysis laid down also some rules about the proper exercise
of authority. Thus some Parliamentarians, notably Charles Herle,
developed a clearer account of the English *constitution* than any to be
found before 1640. In this they were much assisted by the king's own
propagandists, Falkland and Culpepper, whose *Answer to the xix
Propositions* (June 1642) provided, in useful form, a language of constitutional analysis that could be exploited for a variety of ends. The
language concerned was that of the three estates and of mixed
government, resurgent again following its eclipse from the 1590s. It
had a complex history, and the king's *Answer*, in employing it, was only
using a terminology that had already been employed by Henry Parker
(and others).[36] Falkland and Culpepper used the language to claim a
moderate position for the king's supporters, more concretely to assert
that the king was the protector of law and custom, that he could not
and would not misgovern, and that it was the two Houses who were
guilty of innovatory and uncustomary actions. England was declared
to possess a constitution blended of the three 'good' forms of government (monarchy, aristocracy, and democracy), represented in turn by
the three estates of king, Lords and Commons. The Commons, while
'an excellent Conserver of Libertie . . . [was] never intended for any
share of Government'. Its functions were consenting to taxation and
impeaching erring ministers. The Lords maintained the balance
between monarch and people, prerogatives and liberties. It followed
from this analysis that:

> the Power Legally placed in both Houses is more than sufficient to
> prevent and restrain the power of Tyrannie, and without the power
> which is now asked from Us, we shall not be able to discharge that
> Trust which is the end of Monarchie, since this would be a totall
> Subversion of the Fundamentall Laws, and that excellent
> Constitution of this Kingdom, which hath made this Nation so many
> yeers both famous and happie to a great degree of Envie.[37]

The king could then employ one of the great slogans of ancient consti-
tutionalism: *Nolumus Leges Angliae mutari* (we do not wish laws of
England to change) (171). To accede to the demands of the two
Houses would be to consent to the destruction of the English polity.

The king's *Answer* was a short-hand restatement of the ancient
constitution, onto which had been grafted the language of the three
estates and of the classical mixed polity, a language only marginally
present in early Stuart England. It emphasised that the polity was a
self-regulating mechanism. The uses made of these concepts by

Parliamentarians moved to a very different sort of constitutionalism, one that blended together the idea of *enforceable limitation* and the idea of the legitimacy of *violent resistance*. This emphasis on violence grew during the 1640s, and persists as a feature of English political discourse through the seventeenth century. Parliamentarian thought was a *depacification* of the ancient constitution, and it was interested in exploring violent rather than constitutional limitations on royal power. Parliamentarian thought thus, paradoxically, became more obviously constitutionalist, in the sense of possessing a clear theory of the nature, location and limits of governmental authority, at the same time that it became more wedded to normalising the use of political violence as a tool for enforcing constitutional limitations on rulers.

This pattern is perhaps clearest in the case of Charles Herle.[38] His use of the language of the three estates not only reduced the king's role in the polity – in effect, making the king one of three (equal) estates rather than 'the head and sovereign of the whole' that Edward Hyde had warned about even before the king's *Answer* was printed[39] – but formed one component in a new analysis of the English *constitution*. To defend parliament's resistance, Herle needed to show 'what kinde of Government this of Englands is'. The answer was simple: 'a Coordinative, and mixt Monarchy'. It was mixed:

> in the very supremacy of power it selfe, otherwise the Monarchy were not mixt: all Monarchies have a mixture, or composition of subordinate, and under-officers in them, but here the Monarchy, or highest power is it selfe compounded of 3. Coordinate Estates, a *King*, and two *Houses* of Parliament; unto this mixt power no subordinate authority may in any case make resistance.[40]

But though subordinates could not resist, the relationship between co-ordinates (king, Lords and Commons) was one of equals: 'Coordinates supply each other.' Defending Parker's claim that the king was *universis minor* (inferior in authority to the whole realm),[41] Herle advanced the stark and striking proposition that: 'if the temper ... of this Government be of three Estates ... [nobody needs to] buy an Almanick ... to reckon by, that one is less than three' (3). One is less than three, Herle taunted; but one is also less than two. The two Houses were not the king's subjects or subordinates, and might act together to correct his failings. Even the king's right to summon parliament by writ was deemed to be no more than an ordinary conventional practice, for it was 'the Constitution of the government [that] designes them to it' (4). Thus, while government is ordinarily betrusted to the King . . . [nevertheless] if he faile and refuse, either to follow the *rule* Law, or to it's *end* safety, his *coordinates* in this mixture of the supreame power must according to their trusts supply.   (8)

'Supply' might be considered a euphemism. When the king by his personal command raised an army to pursue actions against the public interest, then supplying his deficiencies meant raising an army to fight him.

because they [i.e. Royalits] are in Armes against *Law* and so against the *Kingdom*, and so against *him as King*. . . . [N]ay, they are not only in Armes against *Law* without its authority, but against the very being of it which depends on Parliament. What shall the two other *Estates doe?* Nothing but an *Army* is left whereby to represse these enemies of *King* and *Kingdome*.   (10)

It was an odd constitution that made civil war the very stuff of consti-tutional politics.

The most interesting feature of the argument was, however, its elab-orated conception of a constitution. Herle expressed it in the termi-nology of fundamental law. '[Y]ou'l say', he said to his critics,

there is no written of *fundamentall* Law for this. I answer (to speake properly) if it be written it is *superstructive* and not *fundamentall*, written Laws, that were not Lawes before written, are repealable and alterable, even while the government remaines the same, funda-mentals cannot: a foundation must not be stirr'd while the building stands.   (8)

The fundamental laws formed a set of constitutional principles, acting as the basis for governmental authority and ordinary law.

At least one of Herle's contemporaries could perceive the oddity of this argument. Philip Hunton exposed clearly the fact that Parliamentarian propagandists like Herle had produced a constitu-tional defence of resistance only at the cost of abandoning the view that had prevailed before the Civil War, that violence must always be kept at arm's length, and that kingship and the rule of law should be seen as compatible. The laws kept prerogative and liberty in balance, so that resistance was scarcely needed. When the balance was upset, it was still better to keep the peace than to resort to violence.

Hunton was as willing as Herle to adopt the 'mixed monarchy' theory of the king's *Answer* as a model of the English constitution.[42] He was not, however, of the opinion that two were greater than one – or, at any rate, he believed along Bodinian lines that on important matters sovereignty was not divisible. In three areas of decision-making, the three estates had to act as one: in making laws, in imposing taxes, and in deciding certain matters 'of greatest difficulty and weight, the *ardua regni*' (46–8). Hunton was prepared to admit that 'the two Estates in Parliament may lawfully by force of Armes resist any persons or number of persons advising or assisting the King in the performance of a command illegal and destructive to themselves, or the publique' (52), though force ought *never* to be used against the person of the sovereign (50). There were even circumstances in which the two Houses might legitimately 'assume the Armes of the Kingdome' (63–7).

Yet, in the end, Hunton faced squarely the implications of his theory of mixed but undivided sovereignty. Of disputes between the three Estates there could be 'no legal constituted Judge', for if there were, then government was not mixed but dominated by that part of it with the authority to judge of these matters (69). Both Royalists and Parliamentarians had wrongly claimed such a power to judge for, respectively, the king and the two Houses; and Hunton was scathing about the sorts of claims made for Parliament by men like Herle and Parker. In fact, only individual consciences could decide the matter: 'every Person must aide that Part, which in his best Reason and Judgement stands for publicke good, against the destructive' (73). If Parliament's judgement in the disputes of 1642–3 was sound – as Hunton intimated – then it was so because of the quality of evidence and reason that lay behind the judgement, not because parliament possessed an authority to make binding judgements in matters disputed with the king. In short, when the component parts of the supreme power fell apart, then violence might be the result. But this violence was not, for Hunton, the fulfilment of constitutional order; it was its negation. England's legal, pacified polity had *failed*, and in consequence England was without a legal solution to her difficulties. Those, like Herle and Parker, who tried hard to make violent resistance continuous with legal order failed to understand what a mixed monarchy really was, and failed to understand the constitutional principle of sovereignty.

Profound as Hunton's insights were, most Parliamentarians accepted that the two Houses had a legal or constitutional right to resist. It remains for us to consider the character of the particular arguments used in justification of this right. As we should expect, the case was made (so far as possible) by building upon traditional conceptions of parliament's role and nature. William Prynne in 1654 quoted the view that parliament could be seen in three ways: as a *council* giving advice, as a *court* rendering judgement, and as a *representative body* called to give consent to the alteration and repeal of laws or to the imposition of taxes.[43] John Pym, in a speech to the Short Parliament (1640), had produced a similar analysis. Of parliament he said:

> This is the fountaine of law, the great Councell of the kingdom, the highest Court: this is inabled by the Legislative and Conciliary power, to prevent evils to come; by the Judiciary power, to suppresse and remove evils present.[44]

Parliament was a council, a court, and a representative legislature. All three roles were exploited in Parliamentary propaganda, though in the early 1640s it was the first two that were more important. In emphasising their roles as counsellors and judges, the two Houses were participating in the habit identified by Conal Condren by which those defending resistance found a way of redescribing their actions in traditional terms. Indeed, they usually sought to avoid mention of resistance (still more of rebellion) altogether, and to portray their actions as something else.[45] This was, in essence, a casuistry of obedience.

In the series of statements and demands (or 'laws' made without the king's assent) issued before the Civil War, the two Houses had already made much of their role as the king's Great Council. At least from the time of Pym's Ten Propositions (24 June 1641), Charles's opponents had been insistent that any settlement with him would require his acceptance of parliamentary oversight of the counsel he received.[46] He was 'to remove from him all such counsellors . . . as have been active for the time past in furthering those courses contrary to religion, liberty, [and] good government of the kingdom', and to take counsel only from 'such officers and counsellors as his people and Parliament may have just cause to confide in'.[47] The claims had become more forceful and detailed by the time the two Houses issued the demands for which they were actually to fight, the Nineteen Propositions (1 June 1642);[48] and later proposals for peace settlements kept to similar terms in demanding the exclusion from the king's counsels of all 'malignants'.[49] Mirroring these negative demands were positive ones. The two Houses themselves claimed to be the proper forum for giving counsel to the king. The claim was made in practice by their issuing of executive ordinances tantamount to a claim to take over the Privy Council's function of carrying on the day-to-day running of government in the king's absence (and in his name).[50] But it was made in theory, also, by those pamphleteers who asserted that the king *must* take the advice of his parliament rather than of his chosen private counsellors, or 'privadoes' in Henry Parker's terminology. Henry Marten, precocious as ever, linked this point to the demand that the king had to assent to legislation presented to him as early as 8 February 1642 – 'he thought it sufficient to induce his majesty to pass any bill when the two houses had assented to it because they were his great council, whose advice he was to take and not to have a third house of parliament to counsel him otherways'[51] – but its role in justifying parliament's resistance was perhaps furthest developed in Henry Parker's *Observations*.

At one point, Parker asserted that 'the maine question now is, whether the Court, or the Parliament gives the King the better Councell'.[52] The answer was determined by a simple principle: 'publick advise be commonly better than private' (26). A central claim of the tract was that the public advice of parliament must have precedence over the king's private advisers (evil counsellors), and that without public advice even the wisest kings went astray. Essentially, parliament was fighting in order to have its counsel listened to (25).

This theme – Parliament as council – could easily blend into others. As Charles Herle put it, the two Houses were certainly 'the Kings great Councell' – but their function was not 'onely to *consult* ... but to *consent* with him in the making of Lawes'. For this counsel came not from men to whom the king chose to listen, but from men 'assigned to him by the first constitution of the Government', and representing the people.[53] The constitution *required* the king to listen to parliament. Parker made a similar point. The nature of parliamentary power was 'publicke consent', and 'to consent is more than to counsell, and yet not alwayes so much as to command and controll'.[54] Here we are finding ourselves pushed towards viewing parliament in the third of the senses discriminated by Prynne and Pym. So public was parliament, so fully did it embody the will of the people, that its counsel could not be ignored: it had the right to give consent. What linked together this chain of ideas was the notion that parliament was a *public* body, representing the public, acting for the public weal or commonwealth. The decisions of many were inherently sounder than the decisions of a few; and parliament was the many in a literal sense, for 'the whole Kingdome is not so properly the Author as the essence it selfe of Parliaments' (11, 5). Hence it was that:

> We have ever found enmity and antipathy betwixt the Court and the countrey, but never any till now betwixt the Representatives, and the Body, of the Kingome represented.   (11)

The idea of representation raised acutely the problem of the radical implications of Parliamentarian theory, for it exposed

Parliamentarians to the Royalist jibe that the Commons in fact represented only a tiny proportion of the population (see below). But, in the
first months, even years, of the Civil War, Parliamentarians were largely
oblivious to the risks. Their belief that the people acted only through
parliament, and that parliament, in turn, pursued without hesitation
or corruption the public good, was firmly held.

The third understanding of parliament, that it was a *court* of law,
produced some of the most startling writing of all. The subject was
important, because it was widely held that the debates of the early
1640s did not concern sovereignty and law-making authority, but
judgement. What, on the issues in question, did the law say, and who
had the authority to decide the question? It is here that we get the
strongest sense of the continuities between Parliamentarian propaganda and the common-law political thinking of the preceding
decades. William Bridge can take us right to the heart of the matter.

> Againe, whereas I argue from the being and nature of *Parliament*,
> that if it hath not power to send for by force, those that are accused
> to be tried before them, that should not be a Court of Justice; seeing
> that even inferiour Courts have a power to force those before them
> that are to be tried: and if the Parliament may send one Sergeant at
> Armes, then 20. then 100. then 1000. &c. The Doctor [Henrey
> Ferne] Replies: *Therfore Inferiour Courts have a power to raise Armes.*
> (Answer) this followes not? For though I say every Court hath a
> power to force in the accused; yet it must be in a way suitable: Now
> this raising of Armes is not suitable unto an Inferiour Court, but to
> the Parliament being a more Nationall and publike Court then any
> other is.[55]

It is an extraordinary passage, making every member of the army a
parliamentary sergeant-at-arms! But it takes us directly to the heart of
the constitutional position advanced on parliament's behalf in the
early months of the first Civil War. For many, parliament's claim was
not so much to legislative sovereignty, for the issue at hand was not
deemed to be one of making law. Much more crucial was the authority
to *judge* things to be either for or against the law and the public good.
There was no sustained and clear claim to sovereignty because, in
Parker's words, 'Parliamentary government [was] being used as
Physicke, not dyet.'[56]

It is worth following Parker further, because he shows most clearly
why so much importance was attached to the idea that parliament was
a (sort of) court of law. He made the crucial transition from his
concern with counsel thus:

If there bee any benefit in Lawes to limit Princes when they are seduced by Privadoes, and will not hearken to the Great Councell of the Land, doubtlesse there must be some Court to judge of that seducement, and some authoritie to inforce that judgement, and that Court and authoritie must bee the Parliament, or some higher Tribunall. (30)

There was, of course, no higher tribunal (except God). It was because parliament was the highest court that it could insist that its counsel be followed. Parker was happy to vest legislative sovereignty in the king and two Houses jointly (16); but it was still necessary that in an emergency there be a body capable of giving authoritative judgements applying the laws.

In this Intricacy therefore, where the King and Parliament disagree, and judgement must be supream, either in the one or other, we must retire to ordinary justice, And there we see, if the King consent not with the ordinary Judge, the Law thinks it fit, that the King subscribe, rather than the Judge. (44)

This analysis of parliament's authority was, of course, deeply rooted in the common-law politics of early Stuart England. It stands, perhaps, as the most eloquent testimony to the Parliamentarians' effort to argue at the detailed level from English law and custom, whatever grounding they may have given that law and custom in nature and popular consent.

Varieties of Royalist Propaganda

Much of what has been written about Royalism has focused on moderate or 'constitutional' Royalism.[57] The latter term is not, perhaps, well chosen. On most crucial matters the political thought of James VI's *Trew Law of Free Monarchies* is identical to that of the key work of the 'constitutional' Royalists, Henry Ferne's *Resolving of Conscience*. They agreed about the place of conquest theory, about the nature of the king's coronation oath, about the duties of kings, about the unconscionable illegitimacy of resistance theory; they agreed that all authority flowed outwards from the king, and none was independent of him. No one seems to hesitate in classifying Ferne as a 'constitutionalist', for his thinking is clearly different from that of some of the more extreme defenders of Charles I active in the 1640s, while James VI is routinely thought of as an 'absolutist'. Royalist theory came in several varieties, but it is not apparent that a simple classification into constitutionalists and absolutists is particularly helpful.

Royalism was not, of course, a purely English phenomenon. Especially in the early years, the Scottish Covenanters were opposed in a number of writings by those loyal to the king. This Scottish Royalism antedated that developed in England from 1642, though in both countries much Royalist writing simply continued conformist argument into a new and more pressing context. Perhaps the most important of Scottish Royalist writings were produced by the Aberdeen Doctors. They do not reveal, however, a distinctly Scottish brand of Royalism (nor, indeed, does the work of John Maxwell, a Scottish bishop, discussed below). We can distinguish Scots Covenanters from English Parliamentarians, but Royalist arguments were British. From July 1638 until the meeting of the Glasgow General Assembly in November, the theologians and divinity professors of Aberdeen conducted from the pulpit and in print a campaign of opposition to the Covenant.[58] The published debate began with 14 'demands', or questions, that the Aberdeen Doctors put to the Covenanting ministers, led by Alexander Henderson. The Doctors focused especially on the lack of authority for the National Covenant, arguing that 'subjects may make such a *Covenant* of Mutuall Defence, by Armes, with the consent of the King, who only, under GOD, hath the power of Armes, or of the Sword, in this Kingdome'.[59] This principle had been affirmed by James VI and the Estates in 1585, though it was generally true 'in all *Kingdomes*, and *Monarchies, properly so called*'. Of course, this consent was signally lacking in 1638. In its absence, the Doctors could only condemn the opinions of Buchanan, and affirm that 'it is altogether unlawfull to Subjects in such Kingdomes, to take Armes against their Prince' (7–10; also 87–9). That principle was naturally at the core of all Royalist argument. Obedience was, as the Doctors put it, owed to kings even when 'they embraced not the Trueth; or having before embraced it, yet have fallen from it'; while suffering was the only action allowed under kings 'commanding things unlawfull . . . when we give not active obedience to them' (21–2).

In one respect, though, Scottish Royalists were in a different position from English ones. They were usually, like the Aberdeen Doctors, defenders both of the episcopal structure of the Scottish church, as reconstructed by James VI, and of the five articles of Perth (1618), which introduced rites into the church that many Covenanters saw as idolatrous. They defended these changes to the Reformation settlement, while English royalists were seeking to prevent changes. They tended to assert that the external form of the church was changeable and need not follow a precise scriptural pattern; so did some English

Royalists, though others were *jure divino* episcopalians. For the Doctors, the form was indifferent, and could be altered by lawful authority. And, 'we doe not esteem it lawfull for us, to disobey Authority in things lawfull, though in themselves indifferent: for obedience commanded by the fift Precept of the Decalogue, is not a thing indifferent' (160). Thus the Aberdeen Doctors could not accept the Covenanters' attempt to suggest that the kirk should return to the external from that it had at the time of the Negative Confession (1581). That was 'to make a perpetuall Law, concerning the externall *Rites* of the Church, as if they were unchangeable' (19; also 139–40). They were not. These points are important because they remind us that, in England as in Scotland, Royalists could just as well (and in some cases, rather better) be called Episcopalians; and that many defended episcopacy as an indifferent institution, lawful because allowed, possibly even recommended, by God, and founded on the authority of the Royal Supremacy (or possibly, in Scotland, upon the authority of the General Assembly summoned under the royal prerogative[60]).

Though there is much religious argument specific to Scotland in the writings of the Aberdeen Doctors, their political thought was grounded on these two principles, the irresistibility of kings and their authority to determine, within varying limits, the lawful regiment of the church. Most other Royalists, English and Scottish, built on the same principles, but in a variety of ways. The remainder of this account will assess key themes within that variety.

The ideas developed by Charles I's 'official' propagandists of 1642, Falkland, Hyde and Culpepper, laid down a case for the king that proclaimed loudly its own moderation. Their masterpiece is usually taken to have been the king's *Answer to the xix Propositions*, though Hyde, as we have seen, was not at all happy with the most famous political doctrine advanced in that work. The basic pattern was first set in the King's reply to the Grand Remonstrance and published in early December 1641.[61] The Grand Remonstrance, a 'wildly tendentious document', passed the Commons by eleven votes on 23 November and was never transmitted to the Lords. Instead the Commons decided that it should be 'published' (but not printed), in a blatant and crucial appeal to public opinion.[62] The king's printed reply, written for him by Edward Hyde, has been described as a 'manifesto of good conduct', as the proof that the king had repudiated the bad advice of the past and was now set firmly on the path of legal and moderate government.[63] The typical tone of this argument – which Charles carried with him to the scaffold in 1649 – was quickly sounded in Hyde's claim that 'the prosperity of Our Subjects must be included' in any proper understanding of 'the Peace and happinesse of Our Kingdom'.[64] With

Hyde's pen, the king took full credit for the reforming legislation of 1641, which came from 'Our own Resolution ... to have freed Our Subjects for the future, from those Pressures which were grievous to them if those Laws had not been propounded' (4–5). The legislation of 1641 freed subjects from 'all jealousies and apprehensions of Arbitrary pressures under the Civill or Ecclesiasticall state' (14). The excesses of the Laudian church were quickly abandoned (6–7), but the established church was stoutly defended, and clearly distinguished from popery (7–8). The king was aware that there were those unable to accept all that the Church required, and he therefore declared his willingness to 'comply with the advice of Our Parliament, that some Law may be made for the exemption of tender consciences from punishment, or prosecution for such Ceremonies, and in such cases which by the judgement of most men, are held to be matters indifferent', provided that this was done in a decent and orderly fashion (9–10). The king was ready, too, to leave to 'Publike Justice' any of his counsellors who could be shown to be dishonest (17–18).

Perhaps the single thing that did most to form a moderate Royalist position was commitment to the rule of law. The law guaranteed allegiance to the king, and rights to the subject. Hyde gave a classic expression. Subjects should realise that peace and prosperity depended on their 'yeelding all obedience and due reverence to the Law, which is the inheritance of every subject, and the onely security he can have for his Life, Libertie, or Estate'. For his part, the king declared his resolution 'not onely duly to observe the Laws Our Self, but to maintain them against what opposition soever, though with the hazard of Our being' (19–20). It was this theme, in particular, that later helped to lend such dignity to Charles's scaffold speech, where the link between the king's rights and those of his subjects was made especially clear. The people's freedom consisted in the right to live under 'those laws by which their life and their goods may be most their own', not in 'having share in government'; and the only thing that brought the king to the scaffold was his unwillingness (contrasting with the willingness of his opponents) to accept 'an arbitrary way for to have all laws changed according to the power of the sword'.[65]

Emphasis on the rule of law was at the very core of Hyde's attempt to refashion Charles I's image in 1641/2. All the king wanted to do was 'to defend *The true Protestant Profession, The Law of the Land*, and *The Libertie of the Subject*'.[66] On 4 May, in a defence of the king's right to be admitted to Hull, the king asked, quoting Pym against Strafford, 'what title any subject of his kingdom had to his house or land that he had not to his town of Hull? Or what right any subject had to his money plate, or jewels, that his majesty had not to his magazine or munition there?'

He acknowledged 'the great and unlimited power of a Parliament' – 'but only in that sense as he was a part of Parliament'. The two Houses were a threat to every property-owner, as well as to 'the sovereign legal authority', if they claimed an arbitrary power over property.[67] As the debate unfolded, Hyde directed this charge against the king's opponents with increasing venom, describing them early in June 'as a faction . . . whose Designe is, and alwayes hath been, to alter the whole frame of Government both of Church and State, and to subject both King and People to their own Lawlesse Arbitrary power and Government'.[68] They 'unsettle the Security of all Mens Estates, and . . . expose them to an Arbitrary Power of their own'; they were, in short, tyrants seeking to rule by their own wills (7, 5 / vol. II, 152, 151). In June, subjects were invited to consider 'whether their Estates come to them, and are setled upon them by Orders of both houses, or by that Law which We Defend'. Hyde was implicitly invoking in the king's defence a neo-Roman understanding of liberty as non-dependence on the will of another person, or in this case of another body of persons. Parliament's threat to the king's property enslaved everyone.[69]

Hyde's 1645 pamphlet, *Transcendent and Multiplied Rebellion and Treason Discovered*, reiterated many of the themes he had developed during 1642.[70] Constitutional-legal principle, Hyde argued, was not the real motive for the war against Charles. The king had satisfied by statute all constitutional grievances; he had promised to put the forts and castles of the kingdom in the hands of men trusted by parliament; and he had promised to 'enact whatsoever they did desire against Jesuits, Priests, Papists, and Popery'.[71] How, then, could parliament maintain that its war against the king was a war against tyranny and popery? They could not: 'And so the present Quarrell is, for a . . . *Liberty* against *Monarchy*, not against *Tyrannie*; and for a . . . *Religion* against *Episcopacie* and the *Liturgie*, and not against *Poperie*' (8). Like many Royalists, Hyde drew attention to the wolf in sheep's clothing, to political demands that, however moderately couched, would destroy royal prerogative, and to religious demands that would destroy the established church. Even in the *History* Hyde was prepared to accept of the king's opponents that well into 1642 'they had rather a design of making themselves powerful with the King and great at Court, then of lessening the power of the one or reforming the discipline of the other'.[72] Beyond that, though, the crucial divide was over the origin of kingship and the legitimacy of resistance. Royalists relied fundamentally on a theory of divine right, while their opponents relied on theories of consent. The importance of the difference lay not just in the abstract question of origins itself, nor in the ways in which different accounts of origins might ground different accounts of the extent of royal authority, but also in the remedy available to subjects when their kings overstepped the (largely agreed) limits.

The essentials of the argument were put in place with great economy. It was first emphasised that the king's political authority was 'power . . . over mens Persons and Estates, over their Lives and Fortunes'. It was, however, 'to be exercised by the King according to the Lawes of the Land'. The king could only make laws through parliament:

> he shall enact only such Lawes as the People have chosen, and none other; And it is only a restraint and limitation of that absolutenes in Law-making, exercised by the Kings of *England* formerly; from which they receded by degrees: using first the advice of the Bishops and Barons in making their Lawes, and afterward their Consents also: then not their advice and consent only, but also the advice and consent of the Commons also.   (3)

That did not, of course, mean that the Lords and Commons could legislate without the king. Hyde was as committed as most moderate Parliamentarians to legal and parliamentary kingship. But, for him, this was instituted by the king and did not compromise the duty of absolute obedience owed to him. For parliamentary writers, the *same* system of government was instituted by the people who had an emergency power, exercised through their representatives, to govern without an erring monarch.

Hyde was not the only Royal adviser and publicist. Throughout 1642 he had battled against the uncompromising advice offered to Charles by his wife and Digby; but even the more moderate sometimes held positions uncongenial to him.[73] In particular, as we have seen, Hyde warned against the arguments used in the *Answer to the xix Propositions.* Historians have long wondered whether these arguments presented in the *Answer* were more harmful than beneficial to the king's cause. Certainly, the pamphleteers who supported the king, even the most moderate, seemed to treat the *Answer* as an obstacle to be avoided rather than an opportunity to be exploited. Typical and most important of these moderate Royalist propagandists were Henry Ferne, John Bramhall, and the writers grouped around Viscount Falkland and known, after his country estate, as the Great Tew Circle.

Ferne was the focal point of the early pamphlet exchanges. Most of the major Parliamentarian tracts were produced as responses to his *Resolving of Conscience.* His argument was simple enough, and at its core reiterated the teaching of Romans 13: all forcible resistance was wrong, even in the face of tyranny, 'because resistance (though it be made against abused powers) . . . doth tend to the dissolution of that order, for which the power itself is set up of God'.[74] God commanded unconditional obedience. Ferne denied the popular origin of royal authority, though admitting 'that the designing of the person is sometimes from the people by choice, and that the power of the Prince receiving qualification by joint consent of himselfe and the people, is limited by the laws made with such consent; but the power it self is of God originally' (13). Clearly, the qualifications were important. Ferne was a divine-right theorist who believed that all rulers were irresistible; but he did also think that the king of England was a limited monarch. He was 'limited . . . according to the laws' (15); but that did not mean that the promise made in his coronation oath created a contract with his people whereby he would forfeit authority if he failed to keep his trust (16). In a move seized upon by his opponents, Ferne made use of the Conquest to argue that election had no place in English history, though he made it clear that he was not suggesting that English kings had the rights of conquerors (15). Ferne, at least, was happy to use the language of the king's *Answer*, the language of mixed, moderated kingship. Safety and security were secured in England 'specially in the fundamentalls of this Government, by that excellent temper of the three Estates in Parliament, there being a power of denying in each of them, and no power of enacting in one or two of them without the third' (16).

John Bramhall saw the ideas advanced by Parker (his main target) and other Parliamentarian writers as an outgrowth of Scottish-style Presbyterianism.[75] The case was made with unusual sophistication, and it is a case that many modern historians have themselves advanced. The essential problem was first identified: 'Of all heretics in policy, they are the most dangerous, which make the commonwealth an *amphisbœna*, a serpent with two heads . . . the king and the parliament'. In such a commonwealth all was unstable, for no one knew whom to obey.[76] How did such a conclusion come from ecclesiological premises? Bramhall analysed the argument carefully. First, civil authority was subordinated to the needs of the church. Princes might have 'power . . . to reform the church'; but once it was reformed, they had no 'more to do than execute their [the clergy's] decrees'. This identified their goal: advancement of the true faith. Whatever path seemed to head for that goal, they followed. '[W[here they have hope of the king, there the supreme magistrate may, nay, he ought to reform the Church,' even contrary to the law; 'But what if the king favour them not? Then he is but a conditional trustee, it [authority to reform religion] belongeth to the state and representative body of the kingdom.' If the nobility proved reluctant, appeal could be made to the people. It was this fixture on religious goals and flexibility about means that led to the politics of Buchanan and the Parliamentarians.[77] It led also to a cavalier attitude to legality. In the beginning, the propaganda of the king's enemies spoke 'nothing but encomiums of the law, treason against the fundamental laws, and declarations against Arbitrary government'. But, 'Now the law is become a "formality", a Lesbian rule. Arbitrary government is turned to necessity of state. It is not examined what is just or unjust, but how the part is affected or disaffected, whether the thing be conducible or not conducible to the cause. We are governed, not by the known laws and customs of this realm, but by certain far-fetched, dear-bought conclusions . . . from the law of nature and of nations.' The result? '[F]arewell *Magna Charta* and the laws of England for ever.'[78]

Whatever we make of Bramhall's arguments, they clearly identified the two poles around which much Royalist argument was organised: defence of the king's unmixed and unchallengeable sovereign authority, and defence of governance according to the law of the land (in which was embraced a full acceptance of parliament in its traditional functions). Both of these themes were given particular emphasis in the work of the Great Tew circle; but to them was added (in some cases) a rather less usual willingness to derive royal authority from popular consent. The Great Tew circle took its name from Falkland's country house, where they used to meet; and it included such political writers as Edward Hyde himself, Sir John Spelman and Dudley Digges. Digges's book *The Unlawfulnesse of Subjects Taking up Armes*, of January 1644, was probably their most important product, if we leave aside Hyde's work. Digges gave an account of the emergence of civil society out of something like a state of nature. The natural state was an 'unhappy condition amidst feares and jealousies, wherein each single person look't upon the world as his enemy'.[79] This situation was a product of the fact that 'Freedome is the birth-right of mankinde, and equally common to every one.' It consisted in 'an unlimited power to use our abilities, according as will did prompt', with the result that we have seen (2). To escape from this, men formed communities.

> There being no way to effect this naturally, they reduce themselves into a civill unitie, by placing over them one head, and by making his will the will of them all, to the end that there might be no gap left open by schisme to return to their former condition (4).

This last statement made it clear that, for Digges, this account made resistance to sovereign authority always wrong. This union results in 'the giving up of every mans particular power into his [the sovereign's] disposal'. Men agree to 'not using their naturall power, but onely as

Law shall require, that is, of not resisting that body in which the supreame power is placed' (4). Those who 'allow any power to Subjects against their ruler . . . do thereby dissolve the sinewes of government, by which they were compacted into one' (7). He admitted that it was possible for governments to be founded in such a way that rulers could be disciplined (30–1), though this was not the case in England. Even if it were preferable to allow a constitutional right to resist, those communities who lacked one must accept the fact: 'we may not destroy our Governours out of reason of state; *Machiavell* must not give Law to the Gospell' (31).

This did not, however, make the sovereign absolute. Like so many Royalists, Digges was happy to admit that over time the sovereigns of particular places became limited in various ways. The king was originally 'absolute', but in later times it became common 'to bound his power within the limits of positive Lawes'. Kings so bound were real sovereign monarchs, but being irresistible and 'not responsible for any breaches . . . [they were] supreame, though not absolute' (29). There were those who wished to 'perswade the people, there is not any difference betweene arbitrary government, and government restrained by lawes, if Subjects may not compell their soveraigne to the observation of them' (71). This was absurd. There were in England practical guarantees for the king's observance of the law. First, he 'hath sworne to preserve our Lawes, our Liberties, our Propriety, and our Religion'. Secondly, 'if he should command any illegal things, the executioners of them are responsible, and must make satisfaction to the injur'd party'.[80] And thirdly, the king's interests coincided with those of his subjects anyway, and gave him an incentive to rule lawfully (73–4).

The moderate Royalists of the later 1640s added relatively little that was new. They did, admittedly, write in different circumstances, and were particularly vocal in their attacks on 'parliamentary tyranny'. But this, as we have seen, is a theme that developed as early as 1642. David Jenkins is the best remembered of later constitutional Royalists.[81] His major work, *Lex Terrae*, made plain his intention of demonstrating the illegality of parliament's actions during the 1640s:

> To depose the King, to imprison him untill he assent to certaine demands, a warre to alter the Religion established by Law, or any other Law, or to remove Councellors, to hold a Castle or Fort against the King, are offences against the Lawe declared to be treason.[82]

The king had no superior but God, and all jurisdiction was derived from him. Jenkins repudiated the king's misgovernment of the 1630s (31, *recte* 29). The king was certainly not absolute:

Nothing can be done in this Common-wealth by the Kings grant or any other act of his, as to the Subjects persons, goods, Lands, or liberties, but must be according to established Lawes, which the Judges are sworn to observe and deliver betweene the King and his people impartially to rich and poore.

There was even a practical remedy that fell short of resistance: 'therefore the Justices and the Ministers of Justice are to be questioned and punished, if the Lawes be violated: and no reflection made on the King' (17).

The distinctive feature of Jenkins's work was its attack on the abuses of the law that parliament had committed in its efforts to win the war. Parliament was guilty of all sorts of illegal financial exactions, and deprived subjects of their property without due process; they had acted illegally on the militia, the bishops and on the subject of sovereignty. 'Where is the Covenant? Where is the Petition of Right? Where is the liberty of the Subject?' (36). Yet, in the quarrel between king and parliament, 'what guide had the Subjects of the Land to direct them *but the Lawes*' (42). Surely Parliament's repeated breach of law and due process made it clear which of the parties could claim the sanction of *lex terrae*.

Not all Royalists were interested in claiming the middle ground of constitutional moderation. Historians have suggested, indeed, that Royalism showed a pattern of 'increasing absolutism ... as the 1640s wore on'.[83] That may be so, though extremist voices can be found quite early on in the decade, and not all of the insistent simplifications of more extreme Royalists amounted to an absolutist position. In the replies to Henry Parker we see unmistakable signs that some Royalists impatiently avoided all subtlety of argument. This 'absolutism' was often rooted in a simplistic form of divine-right theory, but the latter does not automatically produce the former. John Jones, in *Christus Dei, The Lords Annoynted*, made it clear that his was 'a theologicall discourse' designed to prove that the authority of kings 'is not of humane, but of divine right, and that God is the sole efficient cause thereof, and not the people. Also that every monarch is above the whole Commonwealth, and is not onely *Major Singulis*, but *Major Universis*'.[84] The ensuing argument stressed the natural incapacity of human beings to fulfil God's purposes, the primary end for which they were put on earth. In any body politic, 'if all members should do what they list, and should not be compelled by some absolute power to contribute their strengths and endevours to the preservation of one another, and the whole Community, it would be but *Regnum in se divisum*, that of necessity must fall to desolation' (p. 7). This absolute power had to be of divine and not human creation, for only such powers could achieve divine ends. Only God could give men a power, such as the sovereign possessed, to put other men to death. The crucial step in the argument lay in seeing human societies as primarily created to worship God. Protection and *salus populi* were secondary ends, important only as necessary adjuncts to the collective worship of God (pp. 2–9). Jones did admit that the people might in some cases appoint the person who exercised this divine authority, and even that they might invest it in more than one person; but in a hereditary and absolute monarchy any such rights of popular election had been altogether lost (pp. 10–11). These absolute kings were 'in power . . . Superiour absolutely over the whole Common-wealth'. All other powers were subordinate to theirs (pp. 12–13). Not a word was said to limit the authority of kings. The need to answer Parker and other Parliamentarian writers could thus push Royalists into simplified versions of divine-right theory, sweeping away all qualifications.

Not unnaturally this path led some to adopt theories of Bodinian sovereignty. This was very evident in the pamphlets published by Sir Robert Filmer in 1648. His *The Necessity of the Absolute Power of all Kings* consisted entirely of passages from Knolles's 1606 translation of Bodin.[85] His own *Anarchy of a Limited or Mixed Monarchy* (a critique of Philip Hunton) boldly began with the assertion that 'we do but flatter ourselves, if we hope ever to be governed without an arbitrary power'. The only question was in whose hands such a power lay.[86] Early on, Bodin was invoked to confute the views of Machiavelli and Contarini concerning the character of the governments of Rome and Venice respectively;[87] and in the course of the pamphlet Filmer argued in Bodinian fashion that any suggestion that monarchical authority was either mixed or limited was a contradiction of the very idea of monarchy itself. *All* monarchies fell within Hunton's definition of absolute monarchy, in which 'the sovereignty is so fully in one, that it hath no limits or bounds under God but his own will'.[88] Monarchs could be bound by no promise to obey and not to alter the law, for their duties might very well require them to take arbitrary measures.[89] Filmer's work was largely negative, ruthlessly and skilfully exposing the contradictions and problems within Hunton's argument. But in making his conclusion Filmer derived from Aristotle the view that it was absurd to suppose either that kings might be limited by law, or that they ruled by anything other than their own will. He supported these contentions by quoting at length from 'the great modern politician Bodin'.[90] He quoted, in particular, Bodin's claim that kings of England were not bound to follow the advice of parliament.

Filmer and Hobbes (in his *Elements*, of 1640) may be the best known Royalists to have advanced an explicitly Bodinian theory of absolute monarchy. But they were not alone.[91] More typical were those writers led to absolutist conclusions through a radical simplification of traditional divine-right theory. Robert Grosse, for example, made a crucial move in his discussion of the biblical text 1 Samuel 8 (discussion of which, it might be remembered, was a crucial part of James VI and I's *Trew Law of Free Monarchies*). Did Samuel's words serve as a pattern for kingship or for tyranny? Both, was Grosse's answer.

> If a King, spurred on by a private desire, and ravenous lust of having, doth claime such things as are there described, he deales unjustly and tyrannically: but if, the safety and necessity of the Commonwealth so requiring, he demands those things; then, he doth not unjustly, if he doth use his Kingly power.[92]

It was not that there were certain things kings could not do; rather they could do whatever was necessary to serve the public good. But the same things done for corrupt purposes were signs of tyranny. Grosse was much less provocative than Filmer, and tried to show that kings would rule well. They 'must not deale with their Subjects as they list'. Kings had to respect their subjects' rights, and subjects their king's prerogatives (p. 21). The *manner* in which they did things was important. They ought to govern legally, so that they might 'command all things which doe not repugne the Law of *God*; the law of *Nature*, and the law of the *Land*' (p. 18). This restriction of the king to legal means might seem a substantial restraint on his capacity to do whatever was necessary for the common good; but it was not so. For Grosse followed these remarks with some strongly Bodinian pages. He seemed, like Bodin, most moderate when talking about the subjects' property rights (p. 22); but his analysis of law-making vested legislative authority in the king alone (in which case the restriction to govern legally could amount to little). A true king had a power of 'making and abrogating Laws at pleasure'; he 'can, when he sees it fitting, whether his Subjects will or no, yea without their consent, either make or abrogate the law'. Not even the promise made in the coronation oath to preserve laws and customs could diminish this authority. Throughout, Grosse referred constantly to Bodin, and he followed Bodin in believing that sovereign authority was summed up in the power of law-making, and that this power could be neither shared nor delegated (pp. 25–32). There was no mention of parliament, except in passing, when it appeared purely as an advisory council (p. 45), and Grosse did not make the point accepted by other Royalists that the king could only make laws that impinged upon his subjects' property rights in parliament. A king who made laws at will was not a king much hindered by the need to rule in accord with law. For Grosse, kings exercised a divinely-instituted authority that retained a protean capacity to do whatever was necessary to serve the common good.

The turn towards starker, simpler theories of divine right is equally evident in the writing of three clerics, often identified (with Hobbes) as theorists of absolutism – John Maxwell, Griffith Williams and Michael Hudson.[93] It is Maxwell's misfortune that he seems usually to be understood as if he really was the figure caricatured in Rutherford's *Lex, Rex* (1644),[94] though he was in reality one of the finest critics of consent theory writing in the 1640s. Maxwell's work, from its dedicatory epistle onwards, relied to an unusual degree on divine-right theory. The classical writers, like modern lawyers, were less well placed than clerics, versed in God's commands, to understand political life. Political duties take on the nature of religious duties, for kings, priests and prophets are the only office-holders anointed by God. Consequently, monarchy 'is the onely government which is most countenanced and magnified in holy Writ'. The ancients did correctly perceive that 'from the happinesse and quiet of Religion issueth forth necessarily the happiness & quiet of the Civil State'. Maxwell's chief enemy was obviously Scottish Presbyterianism, and the view he found in it that kings were subject to the authority of the church's elders. For that reason, he could not agree with those who thought that 'it is enough if the essentials and fundamentals of faith and worship be preserved'. The church, like any other society, needed to be well governed (by episcopacy); and if it was not it could not serve as proper support to the peace and order of the civil state. The result was painfully and dismally obvious. '

[S]ince God and Religion, have been wronged, we will finde we have made an unhappy choice, a miserable change. No man hath protection or direction by Law, no known Law hath place, we are all oppressed and tyrannically over-ruled by an arbitrary power, placed in a wrong and; all Religions (if I may call Sects so) are tolerated, except the true Catholique Reformed Religion, and all Heresies buried long ago in Hell, are revived'.[95]

Maxwell was especially hostile to theories that rooted authority in popular consent, like those Puritans who believed that power was fully retained by the people, who could call their rulers to account and supply any defects in their administration (pp. 7–8). He was aware that even some Royalists (the Great Tew circle) had held that authority was conferred on kings by the people, though never to be revoked. 'I was onetime in love with this opinion,' Maxwell told his readers; 'nor doe

I much condemne it'. Nonetheless, he could no longer avow its truth, for it was incompatible with scripture to suppose that authority first rested in the multitude. Maxwell urged on his readers the same realisation that had come to him: God in scripture tells us that the king holds authority by direct divine institution (pp. 17–19). In his mature political thought, Maxwell affirmed that man was born with freedom (divine and natural) from slavery but into subjection to political authority (pp. 124–5). Though '*the designation of the person*' wielding that authority might be by some human act ('*election, succession, conquest*'), 'yet the *reall constitution, the colation of Soveraignty and Royalty* is immediately from God'.[96] Here in miniature is the shift from complex political theories to simple divine-right argument. '[T]he King and His Power are originally and immediately from God, dependent from him alone, and independent from all others' (p. 24). With particular force, Maxwell was able to point to the contradiction in Parliamentarian theories: if they were right, then they undermined parliamentary authority as much as royal (pp. 101, 129–30). This could be no basis for stable government.

Maxwell was more interested in showing that it was *impossible* for the king's authority to have been derived from the people than in exploring the consequent view that the only possible source of such authority was God. He rested his case on the argument that '*authoritie* and Majestie . . . cannot be found in People', and so cannot be conferred on a king by the people. If you consider the people singly this was obvious, especially on the Parliamentarians' own terms: 'according to our Antimonarchicall Sectaries, all by native right are equally equall borne with a like freedome'. No one has any pre-eminent authority over another; therefore no one could confer such authority on another. Nor could such authority be conferred by the people jointly, for Parliamentarians themselves saw its constitution as coming 'onely by a surrender of the native right every individuall hath in himselfe'. Individuals possessing such rights might contract with one another to create some sort of political community, but those who violated such a contract would not be guilty of disobedience to majesty and sovereignty; they would be guilty only of breaking their promises (p. 48). Such a situation could not be squared with the statements of royal authority in the scriptures, in Romans 13, or 1 Peter 2. The only possible conclusion is that 'in Princes there is . . . something divine, above the reach of man, which cannot be derived from them'. God's direct creation of undivided sovereign authority began with Adam (p. 84). A sovereign possessed the power of life and death, 'which cannot flow or issue from man, for no man hath it'.[97] 'Soveraignty never was, never can be in the Communitie; Soveraignty hath power of life and death, which none hath over himselfe, and the Communitie conceived without government, *all as equall, endowed with natures and native Libertie*, of that Comunitie can have not power over the life of another' (p. 131). Three groups of men were annointed by God, and all derived their authority directly from him, 'Kings, Priests, Prophets' (p. 53).

The kingship and sovereignty that Maxwell defended were not unlimited. It was not 'a *Despoticall Soveraignty* . . . such as the Great Turke this day exercises over his Subjects', but a 'royall paternall Soveraignty [with] . . . Royall Prerogatives inherent naturally in the Crowne, and inseparable from it; so it trencheth not upon the liberty of the person, or the Propriety of the goods of the Subject, but in and by the lawfull and just acts of jurisdiction' (136). Maxwell paraphrased Seneca: 'The sacred Prerogative is the Kings, but it derogateth not from the Liberty and Property of the subjects: it must be entirely secured, that it may secure our Liberty and Property' (171). The king's sovereign power was, as the Roman jurists had it, *legibus solutus*; but for Maxwell that meant only 'subject to no over-ruling power of man'. It was not a claim for an authority over and outside the law. 'Conceive it not so, that Kings are free from the direction of, and obligation to the Law of God, nature, and common equitie; but from *Coercion humane*, or any *humane coactive power*, to punish, censure, or dethrone them' (140).

England was not More's Utopia or Plato's republic. Its government was not perfect; but nonetheless 'we must resolve to endure some inconveniences in the best government, rather than disturb and destroy government' (106). The tone was typical of much Royalist argument, before and after the Civil War. Never forget, they warned, that man is a fallen creature, and that Utopian perfection lies always beyond his grasp. One consequence of this was the strong sense that human society was impossible without the existence of sovereign authority. Men were naturally too corrupted to be able spontaneously to form societies. No human society could be truly perfect, for it would have been made out of sinners – 'while men are, faults will be'. Instead, let us 'endure the tempests of ill government patiently, as we doe other tempests falling from Heaven' (149–50; also 156). So essential was sovereignty in a sinful world, that it was only under its protection that *salus populi* could be achieved. Hence, those who used the maxim *salus populi suprema lex esto* to justify their attack on the prerogatives of kings were, in fact, undermining not only government but *salus populi* itself (159–61). The king 'is the very bottome and foundation upon which the publicke good of the whole state, and the private good of every one is founded and built' (161). And the point was proved by the fact that the arbitrary exactions of the Long Parliament constituted a more obvious threat to liberty and property than the king ever had (173).

Thus Maxwell, despite the ruthless rigour with which he applied the principle of divine right, essentially continued themes developed in Royalist propaganda in 1642. So did others, including Griffith Williams, bishop of Ossory, in the earlier of his three pamphlets, all published within the space of a year or so, notwithstanding his use of Bodin.[98] But he is also interesting in developing (as had Maxwell) another set of Royalist concerns. Arguing that kings were genuinely limited by the liberties they had granted to others, Williams suggested that the king (given the nature of his coronation oath), even as king-in-parliament, could not legitimately deprive bishops of their seat in the Lords, as Charles I had done (albeit under some coercion) on 13 February 1642.[99] He was, in fact, especially concerned to vindicate the ecclesiastical authority of Christian princes, balanced with respect for the rights of an episcopal church, and a number of later Royalists shared in this concern.[100] Williams interpreted the rebellion against Charles I as inspired by religious zealotry. He was (more than most Royalists) willing to confront this on its own terms, rather than to dismiss it as a disguise for wicked political ambition (though he did that on occasion too). Christian kings were in a special position. They shared with other kings the usual duties to administer justice and protect the people. Christian kings, however, had also a second duty peculiar to themselves, a duty '[t]o preserve *true religion*, and to defend the *faith* of Christ, against all Atheists, Hereticks, Schismaticks, and all other adversaries of the Gospell, within their Territories and Dominions'.[101]

This 'Orthodoxall' position on the king's ecclesiastical authority was to be distinguished from the 'Papisticall' and the 'Anabaptisticall'. The Papists denied Christian kings any more authority in religious matters than heathen kings, and assigned it all to the pope. The 'anabaptist' view placed authority over religious matters in the hands of either a consistory of presbyters or a parliament of laymen. Williams traced the latter opinion back to Calvin's opposition to the royal supremacy of Henry VIII.[102] Williams's position was not without its difficulties. In particular, the harder he pushed his argument, the more he risked linking political allegiance and confessional identity together; and in the circumstances of the 1640s that could only have been counterproductive, an unhelpful mirror-image of the argument he assigned to the king's enemies. He had, indeed, already committed himself, in a discussion of the role of English Catholics in supporting Charles I, to the view that 'if Kings cannot perswade their Subjects to embrace the true Faith, they ought not to cut them off, so long as they are true Subjects'.[103] That implied a separation of political and religious allegiances of the sort that had often been attempted in conformist circles since Elizabethan days.

To get around the difficulty, Williams back-pedalled. In fact, even heathen kings had a duty 'to see that their people do *religiously* observe the worship of that God which they adore'. All kings must preserve their people in 'obedience and good manners', and those things were the product of laws and religion. For that reason, many early kings were priests, who well knew that laws and obedience required the support of religion.[104] Christian kings thus shared the general duty of kings to protect and foster the religion they thought best – it just so happened, as luck would have it, that the faith they liked best was the true one.

There was little remarkable in Williams's analysis of the nature of royal authority in the church.[105] He committed to the king only ecclesiastical jurisdiction, and denied him the authority to perform the functions of a priest (instructing the people, administering the sacraments, and the use of the keys of the kingdom of heaven). None of this prevented Williams from referring to the king as not just a layman but *mixta persona* by virtue of his anointing by God. He was thus, as Constantine had claimed, 'the chiefe Christian Bishop among his Bishops'.[106] Notwithstanding this, it was accepted that kings could not preach, but could punish those priests who would not preach or who preached 'false Doctrine'.[107] Kings were not, of course, expected to be learned in religious matters themselves, but should rely upon the advice of the bishops and chaplains that they appointed for this purpose.[108] The position was indeed an 'othodoxicall' one, standard in the English church in Henrician times, and since 1559. More controversially, Williams gave the impression that the king was not alone exercising his ecclesiastical power; rather, he had the authority to call councils and synods to compose matters.[109] Williams devoted a chapter to proving that kings had authority to make laws and canons for the church, with the advice of their bishops and clergy, and without that of their temporal counsellors. Indeed, laymen, that is parliament, were not permitted to make laws for the church at all.[110] Although the church was to be free of secular interference, Williams was perfectly happy to defend the right of the clergy to hold secular office. The interdependence of church and commonwealth seemed to operate to the political advantage of the clergy and to the disadvantage of the laity.[111] Williams defended this view by invoking the principle with which he had begun: the clergy understood better than lawyers and politicians the rights of kings and the duties of subjects. Their participation in civil affairs was essential for the maintenance of obedience in the temporal sphere.[112]

Royalist writers of the Civil War were beginning to explore more forcefully than their predecessors a clericist approach that used the supremacy to guarantee the church's autonomous authority over itself. Williams's argument was a cunning one. Under cover of the royal supremacy, it tied the commonwealth to supporting the authority in the church of the king's clergy. How well had Williams avoided the danger of linking too closely together confessional and political allegiance? An answer can be found in his discussion of toleration. He performed neatly enough the necessary task of allowing a (grudging) toleration for religious diversity while giving no ground to the 'anabaptist' rebels of the 1640s. Williams was clear that toleration was an 'exemption' – he came to the subject through a discussion of the king's power to dispense from ecclesiastical laws – and there was no suggestion either that religious diversity was a good thing, or that there was any *duty* compelling kings to be tolerant. Furthermore, it was to be a private privilege, with no allowance for the public exercise of another faith. Toleration was essentially a matter of political prudence.[113] Williams discussed in turn the situation of Jews, Turks, Papists and Puritans – infidels, heretics and schismatics. The general principle advanced was that 'where the *greater* distance is from the true religion, there the *lesser* familiarity and neernesse should be in conversation, and the *greater* distance in communion'. Nonetheless, it was legitimate to allow even infidels some tolerance, though scarcely mandatory. Papists, part of the same Catholic church as protestants, had an even greater claim to toleration, while schismatics certainly were to be treated not as '*deadly* enemies' but as '*weake* friends'. There was a qualification: schismatics were deserving of toleration provided that 'they proceede not to be *turbulent* and malicious', When they did turn malicious, schismatics were more dangerous than all the others, who professed their religion peaceably.[114] Thus toleration was to be granted or witheld 'not in respect of the *meliority* of their religion, as their peaceable and harmelesse habitation among their neighbours without *rayling* against their faith, or *rebelling* against their Prince'. By this measure, the puritans of the 1640s, though their religion was in itself tolerable, could make no claim to be tolerated. They deserved repression even more than the seditious presbyterians, suppressed by Elizabeth, and attacked in James's *Basilikon Doron*. Catholics were much more loyal to the king than they.[115] Like so many conformists before him, Williams separated confessional and political allegiance. In the 1640s this had an added advantage, because it formed a basis on which to defend the king's willingness to accept the support of Catholics even against his protestant enemies.

Other Royalists would develop ideas on toleration even further, and a lot of work still needs to be done in charting the ecclesiological views of Royalists writers in the later 1640s, such as Michael Hudson, a

Westmorland divine, who had enthusiastically sided with the king from the beginning of the Civil War. Hudson became a royal chaplain early in 1643, and led thereafter a life more incident-packed than that of most ministers. Too incident-packed, perhaps, for it came to a sudden end at Woodcroft House in Northamptonshire, on 6 June 1648, when Hudson became the central character of one of the second Civil War's more appalling atrocity stories. His one published work,[116] *The Divine Right of Government*, gave fair warning of its uncompromising Royalism in its sub-title: monarchy was 'the onely Legitimate and Natural spece of Politique Government'.[117] Subsequently, Hudson made it very clear that monarchy was 'the onely received Policy' in the sacred records of scripture. '[N]o *Polarchie* [literally 'government by several or many'] be honoured with any Divine sanction.' Polarchy was, indeed, 'a meer curse in Nature, inflicted upon a Nation by Divine Malediction for a punishment', though sometimes honoured 'with the humane sanction of practise, Prescription, and Custome'.[118] The priority of a monarchy as a form of government came from the fact that at the Creation, God had invested '*Adam* with a *Monarchicall* Supremacy, not onely *Oeconomicall*, over that one created family in *Paradise*, but *Political* over a society consisting of many families which were to descend of *Adam*'.[119] Paternal and regal government were the same thing, though much of Adam's political authority was only activated after the Fall.[120] In normal circumstances, the true sign of appointment to monarchical authority was birthright and hereditary succession, not popular election, consent, or violent conquest (though conquests could be legitimated retrospectively by God).[121] By this means, monarchy possessed divine right. Polarchy, by contrast, rested on divine malediction, as Old Testament history made manifest.[122] On this basis Hudson felt able to condemn the political principles of the classical world lock, stock and barrel. Aristotle, Plato, Xenophon, Cicero, Livy and Tacitus were alike exposed as mistaken by the evidence of the scriptures.[123] They were all advocates of polarchy, 'a Politick government, invented by the Devill, for the destruction of humane society, by the Administration and exercise of the Supream Power and Authority of a multitude over the rest of the same society'.[124] Many heathen societies that had experienced polarchy (most notably the Roman) later reconstructed monarchical governments, to avoid the anarchy and dissolution that would naturally follow from having a government with no one supreme authority.[125] No Christian society had become a polarchy until very recent times, during which blasphemy and heresy had begun to flourish.[126]

Hudson identified his primary concerns as religious: the true subject of the book was 'the due limitation of Regal Power *in ordine ad extra regalia*'.[127] He began to write in order to defend the freedom of the

conscience from political authority. This he undertook in the belief
that the sacrilegious usurpation of the king's authority undertaken by
parliament was God's punishment of the king's sacrilege in usurping
divine authority. (We will return to this subject later.)

> God hath permitted your Majestyes subjects to possesse themselves of
> your Throne, and act as Kings in those things, whereunto no King
> did ever by any Commission Authorize a subject, because Your
> Majesty hath formerly possessed your self of Gods Throne, and acted
> as a God in those things whereunto God did never by any
> Commission Authorize a King.[128]

The king was, albeit unintentionally, guilty of sacrilege, in which term
Hudson included,

> All usurpation of Power over conscience in the enactment of Lawes
> and Statutes for the Regulation thereof in matters which are not of
> Political congnisance; And under the sanction of Personal or
> Pecuniary mulcts to enjoyn a National conformity in confession of
> Evangelical and Christian Faith, and in Evangelical and Christian
> forms of worship, Government, and Discipline.
>   Which were neither *dutyes*, nor *indeed things in rerum Natura*, when
> Politique Government did first receive it's Institution from God; and
> therefore cannot be directly of Politique cognizance, nor any funda-
> mentall or Essentiall part of the object of Politique Government.[129]

Hudson's account of the powers of a king was built on this principle.
    In secular matters, kings had 'an absolute, and unlimited power,
over both our estates and persons'.[130] Rather like Hobbes, Hudson
believed that although kings could be wicked, they could not in political matters do wicked things: 'in reference to their duty towards us,
(though themselves may be wicked, yet) they cannot doe wicked things
. . . that is, they cannot inflict any thing upon us, but that which God
hath decreed to fall upon us for our sinnes'. Thus, 'we may not thinke
them evill or unjust to us; for the Judgement is not theirs but Gods . . .
who cannot be unjust'.[131] The only significant qualification that
Hudson unequivocally allowed to his absolutism was acceptance of the
principle that 'the King may not breake a Law confirmed by an Oath'.
The point was not much explored, but in view of the king's coronation
oath, might have been of considerable potential significance.[132]
    But the situation was very different with regard to the king's author-
ity in ecclesiastical and religious matters. Hudson was adamant that
nothing could ever legitimate the active resistance or rebellion of

subjects. Nonetheless, he did draw tight limits around the king's authority in the spiritual sphere. He argued for restrictions on royal authority that arose from the fact that God had reserved certain matters to his sole authority, or to that of conscience. The question was to determine what things were '*extra regalia*, and Metapoliticall matters', in which the king could exercise neither his judicial nor his legislative authority.[133] The proper sphere of political authority extends over 'only the Externall duties of the Morall law, consisting in the right use of the Externall blessings of nature'; it extends not at all over 'intrinsecall acts of the soule'.[134] Political government existed under the covenant of works, the requirements of which could be known through nature by all, not by the covenant of grace. Therefore, 'though Heathens cannot be good Christians, they may be good Kings'. If that were so, then 'Evangelicall duties [known only to Christians through revelation] cannot directly and *per se* be the object of Politicall Cognizance, or the subject of any positive Law or Statute, generally obligatory unto all persons.'[135]

However, the matter did not end there. Although evangelical duties could not directly be the object of political authority, they could be so indirectly. Any king who was a Christian was bound in conscience to make laws that ordered the worship of God in ways that the king believed proper – though he was forbidden altogether from making laws 'in matters of faith and doctrine'.[136] Laws made to regulate religious worship, however, bound only those who agreed with him:

> But for other persons, who are not of the same perswasion concerning the Religion of these Evangelicall duties, but beleeve the practise thereof to be superstitious and dishonourable to God, and another forme of worship to be the onely acceptable service unto him: in regard the practise of Evangelicall duties in such persons, cannot proceed from faith and trust in God, whereby they may expect a blessing from him upon their service and devotion, but rather that curse and damnation, which Saint *Paul* affirmeth to be the just merits of all acts of worship which are not of faith, but either of doubtfulness, or (which is worse) of perfect hypocrisie and dissimulation, *Rom.* 14. Last; The enforcement of such a conformity by the Magistrate in Evangelicall worship and service in such persons contrary to their consciences, must necessarily render him guilty, not onely of their sinnes . . . but also of sacrilegious intrusion upon those sacred prerogatives which God hath reserved wholly unto himselfe. . . .[137]

This is a theory of liberty of conscience directly in the line that runs from William Walwyn to John Locke. Any attempts to impose beliefs or forms of religious observance upon another person were a direct intrusion upon that person. All evangelical duties were beyond the sphere of political authority 'because conscience is the onely law and rule whereby the merits of these duties are to be judged', and anyone compelled to participate in religious worship against his conscience is compelled to sin.[138] A compulsive national church was therefore inevitably an illegitimate thing. The king shall not:

> By any positive Lawes and Statutes, determine what points shall be Orthodox, and what Hereticall: neither may he under the sanction of any personall, or pecuniarie mulct, or penalty, enjoyne his Subjects to professe and sweare such Creeds, and Articles of Faith and Religion, as those Laws shall make Orthodox: or by virtue of those Lawes punish any of his subjects, who out of conscience doe professe themselves of another different Faith and Religion.[139]

Many Royalists feared anarchy and disorder, of which religious pluralism was widely taken to be a major cause. Hudson naturally asked, therefore, whether 'preservation of the Common-wealth' required 'Uniformity in matters of Faith and Doctrine'? No. For a start, uniformity 'is more to be desired then hoped for'. But beyond that, differences of opinion among Christians were inevitable and beneficial. They led to 'better information and knowledge in matters of faith', and as a result 'Christians are always best principled in those points which are most controverted.' The argument that religious differences led to political instability was simply swept aside, as constituting an appeal from God to Satan. In any case, the magistrate could make laws to deal with heresy and division 'when they come to be of Politicall Cognizance, i.e. acts of violence and injustice, disturbing the peace of the Common-wealth'.[140] This constituted an acceptance, very rare in the seventeenth century, of religious pluralism as a beneficial thing. Equally remarkable was Hudson's rejection of the view that idolatry ought to be repressed by the magistrate. He accepted that, for Papists, their own 'formes of worship, (how Idolatrous soever in the eyes of Protestants, yet) in their owne eyes appeare to be the onely service acceptable to God'. No coercion could be of use against such sincere errors, and it would therefore be unjust and inequitable for the magistrate to attempt it.[141]

One of the purposes of this extraordinary argument was to defend the autonomy of the clergy against the secular power. The office of minister 'is not subordinate, but of a different degree and nature from the office of Kings, both of them being the Anointed of God, and neither of them depending directly and properly upon the other'.[142] It was thus not only Catholics and Presbyterians who could undermine the foundations of the English church-state, which had rested since the 1530s upon committing to kings the jurisdiction of order within the church. The example of Hudson might lend weight to the argument that the clericist views of the Arminian clergy were a threat to the royal supremacy in the church. Beyond that, it is indicative of the diversity of Royalist response to what many of them perceived to have been a religious war.

Later-Parliamentarian (Independent) Political Thought

From the winter of 1642–3 onwards there were Parliamentarian writers willing to push the arguments used against the king by the two Houses to extremes. Some, most notably Henry Marten, found themselves isolated and criticised for this; but by the mid-1640s more extreme ideas were gaining ground. These could take a number of forms, but particularly important were the Independent ideas advanced by army leaders and used to defend the regicide. Nonetheless, in 1648–9 there were still many who refused to accept the extreme conclusions of the Independents. These political Presbyterians – the term in this context should not be confused with religious Presbyterianism – remained committed to the Parliamentarian ideas of 1642–3. Indeed, in the person and writing of William Prynne there was a very direct continuity between the ideas of the early Parliamentarians and the Presbyterians.

The development of Parliamentarian political ideas, 1643–9

David Wootton has demonstrated that as early as the winter of 1642–3, writers – Royalist and Parliamentarian – began to explore hypothetically the ways in which the arguments deployed against the king could be taken to more extreme conclusions.[143] For Royalists, this was a warning, a *reductio ad absurdum*, and proof that the arguments were inherently unsound. Thus, in 1643 an unknown author inquired 'The people, [Parker says], are the authors and efficient causes of that power that the Parliamentmen have by conveyance from them. May the people therefore conclude themselves to be above Parliament and at their pleasure revoke and control their power?'[144] But what, in Royalist eyes, was a self-evident absurdity sufficient to discredit all challenges to the king in the name of the people, could be hypothetically embraced by others. Edward Bowles, a few days earlier, had inquired:

> whether in case the representative body cannot, or will not, discharge their trust to the satisfaction, not of fancy, but of reason in

the people; they may resume (if ever they parted with a power to their manifest undoing) and use their power so farre as conduces to their safety; and if this doubt cannot be resolved to the advantage of the people but be found either unlawful or otherwise impossible, I know but two waies more betwixt which the choise is very hard, hang or flye.[145]

The earliest work to advance such ideas in earnest has been identified by Wootton as *England's Miserie and Remedie*, which carries the date 14 September 1645. It was a pamphlet, perhaps written by Edward Sexby, in defence of the soon-to-be Leveller leader John Lilburne. The tract began by distinguishing between 'the representative body of the people' (the House of Commons) and 'the represented', divided into 'several shires and boroughs'.[146] The former was the servant of the latter, established only to do those things that the represented 'by reason of their numbers ... cannot conveniently do in their own persons without hazard both of confusion and desolation' (277). That is an important move. One of the major difficulties involved in seeing England as either a republic or a democracy was that both terms implied the direct participation of all citizens or of all people, respectively, in political and civic life. This was inconceivable in any kingdom of reasonable size and population. Only by utilising concepts of representation could ideas of citizenship or democracy be made directly applicable. *England's Remedie* moved towards such a view in that it saw the Commons as a trustee through which the people might conveniently exercise some, but not necessarily all, of their political capacities. In other words, representation was the only practical device by which a sovereign body of numerous citizens could practically exercise its sovereignty. That was the only justification for parliamentary authority.

With help from Buchanan and the example of Rome, Sexby, or whoever wrote *England's Remedie*, explored the response that was due to a parliament that attempted to exercise arbitrary power, contrary to its trust. Oppressed individuals should be allowed 'this last refuge of appeal to the people' (278). All men had freedoms and liberties, and 'let no man dream that the Parliament may trench boldly thereon without check' (279). The interesting question to arise from this is what, exactly, the people might do to check an erring parliament. The answer was unclear. The argument was not constitutional in character; that is to say that there was no formal constitution mechanism by which the people's sovereign power could be exercised. It would appear to be, at best, an irregular and extraordinary power. Indeed, there are indications that it was even less formal than this. Pliny was quoted: 'all lawful empire or sovereign command has its basis or firm foundation in the consent, approbation and good liking of the people'. This led to a position that relied less on attributing to people a right to revolt, and more on a prudential judgement that they would not obey rulers for whom they had no such 'good liking'.

> [T]he multitude touched to the quick in their liberties and means of living, will be easily persuaded to shake off all bonds of obedience, so necessary to the magistrate, and to cast the blame of their sufferings upon the authors, either as false to their trust, or uncapable of the great weight of authority committed unto them. For who but a madman will yield obedience unto those who are regardless of their laws and liberties, or negligent of the means of their subsistence, livelihood, and safety – the main and only ends for which they are convened and called together, and not to provide offices for themselves, or to solicit the cases of their particular friends, sometimes the greatest enemies of the state?   (280–1)

This is a description rather than a recommendation; and it played upon fears of popular rebellion at the same time as it provided some legitimacy for such rebellion.

Others moving in a similar direction included William Ball, who had begun his writing career as a critic of Henry Parker.[147] The criticisms he made were simple enough, mainly protesting that kingly authority came immediately from God and not from the people.[148] At first glance, the ideas that Ball was to espouse two or three years later were startlingly different. By May 1644, when he met Major General Philip Skippon at the siege of Reading he had produced a political paper, which was published in amplified form over a year later as *Tractatus de Jure Regnandi & Regni*. That tract was a work of settlement, attempting to delineate the legitimate powers of king, parliament and people as a step towards their reconciliation. It was in some ways a work of 'radical' populism; yet there was nothing meaningfully described as radical about its purposes. Ball's great insight was to see that, in circumstances in which king and parliament put forward rival and contradictory claims to authority, the people could serve as a device for settling the dispute. He was, perhaps, less concerned to assert the active political rights of the people (though that is the aspect of his work that historians have most noticed), than to exploit popular authority as an intellectual device for the settlement of constitutional discord. Ball now portrayed English government as a mixture of monarchy, aristocracy and democracy. He was still able to incorporate into this framework some essentially Royalist points. In England '*jus Regnandi* is the Kings, he hath it introduced by conquest, which albeit that barely of it selfe it created not a just Title, yet joyned with the consent of the Nation it did'. This authority came from God, not from the people; 'it is our Kings by birthright: neither Nobility, or people can, or ought to deprive him of it, as long as he protecteth them according to the Lawes, and conserveth them (to the utmost of his power) from forraigne slavery or subjection'.[149] But, on the other side, the people also possessed power, a *'Jus Regni Actuale & Potentiale'*, by which they 'have right to their Lawes in *Beeing*, and by their Feoffees, the Knights, Citizens, and Burgesses, whom they intrust to give their consents, they have also right to the Lawes in *Posse*, or to be' (5).

But where was the boundary and relation between these two rights? Again, Ball's tone was balanced and supported Royalist arguments on a number of points. The king had both ordinary and extraordinary powers (the latter called prerogative), 'both limited, and qualified, neither absolute'. By the former he summoned and dissolved parliament, appointed judges and officers, and conferred dignities. In all of these things, he had a duty *in foro conscientiae* to use his authority for the common good (5–6). The extraordinary or prerogative authority of the king was 'a power . . . wherby he may doe good to himselfe, and people, in things wherein the Lawes doe not sufficiently extend'. It is a power *'intra legem, sed non de lege* [within the law, but not of the law], this power is environed by the law'. It consisted chiefly of two things: the power to tax should an invasion occur before parliament could be summoned; and the power in some cases to exempt people from the penalties of the law (6–7). On other particular points, too, Ball defended the king's rights. He accepted that the royal assent, voluntarily given, was necessary for Acts of parliament. The king was not bound in law to consent to whatever was proposed to him by the two Houses (7–8). Ball balanced this, though, with a defence of the authority of the two Houses to legislate by ordinance without the royal assent. In making this case, he recanted on one of the arguments he had earlier deployed against Parker. He now denied that the people's rights and liberties were granted to them by the king in the decades and centuries after the Conquest. In fact 'the Laws and liberties which this Kingdome now enjoyeth were . . . *existent* before the Conquest . . . [and] they are the peoples in generall by right, even as the Crowne, or *Jus Regnandi* is the Kings by birthright' (9–10).

The people's right thus consisted primarily in the protection of laws that the king could not violate unilaterally, and in the right, through their representatives, to consent to the laws that governed them. Law was:

A rule admitted by common consent, by which all men from the highest to the lowest (according to their severall degrees) are to regulate their actions: to this, both King and people have consented; by this, both King and people are preserved; with this, both King and people are united, and as it were linked together. (10)

The people in this formula could, however, be considered in two ways. They formed either 'the Body *essentiall* [of the Kingdom] . . . [including] all naturall or native persons of what degree soever in all Counties, Cities and Towns corporate, and wheresoever within the limits of this Kingdome are comprehended'; or 'the Body representative', parliament. The former was the ultimate *locus* of popular authority. The people elected representatives only because they could not assemble together and make laws 'without confusion or disorder'. But parliament, no more than the king, had an absolute authority over the people at large. King, Lords and Commons could 'enact any thing *in beneficium Regni*, for the benefit of the Kingdome'; but they could do nothing '*in detrimentum libertatis, aut proprietatis generalis subditorum Anglia*', nothing harmful to the liberty or property of subjects. This was so because the English were a people who 'have rather put themselves under a law by common consent, then enforced to undergoe a Law'. In short, 'the King . . . is but in nature of high Steward of the Kingdome by inheritance, and Parliaments feoffees in Trust; and both tyed . . . to conserve the generall liberty and propriety of the people' (11–12).

Ball's argument was an attempt to take the language of the public or common good, so often used in ways too abstract to indicate the institutional and legal ways in which it was to be pursued, and to make it concrete. He accepted many of the king's traditional rights and powers (more than many Parliamentarians), and he had no recourse to the plea of necessity or emergency. The rights of king and people (in and outside parliament) were each inviolable, and their interaction regulated by the public good. In relation to the Civil War, that meant that there was an authority superior to both king and parliament, and capable therefore of settling the dispute between them. In certain circumstances the essential body could act to preserve itself, even against the representative body. What if king and parliament passed an Act allowing themselves to dispose of the property of subjects?

[I]n such cases, the Counties, Cities, and Townes corporate might and ought first to petition against so great an injury, and if not remedied then they might *declare and protest* against such an act; if violated then they might defend themselves by Armes; for if the *Representative*

body of the Kingdome, may in the behalfe of the Kingdome, raise
Arms for the defence of themselves and the Kingdome, may not the
essentiall? . . . Doe not the Counties, Cities and Townes corporate give
being, or a *well-being* to the Knights, Citizens and Burgesses by intrust-
ing their *power Judiciall* to them? And yet by reposing or granting
such Trust, they do not disinvest themselves of their *right naturall* . . .
so that they may defend their liberties and proprieties even by law of
Nature, which no speciall or Nationall Lawes can *nullifie*, unlesse men
will become, or be made slaves, and lose the *right of Nature*.   (13–14)

Ball particularly emphasised that the essential body entrusted to the
representative its judicial power, but not its natural; and even this it did
with the proviso that the power was to be used for good and not harm.
It was also the case that the representatives were allowed to 'judge' the
people only in matters disputable (this included, a marginal note
informs us, religion[150]); but not in matters indisputable. The nature of
representation itself implied the independence of the represented
from their representatives (14–15). It is worth noting that Ball's
defence of popular action did not treat the people as individuals but as
a collection of local communities – counties, cities and towns.

The line of development that has brought us to Ball, appealing to
the people outside of parliament, could lead in various directions, to
the Levellers, on the one hand, and perhaps to the Clubmen on the
other (Ball has been seen as the political voice of Clubmen attitudes).
In neither case did it lead to a politics that placed much reliance on the
direct action of a multitude of individuals. The Levellers actually theo-
rised about extra-parliamentary resistance very little, and aimed
instead at a settlement that would make it unnecessary. So, in a different way, did Ball, using the people as a foundation for a return to the
ancient constitution. And even when Ball did envisage and defend
popular rebellion, he saw it as community-based and not the action of
individuals defending their individual rights. The rights of subjects
were collectively held. By 1649 this line of development had reached its
end, at least as a possible basis for practical politics. The regicidal
Independents, as much as their Presbyterian critics, emphasised
instead the view that the people's sovereignty was in fact *parliamentary*
sovereignty, nothing more. The future prosecutor of Charles I, John
Cook, succinctly noted that '[t]he Parliament is our English *Caesar*,
from whom there is no appeale'.[151] Cook took the trouble to declare
his outrage at the opinions of William Ball. Ball's view that in some
circumstances the counties might defend themselves with arms against
even parliament was 'an expression of more dangerous consequence,
and more derogatory to the just power of that supreme Court then any

thing I have seene or heard this Parliament'. The effect would be to create above the supreme authority 'a higher tribunall, which must bee as prodigious as many Sunnes in one Firmament'. Parliament must determine all property rights, or it will determine none. Without 'one supreame Tribunall . . . Civill Warre must follow inevitably'.[152] Cooke would be able to say as much again in 1649, though by then he might have found more difficulty in defending the claim that Ball,

> mistakes the nature of democracy, where the power resides in the people (as all lawfull power originally is) they may nominate what Governours they please, and may prescribe in what forme they will bee governed, but when they have settled a forme and elected Governours, they may not displace and change that Government.[153]

Ball replied, charging Cook with a failure to see any difference between parliament's authority to determine rights and a power to dispose arbitrarily of men's property. Even Cook admitted that parliament could not contravene divine and natural law, so how could it steal?[154] It was not, then, radical populism that led to legal–constitutional justification of regicide, but a different line of development. This culminated in the belief that the English constitution vested in the people a continuing sovereignty, exercised primarily through their representatives. This sovereignty could be used against all other authority, including the king's; and could even alter the nation's form of government when it was thought desirable to do so. The Assize judge Francis Thorpe, defending the regicide to a grand jury at York on 20 March 1649, argued that all rulers were accountable to the people for their misgovernment, but was careful to add '[I mean] to the People in their Politique Constitution, lawfully assembled by their Representative.'[155] The most precocious and extreme of these Parliamentarians was Henry Marten. He was the first man known to Clarendon to declare his opposition to monarchy, saying in 1641, 'I do not think one man wise enough to govern us all.'[156] Marten continued to be outspokenly provocative, in association with a loose circle of fellow firebrands. Marten's republicanism, if we wish to describe it as such, has rightly been seen as 'an extension of the logic of parliamentary opposition to Charles I'. Royalist newsbooks reported him arguing for the king's deposition as early as 1643.[157] Essentially, Marten seems to have believed in the full legal sovereignty of the House of Commons, in its capacity to perform any acts of government and legislation that hitherto had been performed by the king and his council. The House was none too grateful for this accolade, and in 1643 expelled Marten for over two years when he expressed his hostility to the monarchy once too often.[158] But, though he became for a time a friend of the Levellers, Marten remained throughout an advocate of the sovereignty of the Commons, and not of the active or continuing sovereignty of the people. Unlike the prominent Leveller leaders, he was to be a supporter of the Rump.

After the defeat of the king in 1646 it was to be Marten's friend Thomas Chaloner who did most to focus parliamentary minds on the problem of the monarchy. On 26 October 1646 there appeared in print his speech concerning disposal of the king's person.[159] It became known as the speech-out-of-doors, and led to a considerable pamphlet controversy, in which Chaloner's views were defended by Henry Marten, amongst others.[160] Chaloner was responding to Scottish proposals, which argued that disposal of the king's person could only be by the joint decision of the two kingdoms, he being king of them both. Chaloner's argument rested on a very sharp separation of the king's person from his office. The king, in the abstract sense, was 'the Royall power, Function, and office'. Charles I was two of these, one Scottish and one English; and each of these nations could dispose of the office as it wished, without interference from the other. It was in this sense, too, that 'we fight for King and Parliament' (4). But the person of the king was quite separate, and was to be dealt with according to the laws of the kingdom in which he happened to reside. A king of Scotland resident in England was subject to English laws like any other subject (8). In making this argument, Chaloner treated the conquered king as being entirely at the mercy of his conquerors. All subjects have an interest in the person of the king; but this can be lost. '[A] King . . . by going out of his Kingdome, or by being taken prisoner by his enemies, his subjects lose the interest they had in him, and he is at the disposall of his enemies *Jure belli*' (9). He told the Commons that, on the subject of disposing of the king, 'you onely are to judge of it in England, since being not subordinate to any power on Earth, there is no power under Heaven can judge you'. For good measure, Chaloner expressed his own doubt 'whether . . . his Reception with Honour can stand with the Honour of the Kingdome, whether his safety be not incompatible with the safety of the Commonwealth' (14).

It is important to recognise that this (to a degree, oblique) defence of the right of the English nation to do as it wished with its conquered king, had a powerfully anti-Scottish edge. This helped pave the way for that very English act, the regicide. A year before the execution of his king, Henry Marten made the point unequivocally in his *Independency of England*, exploring what he called at one point 'the nature of confederacies'.[161] Such was the sort of relationship that the Solemn League and Covenant had created between England and Scotland. His key point was that, although confederation made the cause of the two king-doms against their king in some sense a joint cause, fundamentally there were two struggles between a people and their king. Interestingly, the emphasis was on the way in which a community of people formed a nation capable of determining its own political and religious arrangements. The Solemn League and Covenant bound English and Scots to mutual assistance in defence of religion and liberty, but this did not imply they shared the same religion and liber-ties. Rather,

> the native rights of both peoples being the principall, if not the onely thing we looked on, when we swore; we do not keep our oath in preserving those rights, if we do not allow this master-right, to each severall people, namely, to be sole judges within themselves, what Religion they will set up, what kind of Lawes they will have, what size, what number of Magistrates they hold fit to execute those Lawes, and what offenders to be tried by them. Hereupon you know we did not enquire at all how Orthodox your Religion was before we vowed to maintain you in it, that is, in the quiet professing of it, (not in the Theologicall truth of it, a businesse for a University perhaps, not for a Kingdome) being well assured, it was established by them who had all the authority that is visible to chuse for themselves, and could not without apparent breach of order, and injury to fundamentals be disturbed in the exercise of what they had so chosen.   (12).

It did not matter whether the religion for which the Scots or the English fought was the true religion; it did not matter which of them was the better faith. What did matter was that each people was fighting for the right to choose its own laws and religion. The cause could only collapse in self-contradiction if the people of either kingdom had acquired by their confederation a right to interfere with the choices of the other. Marten robustly told the Scots that 'if once you come to fetch away my Liberty from me, I shal not ask you what other thing you wil leave me: and the Liberty of a people governed by Laws consists in living under such Laws as themselves or those whom they depute for that purpose shal make choice of' (23). Indeed, the demands of the Scots were worse than those of the king: he did not ask for a right to impose laws at will, only for his 'negative voyce', the right to refuse his consent to legislation proposed to him (24–5). The point makes it clear that Marten had arrived by this time at the view that the king's traditional role in the parliamentary trinity was incompatible with the liberty of his people.[162] Furthermore, not even the parliament of England could give the Scots the authority they claimed, for it 'hath not in my humble opinion authority enough to erect another author-ity equal to itself' (27).

It is perhaps striking, given the clarity of Marten's position, that similar themes were not more loudly sounded in the regicide debates of early 1649. Though the regicide was certainly an English act, against which the Scots protested, and in defiance of which they crowned Charles II king of Great Britain, it was not, on the whole, proudly proclaimed as such. William Prynne protested that the regicide effec-tively abolished the union of crowns, and (in an interesting inversion of the union debates of 1604) he coupled this with the claim that it destroyed all law and property at the same time.[163] Yet there were surprisingly few explicit attempts by Independents to tap anti-Scottish feelings for propaganda advantage. This was not the only thing that separated Marten from many defenders of the regicide. He was, as remarks already quoted make clear, sceptical in theological matters. Few of those involved in the regicide doubted their knowledge of God's cause. Few of them could have written of God, as Marten did, that 'what ever hath bene said by any yet concerning him is but . . . opinion'.[164] Nonetheless, there were in many other areas clear conti-nuities between the ideas of Chaloner and Marten, and the constitu-tional ideas used a year and more later to justify the sentence of death upon Charles Stuart, tyrant king of England. Both men, as judges of the High Court of Justice, signed the king's death warrant.

Regicidal Independency and Presbyterian Monarchism

Charles I's refusal to plead at his trial deprived his prosecutor, John Cook, of the chance to deliver the case against the king. Undeterred, Cook published an augmented version of his argument early in February 1649. It elaborated a case that had been well summarised in the speech delivered by John Bradshaw, Lord President of the High Court of Justice, at the king's sentencing on 27 January 1649. Bradshaw told the king that 'the law is your superior, that you ought to have ruled according to the law'. Bradshaw then identified as crucial the question 'Who shall be the expositors of this law'? Was it to be 'you and your party, out of courts of justice', or 'the courts . . . nay, the sovereign and highest court of justice, the Parliament of England'? Had he stopped there, we might still have imagined ourselves in 1642. He continued, though, to argue that 'there is something that is superior to the law and that is indeed the parent or author of the law – and that is the people of England'. This is not quite as extreme as it sounds, for Bradshaw appeared to mean by 'the people' 'the people represented in parliament'. His position became more extreme when he argued that the people created kings to secure justice for themselves, and if 'the King will go contrary to the end, or any other governor will go contrary to the end of his government, sir, he must understand that he is but an officer in trust and he ought to discharge that trust, and they are to take order for the animadversion and punishment of such an offending governor'. Parliament was the institution created by the people for this purpose, 'to redress the grievances of the people'. Charles's attempt to subvert Parliament was tantamount to an attempt to subvert fundamental law, and to destroy the liberty and property of England that parliament guarded.

Much use was made of historical precedent, European, Scottish (derived from Buchanan) and English. Bradshaw did not hesitate to label the king a tyrant; nor was he shy in declaring that parliaments had in the past justly 'deposed and deprived' Edward II and Richard II. He also denied that the English monarchy was fully hereditary: of the 24 kings since the Conquest, 'you shall find more than one half of them to come merely from the state and not merely upon the point of descent'. Drawing upon Sir Edward Coke's argument in Calvin's case, and anticipating a key theme of the Engagement Controversy, Bradshaw asserted the historical and legal point that protection and allegiance were reciprocal: 'the one tie, the one bond, is the bond of protection that is due from the sovereign; the other is the bond of subjection that is due from the subject. Sir, if this [former?] bond be once broken, farewell sovereignty.' The essential point was that the royal office was 'an office of trust' rather than an office of inheritance. For breach of trust his people were entitled to punish their king; and this, out of duty to God, they were now doing.[165]

Cook's argument began with a point that Bradshaw had touched on only towards the end of his speech, and then in a relatively restrained way: Charles's 'Blood-guiltiness'.[166] Cook made the most of Charles's 'horid and Barbarous Massacres of Myriades, and legions of Innocent persons'. As a result of the king's actions, '*Anglia* hath been made an *Aceldama*'. (Later Cook spent much time detailing Charles's personal guilt for the massacre of Protestants in Ireland; pp. 28–31.) This was by way of prelude. Cook's case proper began with the claim that 'the kings of England are trusted with a limited power to govern by Law'. He recounted Fortescue's contrast between regal government and 'a Government Politique and mixt' in which kings could only act in ways defined by law (6–7). The coronation oath was cited as proof that the monarchy was really elective – or, at least, that the king's inheritance was not confirmed until the people had given their consent to it (8–9). Underlying this was the principle that 'all power . . . is originally in the people', and 'is given forth for their preservation, nothing for their destruction' (8).

Charles I, however, had betrayed the trust placed in him with 'a Design to alter and subvert the Fundamental Laws, and to introduce an Arbitrary and Tyrannical Government' (7–8). He was accused of tampering with the coronation oath, so that he was freed from the duty to assent to any legislation passed by the two Houses; of altering the terms on which the judges held office, so that they became compliant pawns willing to declare lawful whatever the king might want to do; and of attempting to destroy parliaments (10–12). By these means he would have abolished the three things that were supposed effectively to have limited English kings – their oath, the judicial system and parliament. Instead, with the ship money judgement, the king 'did . . . formalise the people absolute slaves' (13).

One of the things that distinguished Cook and other Independents from the Parliamentarians of 1642–3 was their resolute refusal to allow the king to shelter behind the claim that blame for misgovernment should attach not to him but to the judges and 'evil counsellors'. This helped the regicides to derive from a political theory that differed only in details from that of the early Parliamentarians the argument that the king himself had to be punished. In Cook's eyes the 'evil counsellors' excuse carried no weight at all: the king appointed his own ministers and judges, and he had the authority to prevent their abuses of power. This he had failed to do (13–14). The king was to be held personally accountable for his misgovernment. The supposed principle that the king can do no wrong was no more than blasphemy: only God could not err (25). By his own account, Cook had once given Charles the benefit of the doubt, but since the publication of the 'Naseby Letters' it had become clear that Charles was in fact personally responsible for the actions of his servants, and had often personally commanded their villainy (35).[167]

Another dimension to the extremism of the Independents was that they wished to deprive the king even of those absolute prerogatives that, before the Civil War, he had incontestably held. These were now said to be signs of tyranny, and would reduce a free people to slavery. Thus, Cook interpreted as amounting to 'a perfect Tyranny without maim or blemish' the king's authority to summon and dissolve parliament, to refuse to give his assent to parliamentary bills, to create titles of honour, to pardon, to appoint judges, to raise military force, and to alter the coinage (17–20). These were all 'usurpations', and the king's rights differed from those of 'the meanest man' only in minor ways (20–1). Implicitly, all that was left was a king entirely without discretionary authority; a king whose office would consist only in the duty to do as the people, through parliament, demanded. At this point, one might ask if what was left could reasonably be called kingship at all.

It is not surprising, therefore, that Cook showed little interest in any constitutional theory of shared or mixed ('co-ordinate') sovereignty (21–2). To him, monarchy was so weak that when mixed with any other ingredients it dissolved. Kingship was not sovereign, but simply a revocable office of trust. There could only be one supreme power, and that, in the last resort, was the people represented in parliament. Cook, however, made relatively little use of argument from constitutional theory or positive law. More important was the argument that whatever positive law might say, there were religious and natural law principles that could override it. By nature it was 'the first necessary Fundamental Law of every kingdom' that 'when any man is intrusted with the Sword for the protection and preservation of the people, if this man shall imploy it to their destruction . . . by the Law of the Land he becomes an Enemy to that people, and deserves the most exemplary and severe punishment that can be invented'. More succinctly, 'if a King becomes a Tyrant, he shall dye for it'. This law of nature was God's law and 'hath a suspensive power over all humane Laws'. Without such a principle, societies could not preserve themselves, and men would have given their lives to another, which God forbade (22–3).

As it drew to its close, Cook's argument gave an ever stronger sense of religious purpose. The High Court of Justice was executing God's justice upon a man who had wilfully shed the blood of innocent Protestants. It was plain that 'the prisoner was long since condemned to dye by Gods Law . . . and that this High Court was but to pronounce the Sentence and Judgment written against him' (38). The High Court was itself 'a Resemblance and Representation of the great day of Judgement, when the Saints shall judge all worldly powers, and where thus Judgement will be confirmed and admired' (40).

This religious aspect of the argument, and Cook's obvious hostility to the very institution of monarchy, were to be substantially developed in a subsequent tract, *Monarchy No Creature of Gods Making*. The constitution that England acquired in 1649 was now described as 'that form of Government which was appointed for Gods peculiar people . . . a Commonwealth and free state'.[168] It was important to Cook that the English people had not destroyed monarchy simply because kings were guilty of 'oppressing; burdening, impoverishing, and enslaving the people'. To do so would have been no more than 'an act of self-love to ease themselves'. They had a higher purpose, abolishing kingship 'because God commanded them so to doe' (sigs a3v–a4). Regicide was not an act of popular self-assertion, but a form of humble submission to the divine will and law. In politics, as in other matters, the rules laid down by God in scripture were to be followed; and God had shown himself willing on 3 September 1651 to confound those who thought otherwise (sigs b1v–b2v, b3v–b4). That was, of course, the date of the battle of Worcester, at which the Scottish attempt to make Charles II king of Britain finally foundered.

When kings were the enemies of God, then God's people, following 'the Captains of the men of Warre must put their feet upon the necks of such Kings who ever they be'. And so, 'never did trees in England bring forth such sweet fruit as those wherof the Scaffolds were made at *Whitehall, January* 30. 1648 [i.e. 1649]' (16–19). These events were of apocalyptic significance, for there were 'evident promises for the Churches of Christ in this age of the world to be redeemed out of antichristian bondage'. Though Cook's legal case against the king had rested upon ideas of popular consent, this now appeared less important. '[T]he peoples consent [is something] which no King can plead against Gods people in the matter of their spirituall priviledges' (38–9). Kings were styled defenders of the faith, but 'if they prove offendors of the faithfull; God will take away their kingdomes in a way of Justice, and righteousnes'.[169] Kings who make war on the Saints 'have forfeited their Civill Rights' (39–40). Thus the parliament of England acted rightly in 1649 because 'the Lord hath layd an absolute Command upon' them (42). Even the principle of consent itself was cast into religious form: 'the best goverment is to have Princes of the congregation, godly & righteous men to be chosen governors and Judges' (52).

It has been argued that the essential difference between Presbyterian and Independent political thought at the time of the regicide was that the latter accepted an apocalyptic framework that allowed them to justify the execution of Charles I.[170] John Cook's writings do something to support this claim. But the differences are really more complex, and occur on two fronts. At one front, Independents were divided from Presbyterians by their willingness to argue that all political authority was held in trust from the people, who had authority to discipline and remove their rulers, even to alter the form of government, when they saw fit. In England, this trust was irrevocably held by the House of Commons alone. At the other front, Independents were distinguished from Presbyterians (and Levellers – and many Royalists) by their willingness to resort to arguments (usually religious) that would justify the regicide as an act of higher obedience, an act of God's people executing God's law. This enabled Independents to argue that the niceties of human law were irrelevant. As we have seen, between 1649 and 1651 Cook shifted his activities from one of these fronts to the other.

Both of the fronts are clearly delineated in the first pamphlet (of three) published by London Presbyterian ministers in January 1649.[171] In these were detailed the ministers' reasons for refusing to participate in the Whitehall debates, and for their hostility to the trial of the king. On one front the ministers identified the goal of the army and Independents as 'the Constitution of a new kinde of *Representative* (as you call it) in stead of this and all future Parliaments'. But this was 'manifestly opposite to the lawfull Authority of those Magistrates, which God hath set over us'; it was contrary to the principles enunciated in Romans 13.[172] The men who had purged parliament and were setting out to try the king were acting 'without any Colour of Legall Authoritie'. They presented the spectacle of 'an Armie, raysed by authoritie of Parliament, for the preservation of the Priviledges thereof, and of our Religion, Lawes and Liberties . . . [acting now] contrarie to their trust, and many Ingagements, [to] do that which tends to the manifest Subversion of them all' (5).

On this reading, the Parliamentarian cause had been a limited attempt to preserve the ancient constitution and to prevent misgovernment. England was rightly a mixed monarchy in which the two houses were 'joyntly together with the King, intrusted with the Supreame Authoritie of the Kingdome'. No private individuals, including the army, had any right to meddle in politics. Even parliament itself had been careful throughout to declare the limited and restorative nature of its aims: it 'was not their intention . . . to do violence to the Person of the KING, or devest him of his Regal Authority, and what of right belongeth to him'. 'Much lesse was it their purpose to subvert and overthrowe the whole frame and fundamentall constitution of the Government of the Kingdome, or to give power and authority to any persons whatsoever to do' (6–7). On this analysis, the nature of English government was fixed, and the Civil War a set of emergency measures to restore its normal operation. No one had the authority to subvert the ancient constitution, which existed by divine right. Moreover, all who fought for Parliament had bound themselves in the Protestation of 1641 and the Solemn League and Covenant (1643) to defend the king and the law (8–9). The army's actions amounted to 'mutinous Rebellion' based on Jesuitical principles that had been repudiated by all sensible Protestants (11, 12).

These points were powerfully developed by William Prynne, launched by the unfolding events of 1649 into furious intellectual efforts to demonstrate that the King and Lords were essential components of the ancient constitution, with claims to authority more ancient than those of the Commons.[173] All of this activity was fuelled by his conviction that 'the grosse Ignorance of the ancient constitution of our

English Parliaments, and fanatick dream of A Supreme Parliamentary
and absolute Legislative Authority in THE HOUSE OF COMMONS
ALONE . . . [is] the principal ground-work of all the late unparalleled,
insolent . . . proceedings against the King, the house of Peers, and
secluded Majority of the Late Commons House, by the Army [and
Rump]'.[174] Later, in opposing the oath of Engagement to the
Commonwealth, Prynne identified its intention as a wish to confirm
the suppression of monarch and House of Lords, and so to destroy
'[t]hat Government under which all the Inhabitants of this Isle, since
it was first Peopled, have ever lived, [and] flourished; continuing unal-
terable in all Changes and Successions of those Nations which have
invaded, peopled or Conquered it, as best and most agreeable and
pleasing to the People'.[175] The revolution of 1649 might have been
conducted in the name of the people, but it was not conducted by their
authority or in their interest.

Thus, whatever the popular basis for government might be, the
people had at the least erected a government with which they had no
continuing authority to meddle. Prynne in 1649 remained largely
focused on legal–constitutional matters, though even he took time to
sneer at the 'Saint-seeming Army'.[176] The ministers, however, effectively worked on a second front too, tackling those religious arguments
that might be used to justify constitutional reconstruction. An appeal
to providential direction, they argued, would not help, because 'God
doth not approve the practice of whatsoever his Providence doth
permit' (14). Nor could one appeal to the spirit.

> Nor is it safe to be guided by Impulses of Spirit, or pretended impres-
> sions on your hearts, without or against the rule of Gods written
> Word. For by this means the temptation of Satan, and the motions of
> Gods spirit wil be put in equall ballance.   (15)

(That passage, of course, should remind us that Cook could readily
respond that he was, in fact, doing no more than following the word of
God, which he interpreted in a sense utterly opposed to that of the
London ministers.) Nor, finally, could a plea of necessity be entered:

> If beyond all this you plead Necessity of doing thus, least what you
> pretend as a glorious worke, might else miscarry, and therefore
> venture on these wayes, which are by your selves confessed to be *irreg-
> ular and not justifyable,* We answer, that no necessity can oblige a man
> to sinne; God stands not in need of our sinne to carry on his owne
> worke.   (16)

Thus the Presbyterian case rested on two things. No one had the legal authority to try the king or alter the government; and there could be no religious or conscientious justification for the illegalities necessary for such constitutional change. The difference between this position and Cook's lay less in the area of millenarianism or apocalypticism, and more in their very different readings of scripture and of the duties that God had imposed on men. For Cook, the temporal world must be ruled by Old Testament injunctions which overrode human law and constitution; for Presbyterians, God in Romans 13 and elsewhere had given his continuing protection to whatever political arrangements men might have constructed for themselves.

For all their bluster, it was difficult for Independents to confront these arguments. This is very evident in the writing of one of the key defenders of the regicide and its surrounding events, John Goodwin.[177] His defence of the army's action in purging parliament appeared under the ominous title *Right and Might Well Met*. In it, Goodwin struggled to bring about the meeting to which he had referred, but the participants remained obdurately shy of one another. It exploited the idea of a religious 'calling' to argue that the soldiers of the army were invested with the capacity to judge and deal with enemies of the kingdom, thus to preserve 'the people's good'.[178] Their calling enable Goodwin to defend the soldier's actions in terms, not of law and legality, but of equity. As so often in the 1640s, equity meant necessity. In cases of necessity men were bound in conscience to aid one another, and in such circumstances 'all *callings* are common'. That is to say that, in necessity, the pursuit of equity required that even private men could perform the duties attached to offices (or callings) that were not strictly or legally their own. Thus, for example, where there were no priests, private men could act as priests – and thus, too, 'particular men [might] turne Kings'.[179] To save others against their will was 'a deed of Charity and Christianity', and an example of the principle 'that whatsoever is necessary, is somewhat more than lawfull'.[180] These were dangerous arguments. Goodwin's reply to the objection that it 'is an easie matter to pretend a necessity (almost) for every unjust, and unrighteous thing' was not altogether reassuring. He simply asserted that the use of judgement in such matters was a duty imposed by God on all men, and that it was not difficult to judge clearly.[181] But the controversy in which Goodwin was engaged itself gave the lie to that. His work carried with it, obliquely and in spite of itself, the powerful sense of a man who believed that his faith in himself and in God entitled him to do whatever he judged necessary.

That is equally true of his defence of the regicide against the arguments of the Presbyterian ministers, even though Goodwin did his best to stand on the firmer terrain of consent politics. To launch his case, Goodwin asked the Presbyterian ministers whether they could produce any scriptural grounds for supposing that kings were exempt from God's command that murderers should be punished with death.[182] Even if it could be argued that there was no human law by which kings were punishable for murder (in fact, Goodwin believed that there was), it remained true that 'the *Scripture cannot be dissolved* by the authoritie of any Politick Rule or Maxime whatsoever of humane sanction' (8). From here, the argument moved to constitutional matters. The king was subject to God's laws against murder, but was he also subject to any authority capable of compelling his obedience to those laws? Citing the Presbyterian 'pillars' Rutherford and Prynne, Goodwin claimed 'that the people, or their Representative, are superiour in power or authoritie unto the King' (9–11). It is important to note, then, that this argument developed from a consideration of what authority could enforce scriptural law upon the king. From this point, Goodwin continued to the assertion that:

> The King hath his work of Governing, appointed or set out unto him by the people, in those Laws, which they constitute and make for their own Government, and his, by their Representatives, or Trustees in Parliament. . . . In like manner the people (I mean collectively taken) have no Law of nature, or of God upon them, which prohibiteth them from laying aside a King or Kingly Government, from amongst them, when they have a reasonable cause for it . . . [or when they suspect] that another form of Government will accommodate the Interest of the State upon equall or better terms, with lesse charge and expence. . . . [A] people or State formerly Governed by Kings, may very lawfully turn these servants of theirs out of their doors; as the *Romans* of old, and the *Hollanders* of late (besides many nations more) have done, *and are blamelesse.* (11–12)

More succinctly, 'the people are the makers of Kings, and Kings their creatures, or work-manship' (15). All monarchy was essentially elective, even if election often took the form of a people's refraining from revoking their acceptance of the hereditary principle (27–8). Although authority might have been exercised before the Civil War in the three estates together (king, Lords and Commons), it nonetheless lay fundamentally with the people's representatives alone (39–40). In 'cases extraordinary', furthermore, the people's authority to discipline or depose kings may be exercised by 'such a part of it as shall be spirited and strengthened by God for the atchievement' (32).

Goodwin laboured hard the point that the regicide was the free act of a legally-valid House of Commons, exercising the people's right to preserve themselves as a community. The gap between this theory and the reality of a purged Commons acting outside the law and at the bidding of the Army was such that he could hardly avoid putting in place a safety-net: doing justice (in this instance, on the king) was

> so absolutely and essentially necessary to the preservation and well-being of a State, or body politique, that both the Law of God, and nature, doth not onely allow it in any member, one, or more, of such a body . . . but even calleth them unto it, and requireth it at their hand, in such cases. (40)

The Commons was constitutionally justified. But even if it were not, it should still have executed the king. And if it had refused, any other individual or group was entitled to bring him to justice. Doing justice on murderers was God's work (Genesis, 9.6), and it would not wait for the human niceties to be observed. Where magistrates, superior and inferior, failed, God called all men 'to interpose and act in an extraordinary way, as *viz.* by executing Justice and Judgement in their land, upon the default of those, who *bear the sword in vain* [Romans 13.4], and thereby expose the land unto a curse' (43).

What mattered in this was that the king had done more than break the law: he had committed a *sin* of the most serious sort. 'When a sin, which for the kind of it, and without any aggravating circumstance, deserveth death, is committed with any unnaturall, and execrable aggravation besides, God usually covereth all irregularities, which are found in, or about the Execution of Justice upon the sinner, and justifieth the Execution, though it be not managed in all circumstances according to the standing rules of Justice in ordinary cases' (45). The king had polluted the land with blood, and the nation could only atone for this pollution by shedding the blood of the murderer himself. God, nature and equity, therefore, freed men from their former obligations (such as the oath of allegiance) in order that they bring the king to justice (60–2). To the argument that there was no precedent or previous example for the actions undertaken by the Rump, Goodwin rejoined that 'An example, is no Rule: God made Rules, before that men, yea or himself, made examples.' There was no reason 'for later ages, yea or this present age, not to make presidents for those that are yet to come, as well as it was for former ages, to serve these with the same commoditie' (77). God made the fundamental rules, and human precedents counted for nothing against them.

In the latter part of his tract, Goodwin defended his *Right and Might Well Met* against the criticisms of John Geree. It is here, perhaps more clearly than anywhere else, that he revealed the regicide to have been an act of obedience to God's laws, carried out by men 'who had *ingaged* themselves by many *Religious bands* unto such things' (120). This was characteristic of the regicidal Independents, whose extreme constitutionalism served only to free men to obey God's law more rigorously. Civil freedom, the freedom that allowed communities to change their form of government and allowed individuals in necessity to bring to justice tyrants, was not an end in itself. It was important to Goodwin and others for the way in which it freed men from human ties that might frustrate the operation of their religious ones. Like liberty of conscience, civil liberty could be the handmaid of religious duty. Presbyterians were as uncomfortable with the one liberty as they were with the other.

Not all Independents were of the same stamp. Some could share in the anxieties of Presbyterians, and even try to assuage them. One such was John Sadler, whose *Rights of the Kingdom* gave special attention to Presbyterian fears that the use of necessity to override law and constitution was inherently dangerous. Sadler's title perhaps echoed that of Buchanan's *De Jure Regni*, and Sadler did indeed do for England what Buchanan had done for Scotland. He declared, in ways that avoided Goodwin's extravagant invocations of necessity, 'I am an English Man; and Therefore, am obliged to This Country, and These Laws'.[183] Appeals to necessity, he argued, left us 'in a Dark Chaos'; necessity 'Levels All' (sig. A1v). The justice of the end, the people's safety, was obvious; but it remained necessary to prove the justice of the means that had been used to reach that end. To this purpose, Sadler set out to demonstrate that from the beginning 'All English Kings, had English Bounds, by Law' (p. 12). Beginning with Saxon oaths of fealty, he found that historically English subjects were bound to the kingdom more than to the king, that kings had superiors in the law, parliament and the barons (who could curb and punish their wrong-doing), and that English monarchy was anciently and in essence elective. Furthermore, the House of Commons alone, at least in some circumstances, 'had a Legall right to doe, what All the Kingdom or the Common-wealth of England justly could' (30). Sadler certainly hesitated before affirming that the actions of the army and of a purged parliament were acceptable (56–60, 159–60), and it was his anxiety on this score that no doubt encouraged him to produce a detailed account of the proper procedures that parliament must follow with regard to legal matters. The material was intended, Sadler concluded, 'to minde the Parliament of what their Duty is, and Custome was, in their relation to the Commonwealth' (184). There was more than a hint that, in light of the regicide, they needed such a reminder.

Parliamentarians, Covenanters and Royalists responded to the turmoil of Britain's wars of religion in complicated and cross-cutting ways. All felt the temptations and noticed the risks in using religious arguments to buttress their political cause. For none, was the Revolution *just* a war of religion. Rather, if it was about any one thing at all, it was about the boundaries between religious and civil duties; or, to put the same point another way, it was about competing conceptions of the relationship between divine command and human responsibility. Did God leave humankind free to construct laws and constitutions of their own, giving to these constructions his approbation if they were properly built from consent and reason; or did he command with greater specification of the details, perhaps insisting that only monarchy had his blessing? Did God require unconditional obedience to the powers that be, or did he allow people to act against their rulers, whether for religious or for political reasons? Perhaps, indeed, God might intervene directly in human affairs, with a freedom and an abandon, and a destructiveness, that no human agent could ever contemplate. By the end of the 1640s there were many who thought so, and their ideas will be considered in the next chapter.

6 Religion, 'Radicalism' and the English Revolution

For many historians the most remarkable feature of the English Revolution was the emergence of political 'radicalism', a phenomenon that has attracted considerable attention since the late nineteenth century. It was the subject of one of the finest and most exciting works of scholarship written about the period, Christopher Hill's *The World Turned Upside Down* (1972). During the 1640s, while Independents and Presbyterians argued over the process of reaching settlement with the king, and the army leaders seized control of events from their one-time Parliamentary masters, the presses continued to produce a flood of extraordinary demands and schemes for political, social and religious change. This radical pamphleteering was part of an enormous increase in the output of the printing presses, which, as we have seen, peaked in 1642; it then fell back to climb to another peak in 1648–9.[1] For many, these were years in which millenarian expectation of the world's transformation, and the advent of Christ's rule on earth was at its height. Arguably, this phenomenon constituted an *English* Revolution, a revolution religious in its driving force, and ultimately disappointed in its hopes.[2]

There has been considerable debate about whether the term 'radicalism' really deserves its name.[3] It was coined only in the early nineteenth century, and like most comparable terms risks both misdescription and over-systematising. Though the term is employed here, it is used with reluctance, and because it remains familiar shorthand. But the chapter is concerned to argue that this 'radicalism' must be seen divorced from the anachronistic assumptions and linkages that the term has sometimes been taken to impute. It must be seen as a phenomenon of the Puritan Revolution, and located in relation to contested ideas about the relationships between God and his human creation.

Radicalism and the Political Realm: the Levellers and Henry Ireton

The Levellers occupied a space between Presbyterian intolerance and sectarian enthusiasm. They differed from the former with their insistence on the importance of freedom of conscience, as well as on legal and constitutional matters; and they differed from the latter in their insistence that the political and social world was organised in ways that human beings chose for themselves, not in response to direct divine commands, still less in response to the direct intervention of an active God.

The evidence for the Levellers' distance from the Presbyterians is, of course, obvious and abundant. When the major Leveller pamphleteers coalesced into a loose grouping during 1645–6, they did so in good part thanks to their common interest in supporting religious tolera-tion, though the imprisonment of Lilburne by the Commons for infringing its privileges in 1645 encouraged both him and others to take a stand on legal and constitutional issues too.[4] Lilburne defended himself in *Englands Birthright Justified* (October 1645), in which he partly relied on legalistic and common-law arguments, turning against parliament's its own case against the king. On 'rationall grounds' it was clear that the laws of England were 'binding to the very Parliament themselves as well as others. And though by their legislative power they have Authority to make new Laws, yet no free-man of England is to take notice (or can he) of what they intend till they declare it.' Parliament was bound by the laws which it made, their authority 'limited by those that betrust them; and . . . they are not to doe what they list, but what they ought, namely to provide for the peoples weal'. Drawing the paral-lel explicitly, Lilburne commented 'that unknown Priviledges are as dangerous as unlimited Prerogatives, being both of them secret snares'.[5] These principles were enshrined in Magna Carta, 'which provides for the peoples freedome'.[6]

Dissatisfied with this argument, William Walwyn wrote a short commentary on Lilburne's defence, the first real connection between prominent future Levellers and also the first of Walwyn's writings concerned directly with legal–constitutional matters. His message to Lilburne was simple. Instead of appealing to Magna Carta and to the rights of Freeborn Englishmen, Lilburne would find a more secure basis for his claims in abstract principle, in 'reason, sense, and the common Law of equitie and justice'.[7] The problem with relying on English law and constitutional principle was that it so often began in 'the grants of Conquerours' (148), and contained at best a partial guarantee of what was due to the people. People had trusted in the Long Parliament, believing that it would settle their religious griev-ances. But it was now clear that religion was pre-eminently a matter that could only be dealt with according to the correct general principles:

the Government of the Church is a thing disputable. . . . [N]ow unto things in themselves disputable, and uncertaine, as there is no reason why any man should be bound expresly to any one forme, further then his Judgement and conscience doe agree thereunto, even so ought the whole Nation to be free therein, even to alter and change the publique forme, as may best stand with the safety and freedome of the people. For the Parliament is ever at libertie to make the People more free from burthens and oppressions of any nature, but in things appertaining to the universall rules of common equitie and justice, all men and all Authority in the world are bound.

The only sure foundation was 'open and universall justice', which required 'that none be compelled against Conscience in the worship of God, nor any molested for Conscience sake, the oppression for Conscience, having been the greatest oppression that ever lay on religious people, and therefore except that be removed, the people have some case by removall of the Bishops, but rather will be in greater bondage, if more and worse spirituall taskmasters be set over us' (149–50).

What is interesting in this is that Walwyn, in reflecting on Lilburne's imprisonment, quickly perceived (certainly more quickly than Lilburne) the coherent nexus of principles that was to hold the Levellers together. Support for liberty of conscience or toleration *required* support for the limitation of parliamentary authority, which had the potential to be as dangerous as kingly authority. The view that parliament, the people's representative, had a power 'bound to no rules, nor bounded by any limits . . . accountable to none' (147) gave it impunity to meddle with anything, even individual consciences. Magna Carta might defend John Lilburne, but would it defend the human conscience?

A Remonstrance of Many Thousand Citizens, which appeared in July 1646, is often taken to mark the birth of the Levellers as a group.[8] It elaborated on the themes that Walwyn had raised, informing the Commons that they were entrusted with the task of delivering 'from all kind of Bondage' the people of England. This power was revocable, for 'we possessed you with the same Power that was in our selves, to have done the same; For wee might justly have done it our selves without you, if we had thought it convenient.' The exercise of any power 'that is not derived from our trust and choice' amounts to usurpation and oppression.[9] England's constitutional past was brushed aside in ringing tones, 'for whatever our Fore-fathers were; or whatever they did or suffered, or were enforced to yeeld unto; we are men of the present age, and ought to be absolutely free from all kindes of exorbitancies, molestations or Arbitrary Power, and you wee choose to free us from all without exception or limitation ...' (114). Magna Carta was declared 'a beggarly thing', bearing the marks of the bondage introduced by the Norman Conquest. The core of the problem faced by the English people was identified as being, not the kingship of Charles I and his evil advisers, but the very institution of monarchy itself. Parliament was much too loyal to the king and was wrong to insist on acting in his name. Monarchy should go, and the Lords should be emasculated, leaving legislative sovereignty in the hands of the Commons alone. 'Yee only are chosen by Us the People; and therefore in you onely is the Power of binding the whole Nation, by making, altering, or abolishing of Lawes'. The Commons were wrong to think that they could only make law, under normal circumstances, with the consent of the king and Lords (116). To allow the Lords independent power was to imply that the people were 'their servants and vassalls', and that was just another sort of 'Tyrannicall Power' (117).

The root of the *Remonstrance*'s concern lay in the simple observation that 'neither you, nor none else, can have any into Power at all to conclude the People in matters that concerne the Worship of God, for therein every one of us ought to be fully assured in our owne mindes, and to be sure to Worship him according to our Consciences' (122). Parliament could not compel the people in religious matters,

> for ye have no Power from Us so to doe, *nor could you have*; for we could not conferre a Power that was not in our selves, there being none of us, that can without wilfull sinne binde our selves to worship God after any other way, then what (to a tittle,) in our owne particular understandings, wee approve to be just.   (122 – stress added)

This was the heart of the Leveller position, spelled out at greater length by Overton a few months later (October 1646).

> To every Individuall in nature, is given an individuall property by nature, not to be invaded or usurped by any: for every one as he is himselfe, so he hath a selfe propriety, else could he not be himselfe, and on this no second may presume to deprive any of, without manifest violation and affront to the very principles of nature, and of the Rules of equity and justice between man and man. ... For by naturall birth, all men are equally and alike borne to like propriety, liberty and freedome, and as we are delivered of God by the hand of nature into this world, every one with a naturall, innate freedome and propriety. ... even so are we to live, every one equally and alike to enjoy his Birth-right and priviledge; even all whereof God by nature hath made him free.[10]

As a result, every man is 'by nature . . . a King, Priest and Prophet in his owne naturall circuite and compasse, whereof no second may partake, but by deputation, commission, and free consent from him, whose naturall right and freedome it is'. Consent was thus at the heart of politics. No human being could exercise any sort of authority, temporal or spiritual, over another human being, except with his or her consent.[11]

There was, however, a further restriction. '[N]o more may be communicated then stands for the better being, weale, or safety thereof: and this is mans prerogative and no further.' '[H]e that gives more, sins against his owne flesh' (4). God, indeed, remained the ulti-mate owner of the human person, and to grant to others a power damaging to oneself was an infringement of God's rights as an owner. In 1649 Lilburne restated the basic point: God the sovereign was 'that one, single, individual ALONE (either in heaven or earth) that is to raign, rule, govern, and give a law by his will and pleasure to the sons of men; the absolute workmanship of his hands or power'.[12] God had endowed his creatures with only a *limited* self-ownership. This was stated even more forcefully in July 1647 in another of the great Leveller documents, *An Appeale from the Degenerate Representative Body.*

> For all just humaine powers are but betrusted, confer'd and conveyed by joynt and common consent, for to every individuall in nature, is given an individuall propriety by nature, not to be invaded or usurped by any . . . for everyone as he is himselfe hath a selfe propriety, else could not be himselfe, and on this no second may presume without consent; and by naturall birth, all men are equall and alike borne to like propriety and freedome, every man by natu-rall instinct aiming at his owne safety and weale. . . . Now as no man by nature may abuse, beat, torment or afflict himself, so by nature no man may give that power to another. : . . So that if the betrusted act not for the weal and safety of the betrustyers, they depart from their just power, and act by another, which cannot be tearmed either humaine or divine, but unnaturall and divellish, rendring such usurpers as Monsters amongst men.[13]

One of the things that human beings could *not* do was grant to others any authority over their consciences, as Walwyn had made apparent before his Leveller days, in his anti-Presbyterian toleration tracts. For example, in an attack on William Prynne, Walwyn accepted that not only emperors, kings and popes had 'assumed an absolute power . . . in matters of religion', but also councils and parliaments. Nonetheless, they could not rightly have such power: 'what the people cannot entrust, that they [i.e. parliament] cannot have'. The reason that power over religion could not be acquired by consent was simple:

> the people of a Nation in chusing of a Parliament cannot confer more then that power which was justly in themselves: the plain rule being this. . . . But all things concerning the worship and service of God, and of that nature; that a man cannot without wilfull sin, either binde himselfe to doe any thing therein contrary to his understanding and conscience: nor to forbeare to doe that which his understanding and conscience bindes him to performe: therefore no man can refer matters of Religion to any others regulation.[14]

There was thus an intimate relationship between the Levellers' belief in a politics of consent and their advocacy of religious toleration. It is easy to see why, following Walwyn's lead, it would be argued that consent was the foundation of all authority, and *therefore* that the magistrate could not possibly have coercive powers in religious matters. During 1646 and 1647 Walwyn repeated his case in many tracts, particularly in the course of a lengthy debate with the presbyterian Thomas Edwards, for whom toleration meant the growth of heresy, which he linked in turn to political views 'not consistent with any Civill Government at all, but what necessarily would bring any Common-wealth . . . into a *chaos* and confusion'.[15] One plank of Edwards's attack on the Levellers and toleration was the claim that they were seeking not just tolerance from others, but to exercise a 'Raigne and Domination', and would themselves not extend liberty to others.[16] The Leveller insistence on *universal* principles was an effective reply. Thus Overton's *Araignment of Mr Persecution* (April 1645), one of the finest propaganda pamphlets of the period, pointed out, amid much broad and energetic humour at the expense of the Presbyterians, that to exercise coercive power over consciences was to betray the trust of the people. The first charge levelled against Mr Persecution was that he usurped the sovereignty of God over men's consciences.[17] No one – whether sectary, Leveller, Presbyterian or Anglican – had such authority.[18]

The Levellers had little sympathy with those Parliamentarian arguments which, though relying on a foundation of consent, nonetheless asserted that the people's consent could only be expressed through the institution of parliament, in which all were represented whether they actually participated in politics or not. By 1646 it was clear that their exclusion of religion from the authority of the civil magistrate was part of a general argument that made limited government by consent the only acceptable form of government. Men could not without sin give away authority over their consciences; nor could they give away arbitrary and despotic authority over their lives and estates. God, in a sense, was used to establish the political realm as a realm of freedom dominated by consent. God also determined the boundaries of that realm, protecting human communities against all oppressive and arbitrary authority. Lilburne summed up these core principles of Leveller politics. First, only God can 'make his Will, a rule, and law, unto himself and others'. It followed from this that 'because by nature no man is GOD, or Soveraigne, one over another; Reason tells me, I ought not to have a law imposed upon me, without my consent; the doing of which is meerly tyrannicall, Antichristian, and Diabolicall'. Political authority must be based on 'common consent, in which every individuall is included'. This emphasis on consent led naturally to a contractarian reading of the basis of governmental authority. The king was granted authority by contract and agreement. 'He that by contract and agreement receives a Crown or Kingdome; is bound to that contract and agreement the violating of which, absolves and disengages those, (that made it) from him.' Thus the main point of the tract was to urge the parliament to depose and punish the king for his tyranny. Finally, Lilburne spelt out the crucial theological context of the whole argument. Among 'the Sons of Men' there was a natural equality, 'there is none above another, or over another, against mutuall consent and agreement'. The people themselves, 'knit and joyned together by mutuall consent and agreement', exercise sovereign authority; but within the limits imposed by 'the Law of God, Nature, and Reason', which prohibited any man from enslaving himself. This would be 'against Nature, and the glory of the Image of God, that he created man in ... and so a dishonour to himself, and to his Maker, his absolute and alone Soveraign, cannot justly be done'.[19]

Thus, all political authority was *entrusted* authority, and if misused it returned to the hands of the 'betrusters'.[20] In the *Appeale*, Overton cited his own *Arrow against all Tyrants* in defence of the view that 'all just *humaine powers* are but betrusted, confer'd and conveyed by joynt and common consent'. Every individual has a '*selfe propriety*' on which 'no second may presume without consent'. This self-propriety, created by God, was not, however, absolute, and so the authority created by consent could not be absolute either (162–3). Magistracy was an office. If the persons appointed to that office failed to fulfil its duties, they were no longer magistrates, and the sovereign people could have them replaced (180). Crucial questions remained to be answered – did 'the people' mean *all* of them? Through what agencies could the people exercise their sovereign power, if not through parliament? But the basic principle of popular sovereignty, based on arguments about the inherent nature of the individuality with which God had created human beings, was clearly enunciated by 1647.[21]

The position reached by the Levellers received programmatic statement in their first *Agreement of the People* (1647), a document produced for discussion in the Army Council meeting at Putney in October and November 1647.[22] That document, the first attempt to produce a written constitution for England, was designed to replace the Stuart monarchy with a new political structure, pared down to essentials, based on the consent of the people. It was proposed to redraw the parliamentary electorates 'to be more indifferently proportioned, according to the number of the Inhabitants'. On this basis, once the Long Parliament was to be dissolved (by the end of Septemer 1648, it was said), the people would elect a parliament once every two years on the first Thursday in March. That parliament would sit only from the first Thursday in April until the end of September, and only in the year in which it was elected. (What exactly was to happen for the other 18 of the 24 months between elections was not specified.) The power of this parliament was 'inferiour only to theirs who chuse them', and explicitly encompassed 'enacting, altering, and repealing of Lawes', creating and abolishing 'Offices and Courts', 'appointing, removing, and calling to account Magistrates, and Officers', declaring war and peace, and making treaties with foreign powers. However, explicitly reserved from its authority – for reasons that should by now be obvious – were all 'matters of Religion, and the wayes of Gods Worship', as well as the power to conscript soldiers, to exempt particular people from the general course of law to which others were subject, or to inquire into people's actions during the years of civil war. Finally it was declared, rather vaguely, 'that as the Laws ought to be equall, so they must be good, and not evidently destructive to the safety and well-being of the people'.[23]

The Levellers' insistence that the political realm was shaped, within limits, by human choices was rooted in a view of the relationship of God to his human creatures that distanced the Levellers from those religious enthusiasts who emphasised the *direct* involvement of God in the world. Lilburne had, himself, been one of many people who by the late 1630s was interpreting the struggle against Laud in terms of an eschatological drama,[24] but millenarian elements play no significant role in Leveller argument in the period 1645 to 1649. When touches of apocalyptic language remain, they do little real work. Witness, for example, the opening of Wildman's *Putney Projects*, which announced that 'Gods present designe in the world is, the shaking of the powers of the earth, and marring the pride of all flesh.'[25] It sounds like the beginning of an argument that will invoke an activist God. 'God is humbling the lofty,' we are told. God was responsible for the victories of the New Model Army. That perspective, however, quickly dissolved, and the tract became an attempt to reveal 'the mysterie of deceit, wherein our chiefe Commanders in the Armie walke'. The purpose was to ensure that the people did not put 'their confidence in broken reeds' (1–2). Whatever God was doing, it seems that men still had to make choices. Part of the reason for this, perhaps, lay in the sort of scepticism that informed Leveller defences of toleration (especially Walwyn's). Men had different ideas about what God required, and it was difficult to decide between them. As Wildman himself said at Putney, 'Whatever another man hath received from the Spirit, that man cannot demonstrate to me but by some other way than merely relating to me that which he conceives to be the mind of God.' What other way might there be? '[W]e cannot', he went on, 'find anything in the word of God what is fit to be done in civil matters.' The best we can do is to act 'like unto God – [practising] justice and mercy, to be meek and peaceable'.[26] Failing any direct political guidance from God, the best we could do was attempt to exhibit the virtues that God recommends to us.

Perhaps it was their reluctance to envisage an activist God that contributed to the fact that one of the criticisms most frequently made of the Levellers was that they were irreligious atheists.[27] The Levellers' reply to the charge is a revealing document. In a tract that appeared under the names of Walwyn, Lilburne, Overton and Thomas Prince (but which may have been largely the work of Walwyn), they declared that 'wee beleeve there is one eternall and omnipotent God, the Author and Preserver of all things in the world. To whose will and directions, written first in our hearts, and afterwards in his blessed Word, we ought to square our actions and conversations.'[28] The second sentence was, perhaps, more important than the first, because it amounted to the claim that God interacted with human beings only mediately (through nature primarily, and scripture secondarily) and not directly. To do God's will required involvement in a genuinely *political* world of free human choices, using 'the best care and abilities God hath afforded us' and awaiting the consent of our fellows (283). It is not surprising, then, to find that the relationship between the Levellers and the London sects was a troubled one. During 1647 and into 1648 they could agree to work together for religious toleration, though in other respects their ideas were markedly different from one other. But by 1649, underlying tensions were clearly apparent, as the sects increasingly opted to search for Godly magistracy and the rule of the saints rather than follow the Levellers towards a politics of consent. Sectarian pastors, beginning with the leaders of the particular Baptists, began directly to repudiate the Levellers. In April 1649 there was published under the name of several of them one of the key attacks on Leveller 'irreligion', *Walwins Wiles* (in fact, probably *written* by John Price, associate of John Goodwin).[29] The most distinctive – perhaps the most representative – political grouping to emerge from the sects in 1649 was made up of men devoted to serving as handmaids of the second coming, the Fifth Monarchists; and the contrast between their attitudes and those of the Levellers is stark.[30]

Though this divergence of the Levellers and the Godly enthusiasts was evident only at the end of the 1640s, its roots were clearly deeper. The *Appeale* of July 1647 made clear that civil magistracy was to ensure '*safety* Nationall and generall', thus to ensure that every man, except 'the unnaturall and the inhumane', could 'enjoy his liberty, peace and tranquillity, *civill* and *humane*'. It did not exist only 'for *this opinion*, or that *faction*, this sect or that *sort*, but equally and alike indifferent for all men that are not degenerated from humanity and humane civility'.[31] Thise gives a clear indication of the sort of habitat that the Levellers chose to inhabit, determining that the very essence of their politics would lie in the seeking of *agreement*. They were concerned with the civil rights of men as men; concerned to avoid constructing a politics of merely sectarian appeal. They invested their hope in the possibility of consensus: in their own eyes, they had laid the basis (expressed, though, in gendered language[32]) for a politics of consent that could embrace all of God's human creation.

The Levellers' relationship with the army gave them their opportunities to influence England's constitutional future, but it was also to show that seeking agreement was much easier to talk about than to achieve.[33] Among the most vivid of the records left by the English Revolution is the transcript of the Putney Debates, a meeting of the Army Council during late October and early November 1647, which dramatises precisely this situation. Called to discuss the questions raised by the *Case of the Armie Truly Stated*, a statement of grievances by elements within the army critical of its leadership, the Debates instead discussed the Leveller *Agreement of the People*, probably written by Walwyn or John Wildman. Both documents reflect close links between Levellers and some elements within the army. The *Agreement*, introduced on 28 October, was discussed in earnest in a special committee of the General Council the following day.[34] Commissary-General Henry Ireton (Cromwell's son-in-law) seized upon the *Agreement's* first (vague) clause about reshaping the electorate to accuse the Levellers of advocating universal manhood suffrage. It was the beginning of a debate between Ireton and the Leveller leaders that stretched on into 1649.[35] The logic of Ireton's position at Putney can only be fully appreciated when we remember that central to English thought in the seventeenth century was the idea that the primary function of common law was to defend property. From the common law perspective – Ireton had some training at the Middle Temple – liberty consisted primarily in the protection that human law gave to property rights, though 'property' could be understood in an extended sense to cover not only landed property, wealth and possessions, but also one's entitlement to personal freedom (e.g. from arrest) and even one's entitlement to life.[36] Ireton discerned in the Levellers an appeal to natural rights that, in seeking to go beneath human law, would destroy property and thus destroy the only liberty that men could hope to enjoy. Nature provided almost no political guidance at all. As a result, human beings had considerable latitude to act as they wished; *but* – and here was the crucial point – having made their decisions, they were bound to them. Ireton, indeed, allowed human beings much greater freedom than did the Levellers to shape their own political communities; but he did so because he saw them in these matters unrestricted to any significant degree by divine or natural law. Only upon themselves could they rely; therefore, their decisions must remain inviolable.

> The government of Kings, or of Lords, is as just as any in the world, is the justest government in the world. *Volenti non fit injuria.* Men cannot wrong themselves willingly, and if they will agree to make a King, and his heirs, there's no injustice. They may either make it hereditary or elective. They may give him an absolute power or a limited power. Here hath been agreements of the people that have agreed with this. There hath been such an agreement when the people have fought for their liberty, and have established the King again.[37]

It was on this basis that Ireton launched into an attack on the first clause of the *Agreement.* '[T]his doth make me think that the meaning is, that every man that is an inhabitant is to be equally considered, and to have an equal voice in the election' of representatives. If so, 'then I have something to say against it. But if it be only those people that by the civil constitution of this kingdom, which is original and fundamental,' had the vote, who are to retain it now, then Ireton will be content (52). Faced with this, the Levellers affirmed that it was universal manhood suffrage that they meant. Petty said that 'we judge that all inhabitants that have not lost their birthright should have an equal voice in elections'.[38] Colonel Thomas Rainsborough was more emphatic: 'For really I think that the poorest he that is in England hath a life to live, as the greatest he; and therefore truly, sir, I think it's clear, that every man that is to live under a government ought first by his own consent to put himself under that government; and I do think that the poorest man in England is not at all bound in a strict sense to that government that he hath not had a voice to put himself under' (53). Thus confirmed in his suspicions, Ireton began to explain what was wrong with the position. The ensuing debate is a remarkable document, giving us the chance to experience seventeenth-century political argument with unmatched immediacy

'Give me leave to tell you,' began Ireton, 'that if you make this rule I think you must fly for refuge to an absolute natural right, and you must deny all civil right; and I am sure it will come to that in the consequence' (53). Ireton distinguished between three categories of people in England. First, there were foreigners, not born in England, who had and ought to have no political rights. Secondly, there were the unpropertied English people. Ireton admitted that these men could claim certain things by 'birthright': 'that we should not seclude them out of England, that we should not refuse to give them air and place and ground, and the freedom of the highways and other things to live amongst us'. They might also claim 'the protection of laws', though not any voice in their making. But it was not the case that these men 'shall have a share in that power that shall dispose of the lands here, and of all things here'. Finally there were the propertied, those with 'a permanent fixed interest in this kingdom'. These men 'comprehend the local interest', by owning land and controlling trade; and it was they who participated in elections. To give political rights to those without fixed interest was dangerous. They were excluded by 'what was originally the constitution of this kingdom, upon that which is most radical and fundamental, and which if you take away, there is no man hath any lands, any goods, any civil interest'. Any attempt 'to take away this [civil constitution] . . . shall plainly go to take away all property and interest that any man hath either in land by inheritance, or in estate by possession, or anything else' (53–5).

Controversy focused on the rights of the second of the groups identified by Ireton, the English-born poor. The Leveller spokesmen took Ireton's charges with the utmost seriousness. They did not deny that he had apprehended correctly their actual objectives; but rather, attempted to explain why the consequences that he feared would not come about. Rainsborough's immediate response by-passed the issue of *consequences* by focusing on first principles. He accurately discerned Ireton's drift: 'we must be no freer than the laws will let us be'. But God had given men reason in order for them to better themselves. Unless forbidden to do so, men should use that capacity as they saw fit. Yet there was no principle in divine law to justify denying the franchise to the poor, nor in natural law. That left only English law, but Ireton could not rest his case on that, for 'the foundation of all law lies in the people, and if in the people, I am to seek for this exemption' (55–6).

Ireton was unimpressed by this and other responses, arguing that he was happy to extend the franchise to some degree but that property could only be preserved if some were excluded from it. Otherwise, '[i]t may come to destroy property thus. You may have such men chosen, or at least the major part of them [i.e. the propertyless]. Why may not these men vote against all property?' (63). The propertyless would vote to expropriate the propertied. Colonel Nathaniel Rich added weight to Ireton's reservations by conjuring up an alternative set of fears: rich men would be able to control the votes of their inferiors, and the way would be opened to the establishment of a 'perpetual dictator' as happened to the Romans (64).

John Wildman ably summarised the essence of the Leveller case in two points. First, we could not rely, as Ireton was attempting to do, on the existing constitution and laws, because '[o]ur very laws were made by our conquerors . . . [while] [w]e are now engaged for our freedom'. And, secondly, that freedom required universal manhood suffrage. 'I conceive that's the undeniable maxim of government: that all government is in the free consent of the people. If, then upon that account there is no person that is under a just government, or hath justly his own, unless he by his own free consent be put under that government, that he cannot be unless he be consenting to it' (65–6). The discussion, therefore, had strayed from the point, and so Wildman restated the real question at issue: 'Whether any person can justly be bound by law, who doth not give his consent that such persons shall make laws for him?' (66).

In response, Ireton was compelled to introduce a further crucial distinction, that between tacit and explicit consent. With regard to the foreigner, he ought to be bound by laws to which he has not given his consent, and 'if this man do think himself unsatisfied to be subject to this law he may go into another kingdom'. Essentially, the same was true of the propertyless: 'his money is as good in another place as here; he hath nothing that doth locally fix him to this consent'. Power 'of determining what law shall be law in the land, does lie in the people that are possessed of the permanent interest in the land' (67). Thus those without property consent by remaining in the country; those with property consent by voting for their representatives.

Sexby voiced in reply the view that many of the New Model soldiers must have shared: we believed we fought for liberty; 'I wonder we were so much deceived,' was his sarcastic comment (67, 69). Rainsborough agreed: 'I would fain know what the soldier hath fought for all this while? He hath fought to enslave himself, to give power to men of riches, men of estates, to make him a perpetual slave'. (71). Ireton in reply suggested that men had fought against the principle 'that one man's will must be a law'. Laws were to be made by the representatives of those with an interest in the country, and there was a sense in which this was in everybody's interest, for all would be governed better. Answering Rainsborough's quip that liberty and property could not stand together, Ireton made two points. There was a sense in which the two were compatible, for 'the liberty of all those that have the permanent interest in the kingdom' was provided by the constitution. Equally, however, it was true that 'liberty cannot be provided for in a general sense' because property in itself destroyed the perfect liberty found in nature (72–3).

Eventually voices suggesting compromise positions were heard. Maximilian Petty was one:

> I conceive the reason why we would exclude apprentices, or servants, or those that take alms, is because they depend upon the will of other men and should be afraid to displease. For servants and apprentices, they are included in their masters, and so for those that receive alms from door to door.   (83)

That was a marked change from his initial endorsement of manhood suffrage. It seems to be likely that agreement was reached, with few dissenters, on 29 October to recommend a franchise extended to all save 'servants or beggars'.[39] The Debates left a lasting impression on the Levellers, who had Ireton to thank for instilling at least some political realism into their public statements. After this time they abandoned their earlier straightforward commitment to universal manhood suffrage, and consistently denied that they were advocates of the levelling of men's estates.[40] The petition of 11 September 1648 demanded of the Commons that 'you would have bound your selves and all future Parliaments from abolishing propriety, levelling mens Estats, or making all things common'.[41] In the *Manifestation* Walwyn again responded to the slur, pointing out the statement on the September petition, and denying that the Levellers were interested in 'taking away the proper right and Title that every man has to what is his own'. Authority to do such a thing was reserved from the people's representative, though – less reassuringly – it remained possible if 'there did preced an universall assent thereunto from all and every one of the People'.[42] The idea seems to have been that property rights were of an individuated kind, so that although they could be alienated (unlike, say, one's liberty of conscience), each individual was required explicitly to alienate his or her own right. Thus only universal consent could create genuine social levelling.[43]

The Putney Debates are rare enough as a record of political debate in the seventeenth century; they are even rarer as the record of a group of politicians changing their minds.

Two things, however, conspired to destroy the Levellers' chance of having any influence on a new political settlement for the nation at this time. The increasing threat they posed to army discipline began to encourage the army's leaders to take a much firmer line against them, and alarmed many enough to encourage a closing of ranks against them. But, secondly, on 11 November 1647 the king escaped from army custody at Hampton Court and fled to the Scots. Without the king, the grandees had no one with whom to negotiate a settlement. During 1648, England returned to civil war. But the Levellers' involvement with the army does seem to have encouraged a greater degree of political organisation. Nearly all the evidence we have of the Levellers as an organised political grouping comes from 1648 and 1649.[44] Before that they were at best an association of pamphleteers who wrote in one another's support, and issued occasional petitions together. The army and Putney were not so much subject to Leveller influence as the creators of the Leveller movement.[45] Better organised, the Levellers were able during 1648 to keep up a propaganda and petitioning campaign; but it was after the second defeat of the king that they again found themselves involved in negotiations to settle England's future. Indeed, though 1647 has attracted more attention, it was late in 1648 that the Levellers came closest to success, because the army leadership – above all Ireton – now became willing to endorse their demands with much less equivocation than in 1647.[46] On 15 November 1648 the council of officers agreed to accept Ireton's *Remonstrance* as a collective statement of their position. Its final version was modified slightly in the face of Leveller objections, though not as much as they would have liked; and the debate that followed is particularly helpful in placing the Levellers in relation to the Independency of Ireton, and in assessing their political realism at their moment of highest opportunity.[47]

Remarkable in the *Remonstrance* was the opening willingness to face an unpleasant truth, that if the people were asked to consent to government in 1648 they would be unlikely to support anything acceptable to either the Levellers or the officers of the New Model Army. The *Remonstrance* was, therefore, written in the language of *interest*, opposing the public interest to the interest of particular men, parties or the king, but also suggesting that serving the public interest was, in difficult circumstances, more important than gaining the people's consent.[48] The public interest, 'in relation to common right and reason', required 'a common and supreme council or parliament . . . of deputies or representers, freely chosen by them, with as much equality as may be'. The elections were to be 'successive or renewed', either at fixed intervals or when called by a 'subordinate standing officer or council'. The supreme council was to have sovereign authority in all civil matters, including the power to make and repeal law and the power to make war and peace. There was no appeal beyond its authority to 'any created standing power', such as that of a king. Ordinary government would thus be conducted according to laws made by the people's representatives. Nonetheless, the supreme council would also have certain 'extraordinary or arbitrary powers' (cols 1086–7). Nothing more clearly distinguished Ireton from the Levellers, for whom – as we have seen – *all* arbitrary authority was condemned on theological grounds. In this lay the roots of the Levellers' disillusioned attacks on the new republican Commonwealth during 1649.

The *Remonstrance* was explicit about what that arbitrary power might amount to. The supreme council could exercise its extraordinary powers

> where they shall see cause to assume and exercise the same, in a matter which they find necessary for the safety or well-being of the people. . . . [A]nd especially, since the having of good constitutions and making of good laws, were of little security or avail, without power to punish those that break or go about to overthrow them, and many such cases may happen, wherein the former laws have not prescribed or provided sufficiently for that purpose, or the ordinary officers intrusted therewith may not be faithful, or not able, duly to execute such punishments on many offenders in that kind.

In these circumstances, the supreme council 'may call such offenders to account', even when the offence is not 'provided against by particular laws, yet against the general law of reason or nations, and the vindication of the public interest, to require justice' (cols 1087–8). The way was cleared for the trial of the king by an arbitrary authority executing natural law in order to preserve the public interest. Contrast that with the Leveller view: 'where there is no Law, there can be no Transgression; . . . Can a Law be justified, when made after the offence be committed, to punish the offender?'[49]

There was an element of ruthlessness in this, but it was a ruthlessness that grew out of Ireton's bleak assessment of the particular situation faced by the army in late 1648. The *Remonstrance* lukewarmly endorsed the demands of the Leveller's petition of 11 September 1648 (col. 1126); but it nonetheless embedded the whole scheme of seeking an agreement of the people in a context far different from any hitherto imagined by the Levellers themselves. Certainly, the king's misgovernment had meant that he now forfeited the trust of the people. His actions made him 'guilty of all the innocent blood spilt' in the wars; he had sought to serve not 'the public interest of the people', but 'the interest of his [own] will or power' (cols 1091–3). The people had now won 'a full conquest' over their king, and by right of conquest – one of the king's own principles – they could do with him as they saw proper (col. 1096). There was, however, a catch. Ireton was frank in his assessment of the fact that, amongst that very people in whose name the king had been conquered, he had acquired the reputation of being a lover of peace and freedom who would restore 'trade and plenty'. If Charles were given the chance again to foment civil war, the people might support him, blaming parliament for the excessive exactions they had already borne (cols 1102–4). The risk was that the king could win back all that he had lost, supported by the people (cols 1104–6). Ireton did not shirk from telling parliament that its purpose was to defend liberties, 'for the preservation whereof you will be forced to press upon them in particular matters, against their present ease and freedoms', while knowing that 'the people . . . [are] ordinarily more affected with the latter, as more immediate and sensible, and less with the former, which are more remote and to them less intelligible'. The king might very well be able to exploit this preference for 'present ease' to win popular support (cols 1105–6).

Given that analysis, how was an *agreement of the people* possible? The king had to be brought to justice, that was clear (cols 1110–13, 1120–1); but the problems then began. The *Remonstrance* called, like the Levellers, for parliament to return authority as soon as possible 'into the hands of the people, for and from whom you received it'. Annual or biennial parliaments would be elected on a fairer franchise, though crucially this would exclude those 'who have engaged, or shall engage, in war, against the Right of the parliament, and Interest of the kingdom therein, or have adhered to the enemies thereof' and those 'who shall oppose, or not join in agreement to this Settlement' (col. 1124). Virtually all power, except that to alter the terms of the settlement itself, was to be entrusted to this new representative. The chief exception was that monarchy could only be restored in an explicitly elective form without the power to veto legislation. The people, after the event, would be asked to subscribe to this settlement, put to them in an 'Agreement of the People' by the new representative (cols 1124–5). An executive Council of State would also be appointed by the representative to handle matters too mundane or particular to be suitable matter for the deliberations of a large legislative assembly (col. 1126). There was no provision made for liberty of conscience, and indeed the whole thrust of Ireton's writing was to separate civil from religious demands. The interest of the Godly might coincide with the people's interest in parliament for much of the time, but the two were not the same thing (see especially, cols 1090–1, 1093, 1095).

Ireton's solution had all the virtues and all the vices of simplicity. He would exclude from political rights anyone who would not subscribe the new settlement, and that settlement would only be put to the people after the institutions essential to it were already in place. That was some distance from the sort of agreement imagined by the Levellers, who before this time genuinely hoped to win the consent of a broad spectrum of the political nation. Arguably, though, Ireton's was the only possible 'consent' to be sought – rather, imposed – in a nation as divided as England was at the end of 1648. The army *Remonstrance* was submitted to the Commons on 20 November, but its programme was decisively rejected on 5 December. The inevitable followed, and on the following day, 6 December 1649, the army purged the Commons of members unwilling to support its plans for settlement without the king. In the wake of Pride's Purge, a committee of sixteen (which had been set up in mid-November) – four Levellers, four army officers, four MPs (of whom only Henry Marten regularly attended) and four London Independents – got down to the serious business of drafting the nation's new constitution, a second *Agreement of the People*. The resulting document showed that the Levellers were now prepared to approve an agreement that combined elements of their 1647 programme and elements of Ireton's more ruthless proposals. The Levellers published the committee's draft under the title *Foundations of Freedom* (15 December), but it was at the same time being debated and revised in the imperfectly-recorded Whitehall debates that ran through December and into January 1649.[50] The revised document, known usually as the Officers' *Agreement*, was finished by 15 January, and presented to the Commons on the 20th.[51] It was then published under the title *A Petition from His Excellency Thomas, Lord Fairfax*.

The second *Agreement*, produced by the council of sixteen (but dominated by the Levellers), required that the Long Parliament be dissolved before the end of April 1649. A new Representative (of 300 members) would then be elected, on a franchise redistributed so as to reflect better the geographical distribution of the population. The detailed franchise proposals clearly revealed Ireton's impact. The vote was to be given to male householders over 21, but excluded from it would be servants, wage-earners and those in receipt of arms. Also excluded for a time – as in the *Remonstrance* – were those 'who have adhered to, or assisted the King', and those 'who shall make or joyn in, or abet any forcible opposition against this Agreement'; while those that 'shall not subscribe it [the Agreement] before the time limited, for the end of this Parliament, shall not have a Vote in the next Election'.[52] The practicality of these exclusions was reinforced by a very detailed set of provisions outlining the electoral mechanisms to be employed (297–9). The *Agreement*'s air of hard-headed realism in the search for limited government was further enhanced by a requirement that laws could only be passed with a quorum of at least 153 members present, by the requirement that the Representative appoint a Council of State 'for the managing of publick affairs', and by stipulating that neither those in receipt of public money (including army officers) nor practising lawyers could be elected to the Representative (299). The power of the Representative was supreme – a unicameral sovereign legislature – extending 'to the enacting, altering, repealing and declaring of laws; to the erecting and abolishing Officers of courts of Justice, and to whatsoever is not in this Agreement excepted or reserved from them' (299). Reserved from the Representative's authority, however, was religion: it was forbidden from interfering in any way 'to compel . . . any person to any thing in or about matters of Faith, Religion or Gods Worship', or to restrain people from professing their faith as they saw fit (it was, however, allowed to give non-compulsive guidelines for public worship) (300). There followed prohibitions against impressment, the requirement for equality before the law, and the protection of property rights (300–1).

The reservation guaranteeing liberty of conscience was the subject of debate on the only day of the Whitehall debates for which we have a full account. That discussion, of 14 December, is fully as impressive as the Putney debate on the franchise.[53] The debate presupposed much agreement amongst the debaters (in good part because religious Presbyterians refused to attend). They agreed, in particular, that the civil magistrate did *not* have a *compulsive* authority to force people to worship in the established state church. What they disagreed about was whether or not the magistrate had a *restrictive* authority to forbid religious practices that were sinful or heretical. A start on expressing the Leveller view was made by John Wildman. '[A]ll authority hath been broken in pieces' by God's judgement. What was now needed was 'a new way of settling this nation, which is a new constitution'. As the Agreement was envisaged by the Levellers, it amounted to deciding 'what power the people will agree to give to the magistrates that they will set over them to be their governors' (127–8). The magistrates were not determining the scope of their own authority: they were being told what authority was entrusted to them. That was not good enough for the future regicide Colonel John Hewson. It was not a question of trust, for it was doubtful whether individuals had the capacity to trust the magistrate with religious authority. Rich, supporting him, baldly asserted, 'whether we can empower him [the magistrate] over our consciences; it's impossible'. No, the key question was whether the magistrate might inflict civil punishments for what he took to be religious offences. Of course, such punishments would have no effect on the conscience; but that was no ground on which to welcome them (129). Lilburne, at that point, tried to turn the question back to 'whether it be requisite to express their trust positively in this Agreement, yea or no?' (129).

Ireton adumbrated, in a majestically sweeping statement, what he understood to be at the heart of the contentions of the 1640s. As in the *Remonstrance*, Ireton's argument was one that laid aside religious disagreements, and concentrated on the legal–constitutional. It was a mistake, Ireton argued, to suggest that the struggle in which men had been engaged during the 1640s was one entered into 'for want of knowing what power magistracy hath had'. The real question concerned the purposes to which power was put. All might agree that what Ireton called the 'supreme trust' was the granting to magistrates power in 'all things necessary for the preserving of peace'; but not all realised the further implications of the point. Admittedly, there were also those who saw liberty rather than peace as the chief end of government. They were wrong. Such a perspective implied that 'I am most free when I have nobody to mind me', and that was no foundation for government. You certainly tried to entrust authority to those men best equipped 'for the preserving of peace', and secondarily in ways 'most probable and hopeful for liberty'. But liberty *was* the secondary concern:

> the necessary thing, that which *necessarily* leads all men into civil agreements or contracts, or to make commonwealths, is the necessity of it for preserving peace. Because otherwise, if there were no such thing, but every man left to his own will, men's contrary wills, lusts and passions would lead every one to the destruction of another, and to seek all the ways of fencing himself against the jealousies of another.   (130)

How did that help to resolve the uncertainties surrounding the magistrate's authority in matters of conscience? Ireton suggested that the matter could be resolved by the realisation that the magistrate had to be given whatever power was needed for him to preserve peace; and that the magistrate *could not* have authority over consciences.

> All civil power whatsoever, either in natural or civil things, is not to bind men's judgments. The judgment of the Parliament is the

supremest council in the world, [but] cannot bind my judgment in anything, and whether you limit it to civil things or natural things, the effect of that power is that he hath not power to conclude your inward, but [only] your outward man; the effect of all is but the placing of a power in which we would acquiesce for peace' sake. (130–1)[54]

As his *Remonstrance* had clearly shown, Ireton (like Henry Parker before him[55]) was not particularly concerned about the limits on governmental authority. Rulers sometimes needed to be arbitrary. That did not in any respect mean that they had authority to meddle with men's consciences, for the inner man was in fact beyond the reach of human authority. From such a perspective, the entire debate on liberty of conscience seemed somehow to miss the point. There was no debate over 'limitations' or the character of 'the supreme trust': instead 'we have not known in what persons or parties, or what council, the trust hath lain'. Was it in the king alone, in the king-in-parliament, or in parliament alone? Settlement could be reached when it was clearly laid down 'in what persons, or succession of persons, the supreme trust doth lie' (131).

Ireton accepted that the debate in which he was involved did raise a subsidiary question that he needed to tackle. Even if it was accepted that the civil magistrate was given 'a trust to them for the outward man, and with acquiescence but for peace' sake', it still remained necessary to decide explicitly whether 'it be fit for us to commit a trust . . . for this purpose, concerning spiritual things as concerning civil things'. That is to say, should the civil magistrate be able to punish the outward man for religious offences? Conscience, of course, did not come into it. Having thus narrowed the question, Ireton proceeded to suggest that it should not be answered in the *Agreement*. We should 'make agreement for our civil rights upon those things wherein we are agreed'. No matter what was put about religion in the *Agreement*, it would cause some to refuse to subscribe. In any case it was unnecessary. Men might designate the person who would rule over them; but God determined the scope of his authority. As for power in religious matters, leave it unmentioned, then '[i]f he have it in him of God, then your Agreement cannot take it from him; if he have it not, then it is not in the Agreement' (131–3). Rhetorically, Ireton's position functioned as a way of seeking *settlement*. All the contentious issues could safely be left unmentioned: God would sort them out! While 'it be in man . . . rightfully to elect and designate the persons', their duties in matters of justice and religion 'are not to be determined by those that commit the trust to them'. Just as the extent of the magistrate's civil authority was essentially to be left undetermined in the Agreement, so too his authority in religion should be left to his own 'judgment' and conscience (that is, to his understanding of what God required of him) (133).

Ireton saw matters of conscience and the magistrate's role in policing religion very differently from the Levellers, as was very apparent when a speaker – perhaps Richard Overton – refused to accept Ireton's distinction between the inward and the outward man. '[I]f he [i.e. the magistrate] hath power over my body, he hath power to keep me at home when I should go abroad to serve God' (139). Religion was not just the concern of the inward man. It was essential, therefore, to settle the question immediately. Ireton again tried to clarify matters. He as much as anyone was opposed to any suggestion that magistrates could punish 'any man for his conscience'; that was not the question. The real question was '[w]hether you shall make such a provision for men that are conscientious, that they may serve God according to their light and conscience, as shall necessarily debar any kind of restraint on anything that any man will call religion'. Do we wish to allow men 'to practise idolatry, to practise atheism, and anything that is against the light of God?' (143). That statement does something to substantiate Gentle's claim that Ireton 'was at all times animated by the vision of a godly commonwealth', and opposed religious pluralism on that ground;[56] but it also serves to remind us of Ireton's 'Hobbism'. If you do not allow the magistrate to regulate the public face of religion, then you cripple his capacity to preserve peace and order. What really bothered Ireton was that the magistrate, in trying to preserve peace might be prevented from restraining 'anything which men will *call* religion' (146). There was a risk of giving immunity to men's action whenever they cared to invoke conscience in their defence.

And yet both Ireton and the Levellers found room for an autonomous civil sphere in which men could engage in political life on terms chosen (within limits) by themselves. This view was not, however, shared by all, and the Whitehall debates enable us as well to get a clearer sense of the distance between Levellers (and Independents) and the radicalism of sectarian enthusiasm. Joshua Sprigge insisted that the goal of seeking agreement failed to recognise the primacy of God's activity. 'It is God's design, I say, to bring forth the civil government, and all things here below, in the image and resemblance of things above.' To do as has been done in England, to 'have measured religion and the appearances of God according to rules and ends of policy, it hath been the ruin of all states. I conceive that that is the account that is to be given of the condition that this kingdom is brought unto at this time'. That sort of religious radicalism itself warns us against unmasking, against looking for social, economic or political objectives within the religious language. On the contrary its radicalism arose from the very willingness to sacrifice all worldly institutions before God's wishes. The key thing, now that God had 'thus taken us apieces' and 'brought forth the government of the sword', was to wait, allowing God to act. Men do not have the power to settle things with their Agreements of the People. 'God will bring forth a New Heaven and a New Earth [Revelation, 21.1].' In the meantime the only thing to do was 'restrain the magistrate' so that he could not persecute God's people (134–6). Ireton, Sprigge later said, had forgotten that the only antidote to heresy was 'the breaking forth of Christ, in the minds and spirits of men' (144). Dr Parker suggested that 'under the New testament' it seemed doubtful that Christ had given any power over religion to the magistrate (145), to which Ireton retorted that it was 'not the business of Christ . . . to erect kingdoms of the world'. The Old Testament provided the proper model for a Christian politics (145–6).

The rival claims of Old and New Testament to serve as a basis for political theory merged with a more detailed discussion of the Decalogue. Philip Nye acknowledged that to talk in broad terms of 'matters of conscience' raised exactly the spectre that troubled the Commissary-General. Anything could be defended as a matter of conscience. The discussion should be narrowed to such matters 'as concern the First Table' (i.e. the first four of the Ten Commandments, laying down the duties of man to God, as distinct from the remainder, which laid down the duties of man to man) (146–7). Ireton took up Nye's suggestion (148–9). Another argued that the very nature of the commandments of the First Table required their enforcement by the civil magistrate, 'and therefore it properly concerns the princes of the people, especially those that know God, to restrain corrupt worship' (153). Nye, more guardedly, accepted that the magistrate had no authority relative to true religion, but might restrain false religion (153–4). Ireton supported Gilbert's argument, repeating that the Old Testament provided the proof for his position. Furthermore, he suggested that the New Testament did not alter the situation, for the sins defined in the First Table were understood by men through natural reason, and thus could be committed and restrained at all times (154–6). The Decalogue was thus not simply a set of revealed laws, or God's positive commands to his peculiar people: it was embedded in the law of nature itself, and the commands known to all human peoples. So Ireton's position here was again Hobbesian rather than Mosaic: blasphemy, idolatry and atheism were to be punished because the sovereign enforced the law of nature, not because he was the mediator of specific divine commands.

Hewson among others responded with the view that it was not obvious by the light of nature what exactly constituted offences against the First Table. The magistrate could use any power that he had to punish such offences arbitrarily and extend it at will. Consequently, 'God hath not given a command to all magistrates to destroy idolatry, for in consequence it would destroy the world.' Given that magistrates were as fallible as anyone else, perhaps more so, 'the probability is greater that he will destroy what is good than prevent what is evil' (161). Here is the Leveller distrust of fallible human authority, and its tendency to usurp the place of God. There was no detailed record for later parts of the debate, though we know that on 13 January (just before the Officers' *Agreement* was finalised) Ireton took the opportunity to note again his distance from the enthusiasts. He recognised their millenarian expectation: 'it is not the hand of men that will take away the power of monarchy in the earth, but if ever it be destroyed, it will be by the breaking forth of the power of God amongst men' (172). In the meantime, however, politics was a human business, and magistrates would have their power regulated by consent or by the sword.

In recognition of that fact, the officers presented their revised *Agreement* to the Rump on 20 January 1649.[57] The revisions were numerous, but mainly in the direction of making the proposals more practicable, more specific or more concrete. The vote was no longer denied to any who refused to subscribe the *Agreement*, but only (for seven years) to Royalists.[58] The most significant change occurred as a result of the debates on 14 December. The reserve on religion was dropped, and replaced by a clause specifying the power of the civil magistrate in religious matters. There was to be a state church, maintained from the public treasury rather than from tithes. Its key function was to combat heresy through teaching and instruction. The new representative could construct that state church as it saw fit, save that 'Popery or prelacy be not held forth as the publike way'. No one should be compelled to attend services of the state church. Those who 'professe Faith in God by Jesus Christ . . . shall not be restrained from, but shall be protected in the profession of their Faith and exercise of Religion according to their Consciences in any place', unless they infringed the civil liberty of others, harmed the public peace (one can hear Ireton's voice in this), or were supporters of popery or prelacy (348–9). There was no blanket approval of liberty of conscience. Nonetheless, it does not really make sense to call either the Officers' or the second *Agreement* blueprints for 'a dictatorship of the Godly'.[59] That underestimates the degree to which the two key shapers of the documents, Ireton and the Levellers, were able to envisage a sphere for an autonomous civil politics, and it underestimates too the distance that both kept between themselves and the radical politics of the genuine Godly enthusiasts. If there was to be a dictatorship, it was of the political Independents and their Leveller allies.

That, though, was not to be. The Rump ignored the *Agreement* presented to them, and the officers did not bother to remind them of its existence.[60] John Lilburne, however, was not so coy. He was unhappy with the Officers' *Agreement*, but nonetheless remained wedded to the principle that popular consent, obtained by an agreement of the people, was the only means of legitimating a new political order. His rejection of the execution of the king was derived from just that principle. Lilburne claimed to have been invited to become one of the king's judges. He responded to the invitation:

> arguing . . . very stifly, that upon their own principles, which led them to look upon all legall authority in England as now broken, they could be no better than murderers in taking away the Kings life though never so guilty of the crimes they charged upon him; for as justice ought to be done, especially for bloud, which they then principally charge upon him; so said I, and still say, It ought to be done justly. . . . And therefore I pressed again and again, seeing themselves confess'd all legal Authority in England was broke, that they would stay his triall till a new and equall free Representative upon the Agreement of the well-affected people, that had not fought against their Liberties, rights and Freedoms, could be chosen and sit, and then either try him thereby, or else by their judges sitting in the Court called Kings Bench.[61]

The second of the Levellers' moments had passed. At the end of February 1649 Lilburne's *Englands New Chains Discovered* unleashed their attack on the army grandees, whom they took to be the new rulers of the nation, for their betrayal of the cause. The Levellers had some success in winning support within the army, but the main consequence of that was to precipitate decisive action by the army's leaders. Discipline was restored; the civilian Levellers were arrested.[62] When they issued their third and final *Agreement* (1 May 1649), Lilburne, Walwyn and Overton were all in the Tower. Freed from any need to engage in political compromise, the third *Agreement* was the most extreme set of Leveller demands. In that, it was a document of defeat. Unlike the other *Agreements*, the third incorporated many of the Levellers' social demands, always more prominent when they were more distant from real power. The excise and customs were to be abolished; so too were tithes and imprisonment for debt.[63] Parishioners were now to choose their own ministers, and there was a sweeping commitment to liberty of conscience (408, 405). For the first time they demanded that the Representative be elected annually (404–5). Servants, those in receipt of alms, and Royalists were denied a voice in election (the last group for ten years only) (402–3). That last provision is perhaps the key to the Levellers' failure: consent and free choice were fundamental to Leveller politics, the only way of avoiding arbitrary government; but who could really conceive that any large number of people would consent to Leveller principles in 1649? In a deeply divided nation, how could an agreement of the people be forged? Not even the exclusion of Royalists would be sufficient, as Ireton and many others must have known. The Levellers' best chance of success came when Ireton took up the language of agreement as a basis for settlement; it was gone when he perceived that the Levellers' own intransigence, evident in the Whitehall debates and in the pamphlet campaign of 1649, contributed to making agreement unreachable. They remain the most *political* of the radical groups, eloquent advocates of democratic principles that ensured their defeat in a world hostile to democracy.

Religious Radicalism

Towards the end of the Whitehall debates, the future Fifth Monarchist Colonel Thomas Harrison gave his verdict on the *Agreement* that was about to be submitted to the Rump. Many men, he said, now believe that the time had come when

> the powers of this world shall be given into the hands of the Lord and his Saints, that this is the day, God's own day, wherein he is coming forth in glory in the world, and he doth put forth himself very much by his people, and he says, in that day wherein he will thresh the mountains, he will make use of Jacob as that threshing instrument.[64]

It was hardly to be wondered at, then, if such men thought that the proposals for agreement amongst the people were flawed because they 'seem[ed] to put power into the hands of the men of the world when God doth wrest it out of their hands'. It was clear that Harrison himself, in good part, shared that view. And yet he was still willing to defend the Agreement as showing the world 'that we seek not for ourselves but for [all] men'. Nonetheless, it would fail in its purposes: 'I think that God doth purposely design it shall fall short of that end we look for, because he would have us know our peace, our agreement shall be from God, and not from men' (178).

Embedded in these remarks was the central paradox that structured religious radicalism. A powerful sense of God's activity in the world made it possible for people to envisage radical change; but it simultaneously challenged their sense of the human capacity to bring about change through political activity.[65] No one could resist God's plans. Furthermore, who could be so presumptuous as to assume that God required human help? That did not exhaust the problems faced in attempting to erect a politics on the assumption of an activist God. A contemporary critic of Godly politics raised many of the key questions very effectively.[66] With Hobbesian scepticism, Edward Johnson asked:

> Whether your apprehension of Christ's Kingdom had its beginning in our late Revolutions ... be a sufficient Ground to debarr the Nation from their share in Government? And why our Revolutions of late years are more an evidence of Christ's Kingdom, then those in former years; or the Revolutions in other Nations [like Holland, Poland, Germany and France]?[67]

To the unpersuaded, the claim to privileged religious understanding looked unbearably subjective and arbitrary. Why, in particular, was England to be singled out? 'In what speciall sense can it be said, that the Government of this Nation, more then other Nations is given to Christ, since his Government ... is to be Universall?' (4) Johnson raised, furthermore, the crucial *political* problem of agency, which unsettled Harrison's position at Whitehall: 'Whose work is to take the Government from Men, and give it to Christ, whether the Work of Men, or of God?' If God was the agent of change, then 'what is Man that he should interpose in it?' (5). Questions were raised, as at Whitehall, about the applicability of Old Testament examples to modern politics (5). Johnson's questioning also revealed a major division over the subject of *liberty*. As we shall see, religious radicals could understand that concept in a way that looked to others utterly illiberal. Johnson, from a hostile perspective, suggested that for all their talk of freedom, the Godly would 'impose on most of this nation the greatest violence imaginable, the being ... excluded from all right of Government', treating them as the Israelites did the Gibeonites (5). '[W]hilst you are pleading for the Freedome and Rule of Christians, you adventure their utmost Vassallage' (6). This is an unsympathetic view, but an examination of the radicals' own writings confirms many of Johnson's perceptions.

Religious radicalism was at its height in the years following the execution of the king, the beginning of a period of intense radical millenarian expectation. At least one of the Leveller leaders (William Walwyn), though not a millenarian, shared many of the concerns and attitudes of these radicals, and there are themes that link him firmly to such important radical writers as Abiezer Coppe and other supposed Ranters, Gerrard Winstanley, Lodowicke Muggleton and his ally John Reeve, and Fifth Monarchists like William Aspinwall and John Tillinghast. An attempt can be made to understand the central principles of these religious radicals by examining four such themes: divine agency, antiformalism, practical Christianity, and Christian liberty.

Divine activism

Divine agency was fundamental to religious radicalism. In a world that often favoured renovation over innovation,[68] and in which people had long been encouraged to believe that any effort to destroy the existing social or political order was sinful, the most direct way of legitimating radical change was to argue that it was the work of God. The more extreme an action was, the more likely it was to be defended in terms that invoked divine sovereignty. As we shall see, however, there was a little more to it than this. Radical authors were not interested in taking God's name in vain, employing him as a convenient support for their secular schemes. Divine agency was fundamental above all because radicalism was – more than anything else – *about* doing God's will. Everything else was epiphenomenal.

The languages of providence and millennium were pervasive in the 1640s, and before;[69] but an account focused on radicalism can begin with the defences of Pride's Purge and the regicide. The 'official' Independent justification, especially as represented in the Rump's 22 March 1649 *Declaration*, was conducted largely in legal–constitutional terms; but in the wider body of polemic a quite different tone can gradually be heard.[70] Providentialist themes were common in the writings of the defenders of the Engagement oath required by the Commonwealth,[71] but even in those defences that kept largely to more familiar ground there are attempts at religious justification. John Canne (a millenarian, and later to be a Fifth Monarchist) said of the regicides that 'God doth approve their work, and owns it, so he will defend them.'[72] Another Independent work placed its arguments in broader perspective: 'But the lord is now risen up and doing his great work, throwing down and breaking to pieces the proud powers of the earth, both civil and ecclesiastical.'[73] The 22 March *Declaration* itself noted 'the blessing of God' on republics, and observed that – so far –

he had also 'miraculously owned the justness of their cause'.[74] That perspective was to be further developed in a later *Declaration*, which found 'the good hand of God . . . [to have] been that principally which hath supported us'.[75]

All of these works kept religious argumentation on a close reign, tending to suggest at most that God gave *ex post facto* approval to actions justified on other grounds. But they helped to create a climate in which God was seen to be closely interesting himself in the public affairs of England, and thus a foundation on which radicals might build. Gerrard Winstanley was prepared to encourage men to take the Oath of Engagement to the Commonwealth on the grounds that the Rump, in declaring England 'a free Common-wealth', had promised to restore the English people 'to their Creation right' and was thus committed to ensuring that 'the land of England shall be a common Treasury to all English men without respect of persons: even as the severall portions of Canaan were the proper Birth-right and livelihood of such and such a Tribe'.[76] The full theological underpinnings of this position, however, were revealed only in some of Winstanley's other writings.[77]

Winstanley's language was permeated with a sense of God's activity. As one scholar has recently put it, God was seen by Winstanley as 'an infinite source of power' using man 'as a medium'.[78] That was not only a concept of God that undermined any strong sense of human agency, but one that was also difficult fully to express. As a result, Winstanley's very language itself warns us against the attempt to decode his religion in order to discover underlying political or social slogans.[79] The key question posed by Winstanley is: 'Can the immanence of the spirit be made into a robust and lasting social practice?'[80] – a better way of putting it than was evident in the debate about whether the digging communities, formed by Winstanley and his associates at St George's Hill, Walton and Cobham (both in Surrey) between April 1649 and April 1650, were intended to facilitate social change or were simply symbolic of the spirit rising within individual Diggers.[81] In August 1649 Winstanley himself tried to explain:

> Not a full year since, being quiet at my work, my heart was filled with sweet thoughts, and many things were revealed to me which I never read in books, nor heard from the mouth of any flesh, and when I began to speak of them, some people could not bear my words, and amongst those revelations this was one: that the earth shall be made a common treasury of livelihood to whole mankind, without respect of persons; and I had a voice within me bade me declare it all abroad, which I did obey, for I declared it by word of mouth wheresoever I came. Then I was made to write a little book called *The new Law of*

righteousness, and therein I declared it; yet my mind was not at rest, because nothing was acted, and thoughts run in me that words and writings were all nothing and must die, for action is the life of all, and if thou dost not act, thou dost nothing. Within a little time I was made obedient to the word in that particular likewise; for I took my spade and went and broke the ground upon George Hill in Surrey, thereby declaring freedom to the creation, and that the earth must be set free from entanglements of lords and landlords, and that it shall become a common treasury to all, as it was first made and given to the sons of men.[82]

On this account, Winstanley's digging was a way of *declaring* the commands of God communicated through the indwelling spirit. It was an action continuous with the act of writing, for both were primarily declarations of a message; and it is notable that Winstanley portrayed his compulsion to dig in terms that stressed his own *passivity*: 'I was made obedient to the word.'

That stress on passive obedience is borne out by *The New Law of Righteousnes* itself. Winstanley had announced in it that, 'I heard [in a trance] these words, *Worke together. Eat bread together,* declare this all abroad.'[83] It was in obedience to divine command that Winstanley wrote; and the society produced by this simple new law of righteousness would itself be characterised by perfect obedience. 'For every one shal know the Law, and every one shal obey the Law' (198). Indeed, it was not clear that human agency would be the cause of change at all. Winstanley thus declared his obedience to God's command, and his trust that in some way God would ensure the necessary action. In writing, Winstanley claimed, he 'obeyed the command of the spirit' and 'when the Lord doth show unto me the place and manner, how he wil have us that are called common people, to manure and work upon the common Lands, I wil then go forth and declare it in my action' (194–5).

Winstanley did not have to wait long on his God. The Diggers' initial manifesto took up and clarified a number of the themes already raised. The time had come to undo the Fall; but not by political or military means.

And we shall not do this by force of arms, we abhor it, for that is the work of the Midianites, to kill one another; but by obeying the Lord of Hosts, who hath revealed himself in us and to us, by labouring the earth in righteousness together, to eat our bread with the sweat of our brows, neither giving hire nor taking hire, but working together and eating together as one man or as one house of Israel restored

from bondage. And so by the power of reason, the law of righteousness in us, we endeavour to lift up the creation from that bondage of
civil property which it groans under.[84]

Here (and indeed throughout his writings) Winstanley consistently
embraced two sides of several sets of polarities: God was immanent and
transcendent, 'revealing himself in us and to us'; the Diggers were
obeying the Lord of Hosts *and* removing the bondage of private property from God's creation. That latter duality was replicated in the first of
Winstanley's reasons for undertaking the communal digging of St
George's Hill: 'that we may work in righteousness, and lay the foundation of making the earth a common treasury for all' (84). For
Winstanley, that was *one* reason, not two. As analysed by Winstanley,
private property was chiefly to be condemned because those who
possessed it could not be in a condition of righteousness. Changes to
social relationships and the material fabric of human existence were the
flickering and shadowy reflections of a spiritual drama. Commanded
'by vision, voice and revelation', the Diggers were compelled to live
without private property. If we accept private property, 'we own the
curse'. Three consequences followed from private possession, and they
involved breaches of the Ten Commandments: oppression, murder and
theft. '[L]andlords have thus stolen the earth from their fellow creatures, that have an equal share with them by law of reason and creation'
(84–6). Winstanley thus represented Filmer's flip-side: both of them
believed that if the earth was once held in common, then there was no
morally acceptable method by which the institution of private property
could have come into existence. Only a succession of violent conquests
– the most recent being the Norman – had enabled some men to
possess large tracts of land while others possessed none (86). The
Diggers' hopes for success lay not in the action itself, but in the fact that
'the spirit is upon his resurrection' (91). '[T]he King of Righteousness
is rising to rule in and over the earth' (93).

Private property had to be rejected because those who possessed it,
and indeed those who worked the land for them, accepted the fact of
inequality within God's creation. But God had made all of his human
creation equal, and it was as sinful to accept that one was inferior to
others as to claim superiority. The sin that underlay this view, as
Winstanley's account of the Fall made clear, was *covetousness*. In the
beginning, 'the great creator Reason made the earth to be a common
treasury'. All people were equal, for 'every single man, male and
female, is a perfect creature of himself'. But with time 'human flesh . . .
began to delight himself in the objects of the creation, more than in
the spirit reason and righteousness . . . and he fell into blindness of

mind and weakness of heart'. As a result 'selfish imagination . . . working with covetousness, did set up one man to teach and rule over another; and thereby the spirit was killed'. Private property was a consequence of this spiritual fall: 'hereupon the earth . . . was hedged into enclosures by the teachers and rulers, and the others were made servants and slaves' (77–8).

Winstanley's reference to 'teachers' makes it very plain that at the heart of his view of the Fall was a belief that it consisted in an over-valuation of the external material world: that was what covetousness *meant*. It meant a fascination with the material world, *but also* a willingness to look for the rules of morality in the material husk of a fallen world. That is to say, it meant also the willingness to follow teachers (of which the paramount example was the clergy) rather than the indwelling spirit. '[T]his evil was brought upon us through his own covetousness, whereby he is blinded and made weak, and sees not the law of righteousness in his heart, which is the pure light of reason, but looks abroad for it' (78). The Fall, as he had earlier put it, occurred when man 'sought content from creatures and outward objects'.[85] We hardly do much justice to Winstanley if we, too, locate his priorities somewhere abroad in the world.

This 'radicalism' renders problematic the concept of human political agency, something particularly apparent in Winstanley's *A New-Year's Gift for the Parliament and Army*. In this, his primary stress upon obedience to the instructions of the rising indwelling Christ inhibited his development of any sense of human political capacity. But there was also a tactical element involved, for this helped to portray the Diggers as unthreatening to the interests of property-owners. God, not man, would ensure the success of the Diggers, whose aim was not to transform the world, but to work in righteousness *on land already common or waste*. True Levellers they might have been; but the only land to be levelled was, you might say, already flat.

The main concern of the *New-Year's Gift* was to seek defence against the local landowners who threatened to destroy the digging communities. Certain statements taken in isolation do sound threatening, as when Winstanley urged landlords, 'come, come, love the diggers and make restitution of their land you hold from them'.[86] But the tract did not actually threaten landlords with expropriation. Built into it was a three-part hierarchy of what we might call 'radical activism'.[87] God would in time utterly transform the world; in the meantime the civil authorities could do much to facilitate the process without infringing individual property rights; while individual men must act within the established laws and structures until such time as God altered the conditions of their action. God, rather than man, was the radical activist.

When Winstanley spoke of the universal transformation of the world, he spoke of it as the work of God, who 'is the power of universal love, leading people into all truth, teaching everyone to do as he would be done unto'. Christ himself 'will cast out the curse' (162). Transformation of the earth was not to be achieved – or attempted – by human authorities or individuals. Winstanley addressed his tract to the Commons and the army (many of his Digger writings were addressed to established authorities); but he called upon those bodies not radically to alter the world; instead, they were invited (a) to protect the Diggers' legal rights in the face of threats from local landlords; and (b) to fulfil the promises made during the 1640s, and especially by the two laws of 1649 which abolished kingly power (of the earthly variety) and established England as a 'free commonwealth' (161, 167, 183). Those promises, in Winstanley's reading of them, amounted to allowing the poor to dig the commons and waste land, and required England's new rulers to use confiscated Crown and church lands for the good of the whole community. In making these demands, Winstanley went to some length to make it clear that he was neither asking the state to infringe the legal rights of existing landowners, nor demanding for the Diggers more than they were legally entitled to. Their working of common and waste land was justified 'in England's law'. Because of their involvement in the struggles of the 1640s, the people had 'by a lawful purchase or contract' acquired rights in the waste and confiscated Crown and church lands; they had also acquired such rights by their involvement in the lawful conquest of the king; and such rights had been promised to them by the 'two acts of Parliament' of 1649 (181–3). It was the duty of the state, then, to ensure that these rights were protected, and that the Diggers were unmolested in their activities. Finally, the actions of the individual Diggers were limited by respect for the law. All that they asked for was protection sufficient to enable them to go about their lawful business. The digging was not designed in itself to change the world.[88] '[T]he common land is the poor people's property' (168). They might claim that Crown and church land should be added to the stock of common land; but not land in private hands. Winstanley's attack on existing law was not an attack on the law of landed tenure, but on the laws that allowed persecution of the Diggers (169–72), which was contrary to the proper foundation of law, 'reason and equity' (172, 184). The common people had property in the common land, *and* the landlords had property in their enclosures (181). But even under persecution, Winstanley emphasised, the Diggers remained peaceful, 'their spirits resolved to wait upon God' (179). They fought only 'with the spirit of love and patience' (178). God would do the rest, by regenerating their enemies from within 'till their hearts thereby be softened' (174).

Winstanley imagined radical change as the work of God and not of man. *Human* activity was portrayed in the traditional terms of passivity and legalism. God, though, was 'The great Leveller ... [who] shall cause men to beat their swords into ploughshares and spears into pruning hooks, and nations shall learn war no more; and everyone shall delight to let each other enjoy the pleasures of the earth' (204.) That view of Christ was shared by a radical writer who railed even more bitterly against the rich, Abiezer Coppe. Coppe took to himself the very voice of Christ:

Behold, behold, behold, I am the eternall God, the Lord of Hosts, who am that mighty Leveller, am coming (yea even at the doores) to Levell in good earnest, to Levell to some purpose, to Levell with a witnesse, to Levell the Hills with the Valleyes, and to lay the Mountaines low.[89]

Coppe's writing is such that extended quotation is almost the only way of approaching it. Much of its impact is rhetorical, a product of a language designed to render God's presence with great immediacy, and to use that sense of presence as the core of powerful and reiterated calls to repentance.

1.   Thus saith the Lord: Be wise now therefore, O ye Rulers, &c. Be instructed, &c. Kisse the Sunne, &c. Yea, kisse Beggars, prisoners, warme them, feed them, cloathe them, money them, relieve them, take them into your houses, don't serve them as dogs, without doore, &c.

Own them, they are flesh of your flesh, your owne brethren, your owne Sisters, every whit as good (and if I should stand in competition with you) in some degrees better then your selves.

2.   Once more, I say, own them; they are yourself, make them one with you, or else go howling into hell; howle for the miseries that are coming upon you, howle.

The very shadow of levelling, sword-levelling, man-levelling, frighted you, (and who, like yourselves, can blame you, because it shook your Kingdome?) but now the substantiality of levelling is coming.

The Eternal God, the mighty Leveller is comming, yea come, even at the doore; and what will you do in that day.

Repent, repent, repent, Bow down, bow down, bow down, or howle, resigne, or be damned; Bow downe, bow downe, you sturdy Oakes and Cedars, bow downe.   (89–90)

In Coppe's thought, God was the only active agent of change. The rich and powerful, and all of those who accepted the word of Christ without putting it into practice, were warned that if they did not bow down and abase themselves, then this God would ensure their punishment. Abasement meant, primarily, accepting equality with the poor, and doing all that could be done to help them.

Coppe's emphasis on divine agency is so great that there is little room for any effective human political activity. God would radically transform the social order – he will level it – and all that men and women could do was to show whether they were for him or against him. There was no real concern with human institutions, either; only a thoroughly personal emphasis on repentance and charity. Winstanley retained a political and institutional focus, albeit in tension with his primary stress on divine activism; but Coppe dissolved all human politics in the face of the withering, earth shattering power of Christ the Leveller. In that, if not in all other respects, Coppe's thought resembled that of the most successful of the new Interregnum sects, the Quakers. They too can properly be described as apolitical, in spite of the fact that they were widely feared as a threat to social order.[90] That is not to say that the Quakers were not radical, for their attitudes included hostility to the established Church, to the law, to tithes, and to social hierarchy;[91] but God, as the inner light, was the sole agent of change. 'Now the Lord is coming to teach all his freely; and there is no teacher like him':[92] that certainly meant that one should have nothing to do with the professional clergy. It might even justify harassing them; but it justified no more than that. Very revealing of Quaker attitudes was Edward Burrough's attempt to defend them against the charge that they were a threat to the existing social system, *A Message of Instruction*. Emphasis on the inner light led him to adopt a theoretically antinomian position:

> And they that are reconciled to God, whose consciences are exercised towards God in all things, they are not under the law, nor the law hath no power over them; for the law is fulfilled in them by Christ, who teacheth them in all things to walk without offence towards God and all men, in truth and in righteousness to God, and all men; and such the law of man is to defend, and not to judge them; to justify them, and not to condemn them.

That view, however, was coupled with an acceptance of the principle that magistracy was 'an ordinance of God', established 'for the punishing and suppressing of evil-doers'. Clearly, though, Christ's people were not evil-doers, and ought not to be punished for refusing to pay tithes or to doff their hats to social superiors. One might ask how such people could be recognised: 'such as cannot discern and distinguish in such matters, have not the spirit of God'. If you need to ask, then you are not likely to understand the answer, as Louis Armstrong said in another context. Rulers were exhorted 'to put a difference betwixt the precious and the vile'; but there was no challenge to their authority as such. I 'wish well to magistrates', Burrough concluded.[93] Once again, any broader transformation of the world would be God's doing. In the meantime, the Quakers expected protection – certainly not persecution – from the magistrate, no more. It is misleading to see the Quakers as 'quietist',[94] but not so much because they occasionally embraced bits and pieces of the political programmes of Levellers and others. Rather, their belief in the progressive transformation of the world by the operations of Christ gave a framework to their thought that encouraged a general sense of radical change, while still rendering problematic the role of men and women in bringing about that change. The struggle was essentially spiritual, though it might involve physical actions for which the Quakers were persecuted and hated. Like Winstanley, they were more radical the less they concerned themselves with human agency.[95]

Not all millenarians were as patient as Winstanley and the Quakers. The Fifth Monarchy Men, in particular, have often been portrayed as violent fanatics intent on taking matters out of God's hands. Arguably, though, their thought reinforces the main points being made here. John Tillinghast spoke of the process that would bring into being the Fifth Monarchy in terms of an inevitably successful divine agency that would triumph over human passivity and inadequacy. '[I]t is not for us to struggle against the will of God, and the Covenant of God; it [is] good for us to waite upon God for his will in all thing.'[96] What did it mean to wait upon God?

> [W]e are not to waite as Idlers doe for helpe in a ditch, and cry God helpe us, but we are to wait as if we would have it in by our very strifing & strugling, yet notwithstanding there must be a quiet waiting on God for his time, so it should be with us, for this new Covenant mercy; waite for it patiently, be content with it in Gods own time, when he shall bring it forth. . . . (38–9)

As if: this was not a ringing endorsement of the hope to be expected from human action. Indeed it seemed to render such action pointless, something undertaken *as if* it might achieve a result that God, in fact, would produce in his own good time. A later sermon (the third) did, however, make a much more thorough attempt to reconcile divine agency and human. In it Tillinghast scorned the idea that the Saints had no role but 'to pray and to beleive', an idea that was based on the false view that all change would be achieved by Christ *following* his second coming (59–61). There were, Tillinghast explained, two phases of the Fifth Monarchy, the kingdom of stone (of which the type was David's kingdom) and the kingdom of the mountain (of which the type was Solomon's kingdom) (61–3). In the former, the 'Saints are by their Lord Imployed to do some notable service against his coming; which is, *The breaking downe the great Image, the bringing downe all his Enemies*' (62). When this had happened, when Christ's enemies had 'become his footstoole, then shall he come forth and take his king-dome' (76). In this later kingdom of the mountain, the Saints 'shall not so properly worke, but receive' (162). In a later sermon, Tillinghast made the distinction in terms of an initial coming of the spirit to be followed later by the (second) coming of Christ himself (194–5). The coming of the spirit would involve an internal regeneration of men that presumably made them fit to do God's work (191, 197–9, 202). The language in which this was expressed was the conventional Calvinist language that made even the Saints fully dependent on God's actions for their regeneration.

Notable here are three things. First, the role of the Saints even in the kingdom of stone, was portrayed entirely in *negative* terms. They reduced Christ's enemies to submission. The building of a new kingdom remained the work of Christ alone with the Saints preparing the way for it. Such a vision only ambiguously justified the human task of reconstructing the Old Testament polity that was endorsed by other Fifth Monarchists (especially as Tillinghast could not refrain from saying that even the kingdom of stone 'rose by the hand of God alone' – 63). Secondly, because of this negativity there was little incentive for the development of any very clear conception of what human action was to achieve. God would tidy up the mess: it must have been a comforting thought to men living through a world being turned upside down. Of course, all of this also meant that the Fifth Monarchists had no sense of a civil realm in which men were free to make choices. The 'signs of the times', as Tillinghast had it, showed that the last days of the Fourth Monarchy were at hand. The Saints had no choice but to prepare the way for Christ (81ff.). The Saints were to be instructed in Tillinghast's seventh sermon, that they must ensure that they act not at all in their own interest but 'run along with Gods glory onely' (242). Even the slightest mixture of self-interest would taint the purity of their actions so that, in effect, they were being invited to act *against* their own worldly interests. The ability to act 'contrary to his interest' (243) was a sign that the Saint was on the right path. Nor was it right to be 'a meer Statist, a politick man . . . a man to please all men in all things'; the Saint must undertake all actions so that 'he might gaine some to Christ' (245). And thirdly, when Tillinghast spoke of human action, he spoke (like Winstanley) in very traditional ways. He emphasised patience, obedience (to God), submission, duty. They were the same terms in which conformist divines had long portrayed the political capacities of the king's subjects.

Radical writing was thoroughly grounded in a powerful sense of divine agency. The activities of radical groups were undertaken in a world understood to be subject to the commands of a God now increasingly interventionist. This God was about to transform the social and political world beyond all recognition, and the actions of men were a sign, a token, of their involvement in the process initiated by Christ. It was this sense of divine agency that made radicalism possible. The strong sense of God's activity, however, also made it extremely difficult for radical groups to envisage a political realm that was not utterly dependent on the spiritual realm of divine activity. Men's actions took place in the context of their total subordination to processes and commands of which they were not the author. As a result, radical 'politics' had an unstable existence at best. Men were not responsible for the radical transformation of the world, though they might do what they could to co-operate with it. That was a fact that could, of course, be exploited, as it was by Winstanley, to suggest that men's actions were not threatening at all. In mid-seventeenth-century England, God was the only radical activist; but there was nothing he could not destroy and rebuild. As a result, the radical thought of the English Revolution, because it worked on a fundamentally non-human scale, had little concern with practicality. There were no limits to what could be done – because it was not being done by human action. That fact alone provides us with a powerful reason for avoiding that very common way of evaluating radical ideas in terms of their 'realism'. There was nothing more realistic than God the Great Leveller for the seventeenth century, but it is not the realism of our liberal or post-liberal world, in which politics occurs in more human proportions.[97]

Antiformalism and practical Christianity

Divine intervention provided an essential framework for radical political and social thought. One implication of that framework was that the task of bringing about radical transformation was essentially God's and not man's. Consequently, divine agency had important effects on the *content* of radical thought as well, lending it a curiously negative character. The chief emphasis was on *antiformalism*: existing forms, mainly religious but also political, had to be escaped so that God's actions, his transformation of the world, could take place on a *tabula rasa*. Closely linked to that was an emphasis on the importance of *practising* Christian charity as a way of wriggling free of the grasp of hollow formalities.[98]

At one level these arguments possessed a neat rhetorical or polemical function. They provided a way in which those leading the revolution – parliament, the Rump, the army – could be asked to live up to their own professions.[99] Winstanley's claim that the Rump's commitment to a 'commonwealth' and 'free state' was a commitment to the abolition of private property has already been encountered. It is not surprising, therefore, to find him making the general claim that 'words without action are a cheat and kills the comfort of a righteous spirit'.[100] In 1659 William Covell produced a scheme for communities of the poor, similar to those of the Diggers, in which he made much the same point:. 'Parliament . . . hath declared for a Common-wealth'. Covell was interested in ensuring that this declaration, at bottom religious, was effective; nothing else mattered. '[I]f the work of the Lord be done, (which work is the Restoration of the Creation of God), I care not.' He was insistent '[t]hat a Common-wealth may be really acted; deeds are better than words'.[101] Much of what was required to achieve that goal was negative, requiring that 'all Idols may be destroyed' so that man was able 'to serve his Creator' (10). By taxing the rich (10–11), the means could be acquired to establish communities of the poor on the waste and common lands, where they could work and labour together in God's service. This world was to have four laws and no more, ensuring that the parliament and army would be 'doing the work of Reformation'. Those laws were essentially negative, giving men the space in which to submit to God; and they required that tithes, delinquents' estates and the lands (and fees?) of the inns of court, chancery and the universities be used to pay public debts; that gavelkind replace primogeniture; that waste and common lands be settled forever on the poor; and that the rich should pay for hospitals and other social institutions. By such means the 'Agrarian Law' of republican Rome would be established, and there would occur a restoration of the 'liberty of the people, in a natural equality, ordained from the first Creation of the world' (20–1). Only in such a state could a Christian life be actually *lived*, and a proper submission to God take place.

For Covell, then, a community would have the minimum of legal or religious *forms*,[102] and that would make possible the actual *practice* of Christianity – antiformalism and practical Christianity. These themes were fully developed in the writings of the religious radicals, including this time the Levellers (especially Walwyn), for they were not themes confined only to those with a well developed sense of God's providential or millennial interference in the world. Gerrard Winstanley, even before God had revealed to him the need to dig the commons and waste, stated the basic points. What did it mean, he asked, 'to walke righteously' in the sight of God? The answer: 'When a man lives in all acts of love to his fellow creatures; feeding the hungry; cloathing the naked; relieving the oppressed', and so on. The true Christian 'acts rightly towards that creature in whom he sees the spirit of the Father'.[103] Later, the antiformalist concomitants of this emphasis on practical Christianity were revealed. Winstanley had been accused, he said, of denying God's ordinances. But he scorned the 'hypocrisie' of those who fulfilled ordinances that did not represent Christ's real truth, but were 'their own inventions', empty formalities. 'I doe walke in the dayly practise of such Ordinances of God, as Reason and Scripture doe warrant' (140). Chief among these were praying and testifying, but also '[i]t is my endeavour and practise, to doe to others as I would have them do to me; for this is to act according to the creation of a man, the chief Ordinance'. Later comments spelled out further details of the proper carriage that one Christian ought to show to another. Tolerance was required: 'I can, without grudging, suffer others to walk to that measure of knowledge they have received, though it differ from mine'. Hints of what were to come were revealed in the claim that 'I doe and can break bread, with any in whom I see but the least measure of the Father rising up' (140–1).

In his Digger writings Winstanley expressly portrayed the digging life as a form of practical Christianity entered into by those who wanted to live their faith and not merely to profess it. In the very work that announced the intention of digging, he claimed that 'talking of love is no love, it is acting of love in righteousnesse, which the Spirit Reason, our Father delights in'.[104] '[T]he new commandment that Christ left behind him' was precisely this command to love your enemies. Those 'who say this and does [*sic*] not do this, but acts contrary ... are members that uphold the curse' (175). In short, '[t]rue religion and undefiled is this, to make restitution of the earth, which hath been taken and held from the common people by the power of conquests formerly and so *set the oppressed free*' (185). Sometime before the final failure of the digging communities, Winstanley reproached Presbyterians and Independents for their formalism and failure to practice the faith: 'You speak and preach of the life of love. But you have not the power of it; your verbal profession, without the pure righteous action, shews you generally to be outlandish men.' As a result, 'hypocrisy reigns', 'for you acknowledge Christ [only] in words'.[105] Winstanley envisaged instead a society based on different principles, a society in which God ruled. This 'true government' or Godly magistracy would be characterised by two things: first, 'a great light', the light of peace, reason, love and humility; and secondly by 'the greatest bond . . . [of] universal love'. In such a situation, '[t]he love of Christ in us constrains all men to do his will' (244–5). This was to be a society in which men submitted their wills to Christ. It was to be an institutionalisation of the principle of Christian love, and that encapsulates perfectly what is meant here by 'practical Christianity'. In the absence of any mention of the digging experiments, it was left for Christ, in the form of the spirit of freedom rising within individuals, to bring about this new world (261–3).

The social thought of the Levellers grew also from an attempt to imagine a society in which Christianity was truly practised. Nonetheless, there were important differences between the Levellers and the other antiformalist practical Christians. For many, including in their own way those 'mainstream' puritans who advocated Godly discipline, the new society was something that would be brought about inevitably by God, but possibly also would involve Christian people in acting in ways (sometimes coercive; sometimes more peaceful) likely to facilitate change. The Levellers, however, had left themselves without much of a basis either for expecting the imminent inevitability of a new social order, or for arrogating to themselves any right to force it on people if they failed to choose it for themselves. Thus their practical Christianity was subsidiary to a primary emphasis on the politics of consent, though advocates of a practical Christianity the Levellers certainly were.[106] Like their emphasis on consent, the Levellers derived their social views from nature and the obligations imposed on Christians by their creator, 'to employ our endeavours for the advancement of a commutative Happiness, of equall concernment to others as our selves'. They were not, they admitted, 'so strict upon the formall and Ceremoniall part of' God's service, but emphasised instead 'the practicall and most reall part of Religion'.[107] This practical part of Christianity concerned essentially the implementation of Christian charity. A person's 'personall sins . . . are not of Civill cognizance' but for God to deal with. What mattered publicly was whether someone was 'faithfull and reall to the Common-wealth':

> And till persons professing Religion be brought to this sound temper, they fall far short of Christianity; the spirit of love, brotherly charity, doing to all men as they would be done by, is not in them; without which they are but as a sounding brass, and a tinkling cymball, a whited wall, rottenness and corruption, let their ceremoniall formall practice of Religion be never so Angel-like or specious.[108]

True Christianity did not require that people be persecuted for their private sins. Only the uncivil should be treated uncivilly. There was thus a close connection between liberty of conscience – the willingness not to persecute others for their beliefs and faith – and practical Christianity. The former was the highest expression of the latter. The true Christian practised love and charity more than he cared about taking the sacrament of communion. The most developed Leveller defences of this practical antiformal Christianity were written by Walwyn, at his best perhaps in *A Still and Soft Voice* (1647). He provided therein contrasting characters of the truly religious man and of the superstitious man, each 'best knowne by their effects'. While 'true religion setleth a man in peace and rest: makes him like unto the Angels', superstition 'troubleth and makes a man wilde, a superstitious man suffereth neither God nor man to live in peace'.[109] The chief 'efffect' of true religion can be captured in a single word: charity. Colin Davis has rightly pointed out that the Golden Rule was for the Levellers a summary of their practical Christianity. Walwyn referred to 1 Corinthians 13 as a rather fuller summary: 'Though I speak with the tongues of men and of angels, and have not charity, I am become *as* a sounding brass, or a tinkling cymbal. . . . And now abideth faith, hope, charity, these three; but the greatest of these *is* charity.' Charity it was, then, that led the true Christian to 'Feeding the hungry, Cloathing the naked, Visiting the sick, the Fatherlesse, the widdowes and Prisoners: and in all things walking as becometh the Gospell of Christ'.[110]

The crucial area of overlap between practical Christianity and a politics of consent was liberty of conscience. The widespread radical commitment to liberty of conscience was essentially a type of antiformalism, and not necessarily as 'liberal', in our terms, as it has often been seen. The demand for liberty of conscience was a negative demand; it was demand for the space in which to do the really important things required by service to God. It was not in this context an end in itself, and was therefore very frequently linked to rather 'illiberal' aspirations to Godly rule or subjection to the divine will. What makes a theory of liberty of conscience look liberal is its close structural similarity to liberal theories of negative liberty (i.e. theories that demand a space in which people possess a freedom from interference); but in the seventeenth century theories of this sort could be the servants of a Godly authoritarianism. William Walwyn, the most generous of the theorists of liberty of conscience, does not quite fit that pattern, for his politicals views differed from those of many other religious radicals. Nonetheless, he is absolutely typical in advancing a theory of liberty of conscience that is primarily an outgrowth of the antiformalist impulse.[111]

We have seen that, viewed politically, liberty of conscience was important to the Levellers on the grounds that God had forbidden individuals to alienate control over their own consciences. Thus it was impossible, in a Christian politics of consent, for the civil magistrate or any other human authorities to have power over men's consciences. In the remarkable opening pages of *A Still and Soft Voice*, Walwyn emphasised that for most people religion was a matter of custom and education, not of reflection. Most 'men and women in the world, are drawne into the consideration and Practice of Religion, by education, and custome of the place where they are bred' (265). They loathe those whom custom has led to other beliefs. Custom was a 'fraile foundation' (266). But there were signs of improvement, Walwyn thought, for now men were beginning to think about religion for themselves, and thus to free themselves from the fetters of custom. We are starting, he declared, 'to free our Judgments from absurdityes' (266). Liberty of conscience became the means for freeing religion from the corruptions of custom. Walwyn admitted that in their headlong rush from 'educated and customary religion', men might be too willing to 'fall into new entanglements' (167–8). But that was the price that had to be paid for the reformation of the faith. Thus toleration (a term Walwyn used) was the necessary first step towards the creation of a reformed, ethical Christianity. It would usher in a pristine faith. There may here be a sense that Leveller politics, with its guarantee of liberty of conscience, was the foundation on which the true practice of Christianity could be erected. But even for Walwyn, liberty of conscience was a negative thing, needed to clear the path to the truth, more than it was an end in itself. It was a sustained keeping at arm's length of formalist ties.

In other writings Walwyn developed some elaborate arguments in favour of liberty of conscience, especially in the early works *The Power of Love* (1643) and *The Compassionate Samaratine* (1644). They need to be seen within the framework just provided. That is clearest in *The Power of Love*, in which it was emphasised that 'love makes men to be of one mind'; and from which derived the injunction that '[s]uch opinions as are not destructive to humane society, nor blaspheme the worke of our Redemption, may be peaceably endured and considered in love'.[112] Throughout, the emphasis was on the capacity of love to heal divisions and reintroduce true Christianity. *The Compassionate Samaratine*, however, introduced a slightly different note, and that helps to make it perhaps the most interesting of Walwyn's toleration writings. The most striking feature of the work lies in its combination of scepticism and a stress on the importance of sincerity. Walwyn's scepticism now extended to the possibility of men's being 'of one mind' itself: 'I beleive no man thinkes there will be an agreement of judgement as longe as this World lasts.' Walwyn could not resist adding, 'If ever there be, in all probability it must proceed from the power and efficacie of Truth [discovered in free debate], not from constraint.'[113] Nonetheless, this marks an important shift in Walwyn's thinking, and one which gives us much insight into the Levellers. It amounts to an abandonment of the belief that strict religious uniformity could ever be possible. That combined with the additional belief that diversity of belief was not inevitably destabilising is, essentially, what led to the eventual victory of arguments for toleration. It led also to the perception that persecution was more politically unsettling than toleration. If the Levellers – or one of them, at least – had reached such a perception by the mid-1640s, then it goes a long way towards explaining their divergence from other radical groups. It is hard to imagine most of them accepting Walwyn's contention that it was safe and proper to tolerate both atheists and Catholics,[114] for most of them remained committed to Godly rule and the ideal of diversity only within a more or less tightly-defined unity.

The arguments of *The Compassionate Samaratine* built a powerful and sophisticated case for toleration. They can be grouped into two main divisions. First, there were arguments based on the view that human knowledge could not attain certainty, and – partly for that reason – the only way of persuading people lay in reasoned argument, not compulsion. No one, in other words, could claim a degree of certainty sufficient to compel the minds of others to accept them as guides to be followed blindly. No person or group was sufficiently likely to be infallible for it to be *safe* to trust them as guides to the truth. It was on this basis that Walwyn attacked the claims of the learned and of the clergy to have such superior insight as to justify their right to compel other people to follow their judgements. '[O]f what judgment soever a man is, he cannot chuse but be of that judgement.' It was therefore wrong to punish a man for judgements that he was compelled to make (103). Further, '[t]he uncertainty of knowledg in this life [meant that] no man, nor no sort of man can presume of an unerring spirit' (that included parliaments) (104). It was not only ineffective but also pointless to try to compel men's consciences. From this followed what was essentially a literal application of the doctrine of the priesthood of all believers: every individual Christian was to use his or her *own* judgement and reason in seeking God (esp. 108–9). The second group of arguments focused on the need for *sincerity* in the service of God. God required sincerity before he required to be worshipped according to any particular forms. Built into this was a willingness to accept (formal) diversity in order to place attention where it belonged, on the love that was at the core of Christianity. Walwyn therefore pointed to the Dutch example to show that it was not politically dangerous to allow such diversity (114–15). These arguments were summarised thus:

> Liberty of Conscience is grounded upon these foundations, that whatsoever is not of faith is sin, and that every man ought to be fully perswaded of the truenesse of that way wherein he serveth the Lord: upon which grounds I thus argue, To compell me against my conscience, is to compell me against what I beleive to be true, and so against my faith; now whatsoever is not of faith is sine; To compell me therefore against my conscience, is to compell me to doe that which is sinfull: for though the thing may be in itselfe good, yet if it doe not appeare to be so to my conscience, the practice thereof is in me sinfull, which therefore I ought not to be compelled unto.   (114)

The consequence of this was to accept the fragmentation of faith, and devalue the place of forms of worship. As we have seen, Walwyn had come to doubt that uniformity was a possibility (though he still claimed that 'a compulsion is of all wayes the most unlikely to beget unity of mind, and uniformity of purpose'; 105). That did not mean that toleration was now an end in itself. The goal still remained a reformed pristine Christianity, not uniform at all in doctrine or worship (forms), but focused instead on the living out of the Christian imperatives of love and charity. Liberty of conscience, even for its single greatest spokesman in seventeenth-century England, was an elaboration of the antiformalist impulse. It was, as well, the path, not the destination. If followed, the path would lead to England's abandonment of hypocritical formal religion, embracing in its place a true practical Christianity.

Liberty in the English Revolution

'[L]et the oppressed go free,' William Covell urged; but his understanding of what freedom entailed is one that we might find odd:

> Man is so ignorant, that he centres his happiness in having his own will obeyed, more than in having his will subject to the will of God: he that submits to God is at rest; and in his silent resting in God, and beholding the great wonders, (the workes of God standing firmely,) the wonderful Powers let into that man wisedome, discerning of the things that are, and the things that are to come. But oh man! never do you expect this state, until you have submitted without making conditions.[115]

The understanding of freedom that Covell displayed was common amongst the religious radicals, and contrasted sharply with some other accounts of liberty.[116] There was, emerging from the common-law tradition, the idea of the 'free-born Englishman', whose liberty consisted in the possession of inherited rights that were protected by law. Adaptations of the idea can be found amongst Royalists, Parliamentarians, Levellers and others.[117] Freedom was understood as the opportunity to enjoy in quiet those rights, privileges and property defined by law. People in general could only be free when all obeyed and respected the authority of law; and there was, therefore, a close connection made in this way of thinking between a state of freedom and a state of obedience to legally constituted authority, which was itself expected to obey the law and not to rule arbitrarily. The laws themselves made men free, and so 'the chiefe felicity of a Kingdome [is] when good Lawes are reciprocally of Prince and people . . . duly observed'.[118] The freeman could be dispossessed of rights and property only by legal process, and if that bound the king not to act 'by will and pleasure', then he should see that 'it would be no honour to a king or kingdom, to be a king of bondmen or slaves'.[119] Charles I endorsed the view in the days before his death, while being careful to make it clear that the 'true liberty of . . . subjects . . . consists not in the power of government, but in living under such laws, such a government, as may give themselves the best assurance of their lives, and property of their goods'.[120]

Much explored in recent years has been the humanist and republican understanding of liberty, about which more will be heard in a subsequent chapter. The contrast between jurisprudential and humanist approaches to civil liberty has often been drawn in terms of Isaiah Berlin's famous distinction between 'negative' and 'positive' liberty.[121] While that is undeniably illuminating,[122] it remains a considerable over-simplification. Republican theories of liberty combined both negative and positive elements.[123] For civic humanists, negative liberty was a necessary part of freedom, protecting individuals from the incursions of state authority, but it was also necessary for people not just to guard against *actual* infringements of their property and rights, but to ensure that there was no arbitrary authority with the *capacity*, whether used or not, to take away their freedoms and make them slaves. To avoid this, men were best living in communities in which laws ruled not human will, and these were communities in which citizens shared in their own government. This emphasis on political participation and the *vita activa* was the distinguishing feature of republican thought, in which a free community was a community of citizens who helped to rule themselves and so avoided being subservient to the will of an arbitrary authority. The gap between these two approaches to liberty is, in fact, quite small. English common lawyers had long been of the view that the existence of arbitrary authority was inconsistent with freedom; but during the 1640s republicans pushed this idea to the point of incompatibility with hereditary monarchy.[124] The mere existence of such a ruler made slaves of his subjects: in Charles I's terms, it was precisely having a share in the 'power of government' that gave men 'best assurance' of their liberties.

But amongst the religious radicals like Covell, and indeed amongst many puritans, a different way of understanding liberty was prominent. It drew a close connection between freedom and obedience to true authority, especially that of God. The state of freedom, for the religious radicals, consisted in the destruction of human bonds of obligation in order to clear a proper space for the subjection of men to God. For that reason, amongst radicals a theory of *civil* liberty of the sort discussed above was often in the service of and subservient to a theory of religious liberty. Obstacles to the recognition of divine sovereignty had to be removed, and that could mean a freedom from purely human bonds. Clearly, there was a close connection between such an understanding of liberty and the phenomena of divine activism and antiformalism. The destruction of human forms allowed God to act; and in their obedience to the will governing such activity men found freedom. Colin Davis has identified the signs of such a theory of liberty in a range of thinkers from William Prynne and John Milton to William Walwyn and John Goodwin.[125] In this perspective, to be free was to be God's slave rather than man's.

Richard Baxter articulated the assumptions of many when he asserted that a 'form of Government is not to be judged most for the common good, which giveth the greatest Power to the multitude, but that which provideth them with the greatest advantages to serve and please God, and help their Brethren'.[126] From such a perspective, civil freedom was hardly likely to be important. It comes as no surprise, therefore, to find Baxter declaring that 'a free people should have a free Consent, as from men, though they may be pre-obliged to consent by God'.[127] Thus, although Baxter was prepared to countenance a connection between civil freedom and consent, this was entirely subordinate to the more important concern of ensuring subjection to God. Those who would not consent to such subjection and its requirements were to be forced to do so. True freedom trumped an empty and useless civil freedom. '[S]ometime whole Nations, but commonly a part of every Nation, should be denied the liberty of choosing their Governours, and be compelled to consent.' That 'part' included the unGodly.[128] Later, the desire for civil freedom was to be more directly condemned (124; but cf. 212–13 – Baxter throughout restrains the scope of *civil* freedom by making it purely negative, the preservation of liberties); and freedom yoked to subjection: 'all the free subjects are engaged first to God' (128).

Baxter provides a paradigmatic illustration of the mind-set of those – some radical, some not – who made use of a theory of religious liberty. The anonymous author of the undeniably radical *Tyranipocrit Discovered* (1649) shared Baxter's view that it was important to accept certain theological doctrines about human freedom in order to keep away from Antinomianism. In Baxter's view, God created man 'a Rationall free Agent' (55); the same conception was emphatically endorsed in *Tyranipocrit*. The doctrine of predestination led to the conclusion that 'all meanes tending to salvation, are vaine, then away with Promise, law, prophets, Moses, Christ, Gospel, and all meanes, love, charity, &c.'[129] Predestination undermined the imperative to *practise* the Christian faith, so central to the argument of *Tyranipocrit*. The only satisfactory doctrine was that 'man must bee free to will both good and evil' (9). This theological conception of freedom had direct political consequences. Men must chose to rule themselves 'by the rule of Christ', and not to be ruled 'by wilfully sinful, and partial prerogating respect of persons, tyrants, artificiall theeves, hypocrits, &c.' (5). The consequence must be that individuals required the space to submit their wills to God. Man was 'capable of divine wisdome, not by compulsion, but by reason; not by force, but free-will' (8). God gave men freedom – but he gave it 'to that end that man should give his desire unto God' (37). Those who misused their freedom would suffer the inevitable consequence. Submission to God was primarily a matter of practising Christian love by ensuring an equality of goods in society. It was not a matter of doctrine, forms or even faith. In the end, indeed, it was more important to seek God within oneself than in the world (7). Nonetheless, 'God will not rule men, if they do not chuse him to be their God' (55). Freedom was a matter of making choices; but there was only one choice that you were allowed to make. And so freedom led – or should have led – to a subjection to God and his wishes. Everything that *we* might include in the category of civil freedom was of no more than instrumental significance.

The radicals of the English Revolution were marching – and where necessary frog-marching their neighbours – towards a Christian society. Though for the Levellers the practical priority for human agents, at least, was achieving civil liberty, and using it sensibly, there was still a feeling that sensible use might mean the creation of a Christian society. Nonetheless, there was no real affirmation of the view that this *had* to be the case. They never asked what you should do if free men chose paths other than those of Godliness; still less did they answer it. For the religious radicals, civil liberty was substantially devalued and made a means to allowing (or requiring) people to submit to God. Interestingly, one of them stepped back from this position. Winstanley's *True Law of Freedom in a Platform*, of 1651, understood liberty both as a freedom from economic privation, but also as freedom to participate in a community and its public life. 'What is freedom?', he asked towards the end of the work.

> Every freeman shall have a freedom in the earth, to plant or build, to fetch from the store-houses anything he wants, and shall enjoy the fruits of his labours without restraint from any; he shall not pay rent to any landlord, and he shall be capable to be chosen any officer, so he be above forty years of age, and he shall have a voice to choose officers though he be under forty years of age. If he want any young men to be assistance to him in his trade or household employment, the overseers shall appoint him young men or maids to be his servants in his family.[130]

There is no coincidence in the fact that Winstanley's revised view of liberty coincided with a declining confidence in the likelihood that God would transform the human world.[131] The Diggers would continue to subsist in a world of sin and contingency. In such a world, politics remained necessary; and, like the Levellers, Winstanley came to discover that you cannot have politics when your only concept of liberty is one so deliberately impoverished in its negativity as to be abased before the majesty and sovereignty of God.

It is not surprising that the Godly radicals had a theory of *civil* liberty that was entirely negative. Their concern with politics was entirely a concern with the preliminaries, and even their most characteristic doctrine with political implications – liberty of conscience – was often a pathway to other things. It paved the way; was necessary to protect the Godly from persecution; but in its own right had little significance. Their chief focus lay elsewhere, perhaps on the social requirements of the Christian faith, perhaps on the duty to seek submission to God, occasionally on the possibilities of constructing (with God's essential help) true Godly magistracy; but certainly not with politics considered as the product of human activity in the world. Liberty of conscience was a husk protecting the more precious kernel inside. Henry Stubbe's famous assertion, made in 1659, that the essence of the Good Old Cause for which men had fought in the 1640s and 1650s was 'LIBERTY civill, and spirituall', and that this could be pared down to the simple question 'Whether the Civil Magistrate hath any power in things of

Spiritual concernment?', could have been taken by many as a sign of the failure of the struggle.[132] For liberty of conscience to have become the highest goal, it must be the case that men had lost all hope that the real goals of the 1640s and 1650s could ever be achieved. They had failed even to build the worldly stage on which the divine drama was to be acted out. The God from whom so much had been expected, had turned his back on England.

Radicalism reveals much about the driving and motivating forces compelling the most zealous in the English Revolution. For them this clearly was a war of religion. But for those who wanted to build on earth societies that would achieve human goals – preserving peace, preserving civil liberty – the language of the religious radicals needed to be defused. Among the most effective of those who responded to the Godly impulse were Thomas Hobbes and James Harrington, whom we will consider in subsequent chapters.

7 Thomas Hobbes

Born in 1588, Thomas Hobbes had reached the age of 52 before completing the first version of his mature political theory in 1640. That work, *The Elements of Law*, was prompted by the crisis in the affairs of Charles I that resulted in the calling of the Short Parliament, and so, like all of Hobbes's political writings, it was both an attempt to produce a systematic science of politics and a response to his immediate political environment. It was the work of a man who had behind him many decades of sustained reflection. Sadly the contents of that reflection are now largely beyond our recovery,[1] though it may be that some of his assumptions about the nature of people and politics were grounded in an early acquaintance with Tacitist 'reason of state' ideas.[2] Hobbes's best known political work, *Leviathan*, appeared in 1651 (revised for its Latin translation of 1668). Though the structure of Hobbes's political thinking remained largely unaltered between 1640 and 1651, many of its details (some of them crucially important) were considerably revised. The revisions are important, for they reflect more than a process of intellectual 'tidying-up' and refinement: they show Hobbes's continuing response to and engagement with the course of English political history during the years of Civil War and beyond. Hobbes's diagnosis of the causes of England's mid-century turmoils was a complex one, but religion was never far from his attention. Writing to the earl of Devonshire in mid-1641, he stated his certainty 'that the dispute for [precedence] betwene the *spirituall* and *civill power*, has of late more than any other thing in the world, bene the cause of *civill warres*, in all *places of Christendome*'.[3] In *Leviathan* Hobbes gave a related, though not identical, analysis of the problem of civil war. Again, it was one that put religion at the forefront:

> The most frequent praetext of Sedition, and Civill Warre, in Christian Common-wealths hath a long time proceeded from a difficulty, not yet sufficiently resolved, of obeying at once, both God, and Man, then when their Commandments are one contrary to the other.[4]

In his posthumously published history of the Civil Wars, Hobbes's analysis was broader; yet, still, when he named seven groups of people or sets of misconceptions that caused the English Civil War the list began with Presbyterians, Papists and sectaries, all of whom possessed mistaken beliefs about the proper relationship between civil and eccle-siastical power.[5] Given this, it is fair enough to describe Hobbes's polit-ical thought (especially *Leviathan*) as, in good part, a response in general to an age of religious warfare, and in particular to the threat and the outbreak of religious war in England.

The Development of Hobbes's Political Thought

The first work that Hobbes published (in 1629) was a translation of and short introduction to Thucydides' *History of the Peloponnesian War*. Efforts have been made to draw lines of connection between this work and Hobbes's later thinking, and to make of his interest in Thucydides an oblique comment on English politics of the late 1620s.[6] Hobbes did himself briefly summarise the political lessons to be derived from Thucydides – 'it is manifest that he least of all liked the democracy' and 'best approved of the regal government'[7] – but the comments amount to little, and any attempt to move beyond them is hampered by prob-lems of evidence. We might be best to rest content with Hobbes's own verdict on his translation work, made in his verse autobiography: 'He taught me how stupid democracy is and by how much one man is wiser than an assembly. I made it my business that this author should speak to the English in their own tongue and warn them against the tempta-tion to listen to rhetoric.'[8] The danger posed by rhetoric and rhetori-cians was never to be far from Hobbes's attention.[9] By the time he wrote *Leviathan*, however, Hobbes had revised his attitude to it, and reverted to the more positive view of rhetoric that he had held before writing the *Elements*. His experience of the Civil War led him to believe that reason had only small power over human beings, and that he would need to use the full range of persuasive techniques at his disposal if he were to have any chance of overcoming the insane folly that had gripped his country.[10]

In 1630, soon after his work on Thucydides, and long before the time he finished writing the MS of the *Elements* – the Epistle Dedicatory to which is dated 9 May 1640, though much of the work may be a bit earlier[11] – Hobbes had discovered Euclid, who gave him his initial understanding of scientific method, and he had embarked upon a study of the physical sciences.[12] Undoubtedly this burgeoning interest in the physical world had an impact on his political thinking; but specifying exactly what that impact was is more difficult. Hobbes certainly developed the ambition to produce a complete system of philosophy, of which his political theory would form but a part. The conception of philosophy and its parts that underlay this scheme was to be best and most elegantly expressed in the first chapter of *De Corpore* (Of Body) (Latin, 1655; English, 1656); and Hobbes's conception of the method to be pursued in philosophy was detailed in chapter 6 of the same work. Those wishing to argue for a close association between Hobbes's general philosophy and his political philosophy have tended to focus on two things: his materialist metaphysics and his view of scientific method.[13] For Hobbes, the universe was made up of matter in motion, and philosophy consisted of such knowledge about the 'effects or appearances' of bodies as could be derived 'by true ratiocination from the knowledge we have first of their causes or generation'; or, conversely, of such knowledge of causes or generation as could be derived from a knowledge of effects and appearances.[14] Philosophy was divided into two parts: natural, concerned with the 'generation and properties' of natural bodies; and civil, concerned with artificial bodies, or commonwealths. Civil philosophy was further divided into ethics, 'which treats of men's dispositions and manners', and politics, 'which takes cognizance of their civil duties'.[15] Perhaps the most obvious link to be drawn between Hobbes's materialistic understanding of the world and his civil philosophy lies in the realm of ethics.[16] Because he viewed the human mind and human passions as products of the movement of matter, Hobbes naturally produced a materialistic ethics that drew on the idea of matter in motion not only deductively but (at times) also by analogy and metaphor. The heart of the position Hobbes was to hold for the rest of his life is contained in the seventh chapter of the first part of the *Elements*. Hobbes built on the foundation provided by the view that

> conceptions or apparitions are nothing really, but motion in some internal substance of the head; which motion not stopping there, but proceeding to the heart, of necessity must either help or hinder that motion which is called vital; when it helpeth, it is called DELIGHT, contentment, or pleasure ... but when such motion weakeneth or hindereth the vital motion, then it is called PAIN.[17]

Applied to ethical judgements, this produced the conclusion that

> Every man, for his own part, calleth that which pleaseth, and is delightful to himself GOOD; and that EVIL which displeaseth him: insomuch that while every man differeth from other in constitution, they differ also one from another concerning the common distinction of good and evil. Nor is there any such thing ... simply good.[18]

Because 'all conceptions we have immediately by the sense, are delight or pain, or appetite, or fear',[19] then all moral judgements must be built from these materials. Furthermore, because the senses of delight and pain were not universal – no things delighted or pained everybody – but varied from person to person, then one could expect that there could be no universal set of detailed moral evaluations either. It would then follow that willed human actions, the product of opinions about reward and punishment, were not characterised by much uniformity or pattern.[20]

Thus the foundation of Hobbes's political reflection was a powerful, dismayed recognition of the diversity of all human beliefs, including moral beliefs; and of the immense difficulty of mitigating the effects of that diversity. (As we shall see, however, difficulty does not mean impossibility; and eventually Hobbes found a basis for moral agreement even in nature.) In a sense, then, Hobbes was giving an explanation for the characteristic features of post-Reformation England (and Europe): it was a world of conflicting ideologies, in which groups and individuals held moral beliefs (and the religious beliefs that justified them) in accord with their particular interests. The essential problem was to find ways of preventing the warfare and violence that such ideological conflict seemed inevitably to presage.

Hobbes was as certain in 1640 as he was ever to be that the proper solution to this problem lay in the creation of an absolute sovereign, the necessity for which could be demonstrated *scientifically* so that anyone with *reason* could be made to see that there was no other solution to the problem of human diversity. Such a solution required 'concord', or a situation in which 'all direct their actions to one and the same end'.[21] But, crucially, concord was 'not sufficient security for their common peace, without the erection of some common power, by the fear whereof they may be compelled to keep the peace'. This situation comes about only with 'union', the process of 'including the wills of many in the will of one man'.[22] This man is able to use the strength of the individuals who formed a society to coerce the disobedient few of that society into obedience. Thus a 'body politic', 'civil society' or *polis* 'may be defined to be a multitude of men, united as one person by a common power, for their common peace, defence and benefit'.[23] This union under a common power came about by a *covenant* in which subjects laid down their right to resist the sovereign.[24]

It was clear to Hobbes that a sovereign, or common power, thus created needed to have absolute power; and he set out to make the point as obvious to his readers as it was to himself. All judicial decisions and all decisions about the use of military force were the sovereign's.[25] And, even more importantly: since, all violence proceedeth from controversies that arise between men concerning *meum* and *tuum*, right and wrong, good and bad, and the like, which men use every one to measure by their own judgements; it belongeth also to the judgement of the same sovereign power, to set forth and make known the common measure by which every man is to know what is his, and what another's; what is good, and what bad; and what he ought to do, and what not; and to command the same to be observed.[26]

In this we have the core of Hobbes's political thought. Yet, it should immediately be stressed that when he wrote the *Elements* in 1640 Hobbes was not as aware as he was later to become of just how persistent a problem private *opinions* were. Another way of saying this is to point out that in 1640 Hobbes was not yet concerned centrally and specifically with a civil war in which the participants were motivated by religious opinion, though his *general* awareness of the post-Reformation situation of religious civil war cannot, as we have suggested, be ignored: even in 1640 he believed 'the world is governed by opinion'.[27] As a result, the *Elements* lacked the striking expressions of the sovereign's power to control the public expression of beliefs and opinions that were to be found in *De Cive* and *Leviathan*.[28] The major political thrust of the *Elements* was directed instead at the issues generated by the 1630s: the king's power to tax without consent, and his relationship to the common law. Thus the political parts of Hobbes's *Elements* can be placed squarely in the context of the political conflicts evident in England in 1640.[29]

Later, in 1662, Hobbes was to recall the circumstances in which he wrote the *Elements*: at the time of the Short Parliament,

many points of the regal power, which were necessary for the peace of the kingdom, and the safety of his Majesty's person, were disputed and denied, [so] Mr. Hobbes wrote a little treatise in English, wherein he did set forth and demonstrate, that the said power and rights were inseparably annexed to the sovereignty; which sovereignty they did not *then* deny to be in the King; but it seems understood not, or would not understand that inseparability.[30]

This is not at all a bad summary of the political force of the *Elements*, Hobbes's most Bodinian book.[31] Indeed, it was the only work in which he so much as mentioned Bodin,[32] doing so to support what the *Considerations* was to identify as the central theme of his 1640 work: there can be no commonwealth 'wherein the rights of sovereignty were divided'; all such rights must be inseparably tied to a single sovereign authority.[33] When examining the *Elements* against the background of the politics of 1640 two key arguments about the nature of sovereignty stand out. First, Hobbes tackled the central theme of English common-law thinking, that the king was bound by the law. Though some 'have imagined that a commonwealth may be constituted in such manner, as the sovereign power may be so limited, and moderated, as they shall think fit themselves',[34] the contrary was actually the case. Those who believed sovereigns to be bound by their own laws simply showed that they did not understand what a law was. Laws were *commands*, and logically could not bind him who commanded.[35]

Secondly, the most topical issue in 1640 was that of property and taxation, and it figured heavily in the *Elements*. Hobbes took seriously the fear that one of the disadvantages of government (by which he meant, of absolute sovereignty) for subjects was 'the uncertainty of *meum* and *tuum*', a fear much expressed in England after 1638. His answer to the fear was, however, simple:

> it is . . . none, but in appearance only. It consisteth in this, that the sovereign taketh from him that which he used to enjoy, knowing no other propriety, but use and custom. But without such sovereign power, the right of men is not propriety to any thing, but a community; no better than to have right at all. . . . Propriety therefore being derived from the sovereign power, is not to be pretended against the same; especially when by it every subject hath his propriety against every other subject, which when sovereignty ceaseth, he hath not, because in that case they return to war amongst themselves. Those levies therefore which are made upon men's estates, by the sovereign authority, are no more but the price of that peace and defence which the sovereignty maintaineth for them.[36]

Thus Hobbes was able to assert *both* the sovereign's untrammelled right to tax and dispossess his subjects *and* the contention that there *could* not be any greater security for property rights than in a commonwealth with an absolute sovereign. Those who thought otherwise were no better than deluded.

At no time did Hobbes believe that monarchy was the *only* form that absolute sovereignty could take; yet, at all times, he seems to have thought it preferable to aristocracy or democracy.[37] One of the reasons given in the *Elements* for this preference returns us to the matter of opinion: ruling assemblies tended to be made ineffective by those of their members 'that are of different opinions', whereas in a monarchy 'there is no distraction' of this sort.[38] When he published *De Cive* in April 1642 – it had been written in Paris over the previous year or more

– Hobbes's mind had become much more concerned with opinion, especially religious opinion, than it had been in 1640. It is possible that the change reflected Hobbes's observation of events in and around the Long Parliament,[39] a possibility kept open by the one glimpse we have already had of such observation in mid-1641. In any case, though Hobbes was well aware even in 1640 that the influence an eloquent man had on the opinions of others was politically dangerous,[40] he paid rather more attention to the problem in 1642. *De Cive* in consequence gave specific direction with regard to the authority to determine religious opinions;[41] and added to the list of the sovereign's rights his authority 'to decide which opinions and doctrines are inimical to peace and to forbid their being taught'.[42] Increasingly, Hobbes was coming to write about the problem of religious civil war – conflicts generated by the clash of opinions within a Christian commonwealth.

By the time *Leviathan* was published in 1651 Hobbes had experienced, if only from a distance, the full horror of civil war; and many of the tendencies, especially the growing concern with religious opinion, that can be discerned in *De Cive* are found more fully developed in the later work. In addition, the changing ideological context of the 1640s and early 1650s – Parliamentarian resistance theory, religious radicalism, the theories defending obedience to the Commonwealth after 1649 – drew from Hobbes some response. These responses altered in important ways the detailed context of his political theory; and we shall examine them presently. It remains in this place to jump over the figure of *Leviathan* and ask what further developments are to be found in his political writings between 1651 and his death in 1679.

After the Restoration in 1660 Hobbes came to be accused of heresy – 'atheism, blasphemy and profaneness' – and he naturally turned his attention towards defusing the accusation.[43] Hobbes's later interest in, for example, the English heresy laws was not simply a defensive move; but was also part of a growing engagement with the actual institutions and principles of English public life. Indeed, one scholar has gone so far as to argue that in his later writings Hobbes's growing interest in the specific character of English public life produced a crucial modification in the character and implications of his political thinking.[44] This is a claim worth looking at in some detail. Two passages, one from *Behemoth* (written *c*. 1668, but refused permission to be published until 1679) and one from the *Dialogue between a Philosopher and a Student of the Common Laws of England* (written around 1670 but printed in 1681), prove crucial in this regard.

The dialogue of *Behemoth* came at one point to consider the political doctrine of Richard Allestree's *The Whole Duty of Man*, endorsed as the best available statement of Protestant politics. Yet even it was unsatisfactory,[45] and Hobbes pulled apart the loopholes that it allowed for resistance theory. In the course of the discussion the question of obedience to tyrants was raised. What, it was asked, if one's sovereign 'command me with my own hands to execute my father'? The reply made an interesting distinction:

> We never have read nor heard of any King or tyrant so inhuman as to command it. If any did, we are to consider whether that command were one of his laws. For by disobeying Kings, we mean the disobeying of his laws, those laws that were made before they were applied to any particular person; for the King, though as a father of children, and a master of domestic servants command many things which bind those children and servants yet he commands the people in general never but by a precedent law, and as a politic, not a natural person. And if such a command as you speak of were contrived into a general law ... you were bound to obey it, unless you depart the kingdom after the publication of the law, and before the condemnation of your father.[46]

The distinction drawn here between the king's natural and his politic capacities[47] was discussed more fully in the *Dialogue*, where the lawyer asked the philosopher, 'do you think the distinction between natural and politick capacity is insignificant?' With regard to the ownership of land by a monarch (but not a sovereign assembly) the distinction amounted, or so the philosopher said, to little; but

> as to the Acts and Commands, they may be well distinguished in this manner. Whatsoever a Monarch does Command, or do by consent of the People of his Kingdom may properly be said to be done in his politick Capacity; and whatsoever he Commands by word of Mouth only, or by Letters signed with his hand, or Sealed with any of his private Seals is done in his natural Capacity: Nevertheless, his publick Commands, though they be made in his politick Capacity, have their original from his natural Capacity. For in the making of Law (which necessarily requires his assent) his assent is natural: Also those Acts which are done by the King previously to the passing of them under the Great Seal of *England*, either by word of Mouth, or warrant under his Signet, or privy Seal, are done in his natural Capacity; but when they have past the Seal of *England*, they are to be taken as done in his politick Capacity.[48]

These passages are undoubtedly interesting; but their interest does not lie in any modification of Hobbes's thinking that they might represent.

Even in *Leviathan* Hobbes talked of obedience as being to the sovereign's *laws*, not to any odd remark he might make. The definition of law as command was broad and inclusive – but public promulgation was a requirement.[49] Thus, 'the measure of Good and Evill actions is the Civill Law'.[50]

The importance of those passages in which Hobbes applied this theory to specifically *English* circumstances – including the passages in *Leviathan* – lies in what they tell us of the fundamental character of Hobbes's thinking. *Leviathan* was not a reformist work: Hobbes did not wish to alter English institutions, to reform the law of England, or anything else of this sort. His political writings had little to say about the specific forms and constitutional organisation that a state should adopt, other than a broad recommendation of monarchy. Instead, Hobbes aimed at altering the opinions people held about what underlay English political life. In consequence, *Leviathan* contained two basic lines of argument. The dominant one, addressing itself to the opinions held by subjects, was the demonstration that one should not think that any action of the sovereign could be unjust, or could provide grounds for resistance. It did not matter that the English kings usually ruled with a parliament and in accordance with the common law; it did matter if their subjects had the opinion that a king who broke with parliament or crossed the common law was acting unjustly and could be resisted. The second line of argument in the book was addressed to sovereigns, and it made the point that there were things the sovereign could justly do that he ought not to do as a matter of prudence. Sovereigns who governed contrary to the principles of natural law might in fact create rebellion.[51] Although subjects' actions were thus fundamentally shaped by the civil laws, the Sovereign's were subject to natural law. However, this was not all it seemed. Hobbes, 'at once affirmed the universality of justice and natural law and denied their availability independent of civil law', enabling him both to talk of justice as a duty of sovereigns, while denying that appeals against the sovereign could be made to natural law or the principles of justice.[52] There was for Hobbes no distinction to be drawn between a king and a tyrant, because all sovereign kings were incapable of tyranny: all their actions were by definition lawful.[53]

Leviathan: the Theory of Civil Politics[54]

Hobbes's political theory was constructed to make much the same points in two different ways. He first dealt with civil politics in quite general terms that would be appropriate to any time or place; and he then dealt with the additional problems that arose in commonwealths that were *Christian*. Those additional problems naturally concerned the relationship between civil and ecclesiastical authority, and we shall reserve them for later discussion.

The civil politics of *Leviathan* represent a considerably modified version of the ideas that Hobbes had earlier expressed in 1640 and 1642. Clearly, he had come to see that his earlier formulations contained their hidden problems. The most obvious of these concerned the specific avowal in the *Elements* of the belief that democracy was, in all societies, the first form of government, an argument that came too close for comfort to the view that kings were but the creatures of a sovereign people.[55] In *De Cive*, Hobbes had retained this principle, but had also attempted to defuse its potential for mischief by adding a paragraph that explained how difficult it was for democracy to continue in existence for any length of time.[56] In *Leviathan*, however, the formal structure of Hobbes's theory was recast in such a way as to avoid the idea of aboriginal democracy altogether. The result was that in *Leviathan* sovereignty was instituted by a process of *authorisation*; this authorisation theory, in turn, brought with it a number of further polemical benefits.[57]

An account of Hobbes's argument must begin with the state of nature. As we have seen, Hobbes believed that the individuals who lived in a state of nature lacked a common set of principles upon which they could agree, and which could then serve as a basis for regulating their interactions with one another. *Naturally* the moral principles accepted by each human being were unique to him or herself, and reflected each person's own interests (at least in the broad sense that each person called 'good' that which pleased her). Consequently, when living outside of civil society such people lived in a state of conflict, or continuously-threatened conflict, with one another. Common misconceptions about Hobbes notwithstanding, this situation did not come about because human beings were inherently wicked and unpleasant to one another, or because individuals were incapable always of behaving altruistically. It came about because each person in a state of nature felt *insecure*. Hobbes began his account of the state of nature[58] with an assertion (also found in some radical writers) of human equality. This must not be misunderstood, as it often is, by being linked to later egalitarian theories: Hobbes was concerned to advance the claim that no human being was naturally sufficiently stronger or more intelligent than other human beings to be able to claim authority or continuously to exercise power over them. He thus closed off the obvious response to his account of the origins of society: that, in fact, in nature there would occur a natural process in which power would accumulate in the hands of the best-endowed. '[T]he difference between man and man, is not so considerable, as that one man can thereupon claim to himselfe any benefit to which another may not pretend, as well as he.'[59] Anyone can be killed by anyone else; everyone believes himself wiser than everyone else. The result is that no one is secure from the threat posed by others, yet everyone has sufficient self-conceit to desire things that make them a threat to others.

Upon equality was thus built a 'diffidence of one another': men continually wanted things possessed by others, and were thus always wishing 'to destroy, or subdue one an other'. In a state of constant suspicion of one's fellow human beings, one's natural response is 'Anticipation; that is, by force, or wiles, to master the persons of all men he can, so long, till he see no other power great enough to endanger him.' Not only were men in competition with one another for limited goods and suspicious of one another (diffident), but they all wished for 'glory', a passion which encouraged a man to attempt to force other people to value him as highly as he did himself. Little wonder, then, that Hobbes could conclude:

> Hereby it is manifest, that during the time men live without a common Power to keep them all in awe, they are in that condition which is called Warre, and such a warre, as is of every man, against every man. For WARRE, consisteth not in Battell onely, or the act of fighting; but in a tract of time, wherein the Will to contend by Battell is sufficiently known. . . .[60]

In such a condition of war, none of the benefits of settled civilised life could accrue: 'there is no place for Industry . . . no Culture of the Earth; no Navigation . . . no commodious Building . . . no Knowledge of the face of the Earth; no account of Time; no Arts, no Letters; no Society . . . And the life of man, solitary, poore, nasty, brutish, and short'.[61] And all this chiefly because in a state of war there could be no secure possession of property. Hence no one had a motive to engage in any of the activities that might improve his or her material well-being. In a state of nature, individuals possessed an unbounded liberty to do as they thought best; and it was more or less useless to them.

Nature did not, however, leave men with no means of escape from this condition. Men had reason and passions, both of which pointed towards the doorway to something better. The passions – fear of death, desire for material possessions, and the hope by industry to obtain those possessions – provided a set of motives for escape; while reason suggested the means, 'convenient Articles of Peace, upon which men may be drawn to agreement'. These were the laws of nature.[62]

There is a puzzle in this. If, naturally, men *had* the passions and the reason that enabled them to get out of a state of nature, why were they in it in the first place? This puzzle is often unobserved because it is often assumed that Hobbes's account of how human beings came to call 'good' things that pleased them and 'bad' things that did not meant that he believed that in nature there was no possibility that human beings could reach any *agreement* whatsoever on moral and political principles. But, in fact, Hobbes said the exact opposite of this, in the passage just quoted and elsewhere. The puzzle is solved by the fact that in nature men *could* agree on the basic elements of a moral code; *but* that this was still insufficient for them to be able to escape from the condition of a war of all against all. While remaining outside of civil society, men could progress so far as to *see* the way forward, but no further. Why was this so? There are two reasons. First, agreeing on a moral code was not the same as agreeing to follow one, and the 'diffidence' that men felt toward one another was sufficient for them not to implement their moral consensus under the conditions of nature. And secondly, an agreement about basic moral principles was not a sufficient level of agreement. Human beings were always capable of describing actions that suited their interests in morally acceptable terms, and of condemning actions that harmed them by appealing to agreed moral terms.[63] In short, to escape from nature required more than general agreement. It required the enforcement of a single *detailed* moral code, and the establishment of an authority that could guarantee universal (or sufficiently general) observance of the agreed rules so that diffidence no longer justified non-observance. This authority needed to provide an objective, disinterested implementation of moral principles in order to circumvent each individual's capacity to pervert an agreed moral language into the servant of his or her own interests. Moral agreement of the degree necessary for civil society was thus an artificial thing with natural foundations.

Human opinions were, then, not quite as thoroughly diverse and individual as it might have seemed at first. Indeed, 'all men agree on this, that Peace is Good'.[64] It might seem odd that Hobbes could argue this if he believed that good and evil related only to individual appetites (as he did); but he could do so because in nature the predicament (and thus the appetites) of all human beings had sufficient in common for them to reach an agreement on some basic points. These *shared* opinions formed Hobbes's science of moral philosophy.[65] As Hobbes explained it, men's experience of nature ('where private Appetite is the measure of Good and Evill') itself led them to agree-

ment on the goodness of peace, from which agreement could be
deduced the laws of nature.[66]

But the laws of nature did not tell men how they could *naturally*
escape from a war of all against all: they told them to create an *artificial*
solution. Consequently, though men could apprehend the existence of
natural laws while they were in a natural condition, they could not
safely obey them (which made it pointless to say that they were obliged
by them other than *in foro interno*, i.e. in conscience only).[67]
Nevertheless, like most other natural-law thinkers, Hobbes believed
that the laws of nature were immutable and eternal, and thus existed
prior to the establishment of civil society. Even under the conditions
prevailing in the state of nature they *were* binding *in foro interno*, 'that is
to say, they bind to a desire they should take place'.[68] Indeed, the first
of them essentially reformulated this point: 'every man, ought to
endeavour Peace, *as farre as he has hope of obtaining it*'.[69] Thus, the laws
of nature had a certain circumstantiality built into them: they required
people *always* to look for the opportunity of practising what the laws
demanded, but only bound them actually to such practice when it
could be undertaken with safety. Nevertheless, if Hobbes could show
that there were circumstances in which such practice was safe, then he
could show how men might agree to follow – indeed, be obliged to
follow – the laws of nature out of the state of nature. And, of course, he
could indeed show this.

The argument began with the idea of *natural right*, which was essentially a reformulation in juridical terms of the position in which individuals found themselves in nature. The right of nature (*jus naturale*)

is the liberty each man hath, to use his own power, as he will
himselfe, for the preservation of his own Nature; that is to say, Of his
own Life; and consequently, of doing any thing, which in his own
Judgement and Reason, hee shall conceive to be the aptest means
thereunto.[70]

This formulation *followed* the portrait Hobbes gave of the state of
nature. He did not deduce his portrait of men's natural condition from
the assumption that all men possessed a right to preserve themselves.[71]
That portrait followed from a consideration of what men were in fact
like. The concept of the right of nature, then, resulted from the translation of that naturalistic portrait of natural man, based on observation
and introspection, into legal language, thus enabling it to serve as the
basis for a legal argument. The next stage of that argument required
recognition of the fact that a right and a law were opposite things:
'Right consisteth in liberty to do, or to forbeare; Whereas LAW, deter-

mineth, and bindeth to one of them: so that Law and Right differ as much as Obligation, and Liberty; which in one and the same matter are inconsistent.'[72] The primary obstacle to peace was the retention by all individuals of their natural right. Therefore the laws of nature, discoverable by reason, indicated to men how they might safely divest themselves of that right. If they could indicate the *safety* of this, then it would follow that men were in fact bound actually to follow the 'dictates of natural reason' (i.e. the laws of nature).[73] As we have seen, Hobbes's first law of nature required a disposition towards peace where it could be obtained; the second told men how to act so that peace was in fact attainable. From the first law of nature,

> by which men are commanded to endeavour Peace, is derived this second Law; *That a man be willing, when others are so too, as farre-forth, as for Peace, and defence of himselfe he shall think it necessary, to lay down this right to all things; and be contented with so much liberty against other men, as he would allow other men against himselfe.*[74]

The answer suggested here to the quandary faced by natural man is that he should abandon his natural right when others also were willing to do so. Hobbes explained that this process could lead one to create an artificial 'body' or commonwealth if all men transferred their right, by covenant, to some authority that would represent them all. This authority was the sovereign, which thus gained its power to punish and rule from the transfer of rights by all citizens simultaneously. The sovereign exercised everyone's individual natural right to do all things that in their own judgement furthered their own preservation.[75]

And yet this was not quite the whole story. While it was the case that subjects, in setting him up, gave nothing to the sovereign that he did not already have, they did nonetheless agree to *authorise* his actions, and thus to accept that the sovereign was their *representative*.[76] Hobbes put this point in a variety of ways, but the essential idea was that all the sovereign's commands were to be acknowledged by each individual member of the commonwealth as his or her own. The covenant that produced the commonwealth was carefully worded: each person declared,

> I Authorise and give up my Right of Governing my selfe, to this Man, or to this Assembly of men, on this condition, that thou give up thy Right to him, and Authorise all his Actions in like manner.[77]

Individuals both 'transferred' (in Hobbes's sense) their individual right to the sovereign, *and* authorised his actions – by which Hobbes meant they made themselves each the author of all that he did. This established the 'Mortall God', Leviathan, or the commonwealth, which could in consequence be defined as

> *One Person, of whose Acts a great Multitude, by mutuall Covenants one with*
> *another, have made themselves every one the Author, to the end he may use the*
> *strength and means of them all, as he shall think expedient, for their Peace*
> *and Common Defence.* And he that carryeth this Person, is called
> SOVERAIGNE, and said to have *Soveraigne Power. . . .*[78]

Thus the sovereign representative, though often spoken of by Hobbes in 'personal' terms, was actually an abstract and fictional state.

In this there are a number of things worth stressing. First, Hobbes has here abandoned his earlier two-stage model of the institution of the commonwealth, with its presumption of aboriginal democracy. Now the commonwealth and its sovereign were created simultaneously in one simple act of authorisation. This new way of conceptualising the process had more than just polemical advantages. It also gave a simple answer to the question: How can a man safely divest himself of his right to all things? The answer was: by ensuring that the action needed to divest himself of this right *immediately* created a sovereign authority that could ensure that one's fellow subjects kept their promises to abandon their natural right to all things. It was essential to this argument that sovereignty and society were created simultaneously, for any gap between the natural and artificial situations might lead anyone to ask why they should trust their fellows during this intermediate period. A society without a powerful sovereign was thus inconceivable: unless you created *at once* your sovereign, you would be doomed to live in the state of nature forever. In this way Hobbes could abandon the idea of original democracy, explain why it was safe to abandon one's natural right, and demonstrate the necessity of a sovereign power in the commonwealth, all at the same time.[79]

A second point to note is that a sovereign authority was not a party to the covenant by which it was created. Again there were considerable polemical advantages in this argument: it could accept the idea that government originated in consent, while at the same time denying that sovereigns had entered into any bargain with their subjects. Thus, 'there can happen no breach of Covenant on the part of the Soveraigne; and consequently none of his Subjects, by any pretence of forfeiture, can be freed from his Subjection'.[80] People did indeed create their own sovereign; but not in a way that enabled them to place any conditions upon his exercise of office.

Thirdly, we should note that there were significant qualifications attached to Hobbes's argument. Not all rights could be abandoned by covenant: no one could alienate a right to defend his life against forcible assault, or to defend herself against 'Wounds, and Chayns, and Imprisonment'. More generally, a man's words could not be interpreted to mean that he gave away any right to perform actions necessary for 'the security of a mans person, in his life, and in the means of so preserving life, as not to be weary of it'.[81] Consequently, even in civil society men retained elements of their natural liberty, which meant that there were 'things, which though commanded by the Soveraign, he may nevertheless, without Injustice, refuse to do'.[82] (By 'injustice' Hobbes meant the breaking of covenants, so he was here saying that certain acts of disobedience were not in breach of the covenant that established the commonwealth.)[83] These things included the right to disobey a command to kill (either oneself or anyone else), to refuse to fight as a soldier, not to incriminate oneself, and to refuse an order physically to harm oneself. In addition, individuals were always able to defend themselves from physical harm, a right that extended even to criminals found guilty by due process, who could nevertheless do what was in their power to prevent justice being executed upon them.[84]

Even though this theory of the institution of sovereignty that we have outlined constituted for Hobbes a paradigmatic foundation for his reflections upon politics, he nevertheless did not believe that all sovereigns were instituted in this orderly way. Indeed, 'there is scarce a Common-wealth in the world, whose beginnings can in conscience be justified',[85] for they nearly all actually originated in conquest. Hobbes certainly dealt specifically with conquest in his discussion of the 'Common-wealth by Acquisition ... where the Soveraign Power is acquired by Force',[86] yet little of the discussion of politics in part II of *Leviathan* was closely tied to this material. Presumably, Hobbes, wishing to speak of *authority*, not power, and of *rights* and *duties*, preferred to treat as normative an account of the origins and institution of authority that he admitted to be historically implausible but which could make some claim to being more than a 'might makes right' doctrine.[87] And, in any case, his account of sovereignty acquired by force was designed to show that 'the Rights, and Consequences' of such sovereigns were identical to those of the sovereign by institution.[88] Even the conqueror's rights rested 'on the Consent of the Vanquished',[89] given in a covenant, through one 'which obliges not the Victor longer, than in his own discretion hee shall think fit'.[90]

The rights of all sovereigns were thus identical, regardless of how they had acquired their sovereignty (and regardless of whether they were monarchs, aristocratic councils, or the *demos* itself). Hobbes's adoption of authorisation theory in *Leviathan* allowed him to expound these rights with great polemical force, often in ways that made telling points against the Parliamentarian theorists of the 1640s. The most notable example of this concerned the status of parliament itself. Hobbes's authorisation theory essentially made the sovereign the *representative* of the people. Thus any claim by parliament and the House of Commons to be such a representative[91] was quickly dismissed as a hopeless confusion:

> where there is already erected a Soveraign Power, there can be no other Representative of the same people, but onely to certain particular ends, by the Soveraign limited. For that were to erect two Soveraigns; and every man to have his person represented by two Actors, that by opposing one another, must needs divide that Power, which (if men will live in Peace) is indivisible; and thereby reduce the Multitude into the condition of Warre, contrary to the end for which all Soveraignty is instituted.[92]

Similarly, 'mixed monarchy' theory was condemned by Hobbes as envisaging not 'one Representative Person; but three'. Thus,

> if the King bear the person of the People, and the generall Assembly bear the person of a Part of the people, and another Assembly bear the person of a Part of the people, they are not one Person, nor one Sovereign, but three Persons, and three Soveraigns.[93]

No clearer example could be found of the way in which Hobbes's authorisation theory (and the concept of representation attached to it), built upon the *unitary* notion of a person, could buttress a Bodinian theory of indivisible sovereignty. Only God was capable of being three persons and remaining undivided.

Representativeness was not the only argument used by Parliamentarians to justify their claim that the two Houses had a share in sovereignty. They also appealed to the *public interest*, and contrasted the ability of a representative group to serve it with the inability of a single person. Hobbes's authorisation theory neatly turned the tables; though not altogether convincingly. In monarchies the public and private interest were kept together; in republics they were separated. A monarch could always help himself by helping his subjects; but the members of a ruling council might frequently find that they would personally benefit from acting against the public interest.[94]

While Hobbes's authorisation theory was of particular polemical value against the Parliamentarians, it also enabled Hobbes succinctly to restate the absolutist position that he had first espoused in the *Elements*. The argument now ran that, since the sovereign bore the person of all his subjects, then all the sovereign's acts were the acts of each of his subjects. There was thus nothing that the sovereign might not lawfully and justly do to his subjects. The sovereign's rights were unlimited.

> [B]ecause every Subject is by this Institution Author of all the Actions, and Judgments of the Soveraigne Instituted; it followes, that whatsoever he doth, it can be no injury to any of his Subjects; nor ought he to be by any of them accused of Injustice. For he that doth any thing by authority from another, doth therein no injury to him by whose authority he acteth. . . . [T]o do injury to ones selfe, is impossible.[95]

From which it clearly followed that the Sovereign could never be punished by his subjects for any action.[96] Hobbes clearly said, as he had said before, that the sovereign was in no way subject to the civil laws, and possessed a discretionary right to interfere with his subjects' property.[97] Included in these extensive rights was the sovereign's authority to decide what opinions and doctrines could be spoken in public or published, 'for the Actions of Men proceed from their Opinions; and in the wel governing of Opinions, consisteth the well governing of mens Actions'.[98]

The account of Hobbes's thought given so far captures its dominant flavour. There is, however, a crucial dimension to his political thinking that serves to provide it with an additional degree of complexity and subtlety. This dimension also helps us to understand why Hobbes's thought has been subject to such markedly divergent interpretations; why he has been seen both as a legal positivist with a theory of (absolute) sovereignty that effectively makes him the ancestor of Bentham or Austin, and as a genuine (even Christian) natural-law thinker, which makes him the successor of Thomas Aquinas.

Hobbes was, in a sense, *both* a legal positivist and a natural-law thinker. He reconciled these 'two antithetical currents', each of which was 'the negation of the other',[99] primarily by means of a peculiar but careful use of juridical terms.[100] In particular, one needs to probe carefully what Hobbes meant by a 'right', and a 'duty'. Strictly speaking, a right held by one person (or a 'claim-right') corresponds to a 'duty' imposed on another. If someone has a right to command something, then others have a duty to obey such a command. Hobbes, however, does not necessarily use the term 'right' in this sense. Instead he uses it to mean a 'liberty'. When Hobbes writes of someone having a 'right' he does not always mean that there is any 'duty' corresponding to this. Indeed, it may be that all other people have the same liberty, and no one is at all obliged to respect the rights of another. This is most obviously the case with the Hobbesian concept of 'natural right' (which is really an archetypal example of a 'liberty'). It is also, but less obviously, true of the 'rights' possessed by a civil sovereign, under certain circumstances. In most cases, the sovereign's rights do correspond to duties of the subject;[101] but there are areas in which the sovereign's right is in fact a liberty or privilege, and subjects are under no duty to respect such a 'right' when it is in their interest not to do so. (For example the sovereign had a 'right' to command the executions of criminals but no criminal had a duty to submit to such execution.) There were also peculiarities in Hobbes's use of the term *duty*: though the sovereign had duties, these did not correspond to rights against the sovereign held by other people.[102] This is because these duties were imposed upon the sovereign by the law of nature, which in Hobbes's understanding of it was only enforceable via the civil law, to which the sovereign could not be subject. A person's performance of the duties imposed on him by nature could not be demanded of right by any other person. Also for Hobbes, a (natural) duty did correspond to an absence of liberty in oneself, but not to a right in another person.[103] By using his terms in this way – that is, by separating the terms 'right' and 'duty' – Hobbes was able to construct two parallel languages of political instruction, a natural and a civil one, and to avoid any clash between them.

The central principle of Hobbes's civil politics was, as we have already seen, was that there were no limits on the sovereign's rights. The central principle of his natural politics was that, nevertheless, there were things that a sovereign ought not to do. He had *natural* duties. Furthermore, should he ignore those limitations, the sovereign might well endanger the stability of his own rule.[104] Two points need to be firmly established. First, sovereigns *were*, in Hobbes's view, bound by natural law,[105] though actions against natural law were not unjust, but iniquitous.[106] And, secondly, a sovereign's iniquitous actions had consequences. Even though such actions could not justify a subject's disobedience, they were in actual fact likely to produce rebellion. There were 'Naturall Punishments ... naturally consequent to the breach of the Lawes of Nature'; and 'Negligent government of Princes, [was punished] with Rebellion.'[107] Read in this light, the extensive advice that Hobbes gave to princes throughout part II of *Leviathan* needs to be taken into account. In *De Cive*, indeed, he had explicitly warned sovereigns that where they failed properly to administer justice, 'the commonwealth itself is dissolved, and each man recovers his right to protect himself at his own discretion'.[108] Although he was not so explicit in *Leviathan*, Hobbes seems always to have thought that a sovereign who failed to govern with some minimum (but undefined) level of competence would *de facto* return his (or her, or its) subjects to a state of nature. There came a point when a chaotic judicial system ceased to be much different from a war of all against all.

What things, then, might Hobbes have expected the sovereign to do if he were not to destroy the society over which he ruled?[109] Much of the advice that Hobbes gave on this matter was collected in chapter 30, 'Of the Office of the Sovereign Representative'; and a good deal of it can be construed as a set of instructions about how not to contravene natural law. Some of the advice is obvious: for example, a sovereign was acting against his *duty* (i.e., a duty imposed by natural law, for civil law was not binding on the sovereign; but corresponding to no right in the subject) if he alienated any of the rights of sovereignty. Furthermore, the sovereign failed in his duty if he did not ensure that his subjects were aware of the true basis of sovereign authority.[110] Hobbes's reason for imposing this duty on sovereigns is interesting. It suggests to us that here we have reached the boundary of the artificial civil world, and that that world rests upon natural foundations. The sovereign's rights must be properly understood by the subject, 'because they cannot be maintained by any Civill Law':

> For a Civill Law, that shall forbid Rebellion, (and such is all resistance to the essentiall Rights of Soveraignty,) is not (as a Civill Law) any obligation, but by vertue onely of the Law of Nature, that forbiddeth the violation of Faith; which naturall obligation if men know not, they cannot know the Right of any Law the Sovereign maketh.[111]

As a matter of fact, the sovereign could not command his subjects not to rebel. They needed to be *persuaded* of the duty, or no law against rebellion would be of any effect. That, then, is why control over opinion was such a crucial thing for Hobbes; and why he really meant it when he said that on opinion all government rested. A sovereign could not survive unless enough of his subjects had true opinions about natural law; and it is therefore not surprising to find that Hobbes followed the passage just quoted with a lengthy account of what persuasion was necessary, and how it could be achieved. In the end, not even his supposed monopoly on force could save a ruler who allowed (or whose actions encouraged) subjects to hold the opinion that they could resist him. The foolish opinions of Hobbes's contemporaries needed stern reprimand.[112]

This advice might all be construed in terms of a sovereign's duty to maintain his own absolute sovereignty. The sovereign had a duty to see that his subjects behaved justly to one another;[113] he had a duty equally to administer justice, because he was bound by the natural law requiring equity;[114] he had a duty equally to impose taxes.[115] Above all, the sovereign was required to impose only *good* laws.

> But what is a good law? By a Good Law, I mean not a Just Law: for no Law can be Unjust. The Law is made by the Sovereign Power, and all that is done by such Power, is warranted, and owned by every one of the people; and that which every man will have so, no man can say is unjust. It is in the Lawes of a Common-wealth, as in the Lawes of Gaming: whatsoever the Gamesters all agree on, is Injustice to none of them. A good Law is that, which is *Needfull*, for the *Good of the People*, and withall *Perspicuous*.[116]

A sovereign who neglected such duties clearly committed no injustice, and provided his subjects with no justification for rebellion. This was so because terms like 'injustice' and 'right' took their meaning from a context of civil law. The fact remained that a sovereign who contravened the natural-law restrictions upon his authority might eventually cease to maintain order and thus precipitate the dissolution of society. Thus it was true that the natural punishment for negligent government was 'rebellion' – i.e. the renewal of a state of war.

Thus Hobbes's sovereign did have (natural) duties; and he might be punished (in this world) for ignoring them. Yet, at the same time, he had unlimited (civil) rights over his subjects, and could commit no injustice on them. Furthermore, those subjects never had a (civil) right to rebel, though they did have a (natural) right of individual self-defence; and might even find themselves returned to a state of nature by their sovereign's incompetence (in which case, of course, they had a (natural) right to do as they saw fit). In short, *Leviathan* contained parallel systems of natural rights and duties; and civil rights and duties. Those systems neither clashed nor met, and yet the natural duties that Hobbes imposed on his sovereigns were a little more than just empty attempts to preserve a conventional language of political morality.

Leviathan: the Theory of Ecclesiastical Politics

The place of God in Hobbes's system of politics is a matter fraught with controversy. On the face of it, Hobbes relegated God and religion to a secondary role, only discussing religious matters *after* he had already developed his political thinking along purely – or nearly so – secular lines. However, there are at least two possible reasons that Hobbes might have had for proceeding in this way, and both have a certain plausibility. An 'atheist' reading would maintain that Hobbes *only* discussed religious matters to fulfil the expectations of his audience, and to defuse the political implications of other people's religious beliefs; but that he was himself a thinly-disguised atheist. An alternative reading might accept that Hobbes was a genuine, if unorthodox, Christian believer; but that he first constructed his politics naturalistically because he wished to address people of all and every religious persuasion. He therefore by-passed or bracketed, rather than rejected, religious belief in order to give his ideas an appeal that transcended religious differences. When religion was discussed, the discussion aimed to show that the Christian religion, in particular, taught nothing contrary to the politics derived from nature; and, indeed, that it *reinforced* such politics in a number of ways. This latter view, then, would take Hobbes's seeming relegation of religion as an operative step towards reaching conclusions of general, rather than of religiously partisan, appeal. Given the context of religious civil war within which he wrote, there were good reasons for Hobbes to adopt such a procedure.

On the whole it seems safer to assume the second of these views. Although Hobbes's remarks on religion undoubtedly contain elements that give us cause for some suspicions about the sincerity of his religious professions,[117] we do at least read *Leviathan* in accordance with its persuasive intentions when we lay aside any attempt to uncover its atheism.[118] That remains the best procedure, even though Quentin Skinner has demonstrated convincingly the degree to which Hobbes's writings on the church and religion display satire and ridicule.[119]

Hobbes first mentioned religion as early as chapter 6 of *Leviathan*, in which he offered some terse definitions of the passions. These included:

> *Feare* of power invisible, feigned by the mind, or imagined from tales publiquely allowed, RELIGION; not allowed, SUPERSTITION. And when the power imagined, is truly such as we imagine, TRUE RELIGION.[120]

Reducing religion to the passion of fear, and making the difference between religion and superstition simply one of civil law, were controversial moves; and it was not clear from so brief an introduction to the subject quite how far the definition of true religion went to restoring some acceptability to Hobbes's account. But clearly, he early on struck a naturalistic tone in his discussion of religion, and this was continued in chapter 12, 'Of Religion'. We should not mistake this naturalism as necessarily implying more than it does. Through to the end of part II of *Leviathan*, Hobbes was concerned with taking account only of what could be known of religion through natural reason alone. This was part of his effort to construct a political theory of universal appeal. The first two parts of *Leviathan*, therefore, confined themselves to a discussion of the kingdom of God by nature; and in that kingdom, God ruled by natural law, i.e. by the dictates of natural reason.[121] This ought to mean that God naturally ruled *all* men, Christian, infidel, or atheist, for all men had access to natural law. All that distinguished the Christian from the atheist was the fact that the former was aware, while the latter was not, that the laws of nature by which he was bound were also the commands of God. Nevertheless, the atheist would still be a member of the kingdom of God by nature. At one point, Hobbes said as much.[122] Elsewhere, however, he said the exact opposite: that the atheist, by not recognising God's authority, was *not* a member of the kingdom of God by nature.[123] It is not obvious why this should be so, as all men should have access to the dictates of nature whether or not they recognise them as divine commands.

The crucial question is whether or not the fact that a state accepted 'true religion' altered the situation and character of a civil society initially analysed entirely in terms of natural reason and human passions. As far as the *present* (i.e., the period between the crucifixion and resurrection of Christ and the general resurrection) was concerned, religion had for Hobbes only a minimal political role. This had not always been the case, and would not forever remain the case. From the covenant of Abraham until the election of Saul as King and perhaps beyond into the time of the prophets, the Jews constituted God's 'peculiar people', and he ruled them as a 'prophetic' (not a natural) kingdom.[124] This was most particularly true after Moses had renewed the covenant with God and before the people had asked Samuel for an ordinary secular King, when there was a situation in which God 'governed them [the Jews], and none but them, not onely by naturall Reason, but by Positive Lawes, which he gave them by the mouths of his holy Prophets'.[125] The people of Israel were obliged 'to those Laws which Moses should bring unto them from Mount Sinai; and which afterwards the High Priest for the time being, should deliver to them . . .'.[126] This peculiar people thus formed in this time a literal kingdom of God: God was its sovereign, acknowledged by covenant, though that sovereignty was effectively exercised by Moses and his successors. Moses' authority was itself constituted by the promise of his people to accept always that God spoke directly to him, and to him alone.[127] Thus Moses and his successors, the High Priests were for practical purposes the sovereigns of the kingdom of God, and they derived their sovereignty from popular consent in the form of the people's promise to have faith in their representation of God's will.

This situation – a not altogether happy one[128] – came to an end when the people asked Samuel for a King (Isaiah 8.5), and consequently 'in deposing the High Priest of Royall authority, they deposed that peculiar Government of God', though they did so with God's consent.[129] In the following period, through to the Captivity, God still spoke to the Jews through special prophets, though sovereignty over matters civil and ecclesiastical remained with the kings.[130] This was an unstable situation; but it too was now ended. Prophets had been distinguished by two things: 'One is the doing of miracles; the other is the not teaching any other Religion than that which is already established.'[131] Miracles, however, have ceased; and thus prophecy too has ceased, leaving scripture as the only guide to God's will.[132]

Christ came to renew the covenant, but he did not immediately re-establish God's kingdom on earth. Instead, he promised that there would return at some indeterminate time in the future a literal kingdom of God on earth; and required of Christians only to accept this promise, and to obey God's government. Those who thus had faith were members of the kingdom of Grace, but would not become true subjects of the real kingdom of God (the kingdom of Glory) until after the general resurrection. Following that resurrection (before which the body and soul had together died[133]), Christ would return and rule the world of the saints on earth. They would live forever in a sexless passionless eternity; while the damned (and their progeny) would be condemned to die a second and permanent death. This was the true significance of Hell, and eternal torment.[134]

Thus the past has seen and the future would see a political kingdom of God on earth, a kingdom in basic respects much like any other. Clearly, in those kingdoms there was and would be a direct interpenetration of religion and politics, though at least in the past this had meant little more than the fact that subjects covenanted to give obedience to someone whom all accepted as the mouthpiece of God. But the present was another matter altogether. Christians in the present lived under no *peculiar* kingdom of God at all (though they were under the kingdom of God by nature); but were asked to have faith that there would one day again be such a peculiar kingdom. The crucial political points to follow from this were that for contemporary Christians, the *only* communication they had with God was *via* his word recorded in the scriptures; and consequently that the Christian churches had no direct spiritual contact with God. In no way could they serve as privileged intermediaries between God and the individual Christian. Nor did any Christian individuals, through inspiration or personal revelation, have direct contact with God – or, more exactly, if they did have it no one could be expected to believe them, nor could any *general* communication be made by God through such individuals.[135] Without miracles, no one could prove a claim to be a prophet, and he (or she, given the number of female prophets in the English Revolution) ought properly to be ignored.[136]

It seems fair to say, then, that *the* crucial point made in the third and fourth parts of *Leviathan* was that the phrase 'the kingdom of God', when used in the scriptures, never meant the church. Hobbes used this point to attack both the Catholic Bellarmine and the Calvinist Presbyterian Beza,[137] both of whom used the equation of the church with the kingdom of God to justify its independence from (and interference with) civil sovereignty. They claimed for the church privileged access to the meaning of God's will. But the church instituted by Christ was no more than

> *A company of men professing Christian Religion, united in the person of one Soveraign; at whose command they ought to assemble, and without whose authority they ought not to assemble.* And because in all Commonwealths, that Assembly, which is without warrant from the Civil Sovereign, is unlawful; that Church also, which is assembled in any Common-wealth, that hath forbidden them to assemble, is an unlawful Assembly.[138]

Deprived of any particular spiritual function, the church became a voluntary association of citizens. Like all subordinate associations,[139] the church must remain subject to the civil sovereign. Indeed, in *Leviathan* at least, Hobbes expressed his preference for a decentralised church made up of many voluntary independent congregations – churches rather than a church – each politically unclamorous and recognising its subjection to the civil sovereign. Congregationalism was, in a real sense, the logical end-point of Hobbesian ecclesiology,[140] though his initial definition of a church does appear to be framed with *national* churches, like the Church of England, in mind. Hobbes recognised that most Christian states preferred to have a single national church. National churches were indeed nothing but the Christian commonwealth itself, and the distinction between temporal and spiritual government entirely specious. The church, with no spiritually privileged position, could claim no special spiritual authority. Its chief pastor could be none other than the civil sovereign, who even had authority to baptise and consecrate simply by virtue of being sovereign.[141] The ecclesiastical power possessed by the clergy of any church or churches was no more than a power to teach.[142] Only the sovereign had the power to make religious demands a matter of *law*, and thus to impose their observance on the consciences of his subjects.[143]

Even before he had begun to write of the church and its authority, Hobbes had dealt with the scriptures.[144] As we have seen, his account of sacred history had demonstrated that scripture was the only means of communication that Christians collectively could have with God (until the second coming). Control over its interpretation thus became a crucial matter. Even if the church had no spiritual authority independent of the sovereign, it remained possible that groups or individuals could use scripture and its statements of God's will to legitimate disobedience to the sovereign. In fact, interpretation as such was not the crucial matter; what was important was the authority to impose one particular interpretation of scripture (and its requirements) on the consciences of others. Or, in Hobbes's words, '[t]he question truly stated is, *By what Authority they* [the scriptures] *are made law*'.[145] In so far as the commands contained in scripture were those also of the laws of nature, they 'carry their Authority with them, legible to all men that have the use of naturall reason'; in so far as they were particular commands to certain individuals or groups, they were binding only for those to whom God had immediately communicated them.[146] Otherwise,

> He . . . to whom God hath not supernaturally revealed, that they are his, nor that those that published them, were sent by him, is not obliged to obey them, by any Authority, but his, whose Commands have already the force of Laws; that is to say, by any other Authority, then that of the Common-wealth, residing in the Soveraign, who only has the Legislative power.[147]

This, as Richard Tuck has emphasised, certainly marks a considerable shift of emphasis from *De Cive* in 1642, in which the interpretation of scripture remained in the hands of the clergy, though they were not even there granted any real authority independent of the sovereign.[148] Certainly in *Leviathan*, as Hobbes went on to say, the church had been almost entirely deprived of authority. It was merely a voluntary association of believers. Unless the church was united in the person of the sovereign, it had no power at all.[149] As we have seen, there was no such thing as spiritual authority, distinct from civil: if the scriptures were imposed 'by authority', then between the resurrection of Christ and his second coming there was only *one* locus of authority in all human communities (Christian or infidel, heretic or orthodox) that could make such imposition.

Thus Hobbes radically undercut any argument for religious civil war, and produced in *Leviathan* a masterly explanation of why England's wars of religion ought never to have occurred. Subjects had mistaken opinions about both civil and ecclesiastical politics that Hobbes intended to clear up. In the Christian present, the only kingdom of God on earth was the natural one, so in the Christian present all Christians were in conscience bound to follow strictly the rules of a politics deduced from natural reason. That politics taught an unconditional duty of obedience to an absolute sovereign. It also made the sovereign the arbiter of what opinions could be espoused in public. In the absence of any other immediate communication from God, Christians were bound to obey their sovereign (even when infidel or heretical). To achieve salvation, Christians needed only to practise obedience and believe that Jesus was the Christ.[150] This latter doctrinal requirement was accepted by all Christians, and amounted in practical terms to no more than having faith in an eventual return of Christ to earth and a general resurrection of the dead. For that reason, also, the actual content of scripture was quite unimportant. No Christian needed a 'true' knowledge of scripture, for all that reason told us was that God required us to worship him and do him honour.[151] We could quite satisfactorily do this by following the forms of public worship laid down by the Sovereign; and by believing to be God's word whatever the sovereign told us was God's word. Religion was obedience – but not obedience to anything in particular. As Hobbes was later to put it, 'religion is not philosophy, but law'.[152] It was important to observe its requirements; it was not, however, necessary that any particular thing should be required. Christianity – and here Hobbes was making what is perhaps the most unconventional statement that even he ever made – was not concerned with the advancement of truth-claims other than that Jesus was the Christ. For those still troubled, there was one final let-off: one's *beliefs* were beyond the sovereign's jurisdiction. So long as a person conformed outwardly, he was perfectly free to believe whatever he chose. Should the sovereign command ungodly actions, one was perfectly safe in obeying such commands contrary to one's own private belief. The sin would be entirely the sovereign's responsibility.[153] Indeed, Hobbes went even further on this point, adding one of those warnings to sovereigns against breaking the laws of nature. Imposing unnecessary demands on the conscience was another way in which the sovereign could impose bad (i.e. unnecessary) laws. Such an error could arise from scholastic philosophy:

> another Error in their Civill Philosophy ... [was] to extend the power of the Law, which is the Rule of Actions onely, to the very Thoughts, and Consciences of men, by Examination, and *Inquisition* of what they Hold, notwithstanding the Conformity of their Speech and Actions. ... But to force him to accuse himselfe of Opinions,

when his Actions are not by Law forbidden, is against the Law of Nature. . . .[154]

Religious toleration had a place in Hobbes's thought similar to that of the restrictions imposed on monarchs by the law of nature in the civil sphere.[155] A sovereign would undermine his own authority by seeking to govern the consciences of his subjects (so long as their opinions were not of a sort to encourage seditious or unruly action), because he would unnecessarily push people into disobedience. The sovereign ought, by the dictates of natural law, to tolerate all pacific beliefs – but (the parallel with the civil doctrine, examined above, continues) equally the sovereign had every (civil and legal) right not to be tolerant.

In the end, then, Hobbes's solution to the problem of civil war was the same in both the ecclesiastical and the temporal spheres. The world was so constituted that the sovereign was the only person who could authoritatively interpret natural law to his subjects, and that individuals had no contact with God except through human authority. No prophet, priest or church could claim special insight into God's mind. Subjects must recognise that there were no limits to what their sovereign could justly command; while sovereigns ought to recognise that they would be prudent not to govern their subjects in ways that would lead to the dissolution of society. The main thrust of this argument was certainly to undermine the intellectual foundations of all Parliamentarian, radical and republican argument; but it may also be the case that Hobbes, like a good many other Royalists, was not unaware that Charles I and his supporters might have contributed unwittingly to their own downfall, not least in their promotion of the intolerance and interference of the Laudian clergy. Be that as it may, the enhanced attention given in *Leviathan* to religion is a measure of the degree to which Hobbes saw the conflicts of the English Revolution as, at bottom, religious.

8 Republicanism and the English Commonwealth: Political Thought during the Interregnum

Republicanism arose in the English Revolution because it seemed to some people, at least, to offer ways of healing and settling a nation in which the ancient constitution had been destroyed. In particular, it could come to terms with a situation in which monarchy no longer seemed a viable institution, being more damaging to the nation than beneficial. As a mode of settling the nation, republicanism could be very wary of Godly enthusiasm and zealotry. If it is true that 'almost all republican writing was overtly religiously engaged',[1] then engagement took a variety of forms, and in the case of James Harrington, for example, it was an engagement hostile to the political ideals of radical religion. Political stability required that enthusiasm be contained.

'It can plausibly be argued that English republican theory was far more the effect than the cause of the execution of the king in 1649.'[2] That verdict by Pocock and Schochet, has been much qualified by recent work that has revealed the civic humanist and neo-Roman elements in English political thought in the century and more before 1640. Yet the judgement remains fundamentally sound in one sense: overtly anti-monarchical political programmes were fully developed only after 1649, though some Parliamentarian thinkers might be considered quasi-republicans before that date, and very recent work has even suggested a sort of aristocratic republicanism evident in the early 1640s.[3] Republicanism and the rest of 'the political thought of the Interregnum was an attempt to fill the vacuum' created by the collapse of the traditional order in 1649.[4] Yet in the history of political thought true vacuums never really exist. The political thought of the 1650s was built to confront a new situation, but it was built out of materials already to hand. We shall need to begin with a study of the already existing republican elements in English political thought, before we can study in more detail the birth of a fully articulated republicanism in Commonwealth England.

Republicanism in English Political Thought before 1649

The building blocks of English republicanism include humanist ideas about citizenship and mixed government, and the Roman-law distinction between freedom and slavery, on which much could be built.[5] Late Tudor and early Stuart England witnessed – though very much at the margins – two forms of political argument that historians have been tempted to call 'republican'. There was first the baronial and jurisprudential argument designed to cope with an incapacitated monarch, and which at extremes might envisage a limited period in which the polity continued to exist and operate while the monarch did not. That sort of argument fed also into a broader pattern investigated by Conrad Russell in which the intellectual foundations of Charles I's diminished majesty were laid; and into what Richard Tuck, at least, has discerned as Henry Parker's 'republicanism'.[6] Secondly, there existed throughout the century or so before the Civil War, writers who used classical-humanist language to portray the English monarchy as a classical mixed polity in which a monarch ruled only in co-operation with a wider citizenry, especially a citizenry of senator-notables, giving counsel at court or through parliament. It is never very clear exactly how republican such arguments were. In most cases they amounted to expressions of the king's duty to govern through parliament and the other courts in all matters affecting the private rights (to property and life) of his subjects. Very few, if any, English theorists of classical mixed government seem to have pushed their arguments to the point of reducing the king to purely ministerial functions by trying to see him simply as the creation and agent of a citizen-body. The king of England, even in the eyes of those who did employ classical-humanist language, remained a king and not a republican magistrate. No one, I think, advocated elective monarchy for England after Thomas Starkey (and his *Dialogue* remained, of course, unpublished and unknown throughout this period).

It thus seems that what civic humanist ideas existed before 1640 were of a very muted variety, and similarly constitutional ideals of limited or mixed monarchy were not intended to be anti-monarchical. Some either envisaged the temporary absence of a monarch, and the rule in her or his place of men who were not exactly citizens but subjects briefly and temporarily able to wield royal authority; or alternatively they understood the English polity as a 'mixed government', a reading that often served as much to justify and idealise that polity (and its monarch) as to criticise it. A case could even be made for saying that these supposedly 'republican' elements in political reflection *reinforced* English monarchy as often as they undermined it, though this is a contention that would require further justification. The languages of civic humanism and Roman law, considered already in previous chapters, were multi-valent and not simply (or even primarily) languages of opposition, though clearly in the 1620s and at other times critics of royal policy were able to exploit them in interesting ways, as we have seen. By about 1600 English culture was so imbued with classical and humanist elements, not least because of the nature of grammar school education, that it became an acceptable and unchallenging practice to use them to produce idealised portraits of the English political system that were intended to sustain it as often as to subvert it. Charles I's *Answer to the xix Propositions* remains a classic example, albeit one that was probably seriously misjudged by its authors.

Some Independents and Levellers seem to have been reaching during the 1640s towards the conclusion that monarchy was incompatible with the liberty of the free-born Englishman, whom it inevitably reduced to slavery.[7] Yet Presbyterian, Independent and Leveller political thought drew different political and constitutional conclusions from broadly similar premises, and we should not assume any inevitable move towards the view that the only free polity was one without monarchy. The Levellers certainly developed the idea of the 'free-born' Englishman into a sort of theory of citizenship, but these citizens were primarily possessors of rights that limited governments, rather than rights of participation that might be altogether incompatible with monarchy.[8] What mattered, though, was that the polity was founded on a continuing basis of replenished consent, and they were willing on occasion to envisage the retention of monarchy provided that it was rooted in consent.[9] Consent was not given once the actions concerned were in the past, but all of the actions of a government in the present and future had to be made on a basis of consent. There was a considerable variety of opinions about the exact institutional or constitutional implications of such a view. But the inhabitants of these communities of consent did not necessarily participate in their own government, though they did agree to bestow their consent time and time again on the acts of their rulers. Independents and Levellers could envisage a republic, if we mean by that term a community not ruled by a single person; but they were perhaps more theorists of representative government than theorists of active citizenship.

These, then, were some of the intellectual resources out of which republicanism could be built. We need to examine the uses to which they were put after 1649, when England did indeed become a republic.

The Crucible of Republicanism: the Engagement Controversy and Political Debate in Commonwealth and Protectorate England

In several hesitant steps an English republic was created in the wake of Charles I's execution. The king had been beheaded on 30 January

1649. On 17 and 19 March respectively, monarchy and the House of Lords were abolished. Only on 19 May was England declared a 'Commonwealth and Free State' or republic. This republic would be governed 'by the supreme authority of this nation, the representatives of the people in Parliament' and the officers appointed by that body.[10] Over the following years three ways of defending the legitimacy of this new and non-monarchical régime developed.[11]

The most obvious defence was based on Independent regicidal arguments, themselves an extension of the Parliamentarian resistance theory developed during the first Civil War. This argument did not claim that the new republic was necessarily better than a monarchy. It did not, that is to say, defend the Commonwealth *as* a republic. On the other hand, by 1649 this style of argument had certainly developed into a sustained critique of most actual monarchs. Thus one writer, probably Cuthbert Sydenham, in 1650 admitted 'that there have been some good Kings, yet they have been so few, that as their names from the beginning of the world can hardly make up the Dominical letters in the Almanack [i.e. seven]'.[12] John Milton went even further, suggesting that since kings exercised authority only by consent and for the good of the people, 'then may the people as oft as they shall judge it for the best, either choose him or reject him, retaine him or depose him though no Tyrant, meerly by the liberty and right of free born Men, to be govern'd as seems to them best'.[13]

None of this exactly precluded the legitimacy of monarchy in some form, nor did it do much to develop a sense of citizenship. Milton, admittedly, could get closer, especially to the former. Witness his statement in *Eikonoklastes* – an official reply to Charles I's *Eikon Basilike* – that

> every Common-wealth is in general defin'd, a societie sufficient of it self, in all things conducible to well-being and commodious life. Any of which requisit things if it cannot have without the gift and favour of a single person, or without leave of his privat reason, or his conscience, it cannot be thought sufficient of it self, and by consequence no Common-wealth, nor free; but a multitude of Vassalls in the Possession and domaine of one absolute Lord; and wholly obnoxious to his will.[14]

Milton continued ostensibly to accept the legitimacy of non-tyrannical kingship, as defined by Aristotle and others: 'him who governs to the good and profit of his People, and not for his own ends'.[15] Similarly, in his 1651 official defence of the Commonwealth against Salmasius,[16] *Pro Populo Anglicano Defensio* [defence of the people of England], Milton was careful in 'disclaiming ... any hostility to monarchy as such', though equally he defended the view that a king must be no more than a 'magistrate of the kingdom'.[17] The second thing to note is that Milton's republicanism in 1649–51 was considerably veiled by his appeal to English constitutional and legal precedent. The passage from *Eikonoklastes* quoted above was immediately followed by the suggestion that its muted vision of kingship was simply a deduction from the legal status of English kings:

> for as the King of England can doe no wrong, so neither can he doe right but in his Courts and by his Courts; and what is legally don in them, shall be deem'd the Kings assent . . . so that indeed without his Courts or against them, he is no King. If therefore he obtrude upon us any public mischeif, or withhold from us any general good, which is wrong in the highest degree, he must doe it as a Tyrant, not as a King of England, by the known Maxims of our Law.[18]

In 1651 Milton was to make telling use of the medieval legal authorities Bracton and Fleta to defend the principle that by English law, 'if a king had done wrong to his whole people, he should have persons who cannot only bridle and check him but judge him and punish him too'.[19]

This line of argument was an extrapolation from Parliamentarian resistance theory. As such, it had two serious weaknesses when employed to defend the Commonwealth. First, it brought with it all the conflict of the years of Civil War. Independent arguments were bitterly opposed by those who had stood against the regicide, namely Presbyterians and Royalists. These groups are very likely to have made up a majority of the politically active nation. If it was to survive, the Commowealth needed arguments that could appeal to these groups. It needed something other than Independency. A second weakness was that Independent arguments were entirely negative. They defended the act of regicide well enough, but provided little direct legitimation of the non-monarchical regime established in its wake. It is astonishing that the arguments published by Milton as late as 1651 make so little effort to justify the new régime, except as the product of an act of justice on a tyrant. That is, of course, partly explicable in terms of a polemical style that led Milton to stick very closely to the text of Salmasius to which he was replying; but the work nonetheless gave unmistakably the impression of being an argumentative dead-end.[20]

This Independent way of defending the Commonwealth was not primarily a defence of republicanism. It was instead constructed as an analysis of the nature of monarchy, or of what the people could do in response to tyranny; and it rested on an interpretation of the nature of the historical English monarchy, not on an outright rejection of the legitimacy of that monarchy. Interestingly, however, the Rump Parliament produced a defence of its actions on 22 March 1649 that blended this Independent theory with a more overt republicanism. The parliament of England, 'elected by the people of England whom they represent', had 'long contended against tyranny', and the establishment of a republic was in a sense no more than a development of the need to resist the tyranny of Charles I. But they went further. Kingship was instituted 'by Agreement of the People, who chose one to that office for the protection and good of them who chose him', yet 'very few have performed the trust of that office with righteousness'! None failed in his duty more completely than Charles I. So what was to be done? The same popular authority that instituted kingship could 'change that government for a better; and instead of restoring tyranny, to resolve into a free state'. A defence of republics followed: in them justice was more equally administered and the people less economically oppressed. Republics were also, like Venice, less troubled by internal dissension. A nation was much better without the need to support the 'luxury and prodigality' of a royal court. Wisely, therefore, the commons had 'judged it necessary to change the government of this nation . . . into a Republic, and not to have any more a king to tyrannize over them'.[21]

This defence of the superiority of republics over monarchies was the second way in which the Commonwealth could be defended, and we shall be returning to it presently. But it was a third line of defence, the so-called *de facto* argument developed in the Engagement Controversy,[22] that seems to have been the most telling. During 1649 the Rump gradually extended the range of people who were required to take a loyalty oath (the Engagement) to the Commonwealth. This culminated in an Act of 2 January 1650 which imposed on all adult males the legal duty to swear the Engagement oath: 'I do declare and promise, that I will be true and faithful to the Commonwealth of England as it is now established, without a king or House of Lords.'[23] Already by this time a substantial pamphlet debate (the Engagement Controversy) was developing, particularly over the question of whether or not it was permissible in conscience for men who had in the past sworn oaths of allegiance to Charles I now to swear allegiance to the régime that had executed and replaced him. In defence of taking the allegiance, a number of writers began to make much of the duty of all private subjects to accept allegiance to *de facto* powers, i.e. to any persons or institutions that had in fact the power to govern, regardless of how they had acquired that power. This argument was not, however,

simply a case of 'might makes right', for it advanced what was ultimately a moral case suggesting the legitimacy of *de facto* powers.[24]

The Engagement Controversy was fundamentally an episode in the
history of casuistry. Two chief lines of argument were developed by
those supporting the Engagement. The first was a simple providentialism, developed even before the question of taking the Engagement
had arisen, by Francis Rous, a seventy-year-old puritan divine, MP since
1625, and step-brother to John Pym. His pamphlet *The Lawfulnes of
Obeying the Present Government*, appearing on 25 April 1649, was aimed
at Presbyterians, of whom he claimed to be one. He wanted to
persuade them 'that though the change of a Government were
beleeved not to be lawfull, yet it may lawfully be obeyed'. He therefore
tackled directly a key weakness of the Independent line of defence,
that it offered nothing new to help persuade those who had already
firmly rejected Independent arguments. Rous began his argument
with an exegesis of Romans 13. The Roman emperors who most probably ruled when St Paul penned that Epistle (Claudius or Nero) were
themselves unlawful rulers, yet we were commanded to obey them in
conscience. *All* powers, good and bad, were ordained of God.[25] English
history equally showed that 'many persons have beene setled in
supreame power and authority by meere force without title of inheritance, or just conquest'. But they had been obeyed, and their laws
continued to be obeyed. The lesson was simple: 'the Nation with one
consent seemes to Speake aloud; That those whose Title is held unlawfull, yet being possest of authority, may lawfully be obeyed' (4–6). The
people are incapable of judging titles to authority, but 'th[e]y see who
doth visibly and actually exercise power and authority' (9). The argument was in essence simple: God had commanded obedience to all
those who actually possessed power, regardless of how it had been
acquired.

On that basis others could argue more explicitly that changes of
government were always the work of divine providence, and the more
this was emphasised, the harder it was to maintain that such governments lacked proper title. Would not God's authorisation make up for
any merely human insufficiencies? The anonymous author of *The
Engagement Vindicated* began with a providentialism so broad that it
underlay all changes of government, and legitimated repeated and
sweeping alterations to constitutions. Yet this sat awkwardly alongside
the more Independent argument that changes of government were
legitimated only by consent of the representatives of the people.[26] A
number of works were quite explicit in defending the Commonwealth
from charges of usurpation. In the *Exercitation Answered* it was argued
that the Rump had a legitimate authority in co-ordination with king

and Lords, and could properly fill the gap when king and Lords no longer performed their functions.[27] But the author was taking no risks, and argued that even if the Commonwealth government was guilty of usurpation it was still to be obeyed on providential grounds.[28] Another work which denied that the new régime was founded in usurpation, also returned quickly to the providentialist perspective. It was quick to argue that God instituted 'the Place, Power and Authority of Governing', but not 'the Title of Governour, or the Form of Government'. On that basis a distinction could be drawn between 'Usurpation and Conquest', which were 'not Gods Ordinance', and any conqueror's 'Acts of Government, [which] are Gods Ordinance, and to be obeyed'.[29] Thus the power was always lawful, even though the hand wielding it was not. Such a distinction was, at best, only implicit in Rous. Making it explicit had the curious effect of muddying the argument by means of conceptual clarification. The lines between legitimacy and illegitimacy were even further blurred with the argument 'that the Common-weal be establisht as now it is . . . [by] the determination of providence', which must always be submitted to. The Civil War had been a trial by battle between king and parliament, and parliament's victory came from God himself.[30] The effect of these arguments was to suggest, in fact, that the legitimacy of any government was a matter utterly independent of the legitimacy of the means by which it had acquired authority.

Providential arguments remained prominent through the 1650s in works published in defence of the Protectorate.[31] On 22 November 1655, for example, John Moore's *Protection Proclaimed* appeared. It undertook to prove that the rule of Oliver Cromwell was 'of divine institution', and this it did by a very simple providentialist argument. '[S]uch an extraordinary and unheard-of change of Government in a Christian Nation, could not have been, but by the special hand and determinate counsel of God, who worketh all things after the counsel of his own will.'[32] The Protectorate 'answered the desire of God', and anyone who rejected its authority 'denies the Omniregency of God, and the Ordinance of his will'.[33] Even more than earlier pamphlets, these ones asserted that providence made the Protectorate not just a legitimate but a Godly government. John Hall's interesting attempt to defend the Protectorate on Royalist principles explicitly argued that the workings of providence resulted in 'making him the lawful Governor, whom the present Polity or Law hath set'.[34] Samuel Richardson employed a providential framework to account for 'the many Victories God hath given us'. They might all be taken to show that 'it is the will of god, that we should keep the power he hath given us'.[35] This providentialism certainly supported *de facto* authority, but it did so by denying its illegitimacy. The Cromwellian Protectorate was worthy of obedience because it was a *Godly* government. The wars of the 1640s were primarily 'for freedom in matter of Religion'. That freedom was now best secured by loyalty to Cromwell.[36] The only Saints imprisoned by him, like Christopher Feake the Fifth Monarchist, were so treated 'not for Religion, but for the safety of the Civill peace'.[37] In response to the charge that the Protectorate government was an 'arbitrary' one, Richardson simply replied that all governments were arbitrary. The important matters lay 'not in the having this or that Government, but in the justice and righteousness of those that governe'.[38] Notwithstanding its grounding in providence, Richardson's view was the opposite of any argument that encouraged obedience irrespective of the righteousness of the ruler.

Works published under the Protectorate also showed signs of the influence of the second variety of *de facto* theory developed in the Engagement Controversy. Indeed, one such work developed this line of argument much more single-mindedly than its predecessors. *The Grounds of Obedience and Government* was the work of a Catholic priest, Thomas White. White was quite dismissive of providentialist arguments for submission to government. He argued instead that the only proper way of governing free men was with their consent.[39] The subject's obligation to obey came from the fact that 'hee hath entrusted the Magistrate with the Governement' (180). In exploring the implications of this, and applying them to the circumstances of the 1650s, White argued that if it was to resist a government, then it was also rational 'to break and remove it'. In what circumstances was resistance a sensible course of action? The answer was, at least in principle, simple: 'when the occasion is greater then the value of the publick peace and good of the commonwealth' (109–20). Only the direst threat from a tyrant was sufficient to warrant resistance. Such resistance was never *lawful*, but was nonetheless carried out 'by the force of nature', even though from a legal point of view 'the people hath alienated all right of judging or medling in governement'. (This was a theory that looked back to Hobbes as well as to Hunton.) A tyrant precipitated individuals back into the chaos of nature, and allowed them to act for their own protection (120–3). What would happen, though, if a ruler were dispossessed even though he were no tyrant? It was at this point that White revealed the full extent of his commitment to *de facto* theory. Even after an innocent king had been replaced, 'it is plaine . . . it were better for the common good to stay as they are, then to venture the restoring him, because of the publike hazard'. Indeed, the deposed ruler had a duty 'to renounce all right and claime to Governement' (135–8). Thus subjects were bound always to follow their own collective good, and to obey whatever government was able to foster that good. '[T]heir good stands on the possessours side ... when the Merchant, the Husbandman, and Tradesman ... are in an undisturbed practice of their functions' (153).

Subjects should obey *de facto* powers so long as they were able to provide peace and the benefits of government. Any powers that could guarantee to fulfil the essential purposes of government were to be accepted. The legality of the means by which they had acquired power, like their particular form, was entirely irrelevant, for government was simply something that men created to achieve certain goals. The goals came first, not the interests of the rulers. This was a way of looking at the political world well suited to coping with the aftermath of a religious revolution, for it removed from the equation any need to consider whether rulers were Godly, or whether they passed any other test of legitimacy, save possessing the capacity to maintain peace and order. Rulers did not need to pass religious or moral tests.

This perspective had been extensively explored in the Engagement Controversy, above all by Anthony Ascham.[40] He was probably the author of at least four contributions to the Controversy.[41] He developed an approach that built on a long-standing theme in early modern English political thought – especially a theme in Royalist–conformist thought. That was the claim that in considering whether or not to obey the commands of rulers, 'the things commanded (as they are not in themselves bad) be above the Circumstantiall qualification of the Persons Commanding'.[42] Our obedience to governments is not dependent on the moral quality of the governors. They might be heretics, women, or even usurpers; but their commands were still to be obeyed. It was impossible for subjects to be certain of the moral or legal status of their rulers, and so, therefore, 'it is best and enough for our present Obedience, to informe our selves, Whether the kingdome bee plenarily possest by those who in present exercise immediate command over it. And if so, then we may obey them in ... lawful things ... '.[43] This principle was, however, grounded in the providentialism of Romans 13, which made changes of government the work of God's 'secret disposing', and not of 'meere chance or humane contrivance'.[44]

In his more substantial works Ascham had developed further his discussions of plenary possession, and of the reciprocal relationship between protection and obedience. His case rested on two planks. First, that obedience was always owed to those powers that were able to protect. A 'morall Magistrate' is always 'whoever hath the capacity so to hold inspection over us [and ensure that we live virtuously] ... but that can onely be he under whose full possession we actually are'. But beyond that, 'States cannot look so strictly after vertue, as after publique quiet.' Therefore, 'the chiefe convenience of a State, is, that people might be kept from inconvenience, or incommoding one another'.[45] Thus God set up the world in such a way that men would and should seek to obey whatever power could provide them with peace and order. In obeying that power, we were recognising not its just authority but God's. This was, of course, a not uncommon way of responding to the chaos of religious civil war, by focusing on the minimal purposes of government, and insisting that people act without question in such a way as to ensure that those purposes were achieved. '[R]eason of state is not busied so much about inward piety and vertue, as it is about publique quiet and repose.'[46]

The second plank of Ascham's argument was designed to rebut the charge that he was suggesting anything outrageously new. History demonstrated, he argued, that all governments were of dubious origin. '[W]e and our forefathers for the most part, have liv'd under no better Titles then *Plenary possession*.'[47] There was, indeed, no alternative, and no other way of achieving peace known to men. He asked, 'if . . . we should suspend all obedience till we have infallibly found out that Person who deserves a knowne and an indubitable right from him who was the first in compact . . . then I pray you of what can we resolve lesse, then certainly to extirpate one another?'[48] Unless you accept the government you have, you will keep destroying one another. It was a general law in human affairs that 'the *naked sword permit[s] . . . no nicenesse of obedience*'.[49]

Matters of faith were not the concern of governments, for '[a] Christian may be perfect in any State of Goverment'. But that did not mean that God had left human beings to look after themselves without all guidance in their temporal lives. In fact he commanded obedience to powers in *de facto* possession. Thus,

> our immediate Allegiance is due to those who immediately protect us, and plenarily possesse us, but in and above all to God, the Universall Eternall Magistrate, under whose jurisdiction we are to live eternally in another world.[50]

In obeying the possessor, one obeyed God's command to form societies in the only way possible in this world.

The intellectual origins of the theory lay, at least partly, in Royalist and conformist argument, including the doctrines of allegiance established in Calvin's Case (1608). In the 1640s it was a useful plank in the defence of Charles I. It is therefore not surprising to find that built into the theory of the greatest Royalist writer, Thomas Hobbes,[51] was the principle that '[t]he obligation of subjects to the sovereign is under-stood to last as long, and no longer, than the power lasteth by which he is able to protect them'.[52] But by 1651 that principle no longer worked in support of the Royalist cause. It pointed towards obeying the Commonwealth. John Bradshaw, president of the High Court of Justice which had tried Charles I in January 1649, put it succinctly in his sentencing speech (27 January 1649):

> This we know now – the one tie, the one bond, is the bond of protec-tion that is due from the sovereign; the other is the bond of subjec-tion that is due from the subject. Sir, if this bond be once broken, farewell sovereignty – 'protection entails subjection, subjection entails protection' (Coke in *Calvin's Case*).[53]

The mutual relationship between protection and subjection was no longer an obviously Royalist argument. Hobbes confronted that uncomfortable fact directly in the 'Review and Conclusion' to *Leviathan*. He tried there to ensure that the principle did not confer retrospective legitimacy on the Parliamentarian cause, but he could scarcely avoid accepting that when a ruler has been fully defeated, the subject's duty to obey him must end when 'he hath no longer protec-tion from him'. This was 'a thing inevitable', unpalatable as the fact might be in the present circumstances.[54] Hobbes was scarcely an enthusiastic supporter of the Engagement – he was not explicitly a supporter of it at all – but his writings were quarried by the pro-Engagers, including Ascham. This was a useful propaganda coup, enabling Ascham and others to show that even the jewels in the Royalist crown now twinkled for the Commonwealth. And Hobbes himself accepted, reluctantly or not, that his own theory, built as it was on the principle that men constructed governments to provide them with peace, could not avoid admitting that men could rightly obey whatever authority could provide that peace.

Not surprisingly, opponents of the Engagement were quick to suggest that arguments in defence of obedience to *de facto* authority were a recipe for chaos and immorality. Perhaps the best of the critics was the Presbyterian divine Edward Gee.[55] He was most successful in conjuring up the image of a world ruled by nothing but violence and force.

> If violent occupation made a right; then it were lawfull for any, that could make a sufficient strength for it, to rise up in Arms, invade or seize on any Kingdome or Territory, he can prevail over; yea to kill and destroy men and Countreys for Empire and Dominion.[56]

It did not end there. In a world of violence one could expect no restraint from rulers.

> Where there is no title but power, there can be no rule for Government but power and will: onely that which gives right to Magistracy must set bounds to it; how can they be tyed to Laws, in exercising Government, that are tyed to none in coming by it?[57]

In short, this was a world that made 'every man a Magistrate that will, and every Magistrate a Tyrant, to the height of mis rule, if hee list, and have force so to make himselfe'.[58] Furthermore, the Engagers' principles made a mockery of the principle of government by consent. If usurped governments were accepted, then there was no room for the 'maine and fundamentall Right' of 'the Peoples being Governed by their own legally invested Magistrates, and according to Lawes made by them that are so entrusted'.[59]

The Development of Republican Argument: John Hall and Marchamont Nedham

It is now time to return to those defences of the Commonwealth that relied on arguing for the superiority of republics over monarchies.[60] These arguments had one advantage over *de facto* arguments. If the latter gave the impression of legitimating a political world of continuing and perpetual violence, republican arguments, especially those derived in good part from Machiavelli, were at home in such a world, and suggested a way out of it. They were able to agree that the world was, indeed, one in which violence and force – providential revolutions, perhaps – played a big role. But they were able to argue, in addition, that to some degree it was possible to escape from the chaos of violence, by founding a true republic.

As we have seen, the Rump's *Declaration* of 22 March 1649 had already defended the superiority of republics over monarchies, and it had done so partly because republics were less prone to internal dissension. A number of other works published before 1653 presented similar arguments. On 24 October 1649, for example, there appeared a work, possibly by Henry Robinson,[61] that defended the Commonwealth by arguing that an aristocratic government was inherently superior to a monarchical one. Citing the Roman example, as recorded by Tacitus and Livy, Robinson claimed that 'when Kingly Power began to flourish, LIBERTY decayed, and so *e contra*'. Aristocratic government 'hath many more curbs, and bridles on it to restrain if from Exorbitancy'.[62] But Robinson did not develop the point far. Aristocracy was 'a middle State between Popular anarchy, and Prerogative Tyranny' – between, it emerged, the principles of the Royalists and of the Levellers.[63] It had brought strength and wealth to the Dutch and the Venetians. What Robinson's republicanism lacked, however, was any vision of constitutional refounding or of a thoroughly new beginning. Indeed, he scorned such a thing, associating it with the Levellers' Agreement of the People; and argued that aristocracy was almost a purified form of (traditional) monarchy at its best:

> when we have most solemnly considered Monarchy in its real use and end, it will be found to be in effect but an Aristocracy, though far more dangerous and mischievous; The same things are done, as to the good of the Publique, by States and Councels, which are done by Kings and Councels together; and either the King must rule by his own will, and then he is a profest Tyrant, or else by Counsel of his Parliament, and Publique Senators, and then it's the Councel that rules the Kingdom, who can do it as well, and with less hazard, without him.[64]

Becoming a republic is rather like having your appendix removed: the loss of a bothersome and diseased organ leaves you essentially unchanged. No wonder that John Hall lamented 'how inscrutably Providence carryes on the turns and stops of all Governments, so that most people rather found them then made them'. The implication was that a republican society had to be made, not waited for, a perspective which was some distance from that of the Engagers. Other causes of the persistence of monarchy were 'the constitutions of men . . . some not capable, some not willing' to be masters of their own liberty; and the 'Ambition' of tyrants.[65] Deftly, Hall had sketched a republican problematic: how could the corruption of men be overcome so that they would be fit to found a true republic?

Marchamont Nedham provided some answers, with a boldness that belies his reputation as a cynical conformist. Nedham more than anyone else deserves to be credited with the invention of English classical republicanism. For the first time in England since the early sixteenth century we come across humanist writings that envisage the refounding of the English polity on new principles. Others long before 1640 may have used republican and humanist ideas to analyse and criticise the English monarchy; others since 1645 had explored in various ways the possibility of settling the conflicts of the Civil War in an avowedly non-monarchical way. But it is only in Nedham that we find a broad, classical-humanist programme for the establishment of an English republic.

Nedham's republicanism first received public expression in a contribution to the Engagement Controversy, *The Case of the Commonwealth of England, Stated*, which appeared on 8 May 1650. The opening chapters of the *Case* showed how the world was shaped by 'the perpetual rotation of all things in a circle'.[66] Though Nedham could talk of this rotation in the language of providence (9), he was more interested in exploring the idea that the power of the sword lay at the root of all government. The first and archetypal ruler was Nimrod, a tyrant, who gained power by force (14–15). The history of monarchy was littered with examples of violence and usurpation. All of the kings of Christendom, 'if we trace up to their originals, we shall find to have no other dependence than upon the sword' (19). The same was equally true of republics: 'What title have the Swiss, the Hollanders, Geneva, &c., to their liberty but the sword? On the other side what title have the Medicis to domineer over the free states of Florence and Siena to the utter ruin of their liberties but only force?' (22). Initially, these facts led Nedham to support the necessity of obedience to *de facto* powers. The people always 'paid a patient submission to them [the powers in possession] under their various revolutions'. Indeed, according to civil lawyers the people not only *may* but *must* obey *de facto* powers, for by the *jus gentium* all conquerors were entitled to secure their 'right of dominion' by all means (28). If that was not enough to persuade waverers, then Nedham patiently explained that those who refused submission could expect no protection: 'the throats of every refuser are wholly at their [ruler's] mercy' (30).

Nedham deftly turned thus against monarchy. If there was no difference in inherent legitimacy between the two forms of government, if monarchy could not claim superior moral standing, then the way might be open to a consideration of the merits of republicanism on other grounds. The legitimacy of violent change that Gee so deplored could clear the ground for a new defence of the right of the people to create or found by the sword a free state for themselves. In the final chapter of the *Case*, Nedham provided just such an argument.

Nedham marvelled – like Hall – at 'how lightly men prize this invaluable jewel of liberty', thus making it so difficult for the new republic to survive. Why did men not greet more enthusiastically the establishment of a régime that was in their own interests? For answers, Nedham turned explicitly to Machiavelli (*Discourses*, I, 16–18). The first explanation of the puzzle lay in 'education and custom'. Men reared under monarchy or tyranny were like 'beasts which have been caged or cooped up all their lives in a den where they seem to live in as much pleasure as other beasts that are abroad, and if they be let loose, yet they will return in again because they know not how to value or use

their liberty'. Thus subjects were bred and educated to be 'so enam-
oured of their chains that they admire their own condition above all
others' (111–12).

The second explanation lay in corruption. There was 'a general
corruption and degradation of manners by luxurious courses'. Because
of that, men 'being slaves to their own lusts, they become more easily
enslaved unto the lusts of another'. The history of Rome illustrated this
lesson clearly. When the early republic 'was in its pure estate', then
'virtue begat a desire of liberty, and this desire begat in them an
extraordinary courage and resolution to defend it'. But in time the
Romans 'lost that ancient virtue which purchased their liberty'. And so
'being softened in their manners and conquered by their vices . . . they
soon bowed under the yoke of imperial tyranny' (112–13).

These lessons could easily be applied to the England of 1650. The
people's 'former education under a monarchy' and their 'general
debaucheries' made them lovers of the 'pomp of tyranny' and enemies
to that freedom. The core of the problem was that the people were 'led
with an admiration of old customs to their own hazard rather than they
will steer a new and reasonable course of far more convenience and
commodity'. Thus Nedham was, like Hall, rather gloomy in his estima-
tion of the people's fittedness to be good citizens. That led him to
entrust the commonwealth's safe continuance to a virtuous elite. The
Commonwealth had its own party of 'men of valor and virtue', made
up of 'counselors, grave, serious, abstemious, and vigilant', and an
army led by commanders 'severe and strict in discipline, both moral
and military'. Together they provided an impregnable foundation
(114). The rest of the population, though unworthy, ought at least for
fear or shame to forgo opposition to these virtuous men (115).

Free states were everywhere the oldest forms of government (what
now of Nimrod?). But more than that, free states were superior in that
they enlarged 'wealth and dominion'. Guicciardini had pointed out
that in free states there was more concern for the common good, and
a closer approximation to the equal administration of justice. Though
occasionally monarchies were ruled by a virtuous prince, this situation
never persisted for more than a generation. Virtue was not inheritable.
Therefore Machiavelli most commended those figures who established
free governments rather than those who were virtuous rulers themselves (117–18). This noble person was the founder of a republic.
Again we find it suggested that foundation cannot be the work of a
whole people but must be the work of a public-spirited one or few.

Nedham completed his solution to the problem of refounding
English politics after regicide by making completely clear the subordination of religion to civil politics. He argued for religious toleration.

'[V]ariety of opinions can be no way destructive of public peace'; but also, drawing upon Justus Lipsius, laid down three conditions for it to be beneficial. The rulers must not favour some religions over others; they must punish severely those who disturbed their neighbours for religious reasons; and they must not tolerate evil to be spoken of the state religion. If these rules were followed, then toleration produced public peace and quiet. Persecution, on the other hand, was a major cause of sedition, and those who sought uniformity were 'the greatest disturbers of states and kingdoms' (123–5).

Soon after these words were published, Nedham was appointed editor, under Milton's general supervision, of the Commonwealth's official weekly newsbook, *Mercurius Politicus*. The first issue appeared in June 1650. Nedham was an experienced propagandist, and had edited both Parliamentarian and Royalist newsbooks in the 1640s.[67] From issue 16 of *Mercurius Politicus* (19–26 September 1650) to issue 69 (25 September–2 October 1651), Nedham intermittently serialised the *Case* in the form of short editorials. From issue 70 (2–9 October 1651) to issue 114 (5–12 August 1652) another series of editorials appeared, and these were later published in book form as *The Excellencie of a Free State* (1656).[68]

Nedham's *Excellencie* needs to be read with care. Notwithstanding its official status, the work was implicitly but unmistakably critical of some aspects of the Commonwealth. No English government after 1649 matched the ideal 'free state' that Nedham delineated. Like Harrington, Nedham touched on the importance of a bicameral legislature, and of the need for a rotation of office-holders. On both grounds the Rump was wanting. Especially in those pages which formed the introduction to the *Excellencie* of 1656, Nedham was clearly critical of the Commonwealth government. The Rump itself could be said to be precisely the sort of 'standing Senate' to which Nedham was hostile.[69] But these arguments were not later additions. With minor changes, they are to be found in the corresponding editorials of *Mercurius Politicus*. This forms an important line of connection between Nedham and James Harrington and his *Oceana* of 1656.[70]

Nedham lamented that the English, unlike the people of Athens or Rome, were slow to learn what freedom required, even when presented with the opportunity to have it. He was not slow in helping them out. True freedom, he stated,

consists not in a License to do what you list, but in these few particulars: First, in having wholesome Laws suted to every Mans state and condition; Secondly, in a due and easie course of administration, as to Law and justice, that the Remedies of Evil may be cheap and speedy. Thirdly, in a power of altering Government and Governours upon occasion; Fourthly, in an uninterrupted course of successive Parliaments, or Assemblies of the People. Fifthly, in a free Election of Members to sit in every Parliament, when Rules of Election are once established. By enjoying these onely, a people are said to enjoy their Rights, and to be truely stated in a condition of safety and Freedom. (4–5)

The question that Nedham then went on to raise constituted one of the core themes of his book. How was freedom to be preserved? By a fixed and permanent constitution which committed power 'into the hands of a standing Power'; or 'by placing the Guardianship in the hands of the People, in a constant succession of their supreme Assemblys'? For Nedham, as for Machiavelli, the 'best way to determine this, is by observation out of Romane Stories' (5–6). Roman history showed, in fact, that the 'people never had any real Liberty, till they were posess'd of the power of calling and disssolving the Supreme Assemblies, changing Governments' and making laws, as well as 'chusing and deputing whom they pleased to this work, as often as they should judge expedient, for their own well-being, and the good of the Publike' (6). When they expelled the kings who initially ruled them, the Romans made a mistake. They 'forgat to drive out the Mysteries and inconveniences of kingly power, which were all reserved within the hands of the Senate'. Foolishly, they believed themselves a free state just because they were not ruled by a king. But in reality the Romans, like the Spartans and the Venetians, had aristocratic councillors to 'king' it over them instead. In Venice, the people were free of the Doge, 'but little better than slaves under the power of their Senate' (6–8). Rome was only a free state when the Tribunes were established (12, 15). Then, power was shared by patricians and people, as in Venice (though weighted there too much to the patricians) and the United Provinces (16). Only the Athenians got things right from the beginning, for, though they established a senatorial council, the Areopagus, they left law-making authority still in the hands of popular assemblies (8).

Fundamental to Nedham's own purpose in writing, especially in the *Mercurius Politicus* editorials, was the question of how liberty, once achieved, could be preserved. He was troubled by the fear that a people who had acquired freedom would become corrupt and lose all that they had gained. The *Mercurius Politicus* editorials were, then, efforts to deal with that situation delineated in the *Case*. A people educated under monarchy needed to be re-educated in the means to preserve a republic. Nedham's weekly lessons from Roman history were to provide that education.[71] A people 'bred up and instructed in the brutish Principles of Monarchy' would be led to 'understand what

Commonwealth-Principles are' (81–2). The essential point, as we have seen, was to insist that 'standing' powers of whatever sort were dangerous. We need to explore in detail some of the key arguments with which Nedham surrounded this basic point.

The task facing the English was 'the manner of setling authority upon the close of a Civil Warre, for the recovery of Liberty'. A people 'that have gained it [liberty] by the sword' can only retain it when power is kept in the hands of the people themselves (244). By putting things in this way, Nedham reveals that he has achieved a better resolution than in the *Case*, of the conflict between the idea that all governments are founded in the sword, and the idea that republics based on consent are the best (and earliest) sort of government. Replying in the *Excellencie* to a patriarchal theory very much like that of Sir Robert Filmer,[72] Nedham distinguished between natural or patriarchal government and political government. He agreed that the earliest governments were formed by the rule of patriarchs over an extended family, and that Nimrod, the first tyrant, formed his government by conquering several family groups. He ruled arbitrarily. Political governments appeared only later, when civil societies were formed on the basis of election, consent and mutual compact. The earliest evidence of a people exercising its right to choose its own form of government was when the Israelites rejected theocracy in favour of the monarchy of Saul, foolish though the choice might have been (129–34). The thing that linked together force and consent was Nedham's claim that the people could 'assert their own Rights of Election and Consent (as often as they had opportunity) in the various turns of institution and alteration of Government' (135). This is what the English people were doing: they had won liberty by the sword; they had to secure it by instituting a government that was soundly based on the people's consent. In doing that, they would achieve stability as well as freedom. Implicitly, then, Nedham's final verdict on the ideas of the Engagement Controversy was that a politics based on the sword could be reconciled with a politics based on consent. There was no need to rest content with an amoral acceptance of any *de facto* authority, *provided that* the people took their opportunity to secure the foundations of a free state.

Protection against tyranny and oppression could only be found 'in those States, where all men are brought to taste of Subjection as well as rule, and the Government settled by a due succession of Authority, by consent of the People' (79). This statement is about as precise as Nedham got in delineating the structure that a republic ought to possess. Its central insistence was on 'succession', or a rotation of office, important precisely because it made even the rulers into subjects, essential to the preservation of liberty. Nedham supported the Aristotelian principle (e.g. *Politics*, 1261a, 1279a, 1325b, 1332b: '[political] liberty . . . consists in the interchange of ruling and being ruled', 1317b) that power should rotate amongst the people and not remain permanently in the hands of any individual, family, or faction. It was essential that rulers were also ruled; it was much less important that the ruled were also rulers. That is another way of saying that Nedham did not have a strongly developed sense of active citizenship. Whereas, for Aristotle, the principle of rotation was valuable because it enabled all men to have some share in the most fully human of activities, ruling politically; for Nedham it was important because it ensured that rulers would not be tempted to make laws that were oppressive to others. It guaranteed freedom less as active participation, more as protection from the excesses of government. The crucial thing about republican politics for Nedham was that it kept 'Officers and Governours in an accountable state', something best achieved when there was a 'revolution of Government [i.e. rotation of offices] in the Peoples hands' (79–80). It was 'by [that] . . . means alone, [that] they will be able to know whether they have done well or ill, when they feel the effects of what they have done'. That was the *only* prevention against abuse of power, since there was no appeal against acts of the 'Supreme Body of the People', and a 'due course of Succession' of its members had to be maintained. Those members had therefore to be aware that at some future point they would be fully subject to the laws they imposed on others (101).

Nedham (like Harrington) cast much of his analysis in terms of *interest*, contrasting self-interest or private interest with public interest. It was clear that the way to avoid the subordination of the Commonwealth to some private interest or interests was to ensure rotation in office, and the avoidance of a 'standing senate' (27–9, 32–3). Nedham was an adherent of what Quentin Skinner has called a neo-Roman theory of liberty, and one who gave considerable weight to its negative components.[73] The public interest resolved itself back into private interests. The free state would preserve the negative liberty of its citizens; above all, it would protect their property rights. Nedham could write as if the public interest was something quite apart from private interests, but it was, in fact, the hallmark of a free state that it preserved private interests better than any other political arrangement. The message was that man must be prepared to take at least some share – a fairly minimal one in Nedham's account – in their own government if they wished to preserve their private interests and their rights. Dealing with the argument that popular states would produce the 'levelling' of men's estates, Nedham replied that a 'Free-State, or Government by the People', far from being a threat to property, was its 'only preservative', for in making laws by 'common consent', it was guaranteed that 'every Man's particular Interest must needs be fairly provided for, against the arbitrary disposition of others' (84). It was not private or particular interests themselves that were harmful, but ruling a community in such a way that it served the interests of some rather than others. The problem lay 'in setting up a private Interest of their own, distinct from the Publick' (84). The public interest thus embraced and served all private interests equally. Corruption came when men replaced the public interests (which combined fairly all private interests) with their own interests.

Nedham's concept of liberty was not purely negative. The advantage of a free state was that it gave the people 'a more magnanimous, active, and noble temper of Spirit' (54), arising from the fact that each man has his 'own immediate share in the publick Interest, as well as of that security which he possesses in the enjoyment of his private Fortune, free from the reach of any Arbitrary power'. By active involvement a man is not just made secure but 'he reckons all done for himself', and knows that he can win public reward and office if he merits it (54–5). Republics do more than preserve life and property from encroachment. They involve men in public service, giving all a share in the public good, encouraging noble actions. As a result, republics tend to be militarily expansionist. Rome, for example, built its 'wondrous Empire that overshadowed the whole World' only when in a state of proper liberty. It was an achievement all the greater in that it had to be won on the battlefield against many other free states, all of whom resisted Roman expansion (55–7; on the last point, cf. Machiavelli, *Discourses*, III, 2).

Thus Nedham seemed to embrace the Machiavellian ideal of the commonwealth for expansion (41; Machiavelli, *Discourses*, I, 5). But Nedham also found in Rome's expansion the cause of her inevitable loss of liberty. Nedham shared Machiavelli's preference for a citizen militia over the use of a standing professional army or mercenaries, and noted that Rome's over-expansion had undermined this principle: 'their Empire increasing[,] necessity constrained them to erect a continued stipendary Souldiery. . . . Then Luxury increasing with Dominion, the Strict Rule and Discipline of *Freedome* was soon quitted; forces were kept up at home' (176). Expansion might, within limits, be a sign of health; but too much of it produced ruin. Furthermore, it is worth noting that Nedham's chief reason for favouring a citizen militia was because it maintained *negative* liberty: when they had military power in their own hands, then 'nothing could at any time be imposed upon the people, but by their own consent' (173). 'The Sword, and Soveraignty, ever walk hand in hand together' (173).

A theme around which much else revolved, was Nedham's hostility to the political claims of any hereditary nobility. A political society should confer honour and reward on those who merited such treatment, irrespective of birth or wealth. For Nedham the essence of the Roman republic lay in the fact that it rewarded virtue. '[T]he way . . . [being] open to all without exception, vertue, learning, and good Parts made as speedy a Ladder to climbe unto Honours as Nobility of Birth' (12–13). This was a society, like that of More's *Utopia*, in which true nobility was properly recognised. Experience showed that these free states were the 'most commodious and profitable . . . conducing every way to the enlarging a people in Wealth and Dominion' (19). This was so because free states were 'more tender of the Publick in all their Decrees, than of particular Interests' (20). He therefore recommended such a polity as one in which not equality but 'an Equability of Condition among all the members' was maintained. For this reason it was right that 'any Rank of Men be allowed above the ordinary Standard to assume unto themselves the state and Title of Nobility' (71–2). This emphasis was necessary to protect the people against 'their own Officers', and against those who might 'claim a Prerogative Power, and Greatness above others, by Birth and Inheritance'. Such men could not be tolerated in 'any well-ordered Commonwealth' (72).

A final distinctive feature of Nedham's mature republicanism, in contrast to that of Harrington,[74] was its hostility to a national church. A free state could remove people from the turmoil of civil war; but religion needed to be properly founded if it were not to precipitate a renewal of that war. The first of the errors of government that Nedham identified was the division of the state into civil and ecclesiastical components. By that he meant allowing 'of a National way of Churching' (146). Those Christians who supported the erection of state churches – which included 'our latest Refiners of Political Discourse' (Hobbes?) – failed to understand what Christianity was about. Christ came in order

to set an end to that Pompous Administration of the Jewish Form [in which there was a national church]; that as his Church and People were formerly confined within the Narrow Pale of a particular Nation, so now the Pale should be broken down, and all Nations taken into the Church: Not all Nations in a lump; nor any whole Nations, or National Bodies to be formed into Churches; for his Church or People, now under the gospel, are not to be a Body Political, but Spiritual and Mystical . . . a picking and chusing of such as are called and sanctified; and not a company of men forced in, by Commands and Constitutions of Worldly Powers and Prudence; but of such as are brought in by the Power and Efficacy of *Christs* Word and Spirit.   (148)

It was the work of Antichrist that 'hath twisted the Spiritual Power . . . with the wordly and secular interest of State', by seeking to control heresy, bind men's consciences to orthodoxy, and advance the kingdom of Christ by worldly means (148–9). This error began in the very earliest Christian times, and was further enhanced by the indulgence shown by Constantine and other emperors towards their prelates. From the quarrels of the prelates, emerged the power of the popes. English reformers had done well in reversing some of this trend, but still made the mistake of allowing 'a State Ecclesiastical united with the Civil'. In fact, most of the civil wars in Europe had been caused by 'permitting the settlement of Clergy-Interest, with the Secular, in National Formes, and Churches' (149–52). Nedham's republicanism was thus based on a very thorough repudiation of any suggestion that the state existed to fulfil religious functions – a view shared by many in the Engagement Controversy. A stable polity, one that might avoid civil war, could only be constructed when secular and ecclesiastical concerns were utterly separated from one another.

Nedham returned to the subject of religion in a final editorial for *Mercurius Politicus*, though this one was not reprinted in the *Excellencie*. He there identified a ninth error of policy, 'the persecuting and punishing of men for their opinions in Religion'. This error arose from a prior one, the establishment of an authoritative distinction between orthodoxy and heresy. This pressure towards a 'Nationall Uniformity' arose from the desire to create 'Nationall Churches', which was a goal serving 'the Interest, not of Christ, but the Clergy'. The persecution of men for heresy, schism and sectarianism arose from 'annexing the Spirit to outward formalities'. Presbyterians and Roman Catholics alike held the mistaken belief that there was on earth an authoritative judge of the scriptural canon and its meaning. There was not; and, since there was not, there could be on earth no politics based on the true interpretation of God's will.[75] Nedham urged men to avoid any approach to politics that would link the maintenance of stability and obedience with any particular religious truths. He may or may not have believed that this would enhance the purity of religion; he certainly believed that it was the only way of securing at last the stability of the state.

James Harrington and *Oceana*

Harrington, whose first and major political work, *The Commonwealth of Oceana*, appeared in 1656, had no great faith in people. He tells us clearly that '[t]he spirit of the people is in no wise to be trusted with their liberty, but by stated laws or orders; so the trust is not in the spirit of the people, but in the frame of those orders'.[76] It was not a bad starting point for someone looking to find order in a world disordered by human zeal and consequent civil war.

It is worth contrasting Harrington's approach with that of the Levellers, who were, essentially, exponents of what we might call fundamental-law constitutionalism, in which a sovereign representative was limited only by its lack of authority to contravene basic rights and principles of equity that were enshrined in laws deemed 'fundamental'. This form of constitutionalism was characteristic of all the Agreements of the People, and it was institutionally unelaborated. There was no mechanism provided to ensure that governments respected the restrictions placed on them. It had to be assumed either that violent resistance would curb them, or that their own self-restraint would be effective. This weakness in the Levellers' approach was of some practical significance. In the late 1640s it was likely that a majority of people would have been all too keen to see the sovereign infringe some of those liberties that the Levellers valued, especially freedom of conscience. The Levellers' heavy reliance on consent as a basis for political legitimacy made this very difficult. The very premises on which their Agreement rested would have been unacceptable to many who were supposed to live under its arrangements. Could the Agreement possibly survive in a world where many – perhaps most – would lend their approval to governments that broke its terms? The Levellers' response was to try to define the electorate so that the politically unsound were excluded from it. But that only brought into relief the fact that their own Agreements provided no effective means of enforcing restraints on the representative body, short of a return to civil war. Who could doubt that such a return would soon be precipitated?

The same awareness was present as a tension within the thought of the republican pioneer Marchamont Nedham. How could the people, the citizenry, be trusted to preserve their own liberty? Or, more exactly, what do you do when you know full well that the people *cannot* be so trusted? The question burrows like a worm into the very core of republican political thought, drawing a final bitter outburst in 1660 from John Milton. Harrington, more than anyone else, found an answer – and he showed no coyness in revealing that he knew it. While other republicans – Vane and Milton – seemed to offer as a solution to this problem the rule of virtuous men (and in so doing, took republicanism into the ambit of Godly radicalism), Harrington trusted in rule according to virtuous constitutional laws, or (in his terms) *orders*. The result was a republicanism unusual for its emphasis on detailed institutional and constitutional arrangements. '[T]he people are not to be trusted, while certain it is that in a commonwealth rightly ordered they can have no other motion than according unto the orders of their commonwealth.'[77] Harrington's confidence in the infallibility of his orders was sublime.[78] He recounted a pageant he had witnessed at an Italian Shrovetide carnival. In it

> [was] represented a kitchen, with all the proper utensils in use and action. The cooks were all cats and kitlings, set in such frames, so tied and so ordered, that the poor creatures could make no motion to get loose, but the same caused one to turn the spit, another to baste the meat, a third to skim the pot and a fourth to make green sauce. If the frame of your commonwealth be not such as causeth everyone to perform his certain function as necessarily as this did the cat to make green sauce, it is not right.[79]

Harrington openly contrasted his approach to politics with that of the Levellers, in response to having some of his own ideas presented to the public in an anonymous pamphlet *The Leveller, or the Principles and Maxims Concerning Government and Religion, which are Asserted by Those that are Commonly Called Levellers* (1659). To show how his principles differed from those of the Levellers, Harrington wrote an analysis of the so-called Officers' Agreement of the People, which was the version of the Levellers' second Agreement that had been amended in debates of the army council at Whitehall (December–January 1648–9), and which was presented by the army to the Rump on 20 January 1649. Harrington quoted the Agreement as asserting 'That these representatives [of the people] have sovereign power, save that in some things the people may resist them by arms'.[80] Neither the Leveller's (second) Agreement nor the Officers' Agreement said exactly that, but both allowed some latitude for resistance to the Representative, the latter specifying that it was legitimate 'where such Representative shall evidently render up, or give, or take away the foundations of common right, liberty and safety contained in this Agreement'.[81]

Harrington astutely recognised in this the intellectual failure of Leveller constitutionalism. Referring to his own summary, he noted that the statement was both 'a flat contradiction' and 'downright anarchy'. It was the former because the Representative did *not* have genuine sovereign power: 'Where the sovereign power is not as entire and absolute as in monarchy itself, there can be no government at all.' The entire Leveller strategy of ruling out-of-bounds certain powers could only deprive the sovereign Representative of the authority it needed to govern, and encourage the anarchy to which he also referred. This was the wrong path altogether:

It is not the limitation of sovereign power that is the cause of a commonwealth, but such a *libration or poise of orders, that there can be in the same no number of men, having the interest, that can have the power, nor any number of men, having the power, that can have the interest, to invade or disturb the government.* As the orders of commonwealth are more approaching to or remote from this maxim (of which this of the Levellers have nothing), so are they more quiet or turbulent.[82]

The Levellers were wrong to try to limit governments. Sovereign power was by definition unlimited – it *needed* to be unlimited. The correct solution to the problem of misgovernment was to constitute authority so that its component parts balanced one another, and thus rendered impossible the abuse of authority.

Harrington's solution was rooted in a very detailed historical analysis of the problem itself. He focused especially on the relationship between social power and political authority. The 'Preliminaries' to *Oceana* laid down the proper principles of politics, discovered and practised in the ancient world and revived in the Renaissance (Harrington called this 'ancient prudence'); and they cast a cold eye over the very different and much less adequate principles and practices that had followed the collapse of classical civilisation ('modern prudence'). There were both normative and pragmatic dimensions to these discussions, but happily the two coincided in suggesting a solution to the problems faced by England in the mid-seventeenth century.

Ancient prudence provided the key to political stability, and it did so by revealing the correct linkage between *authority* and *power*,[83] or – in Harrington's terms – between two categories into which the principles of government fell, 'internal, or the goods of the mind; and external, or the goods of fortune'.[84] The former, goods of the mind or authority, were derived from virtue (wisdom, prudence, courage). We shall return to this subject later. The goods of fortune or power derived essentially from 'riches', especially but not exclusively land,[85] because it was wealth that gave men control of the sword and thus gave them the power to compel the obedience of others.[86] It followed from this that the three basic forms of government were determined by the underlying balance of property. Government was 'absolute monarchy' when one man owned all the land, or a vast preponderance of it (three-quarters, Harrington specified in *Oceana*; later he reduced it to two-thirds[87]). If a nobility owned the preponderance of land (Harrington called this situation 'the Gothic balance'), then the government was a mixed monarchy. But:

if the whole people be landlords, or hold the lands so divided among them, that no one man, or number of men, within the compass of the few or aristocracy, overbalance them, the empire (without the interposition of force) is a commonwealth.   (163–4)

The link between property and domestic government, 'dominion' and 'empire', was not automatic. It was possible to govern against the balance. Government against the balance, at least when no effort was made to bring the property foundation and the form of government into kilter, was 'not natural but violent'. These violent forms – tyranny, oligarchy, anarchy – were all confused and 'of short continuance' (164). Harrington's analysis, in contrast to traditional views, essentially took anarchy rather than tyranny as the paradigm of misgovernment. What characterised these forms was not oppression so much as a futile and unstable effort by one, few, or many men to govern in the teeth of an unfavourable balance of property. Like Hobbes's, Harrington's experience of civil war led him to value the maintenance of peace and order as the highest political goal; and therefore his analysis was directed to diagnosing the causes of instability, not the cause of 'tyranny' in the traditional sense.[88]

For political stability to be achieved, however, it was not enough to ensure that government contrary to that compatible with the balance of land was avoided. It was necessary, as well, to ensure that the balance of land did not alter over the long term, so that a government initially well-founded ceased to be so. To confront this danger, Harrington produced one of the defining features of his political theory, the agrarian law. Provided that the balance of land was sound (i.e. there was a clear preponderance of land in the hands of one group, king, nobility or people), stability could only be ensured when that balance was 'fixed' by law. That was achieved, for example, in Turkey, where the law prevented anyone but the Sultan from owning land. Agrarian law 'was first introduced by God himself' in Canaan (164).

The first part of ancient prudence, then, directed that political stability could be achieved by perpetuating a sound balance in landed property, which would provide an enduring foundation for government of the matching form. Such a government would possess power, which is to say that it would have sufficient control over military force to ensure that it possessed the coercive capacity to maintain order. This came about because military force was raised and supported on landed estates. Stability, therefore, required that the group owning the preponderance of land should have a preponderant voice in government. That way, those commanding would also be those controlling military force. The agrarian law ensured that no changes to the balance of landholding could undermine this relationship.

All of this was necessary to stable government, but it was not suffi-cient. Harrington also paid attention to authority, the goods of the mind, as well as to power; and he paid attention to how, according to ancient prudence, power and authority could be brought together. At the very beginning of his discussion of the goods of the mind, Harrington gave voice to a powerful plea for the reconciliation of authority and power. He quoted from Ecclesiastes, 10.5–7 Solomon's '[s]ad complaints, that the principles of power and authority, the goods of the mind and of fortune, do not meet and twine in the wreath or crown of empire!' The fault arose:

> from those principles of power which, balanced upon earthly trash, exclude the heavenly treasures of virtue, and that influence of it upon government which is authority. We have wandered the earth to find out the balance of power; but to find out that of authority we must ascend, as I said, nearer heaven, or to the image of God which is the soul of man. (169)

It seems, then, that not every 'balance of power' was a good one. Harrington appears to mean that, while things could be done to preserve absolute monarchies and mixed monarchies, neither could achieve that perfect stability that enabled a political society to partake of the immutability of the divinity himself. To understand why this was so, we need to explore the principles of authority as well as those of power.

The soul of man, to which Harrington directed our attention, turns out to be the site of an on-going contest between passion and reason. The outcome of the struggle determined whether men's actions were vicious or virtuous. Actions rooted in passion were 'vice and the bondage of sin'; those rooted in reason represented 'virtue and the freedom of soul' (169). Vicious actions naturally drew down upon a man 'scorn or pity', 'so those actions of a man that are virtue, acquire unto himself honour, and upon others authority' (170). Thus author-ity could be defined as the respect and obedience that men displayed towards the virtuous actions of others.

The proper relationship between empire and authority in the commonwealth could be understood analogously.

> Now government is no other than the soul of a nation or city; where-fore that which was reason in the debate of a commonwealth, being brought forth by the result, must be virtue; and for as much as the soul of a city or nation is the sovereign power, her virtue must be law. But the government whose law is virtue, and whose virtue is law, is the same whose empire is authority, and whose authority is empire. (170)

The virtuous actions of the commonwealth were the rational laws made by the sovereign. The implicit contrast being drawn by Harrington was between rule by (rational) law and rule by (passionate) will, as is revealed by his statement that 'the liberty of a commonwealth consisteth in the empire of her laws, the absence whereof would betray her unto the lusts of tyrants' (170). It followed that a government that ruled by law – Harrington meant a government founded on an appropriate balance of property – was able to combine empire (power) and authority (virtue).

It was on this basis that Harrington attempted to rebut Hobbes's approach to liberty.[89] Hobbes had claimed that the freedom of citizens was the same, whether they lived in a monarchy or commonwealth, for no government of whatever form allowed its citizens immunity from the laws and burdens that it imposed. To this Harrington replied that there was a crucial difference between 'immunity from the laws' (which was uniform) and liberty 'by the laws', which was everywhere different. This latter type of liberty was greatest in republics, in which every man was 'a freeholder of both [his person and his land], and not to be controlled but by the law; and that framed by every private man unto no other end . . . than to protect the liberty of every private man, which by that means comes to be the liberty of the commonwealth' (170–1). Thus, in a republic, citizens themselves were actively involved in making the laws that protected them, and their involvement ensured that the commonwealth as a whole functioned to protect the 'freehold' of all individuals in their person and possessions. Liberty could be defined negatively as protection of an individual's property rights (in the broadest sense); but this 'negative' liberty only flourished where the citizens themselves 'positively' participated in the making of law.[90]

His engagement with the sardonic wit of Thomas Hobbes took Harrington even further.

> But seeing they that make the laws in commonwealths are but men [a point that Harrington has emphasised in his reply to Hobbes on liberty], the *main question* seems to be how a commonwealth comes to be an empire of laws and not of men? Or how the debate or result of a commonwealth is so sure to be according unto reason, seeing they who debate and they who resolve be but men. And 'as often as reason is against a man, so often will a man be against reason'. (171, emphasis added)[91]

Hobbes had identified a conflict between reason and interest. A man would follow reason only so long as it served his interest. Harrington found his way around this problem with insouciance: reason and interest were the same thing. A man who followed his interest followed his reason. One scholar has recently declared that interest theory was really peripheral to Harrington;[92] but, if anything, it was reason that was peripheral and interest that was central. For Harrington, to follow reason did not mean to follow the one true and moral path, valid for all men at all times, as individuals or collectively; it meant following a path that your interest gave you reason to consider good for yourself. Thus he could distinguish between different types of reason: 'there be divers interests, and so divers reasons'. He identified three categories: (1) the 'private reason' or the interest of 'private men'; (2) 'reason of state', which was the interest of the rulers; and (3) 'that reason which is the interest of mankind or of the whole' (171). Harrington did not assume that it was possible to harmonise these various interests or reasons; but he did assume that even private men could recognise that the interest of the whole was more important than the interest of the parts. The whole in this argument was, of course, mankind, rather than the commonwealth or body politic. That still left Harrington with work to do.

> Mankind . . . must . . . acknowledge also his common interest to be common right. And if reason be nothing else but interest, and the interest of mankind be the right interest, then the reason of mankind must be right reason. Now compute well, for if the interest of popular government come the nearest unto the interest of mankind, then the reason of popular government must come the nearest unto reason. (171–2)

'Compute well': though it has been denied,[93] Harrington's words suggest that at this point he relied on the rather crude argument that the more people there were, the more their reason/interest was likely to coincide with the reason/interest of the whole. Even so, he had not arrived at his destination, for all he could do was to restate the problem. How could men, all pursuing their own interest, be made to act for the common interest? They might, in principle, recognise its superiority; but in fact they still pursued their private interest. But men could perhaps be *constrained* into choosing the common interest.

Partly, Harrington simply *defined* common interest as the actions of the people ('the people, taken apart, are but so many private interests, but if you take them together they are the public interest'; 280). But there is more to it than that, for he recognised also that common interest was different in kind from private interest. It might require things that were in the interest of no individual. The public interest 'is none other than common right and justice, *excluding* all partiality or private interest'. By that Harrington did not mean that public interest must deny private. It was actually constructed from private interest: 'every man hath an interest what to choose, and that choice which suiteth with every man's interest excludeth the distinct or private interest or passion of any man, and so cometh up unto the common and public interest or reason'.[94] Harrington did not always use words carefully, and we can see in this passage that, notwithstanding his usual equation of reason and interest, Harrington has referred to a form of interest that reflects 'passion'. The thought that appears to underlie this appears to be that men following their rational interests can be constrained to achieve the common interest; but all passion must be excluded from the process. That leads directly to his discussion of constitutional mechanisms, for their essential function was *negative*. They sifted out from private interests the things men did passionately, or the things that could not be generalised. By this means, a common interest was formed which was built from but did not coincide with the private interests of the individual citizens.

Men could be trusted to follow their own interest. By his cunning equation of interest, reason and virtue, Harrington was able to advance the rather less plausible view that men will behave rationally, which makes it more plausible for him to assume that from their rational actions rational consequences might accrue. The pivotal passage in which Harrington made these points was the story of the two girls and the cake in *Oceana*.

> But that such orders may be established as may, nay must, give the upper hand in all cases unto common right or interest, notwithstanding the nearness of that which sticks unto every man in private, and this in a way of equal certainty and facility, is known even unto girls, being no other than those that are of common practice with them in divers cases. For example, two of them have a cake yet undivided, which was given between them. That each of them may therefore have that which is due, 'Divide', says one unto the other, 'and I will choose; or let me divide, and you shall choose'. If this be but once agreed upon, it is enough; for the divident dividing unequally loses, in regard that the other takes the better half; wherefore she divides equally, and so both have right.   (172)

The second girl, the one who chooses, can be relied upon, no matter what options are put to her by the cutter of the cake, to follow her private interest and choose the bigger or better part. However, the cutter knows that her friend will follow her own interest, and therefore does her utmost to cut the cake into equal halves. In doing so, she follows her interest by maximising the size of her portion of cake. The plausibility of this scenario rests upon the fact that it does not require either girl to pursue 'the good'; each behaves selfishly. But there is another dimension to the matter: the situation also relies upon the fact that each is *aware of* the other's selfishness. Thus Harrington's system of government rests upon the plausible assumptions that all people are (rationally) selfish, and known to be so by others; and that the shared knowledge of human selfishness can be exploited so that one's own selfishness is balanced by one's awareness of the selfishness of others. In such a situation a selfish person, pursuing private interest, will in fact pursue her or his interest in such a way as to serve the common interest. No one would be made good, in the sense that he or she would become motivated to pursue public over private interest; but, in certain institutionally-contrived circumstances, pursuit of the private would be tempered and brought into line with the public, and green sauce would be produced. Interest theory was crucial to Harrington, because of its insight into human awareness of the selfishness of others.

Constitutionally, the result of these perceptions was the principle that genuine moral authority was possessed by a government only when the common interest was pursued. That required the involvement in politics of the citizens at large, primarily through a representative assembly of the people. This body decided upon proposals for legislation put to it by a senate. The representative was the second girl. Its members, acting selfishly, decided whether to support proposals – that is, each individual decided whether the proposal was in his interest. Only those proposals that were in the interest of all (or a majority, in fact) were approved. In that way the common interest was pursued. But we must remember that, as in the cake-cutting, the individuals acting selfishly did so in the awareness that all those around them were also acting selfishly. In such circumstances their pursuit of their private interest would be qualitatively different, for it would need to balance the *maximising* of benefit to oneself with the *minimising* of harm from others. It is from this calculus that there emerged legislation for the public interest. '[T]he interest of the commonwealth is in the whole body of the people', but, where that body is too large to be assembled, the 'choosing' must be done by a representative assembly 'so constituted as [it] can never contract any other interest than that of the whole people' (173).

One thing remains unclear in this account. Harrington argued that the public interest might contain elements that were not derived from the private interest of citizens. How could elements not present in private interest be fed into the common interest? The answer is found in Harrington's treatment of wisdom and aristocracy. The first of the two cake-cutting girls, it turns out, must have been a noblewoman, and her aristocratic wisdom formed an essential element in Harrington's perfect commonwealth.[95] As he put it, 'a nobility or gentry in a popular government, not overbalancing it, is the very life and soul of it' (167). Harrington's view of nobility was a quintessentially civic humanist one. There was such a thing as a 'natural aristocracy', the members of which ought to be entitled to sit in a senate, 'not by hereditary right, nor in regard of the greatness of their estates only . . . but by election for their excellent parts, which tendeth unto the advancement of the influence of their virtue or authority that leads the people' (173). The importance of nobility lay in its possession of virtue and wisdom, through which was introduced into the commonwealth a degree of far-sighted and public-spirited statesmanship that the people alone, fit only to be judges of their own interest, were unable to provide. Their wisdom enabled an aristocracy to 'discover things that . . . [the rest] never thought on' (172). There was an important difference between the social distribution of wisdom and of reason: 'The wisdom of the few may be the light of mankind, but the interest of the few is not the profit of mankind.' For that reason, the 'wisdom of the commonwealth is in the aristocracy' (173). It is important to note that Harrington distinguished between reason and wisdom: all men could reason about their interests; but only a few had the wisdom and virtue needed to propose wise legislation. In *Oceana* a Senate of the wise would debate and propose laws, and a Representative of the many would decide, without debate, whether to enact them.

There is in Harrington clear trace of the republican citizen; but that citizen has been fractured by Harrington's strong sense of human selfishness, a sense that appears to have been heightened by his reading of Hobbes. His way of dealing with what we might call Hobbesian man (the man involved in civil war) was not to abandon republican ideals of citizenship. Rather, citizens were not required to possess the full extent of virtue that many others demanded of them. Citizenship was made easy (even a cat could produce green sauce), not austerely demanding. Even the virtue of the nobility was not inexhaustible. Ruin would follow if they were left to decide as well as deliberate, for they would inevitably decide on measures that served their own interests not those of the people at large. Wisdom, virtue and reason ruled only when the elements present in different social groups were combined through complex institutional machinery into a whole.

Harrington went so far as to say that a 'commonwealth' – meaning a community that put the common wealth or interest first – *only* existed when there was a mixed government of the sort that Machiavelli and other republicans had praised. This mixed government consisted of an aristocratic senate that proposed legislation, a democratic representa-tive that decided which proposals to accept, and a 'monarchical' magis-tracy that executed these laws (174). The magistracy was essentially a subordinate thing. It could be in various forms, provided that it was 'answerable to the people' and acted 'according unto the law'. It must always enforce existing laws, made by the reason of the people, and not act above the law (174). This was Harrington's answer to the question of what form of government possessed real moral authority: a govern-ment that served the common interest, or a genuine commonwealth, with the basic structure just outlined. It was only in such a society that the laws were rational to the fullest extent – i.e., in Harrington's terms, they served the interest of the whole and not a part – and only rational laws could be virtuous. Authority was gained by the respect that citizens had for the virtue displayed in these laws. In short, the citizens of a commonwealth could be expected to be pacific and obedient because they knew that they were ruled by virtuous laws made to serve their own interest, in so far as it *could* be served in a world full of selfish people.

There was one further ingredient needed to complete this picture. It was not enough to have a commonwealth: perfect stability required an *equal* commonwealth. In an equal commonwealth, power and authority were conjoined. After considering a whole range of historical examples, and giving particular attention to the things that distin-guished more stable commonwealths (ancient Israel, Sparta, Venice) from less stable ones (Athens, Rome), Harrington was able to distil the form of a perfect commonwealth. The crucial distinction – more important than the one drawn by Machiavelli between commonwealths for preservation and for increase – was between unequal and equal commonwealths. It was this distinction that was fundamental for Harrington's pre-eminent concern, 'domestic peace and tranquillity'. An unequal commonwealth was divided into parties or factions 'at perpetual variance'. In an equal commonwealth 'there can be no more strife than there can be overbalance in equal weights' (180). It is apparent here that the word 'equal' is misleading. 'Balanced' would have been better, because the essential thing about an equal common-wealth was that it balanced social groups by ensuring that the wealthier part was never so wealthy that it naturally possessed overwhelming power. Institutional mechanisms ensured that this social balance produced harmony rather than anarchy. Thus Harrington's 'equality' was actually a balanced social inequality, which does make one wonder why he chose to make so much of a term that his contemporaries viewed so negatively.[96] Nonetheless, Harrington's equality is funda-mental, for an equal commonwealth was one in which power and authority were in line with one another.

An equal commonwealth ... is a government established upon an
equal agrarian, arising into the superstructures or three orders, the
senate debating and proposing, the people resolving, and the magistracy executing by an equal rotation through the suffrage of the
people given by the ballot.   (181)

Such were the ingredients of political perfection. By 'an equal agrarian', Harrington meant one that would ensure that 'no one man or
number of men within the compass of the few of aristocracy can come
to overpower the whole people by their possession in lands'. Although
an agrarian could render any form of 'empire' more stable than it
would otherwise be, permanent stability would be ensured only when
an equal agrarian fixed a property balance appropriate for a popular
commonwealth. That provided the foundation for the 'superstructure'
of a commonwealth that would possess true moral authority, because it
made laws in the common interest. To achieve that, as we have seen,
the minimum requirements were a bicameral legislature; and, it was
now emphasised, a magistracy to execute the laws, filled by different
people in rotation, the choice being made by election using a secret
ballot. The rotation was necessary to avoid 'prolongation of magistracy', which might create a permanent elite of rulers governing in
their own interest. The secret ballot similarly freed the people's choice
from partiality: 'election ... is freest where it is made or given in such
a manner that it can neither oblige ... nor disoblige another, or
through fear of an enemy, or bashfulness towards a friend, impair a
man's liberty' (180–1).

There was, however, one other thing to take into account. The
construction of an equal commonwealth was not possible in all places
at all times. Its reliance on the right balance of property meant that
unless such a balance existed, you could not have an equal commonwealth. And, of course, where it did exist, nothing but a commonwealth could be stable. The agrarian could fix the balance in place; but
it could not create it. Historically, Harrington argued, it was impossible
to put in practice the secrets of political stability contained in 'ancient
prudence' in the centuries that followed the fall of the Roman Empire.
Those centuries saw instead the persistence of the 'Gothic balance',
and were in consequence dominated by 'modern prudence'. The
Roman emperors were forced to call modern prudence into existence,
after the sustained failure of Rome to produce adequate agrarian laws.
The original 'popular' balance of land made Rome a commonwealth,
but its military conquests were handled in such a way as to give more
and more land to the nobility, which then destroyed the commonwealth. The emperors in their turn tried to create a soldiery loyal only

to themselves, the Pretorian guard, as a counterweight; but eventually these soldiers acquired land upon hereditary tenures and their support for the emperors could no longer be relied upon. Imperial Rome was thus 'neither hawk nor buzzard, [and] made a flight accordingly'. It suffered from what Harrington later called the 'privation of government',[97] for imperial rule could be grounded on neither the nobility (hostile to the landholding soldiery), nor the soldiery (now guardians only of their own interest). No stable government was possible (188–90).

In a last effort, the emperors tried 'stipendiating the Goths'. These peoples from outside the northern boundaries of the Empire were used as mercenaries to sustain imperial authority, but they came increasingly to take their payment for military service by force, sacking Rome itself, and eventually flooding into the Empire and destroying ancient civilisation (190). By this process, 'all the kingdoms this day in Christendom were at first erected' (191). They were erected on the basis of 'the gothic balance', by which lands, in the form of the feud, were given upon condition of loyalty and service by kings to their higher nobility, then by these 'feudatory princes' to inferior men ('barons'), and by barons to other 'private men' who were called 'vavasors'. This created a feudal hierarchy based on the close link between land and service.

This feudal or Gothic balance was one that made a commonwealth, equal or not, a flat impossibility. The characteristic constitution of government under the Gothic balance was mixed monarchy,[98] in which a king ruled by the advice and through the assent of a parliament representing the nobility. Harrington was bitter in his condemnation of the Gothic polity, of England's ancient constitution, and of those who eulogised it:

> [T]his government, being indeed the masterpiece of modern prudence, hath been cried up to the skies as the only invention whereby at once to maintain the sovereignty of a prince and the liberty of the people; whereas indeed it hath been no other than a wrestling match, wherein the nobility, as they have been stronger, have thrown the king, or the king, if he have been stronger, hath thrown the nobility; or the king, where he hath had a nobility and could bring them to his party hath thrown the people ... or the people, where they have had no nobility, or could get them to be of their party, have thrown the king, as in Holland and of latter times in Oceana [i.e. England].   (196)

Modern prudence was a political culture that did not value the common interest, but defined government as 'an art whereby some man, or some few men, subject a city or a nation, and rule it according unto his or their private interest'. Whereas a genuine commonwealth was marked by the empire of laws and not of men, in modern prudence men and not laws ruled (161).[99] The Gothic balance, as Harrington was later to say, was 'a state of war'. Yet Harrington acknowledged that efforts were made to regulate it by laws and constitutional orders. 'The monarchy of England was not a government by arms, but a government by laws, though imperfect or ineffectual laws.'[100] But in any case, things had moved on, leaving Oceana – England – at a turning-point. Drawing heavily on Francis Bacon's *History of King Henry VII*, Harrington portrayed a king whose reflections on the violent prelude to his own accession had taught him that 'a throne supported by a nobility is not so hard to be ascended, as kept warm'.[101] Acting on that thought, Henry VII sought to disable his nobility, using parliamentary legislation both to undermine their landholding and to remove their private military might. It was a mistake, for by these means the king 'began to open those sluices that have since overwhelmed ... the throne'. The balance shifted from the nobility, which preserved the throne even when it struck down individual monarchs, to the 'people', who 'striketh through the king at the throne, as that which is incompatible with it' (197). Later monarchs fuelled the fires that were to consume the crown in the reign of Charles I. Henry VIII's dissolution of the monasteries increased the landed wealth of the people, while Elizabeth's successful use of 'love tricks' to win over the people led her to neglect to maintain the position of the nobility. The result was that as soon as the people, represented in the House of Commons, realised their own strength they began to challenge the crown, a challenge that culminated in the Civil War. '[A] monarchy divested of her nobility hath no refuge under heaven but an army. *Wherefore the dissolution of this government caused the war, not the war the dissolution of this government*' (197–8). That is, Charles could, once the truth was out, govern only by force against the balance; and in any sustained trial of strength was bound to lose. The abolition of the monarchy naturally followed.

'[W]hat is there in nature that can arise out of these ashes but a popular government, or a new monarchy to be erected by the victorious army?' (198). The possibility now existed, if only it could be seized, to revive the principles of ancient prudence, and to build in England a perfect equal commonwealth. Conditions were right, but it nonetheless required the constructive efforts of men to bring it about. This was, in itself, a problem for Harrington, and one that he solved by inviting Oliver Cromwell to step into the role of a republican legislator, and warning him of the inevitable failure of any attempt to use the sword to re-establish a monarchy (Cromwellian as much as Stuart). *Oceana,* like republicanism in general, is usually read as a thinly disguised critique, oblique but uncompromising, of the Cromwellian Protectorate. No doubt it was; but Harrington's attitude to Cromwell was perhaps more complex. Harrington endorsed the Machiavellian (*Discorsi,* I, 9) and classical contentions that a commonwealth was best established by a 'legislator', who could construct it and then leave it to run according to its own orders and laws; and that 'the legislator should be one man', public-spirited but willing to use extraordinary means to gain the power needed for him to perform the legislator's function. The Cromwell-figure who is the legislator of Oceana, the Lord Archon, Olphaus Megaletor, certainly had a council to advise him, but he remained its 'sole director and president' (206–7). It was the Lord Archon, and not his council of legislators, who 'framed the model of the commonwealth of Oceana' (209).[102]

The purpose of *Oceana* was as much persuasion as critique. For all its suspicion of political discussion, it was itself a well-wrought rhetorical artefact intended to make concrete and tangible the only stable future England could have. Implicitly, it constructed a Cromwell who firmly grasped the sword, and was poised between using it to create a commonwealth and using it to create a monarchy. The rhetorical task was to persuade him that only the former option was viable. It may have been a critique of the Protectorate, but Harrington was not so foolish as to make it a critique of the Protector, who was its main audience as much as its dedicatee. Above all, it was addressed to the Cromwell whose political uncertainties were painfully worked over in public. Cromwell conceived the Protectorate, as Harrington conceived Oceana, to be an attempt to construct a civil government that would allow the sword to be sheathed. England had arrived in 1653 at a point that gave to Cromwell, as Lord General, an awesome arbitrary power, acquired in attempts to deny arbitrary power to a unicameral sovereign parliament (the Rump) and to the self-appointed Godly.[103] The task was to construct a polity in which arbitrary power played no role – in Harringtonian terms, to convert power into authority. Marchamont Nedham, writing in defence of the Protectorate, defended it as a classical mixed government, one that 'had taken in the good of all the three sorts of Government, and bound them all in one. If War be, here is the Unitive vertue (but nothing else) of *Monarchy* to encounter it; and here is the admirable Counsel of *Aristocracie* to manage it: If Peace be, here is the industry and courage of *Democracie* to improve it.' Nedham portrayed the Protector not as a king but as an elective magistrate, perhaps trying to reinvent the institution that he ostensibly defended. This clearly was a polity without arbitrary power, the rule of laws and not of men.[104] *Oceana* took the reinvention a stage further, by constructing Cromwell as legislator and not as magistrate. In doing so, Harrington might be read as rescuing Cromwell from the predicament in which he found himself in 1654: he was then both part of the machinery of government that had been established in the Instrument of Government; and the ultimate authority, or rather power, on which the Instrument rested. He was, that is, both magistrate and legislator; and therefore any discussion of his role as magistrate could be construed as a refusal to recognise the power of the 'legislator' who had established the constitution. Cromwell's response was, figuratively, to take the sword back out of its sheath. If he could not get his way as a magistrate, he would, if not exactly *as* legislator, then still using the sort of arbitrary power backed by the sword that a legislator needed, continue to use what means he could to preserve the ends for which he ruled.[105] Naturally, republicans were provoked; and Harrington in particular was provoked to argue that Cromwell ought to wield the sword *only* as legislator, and in such a way that no one need ever unsheathe the sword again. But, the condition for success was that the legislator's role be separated from the magistrate's.

Harrington's *Commonwealth of Oceana* fleshed out these principles with a Utopian model for the republic he envisaged, a model constructed in quite incredible (and rather numbing) detail. Little was left to chance. The institutions of local and regional, as well as of national, government were specified; social groups were delineated on the basis of landownership; these groups, along with age, determined the military and civil offices that men could fill; details of the operations of the bicameral legislature and of the magistracy and councils were specified. There were two crucial fundamental laws, the agrarian, which ensured 'equality in the root', and 'the ballot by an equal rotation conveying it into the branch' or superstructure (230–1). We need not fill out the details, but one more thing needs to be considered: religion.

Harrington's chief prescription for the disease of civil war was to seek an understanding of the principles that would enable a civil polity to endure in (internal) peace. In his analysis of the religious 'parties' contending with one another, Harrington showed particular alarm at the Godly radicals, those 'who holding that the saints must govern, go about to reduce the commonwealth unto a party' (204). In fact, God commanded his followers 'to submit unto the higher powers, and be subject unto the ordinance of man'. Those 'pretending under the notion of saints or religion unto civil power' were replacing the rule of laws with the rule of men. Truly Godly government did not rely on sinful men:

The saintship of a people as to government consisteth in the election of magistrates fearing God and hating covetousness, and not in their confining themselves or being confined unto men of this or that party or profession. It consisteth in making the most prudent and religious choice that they can, but not in trusting unto men but, next God, in their orders. 'Give us good men and they will make us good laws' is the maxim of the demagogue, and . . . exceeding fallible. But 'give us good orders, and they will make us good men' is the maxim of a legislator and the most infallible in the politics.   (204–5)

In a stable polity, religion would not be a problem. But a stable polity needed to be organised properly, and that required in religious matters that the church be subject to the state. After reviewing the historical record, Harrington wondered how it could ever have been believed that 'ecclesiastical government [was] . . . distinct from civil power' (308). In all well-ordered polities, the civil power ruled the church. Even the ordination of the clergy was by civil authority, not a spiritual power inherent only in churches. As in ancient Israel, ordination was just 'election of magistrates' (384). Alongside this powerful, indeed Hobbesian, attack on the independent power of the clergy and of churches, Harrington insisted on liberty of conscience too. In Oceana there would be a (civil) council of religion entrusted with 'the care of the national religion and the protection of liberty of conscience'. This arrangement has been termed a 'civil religion' with an Erastian church subject to civil control, and to the demand that 'no coercive power in the matter of religion . . . be exercised in this nation'. Congregations could go their own way unmolested if unpersuaded by ministers of the church (251).[106] This would complete England's escape from the ravages of wars of religion.

Republicanism and the Crisis of 1659–60

The years 1659–1660 produced an astonishing outpouring of political writing, as the Protectorate and then the restored Commonwealth fell apart in anarchy.[107] Not all of these works were republican. Richard Baxter produced a detailed plan of a *Holy Commonwealth*, which included a lengthy critique of Harringtonian republicanism, while George Lawson attempted to write an account of the political world that would provide the intellectual tools for escaping the chaos that had overrun the nation since the death of Oliver Cromwell.[108] The republicans, though, were naturally keen to stave off the Restoration of the Stuart monarchy, which looked more and more like the only way of

rescuing the nation from anarchy. Harrington and his supporters in
the Rota club advanced simplified versions of his model for republican
government, the chief of which was his *Art of Lawgiving*. The
Harringtonian constitutional model, though, jostled with alternative
republican schemes in these desperate years, most notably with the
proposal associated with Sir Henry Vane and his *Healing Question*,
printed first in 1656 and reprinted in 1659, that the nation should be
settled by agreement among the virtuous and the Godly men. The
problem faced, as Vane expressed it in debate with Harrington, was
'the practicableness of introducing and settling the exercise of the
supreme Power, by the free and common consent of the Citizens,
whose equality in power is apt to make their tempers luxuriant and
immoderate, and keep them from coming rightly to agree'.[109] The
only solution was the 'Spirit of God', which could make men less frac-
tious; but this was not a solution that was accessible at will by human
beings. In the meantime, the only solution lay in ensuring that in the
decision-making that would result in the 'Common-wealths constituting', 'none be admitted to the exercise of the right and priviledge of a
free Citizen' except those 'as are free born, in respect of their holy and
righteous principles, flowing from the birth of the spirit of God in
them', or those whose record of faithfulness to the cause showed that
they could be trusted. These people could be trusted to elect a 'Ruling
Senate' which would govern under Christ.[110]

Something like Vane's proposals were supported by John Milton,
writing desperately in a world that appeared to be returning to monarchy. It was an approach to politics similar to that of many religious radicals, fusing ideas of popular consent (admitted to be *in principle* widely
inclusive) with the exclusivity of the Godly. Milton's *Ready and Easy Way
to Establish a Free Commonwealth* thus presented a republicanism very
different from and more Godly than Harrington's. It was pervaded by
a desperate sense of time running out, and by the fear – a persistent
theme in Milton's writings, and in that of some other republicans –
that the English people had not proved fit for the world of freedom. In
that sense, Milton's work was Nedham's in pessimistic voice and times.
There was the same question about whether a people could be made
fit for freedom; but, while Nedham answered with some optimism,
Milton had an awareness of imminent failure. Milton's solution to the
problem was itself desperate, and should not be taken as anything
other than a last hope for staving off the inevitable. He quite explicitly
said that his very simple proposals were suited to times of tumult, and
might eventually be replaced by something better. He looked to the
formation of a 'general councel of ablest men, chosen by the people'.
This body, 'being well chosen, should be perpetual'.[111] This 'Senat of

principal men' was to be preferred to a popular assembly (438). Though chosen 'by the people', the Senate would not be chosen by everyone. It was not a 'rude multitude' but those who were 'rightly qualifi'd' who would nominate representatives, and 'out of that number others of a better breeding' would choose a smaller group; and this number would be reduced by further rounds of sifting, until only the worthiest were left (443).[112] Essentially, this was a preference for the rule of virtue taken to its extreme: identify the virtuous and let them rule. It marked an approach to republican politics quite at odds with Harrington's highly institutionalised vision, and it marked as the essential thing not the rule of laws but the rule of men – the right sort of men. This was a sort of Godly republicanism, curiously blind to the fact that the perpetual rule of the virtuous seemed to risk the same dangers of slavery inherent in arbitrary monarchy.

And of these, Milton had become at last a powerful and eloquent critic.[113] In 1649 he had insinuated republican principles rather than declaring them; now, in 1660, while he might hesitate to declare his faith in the people's capacity to produce a free commonwealth by unfettered consent, he did not hesitate to declare forcefully that monarchy was altogether incompatible with a free state. The superiority of republics could be seen in the fact that their rulers were 'perpetual servants and drudges to the public', men who 'live soberly in thir families, walk the streets as other men, may be spoken to freely, familiarly, friendly, without adoration'. How different from kings! They 'must be ador'd like a Demigod, with a dissolute and haughtie court about' them. This court was marked by 'vast expence and luxurie' and the presence of a 'servile crew'. A king liked nothing better than 'to pageant himself up and down in progress among the perpetual bowings and cringings of an abject people, on either side deifying and adoring him' (425–6). It was particularly dangerous to readmit an expelled king, for he would make sure that the people could never 'free themselves from any yoke impos'd upon them' (449). No wonder Milton could declare: 'It may be well wonderd that any Nation styling themselves free, can suffer any man to pretend hereditary right over them as thir lord; when as by acknowledging that right, they conclude themselves his servants and vassals, and so renounce their own freedom' (427–8). This was the nub of the matter. To be ruled by a king was to be subject to his will, and that made you a slave. Monarchs could not be trusted to allow liberty of conscience (456–8), and they undermined the foundations of civil freedom in order to make their people 'softest, basest, vitiousest, servilest, easiest to be kept under . . . but in minde also, sheepishest' (460).

It was not enough. The Stuart monarchy was restored in May 1660. James Harrington had such sublime faith in his own correctness that, at the time of the Restoration, he is reported to have remarked, 'Well, the King will come in. Let him come-in, and call a Parliament of the greatest Cavaliers in England, so they be men of Estates, and let them sett but 7 yeares, and they will all turn Common-wealthe's men.'[114] The balance, he believed, doomed the Restoration monarchy from the start. As it happened, though, it was not the cavaliers who turned republican, but republicans who turned monarchist.

Epilogue: Ending Wars of Religion?

In 1660 the Stuart monarchy was restored, seemingly with enthusiasm, seemingly to a position little different from that of Charles I immediately before the Civil War. Only twenty-eight years later, however, another Stuart king lost the throne, in good part because of his Catholicism, this time to a Dutch invader rather than an English conqueror. In England the events of the Glorious Revolution were seemingly both peaceful and restrained, but they were less so in Scotland (and even less so in Ireland). The Scots went on in the early eighteenth century to challenge the so-called Revolution Settlement of 1688-9, provoking their neighbours into the policies that culminated in the 1707 union of England and Scotland. England did not again face religious war, though in Scotland the Jacobite cause remained alive, to bring about violence in 1715 and 1745. Indeed, if we accept the peacefulness of the Glorious Revolution within England itself, England did not suffer significant religious or political violence after 1660.

Does the history of political thought throw any light on either the differences between Scotland and England after 1660, or the more effective containment of religious violence after the Restoration?

English and Scottish political thought developed very differently in the 1640s and 1650s. It is possible that some of these differences are illusory, a product of the fact that much more attention has been paid to England than to Scotland, and very little indeed has been written about Scottish political thought other than that of the Covenanters. It will be apparent to anyone reading the second part of this book, that Scotland has largely been absent, once the thought of the Covenanters and their Royalist opponents had been explored. It may be that there is a Scottish radicalism and a Scottish republicanism to explore, but I am not aware of it. What is significant, it would seem, is that whereas both Puritans and Covenanters sought power in order to put in place a Godly society, one of religious and moral discipline, the process seems to have been much more contested in print in England than in Scotland.[1] It was both driven to extremes by religious radicals, and seen as a threat to peace by their opponents. In England, the pursuit of Godliness and Reformation produced articulate opponents as well as enthusiastic supporters (themselves divided). The key divisions in Scotland, from the 1640s onwards, were primarily related to the question of whether the English parliament or Charles I – after 1649, Charles II or the English republic – were likely to prove the better agents of the Scottish wish to ensure the security of Presbyterianism throughout Britain. The fateful decision to crown Charles II king of Britain in January 1651 prompted English conquest and the negotiation of a union that incorporated Scotland into a single state with England in 1653. There were, it now seems, some important religious dimensions to this, and the Scottish people were not as impervious to the attempts by English religious radicals to loosen the hold of the kirk as previously thought.[2]

Nonetheless the cohesiveness of the Godly cause in Scotland, and the persistent insistence on the centrality of Presbyterianism to Scottish identity (which successfully led to the full legal acceptance of a Presbyterian kirk in 1707), along with its persistent denial by the English, may be part of the explanation for the divergences between the two countries after 1660. The Presbyterian cause was kept alive by the Restoration of Scottish episcopacy after 1660; and perhaps the policies of Presbyterians – and even their pursuit by violence – were less discredited by the experience of religious revolution in the 1640s and 1650s than were the aspirations of English puritans. It would be wrong – certainly highly misleading – to suggest that after 1660 the English turned their backs on enthusiasm; but England certainly generated a large body of ideas hostile to it.

The English Revolution might be understood in the realm of ideas as a contest between those who attached paramount value to (religious) truth and those who attached paramount value to peace. The dividing line is not a simple one – it is easy to place Winstanley in the former camp and Hobbes in the latter, but the dividing line separates some republicans from others, and probably does the same with Royalists. The contest between the two values did not disappear in 1660, and religious/confessional difference and discord remained central to English politics and political thought throughout the eighteenth century, at least, as did the various attempts to think through the problem and find ways of ensuring that the pursuit of religious truth in the public realm did not endanger peace. People who pursued that line – making the world safe from religious war – are often considered to constitute the Enlightenment in its English form.

Yet, there were *two* broad responses possible, not one, in the wake of the English Revolution and the wider British experience of religious and civil turmoil. One, certainly, was what we might call the Enlightened or proto-Enlightened response: coming to terms with religious diversity by tolerating it, while at the same time maintaining an alert suspicion of clerical authority and 'priestcraft' sufficient to prevent the church ever being sufficiently powerful to persecute, to perpetrate political violence, or to impede intellectual progress. This process might be understood, at least with certain caveats, as a process of secularisation, separating politics from religion (and from science and other intellectual activities too, for that matter).[3] What is interesting in the history of Britain through the eighteenth century is less the simple triumph of this Enlightenment solution, and more the way in which it was intertwined with a second response. Britain became a united political entity in 1707, but one made up of two paradoxically Enlightened *confessional* states.

This second response, evident immediately following the Restoration of monarchy, was to reconstruct with determination and system a confessional state of sufficient power to stand against its critics.[4] Arguably the blueprint for such a solution developed in the 1660s would have made England a more overtly confessional state than it had ever been, and was not simply a re-creation of the pre-1640 church-state. It demanded Scottish acceptance of an Episcopal church (the hope of Scots that the Solemn League and Covenant might underpin a Presbyterian Restoration in 1660 came to nothing). In England, the Test Acts in particular drew a very neat connection between holding political office and being a communicating member of the Church of England. The confessional state in this form did not work, though it seemed, until 1675, to be successful in establishing its intellectual credentials in England. Certainly, in the 1660s the republican radical Algernon Sidney was busily writing his *Court Maxims* (in exile); and Richard Greaves has revealed the full extent of the plotting and subversion engaged in by the ex-republicans and others, not least in Scotland.[5] John Milton, more quietly, was still at work encoding republican principles into *Paradise Lost*, to be published in 1667. The Good Old Cause was not dead, but perhaps it was to be numbered only amongst the living dead, and had it not been for the inability of both Charles II and James VII & II to refrain from insulting the religious sensibilities of their subjects, things might have gone differently.

From 1660 there was an emphatic rejection of the recent past. On 1 May the Convention parliament resolved that 'according to the ancient and fundamental laws of this kingdom, the government is, and ought to be, by king, lords and commons'.[6] While that statement may bear the impress of the 1640s and 1650s, suggesting that the king shared sovereignty with parliament, the intention behind it was surely to reassert the principles of the old constitution. The king's highest powers were exercised as king-in-parliament. The Cavalier parliament, as Clarendon reported, even more emphatically

pulled up all those principles of sedition and rebellion by the roots, which in their own observation had been the ground of or

contributed to the odious and infamous rebellion in the long parliament. They declared, 'that sottish distinction between the king's
person and his office to be treason; that his negative voice could not
be taken from him, and was so essential to the making of a law, that
no order or ordinance of either house could be binding to the
subject without it; that the militia was inseparably vested in his
majesty, and that it was high treason to raise or levy soldiers without
the king's commission'.

'In a word,' Clarendon added, 'they vindicated all his regalities and
royal prerogatives'; but they were also aware that casting personal
aspersions on the king had been a major cause of the Civil War. And so
they also declared 'that the raising any calumnies of that kind upon the
king, as saying "that he is a papist, or popishly affected", or the like
should be felony'.[7] The past was condemned, consigned to oblivion,
and 'the cult of kingship flourished as never before'.[8]

But the loyalist gentry who dominated the Cavalier parliament were
concerned to restore more than the monarchy: parliament, law and
church were as important. Restoration loyalism, both in the 1660s and
later in its more embattled Tory form, never lost a concern with
nurturing the harmony between king, law, parliament and church. In
that respect there is a very obvious long-term continuity between the
political thought of Elizabethan and Jacobean conformists, constitutional Royalists and many Tories. Of particular importance was the
relationship between the king and the church. The English gentry had
not lost their Erastian instincts; but the church was able to develop a
broadly-shared ecclesiology that defended both the royal supremacy
and the autonomy of national churches under episcopal authority.[9]
Even though, for many of the laity, the return of the church represented 'a prop of the old order, a visible sign of the restoration of the
ancien régime, and a bulwark against sectarianism',[10] they could
nonetheless find common cause with the clergy. Gentry and clergy
supported episcopacy and conformity to the Prayer Book, and loathed
sectarianism and religious sedition, even if for different reasons. The
clergy soon came to reinforce the desire of loyalist gentry to repudiate
the past. The Act of Uniformity (1662) required full acceptance of the
Prayer Book and the 39 Articles; it created a clear legal division
between conformist and nonconformist. In its wake, Sheldon (soon to
succeed Juxon as Archbishop of Canterbury) wrote of the sectarianism
that now flourished:

Tis only a resolute execution of the law that must cure this disease,
all other remedies serve and will increase it; and it's necessary that

they who will not be governed as men by reason and persuasions should be governed as beasts by power and force, all other course will be ineffectual, ever have been so, ever will be. . . .[11]

Clergy and laity together emphasised that monarchy and religious uniformity were mutually supporting, and equally necessary to social and political order, though it must be added that this alliance was in part created by Sheldon and the church. They were able to exploit fear of subversion and hatred for the recent past to create gentry support for the church.[12] The result was that body of persecuting legislation known as 'the Clarendon code'. To bolster the workings of the law, Sheldon sponsored a propaganda campaign in defence of uniformity.[13] Its best-known product was Samuel Parker's *Discourse of Ecclesiastical Politie* (1669). This work gives, perhaps, some idea of the political–religious order that might have been, if only the king had been a more thorough supporter of it. It developed a high view, typical of later Tory argument, of both temporal and ecclesiastical authority.[14]

In Scotland the 1660s tell a different story. Scottish religious traditions had since the Reformation been more congenial to the development and transmission of resistance theories, and this remained the case even in that most monarchical of decades, the 1660s. In 1667 there appeared an anonymous tract, published we assume in the Netherlands, called *Naphtali, or The Wrestlings of the Church of Scotland, for the Kingdom of Christ.* The work had been written by James Stewart and James Stirling, the former a lawyer who was to become Lord Advocate after the expulsion of James VII, and the latter a presbyterian minister. It is a remarkable book, a long record of the sufferings of Scottish Presbyterians, very typical of Covenanter thought in its willingness to make plain the religious cause in which rights to resist secular rulers could be invoked.[15] That right was made even plainer in Steuart's *Jus Populi Vindicatum, or, The Peoples Right to Defend Themselves and Their Covenanted Religion Vindicated* (1669), a work in the tradition of Buchanan and Rutherford. Naturally *Naphtali* aroused considerable hostility and in 1684 Sir George Mackenzie replied with *Jus Regium*, written at a time when the English, too, were compelled by events to look again into the face of chaos and civil war. It appeared in the wake of the Pentland Rising of 1666, the first of two rebellions induced by the persecution of those presbyterians who refused to accept the return of episcopacy and attempted instead to worship in illegal conventicles. The second and more serious was to occur in 1679.[16]

But it was ultimately in England that the attempts to impose an intolerant, exclusive Anglican confessional state failed, notwithstanding the intellectual capital that loyalists could draw upon. That capital

was soon spent by Charles II and James II, whose (respectively) covert
and open support for Catholicism made enemies even of their friends
(but sadly, friends of only very few enemies). The result was the
Glorious Revolution, in which even many Tory-Anglicans felt impelled
to support church ahead of state – another episode in the history of
the casuistry of obedience. It is not surprising to find that the
Allegiance Controversy, which followed the Glorious Revolution, was,
in many respects, a repeat of the earlier Engagement Controversy. An
explicitly casuistical debate naturally followed events of dubious legality as men came to ask whether they could in conscience accept a duty
of allegiance to William III.[17] Among works from the 1650s repub-
lished at this time were Ascham's *Confusions and Revolutions* and Henry
Hammond's *Brief Resolution of the Grand Case of Conscience.*[18] Hammond
was willing to say that in order for men to enjoy 'the solaces of a good
conscience' it was quite proper to act in such a way 'that great disorder
must necessarily continue in such a broken Kingdome'.[19] But what
distinguished 1689 from 1649 was the fact that at the later date the
natural constituency for ideas of conscientious refusal to swear allegiance was so much less resolute. Jacobite and non-juror voices were
certainly loud enough;[20] but most Tories accepted the legitimacy or
necessity of the Glorious Revolution. One could scarcely say that of
Royalist reaction to the regicide. The Tory reaction to James VII & II
was a product of a casuistical defence of resistance to royal command.
Loyalty to the church overrode loyalty to the king, and thus the most
Royalist of all seventeenth-century political groups helped to usher
James VII & II into exile, and to shut the door behind him.[21]

The Restoration attempt to restore politico-religious order failed;
but – crucially – it failed only in part. The Test Acts, which connected
political office to being a communicating Anglican, were not repealed
after 1688. Rather, the confessional state was paradoxically made fit for
an Enlightenment world – from a position of strength, the Church of
England tolerated (explicitly by statute) Protestant dissent, and (in
practice) others too. At the same time the Act of Settlement (1701)
effectively required the monarch to be a communicating Anglican, and
determined a religiously safe line of succession (to be questioned
briefly by the Scots), thus extending the principles of the confessional
state to embrace the highest of all political offices. There emerged a
curious entity, the tolerant confessional state, which was able to bring
a degree of peace to religious conflict, within England, though it did
not reduce the centrality of conflict between confessional groups
passionate in their pursuit of truth.

Notes

Notes to the Introduction

1. Hans Meyerhoff (ed.), *The Philosophy of History in Our Time: An Anthology* (New York, 1959), p. 46; Benedetto Croce, *History as the Story of Liberty*, trans. Sylvia Sprigge (London, 1941), p. 19.
2. Notably perhaps, James Simpson, *Burning to Read: English Fundamentalism and its Reformation Opponents* (Cambridge, MA, 2007).
3. Ivan Roots (ed.), *Speeches of Oliver Cromwell* (London, 1989), p. 67.
4. Some of the reasons for this change of mind are to be found in Glenn Burgess, 'Scottish or British? Politics and Political Thought in Scotland', *Historical Journal*, 41 (1998), pp. 579–90; and Burgess, 'Introduction – the new British History', in Burgess (ed.), *The New British History: Founding a Modern State, 1603–1715* (London, 1999), pp. 1–29.
5. Peter McNeil, '"Our Religion, Established Neither by Law nor Parliament": Was the Reformation Legislation of 1560 Valid?', *Records of the Scottish Church History Society*, 35 (2005), pp. 68–89.
6. See especially, among recent work, Alan Cromartie, *The Constitutionalist Revolution: An Essay on the History of England, 1450–1642* (Cambridge, 2006). This work appeared after the present work was in all essentials complete, and I have resisted the temptation to engage with it extensively in what follows.

Notes to the Prologue

1. Quentin Skinner, *Liberty before Liberalism* (Cambridge, 1998).
2. Quentin Skinner, *The Foundations of Modern Political Thought*, 2 vols (Cambridge, 1978), vol. I, part 3.
3. See especially Eric Nelson, *The Greek Tradition in Republican Thought* (Cambridge, 2004).
4. Thomas More, *Utopia: Latin Text and English Translation*, ed. George M. Logan, Robert M. Adams and Clarence H. Miller (Cambridge, 1995), pp. 2–3. References will be given in the text in parentheses. I have relied heavily on the notes to this edition, and on those of *The Yale Edition of the Complete Works of St Thomas More*, vol. IV, ed. Edward Surtz and J. H. Hexter (New Haven, CT, 1965).
5. More, *Utopia*, 81–3.
6. Alistair Fox, 'English Humanism and the Body Politic', in Fox and John Guy, *Reassessing the Henrician Age: Humanism, Politics and Reform, 1500–1550* (Oxford, 1986), ch. 2, p. 38.
7. On the relationship of More and Erasmus see J. H. Hexter, *More's Utopia: The Biography of an Idea* (New York, 1965), pp. 110–11; George M. Logan, *The Meaning of More's 'Utopia'* (Princeton, NJ, 1983), pp. 58–9; Fox, 'English Humanism and the Body Politic', p. 36. More generally, see Skinner, *Foundations*, I, pp. 213–21; Brendan Bradshaw, 'Transalpine Humanism', in J. H. Burns and Mark Goldie (eds), *The Cambridge History of Political Thought, 1450–1700* (Cambridge, 1991), ch. 4, pp. 126–8.
8. Logan, *Meaning of More's 'Utopia'*, p. 118 n. 76.
9. Hexter, *More's Utopia*.
10. Desiderius Erasmus, *The Education of a Christian Prince*, ed. Lisa Jardine (Cambridge, 1997), pp. 15, 54–65.
11. A. A. Long, 'Cicero's Politics in *De Officiis*', in André Laks and Malcolm Schofield (eds), *Justice and Generosity: Studies in Hellenistic Social and Political Philosophy* (Cambridge, 1995), p. 238.
12. Desiderius Erasmus, *The Adages of Erasmus*, ed. William Barker (Toronto, 2001), p. 29.
13. Erasmus, *Adages*, p. 13; John C. Olin, 'Erasmus's *Adagia* and More's *Utopia*', in C. Murphy, A. Gibaud and M. Di Cesare (eds), *Miscellanea Moreana: Essays For Germain Marc' hadour* (Binghainton, NY, 1989).
14. J. H. Hexter, *The Vision of Politics on the Eve of the Reformation: More, Machiavelli, and Seyssel*

(London, 1973), pp. 138–46. Hexter's brilliant reconstruction of the composition of *Utopia* was first presented in his *More's Utopia*.

15. For these strains in Erasmian thought see the brief but enlightening comment of Brendan Bradshaw, 'More on Utopia', *Historical Journal*, 24 (1981), pp. 1–27, at p. 23 n. 62. For a strongly Greek-Platonic reading of the work, see Eric Nelson, 'Greek Nonsense in More's *Utopia*', *Historical Journal*, 44 (2001), pp. 889–917.

16. This account follows Quentin Skinner, 'Sir Thomas More's *Utopia* and the Language of Renaissance Humanism', in Anthony Pagden (ed.), *The Languages of Political Theory in Early-Modern Europe* (Cambridge, 1987), pp, 125–35, against the criticisms in George M. Logan, 'Interpreting *Utopia*: Ten Recent Studies and the Modern Critical Traditions', *Moreana*, 32: 118/119 (1994), pp. 203–58, esp. 209–11. Skinner's essay is also available in a revised edition as 'Thomas More's *Utopia* and the Virtue of True Nobility', in Skinner, *Visions of Politics*, 3 vols (Cambridge, 2002), vol. II, ch. 8.

17. Skinner, 'Sir Thomas More's *Utopia*', p. 133; cf. George M. Logan, '*Utopia* and Deliberative Rhetoric', *Moreana*, 31: 118/119 (1994), p. 107, which finds Giles appealing only to the crudest from of *utilitas*, benefit to oneself.

18. It is possible that Morus was here reminding both Hythlodaeus and Giles of the arguments of Plato, *Republic*, 519d–521b. There is an irony here: both Giles and Hythlodaeus, in very different ways, assume the identity of the moral and the expedient, of *honestas* and *utilitas*; while Morus, not usually the Platonist, accepts Plato's view that the citizen philosopher may be required to sacrifice his personal good for that of the public. Throughout the debate on counsel the arguments and counter-arguments (including on this point) match very closely the discussion in Cicero, *De Officiis*, I, 69–73 (pp. 28–9, Cambridge edn).

19. Logan, *Meaning of More's 'Utopia'*, pp. 55–83, drawing ultimately on Hexter, *More's Utopia*.

20. This may be a point of some interpretative significance, for Hythlodaeus, *in spite of himself*, may be said to represent a Ciceronian union of eloquence and philosophy, rather than a Platonic adherence to philosophy against eloquence. On the contrast, see Brian Vickers, *In Defence of Rhetoric* (Oxford, 1988), pp. 163–6.

21. Richard Marius, *Thomas More: A Biography* (London, 1984), pp. 20–4. Important accounts of the Morton episode and of the dialogue on counsel of which it forms a part are J. C. Davis, 'More, Morton, and the Politics of Accommodation', *Journal of British Studies*, 9: 2 (1970), pp. 27–49; David M. Bevington, 'The Dialogue in *Utopia*: Two Sides to the Question', *Studies in Philology*, 58 (1961), pp. 496–509; and Arthur J. Slavin, 'Platonism and the Problem of Counsel in *Utopia*', in Gordon Schochet (ed.), *Reformation, Humanism, and 'Revolution'*, The Folger Institute Center for the History of British Political Thought Proceedings, Volume 1 (Washington DC, 1990), pp. 207–34.

22. On this speech (and Book I) as an exercise in deliberative rhetoric, conducted in terms of the *topoi* presented in Cicero's *De Officiis*, the rival claims of the honourable or moral (*honestas*) and the beneficial or expedient (*utilitas*), see Logan, '*Utopia* and Deliberative Rhetoric', pp. 103–20.

23. Skinner, *Foundations*, I, pp. 257–60; Skinner, 'Sir Thomas More's *Utopia*', pp. 135–47.

24. These remarks are based on D. M. Palliser, *The Age of Elizabeth: England under the Later Tudors, 1547–1603*, 2nd edn (London, 1992), pp. 206–15.

25. Contrast the reading of the 'debate on counsel', Hexter's label for Book I, given in Hexter, *More's Utopia*, p. 132–8.

26. It is often pointed out that in the *Republic* communal ownership was practised only by the ruling elite (the Guardians), not by the whole community. However, in the *Laws* Plato did suggest that in a perfect society property-sharing 'is put into practice as widely as possible throughout the entire state', a society in which the very notion of private property is eliminated (*Laws*, 739b–c; Penguin translation, T. J. Saunders). Significantly it was suggested that such a situation might never exist and that this perfect society existed not as a blueprint to implement but as a yardstick by which to measure actual societies.

27. The Aristotelian defence of private property was also in St Thomas Aquinas, *Summa Theologica*, 2a 2ae, qu. 66, art. 2 (A. P. d'Entrèves (ed.), *Aquinas: Selected Political Writings* (Oxford, 1954), pp. 168–9).

28. For a powerful reading of the controlled and disciplined nature of Utopian society see J. C. Davis, *Utopia and the Ideal Society: A Study of English Utopian Writing, 1516–1700* (Cambridge, 1981), ch. 2.

29. As in Shlomo Avineri, 'War and Slavery in More's *Utopia*', *International Review of Social History*, 7 (1962), pp. 260–90. This article might be judged to respond anachronistically to the text, but it nonetheless raises acutely the interpretative problem posed by the passages on warfare. Important also are Robert P. Adams, *The Better Part of Valor: More, Erasmus, Colet and Vives on Humanism, War, and Peace, 1496–1535* (Seattle, 1962), esp. ch. 9; Hexter, *Vision of Politics*, pp 48–54; Skinner, *Foundations*, I, pp. 244–8; and Logan, *Meaning of More's 'Utopia'*, pp. 215–16, 221–9, 238–40.

30. A fact revealed most clearly in his emphasis on the importance of Christian unity to ward off Turkish attack, *Complaint of Peace* (1517), in John P. Dolan (ed.), *The Essential Erasmus* (New York, 1964), pp. 192, 195–6. For a good statement of hostility to national divisions amongst Christians, see pp. 196–7.

31. The liberation of oppressed peoples may sound a little suspicious to the modern reader, but Skinner has pointed out that this was a justification for war acceptable in civic humanist circles: Skinner, *Foundations*, I, pp. 77–8; cf. Logan, *Meaning of More's 'Utopia'*, p. 222.

32. I am indebted to the discussion of this passage in Logan, *Meaning of More's 'Utopia'*, pp. 239–40.

33. Such a view has been most influentially advanced by Hexter (*Vision of Politics*, esp. pp. 65–82, 94–107). For powerful counter-arguments see D. B. Fenlon, 'England and Europe: *Utopia* and its Aftermath, *Transactions of the Royal Historical Society*, 5th series, vol. 25 (1975), pp. 113–35; and, above all, Bradshaw, 'More on Utopia'. There is a useful survey of the trend away from Hexter to the older view that Utopia was a satire, contrasting the considerable achievements of a pagan people with the failures of Christian Europe, in William G. Palmer, 'Still More on *Utopia*: a Revival of the Catholic Interpretation? A Review Essay', *Southern Humanities Review*, 19 (1985), pp. 347–58; also Logan, 'Interpreting *Utopia*'. Skinner, who originally endorsed Hexter's view, has now explicitly modified his views on this subject, and agrees that Utopia was not a truly Christian community (contrast Skinner, *Foundations*, I, p. 233, with Hexter, 'Sir Thomas More's *Utopia*', pp. 148–52).

34. Skinner, 'Sir Thomas More's *Utopia*', pp. 149–50.

35. It might be argued that the tolerance of Utopia was matched by the tolerance of Erasmian humanism, but there was a considerable gap between the broad tolerance of all varieties of belief, and very limited punishment even of atheism to be found in Utopia, and the Erasmian concentration on agreed Christian essentials. For a recent account of Erasmian toleration see Gary Remer, 'Rhetoric and the Erasmian Defence of Religious Toleration', *History of Political Thought*, 10 (1989), pp. 377–403.

36. It has long been recognised that interpretation of the very brief closing dialogue of *Utopia* is central to an assessment of the validity of Hexter's view that Utopia was, as Hythlodaeus said, the best state of a commonwealth. Important contributions to the debate are J. H. Hexter, 'Intention, Words, and Meaning: the Case of More's '*Utopia*', *New Literary History*, 6 (1974–5), pp. 529–41; and Ward S. Allen, 'The Tone of More's Farewell to *Utopia*: a Reply to J. H. Hexter', *Moreana*, 13 (1976), pp. 108–18.

37. Skinner, 'Sir Thomas More's *Utopia*', pp. 152–7, to which the account here is greatly indebted.

38. R. W. Chambers, *Thomas More* (London, 1938), p. 128.

39. Thus while, in Book I, More endorsed Cicero's view that citizens should lead an active political life (as counsellors in this case), in Book II he rejected the Ciceronian view that the commonwealth existed on the basis of and in order to protect private property (Cicero, *De Officiis*, I, 20–21; II, 73 (Cambridge, 1991), pp. 9, 92–3).

40. The work was received by its earlier readers as a critique of neo-Roman values: Eric Nelson, 'Utopia through Italian Eyes: Thomas More and the Critics of Civic Humanism', *Renaissance Quarterly*, 59 (2006), pp. 1029–57.

41. Very good on this is Skinner, *Foundations*, I, pp. 258–62.

42. Alistair Fox, *Thomas More: History and Providence* (Oxford, 1982), pp. 65, 68.

43. Fox and Guy, *Reassessing the Henrician Age*, p. 39.

44. G. R. Elton, 'Persecution and Toleration in the English Reformation', in W. J. Sheils (ed.), *Persecution and Toleration*, Studies in Church History, 21 (Oxford, 1984), pp. 163–87.

45. For the latter see Karl Gunther and Ethan Shagan, 'Protestant Radicalism and Political Thought in the Reign of Henry VIII', *Past & Present*, 194 (2007), pp. 35–74.

46. For this subject, see especially Conrad Russell, 'Arguments for Religious Unity in England, 1530–1650', in Russell, *Unrevolutionary England, 1603–42* (London, 1990), ch. 11 (originally *Journal of Ecclesiastical History*, 18 (1967), pp. 201–26).

47. For a good discussion see Richard Marius, 'Thomas More's View of the Church', in Louis A. Schuster et al. (eds), *The Complete Works of St Thomas More*, volume 8 (in 3 parts) (New Haven, CT, 1973), part iii, pp. 1269–1363, esp. pp. 1335–48.

48. Thomas More, *The Confutacyon of Tyndales Answere* (1532–3), in *Complete Works*, 8(i), pp. 28–9.

49. Ibid., p. 30.

50. Thomas More, *A Dialogue Concerning Heresies* (1529), in Thomas M. C. Lawler et al. (eds), *The Complete Works of St Thomas More*, volume 6 (in 2 parts) (New Haven, CT, 1981), part i, p. 406.

51. Ibid., p. 410.

52. Ibid., p. 411.

53. Ibid., p. 359.

54. Sir Thomas Elyot, *The Book Named the Governor*, ed. S. E. Lehmberg (London, 1962), pp. 1–2. For other later discussions showing anxiety or controversy about the term 'commonwealth', see Edward Forsett, *A Comparative Discourse of the Bodies Natural and Politique* (London, 1606), p. 48; Sir Robert Filmer, *Observations Concerning the Original of Government* (1652), in Filmer, *Patriarcha and Other Writings*, ed. J. P. Sommerville (Cambridge, 1991), p. 186; [Algernon Sidney?], *A Just and Modest Vindication of the Proceedings of the Two Last Parliaments of King Charles II* (London, 1681), in *State Tracts of the Reign of Charles II* (London, 1689), vol. IV, app. xv, cols clxviii–clxix; and John Locke, *Two Treatises of Government*, ed. Peter Laslett (Cambridge, 1967), vol. II, 10, § 133, p. 373.

55. See the excellent discussion in John M. Major, *Sir Thomas Elyot and Renaissance Humanism* (Lincoln, NE, 1964), pp. 109–23. The humanist Richard Morison may have reacted in a similar way to *Utopia*, arguing in 1536 that private property was essential to the order of a commonwealth: see Arthur J. Slavin, '"Tis Rather Far Off, and Rather Like a Dream": Common Weal, Common Woe and Commonwealth', *Explorations in Renaissance Culture*, 14 (1988), pp. 1–27.

56. In this respect also, Hexter and Skinner, rather than the so-called 'medieval' or 'Catholic' interpreters, are correct, for the latter generally argue that More did not intend us to take Utopian communism seriously. For a classic statement of this view see Edward Surtz, *The Praise of Pleasure: Philosophy, Education, and Communism in More's Utopia* (Cambridge, MA, 1957).

57. Fox and Guy, *Reassessing the Henrician Age*, ch. 2.

58. David Starkey, 'Which Age of Reform?', in Christopher Coleman and David Starkey (eds), *Revolution Reassessed: Revisions in the History of Tudor Government and Administration* (Oxford, 1986), ch. 1, pp. 19–27. The fullest surveys of 'commonwealth' thinking are Arthur B. Ferguson, *The Articulate Citizen and the English Renaissance* (Durham, NC, 1965); and Whitney R. D. Jones, *The Tudor Commonwealth, 1529–1559: A Study of the Impact of Social and Economic Developments of Mid-Tudor England upon Contemporary Concepts of the Nature and Duties of the Commonwealth* (London, 1970). They should be read in the light of the more recent historiographical perspectives summarised in Raymond Lurie, 'Some Ideas of Commonwealth in Early Modern England', in Schochet (ed.), *Reformation, Humanism, and 'Revolution'*, pp. 293–306.

59. Thomas F. Mayer, *Thomas Starkey and the Commonweal: Humanist Politics and Religion in the Reign of Henry VIII* (Cambridge, 1989), ch. 3.

60. A good general discussion of the theme in More, Elyot and Starkey is Stanford E. Lehmberg, 'English Humanism, the Reformation, and the Problem of Counsel', *Archiv für Reformationsgeschichte*, 52 (1961), pp. 74–90. Elyot's lesser-known works on counsel are also discussed in Alistair Fox, 'Sir Thomas Elyot and the Humanist Dilemma', in Fox and Guy, *Reassessing the Henrician Age*, ch. 3; and F. W. Conrad, 'The Problem of Counsel Reconsidered: the Case of Sir Thomas Elyot', in Paul A. Fideler and T. F. Mayer (eds), *Political Thought and the Tudor Commonwealth: Deep Structure, Discourse and Disguise* (London, 1992), ch. 3.

61. Thomas Starkey, *A Dialogue between Pole and Lupset*, ed. T. F. Mayer, Camden Society, 4th series, vol. 37 (London, 1989), p. 1. References to this work are hereafter given parenthetically. In quotations I have removed the editor's markings indicating interlinear insertions, etc.

62. Quoted in Mayer, *Thomas Starkey and the Commonweal*, p. 96.
63. G. R. Elton, 'Reform by Statute: Thomas Starkey's *Dialogue* and Thomas Cromwell's Policy', in Elton, *Studies in Tudor and Stuart Politics and Government*, 4 vols (Cambridge, 1974–92), vol. II, ch. 32; also G. R. Elton, *Reform and Renewal: Thomas Cromwell and the Common Weal* (Cambridge, 1973).
64. Elyot, *Book Named the Governor*, pp. 103–6.
65. Mayer, *Thomas Starkey and the Commonweal*, chs 2 and 3, and pp. 153–60.
66. Alternatively given as six men, two of each learned in civil, canon and common law, plus four noblemen (p. 122).
67. The socio-economic aspects of commonwealth thought are explored especially in Jones, *Tudor Commonwealth*.
68. Brendan Bradshaw, 'The Tudor Commonwealth: Reform and Revision', *Historical Journal*, 22 (1979), pp. 455–76.
69. Sir Richard Morison, *A Remedy for Sedition Wherein Are Contained Many Things Concerning the True and Loyal Obeisance That Commons Owe unto Their Prince and Sovereign Lord the King* (1536), in David Sandler Berkowitz (ed.), *Humanist Scholarship and Public Order: Two Tracts against the Pilgrimage of Grace* (Washington DC, 1984), pp. 116–17.
70. Ibid., p. 113.
71. Ibid., p. 110.
72. Edmund Dudley, *Tree of Commonwealth*, ed. D. M. Brodie (Cambridge, 1948), p. 32. Dudley did express the belief that kings should rule by law and not by extraordinary means, but more as a moral platitude than as a criticism of existing practice (pp. 36–7).
73. See especially Ethan Shagan, *Popular Politics and the English Reformation* (Cambridge, 2003), ch. 8; Andy Wood, *Riot, Rebellion and Popular Politics in Early Modern England* (Basingstoke, 2002), pp. 54–60.
74. Gunther and Shagan, 'Protestant Radicalism and Political Thought in the Reign of Henry VIII'.
75. The key work is Markku Peltonen, *Classical Humanism and Republicanism in English Political Thought, 1570–1640* (Cambridge, 1995). Also Patrick Collinson, 'The Elizabethan Exclusion Crisis and the Elizabethan Polity', *Proceedings of the British Academy*, 84 (1994), pp. 51–92.

Notes to Chapter 1

1. G. R. Elton, *The Tudor Constitution: Documents and Commentary*, 2nd edn (Cambridge, 1982), pp. 364–7.
2. Ibid., p. 353.
3. J. G. A. Pocock, 'A Discourse of Sovereignty: Observations of the Work in Progress', in Nicholas Phillipson and Quentin Skinner (eds), *Political Discourse in Early Modern Britain* (Cambridge, 1993), ch. 17, at p. 381.
4. On the development of arguments in favour of the divorce, see George Bernard, *The King's Reformation: Henry VIII and the Remaking of the English Church* (New Haven, CT, 2005), pp. 14–50.
5. The *Collectanea* is now B.L. Cotton MS Cleopatra E 6, fols 16–135.
6. The *Gravissimae Censurae* and the *Determinations* are now available in a parallel edition: Edward Surtz and Virginia Murphy (eds), *The Divorce Tracts of Henry VIII* (Angers, 1988).
7. Bernard, *King's Reformation*, pp. 26–7.
8. On the propaganda campaign see especially G. R. Elton, *Policy and Police: The Enforcement of the Reformation in the Age of Thomas Cromwell* (Cambridge, 1972), ch. 4; and Bernard, *King's Reformation*, pp. 224–8; also Franklin L. Baumer, *The Early Tudor Theory of Kingship* (New York, 1966; orig. edn 1940), ch. 3, and appendix A, pp. 211–24. This paragraph is based on standard sources, mainly John Guy, *Tudor England* (Oxford, 1988); G. R. Elton, *Reform and Reformation: England 1509–1558* (London, 1977); Christopher Haigh, *English Reformations: Religion, Politics, and Society under the Tudors* (Oxford, 1993); and Diarmaid MacCulloch, *Thomas Cranmer: A Life* (New Haven, CT, 1996). Of particular importance, however, are Graham Nicholson, 'The Act of Appeals and the English Reformation', in Claire Cross, David Loades and J. J. Scarisbrick (eds), *Law and Government under the Tudors: Essays Presented to Sir Geoffrey Elton . . . on the Occasion of his Retirement* (Cambridge, 1988), pp. 19–30; and John Guy, 'Thomas Cromwell and the Intellectual Origins of the Henrician Revolution', in Alistair Fox and John Guy, *Reassessing the Henrician Age:*

Humanism, Politics and Reform, 1500–1550 (Oxford, 1986), ch. 7; and the latest account in Bernard, *King's Reformation.*

9. Steven W. Haas, 'The *Disputatio Inter Clericum et Militem*: Was Berthelet's 1531 Edition the First Henrician Polemic of Thomas Cromwell?', *Moreana*, 14 (1977), pp. 65–72; Steven W. Haas, 'Henry VII's *Glasse of Truthe*'; Steven W. Haas, 'Martin Luther's "Divine Right" Kingship and the Royal Supremacy: Two Tracts from the 1531 Parliament and the Convocation of the Clergy', *Journal of Ecclesiastical History*, 31 (1980), pp. 317–25; Quentin Skinner, *The Foundations of Modern Political Thought*, 2 vols (Cambridge, 1978), vol. II, pp. 66–73, 84–9, 91–108; and Francis Oakley, 'Christian Obedience and Authority, 1520–1550', in J. H. Burns and Mark Goldie (eds), *Cambridge History of Political Thought, 1450–1700* (Cambridge, 1991), ch. 6, esp. pp. 174–82.

10. Ibid., pp. 81–2.

11. Ibid., pp. 84–5.

12. Bernard, *King's Reformation*, p. 225.

13. Cf. Richard Rex, 'Crisis of Obedience: God's Word and Henry's Reformation', *Historical Journal*, 39 (1996), pp. 863–94.

14. Alex Ryrie, 'Divine Kingship and Royal Theology in Henry VIII's Reformation', *Reformation*, 7 (2002), pp. 49–77.

15. Cf. John Guy, 'The Henrician Age', in J. G. A. Pocock (ed.), *The Varieties of British Political Thought, 1500–1800* (Cambridge, 1993), p. 38.

16. Cranmer held a conciliar view of the universal Catholic church from his Cambridge days as a Catholic humanist: MacCulloch, *Thomas Cranmer*, pp. 27–30, 151.

17. Walter Ullmann, ' "This Realm of England is an Empire" ', *Journal of Ecclesiastical History*, 30 (1979), pp. 175–203; Henry Chadwick, 'Royal Ecclesiastical Supremacy', in Brendan Bradshaw and Eamon Duffy (eds), *Humanism, Reform and the Reformation: The Career of Bishop John Fisher* (Cambridge, 1989). Cf. the earlier account of the imperial crown in Richard Koebner, ' "The Imperial Crown of England": Henry VIII, Constantine the Great, and Polydore Vergil', *Bulletin of the Institute of Historical Research*, 26 (1953), pp. 29–52.

18. Guy, 'Thomas Cromwell and the Intellectual Origins of the Henrician Revolution', esp. pp. 164–75; and Guy, 'Henrician Age', esp. pp. 22–30. Also John Guy, 'Law, Equity and Conscience in Henrician Jurisitic Thought', in Fox and Guy, *Reassessing the Henrician Age*, ch. 8.

19. Christopher St German, *Dialogus de Fundamentis Legum Anglie et de Conscientia* (1528); English edn, *Dyaloge . . . betwyxte a Doctour of Dyvynytye and a Student in the Lawes of Englande* (1531); and *The Secunde Dyaloge* (1530); known collectively as *Doctor and Student*. Best edition is *St German's Doctor and Student*, ed. T. F. T. Plucknett and J. L. Barton (London: Selden Soc., 1974).

20. Guy, 'Thomas Cromwell and the Intellectual Origins of the Henrician Revolution', pp. 157–61.

21. Ibid., pp. 418–19.

22. Reprinted in John Strype, *Ecclesiastical Memorials*, 3 vols in 6 parts (Oxford, 1820–40), vol. I, part ii, pp. 162–75; vol I, part i, pp. 237–44 gives a very inadequate English paraphrase.

23. English version: Foxe, *The True Dyfferens betwen the Regall Power and the Ecclesiasticall Power* (London, 1548).

24. Translated into English in 1553. All references are to the parallel Latin–English texts in Pierre Janelle (ed.), *Obedience in Church and State: Three Political Tracts* (Cambridge, 1930).

25. Sampson, *Oratio*, p. 167: 'In Anglia plus potestatis non habet, quam habeat Cantuariensis Episcopus Romae.'

26. Ibid., pp. 166–7.

27. Ibid., p. 175: 'Verbum dei est, obedire Regi, non Episcopo Romano.'

28. Ibid., p. 175: 'Hoc [i.e. the ending of all papal jurisdiction in England] mandat Deus, quia Rex Dei in terris minister; cui verbo Dei suprema potestas datur, hoc praecipit.'

29. Foxe, *True Dyfferens*, fols x^v–xi.

30. Ibid., fols xiv, xv.

31. Ibid., fol. xxvi^v; also lix^v.

32. Ibid., fols xxxi^v, xxxiiii.

33. Ibid., fol. xxxvii^v.

34. Ibid., fol. xxxiii^v.

35. Ibid., fols xxxv^v, xxxvi.

36. Ibid., fols l–l^v.

37. Ibid., fol. lvi^v.
38. Ibid., fols lxxx, lxxxiv–lxxxv; see also fols lxiiii, lxv^v, lxxvi. The statement on fol. lxxxiv–fol. lxxxiiii^v about kings consecrating bishops will be discussed later, when we come back to take stock of the exact scope of the royal supremacy that Foxe and others defended.
39. There is a good summary of the work in James A. Muller, *Stephen Gardiner and the Tudor Reaction* (London, 1926), ch. xi, pp. 61–5; and an appreciation of the personal circumstances in which it was written, in Glyn Redworth, *In Defence of the Church Catholic: The Life of Stephen Gardiner* (Oxford, 1990), ch. 3.
40. Gardiner, *De Vera Obedientia*, in Janelle (ed.), *Obedience in Church and State*, p. 73.
41. Ibid., pp. 75, 77.
42. Ibid., p. 87.
43. Ibid., p. 89.
44. Ibid., p. 91.
45. Ibid., pp. 91, 93.
46. Ibid., p. 115.
47. Ibid., pp. 93, 95.
48. Ibid., p. 99.
49. Ibid., p. 101.
50. Ibid., pp. 103–7.
51. Ibid., p. 109.
52. Ibid., pp. 111–13.
53. Ibid., pp, 117–19.
54. Ibid., pp. 119–21.
55. Ibid., pp. 121–7.
56. Ibid., p. 129.
57. Ibid., p. 131.
58. Ibid., pp. 131–3.
59 Ibid., pp. 139–43, 153.
60. Ibid., pp. 143–7.
61. Ibid., p. 157.
62. On this subject see Baumer, *Early Tudor Theory of Kingship*, pp. 49–56; and P. A. Sawada, 'Two Anonymous Tudor Treatises on the General Council', *Journal of Ecclesiastical History*, 12 (1961), pp. 196–214.
63. *A Treatise Concernynge Generall Councilles, the Byshoppes of Rome, and the Clergy* (London, 1538), sigs B6v–B7.
64. Ibid., sigs B7v–C1.
65. Ibid., sigs C1–C1v.
66. Ibid., sig. C2v–C3.
67. Ibid., sigs D3–D4.
68. Thomas Starkey, *An Exhortation to the People, Instructynge Theym to Unitie and Obedience* (London, 1536), fols 8b–9.
69. Ibid., fol. 9b.
70. For the Elizabethan church, see the 39 Articles (1563), art. 21, in David Cressy and Lori Anne Ferrell (eds), *Religion and Society in Early Modern England: A Sourcebook* (London, 1996), p. 65.
71. Charles Lloyd, *Formularies of Faith Put Forth by Authority during the Reign of Henry VIII* (Oxford, 1825), pp. 52–7.
72. Ibid., pp. 246, 248.
73. Baumer, *Early Tudor Theory of Kingship*, pp. 32–4; Francis Oakley, 'Edward Foxe, Matthew Paris and the Royal *Potestas Ordinis*', *Sixteenth Century Journal*, 18 (1987), pp. 347–53; also Felix Markower, *Constitutional History of the Church of England* (London, 1895), pp. 251–9.
74. *The Bishops' Book*, in Lloyd, *Formularies of Faith*, pp. 102–3, 107–11.
75. Ibid., pp. 112–14.
76. Ibid., p. 121; and Oakley, 'Edward Foxe . . . and the Royal *Potestas Ordinis*', pp. 349–50.
77. See Martin Luther, *Secular Authority* (1523), in John Dillinberger (ed.), *Martin Luther: Selections from His Writings* (New York, 1961), pp. 389–90. For a concise discussion see Harro Höpfl, *The Christian Polity of John Calvin* (Cambridge, 1982), pp. 28–30.
78. The most powerful argument to toy with the idea that there were hints of such a high view of the supremacy is put by J. J. Scarisbrick, *Henry VIII* (London, 1968), ch. 12, esp. pp. 416–17.

79. Lloyd, *Formularies of Faith*, p. 121.

80. Oakley, 'Edward Foxe . . . and the Royal *Potestas Ordinis*', pp. 351–3.

81. The full set of answers is reprinted in Gilbert Burnet, *The History of the Reformation of the Church of England*, ed. Nicholas Pocock, 7 vols (Oxford, 1865), vol. IV, pp. 443–96; Cranmer's alone are in Thomas Cranmer, *Miscellaneous Writings and Letters*, ed. John E. Cox (Cambridge, 1846), pp. 114–17. See discussion in Baumer, *Early Tudor Theory of Kingship*, pp. 79–82.

82. MacCulloch, *Thomas Cranmer*, pp. 280–2; Cranmer, *Miscellaneous Writings*, ed. Cox, p. 116.

83. Ibid., pp. 116–17.

84. Ibid., p. 117.

85. The argument is particularly associated with Elton. See, e.g., Elton, *Reform and Reformation*, pp. 197–200; Elton, *Tudor Constitution*, pp. 12–14, 234–40, 342–5.

86. Baumer, *Early Tudor Theory of Kingship*, p. 57. Baumer gives a good concise discussion of this subject (pp. 56–62).

87. See especially F. D. Logan, 'Thomas Cromwell and the Vicegerency in Spirituals: a Revisitation', *English Historical Review*, 103 (1988), pp. 658–67.

88. Guy, 'Thomas Cromwell and the Intellectual Origins of the Henrician Revolution', in Fox and Guy, *Reassessing the Henrician Age*, p. 159, n. 19.

89. *The Letters of Stephen Gardiner*, ed. James Arthur Muller (Westport, CT, 1970; orig. edn 1933), pp. 390, 391, 399.

90. *St German's Doctor and Student*, p. 315.

91. John Guy, *St German on Chancery and Statute* (London, 1985), pp. 41–4; also Franklin Le Van Baumer, 'Christopher St German: the Political Philosophy of a Tudor Lawyer', *American Historical Review*, 42 (1937), pp. 631–51; and now Alan Cromartie, *The Constitutionalist Revolution: An Essay on the History of England, 1450–1642* (Cambridge, 2006), ch. 2; and Daniel Appley, *Defending Royal Supremacy and Discerning God's Will in Tudor England* (Aldershot, 2007), ch. 3.

92. Christopher St German, *An Answere to a Letter* (London, 1535), sig A2v.

93. Ibid., sig. B3.

94. Ibid., sig. B6.

95. Ibid., sigs A3–A4v.

96. Ibid., sig. A7.

97. Ibid., sig. B6v.

98. Ibid., sigs F8v–G1.

99. Ibid., sigs G1–G2v.

100. Ibid., sigs G2v–G3.

101. St German, *Answere to a Letter*, sigs G4v–G5 (emphasis added to last quotation).

102. Ibid., sig. G5.

103. Ibid., sigs G5–G5v.

104. In the microfilmed copy I have used, the words in square brackets appear to have been deleted by hand.

105. St German, *Answere to a Letter*, sigs G5v–G6.

106. See, e.g., Baumer, *Early Tudor Theory of Kingship*, ch. 5; Elton, *Tudor Constitution*, pp. 13–14, 17–18; G. R. Elton, 'The Rule of Law in Sixteenth-Century England', in Elton, *Studies in Tudor and Stuart Politics and Government* (Cambridge, 1974–92), 4 vols, vol. I, i, ch. 14.

107. Elton, *Tudor Constitution*, p. 277 (Ferrers' Case).

108. On the expansion in authority of the early Tudor state, which occurred without recourse to a doctrine of absolutism, see S. J. Gunn, *Early Tudor Government, 1485–1558* (Basingstoke, 1995), ch. 4.

109. There is an extensive literature on humanism and the Reformation, but particularly useful in this context is Richard Rex, 'The Role of English Humanists in the Reformation up to 1559', in N. Scott Amos, Andrew Pettegree and Henk van Nierop (eds), *The Education of A Christian Society: Humanism and the Reformation in Britain and the Netherlands* (Aldershot, 1999), ch. 2.

110. On this group, see Skinner, *Foundations*, vol. II, pp. 100–7; and W. Gordon Zeeveld, *Foundations of Tudor Policy* (London, 1948, 1969).

111. For a concise account of his ideas, see Anthony Black, *Political Thought in Europe, 1250–1450* (Cambridge, 1992), pp. 58–71.

112. Shelley Lockwood, 'Marsilius of Padua and the Case for the Royal Ecclesiastical

Supremacy', *Transactions of the Royal Historical Society*, 6th series, 1 (1991), pp. 89–119 (quotation from p. 97).

113. Starkey, *Exhortation*, sigs a2v–a3.

114. On this work, see Thomas Mayer, *Thomas Starkey and the Commonwealth: Humanist Politics and Religion in the Reign of Henry VIII* (Cambridge, 1989), pp. 216–27. My account should not be taken to suggest Marsilian 'influence' on Starkey, on which subject see Mayer, pp. 226–7.

115. Starkey, *Exhortation*, fol. 6b. The category explicitly included papal supremacy, which was neither necessary to salvation nor damnable to accept.

116. For the contrast see Thomas F. Mayer, 'Starkey and Melanchthon on Adiaphora: a Critique of W. Gordon Zeeveld', *Sixteenth Century Journal*, 11 (1980), pp. 39–49. Mayer shows that the near-universal view, established by Zeeveld, that Starkey introduced a Lutheran concept of *adiaphora* into English thought, and thus founded an Anglican liberal tradition, is wrong. His use of the concept was unLutheran, and he was not a pioneer. The concept was 'a commonplace' (p. 46). See at greater length, Bernard J. Verkamp, *The Indifferent Mean: Adiaphorism in the English Reformation to 1554* (Athens, OH, 1977).

117. Starkey, *Exhortation*, fol. 7.

118. Ibid., fols 7–7b.

119. Ibid., fol. 7b.

120. Ibid., fols 27b–28b.

121. Ibid., fols 10b–11.

122. Ibid., fol. 8b.

123. Ibid., fols 38b–39. Cf. fols 64b–65b on two types of unity, civil and spiritual.

124. Ibid., fols 40–40b.

125. Ibid., fol 40.

126. Ibid., fol. 41.

127. Ibid., fols 42–3.

128. Ibid., fol. 47 (I have corrected the word order).

129. Ibid., fol. 69.

130. See also Glenn Burgess, 'Patriotism in English Political Thought 1530–1660', in Robert von Friedeburg (ed.), *Patria und Patrioten vor dem Patriotismus* (Wiesbaden, 2005), pp. 215–41.

131. Sir Richard Morison, *An Exhortation to Styre All Englyshe Men to the Defence of Theyr Countreye* (London, 1539), sig. A4.

132. Ibid., sig. D1.

133. Ibid., sig. B2.

134. Ibid., sigs C3–C4v.

135. Ibid., sig B5.

136. Ibid., sig. B7v.

137. Ibid., sig C1.

138. Ibid., sig. C2v.

139. Ibid., fol. C5v.

140. Ibid., sig. D4.

141. Ibid., sig. D8.

142. The standard work on the English influence of Machiavelli is Felix Raab, *The English Face of Machiavelli: A Changing Interpretation, 1500–1700* (London, 1964); on Morison see pp. 34–40. It should be read in the light of Sydney Anglo, 'The Reception of Machiavelli in Tudor England: a Reassessment', *Il Politico*, 31 (1966), pp. 127–38. For Morison's (lack of) Machiavellianism, see David S. Berkowitz (ed.), *Humanist Scholarship and Public Order: Two Tracts against the Pilgramage of Grace* (Washington, DC, 1984), pp. 70–80. See further Sydney Anglo, *Machiavelli – The First Century: Studies in Enthusiasm, Hostility, and Irrelevance* (Oxford, 2005).

143. It might be added that it has been claimed that the most elaborate use of Machiavelli in Tudor England was the work of none other than Stephen Gardiner: see Peter Donaldson, 'Bishop Gardiner, Machiavellian', *Historical Journal*, 23 (1980), pp. 1–16; and Donaldson (ed.), *A Machiavellian Treatise by Stephen Gardiner* (Cambridge, 1975). However, the attribution of the work in question, which gave advice to Philip of Spain on governing the English kingdom of his wife Mary, to Gardiner cannot be justified. See Dermot Fenlon, review in *Historical Journal*, 19 (1976), pp. 1019–23; Sydney Anglo, 'Crypto-Machiavellism

in Early Tudor England: the Problem of the *Regionamento dell'Advenimento delli Inglesi, et Normanni in Britannia'*, *Renaissance and Reformation*, n.s. 2 (= o.s. 14) (1978), pp. 182–93; and Redworth, *In Defence of the Church Catholic*, p. 308, n. 93.

144. On this subject, see the classic account of John Neville Figgis, *The Divine Right of Kings*, 2nd edn (Cambridge, 1922), esp. ch. 5; also John Neville Figgis, *Studies of Political Thought from Gerson to Grotius, 1414–1625*, 2nd edn (Cambridge, 1931), lect. 3. There are interesting reflections on the theme, relevant to the present chapter, in Edward Allen Whitney, 'Erastianism and Divine Right', *Huntington Library Quarterly*, 2 (1939), pp. 373–98.

145. Sir Richard Morison, *An Invective Ayenste the Great and Detestable Vice, Treason* (London, 1539), sigs. D5–D5v.

146. Diarmaid MacCulloch, *Tudor Church Militant: Edward VI and the Protestant Reformation* (London, 1999).

147. My account is indebted to Catharine Davies, *A Religion of the Word: The Defence of the Reformation in the Reign of Edward VI* (Manchester, 2002), ch. 4.

148. John Hooper, 'A Declaration of the Holy Commandments' (1550), in *Early Writings of John Hooper D.D.*, ed. Samuel Carr (Cambridge, 1843), p. 362.

149. John Hooper, ' Annotations on Romans XIII' (1551), in Hooper, *Later Writings of Bishop Hooper*, ed. Charles Nevinson (Cambridge, 1852), pp. 111–12.

150. Hugh Latimer, 'Certain Sermons [on the Lord's Prayer]' [1552], in Latimer, *Sermons by Hugh Latimer*, ed. George Elwes Corrie (Cambridge, 1844), p. 406.

151. Davies, *Religion of the Word*, pp. 161–2.

152. Anthony Fletcher and Diarmaid MacCulloch, *Tudor Rebellions*, 5th edn (Harlow, 2004), ch. 6; also Ethan Shagan, *Popular Politics and the English Reformation* (Cambridge, 2003), ch. 8.

153. W. D. J. Cargill Thompson, 'The Two Regiments: the Continental Setting of William Tyndale's Political Thought', in Derek Baker (ed.), *Reform and Reformation: England and the Continent, c.1500–c.1750* (Oxford, 1979), pp. 17–33.

154. William Tyndale, 'The Obedience of a Christian Man' (1528), in Tyndale, *Doctrinal Treatises*, ed. Henry Walter (Cambridge, 1848), p. 177.

155. *Miscellaneous Writings and Letters of Thomas Cranmer*, ed. John Edmund Cox (Cambridge, 1846), pp. 126–7.

156. Ibid., p. 188 (see also the sermon attributed to Cranmer and based on notes by Peter Martyr Vermigli, p. 193).

157. Hooper, 'Annotations on Romans XIII', pp. 101, 103.

158. Ibid., p. 104.

159. Ibid., p. 107.

160. John Cheke, *The Hurt of Sedicion Howe Greveous it is to a Commune Wealth* (London, 1549), sig. A2v.

161. Ibid., sigs A6v, A7, A3v.

Notes to Chapter 2

1. Donald Kelley, 'Ideas of Resistance before Elizabeth', in Gordon Schochet (ed.), *Law, Literature, and the Settlement of Regimes*, Proceedings of the Folger Institute Center for the History of British Political Thought, Volume 2 (Washington DC, 1990), p. 5. For a general introduction: Quentin Skinner, *Foundations of Modern Political Thought*, 2 vols (Cambridge, 1978), vol. II, chs 7–9.

2. For recent work that stresses the slow headway made by Protestantism until the middle decades of Elizabeth's reign, see Christopher Haigh, *English Reformations: Religion, Politics and Society under the Tudors* (Oxford, 1993), ch. 11; Eamon Duffy, *The Stripping of the Altars: Traditional Religion in England, 1400–1580* (New Haven, CT, 1992), chs 13–15. For a reasonably balanced assessment of the state of the debate immediately prior to the publication of these works see David Loades, *The Mid-Tudor Crisis, 1545–1565* (Basingstoke, 1992), ch. 6.

3. The figure (which includes women and children) was first calculated in Christina Hallowell Garrett, *The Marian Exiles: A Study in the Origins of Elizabethan Puritanism* (Cambridge, 1938; reprinted 1966), pp. 30–2, and matches the near-contemporary estimate of John Foxe. More recent historians have not improved on it: see, e.g., John Guy, *Tudor England* (Oxford, 1988), p. 238; Haigh, *English Reformations*, p. 228.

4. There is some room for debate about the exact character of what opposition Mary's religious policies encountered. See Jennifer Loach, 'Conservatism and Consent in Parliament, 1547–59', in Jennifer Loach and Robert Tittler (eds), *The Mid-Tudor Polity, c.1540–1560* (Basingstoke, 1990), ch. 1; and Loach, *Parliament under the Tudors* (Oxford, 1991), pp. 82–4, for a view that plays down the extent of *religious* opposition. What opposition there was concerned fears about property rights, especially with regard to property acquired from the dissolution of the monasteries.

5. Calvin, *Institutes*, IV, xx, 23, in Harro Höpfl (ed.), *Luther and Calvin on Secular Authority* (Cambridge, 1991), pp. 74–5.

6. Ibid., IV, xx, 25, pp. 76–7.

7. Ibid., IV, xx, 32, pp. 83–4.

8. Ibid., IV, xx, 31, pp. 82–3.

9. *The Works of John Knox*, ed. David Laing, 6 vols (Edinburgh, 1846–64), vol. III, pp. 217–26; J. H. Burns, 'Knox and Bullinger', *Scottish Historical Review*, 34 (1955), pp. 90–1.

10. E.g. John Calvin, *Original Letters Relative to the English Reformation*, ed. Hastings Robinson, 2 vols (Cambridge, 1846–7), vol. II, p. 771; Calvin to Bullinger, 29 April 1554, *Corpus Reformatorum*, vol. XLIII, pp. 123–6.

11. *The Zurich Letters*, ed. Hastings Robinson, 2 vols (Cambridge, 1842–5), vol. II, pp. 34–6, 131; also Calvin to Cecil, 29 January 1559. See also Andrew Pettegree, *Marian Protestantism: Six Studies* (Aldershot, 1995).

12. John Knox, *History of the Reformation in Scotland*, ed. William Croft Dickinson, 2 vols (London, 1949), vol. II, pp. 133–4; also vol. II, p. 23 and n. 6; John Knox, *On Rebellion*, ed. Roger Mason (Cambridge, 1994), pp. 208–9.

13. Skinner, *Foundations*, vol. II, pp. 191–206. Also R. M. Kingdon, 'Calvinism and Resistance Theory, 1550–1580', in J. H. Burns and Mark Goldie (eds), *The Cambridge History of Political Thought, 1450–1700* (Cambridge, 1991), ch. 7, esp. pp. 200–3; Cynthia Grant Shoenberger, 'Luther and the Justifiability of Resistance to Legitimate Authority', *Journal of the History of Ideas*, 40 (1979), pp. 3–20; Shoenberger, 'The Development of the Lutheran Theory of Resistance: 1523–1530', *Sixteenth Century Journal*, 8 (1977), pp. 61–76; Richard R. Benert, 'Lutheran Resistance Theory and the Imperial Constitution', *Il Pensiero Politico*, 6 (1973), pp. 17–36; Robert von Friedeburg, *Self-Defence and Religious Strife in Early Modern Europe: England and Germany, 1530–1680* (Aldershot, 2002).

14. Oliver K. Olson, 'Theology of Revolution: Magdeburg, 1550–1551', *Sixteenth Century Journal*, 3 (1972), pp. 56–79.

15. Skinner, *Foundations*, vol. II, pp. 206–38; Olson, 'Theology of Revolution', p. 79; Esther Hildebrandt, 'The Magdeburg Bekenntnis as a Possible Link between German and English Resistance Theories in the Sixteenth Century', *Archiv für Reformationsgeschichte*, 71 (1980), pp. 227–53. In contrast, Kingdon's account portrays the Marian exiles as a 'stand alone' group, whose ideas developed in relative isolation: Kingdon, 'Calvinism and Resistance Theory', pp. 194–200. See von Friedeburg, *Self-Defence*, ch. 5, for the British reception of Lutheran thought.

16. Knox, *History*, vol. II, pp. 129–30; Knox, *On Rebellion*, p. 204.

17. Skinner, *Foundations*, vol. II, pp. 197–204.

18. For the social composition of the Marian martyrs, see David Loades, *The Reign of Mary Tudor: Politics, Government and Religion in England, 1553–1558* (London, 1979), pp. 273–4; Guy, *Tudor England*, p. 238; G. R. Elton, *Reform and Reformation: England, 1509–1558* (London, 1977), pp. 386–7.

19. For recent discussions of the whole body of Marian resistance literature, see Skinner, *Foundations*, vol. II, pp. 221–38; Michael Walzer, *The Revolution of the Saints: A Study in the Origins of Radical Politics* (Cambridge, MA, 1965), pp. 92–113; Donald Kelley, 'Ideas of Resistance before Elizabeth', in Heather Dubrow and Richard Strier (eds), *The Historical Renaissance: New Essays on Tudor and Stuart Literature and Culture* (Chicago, 1988), pp. 48–76; Gerry Bowler, 'Marian Protestants and the Idea of Violent Resistance to Tyranny', in Peter Lake and Maria Dowling (eds), *Protestantism and the National Church in Sixteenth Century England* (London, 1987), ch. 5; Jane Dawson, 'Revolutionary Conclusions: the Case of the Marian Exiles', *History of Political Thought*, 11 (1990), pp. 257–72; and Dan Danner, *Pilgrimage to Puritanism: History and Theology of the Marian Exiles at Geneva, 1555–1560* (New York, 1999); more generally, Pettegree, *Marian Protestantism: Six Studies*.

20. The standard work on Ponet remains Winthrop S. Hudson, *John Ponet (1516?–1556): Advocate of Limited Monarchy* (Chicago, 1942). It contains a facsimile reprint of the *Shorte*

Treatise. See also David H. Wollman, 'The Biblical Justification for Resistance to Authority in Ponet's and Goodman's Polemics', *Sixteenth Century Journal,* 13 (1982), pp. 29–41; Barbara Peardon, 'The Politics of Polemic: John Ponet's *Short Treatise of Politic Power* and Contemporary Circumstance 1553–1556', *Journal of British Studies,* 22 (1982–3), pp. 35–49; Barrett L. Beer, 'John Ponet's *Short Treatise of Politike Power* Reassessed', *Sixteenth Century Journal,* 21 (1990), pp. 373–83; and Walter Lim, 'Radical Politics in Ponet's *A Shorte Treatise of Politike Power* and Milton's *Tenure of Kings and Magistrates*', *Prose Studies,* 23 (2000), pp. 101–20.

21. John Ponet, *A Shorte Treatise of Politicke Power* ([Strasburg], 1556), sigs A4v–A5.
22. Ibid., sigs A6v–A7.
23. Ibid., sig. B1v.
24. There was an alternative (non-violent) remedy: excommunication, as shown particularly by the example of St Ambrose's excommunication of the Emperor Theodosius (sigs H3–H5). Failing that, the Commons were left with the remedies provided by penance and prayer (sig. H6v).
25. John Hooper, *Later Writings of Bishop Hooper,* ed. Charles Nevinson (Cambridge, 1852), p. 102.
26. The best introductions to Goodman are Jane Dawson, 'Resistance and Revolution in Sixteenth-Century Thought: the Case of Christopher Goodman', in J. van den Berg and P. G. Hoftijzer (eds), *Church, Change and Revolution: Transactions of the Fourth Anglo-Dutch Church History Colloquium (Exeter, 30 August – 3 September, 1988)* (Leiden, 1991), pp. 69–79; Dan G. Danner, 'Christopher Goodman and the English Protestant Tradition of Civil Disobedience', *Sixteenth Century Journal,* 8 (1977), pp. 61–73; Wollman, 'Biblical Justification for Resistance'; and Jane Dawson, 'Trumpeting Resistance: Christopher Goodman and John Knox', in Roger Mason. (ed.), *John Knox and the British Reformations* (Aldershot, 1998), ch. 7.
27. Christopher Goodman, *How Superior Powers Oght to be Obeyd of Their Subjects: and Wherin They May Lawfully by Gods Worde be Disobeyed and Resisted* (Geneva, 1558), pp. 187–8; also pp. 118–19.
28. For the theological background, see Michael McGiffert, 'From Moses to Adam: the Making of the Covenant of Works', *Sixteenth Century Journal,* 19 (1988), pp. 131–55.
29. Useful discussions of Knox, in addition to those cited earlier in the chapter, include especially John R. Gray, 'The Political Theory of John Knox', *Church History,* 8 (1939), pp. 132–47; J. H. Burns, 'John Knox and Revolution, 1558', *History Today,* 8 (1958), pp. 565–73; Richard Greaves, *Theology and Revolution in the Scottish Reformation: Studies in the Thought of John Knox* (Grand Rapids, MI, 1980), sect. 3; W. Stanford Reid, 'John Knox's Theology of Political Government', *Sixteenth Century Journal,* 19 (1988), pp. 529–40; Jane Dawson, 'The Two John Knoxes: England, Scotland and the 1558 Tracts', *Journal of Ecclesiastical History,* 42 (1991), pp. 555–76; Roger Mason, *Kingship and the Commonweal: Political Thought in Renaissance and Reformation Scotland* (East Linton, 1998), ch. 5; and Mason (ed.), *John Knox and the British Reformations.*
30. John Knox, 'The First Blast of the Trumpet against the Monstrous Regiment of Women' (1558), in Knox, *On Rebellion,* p. 14; cf. pp. 4–5, 8 (from the Preface), in which this line is strongly proclaimed.
31. See also Roger Mason, 'Knox, Resistance and the Royal Supremacy', in Mason (ed.), *John Knox and the British Reformations,* ch. 8.
32. There has been much attention given to the misogynistic aspects of Knox's argument. The fullest guide is now Amanda Shephard, *Gender and Authority in Sixteenth-Century England: The Knox Debate* (Keele, 1994); on Knox's attitude to women generally, see Maureen Meikle, 'John Knox and Womankind: a Reappraisal', *The Historian,* 79 (Autumn 2003), pp. 9–14.
33. John Knox, appendix to 'The Letter to the Commonalty' (1558), in Knox, *On Rebellion,* ed. Mason, pp. 128–9.
34. For a recent general account see Jane Dawson, *Scotland Re-Formed, 1488–1587* (Edinburgh, 2007). Also Jenny Wormald, *Court, Kirk and Community: Scotland, 1470–1625* (London, 1981), chs 6 and 7; Gordon Donaldson, *Scotland: James V to James VII* (New York, 1966), chs 5–8.
35. Knox, *History,* extracts in Knox, *On Rebellion,* ed. Mason, p. 138.
36. These remarks summarise Roger Mason, 'Kingship, Tyranny and the Right to Resist in Fifteenth Century Scotland', *Scottish Historical Review,* 66 (1987), pp. 125–51; and Roger

Mason, 'Imagining Scotland: Scottish Political Thought and the Problem of Britain 1560–1650', in Mason (ed.), *Scots and Britons: Scottish Political Thought and the Union of 1603* (Cambridge, 1994), introduction, pp. 6–7. On the imperial aspirations of the Scottish monarchy, see Roger Mason, 'The Scottish Reformation and the Origins of Anglo-British Imperialism', in Mason (ed.), *Scots and Britons*, ch. 7, p. 183. Some of these essays and others cited below are reprinted in Roger Mason, *Kingship and the Commonweal: Political Thought in Renaissance Scotland* (East Linton, 1998).

37. See J. H. Burns, 'The Conciliarist Tradition in Scotland', *Scottish Historical Review*, 42 (1963), pp. 89–104. For some thoughts on its influence on Reformation thought, see pp. 101–4. The matter is also discussed in J. H. Burns, 'Political Ideas of the Scottish Reformation', *Aberdeen University Review*, 36 (1956), pp. 251–68; and – for Knox – in Greaves, *Theology and Revolution*, ch. 7.

38. Anthony Black, 'The Conciliar Movement', in J. H. Burns (ed.), *The Cambridge History of Medieval Political Thought, c.350–c.1450* (Cambridge, 1988), vol. II, ch. 17.

39. For late Scholastic conciliarism see J. H. Burns, 'Scholasticism: Survival and Revival', in Burns and Goldie (eds), *Cambridge History of Political Thought, 1450–1700*, ch. 5 (esp. pp. 146–55); and Skinner, *Foundations*, vol. II, pp. 114–23. Skinner's views on the origins of Calvinist resistance theories are elegantly expounded in Skinner, 'The Origins of the Calvinist Theory of Revolution', in Barbara Malament (ed.), *After the Reformation: Essays in Honor of J. H. Hexter* (Philadelphia, PA, 1980), pp. 309–30, revised as 'Humanism, Scholasticism and Popular Sovereignty', in Skinner, *Visions of Politics: Volume II – Renaissance Virtues* (Cambridge, 2002), ch. 9.

40. Francis Oakley, 'Almain and Major: Conciliar Theory on the Eve of the Reformation', *American Historical Review*, 70 (1964/5), pp. 673–90.

41. J. H. Burns, '*Politia Regalis et Optima*: the Political Ideas of John Mair', *History of Political Thought*, 2 (1981), pp. 31–61; also Roger Mason, 'Kingship, Nobility and Anglo-Scottish Union: John Mair's *History of Greater Britain* (1521)', *Innes Review*, 41 (1990), pp. 182–222, esp. pp. 205–12; Francis Oakley, 'On the Road from Constance to 1688: the Political Thought of John Major and George Buchanan', *Journal of British Studies*, 1: 2 (1962), pp. 1–31; and J. H. Burns and Thomas M. Izbicki (eds), *Conciliarism and Papalism* (Cambridge, 1997).

42. John Mair, *A History of Greater Britain*, ed. and trans. Archibald Constable, Publications of the Scottish History Society, vol. X (Edinburgh, 1892), p. 213.

43. From his other writings we can see that Mair thought the community's power to depose its rulers was something exercised only *casualiter* (i.e. intermittently in special circumstances), whereas the king's authority over his subjects was exercised *regulariter* (i.e. continuously in normal circumstances). See Burns, '*Politia Regalis et Optima*', pp. 38–40.

44. John Knox, 'The Copy of a Letter Delivered to the Lady Mary, Regent of Scotland' (1558), in Knox, *On Rebellion*, ed. Mason, p. 59.

45. John Knox, 'The Appellation of John Knox from the Cruel and Most Injust Sentence Pronounced Against Him by the False Bishops and Clergy of Scotland' (1558), in Knox, *On Rebellion*, ed. Mason, pp. 74–5, 83, 111.

46. Though Roger Mason has collected Knox's political writings under the title *On Rebellion*, Knox himself reserved the word 'rebellion' in all of them for acts of disobedience to God. For him, anything termed 'rebellion' was automatically illegitimate, and (like Goodman) he spent much time in accusing others of rebellion, and himself of obedience.

47. Dawson, 'The Two John Knoxes'; modified by Scott Dolff, 'The Two John Knoxes and the Justification of Non-Revolution: a Response to Dawson's Argument from Covenant', *Journal of Ecclesiastical History*, 55 (2004), pp. 58–74.

48. John Knox, 'To His Beloved Brethren the Commonalty of Scotland' (1558), in Knox, *On Rebellion*, ed. Mason, pp. 123–5.

49. Cf. Richard Kyle, 'The Nature of the Church in the Thought of John Knox', *Scottish Journal of Theology*, 37 (1984), pp. 485–501; and Kyle, 'The Church–State Patterns in the Thought of John Knox', *Journal of Church and State*, 30 (1988), pp. 71–87; and the guarded analysis in J. H. Burns, 'Knox: Scholastic and Canonistic Echoes', in Mason (ed.), *John Knox and the British Reformations*, ch. 6.

50. The account below is heavily indebted to Roger Mason, 'Covenant and Commonweal: the Language of Politics in Reformation Scotland', in Norman Macdougall (ed.), *Church, Politics and Society: Scotland, 1408–1929* (Edinburgh, 1983), ch. 6.

51. Knox, *History*, extracts in Knox, *On Rebellion*, ed. Mason, pp. 149–50.

52. For this, see Mason, 'Covenant and Commonweal', pp. 108–10. On the development of 'commonwealth' in Scotland, a process paralleling its development in England, see Roger Mason, 'Aspects of National Identity in Renaissance Scotland', in Mason, *Kingship and the Commonweal*, ch. 3, esp. pp. 91–100.

53. Cf. ibid., pp. 110–11.

54. Roger Mason, 'George Buchanan, James VI and the Presbyterians', in Mason (ed.), *Scots and Britons*, ch. 5, esp. pp. 124–5; also W. S. McKechnie, '*De Jure Regni apud Scotos*', in *George Buchanan, Glasgow Quatercentenary Studies*, 1906 (Glasgow, 1907), pp. 211–96, esp. pp. 211–13.

55. David Hume of Godscroft, *The British Union: A Critical Edition and Translation of . . . De Unione Insulae Britannicae*, ed. P. J. McGinnis and A. H. Williamson (Aldershot, 2002).

56. I. D. McFarlane, *Buchanan* (London, 1981), pp. 392–3. At least one of the reasons for the delay in publication may have been the wish to avoid offending Elizabeth I, on whose support the opponents of Mary relied (pp. 393–4).

57. McKechnie, '*De Jure Regni apud Scotos*', pp. 274–6. On Buchanan's thought, see J. H. Burns, 'The Political Ideas of George Buchanan', *Scottish Historical Review*, 30 (1951), pp. 60–8; Skinner, *Foundations*, vol. II. pp. 338–45; Roger Mason, '*Rex Stoicus*: George Buchanan, James VI and the Scottish Polity', in John Dwyer, Roger Mason and Alexander Murdoch (eds), *New Perspectives on the Politics and Culture of Early Modern Scotland* (Edinburgh, 1982), pp. 9–33; J. H. M. Salmon, 'An Alternative Theory of Popular Resistance: Buchanan, Rossaeus, and Locke', in Salmon, *Renaissance and Revolt: Essays in the Intellectual and Social History of Early Modern France* (Cambridge, 1987), ch. 6; and J. H. Burns, 'George Buchanan and the Anti-Monarchomachs', in Mason (ed.), *Scots and Britons*, ch. 6.

58. See also, Arthur H. Williamson, *Scottish National Consciousness in the Age of James VI* (Edinburgh, 1979), pp. 107–16; also ch. 6. Cf. the contrast drawn between Calvinists like Buchanan and proper republicans, in Richard Tuck, *Philosophy and Government, 1572–1651* (Cambridge, 1993), p. 233.

59. George Buchanan, *A Dialogue on the Law of Kingship among the Scots: A Critical Edition and Translation of George Buchanan's De Iure Regni apud Scotos Dialogus*, ed. Roger A. Mason and Martin S. Smith (Aldershot, 2004), p. 163, quoting Seneca, *Thyestes*, ll. 344–90.

60. What follows here is heavily indebted to Mason, '*Rex Stoicus*', and his introduction to Buchanan, *Dialogue*.

61. Ibid., p. 157.

62. Ibid., p. 53.

63. Ibid., p. 131. Buchanan's immediate source for this was Aristotle, *The Politics*, 1287a, ed. Ernest Barker (Oxford, 1958), p. 146. Aristotle's definition of law as reason without passion, of course, harmonised well with Buchanan's Stoic sources.

64. Buchanan, *Dialogue*, p. 33.

65. Ibid., pp. 39–41.

66. Ibid., p. 35.

67. Ibid., p. 35.

68. Ibid., p. 65.

69. Ibid., p. 125.

70. Ibid., p. 157.

71. Ibid., p. 161.

72. The 1680 translator of the *De Jure Regni*, rendering Buchanan relevantly for a later Stuart English audience, translated *civitas* (not unreasonably) as 'commonwealth'; but also rendered *civis* with the misleading 'subject'.

73. Buchanan, *Dialogue*, p. 15.

74. Ibid., pp. 17–19.

75. Ibid., p. 19.

76. Ibid., p. 21.

77. On how the Ciceronian account of man's sociableness differed from the Aristotelian, in Cary J. Nederman, 'Nature, Sin and the Origins of Society: the Ciceronian Tradition in Medieval Political Thought', *Journal of the History of Ideas* (1988), pp. 3–26.

78. Ibid., p. 57; Cicero, *De Legibus*, III.iii.8 (ed. and transl. C. W. Keyes, Loeb Classical Library, pp. 466/7).

79. Buchanan, *Dialogue*, p. 23.

80. E.g. Cicero, *De Legibus*, III.ii.4–5 (Loeb edn, pp. 460/1).

81. Buchanan, *Dialogue*, p. 39, quoting Cicero, *De Officiis*, II.41–2.
82. Ibid., p. 59.
83. Ibid., p. 23.
84. Ibid., pp. 23–7.
85. Ibid., pp. 27–9.
86. Ibid., pp. 27–33.
87. Ibid., p. 33.
88. Summarising ibid., pp. 41–69.
89. Ibid., p. 105; also p. 133.
90. Ibid., p. 55.
91. Ibid., p. 55.
92. Ibid., p. 55.
93. McKechnie, '*De Jure Regni apud Scotos*', pp. 241–4; Burns, 'Political Ideas of George Buchanan', p. 64; Julian Goodare, 'The Estates in the Scottish Parliament, 1286–1707', *Parliamentary History*, 15 (1996), pp. 11–32.
94. My interpretation is indebted to Mason, '*Rex Stoicus*', pp. 19–20, and Mason's introduction to Buchanan, *Dialogue*, pp. lix–lx; also Williamson, *Scottish National Consciousness*, p. 116.
95. The definition, along with many of the details of Buchanan's portrait of the tyrant, derives from Aristotle, *Ethics*, 1160b.
96. Buchanan, *Dialogue*, p. 87.
97. Ibid., p. 89.
98. Ibid., p. 151.
99. See especially, Oakley, 'On the Road from Constance', pp. 24–6; Salmon, 'Alternative Theory of Popular Resistance', pp. 142–3.
100. Buchanan, *Dialogue*, p. 137.
101. Ibid., p. 141.
102. Ibid., pp. 151–3.
103. Ibid., pp. 153–5.
104. Markku Peltonen, *Classical Humanism and Republicanism in English Political Thought, 1570–1640* (Cambridge, 1995), p. 185; David Wootton, Introduction, in Wootton (ed.), *Republicanism, Liberty and Commercial Society, 1649–1776* (Stanford, CA, 1994), pp. 26, 30–1; Algernon Sidney, *Court Maxims*, ed. Hans W. Blom, Eco Haitsma Mulier and Ronald Janse (Cambridge, 1996), pp. 31, 203.

Notes to Chapter 3

1. The phrase is from Knox's unhappy attempt, in his 1561 discussions with Mary Stewart, to explain away the full extent of his attack on female rulers: John Knox, *On Rebellion*, ed. Roger A. Mason (Cambridge, 1994), pp. 176–7.
2. John Knox, *The Works of John Knox*, ed. David Laing, 6 vols (Edinburgh, 1846–64), vol. VI, pp. 48–9. For an account of the general repudiation of Knox, see Jane E. Dawson, 'The Two John Knoxes: England, Scotland and the 1558 Tracts', *Journal of Ecclesiastical History*, 42 (1991), pp. 555–76, at 560–1.
3. See especially A. N. McLaren, 'Delineating the Elizabethan Body Politic: Knox, Aylmer and the Definition of Counsel, 1558–88', *History of Political Thought*, 17 (1996), pp. 224–52; A. N. McLaren, *Political Culture in the Reign of Elizabeth I: Queen and Commonwealth, 1558–1585* (Cambridge, 1999), ch. 2.
4. Two statements by Goodman are recorded by Strype, one of them (and perhaps both) certainly from 1571: John Strype, *Annals of the Reformation and Establishment of Religion*, 4 vols in 7 parts (Oxford, 1820–40), I, i, pp. 184–5; vol. II, part 1, p. 141. Cf. Dan G. Danner, 'Christopher Goodman and the English Protestant Tradition of Civil Disobedience', *Sixteenth Century Journal*, 8 (1977), pp. 60–73, esp. pp. 65–6.
5. J. Martial, *A Reply to M. Calfhills Blasphemous Answer* (1566), p. sig. **v, quoted in Peter Holmes, *Resistance and Compromise: The Political Thought of the Elizabethan Catholics* (Cambridge, 1982), p. 16, and see pp. 68–78 for Catholic critiques of protestant political thought.
6. Key accounts of the debate about female rule are Amanda Shephard, *Gender and Authority in Sixteenth-Century England* (Keele, 1994); and McLaren's works cited at n. 3 above. Additionally, Paula Louise Scalingi, 'The Scepter or the Distaff: the Question of Female

Sovereignty, 1516–1607', *The Historian*, 41 (1978), pp. 59–75; Richard L. Greaves, *Theology and Revolution in the Scottish Reformation: Studies in the Thought of John Knox* (Grand Rapids, MI, 1980), ch. 8; Constance Jordan, 'Woman's Rule in Sixteenth-Century British Political Thought', *Renaissance Quarterly*, 40 (1987), pp. 421–51; Patricia-Ann Lee, 'A Bodye Politique to Governe: Knox and the Debate on Queenship', *The Historian*, 52 (1990), pp. 242–61; Maria Zina Gonçalves de Abreu, 'John Knox: Gynaecocracy, "The Monstrous Empire of Women"', *Reformation and Renaissance Review*, 5 (2003), pp. 167–88; and Maureen Meikle, 'John Knox and Womankind: a Reappraisal', *The Historian*, 79 (Autumn 2003), pp. 9–14.

7. Cf. Shephard, *Gender and Authority*, pp. 99–100, 127; McLaren, 'Delineating the Elizabethan Body Politic', pp. 232–4.
8. John Aylmer, *An Harborowe for Faithfull and Trewe Subjectes* (Strasbourg, 1559), sig. H4.
9. Cf. Michael Mendle, *Dangerous Positions: Mixed Government, the Estates of the Realm, and the Making of the Answer to the xix Propositions*, (Alabama University, AL, 1985), pp. 38–51.
10. Aylmer, *An Harborowe*, sigs H2–H2v.
11. Ibid., sigs H2v–H3.
12. Cf. the brilliant discussion of this and related themes in Patrick Collinson, 'The Monarchical Republic of Queen Elizabeth I', in Collnson, *Elizabethans* [originally *Elizabethan Essays*] (Hambledon, 2003), ch. 2.
13. McLaren, 'Delineating the Elizabethan Body Politic'; McLaren, *Political Culture in the Reign of Elizabeth*.
14. Patrick Collinson, '*De Republica Anglorum*: or History with the Politics Back', in his *Elizabethans*, ch. 1; Stephen Alford, *The Early Elizabethan Polity: William Cecil and the British Succession Crisis, 1558–1569* (Cambridge, 1998). The important material in John F. McDiarmid (ed.), *The Monarchical Republic of Early Modern England: Essays in Response to Patrick Collinson* (Aldershot, 2007), appeared too recently to be taken into account here. A contrasting account of the early Elizabethan period, stressing the importance of personal 'imperial' sovereignty over mixed polity, is Natalie Mears, *Queenship and Political Discourse in the Elizabethan Realms* (Cambridge, 2005).
15. John Guy, 'Introduction', in Guy (ed.), *The Reign of Elizabeth I: Court and Culture in the Last Decade* (Cambridge, 1995), pp. 1–19.
16. Sir Thomas Smith, *De Republica Anglorum*, ed Mary Dewar (Cambridge, 1982), p. 52. See also David Harris Sacks, 'The Prudence of Thasymachus: Sir Thomas Smith and the Commonwealth of England', in Anthony Grafton and J. H. M. Salmon (eds), *Historians and Ideologies: Essays in Honor of Donald R. Kelly* (Rochester, NY, 2001), ch. 6.
17. A. N. McLaren, 'Reading Sir Thomas Smith's *De Republica Anglorum* as Protestant Apologetic', *Historical Journal*, 42 (1999), pp. 911–39; McLaren, *Political Culture in the Reign of Elizabeth I*, ch. 7.
18. Richard L. Greaves, 'Concepts of Political Obedience in Late Tudor England: Conflicting Perspectives', *Journal of British Studies*, 22 (1982–3), pp. 23–34.
19. Aylmer, *An Harborowe*, sigs Q3–Q3v.
20. Thomas Norton, *To the Quenes Majesties Poore Deceyved Subjectes of the North Countrey* (London, 1569), sig. Ciiv.
21. 'An Homilie against Disobedience and Wilfull Rebellion', *Certaine Sermons or Homilies Appointed to be Read in Churches in the Time of Queen Elizabeth*, ed. Mary Ellen Rickey and Thomas B. Stroup, 2 vols in 1 (Gainesville, FL, 1968), vol. II, p. 279.
22. 'An Exhortation Concerning Good Order, and Obedience to Rulers and Magistrates' [originally 1547], in *Certaine Sermons*, vol. I, pp. 69–70.
23. Richard Crompton, *A Short Declaration of the Ende of Traytors, and False Conspirators against the State* (London, 1587), sig. Eii, translating Cicero, *De Legibus*, III.i.3.
24. Norton, *To the Quenes Majesties Poore Deceyved Subjectes*, sigs Gi, Eiiv.
25. 'An Exhortation', in *Certaine Sermons*, vol. I, pp. 70–1. Also on the crucial importance of Romans 13, see the 'Homilie against Disobedience', ibid., vol. II, p. 277.
26. Crompton, *A Short Declaration*, sig. D4v. For a clerical expression of the same point see Thomas Bilson, *A Sermon Preached at Westminster before the King and Queenes Majesties at their Coronations* (London, 1603), esp. sigs C4v–C5.
27. See J. E. Booty, *John Jewel as Apologist of the Church of England* (London, 1963); W. M. Southgate, *John Jewel and the Problem of Doctrinal Authority* (Cambridge, MA, 1962); and Gary W. Jenkins, *John Jewel and the English National Church: The Dilemmas of an Erastian Reformer* (Aldershot, 2005).

28. John Jewel, *An Apology of the Church of England* [1564 translation by Lady Anne Bacon], ed. J. E. Booty (Charlottesville, VA, 1963), p. 56.
29. 'An Exhortation', in *Certaine Sermons*, vol. I, pp. 72, 69.
30. Ibid., vol. I, p. 70.
31. Ibid., vol. I, p. 72.
32. Homilie against Disobedience', ibid., vol. II, p. 279.
33. George Whetstone, *The English Myrror* (London, 1586), p. 210.
34. Ibid., pp. 213, 202.
35. Peter Lake, *Anglicans and Puritans? Presbyterianism and English Conformist Thought from Whitgift to Hooker* (London, 1988), esp. pp. 53–64, 97–101, 129–39; Daniel Eppley, 'Defender of the Peace: John Whitgift's Proactive Defense of the Polity of the Church of England in the Admonition Controversy', *Anglican and Episcopal History*, 68 (1999), pp. 312–35.
36. *The Works of John Whitgift, D.D.*, ed. John Ayre, 3 vols (Cambridge, 1851–3), vol. II, pp. 238–40.
37. E.g. ibid., vol. I, p. 467: popular government 'is the worse kind . . . that can be'.
38. Ibid., vol. I, pp. 390 (Cartwright), 393 (Whitgift).
39. Ibid., vol. III, p. 310.
40. For a discussion of this concept, see Glenn Burgess, *Absolute Monarchy and the Stuart Constitution* (New Haven, CT, 1996), part ii; also now Alan Cromartie, *The Constitutionalist Revolution: An Essay on the History of England, 1450–1642* (Cambridge, 2006), esp. here, ch. 5.
41. Bilson, *Sermon Preached at Westminster*, sigs A6, B3–B3v, B8–C1v.
42. Thomas Bilson, *The True Difference betweene Christian Subjection and Unchristian Rebellion* (Oxford, 1585), pp. 147, 256.
43. A residue of this remains even in the more ruthless anti-puritan polemic of Richard Bancroft: see Bancroft, *Dangerous Positions and Proceedings, Published and Practised within this Iland of Brytaine, under Pretence of Reformation, and for the Presbiteriall Position* (London, 1593), pp. 32–3.
44. Christopher Morris, *Political Thought in England: Tyndale to Hooker* (Oxford, 1953), chs 7 and 8, gives a measured account of puritan political thought, and is especially strong in its emphasis on their 'extremely high view of the civil power' (p. 161). These views fit well with the emphasis on the hopes and trust placed by puritans in the figure of the 'godly prince' in William Lamont, *Godly Rule: Politics and Religion 1603–60* (London, 1969), pp. 24–5 and ch. 2, though many seventeenth-century puritans (including Prynne and Baxter) identified more with Elizabethan conformists than with Elizabethan puritans.
45. Richard L. Greaves, 'Traditionalism and the Seeds of Revolution in the Social Principles of the Geneva Bible', *Sixteenth Century Journal*, 7: 2 (1976), pp. 94–109.
46. The complexities are well explored in Michael Questier, 'Elizabeth and the Catholics', in Ethan Shagan (ed.), *Catholics and the 'Protestant Nation': Religious Politics and Identity in Early Modern England* (Manchester, 2005), ch. 4.
47. John Floyd, *God and the King* (Cullen, 1620), pp. 139–40. Cf. Thomas H. Clancy, SJ, 'Papist – Protestant – Puritan: English Religious Taxonomy, 1565–1665', *Recusant History*, 13 (1975–6), pp. 227–53.
48. William Cecil, *The Execution of Justice in England* (2nd edn, 1584), edited [with Allen's *True, Sincere, and Modest Defense*] by R. M. Kingdon (Ithaca, NY, 1965), pp. 5–7.
49. Francis Bacon, *Certain Observations upon a Libel* (1592), in James Spedding (ed.), *The Letters and Life of Francis Bacon*, 7 vols (London, 1861–74), vol. I, p. 178.
50. Ibid., vol. I, pp. 163–4.
51. Cf. Patrick Collinson, 'The Politics of Religion and the Religion of Politics', *Historical Research* (forthcoming); Ethan Shagan, 'The English Inquisition: Constitutional Conflict and Ecclesiastical Law in the 1590s', *Historical Journal*, 47 (2004), pp. 541–65.
52. Thomas Norton, *A Warning Agaynst the Dangerous Practises of Papistes, and Specially the Parteners of the Late Rebellion* (London, 1569), sigs Dii–Dii^v.
53. Though Cecil did admit that Pius V's successor, Gregory XIII, had temporarily suspended operation of the bull *Regnans in excelsis*, so that, for the time being, Catholic subjects of the queen could obey her without risking excommunication (p. 19).
54. Cecil, *Execution of Justice*, p. 21.
55. On the Cecil–Allen debate, see the accounts in: Thomas H. Clancy, SJ, *Papist Pamphleteers: The Allen–Persons Party and the Political Thought of the Counter-Reformation in England,*

1572–1615 (Chicago, 1964), pp. 49–55; and Peter Holmes, *Resistance and Compromise: The Political Thought of the Elizabethan Catholics* (Cambridge, 1982), pp. 131–4, 152–3, 157–9.

56. William Allen, *A True, Sincere, and Modest Defense of English Catholics that Suffer for Their Faith Both at Home and Abroad* (1584), ed. R. M. Kingdon [with Cecil's *Execution of Justice*] (Ithaca, NY, 1965), pp. 68–9.

57. Cf. Garrett Mattingly, 'William Allen and Catholic Propaganda in England', in Henri Meylan (ed.), *Aspects de la propagande religieuse* (Geneva, 1957), pp. 325–39.

58. On the debate over whether or not Allen accepted a theory of the indirect deposing power similar to that of Bellarmine's, see Clancy, *Papist Pamphleteers*, pp. 53–4; Thomas Clancy, SJ, 'English Catholics and the Papal Deposing Power 1570–1640, parts I–III', *Recusant History*, 6 (1961–2), pp. 114–40, 205–27; 7 (1963–4), pp. 2–10, at part I, pp. 120–3; Holmes, *Resistance and Compromise*, p. 153.

59. Michael Questier, *Catholicism and Community in Early Modern England: Politics, Aristocratic Patronage and Religion, c.1550–1640* (Cambridge, 2006), pp. 157–69; and the essays in section 3 of Peter Lake and Michael Questier (eds), *Conformity and Orthodoxy in the English Church, c.1560–1660* (Woodbridge, 2000). For the complexities of the conforming church-papist, see also Questier and Simon Healy, '"What's in a Name?" A Papist's Perception of Puritanism and Conformity in the Early Seventeenth Century', in Arthur F. Marotti (ed.), *Catholicism and Anti-Catholicism in Early Modern Texts* (Basingstoke, 1999), ch. 6.

60. Cf. Joseph Lecler, *Toleration and the Reformation*, 2 vols (New York, 1960), vol. II, pp. 374–5.

61. One of those whose guilt was admitted was Nicholas Sander. See the account of his political thought in Holmes, *Resistance and Compromise*, pp. 26–9.

62. John Bishop, *A Courteous Conference with the English Catholickes Romane* (London, 1598), p. 80.

63. Holmes, *Resistance and Compromise*, p. 175; Clancy, 'English Catholics and the Papal Deposing Power (part II)', pp. 205–6.

64. See generally, Michael Carrafiello, *Robert Parsons and English Catholicism, 1580–1610* (Selinsgrove, PA, 1998); and Victor Houliston, *Catholic Resistance in Elizabethan England: Robert Persons' Jesuit Polemic, 1580–1610* (Aldershot, 2007).

65. Robert Persons, *Philopater* (1592), trans. Henry Foulis (1681), quoted in Clancy, *Papist Pamphleteers*, p. 74; Clancy, 'English Catholics and the Papal Deposing Power (part I)', p. 131.

66. Holmes, *Resistance and Compromise*, p. 135.

67. Following criticism of his work at Rome, Persons included in the Latin edition of the *Conference* (1596) a full defence of papal political power: see Holmes, *Resistance and Compromise*, pp. 152–7.

68. Robert Persons, *A Conference about the Next Succession to the Crowne of Ingland* (Antwerp, 1594), vol. i, sigs B4v–B5, p. 1. Peter Holmes, 'The Authorship and Early Reception of *A Conference about the Next Succession to the Crown of England*', *Historical Journal*, 23 (1980), pp. 415–29; Houliston, *Catholic Resistance*, pp. 72–92.

69. Peter Lake, '"A Charitable Christian Hatred": the Godly and their Enemies in the 1630s', in Christopher Durston and Jacqueline Eales (eds), *The Culture of English Puritanism, 1560–1700* (Basingstoke, 1996), ch. 5, p. 178. The most famous radical reading of puritanism is Michael Walzer, *The Revolution of the Saints: A Study in the Origins of Radical Politics* (Cambridge, MA, 1965). His argument is not dependent on demonstrating a continuous puritan commitment to resistance theory; but he does stress the way in which resistance always remains a possible option for them, and his early construction of the Calvinist–puritan 'type' is heavily dependent on two groups that included resistance theorists (Huguenots and Marian exiles). See esp. pp. 57–65, and ch. 3; but note his contrast between 'resistance' and 'revolution', pp. 110–12.

70. Jacqueline Eales, 'A Road to Revolution: the Continuity of Puritanism, 1559–1642', in Durston and Eales, *Culture of English Puritanism*, ch. 6, p. 208.

71. Cf. Lamont, *Godly Rule*.

72. Patrick Collinson's work is crucial here. In addition to material cited above, see also 'If Constantine, then also Theodosius: St Ambrose and the Integrity of the Elizabethan Ecclesia Anglicana', *Journal of Ecclesiastical History*, 30 (1979), pp. 205–29; and 'The Elizabethan Exclusion Crisis and the Elizabethan Polity', *Proceedings of the British Academy*, 84 (1994), pp. 51–92.

73. E.g. Herbert L. Osgood, 'The Political Ideas of the Puritans', *Political Science Quarterly*, 6 (1891), pp. 1–28; Herbert Darling Foster, 'The Political Theories of Calvinists before the Puritan Exodus to America', *American Historical Review*, 21 (1915–16), pp. 481–503.

74. Michael McGiffert, 'Covenant, Crown, and Commons in Elizabethan Puritanism', *Journal of British Studies*, 20 (1980–1), pp. 32–52, esp. 37–9.

75. Seminal work is William Haller, *Foxe's Book of Martyrs and the Elect Nation* (London, 1963). For a conspectus of more recent views, see Christopher Highley and John N. King (eds), *John Foxe and His World* (Aldershot, 2002); and for the texts of Foxe's editions see *Foxe's Book of Martyrs Variorum Edition Online* (www.hrionline.ac.uk/johnfoxe/index.html).

76. Laurence Humphrey, *De Religionis Conservatione et Reformatione Vera* (London, 1559), p. 99; translated in Janet Karen Kemp, 'Laurence Humphrey, Elizabethan Puritan: His Life and Political Theories' (unpublished PhD dissertation, West Virginia University, 1978), pp. 224–5; M. M. Knappen, *Tudor Puritanism: A Chapter in the History of Ideas* (Chicago, 1939) pp. 174–8; McLaren, *Political Culture in the Reign of Elizabeth I*, pp. 120–31.

77. Laurence Humphrey, *The Nobles or Of Nobilitye* (London, 1563; original Latin edn, 1559), sigs. Di–Di^v.

78. Dudley Fenner, *Sacra Theologia* (London, 1586), pp. 184–7; English translation from BL Harleian MS 6879, fols 87–89.

79. I have followed in this paragraph Richard L. Greaves, 'The Nature and Intellectual Milieu of the Political Principles of the Geneva Bible Marginalia', *Journal of Church and State*, 22 (1980), pp. 233–49. See also Hardin Craig, 'The Geneva Bible as a Political Document', *Pacific Historical Review*, 7 (1938), pp. 40–9; and Dan G. Danner, 'The Contribution of the Geneva Bible of 1560 to the English Protestant Tradition', *Sixteenth Century Journal*, 12: 3 (1981), pp. 5–18.

80. Gerald Bowler, '"An Axe or an Acte": the Parliament of 1572 and Resistance Theory in Early Elizabethan England', *Canadian Journal of History*, 19 (1984), pp. 349–59, at 357–8. In the evidence examined by Bowler the target was Mary, Queen of Scots.

81. W. H. Frere and C. E. Douglas (eds), *Puritan Manifestoes: A Study of the Origin of the Puritan Revolt* (London, 1954), p. 130.

82. *Works of John Whitgift*, vol. III, p. 189.

83. Ibid., vol. III, pp. 197–8.

84. Ibid., vol. III. p. 189.

85. Ibid., vol. I, pp. 389–90.

86. Mendle, *Dangerous Positions*, p. 67.

87. Walter Travers, *A Full and Plaine Declaration of Ecclesiasticall Discipline owt of the Word of God / and off the Declininge off the Church of England from the Same* (London, 1574), sigs a3v–a4.

88. Ibid., pp. 1–3.

89. Machiavelli, *Discourses*, vol. III: I.

90. Travers, *Full and Plaine Declaration*, pp. 83–4.

91. Ibid., pp. 162–3.

92. Walter Travers, *A Defence of the Ecclesiastical Regiment Ordayned of God to be Used in his Church* (London, 1588), p. 167.

93. Travers, *Full and Plaine Declaration*, pp. 84–5.

94. Ibid., p. 86.

95. Ibid., pp. 177–9.

96. Travers, *Defence of the Ecclesiastical Regiment*, p. 175.

97. Travers, *Full and Plaine Declaration*, p. 187; Travers, *Defence of the Ecclesiastical Discipline*, pp. 146–53.

98. Ibid., p. 195.

99. See Collinson, 'If Constantine, then also Theodosius'.

100. Travers, *Full and Plaine Declaration*, pp. 85, 186–7.

101. For a sample statement of the latter claim, see Travers, *Defence of the Ecclesiastical Discipline*, pp. 156–7; see also pp. 179–80, 190, replying to the charge that the presbyterians used the same anti-monarchical arguments as the anabaptists.

102. See Chapter 5 below; and Glenn Burgess, 'Religious War and Constitutional Defence: Justifications of Resistance in English Puritan Thought, 1590–1643', in Robert von Friedeburg (ed.), *Widerstandsrecht in der frühen Neuzeit: Erträge und Perspectiven der Forschung im deutsch-britische Vergleich* (Berlin, 2001), pp. 185–206.

103. Cf. Elliot Rose, *Cases of Conscience: Alternatives Open to Recusants and Puritans under Elizabeth I and James I* (Cambridge, 1975), p. 93.

104. Margaret Sampson, 'Laxity and Liberty in Seventeenth-Century English Political Thought', in Edmund Leites (ed.), *Conscience and Casuistry in Early Modern Europe* (Cambridge, 1988), ch. 2, p. 98.

105. Harald Braun and Edward Vallance (eds), *Contexts of Conscience in Early Modern Europe, 1500–1700* (Basingstoke, 2004).

106. Peter J. Holmes, *Elizabethan Casuistry*, Catholic Records Society Publications, Records Series, vol. 67 (1981), p. 5. For fuller surveys see Rose, *Cases of Conscience*, ch. 6; Holmes, *Resistance and Compromise*, chs 9 and 10; and Perez Zagorin, *Ways of Lying: Dissimulation, Persecution and Conformity in Early Modern Europe* (Cambridge, MA, 1990), chs 7–9.

107. Zagorin, *Ways of Lying*, p. 140; Alexandra Walsham, *Church Papists: Catholicism, Conformity and Confessional Polemic in Early Modern England* (Woodbridge, 1993).

108. For the debate on this subject, see J. P. Sommerville, 'The "New Art of Lying": Equivocation, Mental Reservation, and Casuistry', in Leites (ed.), *Conscience and Casuistry*, ch. 5.

109. Rose, *Cases of Conscience*, p. 89.

110. Ibid., pp. 97–101.

111. Holmes, *Elizabethan Casuistry*, pp. 101–3.

112. Ibid., pp. 50–1 (this case is more positive about holding office, declaring it not unlawful provided no anti-Catholic action is required of the incumbent), pp. 120, 121.

113. Quoted in Zagorin, *Ways of Lying*, p. 191.

114. Cf also, ibid., pp. 197–8, a case in the Irish court of Castle Chamber in 1613. Cf. Shagan, 'English Inquisition'.

115. A basic account of English protestant casuistry is to be found in Thomas Wood, *English Casuistical Divinity during the Seventeenth Century* (London, 1952). Also Rose, *Cases of Conscience*, ch. 11; Zagorin, *Ways of Lying*, ch. 10; and, for a slightly later period, H. R. McAdoo, *The Structure of Caroline Moral Theology* (London, 1949).

116. These two works are reprinted, with some abridgement, in Thomas F. Merrill, *William Perkins, 1558–1602: English Puritanist* (Nieuwkoop, 1966). Page references in the text are all to this volume.

117. For some useful thoughts on the pre-Perkins history of puritan casuistry, see Zagorin, *Ways of Lying*, pp. 221–35.

118. Cf. also the account in the *Whole Treatise*, I, iii (99–101).

119. Ibid., p. 484.

120. The editor of Perkins' posthumous *Whole Treatise*, Thomas Pickering, used this same terminology to explain the difference drawn by Catholics between venial and mortal sins: the former 'are onely besides the Law of God, not against it' (84). Perkins himself used the distinction again at III, iv (199–200).

121. Zagorin, *Ways of Lying*, p. 239.

122. The best introduction is Sampson, 'Laxity and Liberty'.

123. Patrick Collinson, *Archbishop Grindal, 1519–1583: The Struggle for a Reformed Church* (London, 1979), pp. 242–6.

124. Ibid., p. 260.

125. Collinson, 'Monarchical Republic', pp. 413–17; Patrick Collinson, 'The Elizabethan Exclusion Crisis and the Elizabethan Polity'; David Cressy, 'Binding the Nation: the Bonds of Association, 1584–1696', in Delloyd J. Guth and John W. McKenna (eds), *Tudor Rule and Revolution: Essays for G. R. Elton from his American Friends* (Cambridge, 1982), pp. 217–34; Edward Vallance, 'Loyal or Rebellious? Protestant Associations in England 1584–1696', *Seventeenth Century*, 17 (2002), pp. 1–23.

126. *The Egerton Papers*, ed. J. Payne Collier, Camden 1st series, 12 (London, 1840), pp. 108–9.

127. Collinson, 'Elizabethan Exclusion Crisis', pp. 65–7, 87–92; Collinson, 'Monarchical Republic', pp. 417–24.

128. The seminal work here is John M. Wallace, *Destiny His Choice: The Loyalism of Andrew Marvell* (Cambridge, 1968), ch. 1; also Sampson, 'Laxity and Liberty', pp. 109–11; Edward Vallance, 'The Kingdom's Case: the Use of Casuistry as a Political Language, 1640–1692', *Albion*, 34: 4 (2002), pp. 557–83.

129. Mark Goldie, 'The Political Thought of the Anglican Revolution', in Robert Beddard (ed.), *The Revolutions of 1688: The Andrew Browning Lectures, 1988* (Oxford, 1991), ch. 2.

130. Richard Bancroft, *A Survey of the Pretended Holy Discipline* (London, 1593), pp. 7–8.

131. Ibid., pp. 48–9, 154–7; Bancroft, *Dangerous Positions and Proceedings*, pp. 9, 29 and passim – this latter work has a particular interest in showing that Reformation Scottish-style was a threat to secular authority.

132. Guy (ed.), *Reign of Elizabeth I*; Shagan, 'English Inquisition'.
133. Cromartie, *Constitutionalist Revolution*, p. 141. See also Alan Cromartie, 'Theology and Politics in Richard Hooker's Thought', *History of Political Thought*, 21 (2000), pp. 41–66.
134. Patrick Collinson, 'Hooker and the Elizabethan Establishment', in Arthur Stephen McGrade (ed.), *Richard Hooker and the Construction of Christian Community* (Tempe, AZ, 1997), pp. 149–81, at pp. 153, 178.
135. Cf. M. E. C. Perrott, 'Richard Hooker and the Problem of Authority in the Elizabethan Church', *Journal of Ecclesiastical History*, 49 (1998), pp. 29–60, at p. 39.
136. *The Works of . . . Mr Richard Hooker*, ed John Keble, rev. R. W. Church and F. Paget, 3 vols, 7th edn (Oxford, 1888), vol. I, p. 132. Further references are to this edition, to which I remain attached, though the standard edition is now *The Folger Library Edition of the Works of Richard Hooker*, ed. W. Speed Hill, 7 vols in 8 parts (Cambridge, MA, 1977–98). References to the *Laws* are in the form 'book.chapter.section' followed by the page number in the relevant value of the *Works*.
137. *Works*, vol. III, pp. 600–1.
138. In his actual treatment of laws, Hooker often follows his more complex but less clear enumeration at I.iii.1, p. 205.
139. J. W. Gough, *The Social Contract: A Critical Study of its Development*, 2nd edn (Oxford, 1957); but see also the ever-careful judgement on these matters of E. T. Davies, *The Political Ideas of Richard Hooker* (London, 1946), pp. 66–7.
140. W. D. J. Cargill Thompson, 'The Philosopher of the "Politic Society": Richard Hooker as a Political Thinker', in Cargill Thompson, *Studies in the Reformation* (London, 1980), pp. 42–3.
141. The issues are explored in Davies, *Political Ideas of Richard Hooker*, pp. 87–9; Lake, *Anglicans and Puritans?*, pp. 220–4; Margaret Sommerville, 'Richard Hooker and His Contemporaries on Episcopacy: an Elizabethan Consensus', *Journal of Ecclesiastical History*, 35 (1984), pp. 177–87; Anthony Milton, *Catholic and Reformed: The Roman and Protestant Churches in English Protestant Thought, 1600–1640* (Cambridge, 1995), pp. 454–75.
142. See below, Chapter 8. For Hobbes and corporation theory, see especially Patricia Springborg, '*Leviathan*, the Christian Commonwealth Incorporated', *Political Studies*, 24 (1976), pp. 171–83. For Hooker, see the suggestive remarks in Arthur B. Ferguson, 'The Historical Perspective of Richard Hooker: a Renaissance Paradox', *Journal of Medieval and Renaissance Studies*, 3 (1973), pp. 17–49, esp. 46–7.
143. An important account of Hooker's view of the royal supremacy, perhaps allowing more authority over doctrine than my account, is Daniel Eppley, *Defending Royal Supremacy and Discerning God's Will in Tudor England* (Aldershot, 2007), ch. 5.
144. On this theme, see especially A. S. McGrade, 'Constitutionalism Late Medieval and Early Modern – *Lex Facit Regem*: Hooker's Use of Bracton', in R. J. Schoeck (ed.), *Acta Conventus Neo-Latini Bononiensis: Proceedings of the Fourth International Congress of Neo-Latin Studies* (Binghamton, NY, 1985), pp. 116–23; and A. S. McGrade, 'Richard Hooker on the Lawful Ministry of Bishops and Kings', in W. J. Sheils and Diana Wood (eds), *The Ministry: Clerical and Law*, Studies in Church History, 26 (Oxford, 1989), pp. 177–84.
145. Cf. Johann P. Sommerville, 'Richard Hooker, Hadrian Saravia, and the Advent of the Divine Right of Kings', *History of Political Thought*, 4 (1983), pp. 229–45.
146. Lake, *Anglicans and Puritans?*
147. Mendle, *Dangerous Positions*.

Notes to Chapter 4

1. Important contextual analyses are Jenny Wormald, 'James VI and I, *Basilikon Doron* and *The Trew Law of Free Monarchies*: the Scottish Context and the English Translation', in Linda Levy Peck (ed.), *The Mental World of the Jacobean Court* (Cambridge, 1991), ch. 3; Roger Mason, *Kingship and the Commonweal: Political Thought in Renaissance and Reformation Scotland* (East Linton, 1998), chs 7–8; J. H. Burns, *The True Law of Kingship: Concepts of Monarchy in Early Modern Scotland* (Oxford, 1996), chs 7 and 8; W. B. Patterson, *James VI & I and the Reunion of Christendom* (Cambridge, 1997); Peter Lake, 'The King (the Queen) and the Jesuit: James Stuart's *True Law of Free Monarchies* in Context/s', *Transactions of the Royal Historical Society*, 6th ser., 14 (2004), pp. 243–60; Glenn Burgess, 'Becoming English? Becoming British? The Political Thought of James VI and I Before

and After 1603', in Jean-Christophe Mayer (ed.), *The Struggle for the Succession in Late Elizabethan England: Politics, Polemics and Cultural Representations* (Montpellier, 2004), pp. 143–75; Maurice Lee, Jr, *Great Britain's Solomon: James VI and I in His Three Kingdoms* (Urbana, IL, 1990), ch. 3; Daniel Fischlin and Mark Fortier (eds), *Royal Subjects: Essays on the Writings of James VI & I* (Detroit, 2002).

2.   J. Craigie (ed.), *Minor Prose Works of James VI and I* (Edinburgh, 1982), pp. 193–7; cf. Burns, *True Law of Kingship*, pp. 233–4, 237.

3.   J. Craigie (ed.), *The Basilicon Doron of King James VI*, 2 vols (Edinburgh, 1944, 1950), vol. II, pp. 9–14. (Further references to this edition are given in the text.) The king's 'Anglo–pisco–papisticall Conclusionnes' were adjudged 'treasonable, seditius, and wicked' by the synod: *The Autobiography and Diary of Mr James Melville*, ed. Robert Pitcairn (Edinburgh: Wodrow Society, 1842), p. 444.

4.   *Diary . . . of Mr James Melville*, p. 370.

5.   In the 1603 edition, James added passages to make it clear that he nonetheless believed the reformation of the Scottish church to have been God's work: it was 'extraordinarily wrought by God . . . of such as blindly were doing the work of God, but clogged with their owne passions & particular respects' (75).

6.   In 1603 this became 'can neither stand with the ordour of the Churche, nor the peace of a common-weale and well ruled Monarchie' (81).

7.   William Barlow, *The Summe and Substance of the Conference . . . at Hampton Court* (London, 1604), pp. 36, 82.

8.   Craigie (ed.), *Minor Prose Works*, p. 60.

9.   J. P. Sommerville, 'Papalist Political Thought and the Controversy over the Jacobean Oath of Allegiance', in Ethan Shagan (ed.), *Catholics and the 'Protestant Nation': Religious Politics and Identity in Early Modern England* (Manchester, 2005), ch. 7.

10. William Goodwin, *A Sermon Preached before the Kings Most Excellent Maiestie at Woodstocke, Aug. 28. 1614* [1614], in Joyce Lee Malcolm (ed.), *The Struggle for Sovereignty: Seventeenth-Century English Political Tracts*, 2 vols (Indianapolis, IN, 1999), vol. I, p. 34. (Further references will be given in the text in parentheses.)

11. James F. Larkin and Paul L. Hughes (eds), *Stuart Royal Proclamations: Volume I, Royal Proclamations of King James I, 1603–1625* (Oxford, 1975), pp. 355–6.

12. Richard Mocket [?], *God and the King: or, A Dialogue Shewing that Our Soveraigne Lord King James . . . Doth Rightfully Claime Whatsoever is Required by the Oath of Allegeance* (London, 1615), pp. 6–17. (Further references will be given in the text in parentheses.)

13. John Floyd, *God and the King, or A Dialogue Wherein is Treated of Allegiance Due to Our Most Gracious Lord King James Within His Dominions* (London, 1620), pp. 6–7.

14. See my account of the 'parliamentarian hermeneutic' in Glenn Burgess, *Absolute Monarchy and the Stuart Constitution* (New Haven, CT, 1996), ch. 2.

15. See J. G. A. Pocock, *The Ancient Constitution and the Feudal Law: A Study of English Historical Thought in the Seventeenth Century*, revised edition (Cambridge, 1987), pp. 79–90; John W. Cairns, T. David Fergus and Hector L. MacQueen, 'Legal Humanism and the History of Scots Law: John Skene and Thomas Craig', in John MacQueen (ed.), *Humanism in Renaissance Scotland* (Edinburgh, 1990), pp. 48–74 [also in *Journal of Legal History*, 11 (1990), pp. 40–69]; Brian P. Levack, 'Law, Sovereignty and the Union', in Roger Mason (ed.), *Scots and Britons: Scottish Political Thought and the Union of 1603* (Cambridge, 1994), ch. 9; and (though it appeared after my account was written) Anne McLaren, 'Challenging the Monarchical Republic: James I's Articulation of Kingship', in John F. McDiarmid (ed.), *The Monarchical Republic of Early Modern England: Essays in Response to Patrick Collinson* (Aldershot, 2007), ch. 9.

16. Thomas Craig, *The Jus Feudale of Sir Thomas Craig of Riccarton*, ed. and translated James Avon Clyde, 2 vols (Edinburgh, 1934), I.1.4 (pp. 3–4). Page references are all to the first volume of the translation.

17. Thomas Craig, *De Unione Regnorum Brittaniae Tractatus*, ed. C. Sanford Terry (Edinburgh, 1909), p. 231.

18. Thomas Craig, *The Right of Succession to the Kingdom of England* (London, 1703), pp. 11–12, 15.

19. Craig, *De Unione*, p. 239.

20. Craig, *Right of Succession*, p. 78.

21. Ibid., sig. b2.

22. Craig, *De Unione*, p. 240.

23. Ibid., pp. 328, 90 (Latin). Cf. here Burns, *True Law of Kingship*, pp. 263–4.
24. Craig, *De Unione*, pp. 281, 56 (Latin), Terry translates 'the fusion of two sovereign states into a single realm'; Burns, *True Law of Kingship*, p. 263.
25. Craig, *De Unione*, pp. 297, 68 (Latin). The translation does render the Latin into making the laws 'identical'; again, the corrective is Burns, *True Law of Monarchies*, p. 264.
26. Sir Henry Spelman, 'Of the Union', in Bruce R. Galloway and Brian P. Levack (eds), *The Jacobean Union: Six Tracts of 1604* (Edinburgh, 1985), p. 181.
27. John Dodderidge, 'A Breif Consideracion of the Unyon', in Galloway and Levack (eds), *Jacobean Union*, p. 146.
28. Sir John Hayward, *A Treatise of Union of the Two Realmes of England and Scotland* (London, 1604), pp. 11–16.
29. Sir Francis Bacon, 'A Brief Discourse Touching the Happy Union of the Kingdoms of England and Scotland', in James Spedding (ed.), *The Letters and the Life of Francis Bacon*, 7 vols (London, 1861–74), vol. III, pp. 97–8.
30. Sir Francis Bacon, 'Certain Articles or Considerations Touching the Union', in Spedding (ed.), *Letters and Life*, vol. III, pp. 230–1.
31. The influence of the account is explored in John W. Cairns and Grant McLeod, 'Thomas Craig, Sir Martin Wright and Sir William Blackstone: the English Discovery of Feudalism', *Journal of Legal History*, 21 (2000), pp. 54–66.
32. Craig, *Jus Feudale*, I.4.4–13; I.5.8–9 (pp. 53–64, 69–70).
33. Cf. Burns, *True Law of Kingship*, p. 264.
34. In the Prefaces to the 2nd and 3rd parts of his *Reports*: Steve Sheppard (ed.), *The Selected Writings of Sir Edward Coke*, 3 vols (Indianapolis, 2003), vol. I, pp. 39–41, 68–9.
35. Coke, Preface to 6th part of *Reports*: *Selected Writings*, vol. I, p. 150.
36. Hayward, *Treatise of Union*, p. 11.
37. See further Glenn Burgess, 'Pocock's History of Political Thought, the Ancient Constitution and Early Stuart England', in D. N. DeLuna (ed.), *The Political Imagination in History: Essays Concerning J. G. A. Pocock* (Baltimore, MD, 2006), ch. 2; also Christopher Brooks, 'The Place of Magna Carta and the Ancient Constitution in Sixteenth-Century English Legal Thought', in Ellis Sandoz (ed.), *The Roots of Liberty: Magna Carta, Ancient Constitution, and the Anglo-American Tradition of Rule of Law* (Columbia, MO, 1993), ch. 2, pp. 83–8.
38. John Selden, 'Nores upon Sir John Fortescue', in Fortescue, *De Laudibus Legum Angliae* (London, 1616), p. 7.
39. See further the discussion of this theme throughout the excellent account of Selden in Paul Christianson, *Discourse on History, Law, and Governance in the Public Career of John Selden, 1610–1635* (Toronto, 1996).
40. Burgess, *Absolute Monarchy and the Stuart Constitution*, pp. 204–7.
41. Sir Edward Coke, *The First Part of the Institutes of the Lawes of England* (London, 1628), fol. 97b; also in *Selected Writings*, vol. II, p. 701.
42. Cf. Richard Helgerson, *Forms of Nationhood: The Elizabethan Writing of England* (Chicago, 1992), ch. 2.
43. Coke, *Selected Writings*, vol. I, pp. 479–81 [12 *Rep.*, 64–5].
44. Craig, *De Unione*, p. 321.
45. James VI & I, *Political Writings*, ed. J. P. Sommerville (Cambridge, 1994), p. 172.
46. See further Glenn Burgess, 'Becoming English? Becoming British?'.
47. James VI & I, *Political Writings*, pp. 184–5.
48. For a different emphasis on this matter, see also J. W. Tubbs, *The Common Law Mind: Medieval and Early Modern Conceptions* (Baltimore, MD, 2000), chs 7–8. Also on Davies, see H. S. Pawlisch, 'Sir John Davies, the Ancient Constitution and Civil Law', *Historical Journal*, 23 (1980), pp. 689–702.
49. Sir John Davies, *Le Primer Report des Cases & Matters en Ley Resolves & Adiudges en les Courts del Roy en Ireland* (Dublin, 1615), Preface Dedicatory, sig. *2.
50. Glenn Burgess, *The Politics of the Ancient Constitution* (Basingstoke, 1992), pp. 145–7; contrasting views in J. P. Sommerville, 'English and European Political Ideas in the Early Seventeenth Century: Revisionism and the Case of Absolutism', *Journal of British Studies*, 35 (1996), pp. 168–94; Sommerville, *Royalists and Patriots: Politics and Ideology in England, 1603–1640* (Harlow, 1999), pp. 248–9; Tubbs, *Common Law Mind*, ch. 6.
51. Sir John Davies, *The Question Concerning Impositions, Tonnage, Poundage, Prizage, Customs, &c. Fully Stated and Argued, from Reason, Law, and Policy* (London, 1656), pp. 1–2.

52. Cf. Sommerville, 'English and European Political Ideas', p. 182, n. 46.
53. Burgess, *Absolute Monarchy and the Stuart Constitution*, pp. 198–200.
54. S. R. Gardiner (ed.), *Parliamentary Debates in 1610* (London, 1862), p. 72. This report of the speech emphasises its common-law elements.
55. Elizabeth Read Foster (ed.), *Proceedings in Parliament, 1610*, 2 vols (New Haven, CT, 1966), vol. II, p. 175.
56. Tubbs, *Common Law Mind*, pp. 149–51; Burgess, *Politics of the Ancient Constitution*, pp. 46–8.
57. Foster (ed.), *Proceedings*, vol. II, pp. 190–1.
58. Ibid., p. 192.
59. Ibid., pp. 194–6.
60. Markku Peltonen, *Classical Humanism and Republicanism in English Political Thought, 1570–1640* (Cambridge, 1995), pp. 222–6.
61. This is indebted to Quentin Skinner, 'Classical Liberty, Renaissance Translation and the English Civil War', in Skinner, *Visions of Politics*, 3 vols (Cambridge, 2002), vol. III, ch. 12, esp. p. 320.
62. Foster (ed.), *Proceedings*, vol. II, p. 196.
63. Ibid., p. 197.
64. Brian Vickers (ed.), *Francis Bacon*, The Oxford Authors (Oxford, 1996), p. 246 [James Spedding et al. (eds), *The Works of Francis Bacon*, 7 vols (London, 1857–9), vol. III, pp. 420–1].
65. Vickers (ed.), *Bacon*, pp. 246–7 [*Works*, vol. III, p. 421].
66. Vickers (ed.), *Bacon*, p. 248 [*Works*, vol. III, p. 423].
67. Vickers (ed.), *Bacon*, p. 254 [*Works*, vol. III, pp. 430–1]
68. Vickers (ed.), *Bacon*, p. 401 [*Works*, vol. VI, p. 450]. For contrasting interpretations of this essay see Peltonen, *Classical Humanism and Republicanism*, pp. 139–45; and Richard Tuck, *Philosophy and Government, 1572–1651* (Cambridge, 1993), pp. 108–13.
69. Thomas Scott, *The Belgicke Pismire* (London, 1622), pp. 90–1; Thomas Scott, *A Tongue-Combat Lately Happening* (London, 1623), pp. 13–14. See further Peltonen, *Classical Humanism and Republicanism*, ch. 5; and Peter Lake, 'Constitutional Consensus and Puritan Opposition in the 1620s: Thomas Scott and the Spanish Match', *Historical Journal*, 25 (1982), pp. 805–25.
70. Margo Todd, 'Anti-Calvinists and the Republican Threat in Early Stuart Cambridge', in Laura Lunger Knoppers (ed.), *Puritanism and Its Discontents* (Newark, NJ, 2003), pp. 85–105.
71. *The Vindication of the Parliament and their Proceedings* (London, 1642), p. 34. This work is discussed in Skinner, 'Classical Liberty', pp. 340–2.
72. *Vindication*, pp. 28, 30.
73. Cf. Burgess, *Politics of the Ancient Constitution*, chs 7–8. On the further deployment of arguments about slavery and liberty, see Quentin Skinner, 'John Milton and the Politics of Slavery', in Skinner, *Visions*, vol. II, ch. 11; and Skinner, 'Rethinking Political Liberty', *History Workshop Journal*, 61 (2006), pp. 156–70.
74. See Linda Levy Peck, 'Beyond the Pale: John Cusacke and the Language of Absolutism in Early Stuart Britain', *Historical Journal*, 41 (1998), pp. 121–49; also Burgess, *Absolute Monarchy and the Stuart Constitution*, pp. 37ff.
75. Peltonen, *Classical Humanism and Republicanism*, pp. 305–7.
76. Burgess, *Absolute Monarchy and the Stuart Constitution*, ch. 5.
77. Ibid., pp. 110–11.
78. On Manwaring, see especially Harry F. Snapp, 'The Impeachment of Roger Maynwaring', *Huntington Library Quarterly*, 30 (1966–7), pp. 217–32.
79. Roger Manwaring, *Religion and Allegiance: In Two Sermons Preached before the Kings Majestie* (1627), first sermon, in Malcolm (ed.), *Struggle for Sovereignty*, vol. I, pp. 64–5.
80. Robert Sibthorpe, *Apostolike Obedience* (London, 1627), p. 10.
81. 'Archbishop Abbot his Narrative', in John Rushworth, *Historical Collections*, vol. I (London, 1682), p. 439.
82. Ibid., p. 442. The reference was to James's speech of March 1610, in part occasioned by Harsnett's sermon, see James VI & I, *Political Writings*, ed. Sommerville, pp. 181–2.
83. The pioneering study of Filmer's background is Peter Laslett, 'Sir Robert Filmer: the Man versus the Whig Myth', *William and Mary Quarterly*, series 3, 5 (1948), pp. 523–46.
84. Cesare Cuttica, 'Kentish Cousins at Odds: Filmer's *Patriarcha* and Thomas Scott's *Defence of Freeborn Englishmen*', *History of Political Thought*, 28 (2007), pp. 599–616.
85. On these matters see the editor's comments in Sir Robert Filmer, *Patriarcha and Other*

Writings, ed. J. P. Sommerville (Cambridge, 1991), pp. viii, xxxii–xxxiv; Anthony B. Thompson, 'Licensing the Press: the Career of G. R. Weckherlin during the Personal Rule of Charles I', *Historical Journal*, 41 (1998), pp. 653–78.

86. Sir Robert Filmer, *Patriarcha*, in Filmer, *Patriarcha and Other Writings*, ed. Sommerville, p. 2.

87. For good accounts, see James Daly, *Sir Robert Filmer and English Political Thought* (Toronto, 1979), ch. 4; and Gordon Schochet, *Patriarchalism in Political Thought* (Oxford, 1975), ch. 7.

88. J. P. Sommerville, 'From Suarez to Filmer: a Reappraisal', *Historical Journal*, 25 (1982), pp. 525–40; and the editor's introduction to Filmer, *Patriarcha and Other Writings*, pp. xiv–xviii.

89. James VI & I, *A Meditation Upon the 27. 28. 29 Verses of the XXVII Chapter of Saint Matthew* (1620), in James VI & I, *Political Writings*, ed. J. P. Sommerville (Cambridge, 1994), p. 237.

90. James VI & I, *Triplici Nodo, Triplex Cuneus* (1608), in James VI & I, *Political Writings*, p. 110.

91. Ibid., p. 129.

92. Richard Field, *Of the Church, Five Books* (Oxford, 1628), V.53, p. 681.

93. See especially, Alan R. MacDonald, *The Jacobean Kirk, 1567–1625: Sovereignty, Polity and Liturgy* (Aldershot, 1998).

94. For some perspectives on this, see D. Alan Orr, 'Sovereignty, Supremacy and the Origins of the English Civil War', *History*, 87 (2002), pp. 474–90; and Paul S. Seaver, 'State Religion and Puritan Resistance in Early Seventeenth-Century England, in J. D. Tracey and M. Ragnow (eds), *Religion and the Early Modern State: Views from China, Russia, and the West* (Cambridge, 2004), ch. 8.

95. Peter Heylyn, *A Briefe and Moderate Answer* [1637], in Malcolm (ed.), *Struggle for Sovereignty*, vol. I, pp. 73–89. See now Anthony Milton, *Laudian and Royalist Polemic in Seventeenth-Century England: The Career and Writings of Peter Heylyn* (Manchester, 2007), ch. 2.

96. Henry Burton, *For God, and the King: The Summe of Two Sermons Preached on the Fifth of November Last in St. Matthewes Friday-Streete, 1636* (Amsterdam, 1636), p. 40. Such citation is, however, not necessarily innocuous: see Joseph Marshall, 'Recycling and Originality in the Pamphlet Wars: Republishing Jacobean Texts in the 1640s', *Transactions of the Cambridge Bibliographical Society*, 12 (2000), pp. 55–85.

97. Margaret Steele, 'The "Politic Christian": the Theological Background to the National Covenant', in J. S. Morrill (ed.), *The Scottish National Covenant in its British Context, 1638–51* (Edinburgh, 1990), ch. 2, p. 56.

98. S. R. Gardiner, *Constitutional Documents of the Puritan Revolution, 1625–1660*, 3rd edn (Oxford, 1906), p. 133.

Notes to Chapter 5

1. Joad Raymond, *Pamphlets and Pamphleteering in Early Modern Britain* (Cambridge, 2003), ch. 5; also David Como, 'Secret Printing: the Crisis of 1640, and the Origins of Civil War Radicalism', *Past & Present*, 196 (2007), pp. 37–82.

2. Ibid., pp. 163–5.

3. Davud Zaret, *Origins of Democratic Culture: Printing, Petitions and the Public Sphere in Early Modern England* (Princeton, NJ, 2000), p. 266.

4. Cf. Jason Peacey, *Politicians and Pamphleteers: Propaganda during the English Civil Wars and Interregnum* (Aldershot, 2004), esp. Epilogue.

5. Ibid., pp. 62–3 and passim.

6. A good account of the consequences is now Michael Braddick, *God's Fury, England's Fire: A New History of the English Civil Wars* (London, 2008), ch. 16. More broadly, David Cressy, *England on Edge: Crisis and Revolution, 1640–1642* (Oxford, 2006), esp. Part III.

7. See generally, Ian Michael Smart, 'The Political Ideas of the Scottish Covenanters, 1638–88', *History of Political Thought*, 1 (1980), pp. 167–93; Alan Macinnes, 'Covenanting Ideology in Seventeenth-Century Scotland', in Jane Ohlmeyer (ed.), *Political Thought in Seventeenth-Century Ireland* (Cambridge, 2000), ch. 9.

8. On the ideological implications of the Covenant, see the essays by Margaret Steele and Edward J. Cowan in John Morrill (ed.), *The Scottish National Covenant in its British Context, 1638–51* (Edinburgh, 1990), chs 2 and 3. For a comparison of Scottish and English Covenanting thought, see Edward Vallance, *Revolutionary England and the National*

Covenant: State Oaths, Protestantism and the Political Nation, 1553–1682 (Woodbridge, 2005), esp. ch. 1.

9. Valuable guidance to these pamphlets is provided by James D. Ogilvie, 'A Bibliography of Glasgow Assembly, 1638', *Records of the Glasgow Bibliographical Society*, 7 (1918–20), pp. 1–12; and Ogilvie, 'A Bibliography of the Bishops' Wars, 1639–40', *Records of the Glasgow Bibliographical Society*, 12 (1936), pp. 21–40.

10. *The Remonstrance of the Nobility, Barrones, Burgesses, Ministers and Commons within the Kingdome of Scotland . . . Feb. 27. 1639* (Edinburgh, 1639), pp. 5, 12.

11. Ibid., pp. 31, 25.

12. [Alexander Henderson], *The Lawfulnesse of Our Expedition into England Manifested* (Edinburgh, 1640), sig. A2.

13. Ibid., sig. A3.

14. [Alexander Henderson], *The Intentions of the Armie of the Kingdome of Scotland* (Amsterdam, 1640), pp. 8–9.

15. See also Henderson, *Lawfulnesse*, sigs A2–A2v.

16. [Alexander Henderson], *Some Speciall Arguments which Warranted the Scottish Subjects Lawfully to Take Up Armes* (n.p., 1642), p. 5.

17. *An Information to all Good Christians within the Kingdome of England* (Edinburgh, 1639), p. 6.

18. David Stevenson, 'The Early Covenanters and the Federal Union of Britain', in Roger A. Mason (ed.), *Scotland and England 1286–1815* (Edinburgh, 1987), ch. 8; Macinnes, 'Covenanting Ideology in Seventeenth-Century Scotland'.

19. Henderson, *Intentions*, p. 2.

20. Ibid., p. 11.

21. *Remonstrance*, p. 24.

22. Henderson, *Lawfulnesse*, sig. A4v.

23. Ibid., sig. A3v.

24. Ibid., sig. A4v.

25. The subject is explored by J. D. Ford, '*Lex, Rex Iusto Posita*: Samuel Rutherford on the Origins of Government', in Roger Mason (ed.), *Scots and Britons: Scottish Political Thought and the Union of 1603* (Cambridge, 1994), ch. 11. On Rutherford generally, see John Coffey, *Politics, Religion and the British Revolutions: The Mind of Samuel Rutherford* (Cambridge, 1997); also Coffey, 'Samuel Rutherford and the Political Thought of the Scottish Covenanters', in John R. Young (ed.), *Celtic Dimensions of the British Civil Wars* (Edinburgh, 1997), ch. 5.

26. Samuel Rutherford, *Lex, Rex: The Law and the Prince* (London, 1644), p. 3; also p. 91.

27. Especially Roland Bainton, 'Congregationalism and the Puritan Revolution from the Just War to the Crusade', in Bainton, *Studies in the Reformation* (London, 1963), ch. 18. See my discussions in Glenn Burgess, 'Was the English Civil War a War of Religion? The Evidence of Political Propaganda', *Huntington Library Quarterly*, 61 (1999), pp. 173–201; and Burgess, 'Religious War and Constitutional Defence: Justifications of Resistance in English Puritan Thought, 1590–1643', in Robert von Friedeburg (ed.), *Widerstandsrecht in der frühen Neuzeit* (Berlin, 2001), pp. 185–206. For counter-argument to the latter, see Edward Vallance, 'Preaching to the Converted: Religious Justifications for the English Civil War', *Huntington Library Quarterly*, 65 (2002), pp. 395–419; and Vallance, *Revolutionary England and the National Covenant*, Part I.

28. Jeremiah Burroughes, 'A Briefe Answer to Doctor Fernes Book', p. 7, appended to Burroughes, *The Glorious Name of God the Lord of Hosts* (London, 1643).

29. Charles Herle, *A Fuller Answer to a Treatise Written by Dr Ferne* (London, 1642), p. 25; Herbert Palmer [et al.?], *Scripture and Reason Pleaded for Defensive Armes* (London, 1643), p. 47.

30. J. G. A. Pocock, *The Ancient Constitution and the Feudal Law: A Study of English Historical Thought in the Seventeenth Century*, revised edition (Cambridge, 1987), pp. 125–7. Cf. Glenn Burgess, *The Politics of the Ancient Constitution: An Introduction to English Political Thought, 1603–1642* (Basingstoke, 1992), pp. 86–99; also Janelle Greenberg, *The Radical Face of the Ancient Constitution: St Edward's 'Laws' in Early Modern Political Thought* (Cambridge, 2001), ch. 5, for a reminder of the radical possibilities that lay in history.

31. Henry Parker, *Observations Upon Some of His Majesties Late Answers and Expresses* (London, 1642), p. 4.

32. Burgess, *Politics of the Ancient Constitution*, ch. 2.

33. Cf. Alan Cromartie, 'The Constitutionalist Revolution: the Transformation of Political Culture in Early Stuart England', *Past & Present*, 163 (May 1999), pp. 76–120: some of the phenomena discerned by Cromartie also have a context in polemical strategy.

34. Edward Husband, *An Exact Collection of all Remonstrances, Declarations, Votes, Orders, Ordinances, Proclamations, Petitions, Messages, Answers, and Other Remarkable Passages betweene the Kings Most Excellent Majesty, and His High Court of Parliament beginning at His Majesties Return from Scotland being in December 1641, and Continued Untill March the 21, 1643* (London, 1643), p. 265; Burgess, *Politics of the Ancient Constitution*, 223–4.

35. Husband, *Exact Collection*, p. 197.

36. Michael Mendle, *Dangerous Position: Mixed Government, the Estates of the Realm, and the Making of the Answer to the xix Propositions* (University, AL, 1985), esp. pp. 128–37.

37. *Answer to the xix Propositions* (1642), in Joyce Lee Malcolm (ed.), *The Struggle for Sovereignty: Seventeenth-Century English Political Tracts*, 2 vols (Indianapolis, 1999), vol. I, pp. 168–9.

38. C. C. Weston and J. R. Greenberg, *Subjects and Sovereigns: The Grand Controversy over Legal Sovereignty in Stuart England* (Cambridge, 1981), chs 3–4; John Sanderson, *'But the People's Creatures': The Philosophical Basis of the English Civil War* (Manchester, 1989), ch. 1.

39. Edward Hyde, earl of Clarendon, *The History of the Rebellion and Civil Wars in England . . . Also His Life Written by Himself* (Oxford, 1843), p. 953.

40. Chartles Herle, *A Fuller Answer to a Treatise Written by Dr Ferne* (London, 1642), p. 3.

41. Parker, *Observations upon Some of his Majesties Late Answers and Expresses*, pp. 1–2.

42. Philip Hunton, *A Treatise of Monarchie* (London, 1643), pp. 40–1.

43. William Prynne, *The First and Second Part of a Seasonable, Legal, and Historicall Vindication, and Chronological Collection of the Good, Old, Fundamentall Liberties, Franchies, Rights, Laws of All English Freemen*, 2nd edn (London, 1655), epistle to the reader; C. H. McIlwain, *The High Court of Parliament and its Supremacy* (New Haven, CT, 1910), p. 158 and n. 2.

44. John Pym, *The Kingdomes Manifestation*, (London, 1643), p. 3 (delivered on 17 April 1640).

45. Conal Condren, *The Language of Politics in Seventeenth-Century England* (Basingstoke, 1994); Condren, 'Liberty of Office and its Defence in Seventeenth-Century Political Argument', *History of Political Thought*, 18 (1997), pp. 460–82; Condren, *Argument and Authority in Early Modern England: The Presupposition of Oaths and Office* (Cambridge, 2006), ch. 9 takes the argument further.

46. John Guy, 'The Rhetoric of Counsel', in Dale Hoak (ed.), *Tudor Political Culture* (Cambridge, 1995), ch. 12.

47. S. R. Gardiner, *Constitutional Documents of the Puritan Revolution, 1625–1660*, 3rd edn (Oxford, 1906), p. 164.

48. Ibid., pp. 249–54.

49. Uxbridge, 24 November 1644; and Newcastle, 13 July 1646 – ibid., pp. 275–86 and 290–306.

50. Michael Mendle, 'The Great Council of Parliament and the first Ordinances: the Constitutional Theory of the Civil War', *Journal of British Studies*, 31 (1992), pp. 133–63; also Mendle, *Henry Parker and the English Civil War: The Political Thought of the Public's 'Privado'* (Cambridge, 1995).

51. *The Private Journals of the Long Parliament: 3 January to 5 March 1642*, ed. Willson H. Coates, Anne Steele Young and Vernon F. Snow (New Haven, CT, 1982), p. 313.

52. Parker, *Observations*, p. 25.

53. Herle, *Fuller Answer*, p. 13.

54. Parker, *Observations*, pp. 13, 9.

55. William Bridge, *The Truth of the Times Vindicated* (London, 1643), p. 27.

56. Parker, *Observations*, p. 24.

57. E.g. James Daly, 'John Bramhall and the Theoretical Problems of Royalist Moderation', *Journal of British Studies*, 11 (1971), pp. 26–44; David L. Smith, *Constitutional Royalism and the Search for Settlement, c.1640–1649* (Cambridge, 1994); more broadly, Robert Wilcher, *The Writing of Royalism 1628–1660* (Cambridge, 2001); Jason McElligott and David L. Smith (eds), *Royalists and Royalism during the English Civil Wars* (Cambridge, 2007), which appeared after my account was written.

58. James D. Ogilvie, 'The Aberdeen Doctors and the National Covenant', *Publications of the Edinburgh Bibliographical Society*, 11: 2 (October 1921), pp. 73–86; more broadly, Martyn Bennett, *The Civil Wars Experienced: Britain and Ireland, 1638–1661* (London, 2000), ch. 1.

59. *The Generall Demands of the Reverend Doctors of Divinitie and Ministers of the Gospell in Aberdene, Concerning the Late Covenant, in Scotland. Together with the Answeres, Replyes, and Duplyes that Followed Thereupon, in the Year, 1638* (Aberdeen, 1663), p. 6 (this is the single most complete reprinting of the 1638 exchanges).

60. The Doctors were notably vague in specifying the *locus* of ecclesiastical authority, though they did say that 'lawfull superioures' consisted of 'the Kings Majesty, the Parliament, the secret Counsell, and other Magistrates, and ecclesiasticall Assemblies' (161), the suggestion being (I think) that all the latter were inferior to the first. A broad discussion of the Doctors' views on church government, resting heavily on the evidence of John Forbes' *Irenicum* of 1629, is in D. Macmillan, *The Aberdeen Doctors* (London, 1909), ch. 3.

61. Clarendon, *History*, vol. I, pp. 492–7; *Life*, pp. 938–9; Graham Roebuck, *Clarendon and Cultural Continuity: A Bibliographical Study* (New York, 1981), pp. 11–12.

62. Austin Woolrych, *Britain in Revolution 1625–1660* (Oxford, 2002), pp. 199–202; Conrad Russell, *Fall of the British Monarchies, 1637–1642* (Oxford, 1991), pp. 424–9.

63. B. H. G. Wormald, *Clarendon: Politics, History, and Religion, 1640–1660* (Chicago, 1976), p. 36.

64. [Edward Hyde], *His Majesties Declaration, To All His Loving Subjects: Published with the Advice of His Privie Councell* (London, 1641), pp. 2–3. Further references are given parenthetically. The circumstances in which this work came to be produced are recounted in Clarendon, *Life*, p. 938, though it was not until late February that Hyde began to write regularly for the king (Clarendon, *Life*, p. 944).

65. David Lagomarsino and Charles T. Wood, *The Trial of Charles I: A Documentary History* (Hanover, NH, 1989), p. 142.

66. [Edward Hyde], *His Majesties Second Message to the Parliament Concerning Sir John Hothams Refusall* (London, 1642); Clarendon, *History*, vol. II, p. 51.

67. Clarendon, *History*, vol. II, pp. 52–3. For another good example see ibid., vol. II, pp. 144–5 (the king's answer to the Lords' and Commons' declaration of 19 May).

68. [Edward Hyde], *His Majesties Answer to a Printed Book, Entituled, A Remonstrance, or, The Declaration of the Lords and Commons Now Assembled in Parliament, May 26. 1642* (London, 1642), p. 2; Clarendon, *History*, vol. II, p. 149.

69. [Edward Hyde], *His Majesties Declaration Concerning Leavies* (London, 1642), pp. 11–12; Clarendon, *History*, vol. II, p. 209; cf. Quentin Skinner, 'Rethinking Political Liberty in the English Revolution', *History Workshop Journal*, 61 (2006), pp. 156–70.

70. On this work see Clarendon, *History*, vol. II, 292, n. 1; and Roebuck, *Clarendon*, pp. 87–8.

71. Edward Hyde, *Transcendent and Multiplied Rebellion and Treason, Discovered by the Lawes of the Land* (Oxford, 1645), p. 7 (further references are given parenthetically).

72. Clarendon, *History*, vol. II, p. 14. See Wormald, *Clarendon*, pp. 82–3.

73. See especially Hyde's own analysis of the differences between himself, Falkland and Culpeper, in Clarendon, *Life*, pp. 939–43.

74. Henry Ferne, *The Resolving of Conscience* (Cambridge, 1642), p. 11.

75. In 1649 Bramhall was to publish a careful attack on the political principles of Scottish Presbyterianism, *A Fair Warning to Take Heed of the Scottish Discipline*, to be found in *The Works of the Most Reverend Father in God, John Bramhall, D.D.*, ed. A. W. Haddan, 5 vols (Oxford, 1842–5), vol. III, pp. 235–87. See also Nicholas Jackson, *Hobbes, Bramhall and the Politics of Liberty and Necessity: A Quarrel of the Civil Wars and Interregnum* (Cambridge, 2007), ch. 2.

76. John Bramhall, *The Serpent-Salve; or, A Remedy for the Biting of an Asp*, in Bramhall, *Works*, vol. III, p. 297.

77. Ibid., pp. 302–3.

78. Ibid., pp. 303–4.

79. Dudley Digges, *The Unlawfulnesse of Subjects Taking up Armes Against their Soveraigne* (Oxford, 1643), p. 3.

80. Cf. my account of the *potestas irritans* in Glenn Burgess, *Absolute Monarchy and the Stuart Constitution* (New Haven, CT, 1996), ch. 5.

81. For the context in which he wrote, see especially Robert Ashton, *Counter Revolution: The Second Civil War and its Origins, 1646–8* (New Haven, CT, 1994), passim, but pp. 109–14 are specifically on Jenkins; also William Epstein, 'Judge David Jenkins and the Great Civil War', *Journal of Legal History*, 3 (1982), pp. 187–221.

82. David Jenkins, *Lex Terrae*, in *The Works of that Grave and Learned Lawyer Judge Jenkins* (London, 1648), p. 11.

83. John M. Wallace, *Destiny His Choice: The Loyalism of Andrew Marvell* (Cambridge, 1968), p. 14.

84. [John Jones], *Christus Dei, The Lords Annoynted* (Oxford, 1643), t.p.

85. Sir Robert Filmer, *Patriarcha and Other Writings*, ed. J. P. Sommerville (Cambridge, 1991), pp. 172–83.

86. Ibid., p. 132.

87. Ibid., p. 134.

88. Quoted in ibid., p. 146.

89. Ibid., pp. 148–9.

90. Ibid., pp. 157–63.

91. On Filmer's typicality, note James W. Daly, *Sir Robert Filmer and English Political Thought* (Toronto, 1979), pp. 50–5, 173–6, and passim.

92. Robert Grosse, *Royalty and Loyalty. Or a Short Survey of the Power of Kings over their Subjects and the Duty of Subjects to their Kings* (n.p., 1647), pp. 17–18.

93. As in David L. Smith, *Constitutional Royalism and the Search for Settlement, c.1640–1649* (Cambridge, 1994), pp. 244–55.

94. But cf. the cautious remarks in J. W. Allen, *English Political Thought, 1603–1660, Volume I: 1603–1644* (London, 1938), pp. 509–11.

95. John Maxwell, *Sacro-Sancta Regum Majestas: Or, The Sacred and Royall Prerogative of Christian Kings* (Oxford, 1644), ep. ded.

96. Ibid., p. 22; on human designation, see also pp. 120–4. Later, Maxwell made it clear that the people could designate as their rulers more than one person, and so establish aristocracies and democracies (135; though cf. 179).

97. Ibid., p. 49; also p. 132. As did the Levellers, Maxwell held that men did not even possess power over their own lives (p. 52).

98. Griffith Williams, *Vindiciae Regum; or, The Grand Rebellion: That Is, A Looking-Glasse for Rebels* (Oxford, 1643); Williams, *The Discovery of Mysteries: or, The Plots and Practices of a Prevalent Faction in this Present Parliament to Overthrow the Established Religion . . . And also, To Subvert the Fundamentall Lawes* (Oxford, 1643); and Williams, *Jura Majestatis, The Rights of Kings both in Church and State: 1. Granted by God 2. Violated by the Rebels 3. Vindicated by the Truth* (Oxford, 1644). In the same period Williams also produced a sermon delivered to the Royalist Oxford Parliament on 8 March 1644: *A Sermon Preached at the Publique Fast the eighth of March, in St Maries, Oxford, before . . . the Honourable House of Commons* (Oxford, 1644).

99. Williams, *Jura Majestatis*, pp. 158–62.

100. See also Anthony Milton, *Laudian and Royalist Polemic in Seventeenth-Century England: The Career and Writings of Peter Heylyn* (Manchester, 2007), ch. 4.

101. Williams, *Jura Majestatis*, pp. 48–9 (also p. 13).

102. Ibid., pp. 50–4.

103. Williams, *Discovery of Mysteries*, p. 71.

104. Williams, *Jura Majestatis*, p. 54.

105. It was widespread in Royalist circles: for another example, see Maxwell, *Sacro-Sancta Regum Majestas*, pp. 62–7.

106. Williams, *Jura Majestatis*, p. 99.

107. Ibid., pp. 56, 61.

108. Ibid., pp. 63–5.

109. Ibid., pp. 65–6.

110. Ibid., esp. pp. 75–8.

111. Ibid., pp. 82–5, 89–90.

112. Ibid., p. 93.

113. Ibid., pp. 106–7, 113.

114. Ibid., pp. 107–11.

115. Ibid., pp. 111–13.

116. He has also been assigned *The Royall and the Royallists Plea* (1647); but I am not sure on what authority this attribution is made, and the character of that work makes it highly improbable.

117. Michael Hudson, *The Divine Right of Government: 1. Naturall and 2. Politique* (n.p., 1647), t.p.

118. Ibid., p. 63.

119. Ibid., p. 75.

120. Ibid., pp. 147–8.
121. Ibid., pp. 106–26. Where there was no heir to the crown, or where a multitude had come together to form a colony on hitherto uninhabited land, a king ought to be appointed by lot (125–6).
122. Ibid., pp. 84–5.
123. Ibid., p. 87–8. It is worth remembering that this aspect of divine-right royalism was not typical of all Royalist writing. See, for example, *A Paralell of Governments: or, A Political Discourse Upon Seven Positions, Tending to the Peace of England, and Preservation of the Citie of London* (n.p., 1647), remarkable for its total reliance on Machiavellian and classical history as evidence in support of the Royalist cause.
124. Hudson, *Divine Right of Government*, p. 89.
125. Ibid., pp. 95–6.
126. Ibid., p. 92.
127. Hudson, *Divine Right of Government*, sig. (a)2.
128. Ibid., sigs A2–A2v.
129. Hudson, *Divine Right of Government*, sig. A3.
130. Ibid., p. 170.
131. Ibid., p. 178; also pp. 187–8.
132. Ibid., p. 190.
133. Ibid., p. 141.
134. Ibid., pp. 144–5.
135. Ibid., pp. 150–1.
136. Ibid., p. 159.
137. Ibid., pp. 152–3.
138. Ibid., p. 157.
139. Ibid., p. 159.
140. Ibid., pp. 162–4.
141. Ibid., pp. 166–9.
142. Ibid., p. 169.
143. David Wootton, 'From Rebellion to Revolution: the Crisis of the Winter of 1642/3 and the Origins of Civil War Radicalism', *English Historical Review* (1990), pp. 654–69, reprinted in Richard Cust and Ann Hughes, *The English Civil War* (London, 1997), ch. 13. A similar process is explored in Skinner, 'Rethinking Political Liberty in the English Revolution'.
144. *A View of a Printed Book* (Oxford, *recte* London, 1643), in Andrew Sharp (ed.), *Political Ideas of the English Civil Wars, 1641–1649*, (London, 1983), p. 111. Sharp and many others attribute this to Sir John Spelman; but there are good reasons against doing so. See Michael Mendle, *Henry Parker and the English Civil War: The Political Thought of the Public's 'Privado'* (Cambridge, 1995), p. 107.
145. [Edward Bowles], *Plaine English: or, a Discourse Concerning the Accommodation, the Armie, the Association* (London, 1643), p. 20.
146. *England's Miserie and Remedie*, in David Wootton (ed.), *Divine Right and Democracy: An Anthology of Political Writing in Stuart England* (Harmondsworth, 1986), p. 276.
147. Richard Tuck, *Natural Rights Theories: Their Origin and Development* (Cambridge, 1979), p. 148; Tuck, *Philosophy and Government, 1572–1651* (Cambridge, 1993), pp. 242–3; Mendle, *Henry Parker*, p. 10; and Sanderson, *'But the People's Creatures'*, p. 63.
148. William Ball, *A Caveat for Subjects, Moderating the Observator* (London, 1642), pp. 5–6.
149. William Ball, *Tractatus de Jure Regnandi & Regni: Or, The Sphere of Government, According to the Law of God, Nature and Nations* (London, 1645), pp. 4–5. (Further references are given parenthetically in the text.)
150. William Ball elaborates on this subject in his *Constitutio Liberi Populi: Or, The Rule of a Free-Born People* (London, 1646), pp. 17–22.
151. John Cook, *The Vindication of the Professors & Professions of the Law* (London, 1646), sig. A4.
152. Ibid., pp. 87–8.
153. Ibid., pp. 88–9.
154. Ball, *Constitutio Liberi Populi: or, The Rule of a Free-Born People*, pp. 8–12.
155. Francis Thorpe, *Sergeant Thorpe Judge of Assize for the Northern Circuit, His Charge, As It Was Delivered to the Grand-Jury at Yorke Assizes the Twentieth of March, 1648* (London, 1649), p. 3.
156. Clarendon, *The Life*, in Edward Hyde, earl of Clarendon, *The History of the Rebellion . . . Also His Life Written by Himself*, 1 vol. edn (Oxford, 1843), p. 937.

157. C. M. Williams, 'Extremist Tactics in the Long Parliament, 1642–1643', *Historical Studies*, 15 (1971), pp. 136–50, at p. 150.

158. Williams, 'Extremist Tactics', pp. 143–4, 159–50. For his basic ideas, see C. M. Williams, 'The Anatomy of a Radical Gentleman: Henry Marten', in Donald Pennington and Keith Thomas (eds), *Puritans and Revolutionaries: Essays in Seventeenth-Century History Presented to Christopher Hill* (Oxford, 1978), pp. 118–38, esp. pp. 130–6; Sarah Barber, *A Revolutionary Rogue: Henry Marten and the English Republic* (Stroud, 2000), esp. ch. 3. Also Ivor Waters, *Henry Marten and the Long Parliament* (Chepstow, 1973).

159. Thomas Chaloner, *An Answer to the Scotch Papers. Delivered in the House of Commons* (London, 1646).

160. [Henry Marten], *A Corrector of the Answerer to the Speech Out of Doores* (London, 1646).

161. Henry Marten, *The Independency of England Endeavored to be Maintained . . . against the Claims of the Scottish Commissioners* (London, 1648) p. 16.

162. Cf. Skinner, 'Rethinking Political Liberty in the English Revolution'.

163. William Prynne, *A Breife Momento to the Present Unparliamentary Junto* (London, 1649), p. 13.

164. Quoted in Williams, 'Anatomy of a Radical', p. 125. The exact character of Marten's religion remains obscure, as does his relationship to classical republican ideas: see Barber, *Revolutionary Rogue*, pp. 60–8, and ch. 4.

165. David Lagomarsino and Charles T. Wood (eds), *The Trial of Charles I: A Documentary History* (Hanover, NH, 1989), pp. 118–28.

166. John Cook, *King Charls His Case: or, An Appeal to All Rational Men, Concerning His Tryal at the High Court of Justice* (London, 1649), p. 5. For the blood-guilt theme, see especially Patricia Crawford, 'Charles Stuart, That Man of Blood', *Journal of British Studies*, 16 (1977), pp. 41–61. I have also examined patterns of argument around the regicide in Glenn Burgess, 'The English Regicides and the Legitimation of Political Violence', in Brett Bowden and Michael T. Davies (eds), *Terror: From Tyrannicide to Terrorism* (St Lucia, 2008), ch. 4.

167. The reference is, of course, to the revelatory publication of the king's private papers captured at the battle of Naseby. They appeared as *The Kings Cabinet Opened* in 1645, edited by Henry Parker and others.

168. John Cook, *Monarchy No Creature of Gods Making, &c. Wherein is Proved by Scripture and Reason, that Monarchicall Government is Against the Minde of God* (Waterford, 1651), sig. A3.

169. There are marked similarities here with the tensions that have been found to emerge in Rutherford's thinking during the 1650s: see John Coffey, *Politics, Religion and the British Revolutions: The Mind of Samuel Rutherford* (Cambridge, 1997), ch. 8.

170. Noel Henning Mayfield, *Puritans and Regicide: Presbyterian–Independent Differences over the Trial and Execution of Charles (I) Stuart* (Lanham, MD, 1988).

171. For background, see Vernon Elliot, 'The Quarrel of the Covenant: the London Presbyterians and the Regicide', in Jason Peacey (ed.), *The Regicides and the Execution of Charles I* (Basingstoke, 2001), ch. 9.

172. *A Serious and Faithfull Representation of the Judgements of Ministers of the Gospell Within London*, ed. R. W. K. Hinton (Reading, 1949), p. 4. Further references are given parenthetically within the text.

173. There is an excellent account of Prynne's position in 1648–9 in William Lamont, *Marginal Prynne 1600–1669* (London, 1963), ch. 8; and an analysis of his writings on parliamentary authority in C. C. Weston and J. R. Greenberg, *Subjects and Sovereigns: The Grand Controversy over Legal Sovereignty in Stuart England* (Cambridge, 1981), ch. 5.

174. William Prynne, *The First Part of an Historical Collection of the Ancient Parliaments of England* (London, 1649), p. 3.

175. William Prynne, *Summary Reasons against the New Oath & Engagement* (London, 1649), p. 4.

176. Prynne, *Breife Momento*, p. 12.

177. Perez Zagorin, *A History of Political Thought in the English Revolution* (London, 1954), pp. 81–6; and above all, John Coffey, *John Goodwin and the Puritan Revolution: Religion and Intellectual Change in Seventeenth-Century England* (Woodbridge, 2006), esp. ch. 6.

178. John Goodwin, *Right and Might Well Met* (London, 1648/9), pp. 3–5.

179. Ibid., pp. 9–10; cf. also pp. 15–16.

180. Ibid., pp. 16–17.

181. Ibid., pp. 17–18, 23.

182. John Goodwin, *Hybristodikai: The Obstructours of Justice* (London, 1649), p. 3–4.

183. John Sadler, *The Rights of the Kingdom; or, Customs of Our Ancestours* (London, 1649), epistle to the reader.

Notes to Chapter 6

1. Joad Raymond, *Pamphlets and Pamphleteering in Early Modern Britain* (Cambridge, 2003), p. 184.

2. Cf. Jonathan Scott, *England's Troubles: Seventeenth-Century English Political Instability in European Context* (Cambridge, 2000), Part II; more broadly David S. Katz and Richard H. Popkin, *Messianic Revolution: Radical Religious Politics to the End of the Second Millennium* (London, 2000); and Martin Malia, *History's Locomotives: Revolutions and the Making of the Modern World* (New Haven, CT, 2007).

3. See especially, Conal Condren, *The Language of Politics in Seventeenth-Century England* (Basingstoke, 1994), ch. 5; and his earlier article, Condren, 'Radicals, Conservatives and Moderates in Early Modern Political Thought: a Case of the Sandwich Islands Syndrome?', *History of Political Thought*, 10 (1989), pp. 525–42. The subsequent debates are reviewed in Glenn Burgess and Matthew Festenstein (eds), *English Radicalism, 1550–1850* (Cambridge, 2007).

4. Helpful recent work on the Leveller origins is Nicholas McDowell, *The English Radical Imagination: Culture, Religion, and Revolution, 1630–1660* (Oxford, 2003), ch. 3; Benjamin Grob-Fitzgibbon, ' "Whatsoever Yee would That Men Should Doe Unto You, Even So Doe Yee to Them": An Analysis of the Effect of Religious Consciousness on the Origins of the Leveller Movement', *The Historian*, 65 (2003), pp. 901–30; and David Como, 'An Unattributed Pamphlet by William Walwyn: New Light on the Prehistory of the Leveller Movement', *Huntington Library Quarterly*, 69 (2006), pp. 353–82.

5. John Lilburne, *Englands Birth-Right Justified* (London, 1645), pp. 2–3; in William Haller, *Tracts on Liberty*, 3 vols (New York, 1979), vol. III, pp. 260–1.

6. Lilburne, *Englands Birth-Right*, p. 5 (Haller, *Tracts*, vol. III, p. 263).

7. William Walwyn, *Englands Lamentable Slaverie* (1645), in *The Writings of William Walwyn*, ed. Jack R. McMichael and Barbara Taft (Athens, GA, 1989), p. 149.

8. The *Remonstrance* has usually been attributed to Richard Overton, but work by David Adams persuasively questions this: D. R. Adams, 'Religion and Reason in the Thought of Richard Overton, the Leveller', PhD dissertation, University of Cambridge, 2002.

9. *A Remonstrance of Many Thousand Citizens, and other Free-Borne People of England* (1646), in Don M. Wolfe (ed.), *Leveller Manifestoes of the Puritan Revolution* (New York, 1967), p. 113.

10. Richard Overton, *An Arrow against all Tyrants* (London, 1646), p. 3.

11. For context, see Nicholas McDowell, 'Ideas of Creation in the Writings of Richard Overton the Leveller and *Paradise Lost*', *Journal of the History of Ideas*, 66 (2005), pp. 59–78.

12. John Lilburne, *The Legall Fundamentall Liberties of the People of England* (London, 1649), p. 73.

13. Richard Overton, *An Appeale from the Degenerate Representative Body the Commons of England . . . to the Body Represented* (1647), in Wolfe (ed.), *Leveller Manifestoes*, pp. 162–3.

14. William Walwyn, *A Helpe to the Right Understanding of a Discourse concerning Independency, Lately Published by William Pryn* (February 1645), in *Writings*, ed. McMichael and Taft, pp. 137, 140, 136.

15. Thomas Edwards, *The Third Part of Gangraena* (London, 1646), p. 262. Ann Hughes, *Gangraena and the Struggle for the English Revolution* (Oxford, 2004).

16. Edwards, *Third Part*, pp. 270–1.

17. Richard Overton, *The Araignement of Mr. Persecution* (London, 1645), pp. 44, 4 (Haller, *Tracts on Liberty*, vol, III, pp. 254, 214).

18. See further John Coffey, 'The Toleration Controversy during the English Revolution', in Christopher Durston and Judith Maltby (eds), *Religion in Revolutionary England* (Manchester, 2006), ch. 2.

19. John Lilburne, *Regall Tyrannie Discovered* (London, 1647), pp. 9–11.

20. Richard Overton, *An Appeale from the Degenerate Representative Body* (July 1647), in Wolfe (ed.), *Leveller Manifestoes*, p. 162.

21. See further though, Rachel Foxley, 'Problems of Sovereignty in Leveller Writings', *History of Political Thought*, 28 (2007), pp. 642–60.

22. See the important material in Michael Mendle (ed.), *The Putney Debates of 1647: The Army, the Levellers and the English State* (Cambridge, 2001), chs 6 and 8.

23. *The Agreement of the People* (November 1647), in Wolfe (ed.), *Leveller Manifestoes*, pp. 226–8.

24. For a good discussion see Paul Christianson, *Reformers and Babylon: English Apocalyptic Visions from the Reformation to the Eve of the Civil War* (Toronto, 1978), ch. 4.

25. John Wildman, *Putney Projects* (London, 1647), p. 1.

26. A. S. P. Woodhouse (ed.), *Puritanism and Liberty* (London, 1951), pp. 107–8.

27. Margaret Sampson, 'A Story "Too Tedious to Relate at Large"? Response to the Levellers, 1647–1653', *Parergon*, n.s., 5 (1987), pp. 135–54, esp. pp. 138–40.

28. William Walwyn [?], *A Manifestation* (April 1649), in William Haller and Godfrey Davies (eds), *The Leveller Tracts, 1647–1653* (Gloucester, MA, 1964), p. 281.

29. Murray Tolmie, *The Triumph of the Saints: The Separate Churches of London, 1616–1649* (Cambridge, 1977), chs 7 and 8.

30. There are some instructive comments in Bernard S. Capp, *The Fifth Monarchy Men: A Study in Seventeenth-Century Millenarianism* (London, 1972), pp. 89–92.

31. Overton, *An Appeale*, in Wolfe (ed.), *Leveller Manifestoes*, pp. 180–1.

32. On the gendered nature of the argument see Ann Hughes, 'Gender and Politics in Leveller Literature', in Susan Amussen and Mark Kishlansky (eds), *Political Culture and Cultural Politics in England: Essay Presented to David Underdown* (Manchester, 1995), pp. 162–88; more broadly, Patricia Crawford, '"The Poorest She": Women and Citizenship in Early Modern England', in Mendle (ed.), *Putney Debates*, ch. 10.

33. On the Leveller relationship with the army, see especially John Morrill, *The Nature of the English Revolution* (London, 1993), chs 16 and 17; Mark Kishlansky, 'The Army and the Levellers: the Roads to Putney', *Historical Journal*, 22 (1979), pp. 795–824; Kishlansky, *The Rise of the New Model Army* (Cambridge, 1979); Austin Woolrych, *Soldiers and Statesmen: The General Council of the Army and its Debates, 1647–1648* (Oxford, 1987); Ian Gentles, *The New Model Army in England, Ireland and Scotland, 1645–1653* (Oxford, 1992); John Morrill and Philip Baker, 'The Case of the Armie Truly Re-stated', in Mendle (ed.), *Putney Debates*, ch. 6; and Morrill and Baker, 'Oliver Cromwell, the Regicide and the Sons of Zeruiah', in Jason Peacey (ed.), *The Regicides and the Execution of Charles I* (Basingstoke, 2001), pp. 14–35.

34. See Woorych, *Soldiers and Statesmen*, pp. 230–1, for the location and forum of the 29 October debate.

35. On Ireton and his views, see especially David Farr, *Henry Ireton and the English Revolution* (Woodbridge, 2006), esp. ch. 4.

36. On the complexities of the term 'property' see Margaret Sampson, '"Property" in Seventeenth-Century English Political Thought', in Gordon Schochet (ed.), *Religion, Resistance and Civil War*, (*Proceedings of the Folger Institute Center for the History of British Political Thought, Volume 3*) (Washington, DC, 1990) pp. 259–75.

37. A. S. P. Woodhouse (ed.), *Puritanism and Liberty* (London, 1951), p. 122 (in all quotations I have omitted Woodhouse's conjectural emendations; material in square brackets is my own, though it occasionally agrees with Woodhouse's). There is important material on Ireton's attitude to natural rights in Richard Tuck, '"The Ancient Law of Freedom": John Selden and the Civil Law', in John Morrill (ed.), *Reactions to the English Civil Law, 1642–1649* (London, 1982), ch. 6, pp. 156–7; and Tuck, *Natural Rights Theories: Their Origin and Development* (Cambridge, 1979), pp. 150–2.

38. Woodhouse, *Puritanism and Liberty*, p. 53. There has been much debate about Leveller views of the franchise, occasioned by C. B. Macpherson's claim that they intended always to exclude servants and wage-earners (see his *The Political Theory of Possessive Individualism: Hobbes to Locke* (Oxford, 1962), ch. 3). For the counter-argument see especially Keith Thomas, 'The Levellers and the Franchise', in G. E. Aylmer (ed.), *The Interregnum: The Quest for Settlement, 1646–1660* (London, 1972), ch. 2. Also J. C. Davis, 'The Levellers and Democracy', in Charles Webster (ed.), *The Intellectual Revolution of the Seventeenth Century* (London, 1974, 1974), ch. vi. My understanding of the debates generally and of Petty in particular has much in common with Christopher Thompson, 'Maximilian Petty and the Putney Debate on the Franchise', *Past and Present*, 88 (1980), pp. 63–9.

39. Woolrych, *Soldiers and Statesmen*, pp. 243–4.

40. The Levellers' social radicalism is fully explored in Brian Manning, *The English People and the English Revolution* (Harmondsworth, 1978), ch. 10.

41. Petition of 11 September 1648, in Wolfe (ed.), *Leveller Manifestoes*, p. 288.

42. Walwyn, *A Manifestation*, in Haller and Davies (eds), *Leveller Tracts*, p. 279.

43. For further discussion of the charge of 'levelling' see Sampson, 'A Story "Too Tedious . . ."', esp. pp. 140ff.

44. For a summary, see Norah Carlin, 'Leveller Organization in London', *Historical Journal*, 27 (1984), pp. 955–60.

45. Cf. Mark Kishlansky, 'What Must Be', in Schochet (ed.), *Religion, Resistance and Civil War*. Cf. Ian Gentles, 'London Levellers in the English Revolution: the Chidleys and their Circle', *Journal of Ecclesiastical History*, 29 (1978), pp. 281–309. The Chidleys' involvement in organised Leveller politics appears not to pre-date the Putney Debates.

46. For this and the general army background to 1648–9 I am indebted to Gentles, *New Model Army*, ch. 9.

47. The text of the *Remonstrance* is in William Cobbett (ed.), *The Parliamentary History of England*, 36 vols (London, 1806–20), vol. III, cols 1078–127, from which my quotations are taken. See further, Farr, *Henry Ireton*, ch. 6.

48. For the significance of this deployment of interest theory, see Jonathan Scott, *Algernon Sidney and the English Republic, 1623–1677* (Cambridge, 1988), pp. 208–9; and for a context into which to place Ireton's language, see J. A. W. Gunn, *Politics and the Public Interest in the Seventeenth Century* (London, 1969), ch. 1, esp. p. 13 and n. 1.

49. From the Leveller-sympathetic newspaper *The Moderate*, no. 38 (27 March–3 April 1649), p. 385, quoted from Jürgen Diethe, '*The Moderate*: Politics and Allegiances of a Revolutionary Newspaper', *History of Political Thought*, 4 (1983), pp. 247–79, at p. 249. The basic demand that no one should be punished 'for doing of that against which no Law hath bin provided' was in the 11 September 1648 Petition: see Wolfe, *Leveller Manifestoes*, p. 287; see also the Petition of January 1648, in ibid., p. 266.

50. Lilburne's own narrative of these events is in *Legall Fundamentall Liberties* (1649), in Haller and Davies (eds), *Leveller Tracts*, pp. 414ff. See also Barbara Taft, 'The Council of Officers' *Agreement of the People*, 1648/9', *Historical Journal*, 28 (1985), pp. 169–85; Gentles, *New Model Army*, ch. 9; and Farr, *Henry Ireton*, ch. 7.

51. Those confused by the many different *Agreements* will find them clearly sorted out in J. W. Gough, 'The Agreements of the People, 1647–49', *History*, n.s. 15 (1930–1), pp. 334–41; and Ian Gentles, 'The *Agreements of the People* and their Political Contexts, 1647–1649', in Mendle (ed.), *Putney Debates*, ch. 8.

52. *Foundations of Freedom* (1648), in Wolfe (ed.), *Leveller Manifestoes*, p. 297.

53. See Carolyn Polizzotto, 'Liberty of Conscience and the Whitehall Debates of 1648–9', *Journal of Ecclesiastical History*, 26 (1975), pp. 69–82.

54. I should reiterate here that, as before, in quotations from the debates recorded in Woodhouse (ed.), *Puritanism and Liberty*, the occasional interpolations are my own. I have deleted Woodhouse's extensive additions to the text, and occasionally modified his punctuation.

55. There seems to have been some patronage connection between Parker and Ireton from 1649: see Michael Mendle, *Henry Parker and the English Civil War: The Political Thought of the Public's 'Privado'* (Cambridge, 1995), pp. 28, 160, cf. pp. 152–3; Farr, *Henry Ireton*, pp. 231–2. G. E. Aylmer, *The State's Servants: The Civil Service of the English Republic, 1649–1660* (London, 1973), pp. 260–1 gives a brief summary of Parker's public career.

56. Gentles, *New Model Army*, pp. 288–9; see further, Farr, *Henry Ireton*, which throughout emphasises Ireton's godly concerns.

57. The version of the second *Agreement* in Woodhouse (ed.), *Puritanism and Liberty*, pp. 355–67, usefully shows in footnotes what changes were made to it as a result of the Whitehall debates.

58. Wolfe (ed.), *Leveller Manifestoes*, p. 342.

59. Gentles, *New Model Army*, p. 292.

60. Gentles, *New Model Army*, pp. 293–4; Taft, 'Council of Officers' *Agreement*', pp. 182ff.

61. Lilburne, *Legall Fundamentall Liberties*, in Haller and Davies (eds), *Leveller Tracts*, pp. 432–3; see also pp. 422–3. Andrew Sharp, 'The Levellers and the End of Charles I', in Peacey (ed.), *Regicides and the Execution of Charles I*, ch. 8.

62. There is a good account of the Levellers and the army at this time in Gentles, *New Model Army*, ch. 10.

63. Wolfe (ed.), *Leveller Manifestoes*, pp. 407–8.

64. Woodhouse (ed.), *Puritanism and Liberty*, p. 178.

65. Cf. J. C. Davis, 'Radicalism in a Traditional Society: the Evaluation of Radical Thought in the English Commonwealth, 1649–1660', *History of Political Thought*, 3 (1982), pp.

193–213, esp. pp. 206–10; generally J. C. Davis, 'Living with the Living God: Radical Religion and the English Revolution', in Durston and Maltby (eds), *Religion in Revolutionary England*, ch. 1.

66. In spite of its title, the pamphlet was in response to a tract (*An Essay Towards Settlement* – 19 September 1659) that was written not just by Fifth Monarchists, but by Baptists and ex-Levellers as well: see Capp, *Fifth Monarchy Men*, p. 126.

67. Edward Johnson, *An Examination of the Essay: Or, An Answer to the Fifth Monarchy* (London, 1659), p. 4.

68. J. H. Elliott, 'Revolution and Continuity in Early Modern Europe', *Past and Present*, 42 (1969), pp. 35–56; Condren, *Language of Politics*, ch. 5; Condren, 'Radicals, Conservatives and Moderates'; Davis, 'Radicalism in a Traditional Society'.

69. Millenarianism has been much examined; but for an account well geared to the discussion of radicalism, see Christopher Hill, *Antichrist in Seventeenth-Century England* (Oxford, 1971). For a useful summary, see Bernard Capp, 'The Political Dimension of Apocalyptic Thought', in C. A. Patrides and Joseph Wittreich (eds), *The Apocalypse in English Renaissance Thought and Literature* (Manchester, 1984), ch. 4. The best introduction to providentialism is Alexandra Walsham, *Providence in Early Modern England* (Oxford, 1999); also Blair Worden, 'Providence and Politics in Cromwellian England', *Past and Present*, 109 (1985), pp. 55–99.

70. Independent arguments are discussed in the previous chapter. For a general survey of religious arguments in defence of the Commonwealth, see Margaret Judson, *From Tradition to Political Reality: A Study of the Ideas Set Forth in Support of the Commonwealth Government in England, 1649–1653* (Hamden, CT, 1980), ch. 2.

71. Glenn Burgess, 'Usurpation, Obligation and Obedience in the Thought of the Engagement Controversy', *Historical Journal*, 29 (1986), pp. 515–36.

72. John Canne, *The Golden Rule, or Justice Advanced* (London, 1649), p. 36.

73. 'Eleutherius Philodemius', *The Armies Vindication* (London, 1649), 'To the Reader' [the tract is a reply to William Sedgwick].

74. *A Declaration of the Parliament of England, Expressing the Grounds of their Late Proceedings, and of Settling the Present Government in the Way of a Free State* (22 March 1649), in Cobbett (ed.), *Parliamentary History*, vol. III, cols 1298, 1304.

75. *A Declaration of the Parliament of England, in Vindication of their Proceedings* (28 September 1649), in Cobbett (ed.), *Parliamentary History*, vol. III, col. 1319.

76. G. E. Aylmer (ed.), 'England's Spirit Unfoulded, Or An Incouragement to Take the Engagement: A Newly Discovered Pamphlet by Gerrard Winstanley', *Past and Present*, 40 (1968), pp. 3–15, at 9–10. On this theme see also Darren Webb, 'Contract, Covenant and Class-Consciousness: Gerrard Winstanley and the Broken Promises of the English Revolution', *History of Political Thought*, 24 (2003), pp. 577–98.

77. There has been extensive debate over whether Winstanley's thought in the period 1649–52 was primarily theological in nature, or primarily secular–materialist: for a useful survey of the discussion, see Andrew Bradstock, 'Sowing in Hope: the Relevance of Theology to Gerrard Winstanley's Political Programme', *The Seventeenth Century*, 6 (1991), pp. 189–204.

78. Nicola Baxter, 'Gerrard Winstanley's Experimental Knowledge of God (The Perception of the Spirit and the Acting of Reason)', *Journal of Ecclesiastical History*, 39 (1988), pp. 184–201, at 195.

79. Cf. Nigel Smith, *Perfection Proclaimed: Language and Literature in English Radical Religion, 1640–1660* (Oxford, 1989), pp. 229–30 (see also 258–61); and Smith, *Literature and Revolution in England, 1640–1660* (New Haven, CT, 1994), ch. 5 for an account of the intractable problems involved in expressing in writing the relationship between God and the inner man.

80. Smith, *Literature and Revolution*, p. 175.

81. The best account of the Surrey Diggers is now John Gurney, 'Gerrard Winstanley and the Digger Movement in Walton and Cobham', *Historical Journal*, 37 (1994), pp. 775–802; and Andrew Bradstock (ed.), *Winstanley and the Diggers, 1649–1999* (London, 2000).

82. Gerrard Winstanley, *A Watch-Word to the City of London and the Army* (26 August 1649), in Winstanley, *The Law of Freedom and Other Writings*, ed. Christopher Hill (Harmondsworth, 1973), pp. 127–8.

83. Gerrard Winstanley, *The New Law of Righteousnes* (26 January 1649), in *The Works of Gerrard Winstanley*, ed. George H. Sabine (New York, 1965), p. 190.

84. Gerrard Winstanley, *The True Levellers' Standard Advanced* (20 April 1649), in Winstanley, *Law of Freedom*, p. 83.

85. Winstanley, *New Law of Righteousnes*, p. 156.

86. Gerrard Winstanley, *A New-Year's Gift for the Parliament and Army* (1 January 1650), in Winstanley, *Law of Freedom*, p. 172.

87. See J. C. Davis, 'Gerrard Winstanley and the Restoration of True Magistracy', *Past and Present*, 70 (1976), pp. 76–93; L. Mulligan, J. Graham and J. Richards, 'Winstanley: a Case for the Man as He Said He Was', *Journal of Ecclesiastical History*, 28 (1977), pp. 57–75, at p. 61, n. 1. Also J. C. Davis, *Utopia and the Ideal Society: A Study of English Utopian Writing, 1516–1700* (Cambridge, 1981), ch. 7.

88. It should be noted that in *The True Law of Righteousnes*, published on 26 January 1649, before the digging began, Winstanley did imagine a process whereby the whole system of landlordism could be destroyed if the poor withdrew their labour (see Davis, 'Restoration of True Magistracy', pp. 81–3). The argument is almost completely absent from the writings that accompanied the actual digging, suggesting the tactical need to appear unthreatening in such circumstances. See Winstanley, *New Law of Righteousnes*, in *Works of Gerrard Winstanley*, pp. 191–2, 194, 195–6, 200–1.

89. Abiezer Coppe, *A Fiery Flying Roll* (1649 – collected by Thomason on 4 January 1650), in Nigel Smith (ed.), *A Collection of Ranter Writings from the 17th Century* (London, 1983), p. 87. For Coppe's social and political thought see especially J. C. Davis, *Fear, Myth and History: The Ranters and the Historians* (Cambridge, 1986), pp. 48–57; Davis, 'Abiezer Coppe and the Well-Favoured Harlot: the Ranters and the English Revolution', *The Turnbull Library Record*, 20 (1987), pp. 17–30; on his language, see McDowell, *English Radical Imagination*, ch. 4. Davis's work sparked considerable controversy: see especially, Davis, 'Fear, Myth and Furore: Reappraising the "Ranters"', *Past and Present*, 129 (1990), pp. 79–103; and the symposium 'Debate: Fear, Myth and History: Reappraising the Ranters', *Past and Present*, 140 (1993), pp. 155–210.

90. The best introduction is probably Barry Reay, *The Quakers and the English Revolution* (New York, 1985) – N.B. p. 40: 'Quakerism is devoid of any coherent and identifiable political philosophy.' Also Rosemary Moore, *The Light in their Consciences: The Early Quakers in Britain, 1646–1666* (Pittsburgh, PA, 2001).

91. See generally, ibid., pp. 37–45; and Christopher Hill, *The World Turned Upside Down* (London, 1972), ch. 9.

92. Thomas Aldam, *False Prophets and False Teachers Described* (1652), in Hugh Barbour and Arthur Roberts (eds), *Early Quaker Writings, 1650–1700* (Grand Rapids, MI, 1973), p. 360.

93. Edward Burrough, *A Message of Instruction, to All the Rulers, Judges and Magistrates, to Whom the Law Is Committed* (1657), in Barbour and Roberts (eds), *Early Quaker Writings*, pp. 364–71.

94. Cf. Alan Cole, 'The Quakers and the English Revolution', in Trevor Aston (ed.), *Crisis in Europe, 1560–1660* (London, 1965), ch. 14.

95. See T. L. Underwood, 'Early Quaker Eschatology', in Peter Toon (ed.), *Puritans, the Millennium and the Future of Israel: Puritan Eschatology, 1600 to 1660* (Cambridge, 1970), ch. 5, esp. p. 99.

96. John Tillinghast, *Mr. Tillinghasts Eight Last Sermons* (London, 1655), p. 30.

97. On this habit of assessing radicals in terms of their 'realism', see the comments in Davis, 'Radicalism in a Traditional Society', pp. 196–201.

98. The seminal work on the theme is J. C. Davis, 'Against Formality: One Aspect of the English Revolution', *Transactions of the Royal Historical Society*, 6th series, 3 (1993), pp. 265–88. See also Davis, 'Cromwell's Religion', in J. S. Morrill (ed.), *Oliver Cromwell and the English Revolution* (London, 1990), ch. 7, for antiformalism; and Davis, 'The Levellers and Christianity', in Brian Manning (ed.), *Politics, Religion and the Englsih Civil War* (London, 1973), for practical Christianity.

99. I have sketched this perspective on radicalism in Glenn Burgess, 'The Impact on Political Thought: Rhetorics for Troubled Times', in J. S. Morrill (ed.), *The Impact of the English Civil War* (London, 1991), ch. 4.

100. Winstanley, *New Year's Gift*, in Winstanley, *Law of Freedom*, p. 161. Cf. Webb, 'Contract, Covenant and Class-Consciousness'.

101. William Covell, *A Declaration unto the Parliament, Council of State and Army* (London, 1659), pp. 7–8. On Covell's activities at Enfield, see J. Max Patrick, 'William Covell and the Troubles at Enfield in 1659: a Sequel to the Digger Movement', *University of Toronto*

Quarterly, 14 (1944–5), pp. 45–7; and Christopher Hill, *The Experience of Defeat: Milton and Some Contemporaries* (London, 1984), pp. 40–2.

102. He also demanded religious toleration and the abolition of 'ecclesiastical powers': Covell, *Declaration unto the Parliament*, pp. 8–9.

103. Gerrard Winstanley, *Truth Lifting Up its Head Above Scandals* (1649), in *Works of Gerrard Winstanley* (ed. Sabine), p. 111.

104. Winstanley, *New Year's Gift*, in Winstanley, *Law of Freedom*, p. 171.

105. Gerrard Winstanley, *Fire in the Bush* (March 1650), in Winstanley, *Law of Freedom*, pp. 213, 216.

106. The following remarks are indebted to Davis, 'The Levellers and Christianity', in Manning (ed.), *Politics, Religion and the English Civil War*, esp. pp. 234ff. See also Brian Manning, 'The Levellers and Religion', in J. F. McGregor and B. Reay (eds), *Radical Religion in the English Revolution* (Oxford, 1984), ch. 3.

107. Walwyn, et al., *A Manifestation*, in Haller and Davies (eds), *Leveller Tracts*, pp. 277, 281.

108. John Lilburne, et al., *The Picture of the Councel of State* (1649), in Haller and Davies (eds), *Leveller Tracts*, p. 231.

109. William Walwyn, *A Still and Soft Voice from the Scriptures* (March–April 1647), in *Writings of William Walwyn*, ed. McMichael and Taft, pp. 268–9.

110. Ibid., p. 269.

111. For a different emphasis, see John Coffey, 'Puritanism and Liberty Revisited: the Case for Toleration in the English Revolution', *Historical Journal*, 41 (1998), pp. 961–85; and Coffey, 'Toleration Controversy'.

112. William Walwyn, *The Power of Love* (19 September 1643), in *Writings of William Walwyn*, ed. McMichael and Taft, p. 94.

113. William Walwyn, *The Compassionate Samaratine* (2nd edn, July 1644), in *Writings of William Walwyn*, ed. McMichael and Taft, p. 116.

114. For one of the most powerful statements, which imposes no limits on the range of views to be tolerated and explicitly includes atheists, see William Walwyn, *Tolleration Justified* (January 1646), in *Writings of William Walwyn*, ed. McMichael and Taft, p. 164.

115. Covell, *Declaration unto the Parliament*, pp. 14–15.

116. See especially J. C. Davis, 'Religion and the Struggle for Freedom in the English Revolution', *Historical Journal*, 35 (1992), pp. 507–30; also William Lamont, *Puritanism and Historical Controversy* (London, 1996), ch. 6.

117. For the last, Rachel Foxley, 'John Lilburne and the Citizenship of "Free-Born Englishmen"', *Historical Journal*, 47 (2004), pp. 849–74.

118. *The Selected Writings of Sir Edward Coke*, ed. Steve Sheppard, 3 vols (Indianapolis, 2003), vol. II, pp. 912, 758, 851.

119. Ibid., vol. III, pp. 1246–7.

120. S. R. Gardiner (ed.), *The Constitutional Documents of the Puritan Revolution, 1625–1660*, 3rd edn (Oxford, 1906), pp. 374–5.

121. Isaiah Berlin, 'Two Concepts of Liberty', in Berlin, *Four Essays on Liberty* (Oxford, 1969), ch. 3. Negative liberty meant 'not being interfered with by others' (p. 123), while positive liberty 'consists in being one's own master' (p. 131).

122. As in J. G. A. Pocock, 'Virtues, Rights and Manners: a Model for Historians of Political Thought', in Pocock (ed.), *Virtue, Commerce, and History: Essays on Political Thought and History, Chiefly in the Eighteenth Century* (Cambridge, 1985), ch. 2, esp. pp. 40–1.

123. Quentin Skinner, 'The Idea of Negative Liberty: Philosophical and Historical Perspectives', in Richard Rorty, J. B. Schneewind and Quentin Skinner (eds), *Philosophy in History* (Cambridge, 1984), pp. 193–221; Quentin Skinner, 'The Republican Ideal of Political Liberty', in Gisela Bock, Quentin Skinner and Maurizio Viroli (eds), *Machiavelli and Republicanism* (Cambridge, 1990), ch. 15; Skinner, *Liberty Before Liberalism* (Cambidge, 1998); Skinner, *Hobbes and Republican Liberty* (Cambridge, 2008).

124. Cf. Skinner, *Hobbes and Republican Liberty*, Preface; Quentin Skinner, 'Classical Liberty, Renaissance Translation, and the English Civil War', in Skinner, *Visions of Politics*, 3 vols (Cambridge, 2002), vol. II, ch. 12; Skinner, 'Rethinking Political Liberty in the English Revolution', *History Workshop Journal*, 61 (2006), pp. 156–70.

125. Davis, 'Religion and the Struggle for Freedom', passim.

126. Richard Baxter, *A Holy Commonwealth* [1659], ed. William Lamont (Cambridge, 1994), p. 80.

127. Ibid., p. 102.

128. Ibid., pp. 102, 106ff.
129. Anon., *Tyranipocrit Discovered with his Wiles* (Rotterdam, [London?], 1649), p. 43.
130. Gerrard Winstanley, 'The Law of Freedom in a Platform' (1651), in Winstanley, *Law of Freedom*, ed. Hill, pp. 385–6.
131. For a contrasting view, Darren Webb, 'The Bitter Product of Defeat? Reflections on Winstanley's *Law of Freedom*', *Political Studies*, 52 (2004), pp. 199–215.
132. Henry Stubbe, *An Essay in Defence of the Good Old Cause* (London, 1659), sig. *4v, p. 1.

Notes to Chapter 7

1. For a summary of what can be known, see Noel Malcolm, *Reason of State, Propaganda, and the Thirty Years War: An Unknown Translation by Thomas Hobbes* (Oxford, 2007), pp. 82–91. I do not believe that the discourses in Thomas Hobbes, *Three Discourses: A Critical Modern Edition of Newly Identified Work of the Young Hobbes*, ed. Noel B. Reynolds and Arlene W. Saxonhouse (Chicago, 1995) are actually by Hobbes.
2. Malcolm, *Reason of State*, pp. 114–23. Cf. Richard Tuck, 'Hobbes and Tacitus', in G. A. J. Rogers and Tom Sorrell, *Hobbes and History* (London, 2000), based on accepting Hobbes's authorship of the discourses mentioned in n. 1 above; and Kinch Hoekstra, 'The End of Philosophy (the Case of Hobbes)', *Proceedings of the Aristotelian Society*, 106 (2006), pp. 23–48.
3. *The Correspondence of Thomas Hobbes*, ed. Noel Malcolm, 2 vols (Oxford, 1994), vol. I, p. 120.
4. Thomas Hobbes, *Leviathan*, ed. Richard Tuck (Cambridge, 1991), ch. xliii, p. 402.
5. Thomas Hobbes, *Behemoth*, ed. Ferdinand Tönnies (Chicago, 1990), pp. 2–4: the points are much expanded in the immediately following pages. See further, Jeffrey R. Collins, *The Allegiance of Thomas Hobbes* (Oxford, 2005), pp. 82–7.
6. Notably, Richard Schlatter, 'Thomas Hobbes and Thucydides', *Journal of the History of Ideas*, 6 (1945), pp. 350–62; Miriam Reik, *The Golden Lands of Thomas Hobbes* (Detroit, 1977), ch. ii; Jonathan Scott, 'The Peace of Silence: Thucydides and the English Civil War', in Rogers and Sorrell, *Hobbes and History*, ch. 7.
7. Thucydides, *The Peloponnesian War: The Complete Hobbes Translation*, ed. David Grene (Chicago, 1989), pp. 572–3.
8. Thomas Hobbes, 'The Autobiography of Thomas Hobbes', transl. Benjamin Farrington, *The Rationalist Annual* (1958), pp. 22–31, at p. 25.
9. See especially David Johnston, *The Rhetoric of Leviathan* (Princeton, NJ, 1986); William R. Lund, 'Hobbes on Opinion, Private Judgment and Civil War', *History of Political Thought*, 13 (1992), pp. 51–72; Quentin Skinner, *Reason and Rhetoric in the Philosophy of Hobbes* (Cambridge, 1996); Conal Condren, *Thomas Hobbes* (New York, 2000), ch. 6.
10. Skinner, *Reason and Rhetoric*, pp. 426–37.
11. See Deborah Baumgold, 'The Composition of Hobbes's *Elements of Law*', *History of Political Thought*, 25 (2004), pp. 16–43.
12. This and other biographical details are from Noel Malcolm, *Aspects of Hobbes* (Oxford, 2002), ch. 1 [p. 9]; see also A. P. Martinich, *Hobbes: A Biography* (Cambridge, 1999), pp. 84–5.
13. A good introduction to some of the issues is Tom Sorrell, 'Hobbes's Scheme of the Sciences', in Sorrell (ed.), *The Cambridge Companion to Hobbes* (Cambridge, 1996), ch. 2; Condren, *Thomas Hobbes*, ch. 2.
14. Thomas Hobbes, *De Corpore*, i, 2, in Hobbes, *Body, Man, and Citizen*, ed. R. S. Peters (New York, 1962), p. 24.
15. Ibid., i, 9 (p. 30).
16. For an introduction, see Richard Tuck, 'Hobbes's Moral Philosophy', in Sorrell (ed.), *Cambridge Companion to Hobbes*, ch. 8; Tom Sorell, 'Hobbes's Moral Philosophy', in Patricia Springborg (ed.), *The Cambridge Companion to Hobbes's Leviathan* (Cambridge, 2007), ch. 5; more broadly, Susan James, *Passion and Action: The Emotions in Seventeenth-Century Philosophy* (Oxford, 1997), ch. 6.
17. Thomas Hobbes, *Elements of Law Natural and Politic*, ed. Ferdinand Tönnies (London, 1969), I, vii, 1, p. 28.
18. Ibid., I, vii, 3, p. 29.
19. Ibid., I, vii, 4, p. 29.
20. See, e.g., Ibid., I, xii, 6, p. 63; and I, xix, 1, pp. 99–100.

21. Ibid., I, xix, 4, p. 101.
22. Ibid., I, xix, 6–7, p. 103.
23. Ibid., I, xix, 9, p. 104.
24. Ibid., I, xix, 10, p. 104; also II, i, 7, p. 111.
25. Ibid., II, i, 9, p. 112.
26. Ibid., II, i, 10, p. 112.
27. Ibid., II, xii, 6, p. 63.
28. Compare ibid., II, ix, 8, pp. 183–4, and II, x, 8, pp. 188–9, with the statements in Thomas Hobbes, *De Cive*, ch. Vi, sect. 11, ch. Xii, ch. Iii, sect. 5, 9 (I have used throughout this chapter the translation in Thomas Hobbes, *On the Citizen*, ed. Richard Tuck and Michael Silverthorne (Cambridge, 1998)); and Hobbes, *Leviathan*, ch. xviii, pp. 124–5; ch. xxiii, pp. 167–8; and ch. xxx, pp. 233–8.
29. For which, see Glenn Burgess, *The Politics of the Ancient Constitution* (Basingstoke, 1992), ch. viii.
30. Thomas Hobbes, *Considerations upon the Reputation, Loyalty, Manners, and Religion of Thomas Hobbes* (1680; first published in 1662, with a different title), in *The English Works of Thomas Hobbes* [hereafter cited as *E. W.*], ed. William Molesworth (London, 1839–45), iv, p. 414 – stress added.
31. Cf. John Laird, *Hobbes* (London, 1934), pp. 73–81; Baumgold, 'Composition of Hobbes's *Elements*', pp. 30–1.
32. This claim is based on the indexes to *E.W.* and to Hobbes, *Opera Philosophica quae Latine Scripsit Omnia*, ed. William Molesworth, 5 vols (London, 1839–45).
33. Hobbes, *Elements*, II, viii, 7, pp. 172–3, citing Bodin, *Six Livres de la République*, ii, 1. The chapter can conveniently be found translated in Bodin, *On Sovereignty*, ed. Julian Franklin (Cambridge, 1992), pp. 46–88. Note also that Bodin powerfully expressed the notion of inseparability: 'all the jurists agree that the rights of the crown cannot be relinquished or alienated', i, 10, p. 49.
34. Hobbes, *Elements*, II, i, 13, p. 113.
35. Ibid., II, viii, 6, p. 172; also II, i, 7–12, pp. 111–13.
36. Ibid., II, v, 2, pp. 139–40; see also II, viii, 8, p. 174; and II, ix, 5, p. 181, which adds to the picture the point that the sovereign ought clearly to determine his subjects' property rights *vis-à-vis* one another; and ought to 'charge' them 'proportionably'.
37. See his 1647 Preface to *De Cive*, in Hobbes, *On the Citizen*, ed. Tuck and Silverthorne, p. 14.
38. Hobbes, *Elements*, II, v, 8, p. 143, repeating an argument that Hobbes had used in his introduction to Thucydides; see Thucydides, *Peloponnesian War*, pp. 572–3.
39. For this, see esp. John Morrill, *The Nature of the English Revolution* (London, 1993), ch. 4.
40. Hobbes, *Elements*, II, viii, 14, pp. 177–8.
41. Hobbes, *On the Citizen*, xvii, 27–8, pp. 230–2. Contrast Hobbes, *Elements*, I, xi, 9–10, pp. 58–9, where the sovereign's role is not mentioned; though, N.B. II, vii, 11, p. 167.
42. Hobbes, *On the Citizen*, vi, 11, p. 80. There is no direct equivalent of this passage in the *Elements*.
43. The matter is well and succinctly discussed in George Croom Robertson, *Hobbes* (Edinburgh, 1901), pp. 193–6; further, Richard Tuck, *Philosophy and Government, 1572–1651* (Cambridge, 1993), pp. 335–45; Jon Parkin, *Taming the Leviathan: The Reception of the Political and Religious Ideas of Thomas Hobbes in England 1640–1700* (Cambridge, 2007), chs 4 and 5.
44. Susan Moller Okin, 'The Sovereign and his Counsellours: Hobbes's Reevaluation of Parliament', *Political Theory*, 10 (1982), pp. 49–75.
45. Hobbes, *Behemoth*, p. 47.
46. Ibid., p. 51.
47. Compare Hobbes, *Leviathan*, ch. xxiv, p. 173; ch. xix, p. 131.
48. Thomas Hobbes, *A Dialogue between a Philosopher and a Student, of the Common Laws of England*, ed. Alan Cromartie (Oxford, 2005), p. 48.
49. Hobbes, *Leviathan*, ch. xxvi, pp. 183–4, 187–8, 189–90 – also, for a list of the types of law, pp. 196–7, and on the definition of a good law, ch. xxx, pp. 239–40.
50. Ibid., ch. xxix, p. 223.
51. Instructive in this regard is Hobbes's comparison of *Leviathan* with Plato's *Republic* (ch. xxxi, p. 254), which clearly focused on the requirements that each imposes on the sovereign. Sovereigns *needed* to understand 'the Science of Naturall Justice'.

52. Condren, *Thomas Hobbes*, p. 79.
53. But there are complexities: see Kinch Hoekstra, 'Tyrannus Rex *v.* Leviathan', *Pacific Philosophical Quarterly*, 82 (2001), pp. 420–46.
54. For the relationship of *Leviathan* to Hobbes's earlier work, and for its composition, see especially G. A. J. Rogers and Karl Schuhmann (eds), *Thomas Hobbes: Leviathan – A Critical Edition*, 2 vols, pbk edn (London, 2005), vol. I.
55. Hobbes, *Elements*, II, i, 3, p. 109; II, ii, 1, p. 118.
56. Hobbes, *On the Citizen*, vii, 5, p. 94. For the continuing acceptance of aboriginal democracy, see also vii, 11, p. 96: '*Monarchy* . . . is derived from the power of the *people*, viz., by the transfer of its *right* . . . to *one man*', which act makes the people 'no longer one *person*, but a disorganized crowd'.
57. There are a great many hidden complexities in Hobbes's authorisation argument. I am indebted to – though not always in agreement with – discussions in David Gauthier, *The Logic of Leviathan* (Oxford, 1969), pp. 99–177; Jean Hampton, *Hobbes and the Social Contract Tradition* (Cambridge, 1986), ch. v; and Quentin Skinner, 'Hobbes on Persons, Authors and Representatives', in Springborg (ed.), *Cambridge Companion to . . . Leviathan*, ch. 6.
58. Hobbes, *Leviathan*, ch. xiii. See the valuable account in Kinch Hoekstra, 'Hobbes on the Natural Condition of Mankind', in Springborg (ed.), *Cambridge Companion to . . . Leviathan*, ch. 4.
59. Hobbes, *Leviathan*, ch. xiii, p. 87.
60. Ibid., ch. xiii, p. 88.
61. Ibid., ch. xiii, p. 89.
62. Ibid., ch. xiii, p. 90.
63. See Quentin Skinner, 'Hobbes on Rhetoric and the Construction of Morality', in Skinner, *Visions of Politics*, 3 vols (Cambridge, 2002), vol. III, ch. 4 for an account of the importance of the rhetorical figure of *paradiastole* ('the precise purpose of which was to show that any given action can always be redescribed in such a way as to suggest that its moral character may be open to some measure of doubt' – p. 89), for an understanding of Hobbes's thought.
64. Hobbes, *Leviathan*, ch. xv, p. 111.
65. Ibid., ch. xv, p. 110.
66. Ibid., ch. xv, p. 111.
67. Ibid., ch. xv, p. 110.
68. Ibid., ch. xv, p. 110.
69. Ibid., ch. xiv, p. 92, stress added.
70. Ibid., ch. xiv, p. 91.
71. The concept of natural right does not appear in the account of the state of nature in ch. xiii of *Leviathan*.
72. Hobbes, *Leviathan*, ch. xiv, p. 91.
73. See ibid., ch. xxxi, p. 248 for this terminology.
74. Ibid., ch. xiv, p. 92.
75. Ibid., ch. xiv, p. 92; ch. xxviii, p. 214.
76. Hampton, *Hobbes and the Social Contract Tradition*, ch. v, esp. pp. 122ff., asserts that Hobbes here employed a concept of authorisation or representation that was dangerous to him and out of keeping with the legal usage of his day; but cf. Skinner, 'Hobbes on Persons, Authors and Representatives', who rightly emphasises the way in which Hobbes was using the concept in order to undermine the language of Parliamentarians like Parker.
77. Hobbes, *Leviathan*, ch. xvii, p. 120.
78. Ibid., ch. xvii, p. 121.
79. Cf. Hampton, e.g. her short statement in *Noûs*, 22 (1988), pp. 85–6, who seems to me to raise problems that Hobbes would not have seen as such, though they are of interest in their own right.
80. Hobbes, *Leviathan*, ch. xviii, p. 122.
81. Ibid., ch. xiv, pp. 93–4.
82. Ibid., ch. xxi, p. 150. See especially Quentin Skinner, *Hobbes and Republican Liberty* (Cambridge, 2008), esp. pp. 162–73.
83. Hobbes, *Leviathan*, ch. xv, p. 100.
84. Ibid., ch. xxi, pp. 151–2.
85. Ibid., 'Review and Conclusion', p. 486, a statement the chief context of which was the Engagement Controversy: see Quentin Skinner, 'Conquest and Consent: Hobbes and the

Engagement Controversy', in Skinner, *Visions*, vol. III, ch. 10; Glenn Burgess, 'Contexts for the Writing and Publication of Hobbes's *Leviathan*', *History of Political Thought*, 11 (1990), pp. 675–702; Conal Condren, *Argument and Authority in Early Modern England: The Presupposition of Oaths and Offices* (Cambridge, 2006), pp. 308–13; Skinner, *Hobbes and Republican Liberty*, ch. 6.

86. Hobbes, *Leviathan*, ch. xx, p. 138.
87. Cf. Richard Ashcraft, 'Political Theory and Practical Action: a Reconsideration of Hobbes's State of Nature', *Hobbes Studies*, 1 (1988), pp. 63–88; provocative on these matters is Kinch Hoekstra, 'The *De Facto* Turn in Hobbes's Political Philosophy', in Tom Sorrell and Luc Foisneau (eds), *Leviathan after 350 Years* (Oxford, 2004), pp. 330–73; also Charles Tarlton, '"To Avoyd the Present Stroke of Death": Despotical Dominion, Force and Legitimacy in Hobbes's *Leviathan*', *Philosophy*, 74 (1999), pp. 221–45.
88. Hobbes, *Leviathan*, ch. xx, p. 139.
89. Ibid., ch. xx, p. 141, marginal note.
90. Ibid., ch. xx, p. 141.
91. Cf. for example, the view credited to Henry Parker and others, in Tuck, *Philosophy and Government*, pp. 228–40.
92. Hobbes, *Leviathan*, ch. xix, p. 130.
93. Ibid., ch. xxix, p. 228.
94. Ibid., ch. xix, p. 131.
95. Ibid., ch. xviii, p. 124.
96. Ibid., ch. xviii, p. 124.
97. Ibid., ch. xxix, pp. 224–5; also ch. xviii, p. 125.
98. Ibid., ch. xviii, p. 124.
99. Norberto Bobbio, *Hobbes and the Natural Law Tradition* (Chicago, 1993), p. 114.
100. The following paragraph relies heavily on the analysis of legal language in Wesley Newcomb Hohfeld, *Fundamental Legal Conceptions as Applied in Judicial Reasoning* (New Haven, CT, 1919; new edn, 1964); and the excellent summary of Hohfeld in P. J. Fitzgerald, *Salmond on Jurisprudence*, 12th edn(London, 1966), pp. 224ff.
101. Cf. Fitzgerald, *Salmond on Jurisprudence*, p. 226.
102. Some of the oddity of this position is apparent from a comparison with ibid., p. 216.
103. Cf. ibid., p. 232.
104. Cf. Glenn Burgess, 'On Hobbesian Resistance Theory', *Political Studies*, 42 (1994), pp. 62–83.
105. Hobbes, *Leviathan*, ch. xxiv, p. 172; ch. xxx, p. 237.
106. Ibid., ch. xviii, p. 124.
107. Ibid., ch. xxxi, p. 254.
108. Hobbes, *On the Citizen*, xiii, 17, p. 152.
109. For some investigation of this matter, see Charles D. Tarlton, 'The Creation and Maintenance of Government: a Neglected Dimension of Hobbes's *Leviathan*', *Political Studies*, XXVI (1978), pp. 307–27.
110. Hobbes, *Leviathan*, ch. xxx, pp. 231–2.
111. Ibid., ch. xxx, p. 232. Cf. the interesting reading of this passage in Tarlton, 'Creation and Maintenance of Government', pp. 322–3.
112. Hobbes, *Leviathan*, ch. xxx, pp. 232–5.
113. Ibid., ch. xxx, pp. 235–6.
114. Ibid., ch. xxx, p. 237.
115. Ibid., ch. xxx, p. 238.
116. Ibid., ch. xxx, p. 239.
117. Examples of the atheist reading of Hobbes include Leo Strauss, *Natural Right and History* (Chicago, 1950), ch. v; David Berman, *A History of Atheism in Britain* (London, 1988), esp. pp. 57–67; and especially Edwin Curley, '"I Durst Not Write So Boldly': or How to Read Hobbes' Theological–Political Treatise', in Daniela Bostrenghi (ed.), *Hobbes e Spinoza: Scienza e Politica* (Naples, 1992), pp. 497–593. But cf. Condren, *Thomas Hobbes*, pp. 55–7.
118. Cf. the important discussions of J. G. A. Pocock, 'Time, History and Eschatology in the Thought of Thomas Hobbes', in Pocock, *Politics, Language and Time* (London, 1972), ch. v, esp. pp. 160–2, 176–7; and Patricia Springborg, '*Leviathan* and the Problem of Ecclesiastical Authority', *Political Studies*, 3 (1975), pp. 289–303, at 289–90. Of other recent works on Hobbes's religion, particularly important are Richard Tuck, 'The Civil Religion of Thomas Hobbes', in Nicholas Phillipson and Quentin Skinner (eds), *Political*

Discourse in Early Modern Britain (Cambridge, 1993), ch. vi; A. P. Martinich, *The Two Gods of Leviathan* (Cambridge, 1992); Collins, *Allegiance of Thomas Hobbes.*

119. Skinner, *Reason and Rhetoric*, ch. 10.
120. Hobbes, *Leviathan*, ch. vi, p. 42.
121. Ibid., ch. xxxi, p. 246.
122. Ibid., ch. xxvi, p. 198: the atheist rejects all of God's laws '*except* the Laws Naturall' (stress added). This whole passage (pp. 197–9) appears directly to contradict a number of things said elsewhere.
123. Hobbes, *De Cive*, ed. Gert, xv, 2, pp. 290–1; *Leviathan*, ch. xxxi, pp. 245–6. Cf. the discussion in Richard Woodfield, 'Hobbes on the Laws of Nature and the Atheist', *Renaissance and Modern Studies*, 15 (1971), pp. 34–43.
124. Hobbes, *Leviathan*, ch. xxxv, pp. 280–4.
125. Ibid., ch. xxxi, p. 246.
126. Ibid., ch. xxxv, p. 284.
127. Ibid., ch. xl, pp. 324–5.
128. As shown in Joel Schwartz, 'Hobbes and the Two Kingdoms of God', *Polity*, 18 (1985), pp. 7–24 (based, however, on the *De Cive* account).
129. Hobbes, *Leviathan*, ch. xl, p. 328.
130. Ibid., ch. xl, pp. 330–1.
131. Ibid., ch. xxxii, p. 257; but compare the discussion in pp. 256–9 with ch. xxxvi, pp. 297–300, which qualifies the earlier discussion by making, in the Christian present, the civil sovereign God's chief prophet.
132. Ibid., ch. xxxii, p. 259; cf. ch. xxxvii, pp. 305–6, which again could be interpreted as modifying the earlier point.
133. On Hobbes's mortalism, see David Johnston, 'Hobbes's Mortalism', *History of Political Thought*, 10 (1989), pp. 647–63.
134. Hobbes, *Leviathan*, ch. xxxv, p. 284; ch. xxxviii, pp. 311–20; ch. xli, pp. 334–6.
135. Ibid., ch. xxxii, pp. 256–7; ch. xxxi, p. 246.
136. See also Kinch Hoekstra, 'Disarming the Prophets: Thomas Hobbes and Predictive Power', *Rivista di Storia della Filosofia*, 21 (2004), pp. 97–153.
137. Hobbes, *Leviathan*, ch. xliv, pp. 419–22, 426–9; also ch. xlii, pp. 378–402.
138. Ibid., ch. xxxix, p. 321.
139. On which, see ibid., ch. xxii, pp. 155–65.
140. Ibid., ch. xlvii, pp. 479–80. A further strict conclusion from these premises was the doctrine of Christian obedience to infidel rulers: see ch. xlii, pp. 399–400. The church, as an association of subjects like any other, had no rights against *any* sovereign. Hobbes's ecclesiology has recently received some valuable contextual discussion – see especially, Collins, *Allegiance of Thomas Hobbes*; J. P. Sommerville, 'Hobbes and Independency', *Rivista di Storia Filosofia*, 59 (2004), pp. 155–73; and Sommerville, '*Leviathan* and its Anglican Context', in Springborg (ed.), *Cambridge Companion to . . . Leviathan*, ch. 15.
141. Ibid., ch. xxxix, pp. 321–2; ch. xlii, pp. 377–8.
142. Ibid., ch. xlii, p. 341.
143. Ibid., ch. xlii, pp. 356–62.
144. See further on this subject, Malcolm, *Aspects of Hobbes*, ch. 12.
145. Hobbes, *Leviathan*, ch. xxxiv, p. 267.
146. Ibid., ch. xxxiv, p. 268.
147. Ibid., ch. xxxiv, p. 268.
148. His initial statement of the point was in Richard Tuck, 'Warrender's *De Cive*', *Political Studies*, 33 (1985), pp. 308–15; also Richard Tuck, *Hobbes* (Oxford, 1989), pp. 84–8. Contrast Lodi Nauta, 'Hobbes on Religion and the Church between *The Elements of Law* and *Leviathan*: a Dramatic Change of Direction?', *Journal of the History of Ideas*, 63 (2002), pp. 577–98; also Sommerville, '*Leviathan* and its Anglican Context'.
149. Hobbes, *Leviathan*, ch. xxxiv, p. 268.
150. Ibid., ch. xliii, p. 403.
151. Ibid., ch. xxxi, pp. 248–53.
152. Thomas Hobbes, *Seven Philosophical Problems* (1662), Ep. Ded. in *E. W.*, vii, p. 5.
153. Hobbes, *Leviathan*, ch. xlii, p. 343; ch. xliii, pp. 413–14.
154. Ibid., ch. xlvi, p. 471.
155. See esp. Richard Tuck, 'Hobbes and Locke on Toleration', in Mary G. Dietz (ed.), *Thomas Hobbes and Political Theory* (Lawrence, KS, 1990), ch. viii; Alan Ryan, 'Hobbes,

Toleration, and the Inner Life', in David Miller and Larry Siedentop (eds), *The Nature of Political Theory* (Oxford, 1983), pp. 197–218; Ryan, 'A More Tolerant Hobbes?', in Susan Mendus (ed.), *Justifying Toleration* (Cambridge, 1988), ch. ii; J. P. Sommerville, *Thomas Hobbes: Political Ideas in Historical Context* (Basingstoke, 1992), pp. 149–56; and Edwin Curley, 'Hobbes and the Cause of Religious Toleration', in Springborg (ed.), *Cambridge Companion to . . . Leviathan*, ch. 13.

Notes to Chapter 8

1. Jonathan Scott, *Commonwealth Principles: Republican Writing in the English Revolution* (Cambridge, 2004), p. 42.
2. J. G. A. Pocock and Gordon J. Schochet, 'Interregnum and Restoration', in Pocock, et al. (eds), *The Varieties of British Political Thought, 1500–1800* (Cambridge, 1993), ch. 5, p. 147.
3. On this last, see John Adamson, *The Noble Revolt: The Overthrow of Charles I* (London, 2007), esp. pp. 516–18.
4. Pocock and Schochet, 'Interregnum and Restoration', p. 148.
5. The major accounts of the presence of republicanism in pre-Civil War thought are Marku Peltonen, *Classical Humanism and Republicanism in English Political Thought, 1570–1640* (Cambridge, 1995); David Norbrook, *Writing the English Republic: Poetry, Rhetoric and Politics, 1627–1660* (Cambridge, 1999); and Quentin Skinner, 'Classical Liberty and the Coming of the English Civil War', in Skinner and Martin van Gelderen (eds), *Republicanism: A Shared European Heritage*, 2 vols (Cambridge, 2002), vol. II, ch. 1. For a commentary with which I am largely in agreement, see Blair Worden, 'Republicanism, Regicide and Republic: the English Experience', in Skinner and van Gelderen (eds), *Republicanism*, vol. I, ch. 15.
6. Conrad Russell, *The Causes of the English Civil* War (Oxford, 1990), p. 23 and ch. 8; Richard Tuck, *Philosophy and Government, 1572–1651* (Cambridge, 1993), ch. 6.
7. Quentin Skinner, 'Rethinking Political Liberty in the English Revolution', *History Workshop Journal*, 61 (2006), pp. 156–70.
8. Cf. Rachel Foxley, 'John Lilburne and the Citizenship of "Free-Born Englishmen"', *Historical Journal*, 47 (2004), pp. 849–74.
9. For Leveller pragmatic flexibility, see J. C. Davis, 'The Levellers and Democracy', in Charles Webster (ed.), *The Intellectual Revolution of the Seventeenth Century* (London, 1974), ch. vi.
10. S. R. Gardiner (ed.), *Constitutional Documents of the Puritan Revolution, 1625–1660*, 3rd edn (Oxford, 1906), p. 388.
11. On defences of the Commonwealth, see Perez Zagorin, *A History of Political Thought in the English Revolution* (London, 1954), chs 5–6; and Margaret Judson, *From Tradition to Political Reality: A Study of the Ideas Set Forth in Support of the Commonwealth Government in England, 1649–1653* (Hamden, CT, 1980).
12. Cuthbert Sydenham [?], *The True Portraiture of the Kings of England* (London, 1650). On this work and its authorship, often assigned to Henry Parker, see Jason Peacey, 'Henry Parker and Parliamentary Propaganda in the English Civil Wars', unpublished Cambridge PhD thesis, 1994, pp. 137–8, 207–9, 237–8. Cf. Michael Mendle, *Henry Parker and the English Civil War: The Political Thought of the Public's 'Privado'* (Cambridge, 1995), pp. 166–7.
13. John Milton, *The Tenure of Kings and Magistrates* (February 1649), in Milton, *Political Writings*, ed. Martin Dzelzainis (Cambridge, 1991), p. 13.
14. John Milton, *Eikonoklastes* (October 1649), in *Complete Prose Works of John Milton: Volume III, 1648–1649*, ed. Merritt Y. Hughes (New Haven, CT, 962), p. 458.
15. Milton, *Tenure*, p. 11.
16. Salmasius [Claude de Saumaise], *Defensio Regia pro Carolo I* (November 1649).
17. Martin Dzelzainis, in Milton, *Political Writings*, p. xxv; John Milton, *Pro Populo Anglicano Defensio* (1651), in Milton, *Political Writings*, ed. Dzelzainis, p. 202, quoting Salmasius.
18. Milton, *Eikonoklastes*, p. 458; cf. Milton, *Pro Populo Anglicano Defensio*, pp. 203–4, 219–20, 224–5.
19. Milton, *Pro Populo Anglicano Defensio*, pp. 212–14.
20. Witness especially Milton's inadequate comment on the Independents' protestations prior to 1649 that they had no intention of changing the form of government: Milton, *Pro Populo Anglicano Defensio*, pp. 242–3.

21. *A Declaration of the Parliament of England, Expressing the Grounds of Their Late Proceedings* (22 March 1649), in William Cobbett, *The Parliamentary History of England*, 36 vols (London, 1806–20), vol. III, cols 1292–3, 1298–1302.

22. Or so mis-called: see Conal Condren, *Argument and Authority in Early Modern England: The Presupposition of Oaths and Offices* (Cambridge, 2006), ch. 14.

23. J. P. Kenyon, *The Stuart Constitution, 1603–1688: Texts and Commentary*, 2nd edn (Cambridge, 1986), p. 307.

24. The best guide is John M. Wallace, 'The Engagement Controversy, 1649–1652', *Bulletin of the New York Public Library*, 68 (1964), pp. 384–405. For discussion of the debates see especially John M. Wallace, *Destiny His Choice: The Loyalism of Andrew Marvell* (Cambridge, 1968), pp. 43–68; Glenn Burgess, 'Usurpation, Obligation and Obedience in the Thought of the Engagement Controversy', *Historical Journal*, 29 (1986), pp. 515–36; Quentin Skinner, *Visions of Politics*, 3 vols (Cambridge, 2002), vol. III, ch. 10; Edward Vallance, 'Oaths, Casuistry, and Equivocation: Anglican Responses to the Engagement Controversy', *Historical Journal*, 44 (2001), pp. 59–77; and Condren, *Argument and Authority*, ch. 14.

25. [Francis Rous], *The Lawfulnes of Obeying the Present Government* (London, 1649), pp. 1–4.

26. T.B., *The Engagement Vindicated* (London, 1650), pp. 3, 6–7, 9.

27. *The Exercitation Answered* (London, 1650), p. 8.

28. Ibid., p. 45.

29. *A Logical Demonstration of the Lawfulness of Subscribing the New Engagement* (London, 1650), pp. 3–4, 5.

30. Ibid., pp. 5–6.

31. See Blair Worden, 'Providence and Politics in Cromwellian England', *Past and Present*, 109 (1985), pp. 55–99. On Protectorate political thought, see Zagorin, *History of Political Thought in the English Revolution*, ch. 7; also Norbrook, *Writing the English Republic*, ch. 7.

32. John Moore, *Protection Proclaimed (Through the Loving Kindness of God in the Present Government) to the Three Nations of England, Scotland and Ireland* (London, 1655), t.p., epistle to the reader.

33. Ibid., pp. 1–2.

34. John Hall, *The True Cavalier Examined by his Principles* (London, 1656), p. '116' recte 114, 45.

35. Samuel Richardson, *An Apology for the Present Government and Governour* (London, 1654), p. 12.

36. Ibid., pp. 3, 4–5, 13.

37. Ibid., pp. 5–6.

38. Ibid., p. 6.

39. Thomas White, *The Grounds of Obedience and Government* [3 July 1655], 2nd edn (London, 1655), p. 9. See also B. C. Southgate, ' "That Damned Booke": *The Grounds of Obedience and Government* (1655), and the Downfall of Thomas White', *Recusant History*, 17 (1985), pp. 238–53.

40. The fullest treatment of Ascham is in Irene Coltman, *Private Men and Public Causes: Philosophy and Politics in the English Civil War* (London, 1962), part 3; but it should be read in the light of the review by John M. Wallace, *Journal of the History of Ideas*, 24 (1963), pp. 150–4.

41. [Anthony Ascham], *A Combate betweene Two Seconds* (London, 1649); [Ascham], *The Bounds and Bonds of Publique Obedience* (London, 1649); [Ascham], *Of the Confusions and Revolutions of Gover[n]ments* (London, 1649), which is the second edition of *A Discourse, wherein is Examined What is Particularly Lawfull During the Confusions and Revolutions of Government* (London, 1648); and [Ascham], *A Reply to a Paper of Dr Sandersons, Containing a Censure of Mr. A.A. His Booke* (London, 1650).

42. Ascham, *Reply*, p. 2.

43. Ibid., p. 5.

44. Ibid., p. 12.

45. Ascham, *Bounds and Bonds of Publique Obedience*, pp. 18–19.

46. Ascham, *Of the Confusions and Revolutions of Governments*, p. 7.

47. Ascham, *Bounds and Bonds of Publique Obedience*, pp. 15–16.

48. Ibid., p. 26.

49. Ascham, *Of the Confusions and Revolutions of Governments*, p. 3.

50. Ibid., pp. 134, 131.

51. On Hobbes and the Engagement Controversy, see Skinner, *Visions of Politics*, vol. III, chs 7 and 10; J. P. Sommerville, *Thomas Hobbes: Political Ideas in Historical Context* (Basingstoke, 1992), pp. 66–70; Glenn Burgess, 'Contexts for the Writing and Publication of Hobbes's *Leviathan*', *History of Political Thought*, 11 (1990), pp. 675–702; Quentin Skinner, *Hobbes and Republican Liberty* (Cambridge, 2008), ch. 6; Condren, *Argument and Authority*, pp. 308–13.

52. Thomas Hobbes, *Leviathan*, ed. Richard Tuck (Cambridge, 1991), ch. xxi, p. 153; cf. ch. xxix, p. 230.

53. David Lagomarsino and Charles T. Wood, *The Trial of Charles I: A Documentary History* (Hanover, NH, 1989), p. 124. For a useful discussion of Coke's doctrine of allegiance, see David Martin Jones, 'Sir Edward Coke and the Interpretation of Lawful Allegiance in Seventeenth-Century England', *History of Political Thought*, 7 (1986), pp. 321–40, esp. pp. 330–1.

54. Hobbes, *Leviathan*, pp. 484–5.

55. On whom, see Ian Michael Smart, 'Edward Gee and the Matter of Authority', *Journal of Ecclesiastical History*, 27 (1976), pp. 115–27.

56. [Edward Gee], *An Exercitation Concerning Usurped Powers* [18 December 1649] (London, 1649), p. 13.

57. Ibid., p. 15.

58. [Edward Gee], *A Plea for Non-Scribers* [11 June 1650] (London, 1650), p. 28.

59. Ibid., p. 19 (second pagination).

60. For a broad account of the emergence of a republican political culture in the Commonwealth, see Sean Kelsey, *Inventing a Republic: The Political Culture of the English Commonwealth, 1649–1653* (Manchester, 1997). For an overview of republican writing in this period, Jonathan Scott, *Commonwealth Principles: Republican Writing of the English Revolution* (Cambridge, 2004), esp. ch, 12.

61. See Wilbur K. Jordan, *Men of Substance: A Study of the Thought of Two English Revolutionaries* (New York, 1967; orig. edn 1942), pp. 180–7.

62. [Henry Robinson?], *A Short Discourse between Monarchical and Aristocraticall Government* (London, 1649), p. 12.

63. Ibid., pp, 14–15, 20.

64. Ibid., pp. 19, 13.

65. John Hall, *The Grounds and Reasons of Monarchy Considered* (London, 1650), pp. 2–3.

66. Marchamont Nedham, *The Case of the Commonwealth of England, Stated*, ed. Philip A. Knachel (Charlottesville, VA, 1969), p. 7.

67. For accounts of Nedham see Joseph Frank, *Cromwell's Press Agent: A Critical Biography of Marchamont Nedham, 1620–1678* (Lanham, MD, 1980); and Blair Worden, *Literature and Politics in Cromwellian England: John Milton, Andrew Marvell, Marchamont Nedham* (London, 2007), chs 1–3; also Vickie B. Sullivan, *Machiavelli, Hobbes and the Formation of a Liberal Republicanism in England* (Cambridge, 2004), ch. 3.

68. The relationship of *Mercurius Politicus* to Nedham's pamphlets was first laid out in J. Milton French, 'Milton, Nedham, and *Mercurius Politicus*', *Studies in Philology*, 33 (1936), pp. 236–52. Details have been added by Elmer A. Beller, 'Milton and *Mercurius Politicus*', *Huntington Library Quarterly*, 5 (1941–2), pp. 479–87; and H. Sylvia Anthony, '*Mercurius Politicus* under Milton', *Journal of the History of Ideas*, 27 (1966), pp. 593–609. There is a summary table in Frank, *Cromwell's Press Agent*, pp. 182–6.

69. Marchamont Nedham, *The Excellencie of a Free State* (London, 1656), p. 10; Blair Worden, 'Marchamont Nedham and the Beginnings of English Republicanism, 1649–1656', in David Wootton (ed.), *Republicanism, Liberty, and Commercial Society, 1649–1776* (Stanford, CA, 1994), pp. 64–5.

70. This reading of Harrington is especially clearly emphasised in Arihiro Fukuda, *Sovereignty and the Sword: Harrington, Hobbes, and Mixed Government in the English Civil Wars* (Oxford, 1997), chs 5–7.

71. On this see Jonathan Scott, 'The English Republican Imagination', in John Morrill (ed.), *Revolution and Restoration: England in the 1650s* (London, 1992), ch. 2, pp. 44–5.

72. See Jonathan Scott, *Algernon Sidney and the English Republic, 1623–1677* (Cambridge, 1988), pp. 111–12.

73. Quentin Skinner, *Liberty before Liberalism* (Cambridge, 1998).

74. See Mark Goldie, 'The Civil Religion of James Harrington', in Anthony Pagden (ed.), *The Languages of Political Theory in Early-Modern Europe* (Cambridge, 1987), ch. 9.

75. *Mercurius Politicus*, no. 114 (5–12 Aug. 1652), pp. 1785–9. Much of this editorial was taken from an anti-presbyterian sermon by Peter Sterry, preached on 5 November 1651, *England's Deliverance from the Northern Presbytery, Compared with its Deliverance from the Roman Papacy* (London, 1651).

76. James Harrington, 'A Discourse upon this Saying: The Spirit of the Nation is Not Yet to be Trusted with Liberty', in *The Political Works of James Harrington*, ed. J. G. A. Pocock (Cambridge, 1977), p. 737.

77. Harrington, *Political Works*, p. 738.

78. Ibid., p. 740–5.

79. Ibid., p. 744.

80. James Harrington, *The Art of Lawgiving* (1659), in ibid., p. 657.

81. A. S. P. Woodhouse, *Puritanism and Liberty*, 2nd edn (London, 1951), pp. 363–4; Don M. Wolfe, *Leveller Manifestoes of the Puritan Revolution* (New York, 1967), pp. 301, 349.

82. Harrington, *Political Works*, pp. 657–8.

83. On this point I am much indebted to the excellent analysis in Charles Blitzer, *An Immortal Commonwealth: The Political Thought of James Harrington* (New Haven, CT, 1960), ch. 3.

84. James Harrington, 'The Commonwealth of Oceana' (1656), *Political Works*, p. 163.

85. Harrington emphasised particularly, but not exclusively, landed property: for details see Blitzer, *Immortal Commonwealth*, pp. 124–7; J. G. A. Pocock, 'Historical Introduction', in Harrington, *Political Works*, pp. 55–63.

86. Cf. Fukuda, *Sovereignty and the Sword*, pp. 75–82.

87. James Harrington, 'A System of Politics' (*c*.1661), *Political Works*, p. 836. The ratio was still three to one, however, in 1659: 'The Art of Lawgiving', ibid., p. 604. Blitzer, *Immortal Commonwealth*, p. 120, n. 16.

88. Fukuda, *Sovereignty and the Sword*, pp. 80–1.

89. For Hobbes and Harrington, see Jon Parkin, *Taming the Leviathan: The Reception of the Political and Religious Ideas of Thomas Hobbes in England, 1640–1700* (Cambridge, 2007), pp. 177–85; Scott, *Commonwealth Principles*, pp. 162–6; also Sullivan, *Machiavelli, Hobbes and the Formation of a Liberal Republicanism*, pp. 165–73.

90. Skinner, *Liberty before Liberalism*, pp. 66–7, 76–7, 85–6. Also Skinner, *Visions of Politics*, vol. II, ch. 7; and Skinner, *Hobbes and Republican Liberty*, ch. 5.

91. The quotation is from Thomas Hobbes, *Elements of Law Natural and Politic*, ed. Ferdinand Tönnies (London, 1969), ep. ded., p. xv, 'as oft as reason is against a man, so oft will a man be against reason'.

92. Steven Pincus, 'Neither Machiavellian Moment nor Possessive Individualism: Commercial Society and the Defenders of the English Commonwealth', *American Historical Review*, 103 (1998), pp. 705–36, at p. 728, n. 121.

93. Blitzer, *Immortal Commonwealth*, p. 140.

94. James Harrington, 'Prerogative of Popular Government' (1658), in *Political Works*, ed. Pocock, pp. 401, 415–16.

95. See J. C. Davis, 'Equality in an Unequal Commonwealth: James Harrington's Republicanism and the Meaning of Equality', in Ian Gentles, John Morrill and Blair Worden (eds), *Soldiers, Writers and Statesmen of the English Revolution* (Cambridge, 1998), ch. 10.

96. For a discussion of the matter, see Davis, 'Equality in an Unequal Commonwealth'.

97. Harrington, 'System of Politics', p. 836.

98. Cf. also Harrington, *Commonwealth of Oceana*, p. 164.

99. Cf. Fukuda, *Sovereignty and the Sword*, pp. 72–5.

100. James Harrington, 'Aphorisms Political' (1659), in *Political Works*, ed. Pocock, p. 762.

101. The sentence perhaps echoes the message of Machiavelli, *Il Principe*, ch. 4, though Machiavelli was primarily concerned there with external conquest.

102. See also Scott, *Commonwealth Principles*, pp. 286–7; also Norbrook, *Writing the English Republic*, pp. 357–78.

103. See his two speeches to parliament in 1654: W. C. Abbott (ed.), *The Writings and Speeches of Oliver Cromwell*, 4 vols (Oxford, reissued 1988), vol. III, pp. 434–43, 451–62.

104. Nedham, *The Case of the Commonwealth of England, Stated*, p. 51; also pp. 28–9, 46–7. (The book was, of course, endorsed by Cromwell as an authoritative justification of the Protectorate: Abbott (ed.), *Writings and Speeches*, vol. III, p. 587.)

105. See the discussion in Barry Coward, *Oliver Cromwell* (Harlow, 1991), pp. 125–39.

106. See Goldie, 'Civil Religion of James Harrington'.

107. Ruth Mayers, *1659: The Crisis of the Commonwealth* (Woodbridge, 2004).
108. Richard Baxter, *A Holy Commonwealth*, ed. William Lamont (Cambridge, 1994); George Lawson, *Politica Sacra et Civilis*, ed. Conal Condren (Cambridge, 1992). See Condren, *George Lawson's Politica and the English Revolution* (Cambridge, 1989), esp. ch. 10 for the 1659 context.
109. Henry Vane, *A Needful Corrective or Balance in Popular Government* (London, 1660), p. 5.
110. Ibid., pp. 7–8, 10. See further Margaret Judson, *The Political Thought of Sir Henry Vane the Younger* (Philadelphia, PA, 1969).
111. John Milton, *The Readie and Easie Way to Establish a Free Commonwealth* (2nd edn, 1660), in *Complete Prose Works of John Milton: Volume VII, 1659–1660*, rev. edn (New Haven, CT, 1980), pp. 432–3.
112. There was also a localist dimension to the proposal: Milton, *Readie and Easie way*, pp. 458–9.
113. Cf. Frank Lovett, 'Milton's Case for a Free Commonwealth', *American Journal of Political Science*, 49 (2005), pp. 466–78. The character and development of Milton's republicanism remains controversial. For a variety of approaches see Martin Dzelzainis, 'Milton's Classical Republicanism', and Thomas Corns, 'Milton and the Characteristics of a Free Commonwealth', both in David Armitage, Armand Himy and Quentin Skinner (eds), *Milton and Republicanism* (Cambridge, 1995), chs 1 and 2; Skinner, *Visions of Politics*, vol. II, ch. 11; William Walker, '*Paradise Lost* and Forms of Government', *History of Political Thought*, 22 (2001), pp. 270–99; Paul A. Rahe, 'The Classical Republicanism of John Milton', *History of Political Thought*, 25 (2004), pp. 243–75; Worden, *Literature and Politics in Cromwellian England*, chs 7–14.
114. John Aubrey, *Brief Lives*, ed. Oliver Lawson Dick (Penguin edn, Harmondsworth, 1972), p. 209.

Notes to Epilogue

1. For some perspectives on the pursuit of a Godly society, see John R. Young, 'The Scottish Covenanters and the Drive for a Godly Society', *Recherches Anglaises et Nord Américaines*, 40 (2007), pp. 25–35; Derek Hirst, 'The Failure of Godly Rule in the English Republic', *Past & Present*, 132 (1991), pp. 33–66; Ann Hughes, '"The Public Profession of These Nations": the National Church in Interregnum England', in Christopher Durston and Judith Maltby (eds), *Religion in Revolutionary England* (Manchester, 2006), ch. 6.
2. See R. Scott Spurlock, *Cromwell and Scotland: Conquest and Religion, 1650–1660* (Edinburgh, 2007); also F. D. Dow, *Cromwellian Scotland, 1651–1660* (Edinburgh, 1979); Patrick Little, *Lord Broghill and the Cromwellian Union with Ireland and Scotland* (Woodbridge, 2004).
3. For a good recent collection of work broadly sympathetic to this modernising view, see Alan Houston and Steve Pincus, *A Nation Transformed: England After the Restoration* (Cambridge, 2001), especially the introduction. Important also are Justin Champion, *The Pillars of Priestcraft Shaken: The Church of England and its Enemies, 1660–1730* (Cambridge, 1992); and John Marshall, *John Locke, Toleration and Early Enlightenment Culture* (Cambridge, 2006).
4. The chief advocate of this view is J. C. D. Clark, *English Society, 1660–1832*, 2nd edn (Cambridge, 2000).
5. Richard Greaves, *Deliver Us from Evil: The Radical Underground in Britain, 1660–1663* (New York, 1986); Greaves, *Enemies Under his Feet: Radicals and Nonconformists in Britain, 1664–1677* (Stanford, CA, 1990); Greaves, *Secrets of the Kingdom: British Radicals from the Popish Plot to the Revolution of 1688–1689* (Stanford, CA, 1992).
6. Quoted in C. C. Weston and J. R. Greenberg, *Subjects and Sovereigns: The Grand Controversy over Legal Sovereignty in Stuart England* (Cambridge, 1981), p. 149.
7. Edward Hyde, earl of Clarendon, *The History of the Rebellion and Civil Wars in England . . . Also His Life Written by Himself* (Oxford, 1843), p. 1069.
8. Mark Goldie, 'Restoration Political Thought', in Lionel K. J. Glassey, *The Reigns of Charles II and James VII & II* (Basingstoke, 1997), ch. 2, p. 14.
9. John Spurr, *The Restoration Church of England, 1646–1689* (New Haven, CT, 1991), pp. 106–7.
10. Ibid., p. 37.
11. Quoted in ibid., p. 47.

12. Ibid., pp. 48–50.
13. Ibid., pp. 48–9, 58–9.
14. On Parker and the debate on his work, see especially Richard Ashcraft, *Revolutionary Politics and Locke's Two Treatises of Government* (Princeton, NJ, 1986), ch. 2; Gordon J. Schochet, 'Between Lambeth and Leviathan: Samuel Parker on the Church of England and Political Order', in Nicholas T. Phillipson and Quentin Skinner (eds), *Political Discourse in Early Modern Britain* (Cambridge, 1993), pp. 189–208; Schochet, 'Samuel Parker, Religious Diversity, and the Ideology of Persecution', in Roger D. Lund (ed.), *The Margins of Orthodoxy: Heterodox Writing and Cultural Response, 1660–1750* (Cambridge, 1995), pp. 119–48; and Jon Parkin, 'Hobbism in the Later 1660s: Daniel Scargill and Samuel Parker', *Historical Journal*, 42 (1999), pp. 85–108.
15. On this work and the debate it inspired, see especially Robert von Friedeburg, 'From Collective Representation to the Right to Individual Defence: James Steuart's *Ius Populi Vindicatum* and the Use of Johannes Althusius' *Politica* in Restoration Scotland', *History of European Ideas*, 24 (1998), pp. 19–42; and, more broadly, Ian Michael Smart, 'The Political Ideas of the Scottish Covenanters, 1638–88', *History of Political Thought*, 1 (1980), pp. 167–93.
16. See further Clare Jackson, *Restoration Scotland, 1660–1690: Royalist Politics, Religion and Ideas* (Woodbridge, 2003).
17. Mark Goldie, 'The Revolution of 1689 and the Structure of Political Argument: an Essay and an Annotated Bibliography of Pamphlets on the Allegiance Controversy', *Bulletin of Research in the Humanities*, 83: 4 (1980), pp. 473–564. As with the Engagement Controversy, the titles of many pamphlets are alone sufficient to indicate the casuistical nature of the debate.
18. Ibid., pp. 522–3; John William Packer, *The Transformation of Anglicanism, 1643–1660, with Special Reference to Henry Hammond* (Manchester, 1969), pp. 180–1. Neither author is aware that Hammond's contribution to the Engagement Controversy was published anonymously in 1650 as *A Briefe Resolution, Of that Grand Case of Conscience (Necessary for These Times) Concerning the Allegiance Due to a Prince* (London, 1650). The work is discussed in Margaret Sampson, 'Laxity and Liberty in Seventeenth-Century English Political Thought', in Edmund Leites (ed.), *Conscience and Casuistry in Early Modern Europe* (Cambridge, 1988), ch. 2, at p. 189, but she is unaware of Hammond's authorship.
19. Hammond, *Briefe Resolution*, p. 6.
20. Goldie, 'Revolution of 1689', pp. 484–5, 490–1, 507–10; J. P. Kenyon, *Revolution Principles: The Politics of Party, 1689–1720* (Cambridge, 1977), chs 2 and 3.
21. Mark Goldie, 'The Political Thought of the Anglican Revolution', in Robert Beddard (ed.), *The Revolutions of 1688: The Andrew Browning Lectures, 1988* (Oxford, 1991), ch. 2.

Further Reading

There is, not surprisingly, an enormous scholarly literature on the subjects covered by this book. My footnotes are intended to direct readers both to the works that have been important in shaping my reading of the evidence, but also to the most useful secondary sources for further reading. The guidance given here should be read in conjunction with these notes.

British political thought cannot be fully understood in isolation from political thought elsewhere in Europe. On this, see especially Quentin Skinner, *The Foundations of Modern Political Thought*, 2 vols (Cambridge, 1978); J. H. Burns, with Mark Goldie (eds), *The Cambridge History of Political Thought, 1450–1700* (Cambridge, 1991); and Howell Lloyd, Glenn Burgess and Simon Hodson (eds), *European Political Thought, 1450–1700* (New Haven, CT, 2007).

Important general interpretative surveys covering large portions of the period are relatively scarce. The best overall survey (multi-authored) is probably J. G. A. Pocock with Gordon J. Schochet and Lois G. Schwoerer (eds), *The Varieties of British Political Thought, 1500–1800* (Cambridge, 1993). More demanding, but inescapable, are J. G. A. Pocock, *The Machiavellian Moment: Florentine Political Thought and the Atlantic Republican Tradition*, new edn (Princeton, NJ, 2003), primarily about republicans but of much broader significance; Marku Peltonen, *Classical Humanism and Republicanism in English Political Thought, 1570–1640* (Cambridge, 1995); Pocock, *The Ancient Constitution and the Feudal Law*, new edn (Cambridge, 1987); and Alan Cromartie, *The Constitutionalist Revolution: An Essay on the History of England, 1450–1642* (Cambridge, 2006).

There is no recent survey account of Tudor political thought. Some key themes are addressed in Paul A. Fideler and T. F. Mayer (eds), *Political Thought and the Tudor Commonwealth: Deep Structure, Discourse and Disguise* (London, 1992). The most valuable introduction to the intellectual history of the Henrician period probably remains Alistair Fox and John Guy, *Reassessing the Henrician Age: Humanism, Politics and Reform, 1500–1550* (Oxford, 1986). Still useful is Franklin L. Baumer, *The Early Tudor Theory of Kingship* (New Haven, CT, 1949). There is no good survey of mid-century resistance theory, best pursued through the specialised article literature listed in my notes to Chapter 2, or through the three books on European political thought mentioned above. The early Elizabethans are surveyed in A. N. McLaren, *Political*

Culture in the Reign of Elizabeth I: Queen and Commonwealth, 1558–1585 (Cambridge, 1999). The later part of Elizabeth's reign and the political thought of Hooker are probably best approached via Peter Lake's *Anglicans and Puritans: Presbyterianism and English Conformist Thought from Whitgift to Hooker* (London, 1988).

Two very different accounts of early Stuart political thought are Johann P. Sommerville, *Royalists and Patriots: Politics and Ideology in England, 1603–1640*, 2nd edn (Harlow, 1999), known in its first edition only by its sub-title; and Glenn Burgess, *The Politics of the Ancient Constitution: An Introduction to English Political Thought, 1603–1642* (Basingstoke, 1992). Older accounts of the period remain very useful introductions, notably Margaret Judson's *Crisis of the Constitution* (Rutgers, NJ, 1949); and J. W. Allen, *English Political Thought, 1603–1644* (London, 1938).

The political thought of the English Revolution still has only one survey, Perez Zagorin, *A History of Political Thought in the English Revolution* (London, 1954), dated but still useful. A better introduction is Colin Davis's contribution to Barry Coward, *A Companion to Stuart Britain* (Oxford, 2003), which also contains an excellent essay on early Stuart political thought by Malcolm Smuts. There is an enormous body of work on the ideas of the English Revolution, making it hard to single out particular items. On Parliamentarians and Royalists most of the surveys seem unsatisfactory for one reason or another, though John Sanderson, *'But the People's Creatures': The Philosophical Basis of the English Civil War* (Manchester, 1989) is found approachable by my students. More limited in range, but valuable, are Michael Mendle's *Henry Parker and the English Civil War* (Cambridge, 1995); and David Smith's *Constitutional Royalism and the Search for Settlement, c. 1640–1649* (Cambridge, 1994). For the Levellers, I remain attached to Joseph Frank's careful book *The Levellers* (Cambridge, MA, 1955), but more up-to-date are the essays in Michael Mendle (ed.), *The Putney Debates of 1647* (Cambridge, 2001). Important recent work by Rachel Foxley can be traced through my notes. On religious radicalism, see Christopher Hill, *The World Turned Upside Down* (London, 1972); J. F. McGregor and Barry Reay (eds), *Radical Religion in the English Revolution* (Oxford, 1986). The many essays of J. C. [Colin] Davis have been particularly helpful to me and these can be traced via my notes. Valuable introductions to Hobbes in context are J. P. Sommerville, *Thomas Hobbes: Political Ideas in Historical Context* (Basingstoke, 1992); Richard Tuck, *Hobbes* (Oxford, 1989); and Conal Condren, *Thomas Hobbes* (New York, 2000). On republicanism, two different approaches worth exploring are those of Blair Worden, in the form of his contributions to David Wootton (ed.), *Republicanism, Liberty and Commercial Society, 1649–1776*

(Stanford, CA, 1994); and Jonathan Scott, *Commonwealth Principles: Republican Writing of the English Revolution* (Cambridge, 2004). Fundamental on Harrington remains Pocock's work, best approached via his introduction to Harrington's *Political Works* (Cambridge, 1977). Quentin Skinner's work on both republicanism and Hobbes is equally essential, and may be best approached through his collected essays, *Visions of Politics*, 3 vols (Cambridge, 2002).

Scottish political thought has been much less intensively studied than English. The work of Roger Mason is of great importance, especially for the earlier part of this period, and much of it is collected in his *Kingship and the Commonweal: Political Thought in Renaissance and Reformation Scotland* (East Linton, 1998). For the earlier period, see also J. H. Burns, *The True Law of Kingship: Concepts of Monarchy in Early Modern Scotland* (Oxford, 1996). Important in placing a canon of Scottish political thinkers on the map are two collections associated with the Folger Institute's Center for the History of British Political Thought: Roger Mason (ed.) *Scots and Britons: Scottish Political Thought and the Union of 1603* (Cambridge, 1994); the second of them, edited by John Robertson, is centred on the union of 1707, and its contents lie outside the scope of this book.

The Folger Center, led by John Pocock, has been at the heart of much new work on early modern British political thought. A collection of essays exploring the results is David Armitage (ed.), *British Political Thought in History, Literature and Theory, 1500–1800* (Cambridge, 2006).

Index

The titles of book and pamphlets are indexed only when the author's name is unknown.